MOTHER JONES SPEAKS

MOTHER JONES SPEAKS

COLLECTED WRITINGS AND SPEECHES

Edited by Philip S. Foner

MONAD PRESS / NEW YORK

TO BERNIE AND ELLA
Dear Friends and Long-Time Companions

*Publication of this book by the Anchor Foundation
was assisted by a fund established in memory of*
KATE ALDERDICE
1945-1983
*Canadian revolutionary socialist,
feminist, and unionist.*

Library of Congress Catalog Card Number 83-060486
ISBN cloth 0-913460-88-5; ISBN paper 0-913460-89-3

Manufactured in the United States of America
First edition 1983

Published by Monad Press for the Anchor Foundation
Distributed by:
Pathfinder Press
410 West Street
New York, NY 10014

89912

I know of no East or West, North nor South when it comes to my class fighting the battle for justice. If it is my fortune to live to see the industrial chain broken from every workingman's child in America, and if then there is one black child in Africa in bondage, there I shall go.

From speech to miners of northern Colorado, Louisville, Colorado, November 21, 1903

The Chairman: Please take the chair. Where do you live?
Mrs. Jones: I live in the United States, but I do not know exactly in what place, because I am always in the fight against oppression, and wherever a fight is going on I have to jump there, and sometimes I am in Washington, sometimes in Pennsylvania, sometimes in Arizona, sometimes in Texas, and sometimes up in Minnesota, so that really I have no particular residence.
The Chairman: No abiding place?
Mrs. Jones: No abiding place, but wherever a fight is on against wrong, I am always there. It is my pleasure to be in the fray.

From testimony of Mother Jones before House Committee on Rules, Washington, D.C., June 14, 1910

I attribute my good health and unimpaired faculties to the life of activity which I have led. Many people retire from active life at the age of 50 and spend the rest of their years in peace and quietness. They allow their mental faculties to become dulled by not exercising them, and by not continuing to take an energetic interest in affairs.

I was nearly fifty when I took up the business of agitating to improve labor conditions. My mind is kept constantly on the alert coping with difficulties, planning campaigns, organizing work along new lines and with striving to better present-day conditions. I have no time to think about getting old; besides I have a lot to accomplish yet.

Interview at age 83 in Vancouver Daily Province, *British Columbia, June 11, 1914*

It is true I have given most of my time to the miners' organization, but I don't belong to any individual organization or creed; I belong to the workers wherever they are in slavery, regardless of what their trade or craft may be.

From speech of Mother Jones at Third Congress of the Pan-American Federation of Labor, Mexico City, Mexico, January 13, 1921

I wouldn't trade what I've done for what John D. Rockefeller has done. I've done the best I could to make the world a better place for poor, hard-working people.

From statement of Mother Jones to the New York Times *on her one hundredth birthday, May 1, 1930*

CONTENTS

1. SPEECHES

2. TESTIMONY BEFORE CONGRESSIONAL COMMITTEES

3. ARTICLES

4. INTERVIEWS

5. LETTERS

Preface

Along with the Bible, the *Autobiography of Mother Jones* sits on tables in many miners' living rooms. Some also have copies of *Thoughts of Mother Jones,* a 16-page pamphlet.[1] But that is all of Mother Jones's writings and speeches available. One biographer of Mother Jones has written that while her "powerful rhetoric was legendary . . . she left little behind on paper,"[2] thereby implying that a comprehensive collection of Mother Jones's writings and speeches was impossible. It is true that her speeches and letters are widely scattered, and that the only collection bearing her name in the Archives and Manuscripts Department of the library of the Catholic University of America consists largely of materials transferred from the John Mitchell Papers and Terence V. Powderly Papers. But it is also true that there are many other manuscripts of Mother Jones in libraries and historical societies all over the country, and that with these and material in newspapers and union publications, one can put together the comprehensive collection of the writings and speeches of Mother Jones which was deemed impossible. The present collection is intended to fill that vacuum.

In nearly all cases the speeches in this volume have been published as they were recorded or printed. In a few cases, as in the speeches delivered during the 1912-13 strike in West Virginia, they were recorded verbatim on the spot by a court reporter for use in a court injunction against Mother Jones. Some of the speeches which were printed may, as has been charged, have been expurgated or dressed up, although the evidence for the former is nonexistent. But they all reflect the views of Mother Jones. In a few cases, it was necessary to piece together fragmentary accounts in different newspapers of what Mother Jones said. In two or three instances, where only a number of sentences in Mother Jones's own words were printed, I have included the paraphrase of the rest by the newspaper reporter. At least that much was printed. In many instances the newspaper would simply report the fact that Mother Jones had spoken in the community without including anything of what she had said.

It has been asserted that because Mother Jones did not trust the mails, she "carefully left her most pressing thoughts out of her letters," explaining to her correspondent that, "I have so much to tell you when I see you . . . can't write in a letter."[3] But a reading of the letters published below will reveal that this occurred rarely, and that she did not, in most cases, hesitate to set down exactly what she thought. A problem with the letters, however, is that it is very difficult at times to decipher Mother Jones's handwriting, especially those written in her nineties, when rheumatism and arthritis made holding a pen and using the typewriter exceedingly painful. Her spelling is so erratic that if one were to note each instance of misspelling with "sic," the page might become unreadable. "I am not able to do much writing mere scribbling half the time I can't remember how to Spell," she observed in one of her many letters to John H. Walker.[4] I have, therefore, decided to publish the letters as she wrote them, omitting all notices of misspellings. Newspaper articles, documents, transcripts and other materials have also been reproduced as they originally appeared.

Mother Jones Speaks has been divided into five sections: speeches, testimony before Congressional Committees, articles, interviews, and letters. Each speech and each of her testimony before Congressional Committees has been preceded by the editor's introduction so that the reader might fully understand the historical background in which the document is set. It is also followed by the editor's notes explaining references in the document which may not be clear to the present-day reader. The documents in the sections of articles, interviews, and letters omit the introductions, but they do include the explanatory notes.

Along with Mother Jones's own words, I have included tributes to her, a Chronology of Mother Jones, a Selected Bibliography, and a general introduction to the volume. I have also given titles to the speeches of Mother Jones and the interviews with her.

When one considers the subjects dealt with by Mother Jones in this volume from 1900 through the 1920s — struggles of the miners, both coal and metalliferous, the garment workers, street car workers, steel workers, oil workers, textile workers, and numerous other workers engaged in the process of organizing a union or in a strike; Socialist Party activities; farmer-labor political parties; international labor solidarity, especially involving the great Mexican Revolution; the organization of the unorganized through industrial unions, and the battle against an entrenched and corrupt labor bureaucracy — one must conclude that this remarkable American woman has furnished us with an incomparable record of the American labor movement during these crucial decades of its development.

Philip S. Foner
August, 1982
Professor Emeritus of History
Lincoln University, Pennsylvania
Visiting Professor of Economics
Haverford College, Pennsylvania

Notes

1. The pamphlet is edited by Jim Axelrod and published in Charleston, West Virginia. It contains five or six quotations of three or four lines each under headings like "On Organizing the United Mine Workers," "On Leadership," "On Freedom," "On Struggle," "On Capitalism." A strange section of six quotations is arranged under "On Women's Liberation," none of which has any relation to the theme.

2. Review by Priscilla Long of Dale Featherling, *The Miners' Angel: A Portrait* in *Labor History* 7 (Fall, 1974): 425.

3. Priscilla Long, *Mother Jones, Woman Organizer,* Boston, 1976, p. 6.

4. Mother to John H. Hunter, no date, John Hunter Walker Collection, 1911-1953, Illinois Historical Survey, University of Illinois Library.

Acknowledgments

The compilation of this volume would have been impossible without the kind cooperation of many individuals, libraries, and historical societies. I have been fortunate that a group of researchers, academic and nonacademic, engaged in the study of Mother Jones have been generous in sharing their information and material with me. I wish to take this opportunity to express my gratitude to Lois McLean, president of the West Virginia Labor History Association, who is preparing what promises to be the definitive life of Mother Jones, and to Professor Edward M. Steel, Jr. of West Virginia University, who is editing the comprehensive edition of the letters of Mother Jones, for their kind cooperation and assistance. I also wish to thank Anthony Zito, Archivist, Catholic University of America Library, for repeated assistance in making available the papers of Mother Jones in the John Mitchell, Terence V. Powderly, and Mary Harris Jones Collections. I also owe a debt of gratitude to Ann R. Lorentz, Reference Librarian, Parkersburg and Wood County Public Library, Parkersburg, West Virginia, for promptly furnishing me with copies of Mother Jones material in the library. I also wish to thank John Hoffman, Director of the Illinois History Survey, University of Illinois Library at Urbana-Champaign, and his staff for generously furnishing me with copies of the correspondence between Mother Jones and John Hunter Walker in the John Hunter Walker Collection, and the Correspondence of Mother Jones in the Thomas J. Morgan Collection. I also wish to thank Peter Gottlieb, Associate Curator, West Virginia and Regional History Collection, West Virginia University Library, for furnishing me with copies of correspondence of Mother Jones and photographs of Mother Jones. Similarly, I owe thanks to Saundra Taylor, Curator of Manuscripts Department, Lilly Library, Indiana University, Bloomington, Indiana; Charles Jonas, Director, Manuscripts Department, Chicago Historical Society; and John Walker, Director, Manuscripts Department, University Library, Indiana State University, Terre Haute, Indiana, for furnishing me with copies of letters and other writings of Mother Jones in these collections. Itoko McNulty, Library Assistant, Southwest Section, El Paso Public Library, was also very helpful, and I wish to express my gratitude. Paul Estrada of El Paso kindly furnished me with several pages of his unpublished M.A.

19

thesis ("Border Revolution: The Mexican Revolution in the Ciudad Juarez-El Paso Area, 1906-1915") which refer to Mother Jones. Paul Nyden called my attention to copies of speeches of Mother Jones in the collections at West Virginia University Library. I owe them both a debt of gratitude. Fred Longley, Assistant Librarian, Department of Labour, Ottawa, Canada, kindly furnished me with materials in the department. Jeanette C. Parson kindly furnished me with a copy of a letter of Mother Jones in the Pennsylvania Historical Collections and Labor Archives, The University Libraries, Pennsylvania State University.

I wish to thank the staffs of the Western History Department, Denver Public Library; Tamiment Institute, New York University Library; Widener and Lamont Libraries, Harvard University; Duke University Library; University of Victoria Library; New York Public Library; Free Library of Philadelphia; National Archives, Library of Congress; Bancroft Library, University of California, Berkeley; University of Maine, Farmington Library; Bates College Library, Lewiston, Maine; and the interlibrary loan department of Rutgers University, Camden library.

Mildred Chasin, Tillie Pevzner, Thelma Siegel, George Walker, John DeBrizzi, and Professor David Roediger were helpful in checking material in local libraries and historical societies. I owe them a debt of gratitude. My brother Henry Foner read the general introduction, and made several useful suggestions for which I wish to thank him.

Mother Jones:
Dynamic Champion of Oppressed Multitudes

by Philip S. Foner

For her services a world family called her "Mother." In repose, she might be the quiet, gentle essence of the young grandmother, of happy youngsters.

Until she spoke, and then she was the dynamic champion of oppressed multitudes. She was motherhood roused to frenzy against the oppressors of her children. —*Eleanore Meherin in* San Francisco Chronicle, *1919*

In his tribute to Mother Jones, published in the Socialist *Appeal to Reason* on November 23, 1907, Eugene V. Debs predicted that her name would be "lovingly remembered" by the children of those whom she had helped, "and their children's children forever."[1] However, this did not come to pass during Debs's own lifetime. In 1922, George P. West, an important social worker and leading investigator for the U.S. Commission on Industrial Relations, deplored the fact that the life of Mother Jones, which he called "an epic," had "never been told," and attributed this to "our tradition of cheap gentility."[2] Three years later, the *Autobiography of Mother Jones* was published by Charles H. Kerr in Chicago, and the fact that it went through only one edition would seem to indicate that not many of the "children" and "children's children" were interested in her story.[3] To be sure, the *Autobiography* (written with the assistance of [some say ghostwritten by] Mary Field Parton, an experienced magazine author and former social worker) omitted essential aspects of Mother Jones's life. The first two paragraphs sum up the first 30 years of Mother Jones's career, and all references to the IWW have been eliminated, along with any material on the march on Logan, West Virginia. Many other important events are not mentioned and, when discussed, are often misdated. But, as David Montgomery points out, the *Autobiography of Mother Jones* "provides valuable insights into miners' battles, their way of life, and especially the role of women of the mining communities during strikes. Mother Jones' unswerving devotion to her class, her sense of struggle, solidarity, patriotism, and the faith that American democracy ultimately

21

would work make this autobiography worth the careful reading of anyone who would understand the ideology of American workers."[4] One might add anyone who would understand the change in the nature of labor leadership in the twentieth century. For in the last chapter, significantly entitled, "Progress in Spite of Leaders," Mother Jones holds up to scorn the "modern leaders of labor who have wandered far from the thorny path of those early crusaders. Never in the early days of struggle would you find leaders wining and dining with the aristocracy; nor did their wives strut about like diamond-bedecked peacocks, nor were they attended by humiliated, cringing colored servants." She lamented the fact that the "rank and file have let their servants become their masters and dictators. The workers have now to fight not alone their exploiters but likewise their leaders, who often betray them, who sell them out, who put their own advancement ahead of that of the working masses, who make of the rank and file political pawns."[5] It is understandable that these trade union leaders were reluctant to place the personal recollections of Mother Jones in the hands of their memberships.

It was not until more than thirty years after her death, in 1930, that the first serious studies of Mother Jones were written. Sister Joan Francis Raffale's Ph.D. dissertation at Catholic University of America, "Mary Harris Jones and the United Mine Workers of America," appeared in 1964, and Judith Elaine Mikeal's M.A. thesis, at the University of North Carolina, "Mother Mary Jones: The Labor Movement's Impious Joan of Arc," came a year later. Both, however, remained unpublished. Writing in *People's Appalachia* in the summer of 1970, Keith Dix noted sadly that Mary Harris Jones, whom coal miners affectionately called "Mother Jones," "remains a mystery to most people outside of Appalachia (and many within). She has been neglected by the 'ivory towered researchers' whose job it is to report to us about important people in American history." He complained that though she had "earned a reputation equaled by only a few in the annals of labor union history," there were "no in-depth books" about her, and that "only an occasional reference to her will be found in the scholarly journals and standard labor histories. As far as the 'established truth' is concerned it is almost as if Mother Jones had never lived."[6]

But a change was under way. In fact, Dix himself acknowledged as much, noting that "the legend of Mother Jones" was being discovered "by young people in the Movement," that those interested in "the buried history of women as agents for social change" were beginning to be attracted by the same legend, that an academician like Professor Edward Steel of West Virginia University was conducting research on the life of Mother Jones, that her autobiography had been reprinted by Arno Press in New York (the only autobiography of a worker's leader in the entire *American Labor* collection issued by the publisher); that a children's book by Irving Weinstein (*Labor's Defiant Lady*) had appeared in 1969, and that a pamphlet of quotations from Mother Jones had been published in Charleston, West Virginia.[7]

As Keith Dix anticipated, new studies of Mother Jones did appear. In 1974, over forty years after her death, the first biography was published: Dale Featherling's *Mother Jones — The Miners' Angel*. It appeared, moreover, under the scholarly imprint of the Southern Illinois University Press! Although Featherling's work did not claim to be definitive, it did gather together a body of useful information on Mother Jones, based on published and unpublished sources, which proved to be of value both to the historian and the general reader. Yet Featherling's approach to Mother Jones reflected a tendency which was widespread in academic (and even some non-academic) circles, namely, that she was fundamentally a rabble-rouser, lacking ideological depth and contributing heart rather than brains to the labor movement, a "firebrand in industrial troubles" who "possessed no qualities of leadership, but was sort of gadfly sent by the union leaders to annoy the operators."[8] Her role was defined for scholars when, in answer to a college professor who introduced her to an audience as "a great humanitarian," she shot back: "Get it right. I'm not a humanitarian. I'm a hell-raiser."

This then is Featherling's summary of Mother Jones: "Although she often let loose with such strong rhetoric, she just as often contradicted it. Her philosophy of collectivism was a desultory one — to be swept up during a speech or a strike, or to share in comradeship with her more consistently committed friends. All her life, Mother Jones was a doer, not a philosopher. She was a political chameleon whose catechism reddened in relation to her mood and to the moment."[9] Featherling likes her best when her mood is least red.

Other factors limited the appreciation of Mother Jones even as interest in her grew and studies of her career multiplied. Her ambiguous relationship with the Socialist Party and what was viewed as her conservatism as she grew older, tended to alienate a number of the "young people in the Movement," upon whom Keith Dix had counted to lead the way in awakening interest in and respect for Mother Jones. Mother Jones's relationship with the Socialist Party will emerge fully in the course of the sections of her speeches, articles, interviews, and letters. Here, one can note the fact that as early as 1895, she was converting men and women to socialism with speeches on its doctrines in trade union halls; that in 1901, Eugene V. Debs wrote that he was depending on her to assist him in "helping the cause," and that a year later, William Mailly, soon to be Socialist Party national secretary, wrote in the *International Socialist Review* that in the anthracite coal districts, "the way has been prepared for us. 'Mother' Jones had not been through the region for nothing. Everywhere she had left a trail of Socialist books and papers behind her. Few of the officials but had sub-scribed for a paper, and many of the miners received one she had sub-scribed for for them. And 'Mother' Jones' name is a talisman that opens the heart of the anthracite miners to any Socialist that comes to educate and not abuse."[10]

Although she continued to serve the cause of socialism over the years that followed, influencing many, including some who became Socialist Party leaders, to join the ranks of those fighting for a new so-cial system, Mother Jones slowly became disenchanted with the Socialist Party. None of this had anything to do with opposition to the marginal positions and second-class status accorded women in the Party, or with the sexism that manifested itself in the ranks and leadership of the movement. Rather, as we shall see, it had to do with her feeling that the Party had failed to live up to its principles because of the influence of lawyers, clergymen, and other middle-class refor-mers in its leadership. She grew particularly disillusioned with the Party during her imprisonment in the West Virginia coal strike of 1912-13, and felt that the Berger-Hillquit elements in the Party were indifferent to the needs of the miners. In her criticism, she began even, and not without reason as we shall see, to include Eugene V. Debs for whom she had had the greatest admiration.

But all this did not mean that she abandoned her belief in socialism. What she told a reporter for the *Charleston (West Virginia) Gazette* in June, 1912 could be said to sum up her philosophy and her mission:

I am simply a social revolutionist. I believe in collective ownership of the means of wealth. At this time the natural commodities of this country are cor-nered in the hands of a few. The man who owns the means of wealth gets the major profit, and the worker, who produces the wealth from the means in the hands of the capitalist, takes what he can get. Sooner or later, and perhaps sooner than we think, evolution and revolution will have accomplished the overturning of the system under which we now live, and the worker will have gained his own. This change will come as the result of education. My life work has been to try to educate the worker to a sense of the wrongs he has had to suf-fer, and does suffer — and to stir up the oppressed to a point of getting off their knees and demanding that which I believe to be rightfully theirs. . . .[11]

Unfortunately, when Mother Jones died, this and similar state-ments were forgotten by the editorial writers and only her differences with the Socialist Party remembered. The *Burlington (Vermont) Gazette* expressed the common view in its editorial tribute to Mother Jones:

With all her militancy, Mother Jones always was a good American. She frowned upon socialism and communism, her good sense alive to the fallacy of permitting these elements to intrude themselves into the field of American labor. Her heart impulses ever were right, and labor can well cherish her mem-ory.[12]

Even Vern Smith, who should have known better, declared in the *Labor Defender* (organ of the left-wing International Labor Defense) that "Mother Jones was no revolutionist. She was a militant fighter for the working class, in that period when the class struggle was simple, almost entirely within the framework of capitalism. She never tried to overthrow capitalism. All this heroic struggle she led was for amelioration only."[13] One wonders if Smith ever heard Mother Jones speak or read any of her articles in the *Appeal to Reason* or the *International Socialist Review*.

Since, as will become clear below, Mother Jones repeatedly pointed out that socialist ideas were rooted in the principles of Patrick Henry and Thomas Jefferson, and since she proclaimed herself a "Bolshevist from the top of my head to the bottom of my feet" at the age of ninety, it is clear that the editorial writers at her death were doing a good deal of whistling in the dark. But many young people in the movement of the 1960s knew nothing of the real Mother Jones and were influenced by the picture of her as depicted in a number of the obituary editorials.

If the socialist issue was a factor in the limited appreciation of Mother Jones in the 1960s, then her relationship to women and the women's movement was a cause for disillusionment among those who were beginning to unearth "the buried history of women as agents for social change" — especially the feminists. Some of this was fully justified. A number of statements by Mother Jones deriding woman's suffrage and asserting the view that woman's place was in the home, deserve to be criticized. The truth is that Mother Jones belongs to neither of the two categories defined by Gerda Lerner — the women's rights movement and the broader women's emancipation movement. Lerner defines the former as a quest for political and legal equality and the latter as a search for "freedom from oppressive restrictions imposed by sex, self- determination and autonomy . . . financial and cultural independence, freedom to choose one's own life-style regardless of sex."[14]

Yet, as the reader of the pages that follow will quickly discover, one can find elements of both movements in Mother Jones's speeches and writings. Although the opponents of woman's suffrage gleefully publicized Mother Jones's statements opposing granting women the right to vote and her widely quoted remark, "You Don't Need the Vote To Raise Hell," the champions of woman's suffrage did not feature her statements that with women in government, society would be much improved and war abolished. Actually, Mother Jones complained that women who had achieved the right to vote in several states were not using it for social justice. "What good is the ballot, if they don't use it? They put the most infamous men in office," she complained of Colorado women.

During a speech in Seattle on May 30, 1914, she emphasized "that revolution could be affected by the ballot," criticized the I.W.W. sharply for opposing political action and denigrating the value of the ballot box, and praised the American Federation of Labor "as a practical organization" that understood the value of political action. And she expressed joy at the fact that the women of Washington had gained the ballot, but "hoped they would use it more wisely than had their husbands, fathers and sons." Speaking a few days later at Everett, Washington, she urged the women (who had the vote) to cast their ballots, but "to have a care how they cast votes for 'good fellows,' good fellows during election preliminaries, but damn bad ones afterwards."

Mother Jones also complained that not enough working women were getting up and revolting against intolerable conditions, joining organizations with men, or organizing their own. When they did and asked her for assistance, she was always ready to help.[15]

But to a number of feminist scholars, the fact that she devoted so much of her time to assisting male workers to organize is enough to condemn her. Apart from the fact that they seem to be unaware that she often went where no one else was willing to venture, they simply have no understanding that, as David Montgomery pointed out, she had a long-lasting and effective relationship with "women of the mining communities during strikes," that she mobilized them into militant struggle which won the admiration of thousands of Americans, and that she was worshipped by these women. A reporter who accompanied her to a meeting of miners' wives and daughters in Pennsylvania was so overwhelmed by what he saw that he wrote:

In about half an hour a strange audience had assembled. There were old, bent women of 70 and young, fresh-faced girls of 10. There were young matrons with babes in their arms, and women faded before their time. The faces that looked up from the rude benches of the strikers' hall were at first only curious, or somewhat shy and embarrassed.

Walking to the edge of the platform, "Mother" Jones stretched out her arms to them, and in her thrillingly sweet voice said, "Sisters!" A perceptible wave of emotion like that of wind sweeping the long grasses of downs and meadows passed over her audience. Still the women waited, wondered, watched.

The faces awoke, the souls back of them kindled. For an hour the speaker walked to and fro telling the deeds of the mothers of the past and sisters and wives. The listeners drew nearer. They leaned their elbows on the platform and lifted their faces to drink in her words. Their bosoms heaved and the tears rolled unheeded down their cheeks, but quickly the smiles flashed out again at the will of the speaker. She was explaining to them a plan to march by night through the mountains to surprise at dawn the body of workmen who had refused to strike, and by soft words and cajoleries to woo them to make common cause with their fellows. For who would stop a body of women carrying flags and singing.

"To Colerain-ah!" they whispered among themselves, and then broke out tumultuously: "We'll go; yes, tonight; to win the boys of Colerain."

And so, just as the sun broke over the mountains that September morning [1900], 500 women from McAdoo poured down into the village of Colerain, and in spite of deputy sheriffs, special guards and a special trainload of militia, they entered the homes of the workers, or surrounded squads of departing workmen, and by tears and smiles, and kisses and loving words they got their way with the men, took possession of the dinner pails, and held a dance of triumph in the village square. The wives and sisters of the town fell in with them, and nothing but boos and baas of derision greeted the company of soldier bank clerks and bookkeepers from Scranton when they tried to stampede the impromptu picnic, which lasted throughout the day.

This is one of the ways in which "Mother" Jones is most dangerous from the point of view of the capitalist who is at outs with his employes. Her magnetic influence over women is remarkable. Old or young, rich or poor, she understands them and draws them irresistibly. An old colored woman ran in the dust at "Mother" Jones' feet crying: "Lemme jes kiss de hem of your garment." "Not in the dust sister to me, but here on my breast, heart to heart," replied "Mother" Jones, lifting the negress, and the reporter who saw this incident declares that the women went mad with emotion, crying out: "Kiss me, too, Mother."

"When the writer once asked 'Mother' Jones why it was she stirred up the women," the reporter concluded, "she replied that it was because every drop of their blood was precious, that they were the inner life of the race, and that every nation was but the reflex of its women. 'No nation,' said she, 'will ever go beyond the development of its women. Lift up the women, make them intellectual; thus will great sons be born, and men find true comrades in their wives.'"[16]

In her booklet, *Mother Jones, Woman Organizer,* published in 1976, Priscilla Long has demonstrated that she has spent long hours studying the archives for materials about and by Mother Jones. But her discussion is only related to women and the woman question as if male workers in the United States at the time were of absolutely no value or importance. Her attitude toward Mother Jones is dominated by this approach, for while she is aware of her work with the wives of miners and with women workers in various fields, she tends to dismiss these as insignificant and to denigrate her contributions because she spent so much of her time organizing male workers. Actually, she tends to patronize Mother Jones. She writes, for example, that Mother Jones "could not have been expected to have lent her support to a suffrage movement [for women] which lacked any class consciousness. Nor could she really be expected to have been a feminist; that is, to have challenged the prevailing ideas about women in society."[17] Why not? Mother Jones should have been aware that the woman's suffrage movement, while led for a very long time by women of the upper or middle class, had begun by the twentieth century to attract wide support among working-class women who realized, as Mother Jones should have, that without the vote, they were fighting with only one hand, the economic hand, to improve their conditions, and that even that hand was rendered ineffective in many instances by their inability to influence legislation on behalf of working women:[18] A narrow opposition to all upper and middle-class women because of the exploitative and cruel conduct of large numbers of them was an approach which should not be condoned.

Long does, however, sharply criticize Mother Jones for failing to "have encouraged male workers to change their attitudes towards women workers. And she might also have pressured some of the AFL unions which used her, tolerated her, and were open to influence by her, to change their practices toward women workers. These things Mother Jones did not attempt. She shared with male workers and their unions an inability to see women as workers at all, in spite of their growing presence in the work force, and in spite of an organized and articulate women's labor movement embodied in the Women's Trade Union League."[19] Some of this criticism is justified, but to say of Mother Jones who responded many times to pleas from women workers on strike (or about to go on strike) for aid in their struggles, that she did not "see women as workers" is absurd. How absurd the reader will discover upon reading Mother Jones's speeches and articles.

Long also faults Mother Jones for not being interested in cooperating with women in her activities. Yet she herself cites several exceptions to this tendency of self-isolation (as she describes it), and she overlooks a very important one. In 1902, Mother Jones teamed with Kate Richards O'Hare in barnstorming anthracite fields around Hazelton and Wilkes-Barre, Pennsylvania, preaching socialism "every day and every night" to working coal miners and raising money for their relief fund. Both women, one over seventy the other 26, and just married, were exhausted by the grueling work, but they established a wonderful rapport and became long-time friends.[20]

Other women historians are not even as tolerant as Priscilla Long, or as willing to condone certain tendencies in Mother Jones's relationship with the women's movement. In 1976, the first comprehensive documentary history of women workers in the United States was published: *America's Working Women, A Documentary History 1600 to the Present,* compiled and edited by Rosalyn Baxandall, Linda Gordon, Susan Reverby. There is not a single reference to Mother Jones, not a single excerpt from a speech, letter, article, or interview. Here is further justification for Keith Dix's lament that to some it seems as "if she never existed."[21]

Susan Estabrook Kennedy knows that Mother Jones existed, and in her *If All We Did Was To Weep At Home: A History of White Working-Class Women in America,* published in 1979, she writes angrily and foolishly: " . . . the famous 'Mother' Jones was unsympathetic to a women's movement and even exploited miners' wives and children in her efforts to help the men. . . . Mother Jones disliked women in general and saw no reason to support working-class women except by improving the wages and working conditions of their husbands." The sources on which this sweeping and false generalization is based consist of: Priscilla Long's pamphlet, Fetherling's biography, and the *Autobiography of Mother Jones,* none of which would justify such a conclusion. It is to be hoped that if Kennedy takes the trouble to read the speeches, testimony, articles, interviews, and letters of Mother Jones, she will revise her fatuous conclusion. It is also to be hoped that Meredith Tax will find a place for Mother Jones in a revised edition of her book, *The Rising of the Women, Feminist Solidarity and Class Conflict, 1880-1917,* published in 1980.[22]

Fortunately Mother Jones's place in history does not depend on the narrow approach of these feminists. For one thing, the people of Appalachia, among whom she spent so many years, have made a special effort to keep her memory alive. The West Virginia Labor History Society, with Lois Clements McLean as president, has concentrated on gathering newspaper clippings, letters, photographs, and other memorabilia on Mother Jones, as well as the recollections of miners, their wives and daughters who knew her. Ms. McLean is herself engaged in preparing what will probably be the definitive biography of Mother Jones. A notice of her interest in materials about Mother Jones in the *Beckley (West Virginia) Post-Herald* of February 26, 1972, and the *United Mine Workers Journal* of February 15, 1972, brought scores of letters and telephone calls, the main theme of which was "one of love, affection and regard for Mother Jones."[23]

The *Autobiography of Mother Jones* was reissued by Charles H. Kerr and Company in 1972 and 1974 with new introductions by Fred Thompson which fill in some of the gaps in the original edition.[24] The name Mother Jones was bestowed on a splinter group of Students for a Democratic Society (SDS) which called itself the Mother Jones Revolutionary League. More lasting is the name of an independent monthly magazine, *Mother Jones.* To readers for whom the name may not be familiar, there is a familiar photograph on the masthead with the caption: "Pioneer socialist Mary Harris 'Mother' Jones (1837-1930) helped found the IWW; organized miners, maids and railway workers; supported the Mexican Revolution; and was one of the great orators of her day."[25]

On Mother's Day, May 10, 1970, the International Ladies' Garment Workers' Union (whose members she had assisted on several occasions) sponsored a full-page advertisement in the *New York Times* which showed a picture of Mother Jones leading her famous "Children's Crusade" of the summer of 1903, with the caption, "I reside wherever there is a good fight against wrong." The same paper carried a front-page story on April 23, 1972, describing a "pop wall poster" with a picture of Mother Jones, and another of her famous statements, "Pray for the dead but fight like hell for the living." On April 28, 1972, a "Mother Jones Day" was held in Parsglove, West Virginia. The rally was sponsored by the "Miners for Democracy," and its featured speaker was Kenneth "Chip" Yablonski. The organization had been formed three years earlier at the funeral of Joseph "Jock" Yablonski, slain father of Kenneth, murdered in a 1969 plot engineered by the incumbent United Mine Workers president, Tony Boyle. In a December 1972 election ordered by Federal courts, the grassroots movement called "Miners for Democracy" ousted a union bureaucracy entrenched since 1919. One of the movement's most popular symbols was a pamphlet of quotations of Mother Jones.[26]

The climax of the growing interest in Mother Jones was reached in 1980-1981. In 1980, the Pennsylvania Labor History Society commemorated the fiftieth anniversary of the death of Mother Jones. That same year, Patricia Montley's one-person play, *Mother Jones,* had its premiere at the Hartke Theater at the Catholic University of America, Washington, D.C., with Terry Handfield playing the role of Mother Jones.[27] And in 1980, Mary Lee Settle published *The Scapegoat,* a novel in her series on life in West Virginia. Dealing with the 1912-13 miners' strike, *The Scapegoat* has two leading characters: the daughter of a mine operator and Mother Jones. Settle devotes six pages to a speech by Mother Jones to the miners' wives and daughters.[28]

A final tribute of this period, and one which Mother Jones would have most appreciated, came in Mount Olive, Illinois, on May 26, 1981. There, women miners representing over 3,000 coal diggers, opened their third annual conference at the memorial gravesite of Mother Jones. Joining the women coal miners were retired coal miners, their wives and friends. Betty Jean Hall, director of the Coal Employment Project, which organized the conference, said: "It is fitting that we pay tribute to Mother Jones, who spent her life fighting for the rights of coal miners."[29]

The truth is that Mother Jones was a fighter for the working class everywhere. While the full story will unfold below in the various sections of her writings and speeches, we must note that perhaps no other person in the United States did so much to help the Mexican revolution as did Mother Mary Harris Jones. To be sure, there were reasons other than those of international labor solidarity which influenced Mother Jones in her work on behalf of those seeking to overthrow the brutal dictatorship of Porfirio Díaz. The miners, for whom she was a leading spokesperson, faced the competition of Mexican workers more than any other group of organized labor in the United States, and as the Socialist New York *Call* pointed out on April 16, 1910, "an economic menace to American miners is fast developing through the starvation wages paid Mexican miners," whose product competed with the output of American mines. Miners' unions in the United States — the United Mine Workers of America and the Western Federation of Miners — "are well aware that miners in Mexico would immediately organize and raise their standard of living if it were not for the guns of Diaz's rurales ready to shoot them down at the slightest pretext."

While we shall see that Mother Jones did not always agree with the ideology and tactics of some of the leading revolutionists, her support of the Mexican revolution never wavered. Overall, the singlehanded support she gave to the revolutionary cause in Mexico can be matched by few others in the United States. The *Appeal to Reason*, itself a foremost champion of the Mexican revolution and of Mexican revolutionists imprisoned in the United States, described a visit to its office by Mother Jones in the course of her tour raising funds for the Mexican revolutionists in U.S. jails:

Mother Jones has already raised almost four thousand dollars for the Mexican defense fund. To do this has required incessant toil and travel on her part. She has attended a number of conventions and delivered numerous addresses all the way from Indiana to Colorado and when she reached Girard (Kansas) she was almost exhausted, but not in the least cast down. On the contrary she was in the most buoyant spirits. She spoke in the most glowing terms of the reception accorded her and of the eagerness of the wage workers to do their share to rescue the Mexican patriots.

And the *Appeal* concluded:

Mother Jones is in her element working for the Mexican patriots and when they are rescued, as they are sure to be, they will have reason to remember no one more gratefully than this grand old warrior of the social revolution.[30]

In 1890, Mother Jones joined the newly-formed United Mine Workers of America as a paid organizer. She had already been an organizer in the labor movement for almost thirty years — a task which she began shortly after the tragedy of losing her husband (himself a union organizer) and four children in a southern yellow fever epidemic, and her possessions in the Chicago fire. The union with which she was now affiliated was a weak organization, and after an unsuccessful strike in 1894, the UMW was reduced to a virtual nonentity. In 1897 came another strike, this time against a series of wage cuts. With only 3,973 paid-up members, the UMW called a national strike. Much to the surprise of the operators, over 100,000 miners responded to the call.[31]

The amazing show of solidarity by the miners was actually not so amazing, for the miners had good reasons to revolt. The tyranny of the corporations in American society was felt by every worker, but it is doubtful if any felt it as much as the coal miners. Their wages had fallen drastically after the Civil War, and the downward trend continued. Since 65 to 80 percent of the cost of mining coal was labor cost, the more wages were reduced, the greater the profits. Wages were further reduced by the "truck system" which forced the miners to buy at company stores where they were charged exorbitant prices for shoddy goods. Excessive rates for company houses and high rates for the oil

31

and power they were compelled to buy from the operators only added to their discontent. Most grievous of all were the abominable conditions under which the miner worked. Every day he labored deep in water, his head and body drenched by seepage, his vision obscured by thick clouds of powder smoke and coal dust, gouging coal from seams often no more than three feet thick. Miles from the portal and 400 feet below the surface, he toiled in the most dangerous occupation in the nation, constantly risking bodily injury or death.

When a miner left in the morning dark for the mine, neither his wife, nor his children knew if they would ever see him again. In Schuylkill, Pennsylvania, alone, 566 miners were killed and 1,655 seriously injured over a seven-year period. In a single year, 1871, 112 miners of that county were killed and 339 badly injured. Nor was the carnage confined to Pennsylvania. In December 1907, in Monongah, West Virginia, 361 miners died in an explosion in the "safe" Monongah No. 6 and No. 8 mines of the Fairmont Coal Company — the largest coal-mine disaster in American history. That same December, explosions killed 34 at the Naomi mine in Fayette City, Pennsylvania; 57 at the Yolande mine in Yolande, Alabama; 239 at the Dorr mine in Jacobs Creek, Pennsylvania; and 11 at the Bernal mine in Carthage, New Mexico.

Year in and year out there was the grim task of bringing out the corpses. Dead miners were laid out in the mine wash house to be identified by hysterical relatives while other wives and children waited expectantly at the main shaft entrance for word of their loved ones. The dead were buried. Flags in the town were lowered to half-mast while a band marched with the procession. Miners came from the nearby towns to join the crowd. Within days after the explosion, stories would circulate that the miners had complained of gas in the mine at least several days before it blew up. A coroner's inquest might be started, but it usually ended abruptly after it became evident that miners had been afraid to complain of gas in the mine because they feared dismissal. The usual verdict was that explosion was an unavoidable accident, and if avoidable, it was the fault of the miners themselves.

Those who escaped sudden death in the mines often underwent a prolonged period of suffering before they too gave up their lives to the brutal and greedy industry. Breathing coal dust for 20 or 30 years slowly but inexorably strangled miners. Their hardened lung tissue no longer transferred enough oxygen into the blood.[32]

The coal operators were probably the most successful in the entire business community at using the governmental machinery to achieve their own ends. They were also the most arrogant. In 1902, when 150,000 Polish, Hungarian, Lithuanian, Ukranian, and Rumanian workers were idled in a strike, George Baer, the antiunion head of the Philadelphia & Reading Railroad (who won notoriety as "Divine Right Baer") said: "They don't suffer — they can't even speak English."[33]

Miners lived under a feudal-like system of company-owned towns in which the company was not only the employer but also the landlord. A familiar sight during strikes was the eviction of strikers. The evictions also revealed the stark poverty in which the miners lived. A *Charleston (West Virginia) Gazette* reporter wrote in 1902: "Most of them haven't much more furniture than a good stout man could carry out at one load, and there it sat out in the weather, the wife busy trying to cook a little handful of grit got at the commissary."[34] McAlister Coleman gives the following description of the brutal nature of the evictions:

I once drove up on a union truck loaded with tents and food to the outskirts of a town where an hour before sunup six families had been set out. Through slashing rains, our truck sloshed along a valley trail to the coal camp where we found the women in drenched house dresses trying to calm their frightened children. They had taken refuge under the shed back of a small church. The men were standing ankle-deep in the creek water that had overflowed its banks and was swirling past the doorsills of the company houses. In the sulphur-yellow water there was a confusion of broken bedsteads, cribs, chairs, tables, toys.[35]

Whole families spent months in tent colonies erected by the union, and they not only had to combat hunger and cold but hired gunmen and national guardsmen whose salaries were paid by the coal companies.

Mining was not only the most grueling industry in which to labor but it was also the hardest for a union organizer. In no industry was the right to organize more bitterly fought, and union recognition (except in 1900 when political considerations forced an early settlement) most often resulted only after hard, bloody battles between miners, company gunmen, coal and iron police, militiamen, and United States troops. The overwhelming power on the side of mine operators led to the loss of many miners' lives as well as strikes. Union organizers also paid with their lives. There were coal regions union organizers did not dare enter, for it was certain they would never leave alive.

Mother Jones organized miners in Pennsylvania, Ohio, Alabama, Michigan, Arizona, Colorado, and other states. But her longest organizing periods were spent in a state which was the most difficult of all in which to attempt to unionize — West Virginia. A full picture of what it meant to attempt to organize coal miners in the Mountain State will emerge in detail below, but here we should note that bad as were working and living conditions everywhere in mining states, those in West Virginia's coal mining communities were especially scandalous. Low wages, unsafe mines, employment of children, company-owned shanty shacks, company stores, private roads, private police ("the damned Baldwin-Felts thugs") faced the miners from birth to death. Furthermore, as Sheldon Harris notes: "The power structure in West Virginia at the turn of the century was patently frigid in the response to the blandishments of union organizers. West Virginia had long since become a captive victim of northern or foreign economic interest groups. English investors, Philadelphia capitalists, Wall Street tycoons invaded the state's fabulously rich coal lands in the early 1880s. The 1890s witnessed a further consolidation of their grasp over the coal fields." Small wonder that Malcolm Cowley wrote recently: "West Virginia has long been a colony of American imperialism, a sort of Third World nation within our borders."[36]

Union organizers were thus guerrilla fighters against this form of colonialism. During the 1897 strike, John Mitchell, then the UMW vice-president in charge of organizing West Virginia, and a fellow-organizer were "pursued in one company-owned town by armed guards who shot at them . . . [The unionists were forced to] swim in an icy mountain stream in order to escape death."[37]

In a profound statement sixty-three years ago, Mother Jones offered a clear explanation of why the mountains of West Virginia witnessed constant turmoil: "There is never peace in West Virginia because there is never justice. Injunctions and guns, like morphia, produce a temporary quiet . . . The strike is broken. But the next year the miners gathered their breath for another struggle. . . . When I get to the other side, I shall tell God Almighty about West Virginia."[38]

Throughout her career, Mother Jones had to face the cry that she represented anarchy, insurrection, socialism, and violence while the operators and employers in general represented law and order. She was called "the most dangerous woman in America," "a mischief maker worse than Borgia."[39] But the opinion of employers and their agents did not matter to her. She ignored the attacks and went where the danger was greatest — crossing militia lines, spending weeks in damp prisons, incurring the wrath of governors, presidents, and coal operators, as she devoted her life to the American labor movement, helping organize workers all over the United States and even in Canada — child textile workers, street carmen, steel workers, metal miners, women in breweries, and women in the garment trades, but above all her beloved coal miners. She did all this with the only tools she needed: "convictions and a voice."

Mother Jones was a "walking delegate" when labor organizers were given that name, but she was one in more than name. Dressed in black, wearing hip boots, she walked along the railroad tracks and dirt roads, waded or was carried piggyback through icy streams, to reach the coal camps and deliver her speeches. She stayed with miners' families when she was in the mountains of West Virginia or Colorado. She ate what they ate and shared sleeping quarters with the children. It was a hard life for anyone, let alone a woman in her eighties.

But she refused to rest. Again and again she would get a hurried call from some harassed local union official: "For God's sake come over to my area." It might be Roaring Branch or Hazelton, Pennsylvania, or Fairmont, West Virginia, or somewhere in Colorado where the miners were desperate after a long struggle and ready to go back to work or in need of funds which she might be able to raise once she saw the situation at first-hand.[40] It could be a letter, like the following from Thomas Haggerty, reading: ". . . I hope you will see your way clear to come here about Christmas time if So let me know . . . com [sic] if you can as those People is for you & spishely [sic] the textile workers." Or it might be a telegram like the following:

SHAMOKIN,PA.

MOTHER MARY JONES
CARE UNITED MINE WORKERS

MOTHER THERE IS A STRIKE AT THE SILK MILLS HERE WILL YOU COME (A)T ONCE I KNOW YOU CAN DO LOTS OF GOOD COME IF POSSIBLE

FROM A MINER[41]

Wherever or whoever it was, the "Angel of the Miners" would go, and with flaming words and rich wit, she would bolster the lagging courage and help carry on the struggle against starvation, gunmen, and other manifestations of company power. As her reputation grew, appeals came regularly from unions with members on strike and from men imprisoned for union activity, or because they were being framed to eliminate them from the labor scene. She answered all of them. At a time when there were no jet planes, she traveled thousands of miles in dusty trains. To avoid arrest or attacks by company gunmen, after having been alerted by friendly trainmen, she would complete the journey in a baggage car or even a cattle car. Her fame as a strike leader and labor agitator made her a popular speaker with the rank-and-file workers and working-class socialists, although union officials may have sometimes regretted inviting her as she lashed out at their luxurious style of life and their class-collaboration policies, and accused them of exploiting workers instead of helping them combat their employers.

A typical Mother Jones experience is described by her in a letter to Chicago Socialist Thomas J. Morgan:

I have been up to My Ears in a Strike of the Miners here I have not had a moment to Spare 20 thousand men and women are here to be looked after I have not had a moment to Spare for the last Six weeks. I just got back after ten miles going and coming in a blizzard to a house away from civilization. I find the father down with Typhoid fever the Mother and Six children Shivering with cold no clothing not a thing to Eat.[42]

Or when she wrote to William B. Wilson from Helena:

I spoke in Helena on Miners day the 13th of the Month Back to Butte for two more meetings then I go to Coakdale for the Coal Miners then I go East.

She certainly knew how to move workers. The shaming of workers into active commitment to the union cause was a strong feature of her speeches. She would indict the men for their willingness to endure slavery and their cowardice. "If you are too cowardly to fight, there are enough women to come in and beat the hell out of you," she told the Colorado miners to "laughter and applause." But she simultaneously offered them a way through the union to prove their manhood and win their freedom.

Operators referred to Mother Jones's "anarchist speeches," but in actuality, she saw herself as holding the miners in check from wreaking uncontrolled violence. While she encouraged beating of strikebreakers and attacks on police and militia, she also felt that her presence kept the fearfully exploited miners from senseless violence. As she put it: "Men on strike are at a terrible nervous tension. They must give vent to their feelings. Leave them alone [unguided] and they will do murder in their mad, misguided excitement."[43]

Workers responded to Mother Jones as they did to few others. This "little old woman in a black bonnet, with a high falsetto voice and a handsome face framed in curly white hair and lighted by shrewd kindly eyes"[44] was able to move workers as no one else, even including speakers like Eugene V. Debs and "Big Bill" Haywood. There are innumerable reports which testify to her effectiveness. One in the *New York Times* of February 25, 1900, read: "On Saturday night [February 17] Mrs. Jones made her last speech [at Blossberg], and the 'striking' portion of Arnot, together with the citizens of Blossberg, turned out in full force to do honor to the old lady who is generally credited with having won the strike." A typical headline read: " 'Mother' Jones Talks To Miners on Cabin Creek And Strike Will Follow." A correspondent for the *United Mine Workers Journal* who heard the speech wrote: "Mother Jones is worth one hundred agitators in the West Virginia field." He noted that she was especially effective in arousing support for the union among black miners. "Mother Jones spoke of the condition of the negro in slavery times and the present, and was lustily cheered by our colored friends in such language as this: 'Hit 'em again, Mother Jones!' 'Tell it to 'em again.' " He concluded:

Mother Jones is indeed a wonderful woman. She has a great mind and retentive memory. I don't think she ever forgets anything she reads. She is a terror to the operators and their henchmen. Let me say right here Mother Jones is doing a grand and noble work for humanity. It is those who work for suffering humanity that their memory will live in ages to come. It was Lincoln, William Lloyd Garrison and Wendell Phillips who advocated the emancipation of the slaves. Mother Jones advocates the emancipation of the miners and all other wage earners. Long may she live to continue the good work.[45]

Writing in the Vancouver *Daily Province* of June 11, 1914, a reporter described how Mother Jones came across to a Canadian:

Modulating her voice from a low tense murmur, as she narrated some terrible incident of one of the strikes in which she has participated, to a shrill note of frenzy as she condemned in virile terms the forces she considered the enemies of labor, the female orator dramatically appealed to the sympathies of her auditors. She thrilled them one moment by a forceful arraignment of the "bosses," as she called the mine owners and other employers, evoked shudders by detailing some gruesome episode and sent them into gales of laughter soon after with a humorous remark or anecdote. She held her large audience spellbound for nearly two hours.

The headlines in the *Denver Post* of November 22, 1903, testified to the remarkable power Mother Jones had to influence workers. They read:

MOTHER JONES BARS SETTLEMENT PLANS: MITCHELL IS DEFIED

Celebrated Woman Orator of the Mine Workers Professes Knowledge of the Colorado Situation Superior to That of the National President

Arguments of Organizer Ream Proved Ineffective in Checking the Eloquence of "Mother" Jones — Operators Non-Plussed by the Result of Conference at Louisville

The story behind the headlines involved the rejection by the convention representing miners in northern Colorado of a strike settlement recommended by UMW president John Mitchell, after Mother Jones had charged the agreement with abandoning the striking miners in southern Colorado. Mother Jones's speech which caused the convention to reject Mitchell's recommendation appears below, but here it is worth reprinting the account by the amazed reporter for the *Denver Post:*

President John Mitchell of the United Mine Workers of America, the most powerful labor leader in this or any other country, has been defied and defeated by officials in his own organization.

The chief power that accomplished this most remarkable result is "Mother" Jones who heretofore has always worked with Mr. Mitchell, and whose influence over mine workers the country over is nothing less than magical.

Her irresistible power was proved beyond question at the mass meeting of miners in the Northern field yesterday when in spite of the fact that the operators granted every concession demanded by the men, the proposition to return to work was defeated by a vote of 228 to 165.

This rejection of the concessions was voted in the face of a telegram signed by President Mitchell urging the acceptance of the proposition of the operators. . . .[46]

37

Armed with this telegram Mr. [John F.] Ream [Mitchell's representative] went into the mass meeting and made a determined fight to secure an acceptance of the terms and a resumption of work Monday morning. He was ably assisted by M. Grant Hamilton, a Colorado representative of the American Federation of Labor.

All day long Mr. Ream pleaded with the miners to accept the advice of President Mitchell. . . . It was believed that he had won the day and that the men would go to work Monday.

But the pendulum was to swing again. . . . President William Howells of District No. 15, United Mine Workers of America . . . made a calm, cold speech giving the basis of his objection to the settlement, under any terms, of the strike in the Northern field as calculated to injure the chances of success in the South. . . .

While Mr. Howells' address was received with some applause, it was seen clearly that he had not carried the miners with him . . . [and] there was but little doubt that the men would have voted with President Mitchell.

But "Mother" Jones had not been heard. There were loud calls for her, and she was not slow coming to the front of the stage. She saw victory in her deep black eyes and there was a vigor about her step which boded no good for the friends of an acceptance of the operators' terms. She began her speech in a low conversational tone and referred to the miners as "boys." She was quiet and calm at first and smiled now and then, and as she made a humorous reference to the situation or scored a hit on the operators. She was dressed in deep black, with not a single shred of white to relieve the somber effect of her attire. Her snow white hair and her complexion as white as Roman marble contrasted with her attire and made a most striking effect. She did not waste much time with quiet speech. She soon raised her voice to a pitch of fervid eloquence and sent her thrusts home with the dramatic effect of the brilliant orator.

It was her hour. She loves to urge the men to stand firm, and she despises compromise. She said so as often as the rules of repetition would permit.

She had judged her audience well. The men responded to every appeal with enthusiasm, and her magnificent speech made her at once the great hero of the critical hour. She won the men over to her cause. She did more. She brought about the first signal defeat that the hitherto invincible John Mitchell has ever sustained. The man who brought coal barons and Wall Street to his feet was for the time forgotten before the sweeping eloquence of this remarkable woman.[47]

The mesmerized reporter followed as she walked off the platform to the railroad station. "As she stepped on the train," he wrote, "the passengers wishing to get on crowded the stand, and a mother with two small children was hemmed in. In her strong voice she commanded the men to stand back and let the little ones out. They obeyed, and she helped the mother off with her children. "I have no children myself, except all of the toiling thousands of this sad earth," she said, as she handed the two tots down the steps, "but I love children and I sympathize with the dear mothers, bless their hearts, whenever I see them."[48]

The account by the awestruck reporter was accurate except for one error. Mother Jones did not object to the terms of the settlement because "she despises compromise." She opposed them because it would have meant betraying the miners in the southern fields who had struck together with their union brothers in the north, and who would be left at the mercy of the powerful corporations and doomed to defeat without the support of the miners in the northern fields — a prediction that unfortunately came to pass after the union bureaucracy, taking advantage of Mother Jones's absence in the southern field, quickly called another convention in the north and jammed through a resolution approving the settlement and ordering the miners to return to work.[49]

In all other respects, however, the account in the *Denver Post* is completely accurate, and is but one of many testimonials to the ability of Mother Jones to sway a working-class audience. When one realizes, moreover, that many of those in the audiences she addressed were often the "new immigrants" from southeastern Europe, unfamiliar with the English language, and that they told reporters that the language barrier did not keep them from understanding Mother Jones's message,[50] one must agree with the journal bearing her name that she was "one of the great orators of her day."

Mother Jones knew how to make good use of music to entertain and warm up a crowd before she launched into a speech. She once reported to UMW President John Mitchell that she was using a phonograph in her organizing campaign. "I play all kinds of comic pieces and get the crowd in a good humor." In one of her organizing drives, Mother Jones came to the labor rally escorted by a brass band composed of the brothers and sisters of a family sympathetic to the union. After this, the Rhodes Family Band became known as "Mothers Jones's Band" from Coal Run.[51]

The five speeches Mother Jones delivered during the West Virginia strike of 1912-13 (published in their entirety below) reveal a good deal of how she moved the miners to battle and raised their hopes for victory. Though we cannot convey the "Irish lilt" or voice intonations which marked her speeches, we can note the specific points she made again and again. Despite the sometimes rambling style she adopted, these points came through clearly.

Mother Jones made sure the audience knew that she herself, despite her age, was tough and fearless. She used her age to reprove miners for not being involved in changing things in West Virginia. "If you are too cowardly to fight, I will fight. You ought to be ashamed of yourselves, actually to the Lord you ought, just to see an old woman who is not afraid of all the blood-hounds." In each of her five speeches, she related incidents where, despite threats of being shot, she carried out her mission for labor. "I want to tell you something," she said in one of her speeches. "The mine owners nor [Governor] Glasscock haven't enough militia in the state of West Virginia to keep me from talking."

The point was clear. If an old woman could be brave and defiant then so too could the miners. If "one women, eighty years old, with her head grey, can come in and scare hell out of the whole bunch [of bloodhounds and villains]," a bunch of exploited miners could so even more. Her age, in fact, represented a special mission: "I am eighty years old — I have passed the eightieth mile stone in human history. I will be eighty more, for I have got a contract with God Almighty to stay with you until your chains are broken."

When Mother Jones announced that should the time come "in the history of this struggle that a mine owner or Baldwin guards will intimidate me I want to die that hour," miners must have felt that they could do no less.

Mother Jones often made use of the coal operators to make her point. In one speech on the levee at Charleston, she stoped in the midst of her speech and asked a spectator in the crowd: "Say, are you an operator, with that cigar in your grub? Take your medicine, because we are going to get after you, no doubt about it." At one point she called to the operators present in the audience asking if they knew what really went into their profits: "God Almighty, come with me and see the wrecks of women, of babies, then ask yourselves, 'How can I sleep at night?' How can your wife sleep at night?"

She followed this with the tale of a poodle whose "royal dogship" was cared for luxuriously by the wife of an operator. She then explained that the wife "had lived off the blood of women and children, she decorated her neck and hands with the blood of innocent children, and I am here to prove it to the world." Speaking on the day before martial law was declared in the strike area, she warned: "But I want to tell you operators that by the gods you will have to settle with us! We are no slaves, no peons, and we are not going to submit to you." The miners roared their approval.

She told the miners they were not being true to their manhood by tolerating the bestial conditions in mines and the mining communities; that they were the ones really responsible for the terrible lot of their wives and children:

No wonder these mine owners beat your wives, no wonder your children will rise up and curse you. It's time for you to stop it. . . . You are to blame and no one else. You have stood for it. You don't stand in your union. If you would, when you were organized up New River, you wouldn't have this condition today. . . . If you were true to your organizations and true to your manhood, you would not have to bother with the guards.

But in the next breath she would tell the miners that they could change these conditions by fighting. She also told them that they were in a class struggle. "You are not dealing with rotten politics. You are dealing with a system that is old and strong." It was a class war and there would be no peace until the issue was settled, "and settled right . . . until man gets justice." Nor was it a struggle confined to West

Virginia. The miners were not the only ones oppressed by capitalism. Mother Jones told them not to forget that the capitalists sent troops to murder workers in France, Germany, Spain, Italy, Russia, as well as in the United States. And there was "despotic Mexico" under the Czar of the New World, Porfirio Díaz. But at least in those countries the steps of the nation's capitol were not inscribed, as in West Virginia, with the words, "Mountaineers are Free." And Mother Jones bitterly proclaimed the irony of it: "God Almighty, men, go down through this nation and see the damnable, infamous condition that is there. In no nation of the world will you find such a condition. I look with horror when I see these conditions."

Graphically Mother Jones described the "murders" of children toiling in the mines, the wives left alone with children to feed after the husband was killed in the mine. "Look at those little children, the rising generation, yes look at the little ones, yes look at the women assaulted." It was for these children, for the future generations to come, that they would be fighting if they were only true to their manhood.

Finally, she again blamed the miners for electing "company pirates" every time they had "a chance to free themselves." "Elect judges and governors from your ranks," she told them. And: "You can carry a bayonet on November 5th and you can go to the ballot box and put a bayonet in there *and stick it to their very heart*. (Loud applause)." But she made it clear that she put the economic struggle first in the class war:

I want to say that the man who is not true to the economical part of his life is not true to the political. The labor movement has two wings. She has an economic wing and the political wing. When you are organized thoroughly on the economic you can march and make demands of the other fellows you want.[52]

When Mother Jones told a reporter "I love children," she had already demonstrated that fact in deeds as well as words. In the summer of 1903, she led what a paper called "a second 'children's crusade'" from Philadelphia, heading an "army" of "400 striking juvenile textile workers" in a march from the City of Brotherly Love to President Theodore Roosevelt's summer home in Oyster Bay, New York, to call the nation's and the president's attention to the evils of child labor. As she departed with her "army," Mother Jones told the press:

The sight of little children at work in the mills when they ought to be at school or at play always rouses me. I found the conditions in this city (of Philadelphia) deplorable, and I resolved to do what I could do to shorten the hours of toil of the striking textile workers so as to gain more liberty for the children and women. I led a parade of children through this city — the cradle of Liberty — but the citizens were not moved to pity by the object lesson.

The curse of greed so pressed on their hearts that they could not pause to express their pity for future men and women who are being stunted mentally and morally and physically, so that they cannot possibly become good citizens. I

41

cannot believe that the public conscience is so callous that it will not respond. I am going to Philadelphia to see if there are people with human blood in their veins. . . .[53]

We will see below what results followed the "children's crusade" of 1903 led by Mother Jones. But all who witnessed this phenomenal event were impressed by the devotion of the seventy-three-year-old Socialist and trade union organizer for the children of America.

How deeply Mother Jones stirred all women, feminists, Socialists, middle-class reformers, woman suffragists and anti-suffragists, is illustrated by statements made during a meeting called by a coalition of such women's organizations on April 23, 1914, at New York's Cooper Union to protest President Wilson's action invading Mexico and occupying Vera Cruz over a trivial incident judged an insult to American "honor" which had occurred at Tampico. (The meeting was also called to protest the shooting down of men, women, and children in Colorado during the strike of the United Mine Workers culminating in the "Ludlow Massacre," which are discussed below.) In the course of her speech, Florence Kelley, famous correspondent of Frederick Engels, prominent Socialist, anti-child labor, anti-sweatshop champion, and leader of the National Consumers' League, demanded to know what business the United States had introducing "intensive guidance" into Mexico when the government had shown itself so totally incapable "of handling one poor American rebel, the aged Mother Jones, aged, gray haired and bowed down with years of fighting against the men controlling the country." She again referred to Mother Jones, declaring: "We have our own rebels. We have ours right here in the United States. One is a white-haired old woman who spends most of her time going in and out of prison." This was a reference especially to the recent imprisonment of Mother Jones in West Virginia and Colorado for leading the miners' strikes in those states.

During her speech, Helen Todd, a California woman suffrage leader, startled the audience by stating: "There is only one cause for which I would go to war, and that is for the woman I think the greatest in the world — Mother Jones." Among the resolutions unanimously adopted was one denouncing the "treatment generally accorded to miners, and especially the much-beloved woman, Mother Jones, by the officialdom of Colorado."[54]

The love felt by workers for Mother Jones was not confined to the United States. When she visited Mexico in 1921 to attend the Congress of the Pan-American Federation of Labor at the invitation of the newly installed president of Mexico, Alvaro Obregón, her reputation as a fighter for the oppressed in general and the working class in particular, and for the Mexican revolutionaries imprisoned in the United States, produced an amazing outpouring of working-class affection and respect. Fred Mooney, a leader of District 17 UMW accompanied

Mother Jones to Mexico City, and his account of the trip is filled with dramatic incidents of the welcome Mother Jones received from the Mexican workers and trade unions of all persuasions. They traveled in a Pullman car provided by the Mexican government, had all their expenses paid while in Mexico, were given a book of tickets which could be presented for food, lodging and drinks, and had two servants and a taxi available at all times. About forty miles from Mexico City, their train suddenly stopped, and when Mooney looked out he saw a "string of taxi cabs blocking the railroad tracks." About 40 strikers from a jewelry factory had come by auto to meet Mother Jones. "They used red flags to stop the train, then boarded it. . . . They threw crimson carnations and blue violets around Mother until only her head and shoulders could be seen." While throwing the flowers, they continuously yelled "Welcome to Mexico, Madre Juanita" — the name Spanish-speaking workers gave Mother Jones.[55]

But this was only the beginning. When she arrived at the Buena Vista station in Mexico City, there were about 2,000 workers waiting, "among whom," the reporter for *El Universal* of Mexico City wrote, "were outstanding a large feminine contingent from the factories 'El Recuerdo,' 'El Buen Tono,' 'Tabacelera,' 'Cigarrera,' 'La Estrella,' 'Departmentos Fabules,' the Trade Union of Waitresses, etc., all of whom carried, as did the male element, the banners of their respective groups." The reporter continued:

Mother Jones was the object of singular interest. With ninety years on her shoulders, she is one of the most indefatigable fighters for working-class organizations in the United States.

Amidst a veritable shower of flowers, Mother Jones was brought in an auto from the platform of the station to the "Glorieta Cuauhtemos," where another contingent of trade union workers were awaiting her. They applauded her and threw fragrant sprays of roses. In the "Glorieta," a demonstration was organized to honor Mother Jones, and was followed by a parade to the Hotel St. Francis where several Mexican workers spoke, and the guest of honor answered. She did so in virile and intrepid language, saying, in short, that when she first visited Mexico, she never believed the workers' movement in this country would have reached its present numbers and effectiveness; that she had been struggling in the field of ideas and action for years and years, a struggle which would end only with her death; that she had dedicated her existence to seeking the economic, moral, and cultural development of the working class. She ended with a tribute to the Mexican workers affirming that only on the day when a single language and a single nation would exist on earth, would human happiness have been achieved.

Mother Jones is an elderly lady whose appearance is as modest as it is admirable, a woman with a very friendly behavior.[56]

"Tough, fearless old Mother Jones" were words that usually introduced contemporary newspaper accounts, and quite often the word "profane" was added. Of her fearlessness there are so many accounts that it would take a small book merely to reprint them. Here is how John Farrance, author of one of the versions of the ballad, "The Death of Mother Jones," put it in a 1958 letter to labor folklorist Archie Green:

I saw her one time in Monongahela. She was trying to organize the mines. She came down Pike Street in a buggy and horse. Two company thugs grabbed the horse by the bridle and told her to turn around and get down road. She wore a gingham apron and she reached under it and pulled out a special .38 pistol and told them to turn her horse loose, and they sure did. She continued on to the park and spoke to a large crowd of miners. She wasn't afraid of the devil.[57]

Mania Baumgartner, who was born and raised in the mining regions of West Virginia, recently recalled some striking experiences with Mother Jones, which also provide insight into her organizing technique and reveal how shallow is the charge that she had no rapport with women:

I first met Mother Jones at my cousin's home. There was a miners' meeting going on and Mother Jones was there. I was waiting on the front porch when Mrs. Jones came out. She looked at me and then walked up to me. She asked my name and I told her. She asked me where I was from and I told her Pigeon Creek. She asked me what my father did and I told her he was a carpenter. Then she asked me how old I was and I told her I wasn't so old, but old enough. Then she looked at me closer and said: "I'd like to have you go with me sometime," and I told her: "Oh, Mrs. Jones, I can't go along. You ain't afraid and I am." She said: "I'll teach you not to be afraid." But I said: "I'm afraid, Mrs. Jones, I couldn't go."

One day after that, she came driving up to our home in a little one-horse wagon. She stopped and called, "Come with me, I'm just going to make a little talk. We won't be gone long." I asked her: "Now there ain't going to be any danger, is there, Mrs. Jones?" "Not much," she answered.

I went into the house and told my mother I was going with her and my mother said I'd better not go. It was dangerous to be with Mother Jones and I might get killed. But I went on and got in the wagon. . . .

When asked how Mother Jones looked, Mrs. Baumgartner replied, "Why, do you know what she had on from the skirt down? She was wearing a pair of men's overall pants! And a man's shirt! Yes, and some funny looking boots. They were sort of wool, men's kind and they come up high, like they'd protect her if she fell. She had a man's hat, too, pulled down on her head."

When we got to the hollow, I noticed a lot of men alongside the road and I wondered what in the world was Mrs. Jones going to do here. Then she stopped the wagon and told me to get out. She got out and reached under the wagon seat and pulled out a great big club, made like a ball bat, but not so long. I asked her what she was going to do with that. She said that I ought to have sense enough to know what she'd do with that if someone bothered her or me.

Well, we walked into those woods and there were a whole big lot of men standing around. Mrs. Jones climbed up on a stump and she reached down and got a hold of my hand and told me to step up on the rock alongside the stump. Then she went to talking and I never heard such talking in all my life. Brother, she cussed like a drunk man. She said, "You lowdown rascals, you. You know what's good for you and what's bad for you. You looks bad to me already." You see, she was trying to organize the union. She'd say anything. Told them she'd bet they didn't have no breakfast and half of them didn't have no home to live in. That they'd better get someone in there that would do something for them so as they could live neat. Then all at once, KA-WHOOM! A bullet went right between our heads and I'm a-telling you that liked to scare me to death. I said: "Now listen here, old woman, I'm getting out from here."

She didn't do anything, Never a blink. She never paid a bit more attention than nothing. No, not a bit. She just said, "Well, you can shoot again, you — — — . You missed me that time." At that the men got tickled and they got to laughing 'cause the bullet didn't hit her between the eyes. I told her, "Sister, you're gonna be left alone if you don't hurry up and come go with me." I was just about ready to get a start out of that hollow and she seen I was scared. I told her, "Mrs. Jones, you'd better hurry up now. You're gonna be left by yourself. I don't want to leave you and I won't. But I want you to hurry up and come on and go."

Then she turned to those men and she said, "You dirty low down — — — s, you. You know! You know what you're doing. You're rotten. You're lowdown. You go home tonight and sit down with your little children and with your wife. Sit down and take your pencil and clear paper and *write*. Just write how you're living and what you've got. And just let the world know how you're living, and what you could have if you'd do the right thing." Then she jumped off that stump and said, "That's my farewell word to you, but I'll tell you one thing I'll get you in the end."

We walked out of there and she never looked back. When we were in the wagon, she told me: "Now, don't you get scared. Just don't say too much about what was said or nothing. We'll be alright." When we got to my house, Mrs. Jones came in with me and stayed awile. But pretty soon, I could see she was thinking about something and she said she'd better get on. There was something she wanted to check on and she believed she could make it on home. She got up, hugged and kissed me and said, "Now I'm going to come and get you again." I told her, "Yes, you will — if you can catch me."[58]

The events just described occurred in West Virginia in 1919 when Mother Jones was almost ninety years old!

Mother Jones did come back to visit young Monia several times, but she was never able to get her to attend another meeting. The two, however, (and Monia's mother) became good friends.

Mania Baumgartner told Lois C. McLean: "There never was anyone like her." She was correct. In 1922 George P. West nominated Mother Jones for *The Nation*'s "list of the twelve greatest American women."[59] I am confident that readers of *Mother Jones Speaks* will conclude that, with all her inconsistencies and contradictions, Mother Jones deserves a place on any list of the greatest women of all time.

Notes

1. Reprinted in Phil Wagner, editor, *Debs: His Life, Writings and Speeches*, St. Louis, 1908, p. 270.

2. *The Nation*, July 19, 1922, pp. 70-71.

3. It has been estimated that about 10,000 copies of the book were sold by the publisher in the first edition. (Dale Featherling, *Mother Jones—The Miners' Angel*, Carbondale, Ill., 1974, p. 194.)

4. David Montgomery, "The Conventional Wisdom," *Labor History* 13 (Winter, 1972): 132.

5. *Autobiography of Mother Jones*, Chicago, 1925, pp. 240-41.

6. Keith Dix, "Mother Jones," *People's Appalachia* 1 (June-July, 1970): 6. Unaware of the existence of the unpublished studies by Raffale and Mikeal, Dix also complained that "no theses or dissertations have been done on her." (*Ibid.*) Apart from this, however, his complaint was justified. Just a year before his article appeared, Melvyn Dubofsky's *We Shall Be All: A History of the IWW* was published, and it had not a single reference to Mother Jones even though she had been the only woman at the original January conference and one of the delegates to the July, 1905 founding convention. (New York, 1969).

7. *Ibid.*

8. See H. B. Lee, *Bloodletting in Appalachia*, Morgantown, West Virginia, 1969, p. 130.

9. Featherling, *op. cit.*, p. 22. In similar fashion, Professor Hoyt N. Wheeler sums up Mother Jones as an "aged but vigorous and profane labor agitator," "a veteran combatant in the labor wars in which the United Mine Workers became involved." "She is perhaps," he concedes, "the most colorful character of this era of American labor history." ("Mountain Mine Wars: An Analysis of the West Virginia Mine Wars of 1912-1913 and 1920-1921," *Business History Review* 50 (Spring, 1976): 71. At least Featherling, while acknowledging that Mother Jones was colorful, adds that "she cannot be dismissed as merely that. She was also extraordinarily effective in her limited field. Militiamen do not jail women for weeks because they are colorful, governors do not deport them on grounds of quaintness, and mayors do not forbid them to speak. More important, hardbitten miners do not at the risk of eviction, starvation, and death, throw down their tools at the call of an addled old woman. Rather, Mother Jones's involved personality provided the precise psychological support for those who, like her, yearned for both a preindustrial Arcadia and a restructured future." (*Ibid.*, p. 160.) I am not sure when Mother Jones urged the establishment of a "preindustrial Arcadia." On the contrary, she insisted that machinery was inevitable, but had to be owned by the people.

10. Eugene V. Debs to Mother Jones, June 12, 1901, original in William B. Wilson Papers, Historical Society of Pennsylvania; copy in Eugene V. Debs Papers, Indiana State University Library, Terre Haute, Indiana; *International Socialist Review* (September, 1902): 83.

11. *Charleston (West Virginia) Gazette*, June 11, 1912, and reprinted in *International Socialist Review*, March, 1913, pp. 418-19.

12. Reprinted in *Washington Star*, December 11, 1930. The *Star* summed up a whole series of similar obituary editorials under the heading, "Mother Jones Dies Honored By All Americans."

Not included, however, was the obituary editorial of the *New York Times* which applauded Mother Jones for her role "in the great labor troubles beginning with the early '70s," and lauded her as "passionately humane, a hater of injustice," but took great pleasure from the fact "that she and Mr. ROCKEFEL-LER came to know each other better and to recognize each other's merits." It was especially pleased that "the fiery agitator, the 'anarchist' and what not of legend lived to be respected by Presidents." ("Mother Jones," *New York Times,* December 2, 1930.)

13. Vern Smith, "From An Era That Has Passed: Mother Jones," *Labor Defender,* January, 1931, p. 16.

14. Gerda Lerner, "Women's Rights and American Feminism," *American Scholar* 40 (1971): 237.

15. Seattle *Post-Intelligencer,* May 31, 1914, Everett *Daily Herald,* June 5, 1914. *See also* pp. 56, 136-38, 141, 270, 362-63.

It is interesting, in this connection, that Beatrice Webb, the British Fabian Socialist, signed Mrs. Humphrey Ward's petition against votes for women. (Norman and Jeanne MacKenzie, *The Diary of Beatrice Webb,* volume I, 1873-1892, Cambridge, Mass., 1982, p. 122.

16. *Boston Herald,* September 11, 1904, Magazine Section, pp. 1, 3.

17. Priscilla Long, *Mother Jones, Woman Organizer,* Boston, 1976, pp. 35-36.

18. *See* Philip S. Foner, *Women and the American Labor Movement: From Colonial Times to the Eve of World War I,* New York, 1979, pp. 128-47.

19. Long, *op. cit.,* pp. 35-36.

20. Neil K. Basen, "Kate Richards O'Hare: The 'First Lady' of American Socialism, 1901-1917," *Labor History* 21 (Spring, 1980): 172-73. *See also* Philip S. Foner and Sally M. Miller, eds., *Kate Richards O'Hare: Selected Writings and Speeches,* Baton Rouge, La., 1982, pp. 3, 13, 103.

21. Rosalyn Baxandall, Linda Gordon, Susan Reverby, editors, *American Working Women: A Documentary History 1600 to the Present,* New York, 1976.

22. Susan Estabrook Kennedy, *If All We Did Was to Weep At Home: A History of White Working Class Women in America,* Bloomington, Indiana, 1979, pp. 1115-16 and p. 266 n. 6; Meredith Tax, *The Rising of the Women: Feminist Solidarity and Class Conflict, 1880-1917,* New York and London, 1980.

Two recent books dealing with socialism and women which have no room for a discussion of Mother Jones are: Mari Jo Buhle, *Women and American Socialism 1870-1920,* Urbana, Illinois, 1981, and Sally M. Miller, ed., *Flawed Liberation: Socialism and Feminism,* Westport, Conn., 1982. Buhle even sees a virtue in omitting discussion of "leftist heroes like Lucy Parsons, Emma Goldman, 'Mother' Jones, or Elizabeth Gurley Flynn." (p. XII). Of course, Mother Jones was not merely a "leftist hero." She was revered by all workers, Socialist and non-Socialist.

23. In a talk at the May, 1972 meeting of the Raleigh County Historical Society, McLean describes how she discovered Mother Jones and became interested in doing research on her life. (*Beckley (W. Va.) Post-Herald,* May 30, 1972.) I am indebted to Ms. McLean for furnishing me a copy of the report.

24. In a circular issued in June 1972, Charles H. Kerr & Co. announced the reprint of the 1925 edition with a new introduction by Fred Thompson and added: "Wherever men dig coal her name is revered." Thompson's introductions to the 1972 and 1974 editions are useful, but also have to be read with care because of inaccuracies.

25. The date 1837 is based on Lois McLean's estimate that Mother Jones was born seven years later than she asserted in her autobiography.

26. The pamphlet was a 16-page collection entitled *Thoughts of Mother*

Jones compiled from her writings and speeches. There is a copy in the Tamiment Institute Library, New York University.

27. In its review the *Washington Times* called the play "a partial success." Clipping in Mother Mary Harris Jones Papers, Department of Archives and Manuscripts, Catholic University of America, Washington, D.C. A TV documentary film, funded by the National Endowment for the Humanities, is in the making.

Another play of the period is *The Trial of Mother Jones* by Roger Holzberg which is partly factual and part myth. Set during the strike of the United Mine Workers against the Colorado Fuel & Iron Company in 1913-14, in which Mother Jones played a leading part, the play departs from historical events by presenting Mother Jones on trial by a committee of United Mine Workers' officials on the charge that she openly and continuously advanced the use of violence over the objection of union officers. At the end of the trial, the audience is asked to vote on whether or not Mother Jones was guilty or innocent of the charge. For a discussion of the play, *see* Raymond L. Hogler, "Labor History as Drama: *The Trial of Mother Jones,*" *Labor Studies Journal* 5 (1980): 146-49.

28. Mary Lee Settle, *The Scapegoat,* New York, 1980, pp. 196-202. Ms. Settle won the 1978 National Book Award for an earlier novel on West Virginia, *Blood Tie.*

29. *Daily World,* May 27, 1981. While a few women were reported to have worked in family-owned strip mines, the number of women in the mines in 1973 appears to have been close to zero. Five years later, it had increased to 2,000 women among the 200,000 coal miners in the United States — or 1 percent of the total. The figure reached 3,061 in June 1980. The first National Conference of Women Coal Miners took place in June 1979 at West Virginia State College at Institute, West Virginia. For the story of women coal miners and the national conferences, *see* Philip S. Foner, *Women and the American Labor Movement: From World War I to the Present,* New York, 1980, pp. 544-50.

30. *Appeal to Reason,* March 27, 1909.

In his article, "The American Socialists and the Mexican Revolution of 1910," *Southwest Social Science Quarterly* 43 (September, 1962), Ivie E. Caldenhead, Jr. achieves the impossible. He devotes fifteen pages (103-117) to this subject without once mentioning Mother Jones's contributions to the Mexican Revolution.

31. John E. George, "The Coal Miners' Strike of 1897," *Quarterly Journal of Economics,* 12 (January, 1898): 186-208.

32. McAlister Coleman, *Men and Coal,* New York, 1943, pp. 36-68; Arthur Suffern, *The Coal Miners Struggle for Industrial Status,* New York, 1926, pp. 31-72; Isador Lubin, *Miners' Wages and the Cost of Coal,* New York, 1924, pp. 230-38; Andrew Roy, *A History of the Coal Miners of the United States: From the Development of the Mines to the Close of the Anthracite Strike of 1902,* Columbus, 1905, pp. 75, 103-05, 162-64, 217-25, 291-93, 302-06, 326-32; F. D. Tyron, et. al., *What the Coal Commission Found,* Baltimore, 1925, pp. 94-106; William Graebner, "The Coal Mine Operator and Safety: A Study of Business Reform in the Progressive Period," *Labor History* 14 (Fall, 1973): 483-505.

33. Baer's "divine rights" remark went in part: "The rights and interests of the laboring man will be protected and cared for, not by the labor agitators, but by the Christian men to whom God in His infinite wisdom, has given control of the property interests of the country." (*Independent,* August 28, 1902, p. 2043.)

34. *Charleston (W. Va.) Gazette,* September 2, 1907. In his study of socialism

in West Virginia, Frederick Allan Barkey notes that miners who became Socialists often indicated in interviews "that such evictions fixed indelibly on their minds the helplessness of the miner." He cites the case of the miner Gustave Frisk, who was born and raised in Poznan, Poland, and came to work in the mines of West Virginia after working for a few years in the peninsula section of Michigan. During the strike of 1902, Frisk contracted typhoid fever. Despite the warning of the coal company doctor, Frisk was thrown out of his house and onto the public highway. "In a tent colony where he fought a desperate fight against the disease, he became convinced that the American ideal of decency and human dignity could not be achieved under a capitalistic economic system." (Frederick Allan Barkey, "The Socialist Party in West Virginia from 1890 to 1902: A Study in Working Class Radicalism," Unpublished Ph.D. dissertation, University of Pittsburgh, 1971, p. 40.)

35. Coleman, *op. cit.*, pp. 101-02. Lowell Limpus, a reporter for the New York *Daily News* wrote of the conditions following evictions in Pennsylvania coal fields in the 1920s: "We saw thousands of women and children literally starving to death. We found hundreds of destitute families living in crudely bareboard shacks. They had been evicted from their homes by the coal companies. We unearthed a system of despotic tyranny reminiscent of Czar-ridden Siberia at its worst. We found police brutality and industrial slavery. We discovered the wierdest flock of injunctions that ever emanated from American temples of justice." (Reprinted in Irving Bernstein, *A History of the American Worker, 1920-33: The Lean Years,* Boston, 1960, pp. 130-31.)

36. Sheldon Harris, "Letters from West Virginia: Management's Version of the 1902 Coal Strike," *Labor History* 10 (Spring, 1969): 229; Malcolm Cowley in statement printed on jacket of Mary Settle, *The Scapegoat,* New York, 1980.

37. Elsie Gluck, *John Mitchell Miner,* New York, 1929, p. 40.

38. *Autobiography of Mother Jones,* Chicago, 1925, p. 235.

39. "There sits the most dangerous woman in America," declared a West Virginia prosecutor. "She comes into a State where peace and progress reign. She crooks her finger — 20,000 contented men lay down their tools and walk out." (Peter C. Michelson, "Mother Jones," *Delineator,* May, 1915, p. 8.) The "Borgia" reference is in a letter to the *Washington News* which reported having heard Mother Jones speak "some years ago, and this was the verbatim advice she gave to the assembled bricklayers, who at the time were getting $4.50 and $5 per day: 'Strike for $8, and when you get that, strike for $10, and when you get $10, strike for $15, and then strike for $25 a day!' It is surprising that he did not report her as having also said that they should strike for six hours a day and then for four hours. (The complaining letter by R. M. B. is in a clipping, Mother Mary Harris Jones Papers, Catholic University of America, Department of Archives and Manuscripts, Washington, D.C.)

40. On July 1, 1916, John H. Walker wrote to Mother Jones: ". . . Mother, it is a strike that should be won and if it is not, it will be because of lack of a little finance . . . If you could only have gone down there and held one meeting, so that you could understand the situation, I know there would be no trouble for you to raise enough money to enable them to win that strike. . . ." Mother Jones did go and did help raise funds. (John Hunter Walker Collection, Illinois Historical Survey, University of Illinois Library.)

41. Thomas Haggerty to Mother Jones, Reynoldsville, Pa., December 9, 1901, William B. Wilson Papers, Historical Society of Pennsylvania; undated telegram in Mother Mary Harris Jones Papers, Catholic University of

America, Department of Archives and Manuscripts, Washington, D.C.

42. Mother Jones to Thomas J. Morgan, Greensburgh, Pa., December 16, 1910, Thomas J. Morgan Collection, Illinois Historical Survey, University of Illinois.

43. Sheldon Harris, *op. cit.*, p. 238; Michael Nash, *Conflict and Accommodation: Coal Miners, Steel Workers and Socialism, 1890–1920*, Westport, Conn., 1982, p.65.

44. Helen Sumner Woodbury, "Mary Harris Jones," in Dumas Malone, editor, *Dictionary of American Biography*, New York, 1933, vol. X, pp. 195–96.

45. H. M. J. in *United Mine Workers Journal*, September 18, 1902, p. 7.

46. The telegram read: "We urge members in the Northern lignite field to accept the scale offered by the operators in Denver." The telegram was signed by President Mitchell, Vice President T. L. Lewis, and Secretary W. B. Wilson. (*Denver Post*, November 22, 1903.)

47. For evidence that this exaggerates Mitchell's relations with coal barons and Wall Street, *see* pp. 90, 165.

48. *Denver Post*, November 22, 1903.

49. *See* pp. 104-10.

50. *Pittsburgh Press*, August 15, 1919.

51. Lois C. McLean, "Mother Jones Organizer," *Talking Union* 4 (June, 1982): 8.

52. The points from Mother Jones's speeches during the West Virginia strike of 1912-13 are to be found below in the speeches of August 1, 4, 15, September 6, 1912.

53. Philadelphia *North American*, July 7, 1903.

54. New York *Call*, April 23, 1914; *New York Times*, April 23, 1914.

55. Fred Mooney, *Struggle in the Coal Fields*, edited by James W. Hess, Morgantown, West Virginia, 1967, p. 79. Mooney reports that the Mexican workers cried "Madre Yones," but this is a mistake. She was known in Mexico as "Madre Juanita." (*See below* pp. 528-30 for an interview in *Excelsior* where this is made clear.)

56. *El Universal*, January 10, 1921. Translated from the Spanish by Roslyn Held Foner. I am indebted to Enrique Gaona Suarez and his wife Esther Schumacher, president and secretary respectively of ACEHSMO (World Association of Institutes for the Study of Labor History) for furnishing me with a copy of *El Universal* containing this report.

57. *Labor History* (Spring, 1968): 77.

58. I'll Teach You Not to Be Afraid," *Mania Baumgartner Remembers Mother Jones*, by Lois C. McLean, *Goldenseal*, January-March, 1980, pp. 22-23.

59. *The Nation*, July 19, 1922, pp. 70-71.

A Mother Jones Chronology

"It would be almost impossible to write a chronological history of the life of Mother Jones," wrote Bud L. McKillips shortly after her death at the age of one hundred. "She had a vivid memory of events, but got mixed up in dates." This, however, is not the only problem. Mother Jones's reminiscences are often fragmentary and contradictory, and usually say nothing about important events in her life. Only the barest outlines of her early life can be reconstructed. The absence of family records and other vital sources makes it impossible to draw any firm conclusions about her childhood and adolescence. The following is pieced together from a variety of diffuse sources.

1830 — Born Mary Harris near Cork, Ireland, May 1, to Richard and Helen Harris. Lois McLean believes she was probably born in 1839 while Priscilla Long gives her birthdate as 1843.

1835 — Grandfather said to have been hanged in the fight for Irish freedom, and father migrates to United States and obtains work as a construction laborer on canals and railroads. Arranges for his wife and children to follow him.

1838 — Harris family settles in Toronto, Canada, where Richard obtains work as a railroad construction laborer.

1847 — Mary Harris graduates from public school in Toronto.

1858-1859 — Records found by Lois McLean indicate a Maria Harris entered Toronto Normal School at age 18 in 1858 and left in 1859.

1859 — A secular teacher at Saint Mary Convent in Monroe, Michigan at $8.00 a month. Leaves in March 1860, and paid $36.43 for the teaching period.

1860 — Works as dressmaker in Chicago (a skill she learned in Toronto schools) and then returns to teaching in Memphis, Tennessee.

1861 — Marries George Jones, "a staunch member" of the Iron Moulders' Union. Couple has four children, one son and three daughters. Priscilla Long believes she had only one child.

1867 — Husband and four small children die in epidemic of yellow fever that ravaged Memphis. George Jones honored by his union at his death for services to the workers. Mary Harris works as volunteer nurse until the disease is halted. Then returns to Chicago and resumes dressmaking.

1870 — Years of making clothes for wealthy in Chicago creates a sense of great resentment in her towards the inequities in American life.

1871 — Burned out of all her possessions by the great Chicago Fire. Attends meetings at scorched hall of Knights of Labor and picnics of the order. Meets Terence V. Powderly, later to become Grand Master Workman of the Knights of Labor and Mother Jones's life-long friend.

Since the Knights of Labor did not admit women to membership until 1881, the story of Mother Jones' relationship with the K. of L. before that year is confusing and not easy to determine with accuracy.

1877 — The great labor uprising begins in July 1877 with the revolt of the railroad workers and becomes the first nationwide strike in United States history. Mary Harris goes to Pittsburgh because, as she says, the strikers "sent for me." She is present when in Pittsburgh, the major center of the hated Pennsylvania Railroad, the strike took on the character of a popular uprising. Forty-two local residents were killed, and the enraged populace responded with the systematic destruction of Pennsylvania Railroad property, including thirty-nine buildings, 104 engines, forty-six passenger cars, and 1,200 freight cars.

1877 strike ends in defeat after the state and federal governments, working with employers, succeed in crushing the labor uprising with perhaps one hundred lives lost across the nation.

1880-1890 — Mary Harris moves from one industrial area to another, whichever seemed in need of her assistance. Where there was a strike, she organized and aided the workers; where there was none, she held educational meetings. Priscilla Long believes she was associated for a time with the Chinese exclusion movement in California.

1886 — Returns to Chicago and is active in the eight-hour movement. Attends meetings of anarchists, but is not sympathetic to their ideas. Participates in May 1, 1886, first May Day demonstration for eight-hour day, and witnesses reign of terror following the Haymarket affair of May 4, 1886.

1890 — Knights of Labor District 135 and National Union of Miners and Mine Laborers merge to form United Mine Workers of America. Mary Jones becomes paid organizer for UMW.

1894 — In Birmingham, Alabama to aid strike of coal miners in that city. Becomes involved in Pullman strike of American Railway Union.

Visits towns in Alabama, Georgia, and South Carolina to work in cotton mills, and help improve conditions "as intolerable as any Negro slavery which had ever existed in the same Southern States." Associated with the Populist movement.

1895 — J. A. Wayland begins publication of *Appeal to Reason,* socialist weekly on August 30, and Mary Jones sells copies of the paper in Pittsburgh and to soldiers at the army barracks in Omaha, Nebraska. Advocates socialism in her talks.

1896 — Returns to Birmingham area for *Appeal* and helps Eugene V. Debs during speaking tour, after his release from jail for having violated a federal injunction during the Pullman strike.

1897-June 15 — Attends founding convention of Social Democracy of America, which Eugene V. Debs, now a socialist, launched after the loss of the Pullman strike and the destruction of the American Railway Union.

July — Visits Washington to appeal to President William McKinley to pardon S. D. Warden, who was under death sentence in California for train wrecking in the Pullman strike of 1894.

July-September — active in support of 1897 strike of coal miners in response to call of United Mine Workers of America. Addresses 10,000 strikers and sympathizers at Turtle Creek near Pittsburgh where 20,000 miners are out on strike. Urges them to fight for their rights. Approaches farmers in the region and asks them to share their produce with strikers. Escorts farmers and their loaded-down wagons in a parade to "Camp Determination," the strikers' headquarters near Turtle Creek, where the food is distributed. Invites neighborhood women to a "pound party," asking them to bring a pound of food for the strikers' supplies. Invites factory workers to come to camp meetings and donate to the cause. Visits strikers' wives and convinces them to work actively for the cause, and organizes them into battallions of pickets to help strikers. Organizes children of strikers into parades in support of their parents on strike. One parade led by a group of 50 little girls carrying homemade banners, one of which read, "Our Papas Aren't Scared." Wins praise from *National Labor Tribune,* published in Pittsburgh, for her work for the strike in the Pittsburgh district. Works with Eugene V. Debs in campaign to organize miners in West Virginia during the strike, but effort fails. Said by John Mitchell to have been imprisoned in West Virginia for strike activities.

1897 — Attends utopian socialist colony at Pushkin, Tennessee but decides not to continue.

1898 — Attends second convention of Social Democracy of America.

1899 — Strike of miners against Erie Company at Arnot, Pennsylvania for wage increase begins in May. By July 1,000 out on strike but by end of September, they prepare to go back to the mines defeated.

October 1 — Mary Jones arrives, gets farmers to help feed strikers' children, and nearby Blossberg families to house the evicted miners. Leads parades of miners, their wives and children from Arnot to Blossberg. By February, 1900 the defeat is turned into victory.

1900 — Charles Kerr, publisher of *International Socialist Review,* advertises in *United Mine Workers Journal* that "Mother Jones" would write in the *Review.* Signs her first article in the *International Socialist Review,* "Mother Jones." Article deals with her observations on child labor in the South.

September 17 — United Mine Workers calls anthracite miners out on strike.

September 23 — Mother Jones leads army of women, wives and daughters of strikers, in march to Coleraine and Beaver Meadows.

September 25 — Leads march to Coaldale in Panther Creek, of two to three thousand women, to bring out 5,000 men still working in the mines. Women have nothing but brooms and mops. Militia ordered breakfast at hotel, and Mother Jones tells the women to go in and eat their breakfast, and let the state pay for it. Women follow her advice.

October 7 — Leads march of 1,500 women to Lattimer to bring out 3,000 men. Closed the mines. Strike settled through intervention of Mark Hanna, Republican political boss, who fears continuation will aid William J. Bryan in presidential campaign against William McKinley, running for re-election. UMW membership in anthracite field jumps from 8,000 to 100,000.

1901 — Spends good part of the year in Pennsylvania organizing miners still not members of the UMW. Speaks at 1901 UMW convention.

Helps strike of miners' daughters working as silk weavers in Scranton which is won by strikers and assists in formation of union of domestic servants. In December is involved in short strike at the Dietz mines in Norton, Virginia.

1902 — Sent into West Virginia to supervise organizing campaign in the southern part of the state. Works from headquarters in Montgomery and is successful in organizing drive. During 1902 coal strike is sent into the more difficult northern part of West Virginia by UMW president John Mitchell.

June 20 — arrested in Clarksburg, West Virginia for violating injunction issued by Federal Judge Jackson of Parkersburg. Taken to Parkersburg, imprisoned, and released on bond. Attends special UMW convention, and returns to Parkersburg to face Judge Jackson.

July 25 — Sentence suspended by Judge Jackson who advises her to engage in charity work, advice she rejects. Goes to anthracite region to help 1902 strike in that area. Returns to West Virginia in fall of 1902. Strike in West Virginia drags on until July 1903. Agreement won only in the Kanawha district which includes Paint and Cabin Creek valleys. In 1904 UMW loses Cabin Creek in ten day strike and only Paint Creek remains in the union.

1902 strike ended with general settlement that followed President Theodore Roosevelt's intervention, but which did not include union recognition. Mother Jones disapproves of settlement believing that union recognition could have been won.

1903-June-August — Leads march of mill children from Philadelphia to Oyster Bay, New York to demonstrate to the public and to President Theodore Roosevelt the evils of child labor. March is from the textile mills of Kensington to the home of President Roosevelt. Not permitted to see President Roosevelt but march helps develop popular support for child labor legislation.

Speaks at memorial service for miners killed in Virden (Illinois) Massacre of October 12, 1898 to establish miners' own cemetery at Mt. Olive, Illinois. Cemetery established when men killed at Virden not permitted to be buried in town cemetery.

Fall — Sent by John Mitchell to Colorado to see what the situation in the coal mines is. Disguised as a peddler she collects information and when strike is called in northern and southern fields, she aids strikers. Urges northern miners not to sign separate agreement ending strike, thereby abandoning southern miners, and despite Mitchell's support for separate agreement, wins their approval to continue strike. But later northern miners, pressured by Mitchell's machine, reverse stand. Mother Jones quits job as UMW organizer over what she regards as "sellout" by Mitchell who, however, claims she was fired. During strike she is deported from Colorado by Governor Peabody but refuses to leave state and asks him what he plans to do about it. Governor does nothing. But Mother Jones attacked in Denver scandal sheet *Polly Pry* and accused of managing a house of prostitution.

1904 — Supports striking machinists of the Southern Pacific Railroad, and helps organize for Western Federation of Miners.

August — Promotes sale of *Unionism and Socialism* by Eugene V. Debs in New York City trade union circles.

1905 — January and June — participates in founding of Industrial Workers of the World (I.W.W.), but does not remain affiliated with the organization for long.

1906 — Tours the country to raise funds for the defense of Haywood, Moyer, and Pettibone, Western Federation of Miners officials who were indicted for murder in frameup attempt to destroy the militant union. Haywood and Moyer acquitted in trials, and Pettibone never tried. Speaks at rallies of Western Federation of Miners in copper mining regions of Michigan, and urges miners to organize.

1907 — June 30 — while speaking to smelter workers in Douglas, Arizona, becomes involved in case of Manuel Sarabia, leader of the Organizing Junta of the Liberal Party, followers of Flores Magón, who were seeking to overthrow dictator Porfirio Díaz in Mexico. Helps to get him returned to the United States from Mexican prison to which he had been taken after being kidnapped from Arizona.

August — visits Mesabi Range in Minnesota to aid strikers, members of Western Federation of Miners. Helps miners in Westmoreland County, Pennsylvania, urges wives of strikers to take their babies on the picket lines and if arrested and imprisoned, to sing themselves out of jails by making so much noise community would be glad to get rid of them. Women follow her advice.

1909 — Helps striking shirtwaist workers in New York City and speaks against Díaz tyranny at Brooklyn rally. Appeals to UMW convention for financial aid to help Mexican revolutionaries imprisoned in the United States.

1910 — Aids copper miners on strike in Arizona. Helps organize women bottlers in Milwaukee breweries.

1911 — Again on the payroll of UMW and remains either a paid organizer or honorary official of the union until her death in 1930. Leads fight at UMW convention to have John Mitchell resign from the National Civic Federation. Returns to West Virginia to help organize local unions.

Continues fight against Díaz dictatorship in Mexico. Carries cases of Mexican revolutionaries imprisoned in the United States to White House in interview with President William Howard Taft. Aids in securing Congressional inquiry into fate of Mexicans persecuted in the United States and testifies on their behalf.

October — Goes to Mexico City to see President Madero after overthrow of Díaz tyranny to help organize Mexican miners. Madero's assassination cuts short project. Establishes friendship with Francisco "Pancho" Villa while in Mexico.

1912 — Returns to West Virginia to help miners on strike at Paint Creek. In August holds first union meeting in years in Coal Creek. Bluffs mine guards at machine guns to allow union meetings by threatening to bring in hundreds of armed miners from the hills, where none actually were at that time. August 15 delivers speeches to strikers in Charleston.

1912-1913 — Battles feudal conditions and military despotism in West Virginia. Tried by state militia military court, convicted of charge of conspiracy to commit murder, and sentenced to prison for twenty years. Refuses to defend self before the military courts, and smuggles out letters from her "military Bastile" to arouse public indignation against military rule. Senate investigation caused by her imprisonment. Freed by newly elected Governor Hatfield.

1913 — Helps Western Federation of Miners in copper strike in Michigan. Goes to Colorado to aid in UMW strike in southern part of state in drive to organize Colorado Fuel & Iron Company, Rockefeller-owned coal mines.

1913-1914 — Three times coal operators have her imprisoned and deported from Colorado, but each time she returns. Spends months in prison for role in strike. After "Ludlow Massacre" of April 20, 1914, when twenty lives lost, travels across the country telling story of strike and rallying support for miners. Goes to Seattle to speak at first Labor Memorial Day. Goes to British Columbia to participate in strike of Canadian miners. Testifies before House Mines and Mining Committee in Washington on conditions in Colorado, and interviews President Woodrow Wilson to obtain his intervention for settlement of strike. Addresses convention of American Federation of Labor in Philadelphia to rouse support for miners' struggles in Colorado and Michigan.

1915-January — hears John D. Rockefeller, Jr. testify before Commission on Industrial Relations and visits him at his invitation at his office, 26 Broadway, New York City, to try to persuade him to go to Colorado and see conditions for himself. Does not succeed.

May 13-14 — Testifies before Commission on Industrial Relations.

Fall — Helps Western Federation of Miners in Arizona.

1916 — Aids strikes of streetcar workers in El Paso, Texas, and New York City. Aids garment workers in New York City to prepare for battle to end Protocol of Peace.

Supports Senator Kern of Indiana for reelection to U.S. Senate over Eugene V. Debs, Socialist candidate, antagonizing Socialist Party. Relations with Socialist Party deteriorating. Supports Woodrow Wilson for reelection rather than Socialist presidential candidate Allan F. Benson. Stumps Arizona to help reelect Governor George Wiley Paul Hunt for third term.

Active in defense movement to free Thomas J. Mooney and Warren K. Billings, framed in bomb explosion incident during 1916 Preparedness Day Parade in San Francisco.

1917 — Back in West Virginia for short time, traveling and speaking to miners in southern coal fields.

Supports U.S. entrance into World War I and urges miners to produce for victory.

1918 — Addresses West Virginia State Federation of Labor convention and urges workers to buy Liberty Bonds, but also calls for conscription of wealth as well as of men.

1919 — Leads protest against intolerable conditions in the Sissonville Prison, Kanawha County, West Virginia and succeeds in bringing some reforms. Works tirelessly to help workers in steel strike of 1919, and arrested several times during strike for speaking without a permit.

1921-January — Speaks at Third Congress of the Pan-American Federation of Labor in Mexico City at invitation of Mexican government, and hailed by Mexican people for her aid on behalf of Mexicans persecuted in the United States and support for the Mexican revolution.

August — Returns to West Virginia to join march of miners on

Logan County. In effort to halt march and prevent bloodshed reads forged telegram from President Harding assuring support for move to eliminate mine guard system and calling for disbandonment of march. Forgery exposed and leaves West Virginia. Addresses 1921 UMW convention.

1922-June — Addresses UMW convention in support of Alex Howat, Kansas mine leader fighting the John L. Lewis machine.

1923-June — Gets Governor Morgan to release last prisoners among miners arrested for battle connected with March on Logan County.

July 3 — makes last major public address at Farmer-Labor Party convention in Chicago.

1924 — works on *Autobiography* in Chicago with assistance of Mary Field Parton. Book published by Charles H. Kerr in 1925. Helps dressmakers on strike in Chicago. Lives with Terence V. Powderly and with his wife after his death on June 24. Visits President Coolidge in White House to pledge support for his reelection.

1928-May — Starts to live with the Burgess family. Walter Burgess, a painter, operated a truck farm on Old Powder Mill Road in Hyattsville, Maryland, near Washington, D.C. Mother Jones became acquainted with the Burgess family while staying with Terence V. Powderly and his wife at their home.

1930-May 1 — One hundredth birthday celebrated at reception on the lawn of Burgess family home. Talks into Movietone Newsreel camera, delivering her last speech. Thanks John D. Rockefeller, Jr. for message of congratulations. Contributes $1,000 to campaign in United Mine Workers to oust John L. Lewis from union leadership. Expresses disappointment at not hearing word from Governor Young of California on her appeal to free Tom Mooney.

September 14 — Given last rites of the Catholic Church.

November 30 — Dies at Burgess home in Hyattsville, Maryland, at 11:55 p.m. Short service held in the Burgess home, followed by services in St. Gabriel's Church in Washington. Body lies in state for the rest of the day at the Huntemann Funeral Home, and was then carried by a chartered funeral coach, escorted by an honor guard, to Mount Olive, Illinois, for burial.

December 7 — Memorial Service at Mount Olive, broadcast over WCFL, Chicago Federation of Labor's radio station. Memorial address delivered by Reverend John W. F. Magure, president of St. Viator's College in Bourbonnais, Illinois, with whom she had worked during the 1919 steel strike in aid of strikers.

December 8 — Funeral held in Mount Olive Roman Catholic Church of the Ascension. Ten to fifteen thousand people attend the services and surround the church.

At her own request, expressed in letters to Mount Olive miners, is buried in Union Miners Cemetery in Mount Olive, Illinois, near the graves of the victims of the 1898 "Virden Massacre."

On October 11, 1936, a memorial was erected at the Union Miners Cemetery with funds raised by locals of the Progressive Mine Workers of America and their women's auxiliaries. In the center of the shaft is a bronze bas-relief plaque of Mother Jones, and at the base, the center plaque, one of five, commemorates Mary "Mother" Jones. The final speaker at the commemoration was Mrs. Lillie May Burgess of Hyates, Maryland, in whose farm house Mother Jones spent her last days. Burgess told the audience that on the eve of her death, Mother Jones had expressed "the wish that she could live another hundred years in order to fight to the end that there would be no more machine guns and no more sobbing of little children."

MOTHER JONES,

Tributes to Mother Jones

"Of all the subjects that have been discussed the "new woman" has received more severe raps than any that have been discussed in the newspapers for many a day. While we do not approve of the "new woman" that makes a show of herself bicycling up and down the principal thoroughfares of a city in bloomers, but we do approve of the "new women" in affairs that they are more than any one else directly interested. The latest in this line is the women as labor agitators. . . .

"But the woman that we wish to speak of in this article is Mrs. Mary Jones, of Chicago. She has done more missionary work for the miners of the Pittsburg district than any two of the officials, and done it better. She seems to have the gift of talking in that forcible manner that interests you the moment she enters into a conversation with you. To her, more than any one else, the miners owe much of their success in this unpleasantness. She has "roughed" it in this district for the last four weeks, and in all kinds of weather she is ready to take the field and use her persuasive powers on the men that are, in a measure, cutting their own throats. Too much credit cannot be given to this "new woman," and her name will go down in history as one of the martyrs to the cause of oppressed humanity . . . Oh that we only had a few more Mary Jones to lead the men out of the slough of despond that they seem to have fallen into."

National Labor Tribune, *August 26, 1897*

"When the history of these times shall be written by people living under a state of industrial harmony and peace, in the years to come, the name of 'Mother' Mary Jones will occupy a prominent place."

Appeal to Reason, *March 17, 1900*

"There is only one Mother Jones. Clara Barton has her work of mercy. Susan Anthony her equal suffrage. Mother Jones has her 'boys' — the great patient army that sweats and strives and suffers whenever there is work to be done. This is the time of Mother Jones. She has been called the stormy petrel of industry. She is the most successful organizer and sustainer of strikes in the country. Her appearance is a signal for those who grow rich by grinding the faces of the poor to 'go slow,' and if they disregard the warning so much the worse for them and the better for organized labor."

New York World, *November 2, 1900*

"She is the best socialist agitator working among labor unions."
J. A. Wayland in Appeal to Reason, *November 17, 1900*

"Mother Jones is the Jeane d'Arc of workers in their industrial warfare."
John Lopez in Philadelphia North America, *July 15, 1903*

"She has done what is virtually conceded no man would have done."
*Bertha Howell Mailly in dispatch from
southern Colorado,* Appeal to Reason, *January 30, 1904*

"If there is a woman in these modern times worthy of being classed with the grand characters of history, the heroic women of the ages — Hypatia, Deborah, the Mother of the Gracchi, Vernonica, Joan of Arc — that woman, in the minds of thousands of the common people of America, is the good, gray-haired woman affectionately know to them as 'Mother' Jones. . . .

" 'Mother' Jones has been accused of being irreligious. Unorthodox she certainly is, for Jew and Gentile are alike to her; but her speeches are full of religious conviction, and she spends no little time reading her Bible. Next to the book of books, she cherishes the poetry of Robert Burns, and says that the peasant poet felt what he did not understand and sang of the joys and sorrows of the people as no other poet has ever done. Her two other literary favorites are Tolstoi and Wendell Phillips. She carries with her always a worn volume of the great abolitionist's orations. . . .

"When asked recently if she would not soon leave off her arduous work and take some comfort in her old age, "Mother" Jones replied: 'I am not uncomfortable nor weary. I am an extraordinarily happy woman, with just enough pain in my life to keep me true. If I yielded to luxury I might lose myself. And if the world were not so foolishly afraid of pain it might end all its misery. Luxury makes slaves. I prefer the down road, a comrade's greeting and the breath of freedom.'"
Boston Herald, *September 11, 1904, Magazine Section, pp. 1, 3*

"No soldier in the revolutionary cause has a better right to recognition . . . than has Mother Jones

"Her very name expresses the spirit of the Revolution.

"Her striking personality embodies all its principles.

"She has won her way into the hearts of the nation's toilers, and her name is revered at the altars of their humble firesides and will be lovingly remembered by their children and their children's children forever."
Eugene V. Debs in Appeal to Reason, *November 23, 1907*

"Mother Jones improves with age. She has passed the allotted three score and ten, but carries with her the freshness of spring and the virility and enthusiasm of youth. Mother Jones is infectious. Where she appears there is action. The most sluggish respond to her magnetic presence.

"There is not a more unique personality in the movement. She is at once as gentle as a cooing dove, and as fierce as a lioness. She is a grand combination of sweetness and gentility, strength and determination."

Appeal to Reason, *March 17, 1909*

". . . when the history of the labor movement is written and there is recorded the glad tidings of labor's emancipation, the name of 'Mother' Jones will shed a halo of lustre upon every chapter that portrays the struggle of man against the despotism of capitalism."

Miners Magazine, *September 26, 1912*

"For eight months, 'Mother Jones' has been working, speaking and fighting with the West Virginia miners. In spite of her eighty years she has suffered with the miners, their wives and children, sharing every hardship, the cold of winter in the mountains, the coarse food and the insults and brutality of the 'guards' and militiamen.

"Many were the speeches she made and every one a battle cry for class solidarity. The most weary and disheartened group gathered courage and inspiration when she addressed her 'Boys.'

"But it became evident to the mill bosses that the beautiful, white-haired woman was a militant figure that it would be well to eliminate. So, on February 13th, 'Mother Jones' was arrested on a charge of murder. It is claimed that she advised the strikers to arm themselves. Many times the mine 'guards' crept up upon strikers in their mountain retreat, and coldly murdered them. Several 'guards' were discovered and shot by the miners in self defense. An attempt will be made to hold 'Mother Jones' responsible. Evidently the true Progressive believes in murder only where the gun is in the hands of a servant of the owning class and directed against working men."

International Socialist Review, *March, 1913, pp. 648-49*

"History tells of many brave women — Jean d'Arc and Molly Pitcher — many others accomplish some daring feat or made some great sacrifice for a brief period, but you may search the archives of history and you will not find one that has given an entire life's devotion so unfalteringly, uncompromisingly, without any reward, as 'Mother' has. . . . Her only home is among the workers in the thick of the fight. She cares nothing for an individual's nationality, creed or color, if they are fighting for the right and need her, she is there in the battle's thunderous roar — thoughtless of no one — except herself. . . .
She is the worker's refuge and inspiration. 'Mother' is the cry when, overawed by corporation hirelings, they seek to join hands in a com-

mon struggle and again when the troops re-inforced by hunger, are beating them into earth. Often she has changed defeat into victory. Her courage is unconquerable. Words are weak; no one can eulogize this noble soul; her work is her eulogy. Let no granite shaft rest on her, but let the flowers tell the sweetness of her life, and prattling children, wrested from mine, mill and factory and given back to childhood's joys, in all ages yet to come, sing her praise."

Emma F. Langdon in Miners Magazine, *March 20, 1913*

"Wherever the miners have had trouble with the mine-owners in any part of the country during the last thirty years her white hair has been pretty sure to wave like an oriflam of war equal to that famous white plume of Henry of Navarre about which we used to declaim in our school days. Five hundred thousand miners call her 'Mother' Jones. Trouble of an industrial sort has an irresistible attraction for her, and she will pack up her belongings at an hour's notice, chase from Montana to West Virginia to get into it, if she has to walk a hundred miles to reach it. . . . 'The most remarkable woman in America,' is the way a writer in the conservative Brooklyn *Daily Eagle* speaks of her."

"The Indomitable Spirit of Mother Jones," Current Opinion, *July, 1913*

"Ten million fighting-men call her 'Mother.' The Lioness Mother of Ten Million Whelps, The Enraged Protectress of Her Own: That's Mother Mary Jones. She stands forever in the history of this epoch as a vital, dominant force in the greatest struggle of all time. Your grand-children will read of her with awe, history will give over its pages to tell of 'A gray-haired women, burdened with the weight of eighty-three years, leading the forces of labor in the long battle.' She fights hard, fast and furious. She rains blows in the thickest of the fighting, and in the fields of West Virginia and Colorado she has carried the colors in the charge. She puts fear in the souls of the 'ungodly' and lays bare the rotten heart of all who oppose the onward march of truth.

"Impartial but stern; tender-hearted, yet hard-hitting; truth's aide-de-camp in the battle of the ages hurls across the vision of the world in the body of an old woman and the soul of a prophetess-genius. . . . She shocks prudes by the directness of her diction, and warped minds might conceive some of her words to be profane, but it is not so. She is so intense that any thing she says is the essence of spirituality. Spirituality consists of the deepest recesses of the human heart. Mary Jones sanctifies ordinary words by the very fervor of their utterance.

"Her thoughts are vital, her insight takes cognizance of the deeps in the ocean of humanity, and her love embraces the whole human race. 'Her boys' are men who do the great things of the world's program. I verily believe there is not one heart beat in that blessed old body which does not come from deep, intense love for 'her boys and girls.' Her 'boys and girls of Seattle' have heard her say: 'I am a member of Organized Labor regardless of name, claim or banner.' What! Would you shame her by bickering and dickering in our ranks: Let us remember this when the petty jealousies arise and the differences of opinion threaten to disrupt the family of thrice blessed, worshipped Lioness Mother of Ten Million — Mother Mary Jones. — C.E.W.

Seattle Union Record, June 6, 1914

"Mother Jones has won the proudest title that a woman can bear from the labor army of America. She has borne labor's cross for the life of a generation, and the struggling vagrants in the bondage of wage slavery have been her children. . . . Mother Jones . . . is adored and worshiped with a reverence by the hosts of labor. . . . Mother Jones is known from the Atlantic to the Pacific, from Canada to Mexico, and her home is wherever labor unsheathes the sword to give battle to 'predatory wealth' . . . The spot where she is laid to rest . . . shall be sacred to the men and women of a nation, who are marching onward and upward toward that goal where man, woman, and child shall be free."

John M. O'Neill in Miners Magazine, February 4, 1915

"She's a wonder; close to 88 years old and her voice a singing voice; nobody else could give me a thrill just by saying that slow solemn orotund way, 'The kaisers of this country are next, I tell ye.' I put this old lady past Galli-Curci."

Carl Sandburg to Negley D. Cochran,
April 5 (ca. 1918), in Herbert Mitgang, ed.,
The Letters of Carl Sandburg, New York, 1968, p. 128.

"May I nominate Mother Jones for *The Nation's* list of the twelve greatest American women? If we believe that organizing the wage-earners and bringing them into consciousness of their dignity as human beings with something to say about the conditions of their own lives is a job of first-rate importance, then she certainly belongs. . . . She has preached the stamina and self-reliance of the old-time America, and her message has been constructive and wise, not merely inflammatory. She has never lost sight of our common humanity. She has marched up to a machine-gun and talked to the professional gunmen behind it until they became ashamed and quit their jobs. Her shrewdness and wisdom and courage and sincerity have impressed Presidents and Governors. She has gone to jail times without number. She has never surrendered to bitterness. She has been, at past 80, an inspiration to those who were trying to bring a new spirit into the American labor movement, to take it from the control of selfish politicians interested only in the immediate advantage of relatively small groups of skilled workmen. . . . The small salary which for years she has received from the United Mine Workers goes, what she can spare from her simple living, to the needy and the defense of workingmen unjustly accused. She is loved and venerated in ten thousand humble homes. Her life is an epic and it is the shame of American writers that it has never been told. She is a great woman, unsung because of our tradition of cheap gentility."

George P. West in The Nation, *July 19, 1922*

"I who have known her for nearly half a century bear willing testimony to her great work for humanity. All through the years she gave while others got.

"When others were getting millions of dollars for self she was giving of the riches of her great soul in loving service to millions of men and women.

"She does not court the favor of any mortal, high or low. As she sees the truth she speaks it, aye even though it may not be palatable to others or helpful to herself.

"I wish to place the laureled crown of greatness upon the head of *Mother Jones.*"

Terence V. Powderly in Labor, *August 1922*

"Mother Jones is one of the most forceful and picturesque figures of the American labor movement. She is a born crusader. . . . Mother Jones is the Wendell Phillips of the labor movement. Without his education and scholarship, she has the power of moving masses of men by her strong, loving speech and action. She has likewise his disregard for personal safety. . . . In all her career, Mother Jones never quailed or ran away. Her deep convictions and fearless soul always drew her to seek the spot where the fight was hottest and the danger greatest. . . . She was never awed by jails. Over and over she was sentenced by courts; she never ran away. She stayed in prison until her enemies opened the doors. Her personal non-resistance was far more powerful than any appeal to force. . . . "

Clarence Darrow in introduction to
Autobiography of Mother Jones, *Chicago, 1925*

" 'Mother' Jones lived as few humans have dared to, giving of her great heart and courage for the disinherited, accepting in return hardships, danger and the small pay of a union organizer. She was in scores of jails, confined in the 'bull pen' many times, tried often on charges of accessory to murder and similar 'crimes.' Neither courts, nor gunmen, nor prisons, nor militia could stop her. Her name will stand at the head among the great of labor's hall of fame."

United Mine Workers Journal, *January 1931*

"Today in gorgeous mahogany furnished and carefully guarded offices in distant capitols wealthy mine owners and capitalists are breathing sighs of relief. Today upon the plains of Illinois, the hillsides and valleys of Pennsylvania and West Virginia, in California, Colorado and British Columbia, strong men and toil worn women are weeping tears of bitter grief. The reason for this contrasting relief and sorrow is the same. Mother Jones is dead."

> *Father John W. R. Magure at Memorial Meeting,*
> *Sunday, December 7, 1930, Mt. Olive, Illinois*

"No one could flatter her to the point of forgetting her main interest, the freedom of the working class, and there was no price which could have bought her consent to the misery of the many while she shared herself in the perquisites of the privileged few.

"Mother Jones would want no monument to herself. But she would count as a memorial beyond all appreciation such spirit on the part of American labor as will forward and not delay the great consummation toward which she gave her life."

> *Robert Whitaker in* Labor Clarion,
> *San Francisco, December 5, 1930*

"The world today is mourning
The death of Mother Jones;
Grief and sorrow hover
Over the miners' homes;
This grand old champion of labor
Has gone to a better land,
But the hard-working miners,
They miss her guiding hand.

Through the hills and over the valleys,
In every mining town,
Mother Jones was ready to help them —
She never turned them down.
In front with the striking miners
She always could be found,
She fought for right and justice,
She took a noble stand.

With a spirit strong and fearless
She hated that which was wrong;
She never gave up fighting
Until her breath was gone.
May the workers all get together

To carry out her plan,
And bring back better conditions
To every laboring man."

Anonymous.

"Men walk the streets with hunger
 in their eyes.
Beaten by fear and hopelessness
 and cold.
Would God — another Mother Jones
 will soon arise.
To free the nation from its chain
 of gold."

Extract of poem read by Harry E. Scheck,
president, Chicago Trade Union Labor League,
at tribute to Mother Jones on her 102nd Birthday,
Federation News, *May 7, 1932*

"The greatest woman agitator of our time was Mother Jones. Arrested, deported, held in custody by the militia, hunted and threatened by police and gunmen — she carried on fearlessly for sixty years."

Elizabeth Gurley Flynn in
I Speak My Own Piece: Autobiography of "The Rebel Girl,"
New York, 1955.

"It was probably at about this time [in 1899], also, that I first saw Mother Jones. At a mass meeting I heard her rip into the operators for their sins of commission and omission. She came into the mine one day and talked to us in our workplace in the vernacular of the mines. How she got in I don't know; probably just walked in and defied anyone to stop her. When I first knew her, she was in her late middle age, a woman of medium height, very sturdily built but not fat. She dressed conventionally, and was not at all unusual in appearance. But when she started to speak, she could carry an audience of miners with her every time. Her voice was low and pleasant, with great carrying power. She didn't become shrill when she got excited; instead her voice dropped in pitch and the intensity of it became something you could almost feel physically. She would take a drink with the boys and spoke their idiom, including some pretty rough language when she was talking about the bosses. This might have been considered a little fast in ordinary women, but the miners knew and respected her. They might think her a little queer, perhaps — it *was* an odd kind of work for a woman in those days — but they knew she was a good soul and a friend of those who most lacked friends: the down-trodden and oppressed, whoever they might be. The union used her as an organizer, and paid her when it could, but she agitated whether she was paid or not. She had a complete disregard for danger or hardship and would go in wherever she thought she was needed. And she cared no more about approval from union leaders than operators; wherever people were in trouble, she showed up to lead the fight with tireless devotion. With all this, she was no fanatic. She had a lively sense of humor — she could tell wonderful stories, usually at the expense of some boss, for she couldn't resist the temptation to agitate, even in a joke — and she exuded a warm friendliness and human sympathy. The priest who preached at her funeral in the little mining town of Verdon, Illinois, said, with all truth, that she had spent her life in God's work for the poor and oppressed. May her soul rest in peace."

John Brophy, A Miner's Life, *Madison, Wisconsin, 1964, p. 74.*

SPEECHES

The Lives of the Coal Miners

Speech delivered summer 1897, during strike in West Virginia

In 1897 the United Mine Workers conducted a nationwide strike against wage cuts. On July 4, West Virginia miners joined the walkout. UMW President M. D. Ratchford sent Mother Jones into West Virginia to organize miners. She worked with Eugene V. Debs, and together they toured the strike areas until Debs had to halt his work because of sunstroke. Mother Jones continued alone, and when UMW Vice President John Mitchell arrived in West Virginia, he reported finding Mother Jones in jail. If so, she was soon freed, and continued to hold "great meetings" at Monongah, Flemington, and other towns.[1] None of the actual texts of her speeches during this period have come down to us, but one of the two reporters who accompanied her later wrote an account of her speech near the mouth of a mine, delivered with the consent of the operator. It includes extracts of her remarks and a summary of the rest.[2]

In West Virginia, during the first great anthracite strike, the United Mine Workers of America had placed some of its organizers. Among these was "Mother" Jones, the only woman organizer employed by the trades unions.[3] On the way she had traveled through the mountain roads by night and day, toiling in the passes, tramping the railroad tracks, riding in farm wagons, on push carts, or in whatever way seemed easiest to get from camp to camp to preach the doctrine that workingmen must unite, the slogan of the trades unions.

She had a good measure of success, and the fame of her power as a trouble maker had spread among the mine owners. She was detested and feared by half the state, wondered about and gaped over by the other half. She was sleeping under any sort of shelter, eating the coarsest of food, stripping herself of clothing to give away right and left. Though she was earning a fair salary,[4] she could not use it to make life easier for herself in this environment.

Reaching a town one morning which was practically dominated by the influence of a rich young mine owner, she applied for permission to the authorities to hold a mass meeting. She was refused the permit unless she could gain the consent of the mine owner himself, who held a position of local political authority. Two reporters, who had been

73

sent out to watch the progress of events in this part of the state, believed that no speechmaking would occur in this town. "Mother" Jones thought differently. She sought the mine owner in his home. She told him that she had come to make a request which she saw in his face he would grant. He smiled and asked who she was and what she desired. With the benignity of the most gentle kindliness and simple dignity the old lady replied demurely that she was "Mother" Jones, and wished to have a talk with his employees.

"You, 'Mother' Jones," said the rich man, astonished; "you are surely not in earnest?"

"Yes, I am 'Mother' Jones, the wicked old woman," replied the supplicant with her steadfastly radiant expression and her almost subtle smile; so quiet, so gentle, so intelligent it made the words she uttered so whimsically of herself, a patent libel and insult upon her character. It was an irony that disturbed the judgment of the rich young man.

The mine owner studied the fact, the attitude, the folded hands of the woman before him, and then inquired what she would like him to do. "Mother" Jones said she would like him to send word through his mines that she was there, and grant her permission to talk on Sunday in an open space near the pit mouth on his own property. Though it seems incredible, the young mine owner consented. The inscrutable smile had been too much for his resistance.

The word was accordingly sent out through the mines that "Mother" Jones was to speak by permission of the operator. The foreman and bosses could scarcely believe their ears, and the ignorant miners, the foreign element that could scarcely speak English, did not believe. They feared it was some trap to compass their economic ruin, or more simply, to cost them their jobs. On Sunday morning only a few persons gathered at the meeting place designated, and "Mother" Jones seated on a rock, watched and waited.

The Local Labor Leader Surprised.

"This is going to be a frost," said the local labor leader, one John Walker.

"Wait a little," said "Mother" Jones.

Gradually it was apparent what the old lady was watching with her smiling eyes. Men were climbing up through mountain passes and hiding behind huge boulders; they were peeping over the tops and around the sides of their hiding places, and women were lurking in the thickets.

"Come nearer, comrades; don't be afraid, brothers," said "Mother" Jones, standing up, and then she began to talk. In a few minutes about 100 men and women gathered in front of the rocky platform. The mine owner himself sat on a rock some paces away.

"Has any one ever told you, my children, about the lives you are living more so that you may understand how it is you pass your days on earth? Have you told each other about it and thought it over among yourselves, so that you might imagine a brighter day and begin to bring it to pass? If no one has done so I will do it for you today. I want you to see yourselves as you are, Mothers and children, and to think if it is not time you look on yourselves, and upon each other. Let us consider this together, for I am one of you, and I know what it is to suffer."

So the old lady, standing very quietly in her deep, far-reaching voice, painted a picture of the life of a miner from his young boyhood to his old age. It was a vivid picture. She talked of the first introduction a boy had to those dismal caves under the earth, dripping with moisture often so low that he must crawl into the coal veins; most lie on his back to work. She told how miners stood bent over until the back ached too much to straighten, or in sulphur water that ate through the shoes and made sores on the flesh; how their hands became cracked and the nails broken off in the quick; how the bit of bacon and beans in the dinner pail failed to stop the craving of their empty stomachs, and the thought of the barefoot children, at home and the sick mother was all too dreary to make the homegoing a cheerful one.

And at home how often when the wife lay helpless in bed the miner must follow a day's toil by domestic chores. There was no one to rub the linament on the aching back, with Mary sick in bed. He must fetch the water and put the kettle to boil and try to wash off the coal dust that stuck into the pores of the skin. He must search the bare cupboard for a pinch of tea, the end of a stale loaf and the bit of cold potato. He might sit on the doorstep and smoke his pipe for an hour after tending the children, while Mary told him of what the doctor had said she must have for medicine and nourishment, which they both knew they could not afford. Other nights there was no place to go for a bit of amusement but the saloon, and sometimes he was too tired and too poor to go there.

And so, while he smoked, the miner thought how he could never own a home, were it ever so humble; how he could not make his wife happy, or his children any better than himself, and how he must get up in the mornin' and go through it all again; how that some day the fall of rock would come or the rheumatism cripple him; that Mary herself might die and leave him, and some day there would be no longer for him even the job that was so hard and old age and hunger and pain would be his lot. And why, because some other human beings, no more the sons of God than the coal diggers, broke the commandment of God which says, "Thou shalt not steal," and took from the toiler all the wealth which he created, all but enough to keep him alive for a period of years through which he might toil for their advantage.

"You pity yourselves, but you do not pity your brothers, or you would stand together to help one another," said "Mother" Jones. And then in an impassioned vein she called upon them to awaken their minds so that they might live another life. As she ceased speaking men and women looked at each other with shamed faces, for almost every one had been weeping. And suddenly a man pushed his way through the crowd. He was snivelling on his coat sleeve, but he cried out hoarsely:

"You, John Walker; don't you go tell us that 'ere's 'Mother' Jones. That's Jesus Christ come down on earth again, and saying he's an old woman so he can come here and talk to us poor devils. God, God — nobody else knows what the poor suffer that way."

The man was quieted by his wife and led away, while "Mother" Jones looked after him with dilating eyes, and then broke out fiercely in one of her characteristically impassioned appeals for organization. The reporters feared the outbreak was too sacreligious for publication. However that may be, it happened, and if a poor benighted miner thought this old woman a special messenger from God, it is not so strange that many intelligent people regard her as the woman genius of the labor movement.

[Boston Herald, *September 11, 1904, Magazine Section, pp. 1, 3.*]

Notes

1. Charles H. Ambler and Festus P. Summers, *West Virginia: The Mountain State,* Englewood Cliffs, N.J., 1958, pp. 445-46; John M. Barb, "Strikes in the Southern West Virginia Coal Fields, 1912-1922," unpublished M.A. thesis, p. 38; *United Mine Workers Journal,* August 19, 1897; Philip S. Foner, *History of the Labor Movement in the United States,* vol. 2, New York, 1955, pp. 390-91.

2. Linda Atkinson quotes part of the account, but she places it in the spring of 1901. Internal evidence would seem to indicate that it occurred during the 1897 strike. (*See* Linda Atkinson, *Mother Jones: The Most Dangerous Woman in America,* New York, 1978, pp. 103-04.)

3. This is not accurate. There had been several woman organizers for the American Federation of Labor, and at the time this was written (1904), Annie Fitzgerald was listed as "General Organizer, American Federation of Labor." But there were few women organizers even in unions with a large women membership, and none who were as active as Mother Jones.

4. United Mine Workers' records for 1900 state that "Mrs. Mary Jones" was paid a total of $494.81. (Atkinson, *op. cit.,* p. 99.)

My Epitaph

Speech at Convention, United Mine Workers of America,
Indianapolis, January, 1901

Following the 1900 anthracite strike in which Mother Jones played a major role, John Mitchell, now president of the UMW, announced that the union would renew its efforts to organize West Virginia. The campaign began in December 1900, and the union sent experienced organizers to the state from Ohio, Indiana, and Illinois. For nearly a year, the organizers moved through the state in the difficult and often dangerous task of unionizing mine workers. Mother Jones was in charge of the work in southern West Virginia, and she took her job as a "walking delegate" seriously, speaking during December at meetings along the Kanawha River where she helped to organize new locals and reorganize old ones. She then moved into the New River field and spoke at Mount Hope, McDonald, Beury, Glen Jean, and other mining camps.[1]

In January 1901 Mother Jones made her debut at the UMW convention, reporting on conditions in West Virginia. The official minutes of the Twelfth Annual Convention of the United Mine Workers of America, Held at Indianapolis, Ind., January 21 to 30 (Inclusive) 1901 *(p. 9) carries the notice for the ninth session: "At 2 o'clock 'Mother' Jones addressed the Convention. She spoke for nearly an hour, and was received with enthusiasm and loudly applauded." Thus though her address was noted, no text was printed. However, in 1978 Lois McLean published this excerpt from the speech.*

Any man or woman who witnessed the scenes [I] saw in that state would betray God Almighty if he betrayed those people. My brothers, I shall consider it an honor if when you write my epitaph upon my tombstone, you say "Died fighting their battles in West Virginia." You may say what you please about the West Virginia miners being "no good" [but] every dirty old miner out there is not a Virginian. He is very apt to be an old scab that the rest of you hounded out of your fields. I met in Virginia some of the noblest men I have met in all the country. . . . These poor fellows realize that they have been neglected. You have not dealt fairly with them. I wish you could see how some of them live. The conditions that surround them are wretched. They have pluck-me stores[2] and every invention known to robbery and rascality to contend with. Why, the Czar of Russia, tyrant that he is, is a gentleman compared with some of the fellows there who oppress these people. . . . I AM GOING BACK THERE!

[Lois McLean, "Mother Jones in West Virginia,"
Goldenseal 4 *(January-March, 1978): 15-16.]*

Notes

1. Lois McLean, "Mother Jones in West Virginia," *Goldenseal* (January-March, 1978): 15.
2. A derisive epithet used for company stores.

Lay Down Your Picks and Shovels and Quit Work!

Reports of speech to miners at Clarksburg,
West Virginia, June 20, 1902
in defiance of injunction issued by Judge John Jay Jackson

On June 21, 1902, the Parkersburg Sentinel *of West Virginia reported on its front page: "Mother Jones and a Dozen Strike Agitators Arrested." The arrests were for violating a sweeping injunction issued by Judge John Jay Jackson of the federal court in Parkersburg which at the request of the Guaranty Trust Company of New York, the holder of bonds of the Clarksburg Fuel Company in West Virginia, served notice that it was unlawful to interfere "with the employes of said company in their mining operations, either within the mines or passing from their homes to the mines . . . and from unlawfully inciting persons who are engaged in working in the mines from ceasing to work in and about the mines. . . ." This ban even included holding a meeting on land leased by the union. For violating this injunction in an address to miners near the Pinnickkinnick mines of the Clarksburg Fuel Company, Mother Jones was arrested, and together with several other UMW organizers, taken to Parkersburg, eighty-four miles from Clarksburg.[1]*

There is, unfortunately, no copy of the speech Mother Jones delivered before her arrest. But the following is pieced together from the report in the Parkersburg Daily News, *the* Autobiography of Mother Jones, *and the statement of Judge Jackson.*

Mother Jones' address this afternoon [to the strikers at Clarkesburg] was more than ordinarily bitter. She has good command of language and a powerful voice, which combine with her grey hair and commanding bearing & pleasant face give her undoubtedly much influence. She understands her power & how to use it, and while in private conversation shows a surprisingly cultivated manner & correct speech. Her language, when addressing a crowd of miners, is much after their common style and is thickly interspersed with slang and homely wit. In her speech today she denounced the mine operators as robbers, and defied Judge Jackson, placing him in the same class, and asserting that he, as well as the newspapers, and even the preachers, are in league with the interests of the mine owners against the mine workers. She was vigorously cheered at different times during her address, and especially at the close while the marshal & his deputies were making their arrests. She closed her address by urging the miners not to work, not to drink, to avoid all lawlessness and to stick together and continue to "agitate."

[Parkersburg Daily Morning News, *June 21, 1902.]*
I wish to thank Ann R. Lorentz, librarian, Parkersburg and Wood County Public Library, Parkersburg, West Virginia, and Lois McLean of Beckley, West Virginia, for furnishing me with the report of this speech.

" 'Mother,' said he [the marshal], "you're under arrest. They've got an injunction against your speaking."
I looked over the United States marshal and I said, "I will be right with you. Wait till I run down." I went on speaking till I had finished. Then I said, "Goodbye, boys; I'm under arrest. I may have to go to jail. I may not see you for a long time. Keep up this fight! Don't surrender! Pay no attention to the injunction machine at Parkersburg. The Federal judge is a scab anyhow.[2] While you starve he plays golf. While you serve humanity, he serves injunctions for the money powers."

[Autobiography of Mother Jones, Chicago, 1925, p. 49.]

Summary of Mother Jones's Speech by District Judge John Jay Jackson

"The utterances of 'Mother' Jones in her public address at or near the Pinnickkinnick mines on the 20th day of June, 1902, should not emanate from a citizen of this country who believes in its institutions. Such utterances are the outgrowth of the sentiments of those who believe in communism and anarchy. . . .

"The evidence shows that Mrs. Jones called the miners slaves and cowards; she criticised the action of the court and said she did not care anything for injunctions; that if they were arrested, or anything done with them, the jails would not hold the agitators that would be there to take their place; that it was the duty of every man there to urge the men to strike; she stated that it was the duty of all of them to influence the men at work to lay down their tools; she further stated that if they would come to Illinois they would be taught how to fight, and then they could come back and take care of themselves; she stated that the judge was a hireling of the coal company, that the coal operators were all robbers, and that the reason that the court stood in with them was that one robber liked another; she said in her speech to pay no attention to Judge Jackson or the court; for them not to listen to Judge Jackson, or any one else, or pay any attention to the court, but just make the miners lay down their tools and come out. This was the concurrent testimony of nine witnesses as to the material facts who were examined upon the rule for contempt, and the evidence was uncontradicted as to those facts; but there was a difference in the recollection of the witnesses as to what 'Mother' Jones said about the court. It is true that 'Mother' Jones denied some of the statements of the witnesses, but her denial was not positive, but equivocal. She admitted on the witness stand that she stated in her speech 'not to fear injunctions.' She admitted in her answer to this question put to her: 'Wasn't your purpose to go as near to those mines as you could to hold that meeting without a violation of the injunction? Were you in your judgment violating the injunction?' Her answer was, 'Perhaps that was.' It must be evident to every unprejudiced mind that the object and purpose of these agitators was to hold a meeting so near the mines of the Clarksburg Fuel Company as to alarm and intimidate the miners that were at work in the Pinnickkinnick mines, and in the language of Mrs. Jones to get them 'to lay down their picks and shovels and quit work.' "

[United States ex rel. Guaranty Trust Co. of New York
v. Haggerty et al., *Circuit Court, N.D. West Virginia,
July 24, 1902, 116 U.S., 517-19 (1902).*]

Notes

1. For further discussion of the injunction, *see* pp. 54, 85-87, 94, 99, 551, 552.

2. In her *Autobiography,* Mother Jones reports the following dialogue caused by this statement between herself and Judge Jackson:

"The Judge said, 'Did you call me a scab?'

" 'I certainly did, judge.'

"He said, 'How came you to call me a scab?'

" 'When you had me arrested I was only talking about the constitution, speaking to a lot of men about life and liberty and a chance for happiness; to men who had been robbed for years by their masters, who had been made industrial slaves. I was thinking of the immortal Lincoln. And it occurred to me that I had read in the papers that when Lincoln made the appointment of Federal judge to this bench, he did not designate senior or junior. Your father was away when the appointment came. You took the appointment. Wasn't that scabbing on your father, judge?' "

" 'I never heard that before,' said he.

"A chap came tiptoing up to me and whispered, 'Madam, don't say 'judge' or 'sir' to the court. Say 'Your Honor.' "

"'Who is the court?' I whispered back.

"'His honor, on the bench,' he said, looking shocked.

"'Are you referring to the old chap behind the justice counter? Well, I can't. call him 'your honor' until I know how honorable he is. You know I took an oath to tell the truth when I took the witness stand.'"

Later, Judge Jackson convinced Mother Jones that she was wrong and that he was no "scab," and she apologized, commenting she was "glad to be tried by so human a judge who resents being called a scab. You probably understand how we working people feel about it.'" (*Autobiography of Mother Jones*, pp. 52-53.)

Dialogue with a Judge

Report of remarks of Judge John Jay Jackson and Mother Jones in federal court, Parkersburg, West Virginia, July 24, 1902

Arrested on June 20, 1902, Mother Jones was released on bond. She was thus able to attend the special convention of the UMW in Indianapolis, and on her return to Parkersburg, she faced Judge Jackson in court.

An unusual incident occurred in the U.S. Court room [in Parkersburg] on Thursday afternoon when there was a spontaneous outburst of applause which lasted for several seconds and which could not be checked by the bailiff.

It was probably the first time that an incident of that kind ever occurred in the august presence of the court and was brought about by remarks that were passed between Judge Jackson and Mother Jones just after the case of the latter had been disposed of.

Judge Jackson in passing on the case said that judging from the interviews with Mrs. Jones that he had seen in the newspapers she desired to go to jail in order to pose as a martyr to the cause, but that he did not propose to send her to jail. The evidence showed that she was guilty of a violation of the injunction and his judgment was that she was guilty, but he would suspend judgment in her case. He hoped she would profit by her experience and would not further attempt to violate the injunction, but that she would devote her time to charitable work, many lines of which were open to her, and wherein she could be very useful. He gave her some further kindly advice.[1]

Mother Jones arose and thanked the Court for his advice. She said she was not responsible for what the newspapers said about her, and that she was not posing as a martyr. She had a duty to perform and proposed to perform it on the lines she had laid out, happen what might, and if she was again arrested it made little difference to her. If she had transgressed the law she thought she deserved the same punishment as her brothers.[2] In conclusion she said that Judge Jackson and herself were old and had not long to stay, but when the end came she hoped they would die good friends.

Judge Jackson replied he hoped they would be good friends and after life's fitful fever was over he hoped they would meet in the same place in the beyond, and that that place would be the right place.

It was at this passage that the outburst of applause occurred.

[Parkersburg Daily Morning News, *July 25, 1902.]*
I wish to thank Ann R. Lorentz, librarian, Parkersburg and Wood County Public Library, Parkersburg, West Virginia with furnishing me with the report of this court session.

Notes

1. The exact words of Judge Jackson were: "I cannot forbear to express my great surprise that a woman of the apparent intelligence of Mrs. Jones should permit herself to be used as an instrument by designing and reckless agitators . . . in accomplishing an object which is entirely unworthy of a good woman. It seems to me that it would have been better far for her to follow the lines and paths which the Allwise Being intended her sex to pursue. There are many charities in life which are open to her in which she could contribute largely to mankind in distress, as well as avocations and pursuits that she could engage in of a lawful character that would be more in keeping with what we have been taught and what experience has shown to be the true sphere of womanhood." (Edward M. Steel, "Mother Jones in the Fairmont Field, 1902," *Journal of American History* 57 (September, 1970): 301; 116 U.S., *op. cit.,* 520.)

2. Six of the strike leaders received 60-day sentences, and Thomas Haggerty received 90 days.

Be True to the Principles of Our Forefathers

Speech at special convention, United Mine Workers of America,
called to consider the strike in the anthracite field,
Indianapolis, July 19, 1902

*In 1902 coal miners affiliated with the United Mine Workers of
America or in sympathy with the union staged one of the greatest strikes
in American labor history. All told, an estimated 200,000 miners were
on strike. In Pennsylvania alone the number of strikers involved was
142,000, as virtually all the anthracite mine workers, as well as many
engineers, firemen, and pumpmen employed in and around the mines
went out on strike. Strikes were also in progress in West Virginia involving 20,000 miners, and in Alabama and Michigan where some
15,000 were out on strike.*

*On May 15, 1902, the United Mine Workers convention at Hazleton,
Pennsylvania which, over the opposition of President John Mitchell,
authorized the strike for union recognition and settlement of grievances,
also directed President Mitchell to call a national convention, the purpose of which was to involve the mine workers of the whole country in
the strike — including bituminous (soft coal) miners who worked under
a trade agreement which was not due to expire until the following year.
Only a general convention, requested by five or more districts, could decide this question.*

*President Mitchell strongly opposed a general strike, and for nearly a
month, he concealed even from associates in the international office, the
fact that he had the five petitions for a general convention. Meanwhile,
he worked behind the scenes, with the assistance of Samuel Gompers,
A.F. of L. president and Ralph M. Easley and Mark Hanna of the National Civic Federation, against a general strike.*

*The special convention met in Indianapolis on July 17, 1902. In his
opening address to the convention, Mitchell urged the delegates to oppose strikes in areas where the union had secured contracts, and to use
the union's financial resources primarily for the striking anthracite
miners. This meant that no additional funds would go to help the strike
in West Virginia's bituminous fields and other areas outside the anthracite districts. When the vote was finally taken, an attempt to spread
the strike to areas under union contract and to commit funds to West
Virginia as well as the anthracite field was defeated.*

*A number of requests were then made for an address by Mother
Jones, who was present, but Mitchell asked that she be excused from
speaking at this time "because she is completely worn out with her work
in West Virginia." (Mother Jones had been in charge of organizing
work in the southern West Virginia fields for over a year, and had been
transferred to the field in Fairmont where she was arrested and jailed*

along with a group of strikers.) On the request of delegate T. D. Nichols, however, Mother Jones was invited to address the convention the following morning.

At ten the next morning, July 19, Mother Jones spoke to the assembled delegates for forty-five minutes, giving a detailed account of the situation in West Virginia and the reasons for her arrest and imprisonment. Although the convention gave her a rising vote of thanks and confidence, it did nothing to change Mitchell's policies which committed the union to massive support only of the anthracite strikers.[1] Not surprisingly the strike in the unorganized bituminous coal fields of West Virginia ended in total failure.

Mother Jones's speech to the 1902 special convention is not included in the printed proceedings which simply note that "Mother Jones spoke." It is published here from the text in the typed copy of the proceedings in the John Mitchell Papers, Department of Archives and Manuscripts, Catholic University of America, Washington, D.C.

FIFTH SESSION
Saturday morning, July 19, 1902

The fifth session was called to order at 10 A.M. July 19th, President Mitchell[2] in the chair.

President Mitchell — The first order of business, under a motion made at the last session yesterday, is an address by Mother Jones.

The work of Mother Jones in the interests of the miners, the sacrifices she has made in their behalf, are so well known to the miners of the United States as to require no repetition from me. I therefore take great great pleasure in introducing to you our friend, Mother Jones.

Mrs. Mary Jones — Mr. Chairman and Fellow Delegates — I have been wondering whether this great gathering of wealth producers thoroughly comprehended the importance of their mission here today; whether they were really clear as to what their real mission was. I realize, my friends, that the eyes of the people of the United States, from one end to the other, are watching you; but you have again given a lesson to the world and a lesson to the statesmen that a general uprising is the last thing you called for; that you will resort to all peaceful, conservative methods before you rise and enter the final protest.[3]

I realize, my friends, what your mission is; but I am one of those who, taking all the conditions into consideration, had I been here would have voted for a gigantic protest. I wanted the powers that be to understand who the miners were; to understand that when they laid down their picks they tied up all other industries, and then the operators would learn what an important factor the miner is toward his support. But, my friends, I believe you have taken the wisest action, that action which the world at large will commend, and which I now commend, believing it is right. I think, my friends, when you go home from this convention it is not the promise you have made here that will be the important thing, but the carrying out of that promise, the doing of your duty in the matter, the fulfillment of your duty as man to man, that is of the greatest importance.

These fights must be won if it costs the whole country to win them. These fights against the oppressor and the capitalists, the ruling classes, must be won if it takes us all to do it. The President said I had made sacrifices. In that I disagree with him, though I do not usually do that, for I hold him very dear. None of us make sacrifices when we do our duty to humanity, and when we neglect that duty to humanity we deserve the greatest condemnation.

There is before you one question, my friends, and you must keep that question before your eyes this fall when you send representatives to the legislative halls. Your instructions to those representatives must be: "Down forever with government by injunction in the American nation."[4] This generation may sleep its slumber quietly, not feeling its mighty duty and responsibility, and may quietly surrender their liberties. And it looks very much as though they were doing so. These liberties are the liberties for which our forefathers fought and bled. Things are happening today that would have aroused our Revolutionary fathers in their graves. People sleep quietly, but it is the sleep of the slave chained closely to his master. If this generation surrenders its liberties, then the work of our forefathers, which we will lose by doing this, will not be resurrected for two generations to come. Then perhaps the people will wake up and say to their feudal lords "We protest," and they will inaugurate one of those revolutions that sometimes come when the slave feels there is no hope, and then proceed to tear society to pieces.

My friends, it is solidarity of labor we want. We do not want to find fault with each other, but to solidify our forces and say to each other: "We must be together; our masters are joined together and we must do the same thing."

I want to explain to some of the delegates here why eleven of my co-workers in the field and myself were arrested and thrown into jail.[5] We had the Fairmount Company practically licked, and as we did our marching and got our camps established the injunction machine began to work, and we had injunctions served against us, and they can grind injunctions out there in daylight and in the dark — it is no trouble to them at all. The Marshall served one on me, and I said to him: "I shall do my duty regardless of injunctions. I am here to do a work and I am going to do it; I think also that my co-workers intend to do their duty." We were not arrested on that injunction, but they served another. You know there is an amendment to every injunction. Well, we discussed the matter, and I said to the boys: "I don't believe there is any government in the world that can make us go blind; and if the company's tipple is a certain distance away I am not going to shut

my eyes and go blind for the sake of the Fairmount Coal Company."
We went to the meeting that was held there. There were eight of the
organizers there. We held our meeting. I was the only speaker there,
and I will confess that I felt particularly irritated that day; in fact, I
felt pretty sore. I shall tell you why. One of our boys was beaten nearly
to death by their bloodhounds as he was coming home from a meeting.
A night or two before that three of our organizers and myself were
coming home, and we met a boy with a buggy. I was tired, so the boy
drove me to the streetcar while the men walked. The company's store
was at the other end of a bridge we had to cross. The guards around the
store asked if that was Mother Jones, and I said, "Yes, boys; be good
and watch the slaves and don't let one of them get away or you will lose
your jobs in the morning." It was a covered bridge, and a very dangerous place. It ought to be torn away. I went through it in the dark and
sat down. It then dawned on me what an unsafe thing I had done.
There isn't a house there, there wasn't a human being with me, and six
thugs there who might have thrown me into the river and no one
would have been the wiser for it or would have known what happened
to me. Just then one of our men came out from the covered bridge yelling, "Murder, Murder!" I said, "What is the matter?" It was Barney
Rice, and I asked him what had happened to the rest of my boys. He
still kept calling for the police, and directly one of the comrades from
Indiana came out, and I said; "Where is Joe and John?" and they said,
"Mother, they are killing Joe." I ran towards the bridge, and Joe stag-
gered out all covered with blood, weak, and almost exhausted from loss
of blood.[6] I put him on the car and asked the car driver to take us to
town as quickly as possible. When we got him to town and examined
his injuries we found that he had eighteen cuts with knuckles on his
head.

I said at that meeting, "We are on a peaceful mission, and I don't see
why the judge should issue injunctions against us. Why does he not
issue injunctions against those thugs who are beating our people to
death? We are not armed; no one carries arms, and yet we have injunctions served on us."

It was weeks before poor Joe was able to get up again. Then we were
arrested and taken to Parkersburg at twelve o'clock at night; and the
Marshal, intending to be very courteous to me, said he had engaged a
room for me at the hotel. I thanked him very kindly, and he told a deputy to go there with me, and when we got to Parkersburg he said,
"Come this way with me," and I said, "Come with me, boys." He said,
"No, they are going to jail, and you are going to the hotel." I said, "No, I
am going wherever my boys go," and we all went to jail.[7] Next day we
were all taken before the judge, and I was kept on the witness stand for
seven long hours, for seven long hours they were questioning me, and
the old judge and I made friends with each other.[8] He asked me: "Did
you say there was an old gray-headed judge on the bench up there at

Parkersburg who thought he was running everything?" I said, "I said to the crowd there is an old gray-headed judge back there in Parkersburg, and he is growing old just as I am myself; we are both getting childish and some day soon we will both die, and then the whole world will miss us."

Then the judge told me that if I would go out of the state and stay out, and be a good girl generally, he would leave me alone. I asked my lawyer to tell him for me that I said all the devils in hell would not get me out of West Virginia while I had my duty there to perform. I said I was there to stay, and if I died in West Virginia in jail it made no difference with my decision. There would be no going out of the state, however; that thing was settled. I was there and I intended to fight whether in jail or out until we won. We all felt the same about that.

Let me warn you right here and now that any fellow who is not willing to go up against all these forces had better stay out of West Virginia; don't go over there, for we don't want you unless you are willing. We want fighters, although we are conducting our business on peaceful lines and according to the Constitution of the United States.

I have wondered many times recently what Patrick Henry would say, Patrick Henry who said, "Give me liberty or give me death," and who also said, "Eternal vigilence is the price of liberty,"[9] if he could witness the things that are done in West Virginia in this day and age, in a state that is supposed to be under the Constitution of the United States? I say with him, "Give me liberty or give me death, for for liberty I shall die, even if they riddle my body with bullets after I am dead."

My friends, you must emancipate the miners of West Virginia; they should be the barometer for you in the future. You have a task; go bravely home and take it up like men. Each one of you should constitute himself a missionary, each one should do his duty as a miner and as a member of this organization. Do your duty also as citizens of the United States, do your duty as men who feel a responsibility upon you, and remember, friends, that it is better to die an uncrowned free man than a crowned slave. You and I must protest against this injustice to the American people that we are suffering under in West Virginia and in Pennsylvania, and in other fields.

In West Virginia the attorney for the company in his argument said, when my case was up, "In strikes of the past we got the deputies, the marshals and the Federal troops out, and still the strikers won the strikes; but the moment the court came out with an injunction, then the strikers were whipped." He said further that the injunction was the barricade behind which the operators can stand.

There is an acknowledgement that we have no show; that the injunction is used for the benefit of the ruling classes. Now remember when your candidates get up and tell you what good friends they are to the laboring class, you ask them to sit right down and take an oath that the first thing they will do when they get to Congress is to introduce a bill entitled, "No government by injunction."[10]

Now I want to say a word about the West Virginia comrades. A great deal has been said for and against them. Perhaps no one there knows them better than I do. No one has mingled with them more than I have, and no one has heard more of their tales of sorrow and their tales of hope. I have sat with them on the sides of the mountains and on the banks of the rivers and listened to their tales. One night a comrade from Illinois was going with me up the mountain side. I said, "John, I believe it is going to be very dark tonight," and he said he thought it was, for only the stars were shining to guide us. When we got to the top of the mountain, besides the stars in the sky we saw other little stars, the miners' lamps, coming from all sides of the mountains. The miners were coming there to attend a meeting in a schoolhouse where we had promised to meet them, and I said to John, "There comes the star of hope, the star of the future, the star that the astronomer will tell nothing about in his great works for the future ages; but that is the star that is lighting up the ages yet to come; there is the star of the true miner laying the foundation for a higher civilization, and that star will shine when all other stars will grow dim."

We held a meeting there that night, and a braver band does not live on the face of this earth today than that band of men up there on the mountain top that night. And in their behalf I stand pleading with you here today. They have their faults, I admit, but no state ever produced nobler, truer, better men under the appalling circumstances and conditions under which they work. It matters not whether a miner is robbed in Illinois or in Virginia, in Indiana or in the anthracite region; they are all ours, and we must fight the battle for all of them. I think we will come out victorious in this fight, but it will only be for a while. Both sides will line up for the final conflict, and you must be ready for the fray. We have no time to lose. There is a peaceful method for settling this conflict. Get books; read at home; read to each other; take your boys that go to school and sit down and discuss the labor problem with them. Teach your women and children to not buy anything that has not a union label on it, to buy nothing that is not made by union men with union principles. You will in that way soon drive scabs and blacklegs out of the market; there will be no room for them.[11]

All of us should do our duty in this matter. Go home from this convention and put every dollar you can spare above your living expenses into this fight. If it costs us every penny we have, if we have to sell our clothes to get money to put into this fight we should do it. We have a class in the two Virginias — and they are the only two states in the Union, perhaps, where you can find them — that do not know what freedom means. They are a species of the human race that for ages have been slaves. They have come down from the Feudal days, they have never known what freedom was; they were sent out here in the time of George III in order to defeat the Colonists who were fighting for the freedom of their country. There are still remnants of them in the two Virginias, and they will work for twenty-five cents a day and be satisfied with it if their masters will give them no more. But they are in the minority. Think of the New River field, of the Kanawha River, of Loop Creek, and think of the work the boys have done there. Every wheel there is closed down, and that shows to you what good material there is there. One of the best elements there, I am here to tell you, are the colored men.[12] One of the best fellows we have is the black man. He knows what liberty is; he knows that in days gone by the bloodhounds went after his father over the mountains and tore him to pieces, and he knows that his own Mammy wept and prayed for liberty. For these reason he prizes his liberty and is ready to fight for it. My friends, the most of us have been told that we have liberty, and we believed the people who told us that!

Now, my friends, we should all work together in harmony to secure our rights. Don't find fault with each other; rather clasp hands and fight the battle together. Be true to the teachings of your forefathers who fought and bled and raised the old flag that we might always shout for liberty. Think, my friends! Did the laborers ever take twenty-two capitalists and riddle their bodies with bullets? Did the laborers ever take twenty thousand men, women and children and lock them up in the Bastille and murder them?[13] No, labor has always advanced Christianity. The history of the miner has been bitter and sore; he has traveled the highways and the byways to build up this magnificent organization, and let me beg of you, in God's holy name and in the name of the old flag, let the organization be used for the uplifting of the human race, but do not use it for the uplifting of yourself. Be true to your manhood; be true to your country; be true to the children yet unborn.

Now I want to say to you here that whether I die in jail or outside, I want to feel in the closing hours of my life that you have been true to each other, that you have been true to the principles of our forefathers. If you are true to these things the battle will end in victory for you.

[Typewritten Document, "Report of Special Convention of the United Mine Workers of America Called to Consider the Strike in the Anthracite Field, Indianapolis, Indiana, July 17-18-19, 1902," pp. 81-91, Department of Archives and Manuscripts, Catholic University of America, Washington, D.C.]

Notes

1. Philip S. Foner, *History of the Labor Movement in the United States,* vol. 3, New York, 1964, pp. 93-95; Edward M. Steel, "Mother Jones in the Fairmont Field, 1902," *Journal of American History* 57 (September, 1970): 298-99; UMW,

Minutes of Special Convention . . . 1902, pp. 38-42, 45-46.

2. John Mitchell (1870-1919), coal miner, member of the Knights of Labor, one of the founders of the United Mine Workers of America and its president, 1898-1908. While conditions of miners improved under his leadership, he was criticized for increasing conservatism and collaboration with big business in the National Civic Federation. Mitchell died a rich man. He was author of *Organized Labor* (1903), and *The Wage Earner and His Problems* (1913).

3. Mother Jones is referring to the rejection of a general strike by the convention. For a discussion which defends Mitchell's decision not to extend the strike into West Virginia, *see* David Alan Corbin, *Life, Work and Rebellion in the Coal Fields: The Southern West Virginia Miners 1880-1922,* Urbana, Illinois, 1981, pp, 47-48.

4. William B. Wilson, UMW secretary, labor congressman from Pennsylvania, and first secretary of labor when the department was created in 1913, expressed the same sentiments, writing to Frank Morrison, A.F. of L. secretary-treasurer: "The paramount issue in American politics in the future must necessarily be the abolishment of Government by injunction." (William B. Wilson to Frank Morrison, Aug. 16, 1902, American Federation of Labor Correspondence.)

5. *See* pp. 54, 78-82, 90, 99, 386, 409-10, 481-82, 551, 552.

6. In her autobiography Mother Jones records the fact that she was able to deceive the assailants and save the lives of the miners by having the gunmen believe that a rescue party was close at hand. She also recalled: "I tore my petticoat into strips, bandaged his [Joe's] head, helped the boys to get him on to the Interurban car, and hurried the car into Fairmont City." (Mary Harris Jones, *Autobiography of Mother Jones,* Chicago, 1925, pp. 43-44.)

7. In indignantly refusing the offer of a hotel room, Mother Jones insisted that as a federal prisoner she should receive the same treatment as her boys. Accordingly she was lodged in the Wood County jail, but the jailer and his wife refused to put her in a cell, and kept her in their quarters, treating her as one of the family. (*Parkersburg Sentinel,* June 21, 1902.)

8. Judge Jackson had received his appointment to the federal bench from Abraham Lincoln, but he was a tough, conservative upholder of law and order. He placed Mother Jones and the others who had been jailed on a bail bond of $300 each and warned them not to engage in any strike activity before the case came to trial. Because she was out on bail, Mother Jones was able to attend the special convention.

9. Patrick Henry (1736-1799), revolutionary statesman and orator of Virginia who in a speech on March 23, 1775, urging strong colonial defense, used the famous phrase, "Give me liberty or give me death." West Virginia was until the Civil War part of Virginia.

10. In 1903 an anti-injunction bill was passed in the House of Representatives, but was defeated in the Senate.

11. At the time Mother Jones made these remarks, the union label was often put forward as the main weapon of the labor movement, and as labor's "battle flag on the industrial field." Armed with the union label, went the argument, trade unions could force all employers to recognize the right of their workers to organize. In achieving the organization of the unorganized, it was "more powerful than strikes and picketing." (*See* Foner, *op. cit.,* vol. 3, pp. 176-77 and *The Union Label: Its History and Aims,* Washington, D.C., 1904.

12. Mother Jones had a definite purpose in making this point. Although Ita-

lians were among the miners in West Virginia most difficult to organize, racism influenced many miners to blame blacks as strikebreakers and threats of lynching were not uncommon. Mother Jones aimed to dispel this anti-Negro propaganda. (For threats of lynching, *see* Sheldon M. Harris, "Letters from West Virginia: Management's Version of the 1902 Coal Strike," *Labor History* 10 (Spring, 1969): 240.)

13. Mother Jones is referring to the ruthless suppression of the Paris Commune and the slaughter of thousands of Communards and their sympathizers after the fall of the commune.

Women Are Fighters

Speech before Central Labor Council of
Cincinnati and Vicinity, July 23, 1902

While she was out on bail for violating an injunction issued by Federal Judge Jackson at Parkersburg, West Virginia, Mother Jones returned to the UMW headquarters in Indianapolis to attend the special convention. After the convention closed, she headed back to Parkersburg for the trial before Judge Jackson on July 24, 1902. En route Mother Jones stopped off at Cincinnati, and, at the invitation of the Central Labor Council, delivered a speech to the body on July 23, parts of which were published in the Chronicle, *the Council's official organ.*

"Mother" Jones, called the sentryman, was at the Central Labor Council meeting Tuesday night. Accompanied by a young miner from the anthracite regions the snow-haired United Mine Worker was admitted. She was greeted with a burst of applause as she walked to a seat beside the presiding officer.

For an hour this quick-eyed, mobile-faced woman sat as an interested auditor to the regular proceedings of the meeting. At 9 o'clock, by resolution of the members, the doors were thrown open to the public. The hallway had been crowded with those patiently waiting to hear and see this eloquent and most court-injuncted labor organizer in the world. For ninety minutes she held her audience by the charm of a well-used voice in words that reached deep into the hearts and minds of the friends present. Humor and pathos, fact and fancy, chased each other in quick succession and were never without their instant response. More than once the expression was heard, "I could listen to her all night." She said in part:

"The greatest industrial conflict in the world's history is now being fought, and if it was not for the wise heads of the United Mine Workers' officials the country would be in the throes of a revolution within a month. By our action in Indianapolis we refute the charge that we are always looking for trouble and ready for war.[1] The miners are showing the world that they are not of the type they are said to be. I call particular attention to the 30,000 anthracite miners in the God-curst monopoly State of West Virginia. There are places there fenced in and guarded like in Siberia. No one is allowed inside, nor are the men permitted to come out. Only one newspaper enters — the *Fairmount Times*, owned by the operators. The least talk against this prison management means discharge. And Patrick Henry, on the same ground, said once, 'Give me liberty or give me death.' For calling a mass meeting there I was put behind the bars. The State law says the men must be paid every two weeks in legal tender money. They are paid when the bosses get good and ready and in soup tickets. The law requires the coal to be weighed fairly. It is misweighed by the operators as they see fit. The law requires 1500 cubic feet of air for each miner. This is not done. Baby boys are compelled to breathe the poisonous air that brings them to disease and early graves. In one place an army of men were thrown out of the company houses. We put them in tents, and for no other reason the men were dragged behind the bars to Parkersburg, thirty miles away. I secured a house for some of the women who were set out one midnight on the road. This was denied in court, but it's God's truth, for I saw them do it.

"There are 30,000 breaker boys in Pennsylvania whose torn and bleeding hands attest the greed of murdering capital.[2] I said in open court to a judge down there who said in low accents, 'labor has its rights,' and in thundering menace, 'and the operators have their rights too, and I am going to see they get them,'[3] I said, 'It is worse than crucifying Christ, because Christ could have helped himself and these babies cannot.'

"On Thursday I expect to go to jail, but I am not afraid of their jails.[4] I go for a principle. There are no convictions except for cowardice when a principle is to be upheld. Men will work together, be enjoined together, will go to jail together, will defend each other, will trust each other, will support each other. Why is it they cannot stand together at the ballot box? No bayonet, no injunction can interfere there. You pay Senators, Governors, Legislators, and then beg on your knees for them to pass a bill in labor's protection. You will never solve the problem until you let in the women. No nation is greater than its women.

"One time this young miner beside me came to me and said that after five months of bitterest hardship they were going back to work in his mine in the morning under the old inhuman conditions. I called a union meeting. The women had never come before. This time they came. They for the first time heard and understood. Instead of returning to work, the women took up the fight and for five months longer the struggle went on, when the company gave in and the fight was won. Women are fighters.

"I appeal to you. We must win in this Miners' fight. Go down in your pockets and raise money and send it to this noble industrial army. If they are whipped you are whipped. It is a duty to yourselves and your children. We are up against it. I work for the children unborn. No children in the mines and mills of the future is my cry.

"Put no faith in the politicians who pat you on the back. Every corruptionist in the Legislature you put there. At the next election be done forever with government by injunction. Thirty-nine years ago the black slaves were freed. Today we are the white slaves to a corrupt judiciary.

"The Chinese bill has a leak in it.[5] Frank Sargeant was appointed Immigration Commissioner, but more paupers are coming into the country than ever before. You have not protested. We are in the majority. Then away with it. Let us have a class conscious proletariat party. The Miners will line up. In '94 the President and both houses of Congress were Democratic. They shot us down in the great A. R. U. strike,[6] and here in Ohio a Republican Governor did the same thing. Don't go off to fight for freedom in a foreign land. There is plenty of fighting to do at home.[7] This is the first time in the world's history that labor is solidifying and I hope Cincinnati will wake up and show the world her force."

On the editorial page:

"Mother" Jones said two things not in type on the first page. We reserved them for this special mention. One was: "You would now have no beer boycott on your hands if you were true to each other. You are not as intelligent as trained monkeys when you drink 'unfair' beer." The other was: "Ask for union-mined coal and help the miners. Don't murder baby boys by being cowards towards yourselves and your own children." Amen.

[The Chronicle, Official paper of Cincinnati and Vicinity,
July 27, 1902. Copy in Cincinnati Historical Society.]
I wish to thank Professor Herbert Shapiro of the University of
Cincinnati for furnishing me with a copy of the Chronicle.

Notes

1. The special convention of the UMW had rejected the call for a general strike, supporting President Mitchell's position on this and other issues.
2. One-sixth of the work force in the mines at this time were boys. In several

states laws existed making it illegal to employ boys under fourteen inside any mine and proscribed employment in surface jobs for those under twelve. The Pennsylvania legislature raised these limits to sixteen and fourteen respectively in 1903. But these laws had little effect. Coal operators, knowing that they could pay the boys the lowest wages — usually well under a dollar a day in the early 1900s — encouraged the parents to file false affidavits with the local magistrates, and the meager income of the miners swept away whatever reluctance they might have had to cooperate.

While boys worked in a number of jobs both above and below ground, most of them separated slate from the coal in the mammoth industrial buildings called breakers. Here the coal was cleaned and sized before its shipment.

3. The judge referred to was Judge John Jay Jackson of the federal court in Parkersburg, West Virginia.

4. At the time Mother Jones was arrested for speaking at a meeting near the Clarksburg Fuel Company's property in violation of the ban imposed by Judge Jackson's injunction, she ended her speech with a farewell in which she used almost the same words: "Goodbye boys; I'm under arrest. I may have to go to jail. I may not see you for a long time. Keep up this fight! Don't surrender!" (Parkersburg *Sentinel,* June 21, 1902; Steel, *op. cit.,* pp. 296-97.)

5. On May 6, 1902 the Greary Act excluding Chinese laborers from the United States expired. It was extended immediately, however, in part as a result of pressure from the A.F. of L., and this time there was added the provision that the immigration and naturalization of Chinese could be prohibited indefinitely. It is not clear, therefore, what the "leak" was referred to by Mother Jones.

6. The reference is to the Pullman strike or boycott called by the American Railway Union in 1894 under the leadership of Eugene V. Debs. During the battle President Grover Cleveland sent federal troops to Chicago to enforce an injunction issued under the Sherman Anti-Trust Act. At least twenty-five workers were killed and sixty injured by the troops. (*See* Philip S. Foner, *History of the Labor Movement in the United States,* vol. 2, New York, 1955, pp. 261-78.)

7. Undoubtedly Mother Jones is referring to the war to crush the Filipino independence movement which was officially terminated by edict of President Theodore Roosevelt on July 4, 1902. It had lasted three years and required the services of 126,468 American soldiers of whom 4,234 were killed and 2,818 wounded. The Filipinos lost their independence: 16,000 Filipino soldiers were killed, and over 200,000 civilians died because of famine and pestilence.

Agitation — The Greatest Factor for Progress

Speech in Memorial Hall, Toledo, March 24, 1903

The anthracite coal strike of 1902 ended after intervention by President Theodore Roosevelt and the appointment of an Anthracite Strike Commission, the arbitration board empowered to review the issues in the strike. Although the degree of "victory" achieved by the anthracite miners as a result of the rulings of the commission[1] is a matter of dispute among labor historians,[2] there is no question that the coal strike among the bituminous miners of West Virginia ended in total failure. Mother Jones did not actually remain in West Virginia for the end of the strike. She was superseded as leader of the strike by Vice-President Tom Lewis, Mitchell's bitter and ambitious rival for control of the union, who had tried to prevent the strike originally and disapproved strenuously of Mother Jones's militant tactics.[3] Mother Jones departed for the anthracite field, but returned to West Virginia after the strike ended, hoping to help if the miners renewed the battle. But in March, 1903, the UMW convention in Huntington voted there would be no strike that year. Again Mother Jones left West Virginia, and spoke on March 23, 1903, in Toledo's "Memorial Hall" to an audience of 1,200, many of them women. While she devoted most of her speech to the struggle in West Virginia against feudal conditions, she also urged women to fight for the right to vote so that they could use the ballot to defeat capitalistic bullets. Excerpts from the speech were published in the To-ledo Bee.

"Mother" Jones, known throughout the country and in fact throughout the world as "The Miners' Angel," addressed a motley gathering of about 1,200 persons in Memorial hall last night. The lower hall was packed. The gallery was full to overflowing and some even crowded the steps leading to the building.

It was truly a motley gathering. The society woman, attracted by mere curiosity to see and hear the woman who has won such fame as the guardian spirit of the miners; the factory girl, the wealthy man and his less fortunate brothers, the black man and the white man, old and young, sat side by side and each came in for a share of criticism.

"Mother" Jones is an eloquent speaker. There is just enough of the down-east accent to her words to make it attractive and she has the faculty of framing pathetic and beautiful word pictures. Despite her sixty years and her gray hairs, she is hale and hearty; has a voice that reaches to the furthermost corner of almost any hall but it is nevertheless anything but harsh.

Her force of character was displayed with her every word spoken. She spared none. She condemned the trades unionist for casting his

95

ballot as he does each year for that system.

Mother Jones was introduced by Chairman Charles Martin. She began deliberately and her address of an hour and a half, interrupted with frequent bursts of applause, was one of the most remarkable heard by local trades unionists in many months.

Wage Slavery.

"Fellow workers," she began, "'tis well for us to be here. Over a hundred years ago men gathered to discuss the vital questions and later fought together for a principle that won for us our civil liberty. Forty years ago men gathered to discuss a growing evil under the old flag and later fought side by side until chattel slavery was abolished. But, by the wiping out of this black stain upon our country another great crime — wage slavery — was fastened upon our people. I stand on this platform ashamed of the conditions existing in this country. I refused to go to England and lecture only a few days ago because I was ashamed, first of all, to make the conditions existing here known to the world and second, because my services were needed here. I have just come from a God-cursed country, known as West Virginia; from a state which has produced some of our best and brightest statesmen; a state where conditions are too awful for your imagination.

"I shall tell you some things tonight that are awful to contemplate; but, perhaps, it is best that you to know of them. They may arouse you from your lethargy if there is any manhood, womanhood or love of country left in you. I have just come from a state which has an injunction on every other foot of ground. Some months ago the president of the United Mine Workers asked me to take a look into the condition of the men in the mines of West Virginia.[4] I went. I would get a gathering of miners in the darkness of the night up on the mountain side. Here I would listen to their tale of woe; here I would try to encourage them. I did not dare to sleep in one of those miner's houses. If I did the poor man would be called to the office in the morning and would be discharged for sheltering old Mother Jones.

Oppression.

"I did my best to drive into the downtrodden men a little spirit, but it was a task. They had been driven so long that they were afraid. I used to sit through the night by a stream of water. I could not go to the miners' hovels so in the morning I would call the ferryman and he would take me across the river to a hotel not owned by the mine operators.

"The men in the anthracite district finally asked for more wages. They were refused. A strike was called. I stayed in West Virginia; held meetings and one day as I stood talking to some break-boys two injunctions were served upon me. I asked the deputy if he had more. We were arrested but we were freed in the morning. I objected to the food in the jail and to my arrest. When I was called up before the judge I called him a czar and he let me go.[5] The other fellows were afraid and they went to jail. I violated injunction after injunction but I wasn't re-arrested. Why? The courts themselves force you to have no respect for that court.

"A few days later that awful wholesale murdering in the quiet little mining camp of Stamford took place. I know those people were law-abiding citizens. I had been there. And their shooting by United States deputy marshals was an atrocious and cold-blooded murder.[6] After the crimes had been committed the marshals — the murderers — were banqueted by the operators in the swellest hotel in Pennsylvania. You have no idea of the awfulness of that wholesale murder. Before daylight broke in the morning in that quiet little mining camp deputies and special officers went into the homes, shot the men down in their beds, and all because the miners wanted to try to induce 'black-legs' to leave the mines.

How It Started.

"I'll tell you how the trouble started. The deputies were bringing these strikebreakers to the mines. The men wanted to talk with them and at last stepped on ground loaded down with an injunction. There were thirty-six or seven in the party of miners. They resisted arrest. They went home finally without being arrested. One of the officials of the miners' unions telegraphed to the men. "Don't resist. Go to jail. We will bail you out." A United States marshall stood in the [illegible] that message was received [illegible] sent back word that the operators would not let them use the telephone to send the message to the little mining camp and that he could not get there before hours had passed. The miners' officials secured the names of the men and gave their representatives authority to bail them out of jail the next morning. But when the next morning arrived they were murdered in cold blood.

"These federal judges, who continue granting injunctions, are appointed by men who have their political standing through the votes of you labor union fellows! You get down on your knees like a lot of Yahoos when you want something. At the same time you haven't sense enough to take peaceably what belongs to you through the ballot. You are chasing a will-o-the-wisp, you measly things, and the bullets which should be sent into your own measly, miserable, dirty carcasses, shoot down innocent men. Women are not responsible because they have no vote. You'd all better put on petticoats. If you like those bullets vote to put them into your own bodies. Don't you think it's about time you began to shoot ballots instead of voting for capitalistic bullets.

A Challenge.

"I hate your political parties, you Republicans and Democrats. I want you to deny if you can what I am going to say. You want an office and must necessarily get into the ring. You must do what that ring says and if you don't you won't be elected. There you are. Each time you do that you are voting for a capitalistic bullet and you get it. I want you to know that this man Jones who is running for mayor of your beautiful city is no relative of mine; no, sir. He belongs to that school of reformers who say capital and labor must join hands.[7] He may be all right. He prays a good deal. But, I wonder if you would shake hands with me if I robbed you. He builds parks to make his workmen contented. But a contented workman is no good. All progress stops in the contented man. I'm for agitation. It's the greater factor for progress."

Here the speaker changed her attention to the society woman. "I see a lot of society women in this audience, attracted here out of a mere curiosity to see 'that old Mother Jones.' I know you better than you do yourselves. I can walk down the aisle and pick everyone of you out. You probably think I am crazy but I know you. And you society dudes — poor creatures. You wear high collars to support your jaw and keep your befuddled brains from oozing out of your mouths. While this commercial cannibalism is reaching into the cradle; pulling girls into the factory to be ruined; pulling children into the factory to be destroyed; you, who are doing all in the name of Christianity, you are at home nursing your poodle dogs. It's high time you got out and worked for humanity. Christianity will take care of itself. I started in a factory. I have traveled through miles and miles of factories and there is not an inch of ground under that flag that is not stained with the blood of children."

Mother Jones then returned to the subject of the miners. She said they were not drunkards. They had neither enough food or enough clothing and the amount they spent for drink would not clothe them. It was no wonder they drank. Their misery was such as to cause them to drown their sorrows for an hour or so. In conclusion, she said: "You may think, as people sometimes do, that my pictures are overdrawn. But if you would come with me I could show you that I have not the power to describe in words the awful conditions existing in some districts and especially in West Virginia. I have not told the half. And, until you labor fellows wake up those conditions will grow from bad to worse."

*[Toledo Bee, March 25, 1903. Clipping in Mother Jones Papers,
Department of Archives and Manuscripts,
Catholic University of America, Washington, D.C.]*

Notes

1. The president's commission handed down its decision on March 22, 1913. The award provided for a ten percent increase in wages, a nine-hour day, and instead of recognition of the union, the creation of a six-man conciliation board on which workers' organizations were to be represented. This board was to adjudicate all disputes arising between miners and their employers. In the section of the award relating to nonunion workmen, the commission stated: "No person shall be refused employment, or in any way discriminated against on account of membership or non-membership in any labor organization; and there shall be no discrimination against or interference with any employee who is not a member of any labor organization by members of such organization." But the report of the commission did not stop here. It went on to emphasize that "the rights and privileges of non-union men are as sacred to them as the rights and privileges of unionists. The contention that a majority in an industry, by voluntarily associating themselves in a union, acquire authority over those who do not so associate themselves in a union is untenable. . . . No one can interfere with their [non-strikers'] conduct in choosing the work upon what terms and what time and for whom it may please them so to do." (*Senate Doc. No. 6*, 58 Cong., Special Session, Washington, D.C., 1903, especially pp. 64-65, 76-78.)

2. The view that the settlement was a "victory" for the strikers is set forth in most labor history works. Philip Taft, for example, hails it as "one of the greatest [victories] in American labor history." (*Organized Labor in American History,* New York, 1964, p. 177.) *See also* Selig Perlman, *A History of Trade Unionism in the United States,* 2nd ed., New York, 1962, p. 170; Foster Rhea Dulles, *Labor in America: A History,* 3rd ed., New York, 1966, pp. 188-93.) On the other hand, Robert H. Wiebe challenges this interpretation as does the present writer, and both view the settlement as a defeat for the strikers and Mitchell as selling out the workers to the operators. (*See* Robert H. Wiebe, "The Anthracite Strike of 1902: A Record of Confusion," *Mississippi Valley Historical Review* 8 (September, 1961): 229-51, and Philip S. Foner, *History of the Labor Movement in the United States,* Vol. 3, New York, 1964, pp. 89-101.) Mother Jones later came to view the settlement as a defeat. (*See Autobiography of Mother Jones,* Chicago, 1925, pp. 58-61.)

3. Years later, Tom Lewis deserted to management and became secretary of the New River, West Virginia Coal Operators' Association (Winthrop D. Lane, *Civil War in West Virginia,* New York, 1921, p. 102).

4. Mother Jones does not mention that President Mitchell also asked her to leave the southern fields of West Virginia and join the campaign to organize the Fairmont field, one of the most difficult in the state. "I think the Fairmont [field]," Mitchell wrote to Mother Jones, "would be the place in which you could do the most good, as the coal companies up there have evidently scared our boys, and of course with good reason, as they have brutally beaten some of them. I dislike to ask you always to take the dangerous fields, but I know that you are willing. . . . " In the Fairmont field, Mother Jones was specially charged with the management of food supplies. (John Mitchell to Mother Jones, May 10, 1902, John Mitchell Papers, Department of Archives and Manuscripts, Catholic University of America, Washington, D.C.) "Her only concession to her seventy-two years," notes Edward M. Steel, "was the buggy in which she rode from Flemington, rather than marching." (*op. cit.,* p. 294.)

5. Judge Jackson actually declared that Mother Jones was guilty, as were

the others, but he would suspend sentence "hoping that she would profit by her experience and would not further attempt to violate the injunction." (Steel, *op. cit.,* p. 301.)

6. A picture headed "Six Killed Outright And A Number Died Afterwards" is included in the Mother Jones Papers, Department of Archives and Manuscripts, Catholic University of America, Washington, D.C. On the reverse, in what is believed to be the handwriting of Mother Jones, is written, "On Standiford Mountain, Raleigh County, West Virginia, Feb. 23, 1903." It is interesting that Mother Jones did not mention the killing of three militant black miners, leaders of the struggle in West Virginia, by Deputy Marshal Dan W. Cunningham and his deputies while they were sleeping. A report of the murders appeared in the *United Mine Workers Journal* of March 5, 1903, in a letter from Chris Evans, sent from Charleston, West Virginia. Evans, a UMW official, was sent to West Virginia "to investigate the killing of colored miners at Atkinsville." (*The Worker,* New York, March 1, 1903.) In her *Autobiography* Mother Jones discusses the murders on Standiford Mountain (pp. 68-70) but again does not mention the murder of the black union miners. (For the role of black miners in West Virginia, *see* Charles W. Simmons, John R. Rankin, and U. G. Carter, "Negro Coal Miners in West Virginia, 1875-1925," *Midwest Journal,* Spring, 1954, pp. 61-86.)

7. The reference is to Samuel Milton Jones (1846-1904), known as "Golden Rule" Jones, a liberal industrialist who ran for mayor of Toledo on the Republican ticket, but with the support of sixty of the city's trade unions. Jones merited the support because he was a liberal industrialist who had instituted the eight-hour day among drillers of his oil wells, and, as president of the Western Oil Men's Association, had gotten a resolution unanimously passed by the organization favoring the eight-hour day. (This was probably the first organization of employers on record to take such a stand.) Jones was a firm believer in trade unionism — although he was critical of unions for organizing only skilled workers (as was Mother Jones), and after he was elected mayor, he infuriated the Republican boss by consulting trade union leaders rather than corporation spokespersons on the needs of the city. He was re-elected, again with trade union support, but as an independent. (*See* Philip S. Foner, *History of the Labor Movement in the United States,* vol. 5, New York, 1980, pp. 62-66.)

The Wail of the Children

Speech at Coney Island, Brooklyn, New York,
during the march of the mill children, July 28, 1903

On May 23, 1903, a hundred thousand textile workers left their jobs at six hundred mills in the Philadelphia area. Over sixteen thousand of *the strikers were children, many of them under twelve years of age. Although the state law prohibited the employment of children under twelve, in Pennsylvania, as in other northern states, only the parents' oath was required to certify a child's age. Poor families perjured themselves in order to keep starvation away from their door. The strikers demanded a reduction in the workweek from sixty to fifty-five hours, even if this meant a decrease in wages, which at the time of the strike ranged from $2 a week for children to $13 a week for adults.[1]*

Although the Philadelphia local of the Socialist Party was critical of the strikers for being willing to decrease their wages in order to obtain a shorter workweek, it rallied to their support. Caroline H. Pemberton, a member of a distinguished Philadelphia family and state secretary of the Socialist Party, published articles in the local press defending the strikers' struggle and calling for aid. Pemberton urged "comrades everywhere . . . to assist in this great work."[2]

Responding to this appeal, Mother Jones arrived in Philadelphia on June 14 from the coal fields of West Virginia. She was appalled by the fact that every day little children, some not more than ten years old, came into union headquarters, "some with their hands off, some with the thumb missing, some with their fingers off at the knuckles. They were stooped little things," she observed, "round shouldered and skinny." When Mother Jones tried to get newspaper publicity about the plight of these children, newspaper men advised her they could not carry the stories because the mill owners held stock in their papers. So she replied: "Well, I've got stock in these little children and I'll arrange a little publicity." She thereupon organized an industrial "army" of child textile workers to march from Philadelphia to President Theodore Roosevelt's summer home at Oyster Bay on Long Island, some 125 miles away, and win the president's support for the abolition of child labor.

On July 7, 1903, the march got under way. About three hundred men, women, and children were led by three children dressed as Revolutionary soldiers, representing the Spirit of '76. The children carried only knapsacks and banners with the slogans, "We Only Ask for Justice," "55 Hours or Nothing," "More Schools, Less Hospitals," "We Want to Go to School," "We Want Time to Play," "Prosperity, Where Is Our Share?"[3]

"Mother Jones's Crusaders" or "Mother Jones's Industrial Army" (names variously bestowed on the marchers by the press[4]) arrived in New York City on July 24.[5] Two days later, Mother Jones took the children to Coney Island for a day's entertainment. But while in the seaside resort, she did not miss an opportunity to emphasize the evils of child labor to the men and women enjoying the sun, sand, surf, and exhibits. Frank Bostock, a sympathetic animal-show owner, invited Mother Jones to use his facilities, and after the barker announced that "Mother Jones will deliver an address at 4:30 o'clock," the crowds gathered and the Bostock Building was filled when she started to speak.

After a long and weary march, with more miles to travel, we are on our way to see President Roosevelt at Oyster Bay. We will ask him to recommend the passage of a bill by Congress to protect children against the greed of the manufacturer. We want him to hear the wail of the children, who never have a chance to go to school, but work from ten to eleven hours a day in the textile mills of Philadelphia, weaving the carpets that he and you walk on, and the curtains and clothes of the people.

Fifty years ago there was a cry against slavery, and the men of the North gave up their lives to stop the selling of black children on the block. To-day the white child is sold for $2 a week, and even by his parents, to the manufacturer.

Fifty years ago the black babies were sold C.O.D. To-day the white baby is sold to the manufacturer on the installment plan. He might die at his tasks and the manufacturer with the automobile and the yacht and the daughter who talks French to a poodle dog, as you can see any day at Twenty-third Street and Broadway when they roll by, could not afford to pay $2 a week for the child that might die, except on the present installment plan. What the President can do is to recommend a measure and send a message to Congress which will break the chains of the white children slaves.

He endorsed a bill for the expenditure of $45,000 to fill the stomach of a Prince who went galivanting about the country.[6] We will ask in the name of the aching hearts of these little ones that they be emancipated. I will tell the President that I saw men in Madison Square last night sleeping on the benches and that the country can have no greatness while one unfortunate lies out at night without a bed to sleep on. I will tell him that the prosperity he boasts of is the prosperity of the rich wrung from the poor.

In Georgia where children work day and night in the cotton mills they have just passed a bill to protect song birds. What about the little children from whom all song is gone?[7]

The trouble is that the fellers in Washington don't care. I saw them last Winter pass three railroad bills in one hour, and when labor cries for aid for the little ones they turn their backs and will not listen to her. I asked a man in prison once how he happened to get there. He had stolen a pair of shoes. I told him that if he had stolen a railroad he could be a United States Senator. One hour of justice is worth an age of praying.

You are told that every American-born male citizen has a chance of being President. I tell you that the hungry man without a bed in the park would sell his chance for a good square meal, and these little toilers, deformed, dwarfed in body, soul, and morality, with nothing but toil before them and no chance for schooling, don't even have the dream that they might some day have a chance at the Presidential chair.

You see those monkeys in the cages.[8] They are trying to teach them to talk. The monkeys are too wise, for they fear that then the manufacturers might buy them for slaves in their factories. In 1860 the workingmen had the advantage in the percentage of the country's wealth. To-day statistics at Washington show that with billions of wealth the wage earners' share is but 10 per cent. We are going to tell the President of these things.[9]

[Brooklyn Daily Eagle, *July 27, 1903;*
New York Times, *July 27, 1903.]*

Notes

1. Philadelphia *North American,* May 24, 25, 1903.
2. *Ibid.,* June 11, 22, 1903; *The Worker,* July 5, 1903.
Until recently Caroline H. Pemberton has been totally neglected. She deserves to be known not only for the fact that she became a Socialist after being brought up in an upper-class family but even more so because she was a leading Socialist in the early years of the party to stand for equality of black Americans. She was critical of the party for its failure to advocate such equality. For a study of Pemberton and especially for her views on the Negro question, *see* Philip S. Foner, "Caroline Hollingsworth Pemberton: Philadelphia Socialist Champion of Black Equality," *Pennsylvania History* 43 (July, 1976): 227-52 and Philip S. Foner, *American Socialism and Black Americans: From the Age of Jackson to World War II,* Westport, Conn., 1978, pp. 180-96.
3. Philadelphia *North American,* July 8, 9, 1903; John Spargo, "Child Slaves of Philadelphia," *Comrade,* August, 1903, p. 253; Russel E. Smith, "The March of the Mill Children," *Social Service* 4 (September, 1967): 300-01; Philip S. Foner, *Women and the American Labor Movement: From Colonial Times to the Eve of World War I,* New York, 1979, pp. 283-85. C. K. McFarland, "Crusade for Child Laborers: 'Mother' Jones and the March of the Mill Children," *Pennsylvania History* 38 (July, 1977): 283-90; Helen Collier Camp, "Mother Jones and the Children's Crusade," unpublished M.A. thesis, Columbia University, 1970, pp. 13-25.
4. The name "Industrial Army" was taken from Coxey's army of the unemployed in 1894, of which Mother Jones was a member.
5. When permission was denied Mother Jones and her children's crusade to march in New York City, she went to Mayor Seth Low and challenged the city's right to deny the marchers access to the streets, when the city had entertained Prince Henry of Germany ("a piece of rotten royalty") and other foreign dignitaries, who added nothing to the nation's well-being. "Well, Mr. Mayor," Mother Jones summed up her tirade, "there are the little citizens of the nation and they also produce its wealth. Aren't we entitled to enter your city?" Low agreed, and the crusaders marched from the Socialist Party headquarters preceded by a band "provided by the Socialists" to an outdoor rally. (*New York Times,* July 24, 1903.)
6. Prince Henry of Germany.
7. Mother Jones had worked in the cotton mills of Alabama and described

her experiences in "Civilization in Southern Mills," *International Socialist Review*, March, 1901, pp. 540-41 and reprinted below pp. 453-55. *See also, The Autobiography of Mother Jones,* pp. 117-19.

8. Mother Jones had been invited to visit Coney Island with the children by the owner of the wild-animal show and after the exhibition of the trained animals, he invited Mother Jones to speak to the audience. She placed the children in the empty iron cages of the animals, and they "clung to the iron bars while I talked." (*Autobiography of Mother Jones,* pp. 79-80.)

9. For Mother Jones's letters to President Roosevelt, *see* pp. 452-55.

We Must Stand Together

Speech at meeting of miners, northern Colorado,
held at Louisville, Colorado, November 21, 1903

Next to West Virginia, Colorado occupied a major part of Mother Jones's organizing activities among the miners. Shortly after the "Children's Crusade," she went to a miners' memorial service for the Virden martyrs in Mt. Olive, Illinois.[1] On the way, she stopped at the UMW national headquarters in Indianapolis, where she found a new assignment awaiting her. President Mitchell sent the seventy-three-year-old national organizer to Colorado to report on the situation in that state where a recent unionization drive had led to the demand for a strike, a policy Mitchell vigorously opposed.[2]

Of the 11,000 coal miners in Colorado only about 15 percent were organized, and the UMW launched a renewed organizing campaign in the spring of 1903. Most of the union's members were in the northern field, mainly in Boulder County, while Huerfano and Las Animas Counties, in the southern and more productive field, were almost entirely unorganized. Here in southern Colorado absentee ownership flourished. All of the coal fields — almost a half million acres — were owned by two companies: the Colorado Fuel and Iron Company (CF&I) under John D. Rockefeller and the Victor-American Company under Jay Gould.

Colorado miners had good reason to strike. They lived in company-owned houses rarely better than crumbling one-room shacks with bare dirt floors and broken windows and they could be evicted at any moment's notice if they dared protest. They were forced to buy at the company stores where, as in West Virginia, the highest prices in the district were charged. Their wages, moreover, were paid in script, not cash, so they had no choice but to buy everything they needed from the company stores. In addition, the coal they dug, on the basis of which they were paid, was weighed at the end of each day by company weighmen who invariably short-changed the miners. The miners themselves had no right to check the measurement.

On top of feudal conditions which rivaled those of West Virginia, the miners were further enraged by the state's failure to enforce the eight-hour-day law adopted by the legislature in 1899. Although the law had been copied almost word for word from a Utah statute, which the state's highest court and the United States Supreme Court had upheld, the Colorado State Supreme Court had ruled the act unconstitutional. As a result the miners continued to work nine, ten, and twelve hours a day.[3] On top of this, in the case of the southern field, the miners complained at the refusal of the mine operators to meet with the union.[4]

Behind the scenes, meanwhile, a bitter dispute was taking place between the militant, pro-socialist Western Federation of Miners and the leadership of the United Mine Workers of America, with Mitchell's growing conservatism and increasing association with big business in the National Civic Federation a major issue in the dispute. This was the situation when Mother Jones arrived in Trinidad, Colorado "unannounced and unattended" on October 26, 1903. Unable and unwilling to see any distinction between the W.F. of M. and the UMW — a miner was a miner to Mother Jones — she cooperated with both organizations. At the advice of W.F. of M. leaders she disguised herself as a peddler and visited the miners in their homes so as to find out for herself what were the real conditions. She found that they "were in practical slavery to the company," and decided that the "time was ripe for revolt against such brutal conditions." She returned to Indianapolis with a recommendation for a strike.[5]

Although Mitchell was anything but pleased by Mother Jones's advice, he was forced to yield to the demand of the Colorado miners in favor of a strike. The walkout was set to begin on November 9, 1903, for an eight-hour day, a check weighman representing the miners, and payment in money instead of script.

The strike covered the entire state. Not a single ton of coal was dug, and the people, feeling the lack of coal in a cold November, put pressure on the operators to settle. By November 15, the operators yielded but only in a way that divided the northern and southern strikers. The offer was for a 15 percent wage increase and an eight-hour day — but only for the northern miners. President Mitchell and his supporters urged acceptance of the offer, and the northern miners met in Louisville to vote on the proposed agreement. Enraged to learn of the impending betrayal of the southern strikers, Mother Jones, accompanied by William Howells, president of UMW District 15, left for Louisville to recommend rejecting the proposed settlement. They were met by a Mitchell lieutenant who bluntly told Mother Jones, "You must not block the settlement of the northern miners because national president, John Mitchell, wants *it, and he pays you." Asking him if he had said all he had to say, Mother Jones shot back:*

> *Then I am going to tell you that if God Almighty wants this strike called off for his benefit and not for the miners, I am going to raise my voice against it. And as to President John paying me . . . he never paid me a penny in his life. It is the hard earned nickels and dimes of the miners that pay me, and it is their interest that I am going to serve.[6]*

Jones and Howells went directly to the Louisville meeting. After Howells spoke against accepting the settlement, there were loud calls for Mother Jones. As the Denver Post, *which we have quoted at length above, noted, she "was not slow coming to the front of the stage," and she "had victory in her deep, black eyes and there was a vigor about her step which boded no good for the friends of an acceptance of the operators' terms."[7] Mother Jones's speech was brief and to the point. Realizing that the operators and Colorado Governor Peabody had spread propaganda against the Italians, who constituted a majority of the miners in the south, and had tried to get the northern miners, who were mainly American-born, to look down upon the Italians "with disdain,"[8] Mother Jones began her speech with a plea for solidarity regardless of language or nationality.*

Brothers, you English speaking miners of the northern fields promised your southern brothers, seventy percent of whom do not speak English, that you would support them to the end. Now you are asked to betray them, to make a separate settlement. You have a common enemy and it is your duty to fight to a finish. Are you brave men? Can you fight as well as you can work?[9] I had rather fall fighting than working. If you go back to work here and your brothers fall in the south, you will be responsible for their defeat.

The enemy seeks to conquer by dividing your ranks, by making distinctions between North and South, between American and foreign. You are all miners, fighting a common cause, a common master. The iron heel feels the same to all flesh.[10] Hunger and suffering and the cause of your children bind more closely than a common tongue. I am accused of helping the Western Federation of Miners, as if that were a crime, by one of the National board members. I plead guilty. I know of no East or West, North nor South when it comes to my class fighting the battle for justice. If it is my fortune to live to see the industrial chain broken from every workingman's child in America, and if then there is one black child in Africa in bondage, there I shall go.

I don't know what you will do, but I know very well what I would do if I were in one of your places. I would stand or fall with this question of eight hours for every worker in every mine in Colorado. I would say we will all go to glory together or we will die and go down together. We must stand together; if we don't there will be no victory for any of us.

I know that President Mitchell has sent a telegram to this meeting endorsing a settlement, but John Mitchell is in Boston, we are here in the field. A general cannot give orders unless he is in the field; unless he is at the battleground. Could a general in Washington give order to an army in Colorado? I know, too, that there are those in our union who would have us to nothing to help our brothers in the Western Federation of Miners now engaged in a life and death struggle with monopoly capitalists at Cripple Creek.[11] I want the world to know, and all the papers to print, that I am going to Cripple Creek to speak there tomorrow for the Western Federation of Miners. I am not afraid to be classed as a friend of this organization and all criticism of me on that account falls flat upon my ears.

Goodbye, boys. I shall leave a happy woman if I know that you have decided to stand by our suffering brothers in the South.[12] I will see you again, boys, after I have licked the CF & I.

[Denver Post, *November 22, 1903;*
Autobiography of Mother Jones, *pp. 99-100.*]

Notes

1. The memorial service was to honor the memory of miners, members of the UMW, who were killed in what came to be known as "the Virden Massacre of 1898." In its struggle with the union, the Chicago-Virden Company recruited Negro strikebreakers from Alabama. Although the Afro-American Labor and Protective Association of Birmingham opposed the hiring of blacks as strikebreakers for the Illinois company, labor agents recruited blacks over its opposition. When the recruited miners arrived and learned that a strike was in effect, they "complained that they had been deceived by the operators, and most of them refused to work." *The Public,* a liberal Chicago weekly, reported on August 27, 1898, that "deputies stationed on the grounds are charged with threatening to shoot Negroes who attempted to leave." The white miners were determined to keep out all black scabs, whether willing or unwilling. Armed with shotguns, revolvers, and rifles, they waited for a train carrying blacks to arrive at Virden. When it did they opened up a steady fire. Deputies guarding the blacks on the train returned the fire. Fourteen white miners lost their lives and twenty-four were wounded. A few blacks were also wounded. Illinois Governor John B. Tanner, a Republican, called out the National Guard, promising the white miners that he would not tolerate the importation of blacks into Virden.

Although the black press did not view the slain white miners as heroes, their white union brothers did, and when four of the dead from Mount Olive were denied burial in the established cemeteries, their comrades bought an acre of their own and created a union miners' cemetery. Although she had not been at Virden during the battle, Mother Jones honored the "Virden martyrs." Years later, she asked to be buried in the cemetery so that she could "sleep under the clay with those brave boys." (*See* Philip S. Foner, *Organized Labor and the Black Worker, 1619-1974,* New York, 1974, pp. 77-79; John H. Keiser, "Black

Strikebreakers and Racism in Illinois, 1865-1900," Journal of the *Illinois State Historical Society* 65 (Autumn, 1972): 324-26, and John Keiser, *The Union Miners Cemetery,* Chicago, 1980). For Mother Jones's request to be buried in Mount Olive cemetery, *see* below, p. 695.

2. Dale Featherling, *Mother Jones: The Miners' Angel,* Carbondale and Edwardsville, 1974, pp. 58-60; *Autobiography of Mother Jones,* pp. 95-96.

3. Ray Stannard Baker, "The Reign of Lawlessness: Anarchy and Despotism in Colorado," *McClure's Magazine,* May, 1904, pp. 43-57; Benjamin M. Rastall, "The Labor History of the Cripple Creek District: A Study in Industrial Evolution," *Bulletin of the University of Wisconsin,* February, 1908, pp. 31-33, 52.

4. Featherling, *op. cit.,* p. 60.

5. *United Mine Workers Journal,* October 29, November 9, 1903; *Autobiography of Mother Jones,* pp. 95-96.

6. *Autobiography of Mother Jones,* p. 98.

7. *Denver Post,* November 22, 1903, and *see* pp. 37-38.

8. George G. Suggs, Jr., "The Colorado Coal Miners' Strike of 1903-1904," *Journal of the West* 12 (January, 1973): 47. Suggs offers evidence showing that Governor Peabody tried to get the leading militants among the Italian miners deported from the United States, and anxious to obtain evidence to justify the deportations, he "turned for help to James McParland, manager of the Denver branch of the Pinkerton Detective Agency, and to Dr. Joseph Cuneo, Italian consul in Denver." However, he was not able to obtain any evidence involving the Italian miners in criminal acts. (*Ibid.,* pp. 47-48.)

9. These words were later twisted by Mrs. George Anthony, publisher of the Denver weekly *Polly Pry,* in her attack on Mother Jones as "a vulgar, heartless creature with a fiery temper and a cold-blooded brutality" who was unfortunately called "Mother" by the "wives and children of the deluded miners. . . ." According to Anthony, Mother Jones's battle cry was: "We'd rather fight than work," and she had employed this effectively in persuading the northern miners in Louisville not to agree to a separate settlement. The article also accused Mother Jones of having been "a prostitute in and around Colorado before going in to work for the miners' union," and that the only reason she had become an organizer was because she wanted power. She already "owned and controlled the United Mine Workers of America and that sister organization, the Western Federation of Miners," and, seeking "new worlds to conquer," she was after "political ownership of the state of Colorado." (*Polly Pry,* January 23, 1904; Linda Atkinson, *Mother Jones: The Most Dangerous Woman in America,* New York, 1978, pp. 147-48.)

Mother Jones made no attempt to defend herself from the vituperative charges, and while the UMW did consider a libel suit, its attorney in Denver advised against it on the grounds that the Colorado laws would operate against Mother Jones. But as George McGovern and Leonard F. Guttridge (who are by no means admirers of Mother Jones) point out, Mitchell "cooly turned down" all private requests for the union to issue "a public rebuttal" as testimony to its "confidence" in Mother Jones. Thus they quote Mitchell as replying to one such request: "I never heard of her prior to 1894," and the charges "regrettably concerned her life before that date, . . . so I am unable to speak on the subject." "And to a New Hampshire cleric seeking to nail the rumors before lecturing about Mother Jones at a women's social club, Mitchell answered, 'I can give you little information . . . except the fact that she has been more or less prominently identified with the labor movement for some years.'" (George P.

McGovern and Leonard F. Guttridge, *The Great Coalfield War,* Boston, 1972, p. 48.)

Mother Jones later told Upton Sinclair that the prostitute charge stemmed from the time she had befriended a woman in Chicago in the 1880's. When she learned this woman had been refused burial in a Catholic cemetery because she had been a prostitute, she wrote a letter to a local newspaper condemning the Church. For this action, she, in turn, was accused of being a prostitute.

10. Use of the expression "the iron heel" was fairly common in radical circles at this time. Jack London, for example, used it as the title of one of his novels, *The Iron Heel,* published in 1908.

11. For a discussion of the Cripple Creek strike and the military despotism established in that section of Colorado to break the strike of the W.F. of M., *see* Foner, *History of the Labor Movement,* vol. 3, pp. 393-400.

12 Although John F. Ream, Mitchell's representative, made a desperate effort to offset the influence of Mother Jones's speech, he was unsuccessful. Not only did she receive a standing ovation from the miners, but the northern miners "voted 228 to 165 to defy John Mitchell and stay on strike." (Featherling, *op. cit.,* p. 62; Rastall, *op. cit.,* pp. 336-36.)

A Tribute to Italian Miners

Speech before New York City Central Federated Union,
August 7, 1904

Mother Jones left the Louisville meeting well satisfied with the vote to reject a separate settlement of the strike. But John Mitchell would not yield to the will of the northern miners, and the machine put pressure on the local officials to force another vote. In Mother Jones's absence, they were able to triumph. On November 30, 1903, the northern miners voted to accept a separate settlement. When the southern miners insisted on continuing their strike, they were forced to face the same type of "military despotism" Cripple Creek strikers, under W.F. of M. leadership, were undergoing. Governor James A. Peabody ordered the militia into the strike zone on March 22, 1904, and it was no sooner in the field than arrests and deportations began. On March 26, 1904, Mother Jones, another UMW organizer, as well as the editor and publisher of a Trinidad newspaper, were deported from Trinidad and ordered never to return. A week later, eight strikers, most of them local union officers, were ejected from Colorado. When the militia commander, Major Hill, was asked if there were any specific charges against the men, he replied: "No, but I believe their absence is better for the people than their pre-

sence.[1]

After writing to Governor Peabody from Denver that he did "not own the state," and that she was "right here . . . four or five blocks from your office," Mother Jones asked the governor: ". . . what in Hell are you going to do about it?"[2] The governor did nothing, and Mother Jones returned to the strike area and continued to deliver speeches to the miners. She also traveled in mid-April 1904 to Helper, Utah, where she lived with an Italian miner's family. On August 7, 1904, she addressed the Central Federated Union of New York City, and delivered a tribute to the Italian miners who were often accused of being "natural scabs," and only useful to help the employers to break unions. At the same time she sold copies of Eugene V. Debs's militant pamphlet, Unionism and Socialism.[3] *Indeed, the excerpt from her speech appeared in the* New York Times *under the heading: " 'MOTHER JONES, BOOK AGENT. Talks to Central Federated Union and Sells Debs's Volume.'"[4]*

"Mother" Jones talked for the most part of the miners in Colorado. "I know something of the conflict in the West," she said, "for I happened to be one of those in the midst of the fight, and I am always happiest when I am in the midst of the gang that is hurting the other fellow. The President of the United States was called on twice to interfere, but the poor fellow said in a helpless way that he could do nothing. But I tell you that when the mine operators began to disobey the law and got into a conflict with the miners, he soon sent troops against the miners.[5] If any of you ever see the President you can tell him I said so.

"I found that the Italians were always the best strikers when it came to a fight, in spite of the low opinion some people have of the Italians. They stood their ground when the National Guard, which I call the Monkey Brigade, was ordered out to shoot the people. It took six of Peabody's lap dogs to take me, a woman of sixty-five, and put me on a train to get out of the country.[6] Imagine six of the Monkey Brigade people being necessary to watch for a Mary Ann like me. When you are casting your ballot you ought to think of these things. If a mule had a vote, he would exercise more sense in voting than you do. A lot of dogs yell and hurrah for freedom every year on the Fourth of July. This is the thing that makes me tired. There is a danger line, and when they pass it the French Revolution will be repeated."

The real mission of "Mother" Jones was then introduced. It was to sell books by Eugene V. Debs on "Unionism and Socialism."[7] It was decided that 250 should be bought, and a vote of thanks was passed to "Mother" Jones for her address.

[New York Times, *August 8, 1904.*]

110

Notes

1. Edmund Philip Willis, "Colorado Industrial Disturbances, 1903-1904," unpublished M.A. thesis, University of Wisconsin, 1955, pp. 78-114; Foner, *op. cit.,* vol. 3, pp. 399-400.

2. For the full text of Mother Jones's letter, *see below* p. 557.

3. *Union and Socialism, A Plea for Both,* one of Eugene V. Debs's chief theoretical works, was first published in *Appeal to Reason* early in 1904 and reprinted shortly afterwards as a pamphlet. Debs emphasized that modern industrial conditions required a modern type of unionism. "This is the industrial plan, the modern method applied to modern conditions, and it will in time prevail." But Debs was convinced that the A.F. of L. could not be quickly converted into a modern type of union, and that a new organization of labor was necessary. Gompers and his lieutenants were completely wedded to the National Civic Federation philosophy of class collaboration. They refused to make any serious efforts to organize unskilled workers, especially Negro, women, and foreign-born workers. They had frequently broken strikes by independent unions. They were unable to make any substantial gains in the face of the open-shop drive, and they absolutely refused to embark upon united economic or political action. They were, in short, committed to the continuation of capitalism with all of its evils. The Socialists inside the A.F. of L. had sought to change these policies through their educational programs. They had not only failed to accomplish their objective, but their outlook was even corrupting segments of the Socialist Party itself. Certain Socialist politicians, trying to win votes at elections from the conservative unionists, were deliberately trimming their own program to conform to the views of Gompers. There was, therefore, only one clear answer to this problem: a new revolutionary industrial union which would organize the unorganized and be "uncompromising" in its attempt to advance the cause of socialism. (*Writings and Speeches of Eugene V. Debs,* New York, 1948, pp. 95-125.)

4. *New York Times* August 8, 1904. The *Times* reported that Mother Jones was "accompanied by ex-Mayor Chase of Haverhill, Mass., but he was not noticed and disappeared soon after 'Mother' Jones began to speak." John Chase was elected the first Socialist mayor of Haverhill, Massachusetts in December, 1898 and was re-elected the following year. But he was defeated for re-election in December 1900. He may have left the meeting because dominant elements in the Socialist Party leadership did not approve of Debs's attack on Gompers and the A.F. of L., believing that the A.F. of L. would soon be transformed, by the education of its membership, into a revolutionary union. Debs's pamphlet, however, impressed the Western Federation of Miners, and played an important role in influencing the union to take steps to establish a new labor organization, an action which helped pave the way for the formation of the Industrial Workers of the World (I.W.W.). The fact that Mother Jones was promoting the sale of Debs's pamphlet indicates that she agreed that a new organization of labor was needed. Hence, as we shall see, it is not surprising that she was involved in the formation of the I.W.W. (For the influence of Debs's pamphlet on the Western Federation of Miners, *see* Philip S. Foner, *History of the Labor Movement in the United States,* vol. 4, New York, 1965, p. 14.)

5. Mother Jones is only partly correct. President Theodore Roosevelt was asked by leaders of both the Western Federation of Miners and the United Mine Workers to intervene in Colorado, and the request was also made that he

send federal troops to prevent further outrages against the miners by the militia and the Citizens' Alliance. But to all requests for intervention, Roosevelt replied that he did not have the power to intercede to protect the rights of Colorado citizens. The president did send a team of investigators to the area, but they reported no justification for federal intervention. Roosevelt followed the advice of Commissioner of Labor Carroll D. Wright, which was to let the public know that he was conducting an investigation, while actually allowing the matter to drift. (*Miners' Magazine,* December 10, 1903, p. 8; Carroll Wright to Theodore Roosevelt, June 21, 1904; Theodore Roosevelt to William H. Moody, August 24, 1904, Theodore Roosevelt Papers, Library of Congress.) Where Mother Jones is mistaken is in her assertion that Roosevelt "sent troops against the miners." No federal troops were sent to Colorado.

6. Mother Jones underestimated her age by at least nine years.

7. In part the sales of the booklet were to enable Debs to support himself. Writing to Mother Jones on January 28, 1901, on the stationery of the Debs Publishing Co., Publishers and Booksellers, Eugene V. Debs pointed out: "I am trying to build up a little book business out of which to make a living so that I shall not have to accept anything from any source for any service I may render the cause. I feel confident you can help me a little and at the same time help yourself as well as the movement." (Original in William B. Wilson Papers, Historical Society of Pennsylvania; copy in Eugene V. Debs Papers, Indiana State University Library, Indiana State University, Terre Haute, Indiana.)

An Appeal to Copper Miners to Organize

Speech at Red Jacket, Michigan, April 18, 1905

Faced with a powerful alliance of corporations and state authorities, and deprived at President Mitchell's insistence of even the meager 63 cents a week in strike benefits from the national office of the UMW, the southern Colorado strikers abandoned the battle on October 12, 1904.[1]

Although hospitalized in Trinidad because of overwork in the cold and snow and arrested and deported several times from Colorado,[2] Mother Jones had tried desperately to keep the strike alive. Her experience in Colorado had intensified a growing hostility towards President John Mitchell for living lavishly at exclusive hotels and at fashionable resorts frequented by the wealthy while many of the miners were having difficulty keeping their families fed.[3] After the defeat of the strike in southern Colorado, Jones condemned Mitchell for traveling in Europe, "staying at fashionable hotels, studying the labor movement" while "the southern miners went out on the bleak mountainside, lived in tents through a horrible winter with 18 inches of snow on the ground. They tied their feet in gunny sacks and lived lean and lank and hungry as timber wolves."[4] Enraged, she resigned from the United Mine Workers shortly after the defeat in Colorado. As she put it tersely: "Poor John, he couldn't stand feasting with the rich. He is no good to his own people any longer."[5]

At the same time, Mother Jones had developed great respect for the militant policies of the Western Federation of Miners, the union's emphasis on the class struggle, labor solidarity, and its endorsement of the Socialist Party.[6] In April 1905, on behalf of the W.F. of M., she went for the first time to the upper Michigan copper country in the hope of aiding the federation's organizing drive which had begun a year before. (She also aimed to aid the strike of the workers of the Houghton County Street Railway Company.) At Red Jacket, Michigan, near Calumet, Mother Jones delivered a speech to copper miners on April 18, 1905, which was described by the Calumet press as "pyrotechnic, enthusiastic, spectacular." But the Daily Morning Gazette, *voice of the mine owners, was anything but enthusiastic in its report. It denounced the seventy-five-year-old agitator as a trouble-maker who threatened to disturb the harmonious relations existing between miners and mine owners. The talk "was not appealing and contained nothing that would make one wish to see the conditions changed that have prevailed in Michigan copper country for half a century."[7] Fortunately, the* Miners' Magazine, *W.F. of M. official journal, thought that the speech would help change these very conditions, and reprinted the account of the talk as it appeared in the* Copper County Evening News *of Calumet.*

"Mother" Jones is raising her voice in behalf of the downtrodden laboring men of the state of Michigan. The *Copper Country Evening News,* published at Calumet, Michigan, gives the following synopsis of her address recently delivered in that city:

"When we look back over the world's history," began Mother Jones, "and go back to the cradle of the race, we try to see how they started out. We can see human beings on the banks of a great river way back in the ages. They could not lisp a language but made known their thoughts by glances and signs. They looked to the opposite bank of the river and beheld trees loaded with fruit. They knew it was there to nourish them, but between them and that wealth stood this tremendous body of water. They began to use their reasoning powers — they were more advanced than we are in some ways — in an effort to find a way to secure this wealth. Finally, one savage saw a branch floating down the stream. It finally decided that the water held up this branch and one savage put his foot on it. By long reasoning he evolved a scheme to ride across the water on the body of a tree. Two other savages then had aspirations. They did not want to see only one of their number over there eating the fruit and by experiments they bound two logs together. But one savage wanted to take his children and they might fall off into the water, so he scooped out the inside of the tree and placed them in it. They reasoned with the brain that nature gave them and took possession of that wealth. They reasoned better than the workingman of to-day. For the great liners which plow the oceans and the locomotives that thunder across the continent are the results of reasoning — all the machinery that produces is the result of that study, and we find that all wealth is in the hands of a few. The other large class must appeal to the few for the right to work, to live, to eat, to be housed.

"Work, work, work is preached from the pulpit, the newspaper and the magazine. The laboring people are anxious to divide the honor, but they won't. You never hear from the pulpit, the magazine or the newspaper headlines, rest, rest, rest. There are men who break their necks to go to work early in the morning and do not know when to quit at night. I don't know about the copper mines, but in the coal mines mules are employed. They kick when it comes time to stop work.

"The machinery which seems so hard for us to claim now will be easy in the future. Look at the great factories. The time of the hand tool is past. We don't work alone now, but collectively, even by thousands. We are brought face to face with a new condition. We work to-day for the great syndicate instead of the single employer. The last war with Spain opened markets which have been locked up for centuries.[8] International armies battered down the walls of Pekin and the American nation took the key.[9] The workingmen have not kept pace with this step. They dream away their days — they dream as they did of old. They do not think. They still slumber. They go on just like dumb animals. It is just as a street railway superintendent said when the men struck: 'The cattle don't know what they're doing.' And the fact is, they did not. They were not organized. They knew that they had cowards to deal with and they used the lash and I give them credit for it. You 'scab' on each other. The capitalists don't scab on each other. They are too honorable."

She told a story about the sugar trust[10] and then cried sarcastically: "But you fellows will 'scab.' Do you wonder that a few own all the Machinery on earth? But your day will come some time. I do not care if it don't though. It is for your children and your children's children that I am fighting.

"In the coal mines and mills some men make good wages, but the average do not. At the end of the month they have nothing and have to ask for help. Is this the condition you boast of in this century? When a human being is killed in a mine, his dead body is hauled up in the cage and the men go back to work laughing. This man was murdered. It is brutal. It is inhuman. It is illustrated by the story of a mine owner who exclaimed every time a miner was killed: 'Was the mule killed?' You see, the mule cost $120 and the miner did not cost anything. He could be replaced."

The speaker referred to the cabled condolences to Russia from Washington when the Grand Duke Sergius was killed,[11] "that murderer of the working people." She said that about the same time 150 miners were killed in a mine in Alabama. "In less than five minutes 150 souls were blown to eternity. Yet there was not one word of condolence, not a single line. If there is any sympathy it must come from our own ranks. What right have you to fear? You say you cannot join the union because you would lose your job. Poor, dreamy wretch. You never owned a job, for those who own the machinery own the job, and you have to get permission to earn your bread and butter. You can change masters, it is true, but you have to hunt your master for that job you call yours.

"I have gotten up at 4:30 in the morning and gone with babies to the factories. They began work at 5:30 and quit at 7 at night. Children six years old going home to lie on a straw pallet until time to resume work the next morning! I have seen the hair torn out of their heads by the machinery, their scalps torn off, and yet not a single tear was shed, while the poodle dogs were loved and caressed and carried to the seashore. And you stand idly by and indorse this thing. If it were you who were going to suffer I would say 'Let it be so.' But it is for your children and your children's children that I do this — that I fight your battles for you.

"A fruit grower in California, after the Chinamen were excluded,[12] sent to South America for 500 monkeys. He trained them to pick the fruit, and for fear they would eat the fruit he muzzled them. Your employers do not have to go to the expense of muzzling you — you are already muzzled."

Mother Jones then began an exhaustive description of the conditions which prevailed in Colorado during the recent labor troubles there, and she said: "Yes, I was in Colorado. I was there seven months and I would be there yet if the military had not put me out in the night." She said that a blacker conspiracy was never put up than there was against the people of that state. "I am not afraid of the pen, the sword or the scaffold. I will tell the truth about it everywhere I please." She reviewed the action which brought about the troubles and paid a tribute to the Western Federation of Miners. She said the people who were sent out of Colorado were inhumanely treated and had to drink out of the place where horses did; that they were placed in cars and unloaded after a long ride miles from any place of shelter, and that they had no food in all the journey.

She appealed to the women to bring up their children in the right way. Then she spoke of the troubles with the miners of West Virginia. "These men were peaceful. They worked in the mines in the mountains and lived in shacks. A marshal came there to arrest them. The people said they had not violated the law and resisted arrest. The next night a United States deputy and a large number of men stole softly up the mountain side and murdered those men while they slept. I am not speaking from what I have read in books; I was there. I took their bleeding heads in my lap and I kissed their dead lips. They are my brothers and sisters. They were murdered for human greed and that is all."

Mother Jones spoke tenderly of the workingman who takes a drink. She said that it is a good thing that he can forget his misery for a few minutes. "It's a wonder that we are not all drunk all the time," she exclaimed. She said she had worked among drunken men for years. She ridiculed the idea of sending missionaries to foreign lands, saying that there is plenty of such work needed here at home.

She closed with an appeal to the men to organize. "Boys, get together and organize. It will make business better for your city. It will end the troubles. It will end the strikes. Down in Illinois they used to have strikes right along, but since the men organized they get together with the mine operators and talk over the matter and arrive at a decision as to their best interests. They never have any trouble there."

[Miners' Magazine 6 *(May 4, 1905), pp. 8–9.]*

Notes

1. Edmund Philip Willis, "Colorado Industrial Disturbances, 1903-1904," unpublished M.A. thesis, University of Wisconsin, 1955, pp. 78-114; Foner, *op. cit.,* vol. 3, pp. 399-400.

2. While Jones was hospitalized in a Trinidad hospital, Bertha Mailly, wife of the national secretary of the Socialist Party, wrote from Trinidad praising Mother Jones's work in Colorado and added "These days men in Trinidad are asking on every hand, 'How is Mother Jones?' or from the poor Italians, 'Mr. Mudder Jones, she well?'" (*Appeal to Reason,* January 30, 1904; Featherling, *op. cit.,* p. 64.)

For Mother Jones's letter to Governor Peabody after he had ordered her deported from Colorado, *see below* p. 557.

3. For a picture of the lavish style in which labor leaders of the period lived, see Foner, *op. cit.,* vol. 3, pp. 146-50.

4. Atkinson, *op. cit.,* pp. 152-53.

5. Eugene V. Debs Clippings, No. 8, p. 248, Tamiment Institute Library of New York University; Foner, *op. cit.,* vol. 3, p. 149.

6. For the policies of the Western Federation of Miners, *see* Foner, *op. cit.,* vol. 3, pp. 400-07. For a somewhat different opinion of Mitchell by Mother Jones around this time as well as a discussion of what she planned to do after she had resigned from the United Mine Workers, *see* her letter to John H. Walker, January 4, 1905, pp. 557-59. For a defense of Mitchell's policies, *see* Joseph M. Gowaskie, "From Conflict to Cooperation: John Mitchell and Bituminous Coal Operators, 1898-1908," *Historian* 38 (August, 1976): 669-88.

7. Quoted in Featherling, *op. cit.,* p. 79.

8. The reference, of course, is to the annexation of Hawaii and Puerto Rico

and the purchase of the Philippines in the period during and after the United States war with Spain in 1898. Cuba also was dominated economically by the United States by means of the Platt Amendment. *See* Philip S. Foner, *The Spanish-Cuban-American War and the Birth of American Imperialism* vol. 2, New York, 1972, pp. 446-84, 668-72.

9. The reference is to the fact that the Chinese people, led by the "Boxers," had risen up against the territorial encroachments upon their country by foreign imperialists, and the division of the thirteen richest, most populous, and most desirable of the eighteen Chinese provinces into "spheres of influence." War was the imperialists' answer to the attempt of the Chinese people to keep their country for themselves. In June 1900, an international fleet bombarded and captured the Tuku forts which commanded the approach to Peking, and the American Admiral Kampff cooperated in the attack. Although the slaying of 242 foreigners, chiefly missionaries, was the excuse for the war against China, the slaying actually did not begin until the opening days of July, three weeks after hostilities had started. Some 18,000 troops of eight different powers, including 2,000 American soldiers, attacked China, plundered the country, executed leaders of the anti-imperialist movement, and imposed a humiliating treaty of peace.

10. The American Sugar Refinery Company, which came to be known as the Sugar Trust, was originally organized in 1887. It controlled all the important refining interests in New York and Brooklyn, fifteen plants in all. Henry D. Havemeyer, its president, was closely linked to Wall Street.

11. Grand Duke Sergius was assassinated by a terrorist in 1903.

12. Congress passed the Chinese Exclusion Act in 1882.

The I.W.W. Convention

Remarks at the Founding Convention of the Industrial
Workers of the World (I.W.W.), Chicago, July 7, 1905

Probably the shortest speeches Mother Jones ever delivered at an important labor conference were those she gave at the founding convention of the Industrial Workers of the World. She was the only woman among the thirty-six persons who were invited by a group of radical labor figures, including Eugene V. Debs, to a secret conference in Chicago on January 2, 1905. The letter of invitation emphasized that the events of the past year had convinced the signers "that craft divisions and political ignorance were doomed to speedily end," and that they were confident in the ability of "the working class, if correctly organized, on both industrial and political fields to take possession of and operate successfully for their own interests, the industries of the country." It continued:

"We invite you . . . to discuss ways and means of uniting the working people of America on correct revolutionary principles, regardless of any general labor organization, past or present, and only restricted by such basic principles as will insure its integrity as a real protector of the interests of the workers."[1]

The invitation received widespread support in left-wing circles. The Western Federation of Miners sent three delegates: Charles H. Moyer, W. D. ("Big Bill") Haywood, and John M. O'Neil, editor of the Miners' Magazine. Mother Jones, the only woman among the thirty-four who met secretly in Chicago, participated in an unofficial capacity as an individual. The conference took on the name of Chicago Conference of Industrial Unionists, and elected William D. Haywood as its permanent chairman. During the three days' session, plans for a new labor organization to be based on the principles of industrial unionism, working-class unity, and recognition of the class struggle were discussed and worked out. This new labor organization would be created at a convention in Chicago on June 27, 1905.[2]

At the founding convention of the new labor organization, Mother Jones was also present but this time she was not the only female delegate. Twelve delegates, including Lucy Parsons (the widow of the Haymarket martyr), Emma F. Langdon of Denver Typographical Union No. 49, and Luella Twining, delegate of Federal Union No. 252 of the American Labor Union, an industrial union movement active mainly in the West, were among the women who joined Mother Jones at the founding convention of the I.W.W. On Mother Jones's nomination, Langdon was appointed assistant secretary of the conference, and Twining served as presiding officer during the closing-day speeches. Lucy Parsons, who was named to the committee in charge of seeing that the minutes of the convention were printed, was the only one of the twelve female delegates who addressed the convention at some length.[3] Apart from nominating Emma Langdon, Mother Jones spoke only twice during the 12-day-long proceedings. She did vote for the I.W.W.'s constitution, but as one of her biographers puts it, "her role and apparently her commitment ended there."[4] In her autobiography, her speeches, interviews, and letters she hardly ever mentions any connection with the I.W.W. She played an active role in the defense of "Big Bill" Haywood, Charles F. Moyer, and George Pettibone, accused of instigating the murder by a bomb explosion of Governor Frank Steunenberg of Idaho. But she did so more in support of the three men as militant labor figures and W.F. of M. leaders than as men associated with the I.W.W.[5] However, Mother Jones did maintain ties with the Industrial Workers of the World in struggles in Texas and Arizona. She assisted, for example, in the strike of El Paso Mexicans and Mexican Americans at the American Smelting and Refining Company's smelter in 1913, where many of the strikers were I.W.W. members.[6]

However, in a speech in Seattle in May 1914, Jones made it clear that

she did not approve of the I.W.W.'s tactics, including opposition to polit-
ical action, and believed the A.F. of L., representing over two million or-
ganized workers, held out more hope for American workers than did the
Wobblies. While she was not a member of the Syndicalist League of
North America, organized by William Z. Foster, she agreed with him
that militants should leave the I.W.W. and work inside the A.F. of L. to
transform the federation into an organization that would organize the
unorganized, especially the unskilled workers.[7]

The Secretary (to Mother Jones): How do you vote on the adoption of the constitution as a whole as amended?

Del. Mother Jones: I was not here when the report of the constitution was read, but I have sufficient confidence in the makeup of the Constitution Committee to commit my destinies to them, and therefore I vote yes. . . .

Compensation of Officers

Del. Mother Jones: Owing to the fact that there is no money in the treasury to start this organization with, it seems to me it would be good policy to leave the decision of the salaries to the incoming officers. I for one am not afraid to trust those officers with fixing the salaries that will compensate the officers, and I think it will be satisfactory to the body as a whole. I do not know that this body here could now decide what is best to do with regard to the salaries, as long as we have no funds to begin with. When the funds grow larger and it is worth while making a decision about that, I believe that is time enough for us to begin. (Motion seconded.)

[Proceedings of the First Convention of the Industrial Workers
of the World. Founded at Chicago, June 27-July 8, 1905,
New York, n.d., pp. 508, 555.]

Notes

1. Philip S. Foner, *History of the Labor Movement in the United States,* vol. 4, New York, 1965, pp. 14-17.
2. *Ibid.,* p. 16.
3. Philip S. Foner, *Women and the American Labor Movement: From Colonial Times to the Eve of World War I,* New York, 1979, pp. 392-93.
4. Featherling, *op. cit.,* p. 72. Featherling cites two reasons for Mother Jones's limited association with the I.W.W. and its struggles, first pointing out that "she did so not out of fear . . . the years between the IWW's founding and America's entry into World War I would be her most perilous ones. She would face dungeons, bayonets, incensed governors, disease, and gunmen unflinchingly." The first reason, as Featherling sees it, was that the factional struggles within the I.W.W. alienated Mother Jones and that when the Western Federa-

tion of Miners abandoned the organization in 1907, a major reason for her initial association departed. The second reason was that Mother Jones "was not as radical as many of the Wobblies. . . . She recoiled from IWW extremism," and looked with disfavor on the I.W.W. tendency to call strikes without first building up strike funds. "To bring in a strike and go back licked by hunger is not progress for labor," she told an interviewer. (Featherling, *op. cit.*, p. 73.)

5. For the story of the Moyer, Haywood, Pettibone case, *see* Foner, *op. cit.*, vol. 4, pp. 40-59. For Mother Jones's comment on the case, *see* her letter to Terence V. Powderly, May 24, 1907, pp. 565-67.

Defended by Clarence Darrow, the labor leaders won an outstanding victory. After 20 hours of deliberation, the jury in the case of Bill Haywood brought in a verdict of "Not Guilty." Pettibone was also acquitted, and Moyer was never tried. The labor movement had won what Eugene V. Debs called "one of the greatest legal battles in American history." (Foner, *op. cit.*, vol. 4, p. 59.)

6. Richard M. Estrada, "Border Revolution: The Mexican Revolution in the Ciudad Juarez-El Paso Area, 1906-1915," Unpublished M.A. thesis, University of Texas, El Paso, 1975, p. 49.

7. *See* p. 660. For the Syndicalist League of North America, *see* Foner, *op. cit.*, vol. 4, pp. 415-34.

A Plea on Behalf of Mexican Revolutionaries Imprisoned in the United States

Speech at annual convention of
United Mine Workers of America, 1909

In 1875 General Porfirio Díaz overthrew the Mexican government and established a dictatorship that lasted until 1911. During the decades of his authoritarian rule, opposition mounted, reaching a high point in the opening decade of the twentieth century. The most vocal and active of the opponents of the Díaz dictatorship were the Magonistas, *the followers of Ricardo Flores Magón, founder of the* Partido Liberal Mexicano.[1] *Forced into exile in the United States, Magón and his followers incited rebellion in their homeland from numerous headquarters in St. Louis, Los Angeles, and cities and towns in the Arizona Territory and Texas. Since leading American capitalists enjoyed a free hand under Díaz to exploit the resources and population of Mexico, it is not surprising that Magón and* Magonistas *served terms of imprisonment for violating the American neutrality laws. As Lowell L. Blaisdell points out, "the severity of the Liberals' harrassment was primarily caused by the American officials' failure to resist the efforts of the Mex-*

ican government at close surveillance over prominent exiles. At various times, the Post Office Department, the Immigration Bureau of the Department of Commerce and Labor, the Department of Justice, the Department of State and various state and territorial authorities seemed to have adopted an overly latitudinarian view of the scope of their functions in an attempt to accede to Mexico's desires."[2] A "latitudinarian view" was part of American foreign policy in the era of "Dollar Diplomacy."[3]

While walking in the streets of Los Angeles in August 1907, Flores Magón and two Magonistas were arrested, and later beaten up by the local police, working hand-in-glove with Mexican agents of Díaz. Earlier, on June 30, 1907, Manuel Sarabia, one of Magón's key disciples and a leader of the Organizing Junta of the Liberal Party, was kidnapped from Douglas, Arizona, and taken to the border where Mexican police led him on a five-day mule-back journey to the Hermosillo, Sonora, jail. But Sarabia remained in a Mexican jail for only eight days after which he was returned to the United States. In Revoltosos: Mexico's Rebels in the United States, 1903-1923, *the most detailed study of the subject, W. Dirk Raat attributes the return of Sarabia to Arizona from the Mexican penitentiary to the "influence" of Mother Jones.[4]*

The successful end of what John Kenneth Turner in his classic Barbarous Mexico *called the "most notable case of refugee kidnapping on record"[5] was largely due to the fact that Mother Jones happened to be in Douglas, Arizona on June 30, 1907, speaking to smelter workers in one of several campaigns to help organize the Arizona copper mines. While she was speaking, Mother Jones was informed of the Sarabia kidnapping a few blocks away, and enraged at the "idea of any bloodthirsty pirate on a throne reaching across these lines and crushing under his feet the Constitution which our forefathers fought and bled for," she launched the first of many activities on behalf of Díaz's opponents, winning in the process the love and admiration of Mexican revolutionaries of all persuasion, from anarchists to liberals, including the daring and controversial revolutionary Francisco (Pancho) Villa. Richard Flores Magón and two of his lieutenants wrote to Mother Jones from the territorial prison in Florence, Arizona, where they were serving an eighteen month sentence for violating the neutrality laws:*

Territorial Prison
Florence Arizona, Nov. 31, 1909
Beloved Mother Jones: —

You will find enclosed a long statement in regard to the Mexican cases. Read it carefully, and kindly do everything in your power to fulfill those of our recommendations you consider practical and well-founded.

Despite all restrictions calculated to keep us from reading Socialist papers, we have succeeded in obtaining information about your splendid work. You are set-

ting a noble example and teaching a lesson humanity should not forget. You, an old woman, are fighting with indomitable courage; you, an American, are devoting your life to free Mexican slaves.

And they will be freed in the near future, and they will learn to call you Mother.

You are confirming the beautiful thought of Lamartine: "There always is a woman at the foundation of every great movement."[7] You are the woman at the foundation of this tremendous struggle for the emancipation of our country and you will live forever in the hearts of all liberty loving Mexicans.

> With best wishes, we are,
> Yours for the Revolution,
> R.F. Magón.
> Antonio I. Villarreal,
> Librado Rivera[8]

On three different occasions Mother Jones described the action she took which led to the rescue of Manuel Sarabia from a Mexican prison — in the course of a speech to the 1909 and 1911 United Mine Workers conventions, reprinted below, during hearings before the House of Representative Rules Committee to investigate the "alleged persecution of Mexican citizens by the Government of Mexico," (see pp. 369-75), and in her Autobiography.[9] *In the speech to the 1909 UMW convention, Mother Jones also appealed on behalf of all Mexican revolutionaries in American prisons. "We have got to get those boys out of jail," she implored. "We have got to let them live in this land; we have got to let them fight Mexico from here." She argued that large American corporations, especially the Rockefellers and Guggenheims, the very capitalists who were oppressing American miners, were behind the kidnappings and jailings. They feared that a Liberal victory would lead to expropriation of their vast holdings in Mexican land and mines. The UMW convention voted to donate $1,000 for the Mexican defense fund, and Mother Jones also raised $3,000 from other miners' groups. Although she was "not in very good health," she told the House Rules Committee, she had joined strenuously in the fund-raising campaign, convinced that the Mexican prisoners "were just like Kosciusko, Carl Schurz, Kossuth, and Garibaldi, and men of that kind who received protection in our country from the tyrannical governments which they fled."[10]*

President Lewis[11] — If there are no objections we will have a short intermission at this time and hear from a visitor we have present.

We have with us this morning a friend with whom many of the delegates are acquainted. The Mine Workers of the country generally know of the work of this friend. In many of the districts in the turbulent times when our men were engaged in a struggle, when men, women and children were suffering all the hardships incident to industrial warfare, she spent her time helping them. This morning she is here in the interest of men who have been persecuted in other countries and have come to this country in the belief that they were coming to the land of the free. We understand that the men in whose interest she is here have not committed any crime, but rather are regarded as political criminals because they believed that all men have certain rights that all other men should respect. She has encouraged our men, women and children, not alone in the mountains of West Virginia and the valleys of Pennsylvania, but on the prairies of some of our states where words of encouragement were needed by those whose spirits were drooping because of surrounding conditions. I therefore take great pleasure in introducing to this convention Mother Jones, who has lost none of her vigor, none of her interest in the cause of organized labor and in the cause of humanity because of her age or her white hair.

Mrs. Mary Jones (Mother Jones) — Permit me to extend to your worthy President my appreciation for his introduction. In the days of old when the revolutionists fought against the conditions that King George III was about to fasten upon them, could he have reached his claws in and have put them around Washington he would no doubt have hung him. Today, after a century or more of history in this nation, we find two diabolically tyrannous governments reaching their hands into this country and asking us to deliver men who have taken refuge here and surrender our rights to the czar of Russia and the military despot of Mexico. You will realize, my friends, that international economic interests are back of all this; you must realize that for this change in our nation's history there is a cause. Economic interests, both in Mexico and Russia, are dictating the policy of our government today — I mean the other fellow's government. As the method of production changes, the policy of the government must change to fit into it. Newspapers, magazines, churches, all must fit into the changed order. It governs home life, it governs national life, it governs the newspapers, it governs all avenues of educating the people.

To prove my statement I am going to give you an illustration, and I don't know of a better one to convince you that they have reached into the avenues of religious life to gain their ends. In Texas we had a fight with the Copper Queen Company. They sent to Joplin, Missouri, for scabs. And I want to say to you Missouri boys that you ought to get those scabs organized or lick hell out of them. They got about forty scabs. They were coming over the Rock Island road. I asked the conductor why the train was rocking so much, and he said there was a bunch of fellows on it going to Bisbee, Arizona. I asked him to take me to them, and he did, and I won over thirty-seven of them. The company had only three left. I sent them into Mexico. I said, "Go in there and earn four or five dollars a day and lick the other fellows who are scabbing." I had to stay in El Paso for a while. While I was there three miners from Mexico came along and they said, "Mother, we haven't had anything to eat today, or yesterday, or the day before, and we are dead broke." I said it would be remarkable to find a miner any other way. I said I had enough money to get them plenty to eat, but to be sure and steer clear of the charity organizations. I said, "I can tell you where you can go and get filled up. Go down to the saloon and get a free lunch, and they will give you a schooner of beer to wash it down. I will have a meeting on the street tonight, and as this is the tourist season the collection will be good and I will give it to you." We had a collection of eighteen dollars that night, and I gave them five dollars apiece and kept three dollars to get something to eat.

Then we saw a gang coming down the street and they were hammering each other. I asked a policeman what the trouble was. He said it was a row about Jesus. I said, "Who is in it?" He said, "The Salvation Army and the Volunteers are fighting about Jesus." I said, "That is a hell of a way to fight for Jesus. Why don't you arrest them?" He said it would not do because they were fighting for Jesus. They had beaten each other and the women had pulled each other's hair out. They were fighting to see which side Jesus belonged to. While they were hammering each other the collection that had been taken up rolled on the street. I jumped in and rescued the coin. When I had some coin I didn't have to fight for or talk for, but got it by bending my back a little, I said to the policeman: "Don't you want a drink on Jesus?" He said, "By God, I do!" so we went to a restaurant and got supper and some beer, and if any fellow wanted to get an extra jag on we were ready to pay for it because we had Jesus's money. When we had had our suppers we asked the restaurant keeper how much we owed him, and he said we didn't have to pay anything.

These things fit into the changed order of things. That month I went up to Douglas, Arizona, to try and organize the smelters for the boys. One evening on the street one of the boys came to me and said, "Mother, there has been some dirty work going on at the jail." I said, "That is none of our business; let the jail take care of itself." Then he said, "But something is going on that is not straight. They brought a fellow there in an automobile and he screamed for his liberty. I think there is something wrong." Then a young fellow came along and said, "My God, Mother, they have kidnapped our young revolutionist, and they have run him across to Mexico and he will be murdered immediately!"[12] We telegraphed to the governor and to Washington. We got Teddy out of bed that night, I can tell you.[13] The next night we proposed to hold a mass meeting. I needn't tell you it is a very hard thing to wake people up in a town. There is a peculiar stupidity about them, and it is hard to wake them up at once to action. I said we would have to get at the papers in some way or put leaflets into the hands of the people.

I went to a fellow who was fighting the Copper Queen and asked if he could get out an extra. He said he hadn't the money, and I gave him twenty dollars and told him to go ahead. He did, and we flooded the town with them, and when we got to the meeting the crowd was dense all around that neighborhood. I needn't tell you, boys, I suppose, or most of you, that I long ago quit praying and took to swearing. If I pray I will have to wait until I am dead to get anything; but when I swear I get things here. Well, I was not very particular what I said at that meeting. I said, "Boys, if you will go with me we will go into Mexico and bring that fellow back; we will make Díaz give him up." They said they would go with me. I said, "There isn't a Pinkerton[14] between here and hell we won't hang," and they went and got the ropes. Well, we got the fellow back.

Here is the question you have to bear in mind, my brothers. Owing to international economic conditions this government is becoming officious in this matter. The Southern Pacific railroad, the Standard Oil and the copper interests are all back of this affair. They know if these men win out their doom is registered. Here are some pictures I wish to send down through the audience. These men were in the battle of Cannanea in 1896 when they drove those poor slaves back. These six were missing. Nobody could tell where they were for three or four weeks afterwards, and then they were found hanging as they appear in the pictures, with their flesh eaten off their bodies. The other two that led the strike in the Green mines of Cannanea were sent to prison at hard labor for fifteen years.[15]

I have a letter here which says: "The cause of liberty is going back here every day. The Mexican who has the courage to speak out is arrested and punished to the limit. The Mexican consul is lying every day to his government in order to hold his dirty job of spy. God only knows what will become of these people. They have incarcerated many workers in Sonora for leading the strike." Talk about Russia! Mexico is worse than Russia, because Russia has a parliament but Mexico has nothing but Díaz! They have reached into St. Louis and have the Jeffries Detective agency to hound those men all over the continent, even into Canada. Those men were behind the bars when I was notified of it. They said they had not a dollar for their trials. One of their lawyers said he had been engaged in the last year fighting the case. He said that when he saw me he would tell me many things that would make my blood boil. He said they needed both money and moral support. He asked that whenever I spoke before a gathering to have a resolution adopted asking the government to intercede in their behalf.

I have a bunch of such letters, but as you have been held here a long time, with someone spouting something to you to make you good or bad, I won't detain you. I am not here to spout something to make you good or bad; I know you are good. I have fought with you long enough to know that you are about the best fighters this country has. You miners can revolutionize this whole country if you want to. I will tell you,

Comrade Wilson, it is not waterways we need, but the ownership of those means so the boys will only work four hours a day. That is what we are after. You have to work too much.

President Lewis — We are willing to work less.

Mother Jones — Send more fighters to congress. I want to tell you, Wilson, you haven't made enough noise in congress.[16] I have been watching you. You must understand that this government is not in Washington; it is in Wall street. That is the trouble with those boys. That is why Russia can enter Sandy Hook and find written on the portals of the city "Leave behind all hope of liberty, you who enter here." Morgan went to Russia last year and made a deal with the czar of Russia, and the czar said: "If you will surrender those refugees we will take care of your interests." Morgan got his order for thousands and thousands of tons of steel rails. Harriman and Morgan were fighting, and Harriman went to Morgan and said: "Let us fix it up," and they did, and instead of charging the Southern Pacific $29.00 a ton for rails they put them down to $23.00 a ton, and reduced the wages of the steel workers. If you fellows cannot make a noise in congress get down and out and we women will go there. If I was in congress I would tell Teddy to shut his mouth, not be lecturing women about race suicide, when his own daughter has been doubled up with a congressman for three years and he hasn't said a word about race suicide to her yet.

Now, boys, remember that back of all these things is the question of economic interests. The Standard Oil owns the Green mines. Green owns seventy-five square miles of the people's land in Arizona. And we haven't an oligarchy in this country! You ought to be looking after these things, Wilson and Nicholls, not looking after waterways. Those little side-show issues don't amount to anything; what we are after today is to shake them up, because president, cabinet, congress, senate and the courts are simply putty in the hands of the Wall street gang of commercial pirates. If they weren't old Joe Cannon would not be boss and shooting off his bazoo. If there was just one woman in that congress old Joe Cannon would shake on his throne.[17]

Now, I will tell you what I am here today for. I am not here to beg. I hate beggars; I don't want any begging machines; I want to do away with every begging parasite in the world. I want to fight and take what belongs to us. What I want here today with you is this: We have got to get those boys out of jail. We have got to let them live in this land; we have got to let them fight Mexico from here. And I am with those boys because Díaz and Harriman and Rockefeller and the whole push are together down there. They were down there wining and dining, and we paid for it. And while I am on this wining and dining subject I am going to say something about the board member from Pennsylvania, Miles Dougherty. I want to talk to you Pennsylvania fellows. You had an awful fight there. I was out West and took up a paper and read of Mr. Miles Dougherty sitting down with his feet under the table look-

126

ing Mrs. Harriman square in the eye and putting a bowl of champagne inside of his stomach — "Here's a health to you, Mr. Belmont; here's a health to you, Miss Morgan, and here's a health to you, Mrs. Harriman." And then, when Mrs. Harriman and Miss Morgan walked down the street with Miles Dougherty the fellows over home in Pennsylvania said, "Don't you see how labor is getting recognized!" How labor is getting recognized! That's true, Mr. Lewis, as sure as you sit there, they said that about labor getting recognized! I want to tell you here the trouble with you is this: your skull hasn't developed only to the third degree. You would consider it an honor to go down the street with Miss Morgan, who never worked a day in her life. You would consider it an honor to dine with those fellows that skinned you and your children and murdered you in the mines, and while they were filling you with champagne they murdered us poor devils with bullets.[18]

Now, I want some money. I am not here begging; I am simply here to wake you up and tell you to tell Mr. Lewis and Mr. Ryan — I am not going to say "brother" to him now because he is leaving me and going over to the other fellows. We fellows have got to stick together and fight, and if we get a jag on us we have to get a ten-cent drink of rotten whisky instead of champagne. And they are even trying to get that away from us! What we want to do is to fix things so we can drink the champagne and make them drink the whisky for a while. As I started out to say, I want you to tell Mr. Lewis and Mr. Ryan to give me this money. I want to get those men out of the clutch of Díaz. Down there in Mexico a Canadian and a British syndicate own all the railroads and street cars and the land is being surrendered to them. You must realize when men and women have the spirit of liberty in their breasts, even though for nineteen hundred years they have been trying to carry out Christ's doctrine, "Peace on earth, good will to men," there can be no peace on earth under present conditions. We have no peace on earth today. You are making an awful fuss about Mr. Gompers and Mr. Mitchell and Mr. Morrison going to jail.[19] What is the matter with you? Didn't you build the jails? Didn't you put the iron bars on them? Didn't you pay the judges, and didn't you tell them when you paid them, "You can send us to jail if you want to?" Don't you know the jail is the national reception parlor for the worker? They didn't put Mr. Lewis in jail because he was a good boy. If you weren't, they would have you locked up, too, wouldn't they, Mr. Lewis? But they are not going to; don't worry. Now, I wouldn't fight that injunction. It was perfectly legitimate. What I would do is to take my medicine and go to jail. I ought not to go because I didn't indorse the building of that jail; but the fellows that did ought to go. Do you think I would say a word to Judge Wright? I called the old judge in Virginia a scab. He said, "Did you call me a scab, Mrs. Jones?" I said, "Yes," and he gave me a document to show he was no scab, and I said I was glad an old scab judge didn't try me.[20]

I read in the paper, Mr. Ryan, what you said about recalling the resolution.[21] I don't know whether that was right, because the papers don't always tell the truth. The boycott is the only weapon left to labor outside of the ballot, and I would not only boycott the Buck Stove and Range Company,[22] but I would boycott every minister that didn't have the union label on the outside of his church. We have nothing to take back. We are giving them everything. The parasites couldn't live on this earth without us; they are too lazy to work. The Rio Grande railroad murdered a lot of people the other day. The officials of the road were too stingy to put a man in the tower and pay him fifty dollars a month to watch the trains. They could not pay that, but they could pay a hundred thousand dollars a week before to fill their own stomachs. That's what you ought to bring up in Congress, Mr. Wilson.

Now, boys, I want you to ask Mr. Ryan to give me a thousand dollars out of the treasury. And, Mr. Lewis, if ever you get hard up I will go out and raise a thousand dollars for you. Lawyers are grafters, and they won't do a thing on God's earth unless you pay for it. They are like a lot of blood-suckers hanging around to see where they can get the blood to suck out of us. We have got to make a fight up there at Washington. We must let those fellows know we are alive. I want to say to you here before I close that they are more afraid of the organized body of workers than they are of all the political bodies of the country. If we can thoroughly organize and educate our people we can stop every wheel in the country and we can make those fellows stop eating. When we do that we will spend what belongs to us and they will work as we will rest. If you cannot give me the money out of your pockets — and I don't believe you can, because those old pauper leeches have been here bleeding you — I will get it from the locals. The mine owners bleed you first, and then the people here begin. I saw one of those leeches over at the hotel last night with a nice little basket shaking at you and asking you to put in. She was dressed like one of those parasites. What I want you to do is to vote me a thousand dollars, and then Mr. Ryan will have to pay it to me whether he wants to or not.

I am not going to hold you here any longer. Say, you ought to be out in the country with me. We have great times out there in the West, and I am going to stay there for quite a while. An old fellow said the other day in Pittsburg, speaking of me, "That old devil ought to die!" What is the matter with him? Why, I am only seventy-three years young and I have a contract with God to let me stay here many more to help clean up that old gang.

Delegate Walker (J.H.) — I move that $1,000 be appropriated out of the International treasury for the purpose of defending the Mexicans referred to by Mother Jones. (Seconded.) . . . .

Mother Jones — When Rudovitz and Puron were being tried a strong committee in Chicago was attending to their affair,[23] but no one was pleading the case of the brave fighters on the border line within the clutches of Díaz and the Standard Oil. Moyer wrote to me and I said, "Which way will I go, east or west, to stir up sentiment?" He told me to go east. I send this money through Brother Germer and every dollar is registered in East St. Louis. Every dollar goes out to Mr. Moyer of the Western Federation of Miners. I would trust them with the United States treasury, and I wish to God we had it! I don't want any of the money; I am responsible for every dollar I collect. If you don't find it recorded in the miners' magazine, call me up and put me in jail if you want to. I am collecting for those boys in the West, and I propose to get them out if I have to go down to Congress and ask for an appropriation. Those boys out on the border line won't go back to Díaz. Now, Mr. Green, if you have any objections to donating the thousand dollars, keep it and I will get the thousand dollars out of your boys in the locals. I have already got $1,200. . . .

President Lewis — . . . Mother Jones would like the floor for a few minutes to express her appreciation of the action of the convention in donating $1,000 for the defense of the Mexican refugees.

Mother Jones — In behalf of our brothers who are lying in the bastile of capitalism because they dared to raise their voices in behalf of their oppressed and murdered brothers in Mexico, I tender to you my deepest and most heartfelt appreciation of the resolution and donation to them. It is not charity; it is our duty even to go with them and give our lives for a cause so great. Never in human history before were men and women called upon to link hands in the mighty battle for the emancipation of the working class from the robbing class. Our brothers are behind the bars, and it lies with you and with me to do our part to free them. I extend to you my deep appreciation for the generous donation you gave to them. And when your turn comes they will be on deck to do their part for you. They will never surrender the rights of labor to the ruling class, even if they die in its defense.

Now, my brothers, you and I are not going to part. We have fought many battles together, and we have marched the highways together. Brave hearts marched with us then. Lying in lonely graves are some of the men who laid the foundation for this great and magnificent organization that you represent here to-day. Let me say to you, my brothers, the hand of capitalism is in your convention. The Standard Oil has its tools on the floor of your convention and they are trying to divide the forces. I intended to bring a letter over with me to read to you. I received the letter some time ago from one within the Standard Oil. In writing that letter he said, speaking of the Western Federation of Miners: "The secret service men of the Standard Oil I know were in that organization and kept the members in a turmoil the whole winter. The miners did get the best of the secret service men, but the machinists fell victims to their wiles." I say to you, my brothers, to-day to be cautious because every eye is on this convention. Down in the state I went to a bank to get a check cashed. I took a miner with me, and the banker said to him, "You are going to have war up there in Indianapolis in your convention, aren't you?" The miner said, "What about?" "Oh, they are going to have a big explosion there." "I don't know," said the miner, "I haven't heard about it." "Yes, they are going to have war." Of course I had to chip in then, and I said, "If we have a family row it is none of your business. We will settle our row ourselves, and after you are through if you begin to attack us we will fight you into hell, for the whole bunch of us will get together to do it."

Now don't give those fellows the satisfaction of seeing you have a row here. We have made mistakes, and we will make them again; we can't help it, but when this convention closes — and I want this registered by your reporters down there — every one here will be united to fight our masters. We are going to settle our difficulties.[24] No family ever succeeded very well that did not hammer one another once in a while. We must hammer President Lewis once in a while to keep him thin or he will get to look like old Taft.[25] When this convention assembles next year I am going to try to be here, and I am going to try to bring your Mexican brothers with me. I am going to present them to this convention and get them acquainted with you.

Now, my boys, I want you to be good. You know there was a time in our convention here when Indianapolis people thought they had to fill the miners with booze. The corridor used to be lined with beer bottles every time they were going to give us a banquet. The banquet they used to give us was to sell beer for a trust. We concluded that didn't pay, so we made them clean out the beer. And we will make them clean out their smokers by and by and put a stop to all this nonsense. We are not going to take any taffy; we are going to get down to solid business.

Now I want to say something to Missouri about this organizing business. Some of the delegates took exceptions to what I said here the other day, and said that Joplin belongs to the Western Federation of Miners. There must be no line drawn. Whenever you can organize a man bring him into the United Mine Workers, bring him into the Western Federation, bring him into the Carpenters' Union — bring him into any union. Whenever you do that you have taken one away from the common enemy and joined him with you to fight the common enemy. When I am on the street cars with organized men I bring up their conditions before them. I make it a point to get on the cars early in the morning and talk to them and show the necessity of getting together. I try to bring the farmers with us also, because the stronger we grow numerically the weaker the other fellow grows. I have got no pet organization. Wherever labor is in a struggle with the enemy, the name of the organization cuts no figure with me, I am there in the fight. I did speak of Joplin the other day. Why? Because in my experience in the West I found the companies could go to Joplin and get scabs and bring them on to break strikes. Because you live in Missouri close

130

to that region you should do what you can to organize Joplin and bring them with us. You must remember it is the unorganized man and the modern machine that will lock you by and by. It is the brain of the genius working out on modern lines that is going to interfere with your prosperity by and by, and every uneducated, every undeveloped worker will be used by that class to fight us. It is no reflection on you brave boys of Missouri. I simply called attention to that nest of scabs, and I advise you to get them organized and educated. And organize and educate them, not only in Joplin, but wherever you find them.

The man who has to be paid for organizing labor — well, I don't care much about him. Each one of us should be an organizer, and we should not wait for any commission from any president. We should all be organizers in every field, and not only organize the workers, but those poor slaves of the pen as well and get them with us. I mean you, you newspaper boys. One of them said the other day he had the headache because he didn't sleep enough. Of course he had, and by and by his skull will get so dumb he won't know what he is writing. Now, boys, I am going down through the State, and probably will go West after awhile. I promised to go to New York State to do some work in some prominent meetings.

In closing I want to say to you, shake hands with each other and let the boys who are here for the paper spread the news that you are the jolliest, most harmonious and loving family there is in the nation. On you and around you are built other organizations.[26] If you become weak the forces of every craft will become weak. When you become strong you strengthen the forces of every other craft. You must not be narrow. For the first time in human history we are able today to touch the wire and even over in Japan we can say, "What are you doing for the workers?" And in the morning you will get the returns, "We held a tremendous meeting last night, and we, too, are marching on to claim our own with you, the workers of America." Don't let the tools of capitalism sit in this convention and tell you to get up and give some one hell! Get up and throw him out! Stop that, my friends. Transact your business and go home. You need the dollars you are spending in Indianapolis. The longer you stay the more the merchants will get and the less you will have. Now, good bye, and God bless you.

A motion was made and seconded that a vote of thanks be tendered Mother Jones.

Mother Jones — You have been trained under the capitalists. We don't owe a vote of thanks to any living being on earth; but we owe a vote of condemnation to every human being that does not rise up and do his duty.

[Minutes of the Annual Convention,
United Mine Workers of America, 1909, *pp. 374-82, 516-19.*]

Notes

1. Daniel Cosío Villegas, *The United States Versus Porfirio Díaz,* translated by Nettie Lee Benson, Lincoln, Nebraska, 1963, pp. 45-46; Ellen Howell Myers, "The Mexican Liberal Party, 1903-1910," unpublished Ph.D. dissertation, University of Virginia, 1970, pp. 38-56; Ward Sloan Albro III, "Ricardo Flores Magón and the Liberal Party: An Inquiry into the Origins of the Mexican Revolution of 1910," unpublished Ph.D. dissertation, University of Arizona, 1967, pp. 120-65; Pedro María Amaya Ibarra, *Precursores de la revolución mexicana,* Mexico City, 1955, pp. 11-35.

2. Lowell L. Blaisdell, *The Desert Revolution: Baja, California, 1911,* Madison, Wisconsin, 1962, p. 9.

3. "Dollar diplomacy" was a concept especially used during President Taft's administration (1909-1913) which involved State Department efforts to increase bankers' loans to specific governments, and the use of financial arrangements to increase American domination of various countries, especially in Central America and the Caribbean, and political influence in the area. (*See* Scott Nearing and Joseph Freeman, *Dollar Diplomacy: A Study in American Imperialism,* New York, 1925.)

4. John Kenneth Turner, *Barbarous Mexico,* Chicago, 1911, p. 239; W. Dirk Raat, *Revoltosos: Mexico's Rebels in the United States, 1903-1923,* College Station, Texas, 1981, pp. 47-48.

5. *Ibid.,* p. 238.

6. On May 25, 1911, Porfirio Díaz resigned and departed for exile in Europe. Soon after his triumph Francisco Madero announced that workers had the right to organize unions, and in October, 1911 Mother Jones went to Mexico City together with an official of the UMW and W. F. of M. to consult on the influx of Mexican miners into the American West. They met with President-elect Madero who pledged to help them organize the Mexican miners. But the offer was nullified by Madero's assassination. However, later Pancho Villa, with whom Mother Jones developed a friendship, also offered to help Mother Jones organize the Mexican miners, but nothing again came of the effort. However, in a letter to the *Appeal to Reason,* Mother Jones reported her agreement with Madero, noting: "This is the first time that any one has ever been granted that privilege in the history of the Mexican nation . . . I am the first person who has been permitted to carry the banner of industrial freedom to the long suffering peons of this nation." (Quoted in Judith Elaine Mikeal, "Mother Mary Jones: The Labor Movement's Impious Joan of Arc," unpublished M.A. thesis, University of North Carolina, 1965, p. 40.) On May 22, 1915, Mother Jones publicly expressed the opinion that she wished "to God that we had two or three [Pancho] Villas in this country." (*New York Times,* May 23, 1915; Featherling, *op. cit.,* p. 82.)

Born into a peasant family in the state of Chihuahua in northern Mexico, Francisco (Pancho) Villa rose to become a leader in the campaign against the regime of Porfirio Díaz. Villa's daring, impetuosity, and horsemanship made him an idol of the masses, especially in northern Mexico. But he was accused of numerous attacks on defenseless people, and was accused by some Mexicans of being a murderer of his own people. In the United States Villa is best known for a raid that some of his men made in March 1916 on Columbus, New Mexico, in which a number of Americans were killed. A punitive expedition led by Gen.

John J. Pershing pursued Villa through Chihuahua for eleven months, but failed to find him.

Villa was assassinated in 1923 in Hidalgo del Parral, Chihuahua. In 1967, the Mexican government officially elevated Villa to the status of hero, and nine years later his remains joined those of four other heroes in a crypt at the Monument to the Revolution in Mexico City. On June 30, 1981, a statue of the Mexican revolutionary, a gift from the Mexican government and a national journalists' association in Mexico, was unveiled in a park in Tucson, Arizona.

7. Alphonse de Lamartine (1790-1869), French poet and statesman, was the author, among other works, of a prose work *Graziella,* dedicated to a working-class girl with whom he had fallen in love.

8. Magón, Villareal, and Rivera to Mother Jones, Nov. 31 (*sic*), 1909, Mother Jones Papers, Department of Archives and Manuscripts, Catholic University of America, Washington, D.C.

Villareal and Rivera were the two men with Magón who had been roughed up by the Los Angeles police. The three were released from prison on August 1, 1910. Less than a year later, Magón was back in jail, having organized a revolutionary movement in Baja, California.

9. *See Autobiography of Mother Jones,* pp. 136-40.

10. U.S. Congress, House Rules Committee, *Hearings for a Joint Committee to Investigate Alleged Persecutions of Mexican Citizens by the Government of Mexico,* 1st Congress, 2nd Session, 1910, p. 92.

Thaddeus Kosciusko (1746-1817) was the Polish hero who served with the American army during the American Revolution, and later led a rebellion in Poland.

Carl Schurz (1829-1906), refugee from the German revolution of 1848, who became a leader of the German-American community; served as a general in the Union army during the Civil War, and was later Secretary of the Interior under President Rutherford B. Hayes in which post he advocated civil service reform.

Louis Kossuth (1802-1891), Hungarian revolutionist who led the unsuccessful attempt to end Russian rule in 1848; was received with acclaim in the United States in 1852, but alienated progressive Americans by refusing to speak out against slavery.

Giuseppe Garibaldi (1807-1882), republican leader of the national liberation movement in Italy, who had to leave his country in 1834 because of his complicity in antimonarchist plotting. He returned in 1848 and was prominent in the revolutionary activities of that year. After their failure, he left once again, this time coming to the United States, but he returned to Italy in 1859. In 1860 he led his victorious expedition to Sicily and Naples, and with his thousand "red shirts" overthrew the Bourbon monarchy and made possible the accession of these states to a United Italy.

11. Tom L. Lewis (no relation to John L. Lewis) succeeded John Mitchell to the United Mine Workers' presidency in 1908 after the former was forced to resign because of growing opposition to his hobnobbing with the business elite in and out of the National Civic Federation and improving himself materially while UMW president. Lewis continued these practices while he was president, and later became a well-paid official of a West Virginia mine owners' association.

12. The reference is to the kidnapping of Manuel Sarabia. *See* Manuel Sarabia, "How I Was Kidnapped," *International Socialist Review* 9 (May, 1909):

853-62.

13. Mother Jones is referring to the fact that she organized telegrams of protest to state and federal officials, including President Theodore Roosevelt. There are, however, no letters or telegrams of Mother Jones in the Roosevelt Papers in the Library of Congress.

14. The Pinkerton Agency was established in 1850 by Allan Pinkerton who had migrated from England to Chicago in 1842. At first the agency specialized in railroad theft cases, but later it specialized in antilabor and antiunion activities, becoming most active in major strikebreaking work. There were few industrial conflicts in which the Pinkertons were not involved. James McParlan, who engineered both the Molly Maguires and Haywood-Moyer-Pettibone frameups, was a Pinkerton labor spy.

15. Mother Jones is referring to the 1906 (not 1896) strike at the American-owned copper mines at Cananea, Sonora, Mexico. The Díaz regime used repressive measures that caused death and injury to many Mexican miners in a move to break the strike, methods which included importation of strikebreakers and state police from Arizona.

16. William B. Wilson, UMW national secretary-treasurer was elected to Congress from Pennsylvania in 1906, and Mother Jones had campaigned for him at the time. Perhaps as a result of Mother Jones' prodding, Congressman Wilson sponsored the hearings by the House Rules Committee in June 1910, for an investigation of "alleged persecution" of Mexicans by the Mexican government.

17. Joseph G. Cannon (1836-1926), known familiarly as "Uncle Joe" and "Czar Cannon," dictatorial and anti-reform Speaker of the House from 1903 to 1910. In the latter year a revolt headed by George W. Norris, progressive Republican from Nebraska, overthrew his control of the powerful Rules Committee in the House, and retired him from the speakership.

Mother Jones' comment about "one woman in that Congress" is another example that she did not invariably oppose participation of women in politics.

18. On August 25, 1909, the Chicago *Examiner* carried in its society columns a report of a dinner given by Mrs. J. Borden Harriman at her home in New York state at which "waiters in gorgeous livery served, pretty misses in costumes led by Miss Edith Harriman, posed in quaint tableaux and sang patriotic songs, and Mrs. Harriman, John Mitchell and Tim Healy (A.F. of L. leader) delivered addresses. . . . The tables were laid upon the lawn in the shape of the letter E. Mrs. Harriman presided at the center table. To the right and left of her sat Mitchell and Healy. Others present were Frank J. McNulty of Springfield, Ill., president of the International Brotherhood of Electrical Workers; Thomas B. Levy of Isaac G. Johnson & Co., of Spuyten Duyvil, N.Y.; Edward A. Moffett (former editor of the *Bricklayers' and Masons' Journal*), Camden, N.J.; C. L. Shamp of Omaha, Neb., secretary of the International Stationary Fireman's Union." The *Industrial Worker,* organ of the I.W.W., commented caustically on September 2, 1909: "Every coal miner's shack should be ornamented with a copy of the photograph which was taken of the revellers." Ann Morgan was the daughter of J. P. Morgan.

19. On December 23, 1908, in a speech replete with bitter invective and abuse, Judge Daniel T. Wright found Samuel Gompers, John Mitchell, and Frank Morrison guilty of contempt for refusing to abide by the injunction issued in the Buck's Stove and Range Co. case. Judge Wright sentenced Morrison to six months in the United States jail in the District of Columbia, Mitchell to

nine months, and Gompers to 12 months. None of the men, however, ever served.

20. *See above* p. 81.

21. The resolution denounced the sentencing of Mitchell, Gompers, and Morrison, noted that "Jan Pouren and Christian Rudovitz, Russian exiles, are about to be turned over to the Russian Czar to be murdered because they had the courage to ask for freedom for labor," and that "Flores Magon, Antonio Villareal and Librada Revera, Mexican patriots, are incarcerated in a United States jail because they spoke and wrote against the tyranny of an unjust government," and urged the president of the United States to take a stand to remedy the actions taken in each case by the courts. Because the resolution dealt with three separate subjects, it was recommended by the Resolutions Committee that no action be taken. The resolution was separated and later adopted by the convention.

22. After going on strike for a nine-hour day against the Bucks' Stove and Range Co., located in St. Louis, the Metal Polishers Local No. 10 declared a boycott against the company. The A.F. of L. Executive Council endorsed the boycott and published the name of the company on the "We Don't Patronize" list of the *American Federationist*. At the request of the American Anti-Boycott Association, the court issued an injunction against both the union and the A.F. of L. leaders associated with the action of the executive council and it was this injunction which Judge Wright had upheld. (*See* Foner, *op. cit.*, vol. 3, pp. 338-78.)

23. Rudowitz, a young Jewish worker, was in danger of being deported to Russia and certain death when Jane Addams and others at Chicago's Hull House organized a Rudowitz Committee to prevent the deportation. Mother Jones spoke at a meeting in Chicago organized by the committee.

24. During these years the United Mine Workers of America was the scene of repeated and heated internal factional struggles as rivals for power and influence battled each other. Mother Jones appealed repeatedly and, in most instances, fruitlessly for unity in the face of attacks from the capitalist enemy. One reason for her failure was that too often the men she appealed to were more interested in advancing themselves materially by collaborating with the "enemy" than in advancing the interests of the workers they represented. (*See*, in this connection, Warren Van Tine, *The Making of the Labor Bureaucrat: Union Leadership in the United States 1870-1920*, Amherst, Mass., 1973, pp. 162-77.)

25. Tall and heavy, William Howard Taft, president from 1909 to 1913, was the biggest man ever to occupy the White House. He weighed between 300 and 350 pounds most of the time and had to have a special bathtub constructed for him when he took up residence in the White House.

26. Whatever its inner conflicts and corruption, the United Mine Workers was noted for its support of other unions in their struggles and of progressive causes in general. It was a bellwether in many instances for American labor advance.

This Is Not a Play, This Is a Fight!

Speech on behalf of the waistmakers on strike
New York City, December 9, 1909

On November 24, 1909, eighteen thousand waistmakers in Manhattan and Brooklyn, New York City, walked out of nearly five hundred shops. By the end of the day, more than twenty thousand workers, the vast majority women, were on strike.[1]

The women working in New York City's dress and waistmaking shops astonished the nation by staging this strike, one of the most dramatic in twentieth century labor history. This great uprising of 20,000 workers (some say 30,000[2]) served as a catalyst for workers in other branches of the needle trades' industry. And it spearheaded the drive that turned the shells of unions like the International Ladies' Garment Workers' Union, the United Garment Workers and the Amalgamated Clothing Workers of America, into mass organizations, thereby laying the foundation for stable and lasting organizations in the women's and men's clothing industries and for the widespread organization of women workers.[3]

The strikers won the support of many sympathizers, outstanding among them being the Women's Trade Union League[4] and the Socialist Party. On December 9, Local New York of the Socialist Party sponsored a meeting at Thalia Theater in Manhattan at which the featured speaker would be Mother Jones. Excerpts from Mother Jones's speech appeared the next day in the Socialist Party organ, the New York Call.

"This is not a play, this is a fight!"

With these ringing words, Mother Jones, the valiant agitator for the freedom of the workers, struck the keynote of the enthusiastic mass meeting, in behalf of the waist workers, held by Local New York of the Socialist Party in Thalia Theater yesterday afternoon. The big crowd applauded this sentiment to the echo. . . .[5]

Mother Jones, the friend of the miners and champion of all oppressed, was greeted with a very hearty reception by the big crowd. She was in excellent condition. As she attacked the system with sledgehammer blows, logic and wit, the enthusiasm of the crowd broke into storms of applause.

"Through all the ages you have built a wonderful monument of civilization, but you don't own it," said Mother Jones, in opening. "You make all the fine waists, but you do not wear them. You work hard and are poorly paid, and now you have been forced to strike for better conditions of labor, shorter hours and higher wages.[6]

"You ought to parade past the shops where you work and up the avenue where the swells who wear the waists you made live.[7] They won't like to see you, they will be afraid of you!

"If I belonged to a union and was on strike, I would insist that we parade past the shops and homes of the masters.

"You must stick together to win. The boss looks for cheap workers. When the child can do the work cheaper he displaces the woman. When the woman can do the work cheaper she displaces the man. But when you are organized you have something to say about the conditions of labor and your wages. You must stand shoulder to shoulder. The woman must fight in the labor movement beside man. Every strike that I have ever been in has been won by the women."

Last Great Fight of Man

"Whether you know it or not, this is the last great fight of man against man. We are fighting for the time when there will be no master and no slave. When the fight of the workers to own the tools with which they toil is won, for the first time in human history man will be free," declared Mother Jones as she concluded amid storms of applause.

[New York Call, *December 10, 1909.]*

Notes

1. For a discussion of the strike, *see* Philip S. Foner, *Women and the American Labor Movement: From Colonial Times to the Eve of World War I*, New York, 1979, pp. 324- 45.

2. The report on the strike in the *Annual Report of the Women's Trade Union League of New York 1909-1910,* is entitled "The League and the Strike of the Thirty Thousand," New York, 1910, p. 11.

3. See, for example, the chapter "Repercussions of the Garment Workers' Uprising" (pp. 346-73) in Foner, *Women and the American Labor Movement*.

4. Formed in 1903 by a number of social workers and trade unionists, who modeled the organization after the one in England, the Women's Trade Union League aimed to "aid women in their effort to organize; to assist already organized women workers to secure better conditions; to start clubs and lunchrooms for women working in big factories; to give and arrange entertainments for them; to notify secretaries of labor organizations whenever an organization was to be formed so as to avoid conflicts in regard to jurisdiction." Activities of the league included organizing, picketing, raising bail, working for remedial protective legislation, and publicizing the need to improve working conditions. The league united upper- and middle-class women and working-class women, although there were strains in this relationship. For the full story of the league, *see* Foner, *Women and the American Labor Movement,* chapters 16, 17, 18, 26.

5. The account then reported the speeches of Carrie W. Allen who was described as "the well known agitator," and chairperson of the meeting, and

Algernon Lee, Socialist Party leader.

6. The strike demands included a union shop, a fifty-two-hour week, limitation of overtime work, and an increase in wages. The strike brought only a partial victory since the settlements did not include a union shop.

7. Mother Jones must have known that a number of the "swells" were helping the strikers through the Women's Trade Union League, picketing with the strikers, and, in some cases, even going to jail with them.

The Tyranny of Mexico

Speech delivered at the People's Forum, Hart's Hall,
Brooklyn, New York, December 12, 1909

While in New York City on behalf of the waistmakers, Mother Jones used the opportunity to organize support for Mexicans imprisoned in the United States for fighting the Díaz dictatorship, and spoke in their behalf at the socialist People's Forum, "to an audience which jammed the hall," reported the New York Call *which published excerpts from her speech.*

Her theme was "The Tyranny of Mexico," and she aroused the indignation of all who heard her arraignment of "Perfidio" Díaz, the autocrat of Mexico, to a very high pitch. At the conclusion of the speech a collection was taken, which netted more than thirty-two dollars for the fight against Diaz.

A petition was also circulated in behalf of Carlo De Fornaro, the artist, who was sentenced by Judge Malone to serve one year at hard labor in the workhouse on the charge of libeling Rafael Espindola, one of Diaz's tools, and about 350 persons signed it. The petition will be sent to Governor Hughes, with a set of resolutions demanding that Fornaro be given a new trial.[1]

Judge Malone was mercilessly flayed by Mother Jones for his treatment of Fornaro, and she also severely criticized the judiciary as a whole. She said: "Over half the judges in this country don't understand, or know anything about law. They're not supposed to, anyway. They are only supposed to do what their capitalist masters want.

"If Jesus Christ were to go before Judge Malone and tell him that he was breaking the Ten Commandments by his action, Malone would tell Jesus that the Ten Commandments are unconstitutional in this country!"

Mother Jones also made a strong appeal to the women to assist in the fight against Diaz, who seeks to make the United States a watchdog to capture such of his subjects as dare to disagree with him. She declared: "Women win all strikes! Women support all strikes! They keep their husbands in good standing in the union; they give them the courage to fight. We need the women in this fight against the tyranny of Mexico."

The conservative labor leaders also came in for some sharp criticism from Mother Jones. She declared vehemently: "Most of them have paunches as big as Taft from sitting down at Civic Federation banquets, Harriman and Belmont dinners, where they have been settling the labor problem to the satisfaction of the master class.[2] They are not fighting the class struggle! But the workers are going ahead in spite of them!"

After the meeting Mother Jones left for Trenton, N.J., where she spoke on the same subject last night. She will speak in Philadelphia tonight, and after that she will start West, where she will continue her work of agitation against the imprisonment of men for criticizing the tyranny of Mexico.

[New York Call, *December 13, 1909.]*

Notes

1. Republican Governor Charles Evans Hughes (1862-1948) ignored the petition. For another statement by Mother Jones on this issue, *see* p. 439.

2. The National Civic Federation, founded in 1900, was an organization of industrialists, labor leaders, and public figures committed to "responsible" labor relations, or as Professor Norman J. Ware put it: "It united A.F. of L. officialdom and powerful financial interests against all aggressive labor leadership in the United States. The A.F. of L. became a 'Morgan partner' in attacking radicalism wherever it appeared." (Quoted in Foner, *op. cit.,* vol. 3, p. 110.) *See* Foner, *op. cit.,* vol. 3, pp. 61-110 for the origins and early history of the National Civic Federation.

Don't Give the Master Class Any Weapon to Strike You With

Speech delivered at 1911 convention of the United Mine Workers of America

The attack Mother Jones leveled at the conservative labor leaders for "sitting down at Civic Federation banquets" in her Brooklyn speech on "The Tyranny of Mexico" became the crucial issue at the 1911 UMW convention as John Mitchell's membership and salaried position in the National Civic Federation dominated convention debate. Speaker after speaker denounced Mitchell and the Federation for "class collaboration" policies against the interests of the labor movement.[1] In addressing the convention, Mother joined in the attacks on the National Civic Federation with relish, denouncing it as "the most diabolical game ever played on labor," cooked up by "the gang of robbers in Wall Street" to emasculate the labor movement.

But Mother Jones also ranged over a wide assortment of topics, covering miners' strikes in Colorado, Arizona, and Pennsylvania, denouncing the death sentence imposed upon labor leaders in Japan, and the action against Fred Warren, editor of the socialist Appeal to Reason *who had been sentenced in the spring of 1909 to six months in jail and fined five thousand dollars for sending "scurrilous, defamatory and threatening" literature through the mails. She also dealt with one of her favorite themes, the battle against the persecution of Mexican revolutionaries in the United States and against the Díaz dictatorship.*

President Lewis — Mother Jones is here. A motion was unanimously adopted yesterday to invite Mother Jones to address this convention at 9 o'clock this morning. That carried with it that it would be any time to suit her convenience. I believe most, if not all, the delegates in this convention know Mother Jones and know of her work in behalf of the mine workers and the wage earners of the entire country. I take pleasure now in both introducing and presenting to you Mother Jones, who will address the convention.

Mother Jones — The time is short and I will not wear you out. I know a lot of you here want to go out and get a drink.

President Lewis — There is no time limit to your speech, and when we adjourn we will convene that much later after dinner.

Mother Jones — Brothers of this convention, perhaps never in the history of the mine workers was there a more important convention than this. The eyes of the world are resting today and all other days you are in session on this hall. The master class is watching your convention with keen interest. And so I say to you, be wise, be prudent in your actions. Think before you act. Don't give the master class any weapon to strike you with and laugh about. Let us have the laugh on them.

Now, my brothers, the last year has been a trying year for organized labor all along the line. There have been some wonderful fights on the industrial field. It has not been alone the miners, it has not been alone the steel workers.[2] For the first time, perhaps, the women in the industrial field have begun to awaken to their condition of slavery.[3] In New York and Philadelphia the women arrayed themselves in battle, and they gave battle fearlessly. They were clubbed, they were jailed, they were insulted, but they bore it all for a principle they believed in.[4] Never can a complete victory be won until the woman awakens to her condition. We must realize that the woman is the foundation of government; that no government is greater or ever can be greater than the woman. It was once asked of Napoleon how the French nation could become a great nation. He considered a moment and then said: "Never until you have a great motherhood. When you have that you have a great nation."

And so it is with us in this nation. Never as long as the women are unorganized, as long as they devote their time to women's clubs and to the ballot, and to a lot of old meow things that don't concern us at all and have no bearing on the industrial battle, can we succeed, and the men will have to make the battle alone. But the century is here when the woman is going to take a mighty hand in these battles, and then we will fight it out and fight it to a finish. Put that down, Mr. Reporter!

Now, I want to call your attention to some things. The industrial war is on in this country. Why? Because modern machinery plays a greater part in the production of wealth in this nation than it does in any other nation of the world. The class that owns the machine owns the government, it owns the governors, it owns the courts and it owns the public officials all along the line. There may be an exception, but on the whole it is true. It certainly owns the Governor of Ohio.[5] Put it down, Mr. Reporter, that I said so! First the Governor of Ohio brought out his dogs of war to turn them on the steel workers. That cost this State $250,000. Then he brought them out and turned them on the street car strikers and undertook to lick them into submission. I want to serve notice on the Governor of Ohio that he has never licked labor into submission and never will, and by the eternal gods we will lick him into submission before we are through!

I have not forgotten Harmon. He brought the bayonets out in '94 — not the state bayonets, but the federal bayonets, to shoot us down in Chicago. He was Attorney-General and Cleveland was President.[6] Cleveland was off on a drunk and the other fellow had the job. I generally keep tab on what these fellows do. Well, the steel workers are not licked yet. They are going to come to the front one of these days, and when they do they will be heard from.

Now, you have a fight of the miners in Colorado. You have got to call

141

a strike in the Southern field and lick the Colorado Fuel and Iron Company out of its boots. You cannot win in the Northern field until you take a hand in the Southern field. You could have won in Colorado at one time. You had the strike in your own hands, but you undertook to make a settlement in the Northern field and left the Southern field to fight the battle alone.[7] Then they were able to turn their batteries. The Northern field furnished coal for the State institutions, and the result was their rotten carcasses got heated up and they could turn the bayonets on you. I am for making a fight on the whole bunch. If you don't want to do it alone, I will go there and take a hand in it and give them hell.

When I heard those fellows talking about a dual organization here on this floor I was disgusted — it was enough to make a dog sick! Let me say to you the only real dual organization there is in the country is the Civic Federation and the gang of robbers in Wall street. That is the dual organization against labor, and I want to tell you fellows in the central field to bury your hatchet, take a day off and get your skulls to working instead of your jaws. I happened to be in the central field a long time ago, before those fellows who are blowing off hot air here were in the union — they were scabbing. I am glad you are in the union, however. I know how a scab is made up. One time there was an old barrel up near heaven, and all of heaven got permeated with the odor. God Almighty said, "What is that stuff that smells so?" He was told it was some rotten chemical down there in a barrel and was asked what could be done with it. He said, "Spill it on a lot of bad clay and maybe you can turn out a scab." That is what a scab is made of, and he has been rotten all down the ages. We have a few scabs in Pennsylvania, Mr. President, and once in a while we get hold of one of them and lick him. I have licked lots of them, and I expect to lick more of them before I die.

Now, I am going to speak to you on this question of machinery, and I want to draw your attention to the fact that they have reached into China and are developing the industries there. Capitalism is in business for profit, and wherever it is going to realize the most profit out of human blood there it is going. So they have reached into China, where they can hire men for eight cents and ten cents a day. The result is we are feeling it here all along the line. The merchants in Westmoreland county, at Greensburg, called the Council together and asked them if they would not pass an ordinance demanding that the mounted constabulary be placed in Greensburg. They wanted one place in each hotel to take care of the hotelkeepers. They said the miners were in a terrible way and the scabs were afraid to come into town. The scabs were not a bit afraid to come into town, but the merchants were so full of greed and avarice they did not realize where they were struck. They wanted the constabulary to protect them against a handful of miners, but they never thought of calling in the constabulary to see after the

Standard Oil, that has taken over eighty-four of the great department stores of this country. It is the onward march of civilization. And so it must be with us; we must centralize our forces in one great, mighty column.

If there is an organization in this land or in any other land the master classes are afraid of, if there is an organization they want to split in two, it is the United Mine Workers of America.[8] They are putting up every sort of game to divide our forces, but they are going to get left, my friends. We may have a little housecleaning, we may have a little jawing and chewing the rag; but when the time comes we will line up and give the master class what they have been looking for. In Colorado you have sixteen men in jail. A distinguished judge, owned body and soul and brains — and he never had any too much brains — by the corporations, has put sixteen of our men in jail. Let me serve notice on the judges of this country that the day is not far distant when we will put every capitalist judge in jail and make a man out of him. That day is coming and it is not far away. Put that down, Mr. Reporter, so the judges will know it!

They take our boys and for no cause on earth put them in jail. In Greensburg they hauled them in all over the county, and gave them nothing to eat until the miners came along, put up their treasury, bailed them out and they went back again to help their brother strikers.[9] They are trying to create a riot. Fellows will go out and say, "Why, the miners are very peaceful." I wonder what those fellows think? We will be peaceful if they give us what belongs to us, but we will not be very peaceful while they are skinning us. We are at war, and there is no war so fierce as an industrial battle. No war on the battle field of the world's history can equal an industrial battle.

Now, I want to speak on the strike in Westmoreland county. I did not go in there until a little late. I was engaged on the Mexican case, and had to carry it to Washington. I forced it myself without any aid from any human being. Nobody else knew anything about it. I spent nights awake and days alone. I knew if I went and secured counsel it might be bought. It was a grave and mighty question, and I knew its importance to the labor movement, so I worked it out as best I could. I got some documents from the federal prison in Arizona. The men had them stolen out to me. They were forwarded to me and I sat up at night to read them. I said to myself that the liberties of the whole American people were at stake if that thing was not brought into the public eye.

Then I went to President Taft. I did not present the documents to him, but I made statements. He said, "Mother, if you bring me some evidence in regard to this I will go over it myself." I said, "Very well, Mr. President; that is all I can expect you to do." Then he said, "They were not anarchists, were they?" They don't know any more about anarchy than a dog does about his father, because the real anarchists of this country are the Supreme Court judges, the Wall street gang and

143

the Governor of Ohio. They don't understand the definition of anarchy. I would have told him something about anarchy, but I had a mission there and I thought I would use a little diplomacy and a little taffy. Even if he is President, he will swallow that as well as the rest of us. His eye was hurt and I said he ought not to use it any more that day. He said he had been out in his automobile and a bug got in his eye. I never get hit in the eye automobiling, because I never go riding. I said: "Mr. President, don't see any more people today; that eye needs a rest. Before you are four years in this office you will need the use of your two eyes and your two ears." He said, "Do you think I will, Mother?" I said, "I am sure of it."[10]

I didn't hear very much from the President. I was telegraphed for to go to San Antonio, where they were arresting a lot of those men. I want to show how closely we are watched. The editor of a paper there came to me in the afternoon and said: "Mother, you had better be careful in your speech tonight. The Mexican government has filled the city with secret service men." "I am much obliged for the information," I said, "but I want to tell you that old Diaz, the bloody murderer, can come here himself and I will talk all I want to." I said I was not going to be careful; that I was going to say what I pleased, and even if they hung me for it I would say it before I was hung.

We held five meetings. I went to the United States marshal to get permission to see some of the revolutionists who were in jail. The marshal and the attorney were in the marshal's office. The marshal gave me a permit to go to the jail. While I was there they got to talking about guns. It seems they went into a little Mexican cabin and found a couple of old broken pistols you couldn't shoot a cat with. I said: "I don't see why you are so afraid of guns. Didn't Washington use guns? Wasn't the victory of this nation won with guns? Didn't we make the Southern Confederacy come back into the Union by the use of guns?" Then I said, "If it is necessary to use guns to protect these revolutionists, we will do it." He said, "That is right." He came to the meetings every night, and he threw money into the collection. The secret service men got all the talk they wanted. The night I closed my meeting I told them in my speech I was going to El Paso. I said, "I want all the dogs of war belonging to Diaz and the secret service men to come down there, because I am going to raise a row with old Diaz."

To tell the truth I was going to the Black Hills to speak on Labor Day, but I thought I would throw them off my track. A fellow has a job on his hands to get the best of a woman, even if he is a slick sleuth of a detective. All my mail went to El Paso and I had to write there to have it forwarded to the Black Hills. When I got to Fort Worth I said to the conductor: "There is a bunch of those corporation dogs on my trail. I am going to the Black Hills, but they expect me to go to El Paso. I have only one satchel. If you will take care of it I will walk about five miles out in the country and get on the train." He said, "All right,

Mother; I will send you out in a buggy."

Then they arrested one of the Mexicans. I went to Texas and they telegraphed me to come to New York. I carried those documents. I remembered we had two miners in Congress, and perhaps they could frame a bill on the question and bring it before the House. The bill was framed by Congressman Nichols, of Scranton, and he fought a brave battle. I want to tell you it is necessary for you to put your clear-cut men in Congress and in the Legislatures. You will not win until you do. I bring this up to impress upon your minds what can be done. The bill was brought up in the House, sent to a committee and pigeon-holed. I wrote to the different labor papers and trades councils asking them to demand of their representatives that that bill be brought out on the floor of the House, where it could be discussed. I went to Washington and the bill was brought up. The Attorney-General, Wickersham, the Wall street representative of the gang of thieves, made a slight excuse. I asked Congressman Wilson to frame a bill appropriating $25,000 to bring lawyers and witnesses there. The bill was framed.

I was sick in Cincinnati when I heard the bill was coming up for a hearing on the following Friday. I went to Washington and talked to Congressman Wilson. He had read the documents I had in my possession. The question came up to the committee. You should have been there before that committee! There were representatives of the Steel Trust, of the Southern Pacific Railway and of other interests. I sat during the hearing and took it in. Congressman Wilson called on me to give my evidence. I got up and related a little history to the committee. I said, "I do not go into the classics after language to express myself when there is a condition that forces me to pray, and it isn't the prayer that will take me to heaven that I use." Dalzell said, "Mother Jones, where do you live?" "I will tell you. I live wherever there is a bunch of workers fighting the robber. My home is with the workers." He didn't ask any more questions, but I related the whole affair. [11]

Now, the miners of this country put up $4,000, and those Mexican refugees are indebted to you for being where they are today. Had we not exposed this affair they would have been arrested again the day they came out of prison. On account of the hearing and the way we exposed it they were not arrested. The morning they came out I sent $75 to each of them. That was your money. I sent $100 later. There is a little more in the treasury of the Western Federation of Miners. We placed the money there because it was nearer the seat of war. That I intend to hold. I have written the warden of the penitentiary to find out when the time of a man who is there now will expire. He has five children and they are without a mother. You have dug down into your treasury and brought out your hard-earned dollars and put them up for that cause. I desire to pay my respects to Comrade Germer, who handled the money and sent it West. [12] Those Mexicans are indebted to the miners of this country for being safe today. A revolution is on in

Mexico, and if we didn't have a revolution of our own I would be down there, because I want to send that bloody thief of a Diaz up to God Almighty in a condition that will show how big a rascal he was down here.

Now, to come back to the Irwin field.[13] I didn't go in there when I should have gone, because I was not well after the spell of sickness I had. I had been up against two governments and it was a great strain. I went to the anthracite and stayed at Charlie Gildea's home, and Andrew Matti, Martin Flyzik and Angelo Gillotti furnished all the beer I needed until I got well. Now, as to the Irwin field. Fourteen years ago I went there with poor Pat Dolan. I think Ed McKay was with us. We pulled out Congressman Huff's mine and the mines all along the line. I said to Pat, "You can get these fellows if we can only take care of them." He said, "That is the trouble; the organization is not in a position to take care of them." I left the Irwin field then and did not go back until last November. Then I surveyed the situation carefully. Now, I am not going to whitewash anything; I am going to tell the delegates to this convention the truth, because you are the men who furnished the hard-earned dollars to win that strike.

No man, no set of men will or ever have owned me except the working class. There is not a more important strike in the history of the Miners' Union than the strike in the Irwin field — not one. I knew that when it started; but the whole industrial body of the miners were in a strike of their own at the time it started. They were not able to take hold of it as they should have done. They have done yeoman work in that field; they are magnificent fighters; but in all strikes there will be the grafters, there will be those who have no conscience, there will be those who sell their homes and come out and live off the organization.

I want to say to you that strike must be won; it will be won, but you have got to center your forces there, and if it takes all the money of your organization, put it there and lick hell out of those operators. Maryland depends on the Irwin field, Central Pennsylvania depends upon it, and the Pittsburg district depends upon it. If you lose the Irwin field the operators of the Pittsburg district will give it to you in the near future. There is the Connellsville field, there is Maryland and West Virginia which you must organize, because that coal comes into competition with yours, and if a fellow goes over there who is afraid to go up those mountains, send him home, put a mother hubbard on him and give him a nursing bottle. Many men have lost their lives. Many men want a job of organizing, but they never did any organizing. Put that down, Mr. President! Don't be watching the salary.[14] For God's sake cut that rotten salary out of the deal. Get into the fight, every one of you, because we are up against it.

They have made a fine fight in the Irwin field, but the men were inexperienced in strikes. I saw that the minute I went in there. I wasn't there four days until I took the whole situation in. I have been in strikes for a good many years — not alone miners' fights, but garment workers' and textile workers' and street car men's strikes. I knew that field could be won if we were able to center our forces there. You must stop all conflict and get down to the fight. Instead of fighting each other, turn all your batteries on the other fellow and lick him; then, if there is any fellow in our own ranks who needs a licking, let us give it to him. Let us be true to the organization; let us fight to a finish. That field must be organized, and the Southern Colorado strike must be won. You cannot win that field in the North until you do. You are wasting money. I know that field thoroughly. I was up against the guns there too many months not to understand the situation.

Now, I am talking to you miners. I am not talking to officers. I am talking to you who put up the money to fight those battles and win them. I knew the men who blazed the way. There was no pay, there was no newspaper eulogy, there were no compliments; they slept by the wayside, but they fought the battle and paved the way for this magnificent organization, and, knowing them as I did, this organization is dear to me. It has been bought with the blood of men who are scarcely known today.

Now, I want to say a few more words. I want to call your attention to that magnificent dope institution that was formed to get labor, that mutual admiration society, the Civic Federation. The biggest, grandest, most diabolical game ever played on labor was played when that was organized. The Civic Federation! It ought to be called the physic federation, because that is what it really is! I know it all! That Civic Federation is strictly a capitalist machine. The men or women who sit down and eat and drink with them and become members of the Belmont-Carnegie cabinet are not true to labor. Tell them I said so! I have a letter I ought to have brought with me. It is from one of the leading lawyers of the city of New York. I got it just a day before I left Greensburg. There were eight pages in the letter. I met him during the protest meeting when I was going after the judge, and he was one of the leading lawyers. He said in that letter: "Mother, I should very much regret that your work would be lost. Why don't you tell the workingmen to pull their leaders out from the Civic Federation?" Labor never will progress; it cannot as long as they sit down and eat and drink and fill their stomachs and get their brains filled with champagne. And then Mrs. Harriman will say: "How deah! I get such an inspiration!" Inspiration from a couple of old labor scavengers! "It is so delightful to have labor and capital coming together in a brotherhood." What do you think of such rot? The robber and the robbed, the fellow who brings the militia out to murder my class and representatives of the workingman! Not on your life!

Let the Civic Federation stop the guns. Thirteen men have been murdered in the Irwin field. What has the Civic Federation done there? Sixteen men are in jail in Colorado. What did the Civic Federation do with Roosevelt when he sent 2,000 guns to the Governor of Colorado to blow your brains out? You have an old Mary Ann of a Governor there now. He hasn't as much backbone as Peabody had. Make me Governor of Pennsylvania or Colorado just one month, and you will find there will be none of those fellows in jail.

That Civic Federation is a menace to the working movement. The Labor Commissioner of Colorado came to Trinidad during our strike and said: "Mother, we had a delightful time in Chicago. You know there was a banquet of the Civic Federation. It was a charming treat. It was delightful to be there. Here was a labor leader, here was a millionaire, here was a labor leader and here was a millionaire. Why, we had drinks that cost 75 cents a drink and cigars that cost 50 cents apiece! I have one here; the odor of it is beautiful." "It ought to be," said I, "when it is stained with the blood of men that you infernal hypocrites, scavengers, robbers and fakers have wrung out of the labor movement! They pay the bills." You can tell old Easley, the secretary of the Civic Federation,[15] that we know his game; that he had been hoodwinking labor, but labor is awakening. This convention must tell those who represent labor in the Civic Federation to get out of it or get out of the labor movement.

You must look after the Irwin field. I went nine miles one day to where we found a woman with a baby wrapped up in a carpet. There were six other children, cold and hungry. The organization sent them clothing. They had built houses, they have done everything that could be done, but now you must do more. You must send your forces in there. I want to say that the secretary of the Labor Temple of Pittsburg is deserving of a great deal of gratitude and appreciation from the organization. Besides doing her other work, she has tramped over that field. She did not go into the newspapers to say what she did, but her work is there. I refer to Miss Pitt, secretary of the Pittsburg Labor Temple Association. We need more women of that type to take up the work.

Now, there is a great deal more I want to say, but I know you want to go to dinner, and I know the newspaper men want to go to the office with their news. Some of you want to go out and get a drink and you wish I would shut up. I am not going to do it for a minute or two. Whatever else you do, keep the fight up in the Irwin field. I want to say to the International that it is the miners' money that is to be spent. I know that many of you put up the assessment when your wives need it at home. I was in West Virginia with Ben Davis when he was a boy. Going down the track one day I saw a poor fellow and a little boy carrying the head of a bedstead up the mountain. I said, "Jack, for God's sake where are you going with that bed?" He said he was going up there to live. "Why," I said, "don't you know the children will roll down the mountain and be killed?" He said: "Mother, I get this place for three dollars a month. The company keeps it off. I haven't a dollar, and

148

I thought maybe I could save the other three dollars I paid for the house down the river. With my assessment and dues I haven't a penny."

Next day I went up there. His wife was dying with consumption. The little boy of ten and the father walked in tired, worn and wet. I gave the little ones a few pennies. One little girl said she would go down to the company's store and get some peanuts. The older girl, the little housekeeper, said: "No, Mamie, you can't spend that; we have got to put it away to buy some things for mamma." I could tell you stories that would take the roof off this building, but many of you know them all without my telling. I know it is these brave men who are digging down into their hard-earned money to pay for the strikes, to pay for this convention and for everything else, and so for their sakes see that the money is judiciously spent; see that there is an accounting for every penny, and that the man who is low enough and mean enough to take money from this organization and rent out houses and draw the rents — well, you may say he will go and scab. Let him do it, but lick him out of his boots before he does it. He is an imposter, a robber and a thief. There is no biger rascal walking. I have some respect for Morgan — he doesn't belong to my class; but when our own people rob us there is nothing to be said for them. What about the men in the Hocking Valley twenty-five years ago?[16] What about the men in Illinois? What about the men who have given up their lives for the organization? Look at those unmarked graves, the graves of men who made it possible for us to be here holding a meeting in the capital city of Ohio today and discussing these mighty questions.

Today twenty-one men are to be hung in Japan — twenty-one revolutionaries, twenty-one brave souls in that nation that has only come from barbarism within the last forty years.[17] Those twenty-one brave men go to the scaffold today, my friends, for a principle in which they believe, the principle of right and justice, and I want this convention to pass resolutions and notify the Japanese consul in Washington that they will hear from us if they hang any more of those men. Today Fred Warren goes to jail for undertaking to save the lives of the men of the Western Federation of Miners when they were behind the bars. I have a letter here I received from a gentleman who wrote me from New York. He said, "I notice in the papers today that one of the *Appeal to Reason* men has been tried on a charge of criminal libel." It was a falsehood, but that is the way the capitalist papers give the news. He was tried because he sent a postcard out. He asked the postmaster several times if it was against the federal laws and the postmaster said it was not. He sent the cards out asking that Taylor of Kentucky, who murdered Boebel, be caught and taken back to Kentucky.[18] It was no crime to hang and starve and shoot workingmen, but it was a crime to dare to do anything to defend our people. He asked me if I could get him the data of the case and a copy of the complaint. It is in this sort of thing he is going to specialize, restrictions of the freedom of speech and of the press. He said: "For years we have been fighting for that. It is the corner stone of our institutions and of all our rights that should be most sacredly guarded." That comes from one of the great attorneys of New York who did not understand the case. I sent for a copy of the complaint and had it forwarded to him. You see how these things are going along.

In reading over the report of the President I noticed statements I want to call you attention to. He said it makes no difference to him if he is the retiring officer,[19] he would stick to the workers anyhow, and would not sell his knowledge and experience and education the miners of the country gave him to the master class. I hope, Mr. President, you will keep your word. That is the particular part of the report I took stock in. It is unfortunate that men whom you have educated and have thrown up against the trained brains of the nation to learn how to benefit labor should give their services to the corporations of the nation. You have paid their salaries, you have paid their expenses, and I can count on my fingers over twenty men that I know have given their experience to the mine owners, to the master class, and are serving them. It is time to call a halt on this thing. You are not educating men to serve the master class. You give them office, you trust them to serve you, and when they do not do so, ostracize them as you would a mad dog. I have gone over this country and I have seen these things until I have become disgusted sometimes with the workers.

You are in the mightiest conflict of the age. Put away your prejudice, grow big and great and mighty in this conflict and you will win. There is no such thing as fail. We have got to win. You have brave fighters, both in Colorado and Pennsylvania. You have warriors there, but you must stand by them. Pay your dues, win that battle in the Irwin field, and then, my friends, turn your batteries on the Colorado Fuel and Iron Company and show them what the United Mine Workers' organization is made of.

President Lewis — In reply to the last statement by Mother Jones, when she said she hoped I would keep my word, I have never knowingly broken my word, and I expect to be back with the next convention of the United Mine Workers, if not in an official capacity, as a delegate from the picks.

On motion a rising vote of thanks was tendered Mother Jones for her address to the convention.

[Minutes of the Annual Convention, United Mine Workers of America, 1911, *pp. 258-70.*]

Notes

1. *United Mine Workers Journal,* Feb. 1, 1912, pp. 2-3; Feb. 8, 1902, p. 2.

2. The reference is to the strike of the steel workers at the Pressed Steel Car Company, led by the I.W.W., and the Bethlehem Steel strike led by the A.F. of L.

3. Having been a member of the Knights of Labor which had a large and militant women membership, it is strange to find Mother Jones referring to the "first time perhaps, the women in the industrial field have begun to awaken to their condition of slavery."

4. The reference is to the uprising of the waistmakers which took place in Philadelphia as well as in New York City.

5. Governor Judgen Harmon was inaugurated chief executive of Ohio for a second term in January 1911.

6. It was Richard B. Olney (1835-1917), not Harmon, who was the attorney-general in President Cleveland's cabinet responsible for the issuance of the sweeping injunction against the American Railway Union and in influencing Cleveland to send federal troops to break the Pullman strike.

7. *See above* pp. 37-39, 104-10.

8. In 1911 the United Mine Workers of America was the largest union in the United States with a membership close to 300,000.

9. The strike in Greensburg, Westmoreland County, Pennsylvania is described by Mother Jones in her *Autobiography* (pp. 145-47). There she also tells of the role played by the miners' wives, under her leadership, who carried on the battle against the scabs after their husbands had been imprisoned. The women also went to jail, and at Mother Jones's advice, took their babies with them, and, at her direction, sang "the whole night long." They caused so much noise that the townspeople could not sleep. "Finally after five days in which every one in town had been kept awake, the judge ordered their release." (*Ibid.,* p. 147.) The same tactic was used by I.W.W. free-speech fighters in their battle for the right to speak on the streetcorners.

10. Later Mother Jones added further details of her interview with President Taft such as the following dialogue:

Taft: "If I put the pardoning power in your hands there would be no one left in the jails."

Mother Jones: "I'm not so sure of that, Mr. President. A lot of those who are in would be out, but a lot of those who are out would be in." (Washington *Daily News,* December 2, 1930.) In any event, President Taft granted Mother Jones's request. There are no letters of Mother Jones in the William Howard Taft Papers in the Library of Congress.

11. Mother Jones's discussion involves the creation of the Committee of Rules of the House of Representatives to investigate "alleged persecutions" of Mexicans by the Mexican government. For Mother Jones's testimony before the committee, *see* pp. 369-75.

12. Adolph Germer was one of the leaders of the United Mine Workers in Illinois and of the Socialist Party in that state.

13. *See above* p. 576.

14. Salary increases for UMW officials took up a good deal of time at the convention.

15. Ralph M. Easley founded the Chicago Civic Federation in 1893, and was founder and leading functionary of the National Civic Federation when it took

on that name in 1900.

16. The reference is to the long, bitter, and unsuccessful struggle of the Hocking Valley miners which began in June 1884, and ended in March 1886, with the miners returning to work at a drastic wage cut of 70 cents a ton, and acceptance of the condition that they resign from the union.

17. On January 24, 1911, twelve labor activists were executed in a Tokyo prison, Japan. For a discussion of whether the executed men were socialists or anarchists, *see, The Agitator*, Home, Washington, March 1, 1911.

18. A former governor, Taylor, was wanted in his native state of Kentucky for questioning in connection with the murder of a political rival. Taylor had fled to Indiana, but the governor of that state refused to extradite him. Warren pointed out that in the Haywood, Moyer, Pettibone case, the men had been kidnapped from Colorado and taken to Idaho for trial. But they had been labor leaders, and Taylor was a capitalist politician. Warren offered a thousand dollars reward to anybody who seized Taylor and turned him over to the Kentucky authorities. The federal government found Warren guilty and he was sentenced to six months prison and five thousand dollars fine. President Taft, yielding to a huge defense movement, headed by Eugene V. Debs, pardoned Warren, removed the six months' sentence, and reduced the fine to a hundred dollars. Warren refused to pay the fine, and never did pay it.

19. Tom Lewis had been defeated for re-election by John P. White in an election which was considered to be fraudulent, a charge leveled against most UMW presidential elections.

Barbarous West Virginia

Five speeches to striking coal miners, Charleston and Montgomery, West Virginia, August 1, 4, 15, September 6, 21, 1912

Probably more than any other important mining state, West Virginia urgently needed effective organization in 1912 to protect the lives and interests of her coal miners. Engaged in one of the most dangerous occupations, they had to endure short coal weights, payments in company scrip, poor housing, low wages, inadequate medical attention, a system of blacklisting, brutal company guards, and high company-store prices which kept them constantly in debt. A state investigating committee found "in many instances an overcharging ranging from ten to twenty-five percent . . . at company stores." One student of the West Virginia mines concludes that for the miners "a system of peonage existed."[1]

When the miners did obtain some relief from the legislative bodies, the courts invariably wiped out their gains. The West Virginia courts denied the miners the right to be paid in cash and refused to uphold the law which prohibited the mine owners from selling to the laborers at higher prices than outsiders. The court stated that these laws represented "unjust interference with private contracts and business," and that they were an "insulting attempt to put the laborer under legislative tutelage," which was "degrading to his manhood" and "suppressive of his rights as a citizen of the United States." So the companies continued to use the scrip-system of wage payment and to compel their employees to trade at company stores. They also continued the practice of "cribbing," constructing wooden cribs on the sides of the mine cars to make them hold more coal and then paying the piecework miner as though the car were of ordinary size.[2]

In March 1913, after a thorough investigation of West Virginia mining operations, the conservative New York Tribune reported:

If anywhere in the world men need organizing to protect their interests it is in the West Virginia mining district. . . .

In the West Virginia coal fields the mine operators are the landlords, the local merchants — for the miners trade at the company stores — and they are very much of the local government so far as there is any in those mountains. Indeed, they have always been a large part of the state government, too. Each way the miner turns, he comes up against the employing corporation. When he rents a house it must be at the company's terms. When he buys food and clothing he must pay the company's prices. And when he seeks his legal rights it must be from the authorities that are likely to be subservient to the great local industries. It is a species of industrial feudalism to which he is subjected.[3]

Exercising the right of private ownership, the operators employed guards who would not permit union organizers to come near the mines and would not even allow meetings of the miners. The guards permitted no one to visit the mines or mine villages or "even to walk along the roads leading to the villages unless his business was known. Strangers were stopped and asked their business."[4] Organizing the miners was made still more difficult by the fact that towns were isolated and often inaccessible because of the rugged terrain, "each constituting a little world within itself."[5] Another factor retarding union growth was the ability of the anti-union employers to capitalize on race prejudice. The United Mine Workers adhered to the policy of organizing both white and black workers into the same local, and this was played up by the companies in order to create hostility to the union among white miners, most of whom were either native mountaineers or recent immigrants. The fact that many blacks were brought into the state from the South as strikebreakers, often without their knowledge, also increased racial friction and antagonism.[6]

The unorganized status of the mines in West Virginia constituted a threat to both the United Mine Workers and the stability of the industry. The state's coal companies competed in both the eastern and Great

Lakes markets. Because of the union, mid-western operators were paying higher wages and had been forced to eliminate many of the miners' long-standing grievances. In West Virginia, on the other hand, the company store, excessive docking, the absence of checkweighmen appointed by the miners, over-sized mine cars, and the longer hours of work — all enabled the operators to sell their coal at a lower price. This, of course, was a constant threat to the organized coal fields. Not only did the nonunion status of the industry attract operators to West Virginia, but even those with UMW contracts made it a practice to own mines in the state, so that they could shift operations from the union mines whenever they were threatened with a strike.[7]

In the great coal strike of 1902, the miners were defeated in all but one section of West Virginia by a combination of eviction of strikers from their homes, the repression by the mine guards and National Guardsmen, the use of strikebreakers and injunctions, the arrest of their national organizers, and the determination of the UMW leadership, pressured by John Mitchell, to confine assistance only to the anthracite strikers. Although the miners of the state lost their strike almost everywhere, those in the Kanawha section managed to win an agreement which included a nine-hour day, the election of checkweighmen to watch the weighing of the coal to see the miners received their fair weight, semi-monthly pay days, a reduction in the price of powder, the right to trade at noncompany stores, and no discrimination in rehiring the strikers or for union affiliation. In addition, the "check-off" was included, and the coal companies agreed to collect dues owed by the miners to their union and transmit them to the UMW.[8]

In 1904, the only organized mining district in West Virginia suffered a setback when a strike over the issue of the "check-off" ended in a defeat.[9] Nevertheless, the union, increasingly threatened by the expanding production in the state, persisted in its efforts to organize. The work had to be conducted in secret, for union organizers were followed and assaulted by guards and detectives. Miners seen talking to organizers were immediately discharged and those who even discussed unionism were dismissed and blacklisted.[10]

Some miners did manage to move through the state with the message that only through organization could the miners improve their conditions, raise their standard of living, and provide safeguards for their protection in the mines. Their activities brought some results, but by 1912 only 12,000 of the 76,000 miners in West Virginia belonged to the UMW, and of these, only 2,494 were paid-up members. Paint Creek in Kanawha County, ten miles from the state capital of Charleston, was the only organized coal field in the state. Four miles away was the unorganized coal field in Cabin Creek. Approximately 35,000 people lived in coal camps located on the two creeks. Fifty-five mines operated on Cabin Creek and forty-one on Paint Creek, employing a total of 7,500 miners.[11]

On April 1, 1912, the contract in the organized Paint Creek district expired. As the expiration date approached, the miners presented new contract terms which included wage scales based on the rates in adjacent coal fields, or increases of 2½ cents per ton, a working day of nine hours, instead of ten, payment of wages fortnightly in cash, improved sanitary conditions in the company houses, the right of miners to trade wherever they pleased without discrimination for not trading at the company store, a "more complete recognition of the union," including the "check-off system," and abolition of the mine guard system.[12]

The operators, fearing that granting the new demands would enable the union to strengthen its position throughout the state, refused to negotiate and withdrew recognition of the union. Indeed, the Cabin Creek miners, stimulated by the action in Paint Creek, submitted to their employers demands for union recognition; rights of free speech and peaceable assembly; an end to blacklisting of union men, an end to compulsory trading at company-owned stores, and other demands including the right to checkweighmen selected and paid by the miners. The operators rejected all these demands.[13]

On April 20, the Paint Creek miners walked off the job and closed down the mines. Soon the strike spread to the Cabin Creek and New River mine districts as nonunion miners voluntarily joined the walkout, bringing the total number of strikers to 4,000 and the number of companies affected to forty.[14]

The Cabin Creek–Paint Creek coal strike of 1912-1913 became one of the most violent labor battles in American history. Since the strikers who lived in company-owned houses were described by the operators as having "no more rights than a domestic servant who occupies a room in the household of the employers,"[15] the mine guards proceeded to forcibly evict the miners and their families. Strike breakers were imported, the company guard was increased, detectives and guards from the notorious Baldwin-Felts agency of Bluefield, West Virginia, which supplied guards (actually thugs) in the coal district were brought in, searchlights were mounted over the collieries, and machine guns were installed. The UMW set up a tent colony for the evicted families at Holly Grove, about fifteen miles from Charleston. The miners and their families in the colony were threatened, beaten, and murdered, and in self-defense, the miners armed themselves with guns, erected forts, and organized armed squads to protect their families and fight back.[16]

"Violence," writes Frederick Allan Barkey, "had been characteristic of West Virginia coal strikes, but the bloodshed which accompanied the Paint Creek–Cabin Creek strike during the summer of 1912 took on the symptoms of a real civil war." For nearly a month, however, the strike was conducted without violence. Then, on May 10, 1912, the coal companies contracted with the Baldwin-Felts Detective Agency for sufficient mine guards to break the strike. Three hundred were brought in. "These guards," Howard B. Lee in his study Bloodletting in Appalachia *points out, "were professional strikebreakers, all tried on a dozen industrial battlefields, and willing to shoot with or without provocation. . . . They immediately began a campaign of assault, intimidation, and terrorism."[17]*

The first action of the mine guards was to evict miners and their families from company-owned houses. Personal belongings were loaded on trains, transported off company property, and dumped beside the railroad tracks. Miners and their families took up residence in tent colonies established by the United Mine Workers.[18]

At this juncture, Mother Jones was brought into the struggle by the union. The eighty-two-year-old organizer was traveling through the Pacific Northwest and California in 1912, assisting striking railway workers and addressing mass meetings. By the first of June she was in Denver, and then moved on to the copper miners in Butte, Montana, just before leaving for San Francisco for a speaking tour. But she never made it to the Pacific Coast again in 1912, for the request came from the union for her to leave for West Virginia and help the hard-pressed strikers. "Now the battle had to be fought all over again," she recalled later, "I cancelled all my speaking dates in California, tied up all my possessions in a black shawl — I like traveling light — and went immediately to West Virginia."[19]

Once in the strike region, Mother Jones worked closely with members of the West Virginia Socialist Party who, as Frederick Allan Barkey points out, "took upon themselves many of the most dangerous tasks, some of which the regular mine worker leadership was not anxious to assume." It was both as a UMW organizer and a Socialist that Mother Jones moved about the coal regions, and by her courage inspired miners to join the strike. She went into the incorporated community of Eskdale of Cabin Creek after Frank Keeney, a miner, had been turned down by union officials who were afraid to enter the "forbidden territory." Keeney told the union officers: "I will find someone with nerve enough to go with me, for if you men are afraid to make the trip, there is a woman who will go." Fred Mooney, who was a participant in the events that followed, recalled later:

He proceeded to locate Mother Jones and after a thorough understanding was reached, a date was set for Mother Jones to go into the forbidden territory.

I was standing on the bridge at Cabin Creek Junction the day Mother Jones entered Cabin Creek.

Her hair was snow white, but she could walk mile after mile and never show fatigue. When we saw her drive by in a horse drawn vehicle we knew the meaning of that visit and we fully expected to hear of her being killed by the gunmen. She arrived at Eskdale without mishap, but after she passed through the business center of town and as she approached the southern residence section a body of gunmen could be seen just ahead.

The morning sun cast its rays on the steel of machine guns, behind which stood creatures that could have been men, and as Mother Jones came near the *frowning muzzles of these death dealing implements of war, some of these gun-men fingered the triggers of the guns and licked their lips as though thirsty to shed human blood.*

But she drove her rig near and one of the miners assisted her to alight. She surveyed the scene with a critical eye and walked straight up to the muzzle of one of the machine guns and patting the muzzle of the gun, said to the gunman be-hind it, "Listen here, you, you fire one shot here today and there are 800 men in those hills (pointing to the almost inaccessible hills to the east) who will not leave one of your gang alive."

The bluff worked; the gunmen ground their teeth in rage. Mother Jones in-formed me afterwards that if there was one man in those hills, she knew nothing of it. Her comment in regard to this day was, in part, as follows:

"I realized that we were up against it, and something had to be done to save the lives of the poor wretches, so I pulled the dramatic stuff on them thugs. Oh! how they shook in their boots, and while they were shaking in their boots I held my meeting and organized the miners who had congregated to hear me."

Having bluffed machine-gun armed mine guards into allowing her to hold a mass meeting, Mother Jones instilled such courage into the miners that not only was the meeting a great success, but the miners of Cabin Creek joined the strike, and Eskdale became a center of militant strike activity.[20]

Throughout July as Mother Jones was "working day and night" en-couraging the miners' resolve, the miners and the Baldwin-Felt guards engaged in pitched battles. On July 26, in a battle at Mucklow, not far from Holly Grove, twelve men, mostly guards, were killed. Governor William E. Glasscock dispatched three companies of the National Guard to the district, and on August 16, he declared a state of martial law in the area. Ten days later, the governor appointed a commission headed by the Most Reverend P. J. Donahue, the Catholic Bishop of Wheeling, to study the dispute and make an impartial report to the state legislature.[21]

But Mother Jones had no patience with such stalling tactics on the part of the governor. On August 1, addressing a meeting of six thousand people in Charleston held to urge Governor Glasscock to remove the mine guards, she made the first of four important speeches during the strike. She stood on the Charleston levee, in her prim, black dress, em-broidered with white lace, with wisps of silvery hair curling around her forehead, and told the miners in a loud voice: "I am not going to say to you don't molest the operators. It is they who hire the dogs to shoot you. (applause) I am not asking you to do it; but if he is going to oppress you, deal with him."[22]

Mother Jones's speeches during the West Virginia strike of 1912-1913 are among the most militant of her entire career. They have been commented on by contemporaries and by recent scholars. In his 1981 study, Life, Work, and Rebellion in the Coal Fields: The Southern West Virginia Miners 1880-1922, *Daniel Alan Corbin notes Jones's* emphasis in these speeches on children, and the point that victory would not be for the miners alone, but for their children. He points out that the "miners agreed with her. When Jones shouted that 'the next generation will not charge us for what we have done; they will charge and condemn us for what we have left undone,' the miners became screaming, 'That is right!'"

Corbin also notes that while Jones repeatedly condemned the company-controlled churches in many mining towns, "her speeches, were filled with religious overtones and biblical references, as she looked, and asked the miners to look, to the heavens for guidance and wisdom. In one sentence Jones could prophesy revolution and urge 'her boys' to buy ammunition and guns for protection and to kill the 'god damn guards,' and in the next sentence refer to her personal connections with the Almighty. 'I have passed the scripture period of three score years and ten,' she declared in one of her most violent speeches during the Paint Creek–Cabin Creek strike. 'I am eighty-one, but I have a contract with God to see you boys through before I go.'"

Corbin calls this "the paradox of Jones." But for the woman who said, "Pray for the dead but fight like hell for the living," there was nothing paradoxical about it. At any rate, her speeches during the strike had a profound effect on the miners. Ralph Chaplin, author of labor's anthem "Solidarity Forever," and future editor of the I.W.W.'s official publication, Industrial Worker, shared the platform with Mother Jones at the meeting on the levee in Charleston, and he recalled later that while he "made a strong appeal from the platform for industrial solidarity,"

no words of mine, however, could compare with the vitriolic wrath of "Mother" Jones on the same subject. She might have been any coal miner's wife ablaze with righteous fury when her brood was in danger. Her voice shrilled as she shook her fist at the coal operators, the mine guards, the union officials, and all others responsible for the situation. She prayed and cursed and pleaded, raising her clenched and trembling hands, asking heaven to bear witness. She wore long, very full skirts and a black shawl, and her tiny bonnet bobbed up and down as she harangued the crowd. The miners loved it and laughed, cheered, hooted, and even cried as she spoke to them.[23]

Writing in the Political Science Quarterly directly after a visit to the strike zones, Lawrence R. Lynch emphasized:

Head and shoulders above all the other agitators in ability and forcefulness stands "Mother" Jones, the heroine of many similar strikes. Her eighty or more years have not dimmed her eye, weakened the strength of her personality or tempered the boldness of her language. She is the woman most loved by the miners and most feared by the operators. Her thoughts are expressed in language both picturesque and striking. She knows no fear and is as much as home in jail as on the platform. In either situation she wields a greater power over the miners than does any other agitator.[24]

Fred Mooney summed it up when he wrote: "The miners loved, worshipped, and adored her. And well they might, because there was no night too dark, no danger too great for her to face, if in her judgment 'her boys' needed her."[25]

In mid-December all four companies of militia were withdrawn from the strike zone and civil law was restored.[26] On December 23, Governor Glasscock granted "Christmas pardons" to seven of the twenty miners sentenced by military commissions to imprisonment for from one to five years. The strike continued during the severe winter season. The union had removed 900 strikers' families from the area, but 600 still remained in the tent colonies.[27]

On the night of February 7, 1913, an armored train equipped with iron plate siding and machine guns — the "Bull Moose Special" — crept slowly toward the tent colony at Holly Grove and stopped outside the first line of tents. Volley after volley of shots poured into the ragged tents of the sleeping miners. Miraculously, there were only a few casualties. One miner was shot dead running away from his dwelling and the wife of another was wounded in her bed.[28]

Three days later, the infuriated miners marched in protest to Mucklow. They were met by a posse of armed guards and a battle began, and before it was over, twelve miners and four guards were dead. Governor Glasscock declared martial law for the third time, ordered six companies of militia to go to the strikebound counties, and reestablished the military commission.[29]

A wave of arrests of strikers and their leaders now followed. Nearly three hundred were arrested and tried by the military commission. On February 12, Mother Jones went to Charleston to consult the governor, but upon her arrival in the state capitol, she was immediately arrested. About 125 of those arrested, including Mother Jones, were taken to Pratt and held for trial by the military court, even though all of the prisoners were civilians and the charges against them were for civilian offenses within the jurisdiction of the civil courts, which were open and functioning in the districts under martial law. As Robert S. Rankin notes in his study, When Law Fails: "In the history of the United States, martial law has never been used on so broad a scale, in so drastic a manner, nor upon such sweeping principles as in West Virginia in 1912-13."[30]

But as Richard D. Lunt points out, the detention of Mother Jones "backfired, making her into a vociferous martyr. With the assistance of sympathetic guards, she communicated her plight and the miners' cause to allies in the outside world."[31] She signaled to the guards by clinking beer bottles together. One of the guards would crawl under the floor to a hole covered by a rug, pick up her messages, crawl back, and then smuggle them out to the recipients. A hastily scribbled letter sent in this manner from the "Military Bastile," West Virginia, went to William B. Wilson who was shortly to become secretary of labor in President

Wilson's cabinet, describing to the labor congressman how she had been picked up on the streets of Charleston, thrown into an auto and brought twenty-two miles to the military prison. She urged Wilson to get her note to Senator William E. Borah, so that he could know the facts about what was happening. A few days later, Senator Borah introduced a resolution in the Senate demanding an investigation of the strike by the federal government. Borah's resolution, however, failed of consideration.[32]

Mother Jones and a number of the other prisoners refused to acknowledge the right of the military courts to try them and declined even to put up a defense. John Brown, a socialist miner and one of the prisoners, explained their reason in a moving letter to his wife on March 9, 1913, written at the military camp in Pratt:

. . . As you have undoubtedly seen by the papers, Boswell, Batley, Parsons, "Mother" Jones, Paulson, and myself have refused to acknowledge the jurisdiction of the military court, and therefore are not putting up any defense. You, perhaps with others, do not see at this time the wisdom in such tactics, seeing that we are wholly at the mercy of this tribunal, but time will tell and justify the position we take.

If it was only myself personally that was concerned, I would, for the sake of gaining my liberty and being free to go to you and the children, go before this court and defend myself. Nor have I the least doubt in my mind that I would come clear. But, my dear, there are principles involved in this case infinitely deeper than the fate of any one citizen. If the capitalist class gets a way with this, then CONSTITUTIONAL GOVERNMENT IS DEAD: AND JUSTICE FOR THE WORKING CLASS IS A THING OF THE PAST. . . .

If we let them get away with it, then in the future wherever and whenever the interests of the working class and the capitalist class reaches an acute stage, out will come the militia, the Courts will be set aside, and the leaders railroaded to the military bull-pens, and thence to the penitentiaries. Here lies the great danger. . . .

As Mother Jones was being led up the steps to the courtroom, she made a short speech to the reporters who had come to interview her. "I am 80 years old and I haven't long to live anyhow," she told them. "Since I have to die I would rather die for the cause to which I have given so much of my life. My death would call the attention of the whole United States to conditions in West Virginia. It would be worthwhile for that reason. I fear, though, that I shall not be executed."[33]

She was not, but the military commission found her and sixty others guilty of murder, conspiracy, and inciting to riot. The tribunal sentenced Mother Jones and the others to twenty years in the penitentiary, and transmitted the findings to Governor Henry D. Hatfield, who had succeeded Governor Glasscock. In late March 1913, the new governor released about 45 of the 65 persons who had been convicted by the military commission, conditioned on their good behavior. But Mother Jones was not released. "I know," she wrote to a friend on April 5 from the

"Military Bastile," "they would let me go if I would go out of the State but I will die before I give them the satisfaction." Among the prisoners released by Governor Hatfield were several UMW organizers who left the district immediately after a private interview with the governor.[34]

What made the new governor's refusal to release Mother Jones especially reprehensible was the fact that he had himself visited the "little shack" in which she was being held and guarded, and he recalled that "when I entered I found her lying on a straw tick on the floor, carrying a temperature of 104, very rapid respiration, and a constant cough. She had pneumonia."[35]

"To the Rescue of Mother Jones and Her Comrades," read the headline in Appeal to Reason on March 29, 1913, and the socialist weekly warned that if Mother Jones "is railroaded by a bunch of military hirelings, there will be something done very speedily in this country." In a May Day article in the Appeal, Debs urged a strike by all United States miners to force the release of Mother Jones, warning that if Mother Jones, "seamed and scarred as she is in her lifelong struggle to break their fetters," died in prison, her death would be "a foul and indelible blot" on the miners' manhood and self-respect.[36]

That same month of May 1913, a resolution was introduced in the Senate by Senator John W. Kern of Indiana, a friend of the UMW, calling for a congressional investigation to determine if a system of peonage existed in the strike zone, if immigration or postal laws were being violated, if strikers were being prosecuted contrary to federal law, and if certain other conditions existed. The night before the resolution came up in the Senate, Kern received a telegram from Mother Jones which had also been smuggled out of military prison. The next day, Senator Kern read the following before an astonished Senate and press:

From out of the military prison wall of Pratt, West Virginia, where I have walked over my eighty-fourth milestone in history, I send you the groans and tears and heartaches of men, women and children as I have heard them in this state. From out these prison walls, I plead with you for the honor of the nation, to push that investigation, and the children yet unborn will rise and call you blessed.[37]

While the debate on Kern's resolution continued in the Senate, Governor Hatfield released Mother Jones on May 10, 1913, after eighty-five days of confinement. Mother Jones then left for Washington to join in the demand for an investigation of the strike, and after conferring with Senator Kern, she left on a speaking tour to win public support for the inquiry.[38] As she left the state, the Huntington Socialist and Labor Star published the lines written by Ralph Chaplin as a "Paint Creek Miner" about "Mother" Jones:

How they fear her, how they hate her — hate her kind and timeworn face.
How they rush armed mobs to meet her when she moves from place to place.

Bristling bayonets and sabers working shameless, deep disgrace.[39]

A West Virginia prosecutor indicated "how they hate her," when pointing to Mother Jones, he said: "There sits the most dangerous woman in America. She comes into a State where peace and prosperity reign. She crooks her finger — 20,000 contented men lay down their tools and walk out."[40] The answer to this childish (but fairly typical) analysis of the reasons for the strike was best given by Ethelbert Stewart after an investigation of similar conditions in the coal mines of Colorado. Stewart denounced the contention that the workers were satisfied and that only "agitators" were responsible for the coal strikes:

> . . . To have a house assigned to you to live in, at a rental determined for you, to have a store furnished you by your employer where you are to buy of him such foodstuffs as he has, at a price he fixes; to have a physician provided by your employer, and have his fees deducted from your pay, whether you are sick or not, or whether you want this particular doctor or not; to have churches, furnished ready-made, supplied by hand-picked preachers whose salary is paid by your employer; with schools ditto, and public halls free for you to use for any purpose except to discuss politics, religion, trade-unionism or industrial conditions; in other words, to have everything handed down to you from the top; to be . . . prohibited from having any thought, voice or care in anything in life but work, and to be assisted in this by gunmen whose function it was, principally, to see that you did not talk labor conditions with another man who might accidentally know your language — this was the contented, happy, prosperous condition out of which this strike grew. . . . That men have rebelled grows out of the fact that they are men. . . .[41]

On May 27, the Senate passed the Kern resolution, and Mother Jones returned to Charleston on June 7. Three days later she listened to the testimony of witnesses before the subcommittee. In West Virginia and later in Washington, the senators heard witnesses whose testimony filled 2,291 pages.[42] But none of it was from Mother Jones. Probably the major reason was that the senators and the UMW leadership feared that Mother Jones would condemn the settlement forced upon the strikers by UMW President John P. White and Governor Hatfield, and which did not include the miners' most important demands — elimination of the hated guard system, payment of the "Kanawha" scale of wages, the "check-off," and reinstatement of all strikers.[43]

Although Mother Jones did not give testimony during the investigation of the West Virginia strike, in which she played a major role, stenographic reports, taken down by a court reporter, of several of her speeches in Charleston and Montgomery are appended to the record of the hearing. Most of them are brief excerpts, although one, delivered on the steps of the capitol on August 15, 1912, appears in full. All of the speeches were deposited in the records of the West Virginia Mining Commission, and the West Virginia Collection of West Virginia Uni-

versity Library was given a copy of the transcribed hearings before the West Virginia Mining Investigation Commission, including the transcribed speeches of Mother Jones, by R. G. Kelley, partner in the Charleston law firm of Jackson, Kelley, Holt and O'Farrell.[44] It is from the material deposited by Mr. Kelley that copies of Mother Jones's five speeches were obtained for inclusion in the present volume.

Speech to striking coal miners, on levee at Charleston, West Virginia, August 1, 1912

(Mother Jones getting up into the back end of a dray wagon, while the crowd were saying first one thing and then another) If you would just use your brains instead of your mouths, but you do not.

(Cries of "Take your time, Mother.")

Don't give me any advice.

I will attend to you; I will stay with you.

(Voice: "I believe you are right.")

Now, you have gathered here today for a purpose. Every movement made in civilization has had an underlying purpose. You have reached the century in human civilization when the charge of human slavery must forever disappear. (Applause)

You, my friends, in my estimation, have stood this insult too long. You have borne the master's venom, his oppression, you have allowed him to oppress you. When we said, "a little more bread" he set out to get the human blood-hounds to murder you. Your Governor has stood for it. He went off to Chicago and left two Gattling guns with the blood-hounds to blow your brains out.

(A voice: "That is what he had done, Mother.")

Yes, that is what he has done. But what did you elect him for?

(A voice: "That is the question.")

Then you elected a sheriff, that began to shake like a poodle dog the night of the trouble on Paint Creek. He began to tremble and ran into a store to be sheltered. I have never in all my life — in all the battles I have had — taken back water, and why should a public officer do it, elected by the people. The best thing you can do is to apply to some scientist to give you some chemicals and put into a nursing bottle, give it to them fellows and tell them to go away back and sit down. (Applause)

This industrial warfare is on. It can't be stopped, it can't be put back, it is breaking out over all the nation from the city of Mexico clean through to the border of Canada, from the Atlantic Ocean clean across the oceans of the world; it is the throbbing of the human heart in the industrial field for relief. They are preaching appeal to the Legislature, they appeal to Congress, and I must give this Congress credit — I always want to give credit where credit is due — you have had more labor bills passed in the last session than in all the days of your Congress.[45]

163

I was in Washington not many weeks ago. I sat up in the gallery watching the voters. I was watching the fellows who would vote against your bill. One fellow, when they asked for roll call, he got up among those who didn't want it, but when the vote came he had to be registered on the Congressional Record, he took mighty good care that his vote was in your favor. Why? Because the whole machine of capitalism realize for the first time in history that there in an intellectual awakening of the dog below, and he is barking. Have you been barking on Paint Creek?

I want to say, without apology, without fear of the courts, without fear of jails, you have done what ought to have been done a long time ago. When men — when a corporation which is bleeding you to death, would go and hire — send over the nation and hire human bloodhounds to abuse your wife, your child, it is time every man in the State should rise.

I saw an inscription on your State house, and looked at it — because I know Virginia. I know the whole machine of capitalism; they locked me up and put me out of the State and shook their fists at me and told me not to come back again. I told them to go to hell, I will be back tomorrow.

You know the trouble with you fellows is that you get weak-kneed, and get a pain in your back, and then go home and are sick for a week.

Now, this fight, the Governor can't stop it, the State militia can't stop it, and I want to say something to you. Don't get into the conflict with the boys in the State militia.

(Cries of "Amen!" "Amen!")

I don't want one single man in the State militia hurt. I know what the militia is for. It is organized to shoot down the workers when they protest, in every nation of the world. But there are many workingmen in the militia, and I always deal with them — they are mine, anyhow. I am going to change them from the capitalists' interest over to my interest.

You know the "two-by-four" governor. (Applause) I am not talking about your governor. He has the Gattling guns. I am talking about the "two-by-four" corporation tool in the State of Pennsylvania.[46]

(A voice: "How about West Virginia?")

I am not talking about West Virginia. When we had a fight in 1900, the Governor was going to clean us up, and four thousand women went down at three o'clock in the morning. They weren't ladies, they were women. A lady, you know was created by the parasitical class; women, God Almighty made them. The crack thirteenth were sent down by that governor to meet those four thousand women. Their sleeves were rolled up on their arms, they walked fifteen miles over mountains. What did those women do? They licked the crack thirteenth of Pennsylvania, the "two-by-four" lawyers, the bank crooks and corporation rats — they don't know how to fight. So the militia begged for mercy. The Colonel says, "Move back, we are going forward in civilization. I will charge bayonets on you people." Not on your life, you don't charge bayonets on us, because if you do — I will tell you now, we are fighting the robbers who take our bread and butter; if you go to shoot us we will clean up the high-way with the whole bunch of you. You ought to have seen them run! Their moustache wasn't curled that day. They went up and hit the pike and didn't bother us any more. The sheriff said to me, "Take these people away." No, I didn't come here to take them away, I came to meet them. He said, "I will have you arrested, I will call on the Governor for the militia." I said, "We will lick the militia." It is the fighting of the classes. You have today in this country two warring forces, the one the lying oligarchy, the other the crush pin, the breath is taken from them.[47]

Go into the mines — I want to say to you, don't let me hear that you have ever injured a single mine in the whole State of Virginia. These mines belong to you. The outside belongs to the operators, the inside is where your property is, your job is inside, that is your property, you go inside and dig down the wealth, and you are generous enough to give three-fourths of it to the other fellows. You give up three-fourths to the other fellows, then if you say you need a little more bread for your children he sends out after the blood-hounds.

I want to say, my friends, in this age of ours, in this modern conflict we are going to prepare you to stop it. I am eighty years old — I have passed the eightieth mile stone in human history. I will be eighty more, for I have got a contract with God Almighty to stay with you until your chains are broken. (Loud applause)

We have broken the chains of chattel slavery, we changed his condition from a chattel slave to a wage slave. But you say we didn't make it any better. Oh, yes, we did, we made it better for the chattel slave. Then we entered into industrial slavery. That was one step in advance. We forever wiped out chattel slavery and came into industrial slavery. Now, industrial slavery is the battle you are in.

Let me say to you, I don't want a single officer of the militia molested in any way. I am not going to say to you don't molest the operators. It is they who hire the dogs to shoot you. (Applause) I am not asking you to do it, but if he is going to oppress you, deal with him. I am not going to take any back water because I am here in the capital. No back water for me. No man lives on the face of God's earth that is oppressing my class that I am afraid of. (Loud applause)

I want to say, my friends, here —

(Here the speaker took time to get up on top of a box which was in the bed of the wagon.) I want to see if the guards are here.

You have inscribed on the steps of your Capitol, "Mountaineers are Free." God Almighty, men, go down through this nation and see the damnable, infamous condition that is there. In no nation of the world will you find such a condition. I look with horror when I see these conditions.

You gather up money to send to China to learn them to know more about Jesus. Jesus don't know any more about you than a dog does about his father. (Loud applause)

I was in church one day when they raked in $1600, and at the same time they were robbing the representatives of Jesus to feed them who robbed them. You build churches and give to the Salvation Army and all the auxiliaries of capitalism and support them, to hoodwink you.

But I want to say they will not be able to get an army in the United States big enough to crush us.

I was speaking to the manager in the ticket office in the Far West, and I said "I am going to West Virginia." I had been in fourteen states with the strikers in each state. I said "I am going into West Virginia, and there will probably be hell." He said, "Be quiet, a great many of us will be with you." Get all you can out of these thieves. I say to the policemen, get all the ammunition you can, get all the ammunition and lie quiet, for one of these days you will come over with us and we are going to give the other fellow hell.

Now my friends, my brothers, this is a new day for me. I can write a new message to the boys in the Far West. I can write a new message even to my boys in Mexico.

I went into Mexico last October. I want to give you a little incident of how things happened over night. I fought Diaz until I had to leave the country. I made it so blamed hot for the tyrant that I had to get up and get away to be safe. I saw the whole administration in Mexico. I had a talk with them. I walked up into that palace where that tyrant had robbed and murdered millions of human beings — I walked up into that palace that he left, and I said "My God! This is making history fast." He went to Santa Cruz and took a steamer to go into exile; the prison doors were opened the same day and four or five of my brothers that he had incarcerated there, went free.

Oh, friends, even castles cannot protect tyranny. Every member of the Mexican administration gave me an audience, and they said to me, "Mother Jones, you can come into Mexico — we want you — and organize the men."[48]

Some one said yesterday in my presence, that when the Panama Canal was finished, their goods would get a tremendous market. Let me say the Panama Canal was not started for your benefit. The gang on Wall Street started the Panama Canal[49] because they said "we will capture Nicaragua and Mexico and get thirty million peons." When the Wall Street oligarchy move, it don't fool me. (Applause)

You held a convention here the other day, to elect him president again. May God Almighty grant that he may die before election comes. He sent two thousand guns in to blow my brains out in Colorado, and I have got it in for him.

(A voice: "Call his name.")

I did call his name, it is Teddy the monkey chaser.[50]

I can give you more.

(From the crowd: "Tell it, tell it.")

I can't tell it from hearing, I can tell it from experience. The Mayor of New York didn't want to let me in, but I got in.[51] A man is a fool to try and play the game on a woman. The Mayor let me in and then I went on to Oyster Bay. He had a secretary, who died since in Washington — I was glad when I heard it — he was afraid I would dynamite him. That fellow Roosevelt had secret service men from his palace down at Oyster Bay, all the way to New York, to watch an old gray-headed woman.[52]

I don't care whether it is Taft or him, the fight is the same. Mr. Policeman, we will give them hell any how.

Now boys, you are in this fight. I want to say to you the Governor is sick, poor fellow. I feel sorry for him.

(From the crowd: "I hope he is dead. I do.")

Let the Governor alone today. We have arranged a mass meeting in Montgomery, also the citizens, merchants, lawyers, doctors and all — in Montgomery for four o'clock Sunday afternoon. Come down there and then we will do business with the Governor. You must have a system, you must have a force behind you. When you are going to do business with those big fellows you have got to have ammunition. (Loud applause)

One day I went to see President Taft, spent nearly forty minutes with him. Teddy was scared of me, but I will give Taft credit,[53] he wasn't, he gave me an audience of forty minutes. I know Taft belongs to the Wall Street crowd, but he shows his hand, but the other fellow will talk about referendum and recall but he will recall you with the militia and bayonets.

And don't trust those judges today. I know them. I went down to see a judge in Colorado. He had fifteen of my boys in jail. I first tackled the sheriff and then went to see the Governor. I gave him some taffy and then he let all my boys out. He said, "Mother, if you would get them to come down and apologize." I said I have been trying to get them to stand up off of their knees for many years, and there is no apology to make. I wouldn't have them to apologize under any circumstances. Seven years ago we went to the Governor and put the whole matter before him, and he said "I can't do anything, I am helpless." Then we went to the sheriff, and he said, "I can't do anything, I am helpless." But the Governor wasn't helpless when the operators asked him for two Gattling guns to murder the miners. (Loud applause) He wasn't helpless then. The sheriff wasn't helpless then, my friends. Are we going to stand for the insults of the governors and the public officers and see our children and wives thrown out and insulted by the corporation blood-hounds? I say, no, fight daily until the last minute. (Prolonged applause)

We are not going to surrender. We are not going to destroy property, but we are going to do business with your blood-hounds. (Applause)

"Mountaineers are always free!" Take that inscription off your State house steps until we have made you free and then you will be free.

I want to say boys, take this advice from "Mother" — I have stood with you in all the years. No Gattling guns, no militia, no courts, have ever intimidated me. There isn't a policeman in any city in America has ever molested me or arrested me. Never! They are every one my friends. When I spoke at the Navy yard at Brooklyn — when I quit talking I went up to four policemen — I said, "Officers, will you kindly tell me where I will get a car to such a place." They said, "We will go with you, 'Mother'." They said, "Come back next week, and give them fellows hell." (Applause)

So, you see we have been educating, we are converting the police, and you (operators and officers) haven't got everything with you. I know the Baldwin guards are here, maybe Baldwin is here. But I want to say, you take back water, or by the Eternal God we will make you do it. (Loud applause) We won't down further. There will be no guards to shoot us down. *We* will watch the property, it is ours, and in a few years we will take it over. And we will say to Taft and Teddy, "You have had a devil of a good time, go in and dig coal."

Boys, go home peacefully (peaceably), and I will go with you. Yes I will go with you.

(A voice from the audience: "Lord help".)

No, we will help ourselves.

I am like a fellow in Pennsylvania. The Salvation Army was whooping for Jesus. Along came a fellow, and one lassie went out and said to him, "Say, brother did you ever work for Jesus?" "Oh, no, I don't know him." "You don't know Jesus?" "No."

She got horrified, she thought everybody ought to know Jesus. She said, "Well come in and work for him."

"How much will you give me a day?"

"He will give you a bed in heaven."

He said, "Give me a bed here."

So we want the bed here, not when we die. There is too much preaching to wait until you die in peace. We don't have any peace, there is industrial war. It isn't politics, it isn't parties, it is industrial war, my friends. There will be no peace until that question is settled and settled right, and until man gets justice.

Look, you operators! You are here. God Almighty, come with me and see the wrecks of women, of babies, then ask yourself "How can I sleep at night?" How can your wife sleep at night? I saw one of them coming down the street the other day in an automobile. She had a poodle dog sitting beside her: I looked at her and then looked at the poodle. I watched the poodle — every now and again the poodle would squint its eye at her and turn up its nose when it got a look at her. (Laughter and applause) He seemed to say, "You corrupt, rotten, decayed piece of humanity, my royal dogship is degraded sitting beside you." She had lived off the blood of women and children, she decorated her neck and hands with the blood of innocent children, and I am here to prove it to the world.

Do you want any more? If you do I will give it to you. I have got the goods, and I will deliver it, and I have no fear of the courts, no fear of the militia, no fear of the mine owners, no fear of Taft, or of Teddy the monkey chaser.

It takes six billion dollars to take care of the criminals which the "system" makes. When Mr. Taft, the president of the United States, said to me, "Mother Jones," said he, "I am afraid if I put the pardoning power in your hands, there wouldn't be anybody left in the prisons!"

(A voice from the audience: "Great God Almighty!")

I said this: "Mr. President, if this nation spent half the money, half the energy, to give her people a chance, that she does to force them into the prisons, I don't think we would need many prisons."

My friends, I stood in the federal prison at Leavenworth, and saw eight hundred men march before me in the corridors. I looked at those men, and said to the warden — the chaplain, who stood with me — I said, "Chaplain, we are not civilized yet, we are not two degrees away from the savages. A pen like that, in a nation which can create more wealth than the world can consume!" There wasn't twenty-five men among that eight hundred that I couldn't take and open wide the Bastile doors, and say to those men, "Go free." "I will break your chains, trust yourselves, and then you will trust me, they wouldn't violate the confidence I placed in them, because if a man can't live without being robbed he is going to rob and murder to do it." (Applause.)

You are today with the guard system. I will say, "Mr. Operators, the day is going to come when you will say you wished you had never seen the face of a guard." We are law-abiding citizens, we will destroy no property, we will take no life, but if a fellow comes to my home and outrages my wife, by the Eternal he will pay the penalty. I will send him to his God in the repair shop. (Loud applause) The man who doesn't do it hasn't a drop of revolutionary blood in his veins.

Now boys, we are approaching the day, we are going on until every man and woman that works, that produces, in this life, he becomes aflame with the same spirit that brought from the brain of England's greatest orator, "Resistance to tyranny is obedience to God."

Now, I want you to be good boys. Don't drink. You haven't got anything to drink on. A good many women will say, "don't drink, then you will have money in the bank."

I would rather drink than let the banker drink. These women howl, "Temperance! Temperance!" The government says for $12 a year for drink — that wouldn't get a jag on a good black cat. Don't drink! No, save it — and the operators will have that much more. You rob them everywhere and then you murder them. Then you think they are going to stand for it? No, by the Eternal God, we are not.

That old fellow Taylor, from Paint Creek, with a couple of guards and a sheriff — if I was that fellow's wife I would lick him every day and on Sunday — he ran into a store and said "Hide me!" Don't touch the sheriff, there isn't enough in him to touch. Let him go, only when he comes up again tell him to take a walk.

I will tell you something. If the Adjutant General had come and said "Mother, will you come with me, we are going to Peytons, the sheriff can't handle the trouble," I would have said "All right." We would have settled that thing in twenty-five minutes.

I will give you an instance. We had a fight with the Erie Company. The company said "Bring the militia, hurry up, they are going to eat us up." We were not going to touch them; their flesh is too rotten to eat. The sheriff met me and wanted us to get off their property. I said they want to take our jobs and we are not going to let them. That is our bread and butter, sheriff. We dig down the wealth and the other fellow isn't satisfied. We want to make a day 8 hours instead of 10. We want to spend a little time with our wives and children, we want to study our affairs. Sheriff, come with me and swear the boys in and it will end in twenty minutes, and the sheriff came, and inside of one hour it was settled.

Out in Colorado, the officers were gambling, and one of them lost seven hundred dollars that night. While they had a corporation jag on them they telephoned for the militia. Some one telephoned to me that they were mobilizing the troops. I said, "Let them mobilize the troops." They had a "Colonel" with them. They always have a title, "Colonel," "Major," or something of that sort, to make you fellows believe they are bigger than you. The boys said to me, "You had better go to Utah." I said "No, I am going to stay and fight it out." Saturday night they pulled me out of bed and landed me out of the state with five cents in my pocket to get a bed and something to eat. Next day the Santa Fe train came along, and I said, "Will you take me into Denver?" When I got there I said, "I am here in the capital, what in the hell are you going to do about it?" When I know I am right fighting for these children of mine, there is no governor, no court, no president will terrify or muzzle me. I see the babies, the children with their hands taken off for profit; I see the profit mongers with their flashing diamonds bought by the blood of children they have wrecked. Then you ask us to be quiet! Men, if you have a bit of human blood, revolutionary blood in your veins and a heart in your breasts, you will rise and protest against it. (Applause.)

I went up where you murder these baby children, and you will see those little boys gather around me in the dead of night and say "Mother, do come back to be with us."

Oh, men of America! Oh, men of human instinct! Oh, men descendants of the great Patrick Henry and Lincoln, will you stand for it?

(Cries from audience: "No, No, No, No.")

The only thing in life is at stake. Put a stop to it. Don't go near the Governor today, he might have a nervous collapse.

Now, like good boys go back home. I will go with you. We won't hurt anybody, we will have a good time, and when we get home, if the operators want to come and have a good time with us, we will be good to him — if he settles with us.

Now, boys, you came up here to the Capital. It was the proper place to come to. This is the chief executive. So you haven't retired, if the chief executive don't do something, if the sheriff don't do something, then the people *must* do something.

I am not going to talk any more today. I am going to talk Sunday at Paint Creek. They said that if I went up there last Sunday they were going to riddle me with bullets. Now, I went, and there wasn't a bullet struck me. I am going next Sunday. I am going with you wherever you are.

[copy missing in original]

The day for the small man is gone, and the day to rise is now here. We want the right to organize. Carnegie said that in a few years — he went into the business with five thousand — he took seven thousand five hundred. He said he knew the time was ripe for steel bridges, and they went into it. He closed out his interest for three hundred million dollars.[55]

Do you wonder that the steel workers are robbed? When one thief alone can take three hundred million dollars and give to a library[56] — to educate your skulls because you didn't get a chance to educate them yourselves.

A fellow said, "I don't think we ought to take those libraries." Yes, take them, and let him build libraries in every town in the country. It is your money. Yet he comes and constructs those libraries as living monuments reddened with the blood of men, women, and children that he robbed.

How did he make three hundred million dollars? Come with me to Homestead, and I will show you the graves reddened with the blood of men, women and children. That is where we fixed the Pinkertons, and they have never rose from that day to this.[57] And we will fix the Baldwins in West Virginia.

The Pinkertons were little poodle dogs for the operators. We will fix the Baldwins just the same.

Some fellow said, "You are talking on the porch of the State House." That is the very place I want to talk, where what I say will not be perverted.

Senator Dick said, when I met him, "I am delighted to see you, 'Mother' Jones." I said, "I am not delighted to see you." He said, "What is the matter?" I said, "You have passed the Dick military bill to shoot my class down, that is why I wouldn't shake hands with you."[58] That is the way to do business with those fellows. All the papers in the country wrote it up, and he was knocked down off his perch. I will knock a few of these Senators down before I die.

(Cries of: "Tell it, 'Mother' I heard it.")

I will tell you. I want you all to be good.

(A voice: "Yes, I will." "We are always good.")

They say you are not, but I know you better than the balance do.

Be good, don't drink, only a glass of beer. The parasite blood-suckers will tell you not to drink beer, because they want to drink it all, you know. They are afraid to tell you to drink, for fear there will not be enough for their carcass.

(Cries of: "The Governor takes champagne.")

He needs it. He gets it from you fellows. He ought to drink it. You pay for it, and as long as he can get it for nothing any fellow would be a fool not to drink it.

But I want you to be good. We are going to give the Governor until tomorrow night. He will not do anything. He could if he would, but the fellows who put him in won't let him.

(Cries of: "Take him out.")

I don't want him out, because I would have to carry him around. (Applause)

I want you to keep the peace until I tell you to move, and when I want you every one will come. (Loud applause)

Now, be good. I don't tell you to go and work for Jesus. Work for yourselves, work for bread. That is the fight we have got. Work for bread. They own our bread.

This fight that you are in is the great industrial revolution that is permeating the heart of men over the world. They see behind the clouds the Star that rose in Bethlehem nineteen hundred years ago, that is bringing the message of a better and nobler civilization. We are facing the hour. We are in it, men, the new day, we are here facing that Star that will free men, and give to the nation a nobler, grander, higher, truer, purer, better manhood. We are standing on the eve of that mighty hour when the motherhood of the nation will rise, and instead of clubs or picture shows or excursions she will devote her life to the training of the human mind, giving to the nation great men and great women.

I see that hour. I see the Star breaking your chains, your chains will be broken, men. You will have to suffer more and more, but it won't be long. There is an awakening among all the nations of the earth.

I want to say, my friends, as Kipling[59] said: He was a military colonel or general in the British army, and he said:

"We have fed you all for thousands of years,
And you hail us yet unfed.

172

There is not a dollar of your stolen wealth
But what marks the graves of workers dead.
We have given our best to give you rest;
You lie on your silken fold.
Oh, God, if that be the price of your stolen wealth,
We have paid it o'er and o'er.

There is never a mine blown skyward now,
But our boys are burned to death for gold;
There is never a wreck on the ocean
But what we are its ghastly crew.
Go count your dead by the forges rail
Of the factories where your children lie,
Oh, God, if that be the price of your stolen wealth,
We pay it a thousand fold.

We have fed you all for thousands of years;
That was our doom, you know.
Since the days they chained us on the field,
Till the fight that is now on over the world.
Aye, you have beaten our lives, our babies and wives,
In chains you naked lie.
Oh, God, if that be the price we pay for your stolen wealth;
We have paid it o'er and o'er."

We are going to stop payment. I want you to quit electing such
judges as you have been. This old judge you had here, he used to be
your lawyer. When this fight was on he was owned by the corporations. When you wanted him he went off fishing, and got a pain in his
back. Elect judges and governors from your own ranks.

A doctor said to me in Cincinnati, "Did you ever graduate from a college, Mother Jones?" I said "I did." He said, "Would you mind telling
me?" "No," I said, "I graduated from the college of hard knocks. That
is my college, I graduated from that college — hunger, persecution and
suffering — and I wouldn't exchange that college for all the university
dudes on the face of God's earth." (Loud applause)

I know of the wrongs of humanity; I know your aching backs; I know
your swimming heads; I know your little children suffer; I know your
wives, when I have gone in and found her dead and found the babe
nursing at the dead breast, and found the little girl eleven years old
taking care of three children. She said, "Mother, will you wake up,
baby is hungry and crying?" When I laid my hand on mamma she
breathed her last. And the child of eleven had to become a mother to
the children.

Oh, men, have you any hearts? Oh, men, do you feel? Oh, men do you
see the judgment day on the throne above, when you will be asked,
"Where did you get your gold?" You stole it from these wretches. You
murdered, you assassinated, you starved, you burned them to death,

that you and your wives might have palaces, and that your wives might go to the seashore. Oh, God, men, when I see the horrible picture, when I see the children with their hands off, when I took an army of babies and walked a hundred and thirty miles with a petition to the president of the United States, to pass a bill in Congress to keep these children from being murdered for profit. He had a secret service then all the way to the palace. And now they want to make a president of that man! What is the American nation coming to?

Manhood, womanhood, can you stand for it? They put reforms in their platforms, but they will get no reform. He promised everything to labor. When we had the strike in Colorado he sent two hundred guns to blow our brains out. I don't forget. You do, but I don't. And our women were kicked out like dogs, at the point of bayonet. That is America. They don't do it in Russia. Some women get up with five dollars worth of paint on their cheeks, and have tooth brushes for their dogs, and say, "Oh, them horrible miners;" "Oh, that horrible old Mother Jones, that horrible old woman."

I am horrible, I admit, and I want to be to you blood-sucking pirates.

I want you, my boys, to buckle on your armor. This is the fighting age, This is not the age for cowards, put them out of the way.

(At this point "Mother" stopped suddenly and said to some one in the crowd: "Say, are you an operator, with that cigar in your grub?")

Take your medicine, because we are going to get after you, no doubt about it.

(Cries from the crowd: "Give it to them.")

Yes, I will. (Cries again: "Give it to them.")

I want you to be good. Give the Governor time until tomorrow night, and if he don't act then it is up to you. We have all day Saturday, all day Sunday, all day Monday, and Tuesday and Wednesday, if we need it.

We are used to living on little, we can take a crust of bread in our hands and go.

When they started that Civic Federation in New York,[60] they got women attached to the Morgan and Rockefeller joint, they wanted to revolutionize the mechanics in Washington. One day I went to their dinner. An Irishman, a machinist, rolled up his sleeves, and ran into a restaurant and got a piece of bologna as long as my arm — you know it is black — he got some bread. He put a chunk of the bologna into his mouth, and put some bread in his mouth, and went out eating. One of these women came along and said, "Oh, my man, don't eat that it will ruin your stomach, it will give you indigestion." He said, "Oh, hell, the trouble with my stomach is I never get enough to digest."

That is the trouble with half our stomachs. We don't get enough to digest, and when we do get something we are afraid to put it in lest it won't digest.

Go to the "pluck-me" store[61] and get all you can eat. Then you say to

"Mirandy" — you say — "Oh, God, I have a pain in my stomach." You wash yourself, and she holds the water. The mine owner's wife don't hold the water. "Oh, Mirandy, bring the linen to take the corporation hump off my back."

I can't get up to you. I would like to be there, I would give you a hump on your back.

Boys, stay quiet until tomorrow night. I think it would be a good thing to work tomorrow, because the mine owners will need it. The mine commissioner will get a pain in his skull tonight, and his wife will give him some "dope." The mine owners wife is away at the seashore. When she finds no more money coming, she will say, "Is there any more money coming?" He will say, "Most of the miners are not working." She will say, "Take the guards and shoot them back into the mines, those horrible fellows."

The Governor says, if you don't go to work, said he, in the mines or on the railroads, I am going to call the militia, and I will shoot you. So we went. I said we can get ready, too. What militia can you get to fight us? Those boys on Paint Creek wouldn't fight us if all the governors in the country wanted you to. I was going yesterday to take dinner with them, but I had something else to do. I am going some day to take dinner with them, and I will convert the whole bunch to my philosophy. I will get them all my way.

Now, be good, boys. Pass the hat around, some of these poor devils want a glass of beer. Get the hat. The mine owner robs them. Get a hat, you fellows of the band.

I want to tell you another thing. These little two-by-four clerks in the Company stores, they sell you five beans for a nickel, sometimes three beans for a nickel. I want to tell you, be civil to those. Don't say anything.

Another thing I want you to do. I want you to go in regular parade, three or four together. The moving picture man wants to get your picture to send over the country.

(Some one in the crowd asks what the collection is being taken for.)

The hat is for the miners who came up here broke, and they want to get a glass of beer. (Loud applause)

And to pay their way back — and to get a glass of beer. I will give you five dollars. Get a move on and get something in it.

This day marks the forward march of the workers in the State of West Virginia. Slavery and oppression will gradually die. The national government will get a record of this meeting. They will say, my friends, this was a peaceful, law-abiding meeting. They will see men of intelligence, that they are not out to destroy but to build. And instead of the horrible homes you have got, we will build on their ruins homes for you and your children to live in, and we will build them on the ruins of the dog kennels which they wouldn't keep their mules in. That will bring forth better ideas than the world has had. The day of oppression will be gone. I will be with you whether true or false. I will be with you at midnight or when the battle rages, when the last bullet ceases, but I will be in my joy, as an old saint said:

Oh, God of the mighty clan,
God grant that the woman who suffered for you,
Suffered not for a coward, but Oh, for a man.
God grant that the woman who suffered for you,
Suffered not for a coward, but Oh, for a *fighting* man.
(Loud applause)

Bring the hat in. Is that all you got? (As the hat was handed to her.) "That is all I got."

Go out and get some more, that is not enough to go on a strike.

Any of you big fellows got any money in your pockets? If you have, shell it out, or we will take it out.

(A man coming up out of the crowd: "Here is ten dollars, I will go and borrow more. Shake hands with me, an old union miner. My children are able to take care of themselves, and I will take care of myself.")

Fight. ("Fight, right. I have a good rifle, and I will get more money. If I don't have enough to pay my railroad fare, I will walk. I don't care if this was the last cent I had, I will give it to 'Mother', and go and get some more.")

Maybe the Governor will give something.

(Cries of: "Call him out.")

("Governor, Governor, Governor.")

The Governor is sick. He can't come out. (Applause)

(Cries of: "Better stay sick.")

Hand in the money. (From some one: "The Governor is sick?")

Mother: Yes. He has got a pain in his stomach.

Go over and form a parade, the moving picture man wants to take a picture. Go ahead and arrange the parade. Get out, and get them in a line.

(Cries of: "Governor Glasscock.")

Hush up, the poor fellow is sick.

(Cries for: "Houston, Houston.")

(Cries of: "Gone to the hospital.")

Now, let us go home. Be good boys. I am coming down to the camps and see you.

(The crowd did not disperse, but waited until some one got up on the box. The writer learned that his name was Walter Deal, who made a speech.)[62]

(At this point "Mother Jones" came out and got upon the box and began to speak.)

My object in coming back to you is this: That this meeting stand adjourned until we hear from the Governor. We are going to have a committee. There is always a lot of hot air orators that like to blow off hot air on occasions like this. There is nothing in what they say. We want brain work, not hands, but brains. There is no more speaking here, this meeting stands adjourned until we hear from the Governor. I told you to organize and march along here.

We will let you know. Go home to your camps. The Governor aint going to come, he is occupied. This meeting stands adjourned, no more hot air here.

You have heard the motion to adjourn, ready to vote. As many as are in favor of adjourning, hold up your hands.

(Very few held up their hands.)

Now you have got to go.

(Calls for the contrary vote.)

Mother don't permit the contrary.

We can't forget that we are men. We have been tendered courteously the ground. It is nothing but right, but if the chief executive wanted to protest he could have done so. He has given us the ground. You have talked the causes of the grievances. Wait until you hear from them. Leave the Capital alone.

(The meeting adjourned.)

Go home, boys, when we need you again I will call on you.

I will be down tomorrow, and if I am not down the telegraph will be going.

*[Typewritten copy in West Virginia Collection, "Coal Strikes,"
West Virginia University, Morgantown, West Virginia.
Extracts published in U.S. Congress, Senate, Subcommittee
on Education and Labor, Conditions in the Paint Creek District,
West Virginia, 63rd Congress, 1st Session, 1914, pp. 2257-58.]*

Speech to striking coal miners,
Baseball park, Montgomery, West Virginia, August 4, 1912

Fellow workers:

Let me say this to you, that no one person wins a strike, that it takes the combined forces of the oppressed, the robbed class to get together and win a strike. The operators, the money power, never in all of human history have won a strike. You have never lost a strike — that is, the workers have not. You have simply rolled up your banners and retreated for awhile until you could solidify your army and then come back and ask the pirates, "What in hell are you going to do about it?"

This hero worship must stop. We don't owe any debt of gratitude individually.

Now, we are here today, as we have been — this is the outcome of an age-long struggle. It did not begin yesterday nor today. It is an age-long struggle, and it has crossed the oceans to you. It is about to crystallize, it is about to close just now. The ship is sailing, it calls for pilots to come aboard. I want to say to you that all the ages of history have been ages of robbery, oppression, of hypocrisy, of lying, and I want to say to you tyrants of the world — (railroad train whistling) — they got that gang to blow off hot air (Applause) — I want to say to you tyrants of the world that all the centuries past have been yours, but we are facing the dawn of the world's greatest century, we are facing the dawn of a separate century.

This, my friends, is indicative of what? No church in the country could get up a crowd like this, because we are doing God's holy work, we are breaking the chains that bind you, we are putting the fear of God into the robbers. All the churches here and in heaven couldn't put the fear of God into them, but our determination has made them tremble.

What happened on Paint Creek? Did the church make the operators run and go into the cellar? (Applause)

I don't know who started the racket, but I know that Mr. Operator began to shake, the marrow in his back melted, and he had to go into the cellar to hide himself.

Now, my friends here, twelve years ago I left the great battle that closed in the State of Pennsylvania, and came in here. We had fought a tremendous battle there. We fought that battle until Mr. Hanna said, "These workers are men and women, we have got to do something, we have got to blind them, we have got to hoodwink them some way. Let us start the Civic Federation." The Republic hurrahed for peace and harmony is coming. Mark Hanna stood at the top of the game. We had them trembling, and they didn't know where to get off at.

And so they got the Civic Federation, they got Morgan, Belmont, and the labor leaders. I said that is only a "physic" Federation, what are you joining it for? There are some fellows in the labor movement, when their heads get swelled, they sit down with the thieves. They had their feet under the table — twenty-six thieves and twelve labor leaders — and you stood for it. I begged them not to join it, and some of them left it. They stuck their feet under the table and drank champagne, and the bloody thieves, when we had the women fighting for bread, that gang of commercial pirates were feasting on our blood in New York. And then we stand for it. And when those fellows comes along you say "hurrah," and the whole gang drunk.

Now that wouldn't do. They got the women so as to keep the labor leaders up in tune. They got women to join. They got a welfare department in their Civic Federation, and after a while the leaders and parasites and blood suckers they thought they would hoodwink us. One went up to Washington — it was — — — Morgan's daughter.[63] I happened to be in Washington. They were running to the free soup bowls to get a lunch. An Irish machinist ran in and had a piece of bologna that long (measuring on her arm about a foot), and a chunk of bread in the other hand. One of the women said to him, "Oh, my dear man, don't eat that, it will give you indigestion." He said, "the trouble with me is I never get enough to digest — indigestion, hell." The half of you fellows never get enough to digest. You never got a good square meal in your life, and you know you never did. But you furnish the square meals for the others who rob and oppress you.

When I came here ten or twelve years ago, we marched those mountains. The mine owners threatened to kill me, to shoot me. I am never much afraid of their shot. We have some men that will run away, but you will never get me to run, don't worry about it at all. They said I ought to be gotten out, I ought to be shot, locked up in the asylum. We marched the mountains, every one who took up Christ's doctrine, not the hypocrites but the fighters. We organized, you organized, we got together, we fought, we got you double what you had. We made a settlement with these operators. You became friends for the time being. But the mine owners have their tools, their paid, lying, treacherous dogs amongst you. And you were betrayed, and you can't deny it for I can prove it. Mind you, I am not looking for office, I am looking for your interests and your children's interests, and when you don't have an office you are watching the pendulum of every fellow that has. When I find out that they are false to you they have to get down and out. I don't care who it is that is at the head of your organization, if I find they are false to you they will get down and out, for I won't let up until they do. (Applause)

You need not give me any advice (to someone in the audience who offered some advice).

It was Aristotle who said to Alexander, many ages ago, he said, "Alexander, don't bother with the outside enemy, your real enemy is inside your own ranks."

And so it is. We could clean up the mine owners overnight if you were true to your standards.

You lost your organization. Scabs and union men work together. You destroyed your charter. Go down to that hellhole, there isn't another like it in the United States. I went up to that hole one night. I looked at the riches, and wondered at the men who call themselves Christians, who give to the Salvation Army, to the church, to the temperance brigade, to every other shouting gang that comes along — I wondered how those blood-sucking pirates could sleep in their beds, with that horrible outcome of their exploitation. Women sat on the porch, and these pirates said "Keep that burning hell before them to keep them in subjection." They said "the more hell you keep, the more of their blood will decorate my head and arms." One woman, the wife of one of the blood-suckers, get diamonds to buckle her shoes with. She went to church and said, "Jesus, I made the other fellows give it up."

(Laughter and applause)

And so, if you, who are here, were true to each other, we would not have to have this meeting today. But you have started, and I want to congratulate you. I want to say here, my friends, that is what brought me into West Virginia. I was in a fight all winter. I traveled fourteen states, and fifteen thousand miles in your behalf, inside of seven months. I went down to Mexico, and I made arrangements with the Mexican Government — I want you to listen, Mr. Operator, get your skull ready because there is a very little will go into it — I had an audience with the Mexican governor, and I said, "I want to come in and organize the men that slave, that have been oppressed, crushed. We want to educate, elevate them." The Mexican governor said, "Mother Jones, you can come into this nation and bring any organizers you want, I will take your word, from my experience with you, you will not work with those who will not do their duty." I said, "I may be rushed with cannon." Immediately he had the wires touched, and said, "If they arrest you or your organizers, they will have to be turned loose." That was in despotic Mexico. We chased the President out because he was a tyrant. Not so long ago in this State — I came into your state and found the Baldwin blood-hounds, and find your wives and children thrown out like dogs on the street. They beat you up, put into their hands weapons to beat you with, to beat any of us, yet I didn't find the courts saying, "stop it." I didn't hear of the Governor saying "stop it." No. Why? Because the powers that be are the courts. I want to say, if the judge is here — I know Judge Bennett is. That judge in Charleston went off on a visit. I guess his skull needed a fish to give it something to do. The Governor went to Chicago, then when he heard there was a racket on Paint Creek, he got sick and went to Huntington. (Applause)

Now, my friends, I want to say here, I have dealt with courts; I have dealt with the detectives and spotters. I have been from one end of the nation to the other, even in Mexico. I have been in Washington fighting for these poor unfortunate wretches — I have seen more freedom in Mexico than I have seen in America under the Stars and Stripes. We appealed seven years ago to the Governor and he said, "I can't do anything." We appealed to the sheriff, and he said "I can't do anything." But the State was in jeopardy. We pictured the guards and the outrages to them. Let me say this to you, when the Governor occupies the chair and can't do anything, he ought to get down and out and put somebody in that can. (Loud applause)

I had business with the Governor in the West. The corporations asked for the militia. The Governor said, "You will get no militia from me." "Give me the job," said I, "and I will attend to them." The Governor said, "You will do it too fast, 'Mother,'" said he. He went down himself and surveyed the whole state of affairs. He went to the miners' union and got their story; then he went to the operators and heard their story — he walked twelve miles in the rain and snow. He called to the militia and said, "Take care of those miners, in their jobs, and if the tools of the corporations dare to raise their hands against them, blow their brains out." They went down and the strike was settled in no time. The sheriff called for the troops, like your sheriff did. When you had the trouble here on Paint Creek he got under a table, and said "For God's sake, hide me." The mine owners, we put the fear of God into their carcass, and they said "hide me" too. Don't you see you have got them, if you will only be wise. I have seen those fellows tremble. I have been in strikes, and I didn't come in yesterday. I worked in the mines, but I didn't dig coal, but I did help to load it. I went in on the morning, on the day shift before daylight, and I went in on the night shift, with those poor slaves. I found the children perishing and the wives dying, there was nothing in the house, the company had stopped everything. They have brought the same thing in here. They have brought on war. The organization was a baby then, and they worked long hours and got poor pay, they didn't get enough to get a jag on when they worked full hours. We began to educate them. I went into the mines to put literature into the hands of those slaves. I was the first one who came over here and put literature into your hands in this class struggle. My friends, I have stuck to the job. I have been maligned, and the women I was fighting for have turned their noses in the air, and have said, "Oh, that horrid old woman." And those women love the dogs better than they love humanity! They decorate themselves in new costumes made of the blood of your children and your wives, and now when you kill a handful of guards they raise a great howl. You are to blame because you didn't clean them up. (Loud applause) When you go at it again, do business. I don't know whether you are an operator or not, but if you are take your medicine. (Loud applause)

One of these cats came down on the train from Cabin Creek the other day. She said, "You are 'Mother' Jones, aren't you?" I said, "Yes, what about it?" She said, "What are they doing on Paint Creek?" I said, "Go up and find out." She was one of those corporation cats.[64]

Now, then, we are here, my friends, in protest against a system of peonage[65] such as the world has not dealt with in all its ages. You are building jails, you are paying millions and billions of dollars to take care of the criminals you have made. You operators rob the workers, and your wives live in luxury, they turn their skirts away from the workers. One poor slave said to me — he was sitting down on the steps of a church — he said, "Mother, I have worked ever since I was a boy, and they have got it all. This is all that is left, this old worn out frame." Just then he saw an operator, his family and wife in a carriage, and he said, "I have got to run, I will be discharged if they see me talking to you." Down in Harrison County, West Virginia, I held a meeting. The operators sent me word, "If you come down to our mining camps, we will have you shot." I said, "Is that so?" "Yes," they said, the mine owners said, they will have you shot. When I got off the train, I said "All right, I will go." I said, "If you are a lap dog for a mine owner, you can be one for me. You go down and tell the operator I am going down to rouse his slaves, and he can shoot me and be damned." Did he shoot me? Not on your life. I told him to come to the meeting. That is the way I pray.

I told Judge Jackson how I prayed. When the time comes in the history of this struggle that a mine owner or Baldwin guards will intimidate me I want to die in that hour.

In the old chattel slavery days the old black mammy took up the battle and dug through the earth, and said to the young slaves, "Come and dig with me." They made a tunnel to get away. Do you black fellows do that today? No, you don't. There are a few of you would do it. But the most of you won't do it. What did your mammy do, what did your fathers do two generations ago? They rose up and defied the law, property rights, courts, and everything. He said, "Bring your bloodhounds, but we are human, we will be free." And they did free themselves. Why? Because the nation rallied to them, the nation saw you were determined to free yourselves.

When you men will rise and say this is our fight, it will be done. We asked the courts and they wouldn't do it; we asked the Governor and he wouldn't do it; we asked the sheriff and he wouldn't do it; we asked the officers of the law, and they wouldn't do it. They said they would do it, and you see how they have been doing it.

The Governor was able to do something when the operators wanted him. The sheriff said, "Oh, God, we are up against it." The mine owners said, "He, Ha, we will get the troops in." They telegraphed to Pennsylvania to accommodate the operators, the Governor and the sheriff telegraphed immediately for them to come back. Can you deny it? No, you can't deny it. I have got the goods on you.

I want to say, men, if you organize to a man — don't the churches have a right to go up Cabin Creek and talk about Jesus? Have you? If the ministers have a right to go and talk about what Jesus did (laughter) — where you have got guards to beat our brains out.

Let me say to you, my friends, let me say to the Governor, let me say to the sheriffs and judges in the State of West Virginia, this fight will not stop until the last guard is disarmed. (Loud applause)

Forty thousand men — forty thousand braves, said to me, "We are ready for battle, 'Mother,' if they don't do business." So we are, my friends, and the day of human slavery has got to end. Talk about a few guards who got a bullet in their skulls! The whole of them ought to have got bullets in their skulls. How many miners do you murder within the walls of your wealth-producing institutions! How many miners get their death in the mines!

A fellow said to an operator, "Why don't you prop the mines?" "Oh," he said, "Dagoes are cheaper than props." Every miner is a Dago in their estimation — every miner that they can rob.

You go into the mines and work ten or twelve hours, ten years ago. We made a fight and brought it down to nine. Up New River you work ten and twelve, and when you get your statement there is nothing on it. You look at it and scratch your head, and say, "Bookkeeper, I dug more coal than this." He will say, "Get to hell out of here." Then you shrug your shoulders and off you go, instead of taking the bookkeeper by the back of the neck and knocking his head against the wall. Oh, that is terrible, I know. I know the *Gazette* and the *Mail* say, "Oh, she is horrible." Yes, but I am dealing with a horrible condition. When you take the conditions from these fields we will be as tame and polite as your wife when she hammers hell out of you. (Applause)

Some of you fellows with only one arm — some of you traitors to your class, with one arm on you — they had taken one off to beat you with — went in and cheered for that gang yesterday. You cheered for McKell.

Let me tell you about McKell. The old man McKell was a pretty decent man. I will give everybody credit whether against me or for me. When you had that strike in 1902 I went up to Glen Jean. The Baldwin guards were at Thurmond. I said to the Baldwin guards, "Don't you come up, I am going up to see McKell to do business with him tonight, don't you come on the train." And the conductor said, "If you do I will tell Bill Baldwin and you will lose your jobs."

I went up to his home. I know your ears are cocked — I know your ears are cocked — to tell him, but tell him to come here and I will tell him. He started a tirade of insult and abuse of the miners. I told him I didn't come there — it was his house — I didn't come there to quarrel, I came to negotiate a settlement. I said, "If we can't discuss this matter in a peaceful, intelligent way, I will go."

I keep a tab on those fellows. I am not like you, take a glass of whisky and say, "Oh, hell, it is all right." (Laughter and applause)

Then they call themselves Independent Republicans! Independent monkey-chasers! (Laughter and applause) They say they will take off the guards and call the legislature in extra session. They need not call the legislature. They know it, but they think you don't know it. All they need is to tell the sheriff to disarm the guards.

I want to call your attention to another fellow. When —— —— was beat up by the Baldwin guards, —— —— who was nominated for sheriff yesterday, had the information right in his hands. Then the miners of the country had to pension him owing to the fact of the brutal assassination of the guards. This man Malone knew it. It was right at his door. I keep an eye on those crooked politicians. He says we will have to do away with the Baldwin guards. He runs a detective agency with Dan Cunningham, who went up to murder the miners at Stanaford Mountain. They went with labels on their breasts. It is enough to make anybody disgusted. No wonder these mine owners beat your wives, no wonder your children will rise up and curse you. It is time for you to stop it. You are not dealing with rotten politics. You are dealing with a system that is old and strong.

Let me say to you it needs men of America, men of a great state, it matters not to me whether you are a judge or whether you are a merchant, you are still a citizen of this state. Let me say to you, my friends, there is a feeling abroad in the land, I have traveled over it, and I know the pulse of the workers. I know the pulse of the intelligent people.

I want to say to you here, my friends — you needn't go so near God Almighty to take a picture, come here to take it. (This was spoken to a young man who went up on top of the grand stand to take a photograph of the crowd.) There is a spirit abroad in the land, there is an under-current going on, and unless the wise men of the nation get together and save her I want to say to you, my friends, a cry in the night from the hungry is an awful teacher, you need but a sword for a judge and a preacher.

Oh, men of America, I want to say to you, we are dealing too much with the intellect. A nation that does not deal with the heart of man will perish. In fifty years you have produced more wealth than it took five hundred years in Babylon, Greece, and Rome to travel the same road you are traveling today. They didn't take warning. What happened?

I went to a place in New York. A lawyer of Wall Street said, "Mother Jones, I would like to show you a picture. Will you go?" I said "I am twenty-one years old, I will take care of myself." There is a place there if you turn your nose inside of it it will be snapped off. The government knows it but you guys don't know anything about it. I went in. It cost $2.50 for hanging your cloak up. I sat down at the table. My cloak wasn't worth $2.50 so I kept it on. We ordered supper. Now this place is where the opera houses and theaters are built and opened. It is supported by the blood-sucking tribe of Wall Street gamblers. There came in a woman between two fellows. The lawyer said to me, "Mother Jones, do you know how much that cloak on that woman cost?" "I don't know," said I, "it looks like Russian sable. If it is it cost twenty thousand dollars." "That cloak," said he, "cost $50,000.00." "Those fellows paid for it and they never worked a day in their lives." I said "They never paid for it." I said "My boys paid for it." (Applause) Then they sat down and feasted like Belshazzar[66] did long ago.

Then came along another gang. They sat down at a table, and got so full and debauched that they upset a table and smashed everything on it. When they did there was a check written out instantly for a thousand dollars. $1.50 will pay for what is on your table. Put that down (to the reporter). Oh, you blood-suckers well know it.

My friends you are exploited, you are robbed, you are plundered. You have submitted to it, you haven't protested. You grunt but you don't fight as you ought to do. You don't have to kill the guards, all you have to do is to go to the ballot box and vote them out of business. (Applause)

Now, my friends, after I left you, before, when I was in Utah a poor ·creature came to me one morning. Her husband was among the revolters. He was carried off to the jail with one hundred and twenty-five or thirty others. The wife came to me, she held in her arms a babe, and said "Mother Jones, do you see my Johnnie?" I said, "Yes, I see your Johnnie." And the tears streamed down her breast. She said "Oh, Mother, you know my Johnnie isn't strong, I was afraid he would get hurt or killed in the mines. We got a lot from the company and I took in boarders. I was trying to pay for a shelter, so if anything happened to John I would have a shelter for the children. Do you see my Johnnie, he was born at 11 o'clock at night, and I got up at half past four in the morning and cooked breakfast for eleven men to go into the mines. Now, they have got my John, my home, my health." She says, "Mother, tell me, My God, what am I going to do?"

I want to say to this audience, I knew at five o'clock in the evening those blood-hounds were coming in to arrest those men next morning. I said to the boys, "Go up in the mountain and bury your guns." I didn't want a clash. "Bury your guns." They said, "No, Mother, we will need them." I said, "No, boys, go and bury them." At half past four in the morning I heard the footsteps. I went to the window. The first I saw was the Mormon sheriff. I said, "What is the trouble?" He said, "We have come to get these dogs." I said, "What have they done?" He said, "They don't go to work." "No, they won't," said I. They arrested those men, that were in tents at the foot of the range, and drove them up the road without a particle of clothing on them.

Put that down (to the reporter). And they know it is true. They hit them with their guns, and their ribs shook like aspen leaves. They begged to put on their clothes. "Oh, no," they said, "go to work." And the profane language that was used was horrifying — they were church members. But if you are working for Jesus you can use any language. The ministers can say "hell-fire" and "damnation," but if you are not a church member you mustn't use it.

Those wretches were taken into court and tried, and that woman perished with her babe and four children. They don't murder, do they? They don't murder, do they?

With the bleached bones of these people you build your churches, your YMCAs and your institutions. You have robbed and plundered these people, and they will build it into churches — and they will be churches too — and the love of God will be there — or will it be the love of capitalism or the operators. Look into the churches, and see the big fellow at the front singing, "All for Jesus." They murder for Jesus, they rob for Jesus, and own the government for Jesus, and scare hell out of the sheriff, for Jesus. (Loud applause and laughter) Get behind those fellows. They say, "Our Father in Heaven." You can hear them forty miles, crying to heaven, "Give us today, Oh, Lord, give thy son his daily bread," and "Oh, Lord Jesus, fix it so I can get three or four other fellows' bread." (Laughter)

Now, my friends, you can't blame those people after all, coming down to it. They couldn't change the system if they wanted to. We, the people, have got to do it.

I will give you an illustration. I want to ask any man here, is this government today the same kind of government it was sixty years ago, when the immortal Lincoln was in Washington?

(Cries from the crowd: "No, No, No, No").

Well, it wouldn't fit in. The government of forty or fifty or sixty years ago, wouldn't fit in.

Government changes as the field of production changes. It has done that all down human history. It had to change with the field of production. Literature changed and the newspapers are more vicious today than they were fifty or sixty years ago. Public opinion is moulded from what you read in the papers and magazines and what you hear in the pulpit. And your religion is not what it was fifty or sixty years ago. Then the Catholic bishops did not visit Washington and wine and dine with the presidents. They do it now. It is essential, because they have got the power, and the people have multiplied. Religion changes without changing the order of production.

I want you to bear in mind, my friends. Your judges are owned and controlled by the ruling classes. You need not expect any justice in the courts, I don't. I don't look for justice.

Did you have a Salvation Army sixty years ago?[67] No, you didn't. Why? They weren't needed. Capitalism hadn't developed. Did you have the Holy Jumpers fifty years ago? No, you didn't. Did you have the Holy Rollers? No. Did you have the Sanctified Saints? No. They weren't needed. Why weren't they needed? Because capitalism hadn't developed. It was when they reached in for the private ownership of the industries that the master class added these auxiliaries to their bulwark.

I have made a great study of those things, my friends, and I will prove it to you. I happened to be in El Paso after a strike. One hundred and fifty of our men were murdered. I was going through Arizona at that time. One hundred and fifty men were murdered. They hung others upon the trees. I went to El Paso. I said to the boys, "I will go down and cross the line from El Paso. I will get the information I want." I went into Mexico, and as I was going in I met three miners coming over the bridge. The boys said to me, "Mother, for God's sake, where did you come from?" I said, "I thought they had you murdered." They said, "No, we have been in the range three days and nights, we haven't had anything to eat." I said, "I will give you some money, go up and make yourselves at home. I am going to hold a meeting on the corner tonight." So I went up, and the boys met me. We got $18.50 collection. I gave them $5.00 apiece, and said, "Now we will go and eat, and while we are eating we will talk things over." So, while we were going down the street there was a mob howling and yelling at each other, calling each other liars. I thought the whole town of El Paso was going to be torn to pieces. So I stuck my head in. Directly I caught on to the game. I said to a policeman, "What is it? They are fighting?" He said, "I know what the fighting is about, it is about Jesus." "What did he do to them? Well, what are they fighting about?" He said "The Salvation Army occupies this corner, the Holy Rollers occupy that corner. There is only two corners. These fellow get all the money. They want to swap corners, and let the Salvation Army take that." I said, "Isn't the money for Jesus? What difference does it make?" He said, "Don't you think Jesus ever sees that money."

I don't know whether you ever watched women when they get religion the first time. They get up to heaven without being sent for. I went in and watched it. It was funny for me. Those things have a wonderful philosophy for me. The Holy Rollers were over there rolling for Jesus, and the Holy Jumpers were over there jumping for Jesus. The money belonged to Jesus. I gathered up all I could. I kept watching. I went to the policeman and said, "I have got a lot of Jesus' money, what shall I do with it?" He said, "You will keep it." I said, "Well, that is what I thought I ought to do." While those people in their hearts meant well, they didn't understand that they were the machine of capitalism hoodwinking the people while the chains of slavery were woven around them.

I know a lot of you will go off and condemn me, but you condemned Christ, you condemned every man and woman that ever dared to raise their voice in behalf of truth and justice, and you will do the same with me. But I don't care what your comments are. There will be a judgment day, and *you will pay the penalty*. (Applause)

I want to tell you that.

I want to say, my friends, it is a fine illustration; every avenue is commercialized today by the ruling class of the age in which we live. We write slander, we rob each other and say it is right; we rent each other out to the ruling class to beat us.

(A voice: "That is what we do.")

I want to say, my friends, it is time to stop it. Say, brave boys, say, the Star that rose in Bethlehem has crossed the world, it has risen here; see it slowly breaking through the clouds. That Star of Bethlehem will usher in the new day and new time and new philosophy, and if you are only true you will be free — if you are only men, if you only go home and leave the saloons alone. "Mother" knows how often you need a drink — (Cheers from the audience and clapping of hands, particularly noticeable of one woman) — you needn't clap your hands. It is to your disgrace. You needn't do it. If you understood the philosophy you would keep your hands down, and use your head to the best interests of the race. If you knew their aching backs, their swimming heads, if you knew the empty stomachs, if you knew the food that goes into their mouths you wouldn't clap your brutal hands like a thug, you wouldn't do it, my sister woman, you wouldn't clap your hands at these poor boys. They often need a drink. Many times they are often worn and exhausted. Like the big brewers in Milwaukee, when I went there to reach out a helping hand to three hundred girls they had enslaved.[68] One of the brewers said to me, "Mother Jones, I saw a terrible picture in Massachusetts, you don't see it here." He said, "I saw a woman on the sidewalk and the little boys and girls were throwing pebbles at her and bullying her. You don't see it here." I said, "There is a cause for that. Don't you know there is an underlying cause for that? Don't you know that Massachusetts has been a manufacturing state for some generations. Wisconsin is an agricultural state," said I. "Don't you know that the grandfather of this woman went into those slave pens of capitalism and in her infancy she was ground into profit, she never had a square meal, never had anything to develop her nerves. All the brutes gave her was to develop the muscle and bones for profit. Don't you know the mother and father of this creature also went into that slave pen? Don't you know we have made a fight to bring the hours down from sixteen to ten, from ten to eight? We have made a fight to give them a little more food to develop them. Don't you know your class have robbed them, and when this woman came into the world she was starved and a nervous wreck? She was robbed by your class, and now you find fault with her. Your own girls here you are robbing, and their children will be the same."

If this woman could stay in her home and plant love there, and girls' instinct, they wouldn't throw stones at this object of pity.

This woman was a nervous wreck. If she didn't get a drink of liquor she would have been in the insane asylum — and us paying six million dollars a year for the support of them!

Look at the class pirates that sail the high seas and don't need the riches. We will stop drinking when you give us what belongs to us. When you take us out of your shacks and give us what belongs to us, we don't need anybody to howl for us.

Often I have had to give my boys a drink, they had to have it. A fellow met me on the street one day — he had asked half a dozen people for a drink. He said, "Give me ten cents, I want to get a drink." I said, "Here is fifty cents, get a couple of good drinks." I said, "You haven't had anything to eat, here is fifty cents, go and get a bed and supper." The man looked at me, and shook hands. Eight years afterwards that man came up to me on the train and said "I believe your name is Mother Jones." I said, "Yes sir, it is. What about it?" He said, "I want to grasp your hand, I would have died one night but for you, I am in business, I am worth over seven hundred thousand dollars today," said he, and he handed me money for the Mexican refugees. If I had let that man go that night he would have stolen, because he had to have that drink. The police would have clubbed him and put him in jail and degraded him.

Let us know the cause of the suffering race. Let us put less feathers on the outside of the skull and a little more intelligence on the inside. (Applause)

Away back in Palestine they were robbing and plundering them. There was a humble carpenter that came.[69] It was not the leaders that came to him, it was not a member of the church that came to him, it was not a society woman — she would shun him then as she would now, if he came to her. It was that woman crushed by economic wrongs that came to wash his feet with her tears and wipe them with her hair, then he gave her the hope, the light of the future economic age. It was she in gratitude that fell at his feet and paid tribute to him, it was on her sacred head he placed his hands.

It has ever been the humble that have done the world's enlightening. It has been those that have been pointed to with scorn that have had to bear the brunt.

I have had to measure steel in the dead of night with the bloodhounds of the ruling class. I have measured steel with them in the lonely hours of night. It is the society women that dragged me out of bed in the night, when fighting for you, and with the bayonets in the hands of seven of them, put me out of the state and told me never to come back. If women were true they wouldn't raise men to do such acts.

(Cries from the crowd: "You are right." "You are right.") No, they wouldn't my friends.

It was Miss Helen Gould,[70] the great philanthropist, that hired blood-hounds to come in in the morning. She took them out of the penitentiary, they came in at 4 o'clock where I was locked up. I never undressed my self for eighteen nights. He planted his gun under my nose and said, "Tell me where I will get three thousand dollars of the miners' money, or I will blow your brains out." I said, "They wouldn't be any use to you after you got them out." I was alone at four o'clock in the morning. He was a big ruffian. Helen Gould took him out of the penitentiary, like those guards up here, to shoot me if I dared to interfere with profit.

He said, "Where is the money?" I said, "Up in Indianapolis." I said, "Write to them. They are good fellows, they will send it to you." He said, "Haven't you got any money here? How do you pay these bills? Haven't you got any money?" I said, "Yes, I have some money." He said, "Out with it or I will blow your brains out." I pulled it out — I am generous — out I came with the money. I took 50 cents out, and says I that is what I have got, but I am not going to give it to you. He said, "Is that all? How are you going to get the money which is in Indianapolis when you get out?" I said, "I will telegraph for it when I need it." He said, "If you don't shell it up I will kill you." I said, "I am not going to shell it up." He said, "Why?" I said, "I have got Helen Goulds smallpox, and when I get out of here I will need the money to get a jag on to roast them off."

I suppose if you were there you would clasp your hands and say, "Shoot her." None of your chatter, blackguards, we don't need it. We will open up without anybody to tell us, when these bloodsucking pirates give you what belongs to you. Now, boys, we are facing the day when human liberty will be yours. I don't care how much martial law the Governor of West Virginia proclaims, I have had martial law proclaimed where I was more than once, but I didn't stop fighting. When he pulled off his martial law I began it again, and he had to bring them back. Do you see how you can do the business. If they proclaim martial law, bury your guns. You can tell him that if you see him. If the Governor proclaims martial law, bury your guns. I have been up against it. They hauled me into court.

Stand by the militia, stand by the boys. Don't allow no guards to attack them. (Cries of: "That is right." "That is right.") Stand shoulder with them.

I want to say here in behalf of General Elliott. I know him well. I have had some experience with his manhood. I want to say to you he will never hurt the workers. He will only do what he is forced to do. But don't you force him to do anything. He won't do it if he can help himself. I will shake his hand every day of the year. I know General Elliott very well. It was General Elliott who arrested me in Clarkesburg when he was United States Marshal, by the order of Judge Jackson. General Elliott did not undertake to send me to jail, nor did he send a deputy with me. There was nine of us. He sent a young man, who is now on the *Evening Mail* in Charleston. When we got off in Parkersburg, the young man and I were going one way, and four or five deputies and eight boys were going another way. I said, the boys are going the wrong way. No, he said, they are going to jail. He said we engaged a room for you at the hotel. I said I would rather go board with Uncle Sam, I have better company than at the hotel. (Laughter and applause) I said my colleagues and I have fought this battle for years, and when they are jailed I will be jailed, and when they are hung I will be hung. So I went to jail. Major Elliott gave the jailer orders, and I was treated courteously. His wife and daughter came down to the trial, and went out with me; they offered their home for me to rest. I shall always remember Major Elliott. I don't care what position he holds he won't hurt you, and he will tell the Governor.

Be true to the boys, we will capture the militia some of these days. We will join the militia and say to the blood-sucking fellows, get off your perch. (Laughter and applause)

I know some very good operators, but they are dictated to by the syndicates, the oligarchy in Washington, so they can't help themselves.

You are to blame and on one else. You have stood for it. You don't stand in your union. If you would, when you were organized up New River, you wouldn't have this condition today. Don't blame the Governor. I blame him for violation of the law, that is what I blame the Governor for. (Applause.)

I am going to be with you, I am going to stay with you, I don't care what the papers say, they can jump on me, but they never weaken me, I am just as strong as ever. One corporation lap dog on Paint Creek — one of the C&O agents — I will clean him up when I get to Huntington. I won't say anything about his generosity. When you give those fellows a little bit of office — What are you looking at that watch? — That will watch you devils well, my boys.

I was in court when the judge condemned a man, and said, "You are a bad fellow." The fellow said, "I am not half as bad not half as mean, nor half as wicked as the judge" — then he stopped, and the judge got furious. The fellow continued — "as he thinks I am." The judge said connect your sentence.

Now, my boys, we are facing a new day. I am one of those who believe, as immortal Hugo did. I read Hugo's works when I was young.[71] Hugo was my idol, he was inspiring. He said so many grand things. I felt that he had the agony of the race in his body.

So, my boys, I said, we are in the early dawn of the world's great century, when crime, brutality and wrong will despair, and man will rise in grander height, and every woman shall sit in her own front yard and sing a lullaby to the happy days of happy childhood, noble manhood of a great nation that is coming. She will look at her mansion and every room will be light and there will be peace and justice.

I see that vision today as I talk to you. Oh, God Almighty grant, Oh, God Almight grant, God grant that the woman who suffers for you suffers not for a coward but for a man. God grant that. He will send us another Lincoln, another Patrick Henry. God grant, my brothers, that you will be men, and the woman who bore you will see her God and say "I raised a man."

(Cries from the audience: "Right," "Right," "Right," and applause.)

Resolution
(Read by "Mother Jones" at the close of
Judge W. R. Bennett's speech, at Montgomery, August 4, 1912.)

Miners and citizens of Fayette and Kanawha Counties, in mass meeting assembled in the Town of Montgomery, West Virginia, make the following resolution:

RESOLVED: That we most earnestly denounce certain officials of Kanawha County, State of West Virginia, because they failed to do their duty under the laws of West Virginia, which has resulted in the most cruel, inhuman treatment of the United Mine Workers, of their wives and children by certain Baldwin guards, in the County of Kanawha. Because we know that if the Judge of the Circuit Court of Kanawha County, and the Judge of the Intermediate Court of said county, had, at the time the oppressions were being committed against defenseless miners, their wives and children, had called a special session of the grand jury to indict certain criminals, that if the prosecuting attorney had prosecuted them as they should have been prosecuted, and as other criminals in said county, and sent them to the penitentiary, the trouble would all have been settled and peace would reign.

We declare that said officials have disregarded their sworn duty, that had they regarded their duty it would have saved the state enormous expense.

We denounce the coal operators of Fayette County as unworthy of confidence by the people. They have met in political conventions and denounced in strong terms the guard system of West Virginia. At the same time they are contributing to the salaries of these guards, who have caused such outrages to be committed on many mine workers of this state.

We denounce the candidates for office who have gone into these conventions, because they have not the courage to demand that there should be steps taken to get rid of the Baldwin guards of West Virginia.

Be It Resolved Further: That we now, seeing as never before the vast importance of the laborers of the country vote as one man to elect the officers of this state, that the laborers meet and organize.

These resolutions are drawn up by the citizens and miners of Montgomery, so that they will go to the Governor and state officials.

(Comments) Now, the Judge said if the operators would quit paying the Baldwin guards they would leave the State. The operators don't pay the Baldwin guards, they don't pay them a penny. If it had to come out of their pockets the Baldwin guards would be gone long ago. The miners are robbed in the weighing of coal, in rent, and in the store, they pay the Baldwin guards. (Applause)

You are the fellows that have got the right to clean up the Baldwin guards, because you are the fellows who pay them.

There was a poor black fellow down here at Nashville who couldn't afford to pay the rent in a rotten shack that you couldn't put a hog in. He said he couldn't do it, and went in a coke oven to sleep, and the company charged him $2.50 for sleeping in the coke oven. (Applause)

What is the matter with you people of West Virginia? What is the matter with the Governor? What is the matter with the whole of you? There isn't another state in the union stands for it — not a one — poor black wretch, just because his skin is black. It was an accident that the lawyer's skin wasn't black. If you work long for the coal companies you won't have any skin about you.

Stand by the guards, be sure to do that, let them hammer you. Let them put your wives into the creek, and make them walk it. One fellow said the guards haven't troubled me, they never bother me, put everybody out of the houses, but let me stay. So his wife was going to give the nation another citizen. They walked in and put the whole bunch out. He was boasting what lovely fellows the Baldwin guards are. Then they gave him a blow. It depends on how you get hit.

They have got to go out of the State. And if the men of the State of West Virginia are too cowardly, if they will give their wives and children up to the blood-hounds to be beaten and abused we will bring enough men in to clean them up, who are not afraid of your guards, who are not afraid of your Governor. When our women are insulted, who are the mothers of the nation, no blackguard will come along to beat them that we will not beat them back. We are not afraid of the Governor.

Don't drink. Go home and be good boys.

Resolved, that a copy be sent to the Governor; a copy to Judge Burdett —

Don't send a copy to the poor sheriff —

(Cries of: "Send him one.")

Oh, the poor fellow, he might take a fit.

Taylor and this Morton up here, who have been telling you what they will do — the dirty cowards — they went into the cellars, and said, "Put the dirty clothes all over my back." God knows there couldn't be anything dirtier than they are.

[Typewritten Copy in West Virginia Collection, "Coal Strikes,"
West Virginia University, Morgantown, West Virginia.
Extracts published in Senate, Subcommittee on Education and Labor,
Conditions in the Paint Creek District, West Virginia,
63rd Congress, 1st Session, 1914, p. 2261.]

Speech at meeting of striking coal miners, held at front steps of capitol, Charleston, West Virginia, August 15, 1912[72]

This, my friends, marks, in my estimation, the most remarkable move ever made in the State of West Virginia. It is a day that will mark history in the long ages to come. What is it? It is an uprising of the oppressed against the master class.

From this day on, my friends, Virginia — West Virginia — shall march in the front of the nation's states. To me, I think, the proper thing to do is to read the purpose of our meeting here today — why these men have laid down their tools, why these men have come to the State House.

"To His Excellency, William E. Glasscock, Governor of the State of West Virginia:

"It is respectfully represented unto your Excellency that the owners of the various coal mines doing business along the valley of Cabin Creek, Kanawha County, West Virginia, are maintaining and have at present in their employ a large force of armed guards, armed with Winchesters, a dangerous and deadly weapon; also having in their possession three gattling guns, which they have stationed at commanding positions overlooking the Cabin Creek Valley, which said weapons said guards use for the purpose of brow-beating, intimidating, and menacing the lives of all the citizens who live in said valley, and whose business call them into said valley, who are not in accord with the management of the coal companies, which guards are cruel and their conduct toward the citizens is such that it would be impossible to give a detailed account of.

"Therefore, suffice it to say, however that they beat, abuse, maim, and hold up citizens without process of law, deny freedom of speech, a provision guaranteed by the Constitution, deny the citizens the right to assemble in a peaceable manner for the purpose of discussing questions in which they are concerned. Said guards also hold up a vast body of laboring men who live at the mines, and so conduct themselves that a great number of men, women and children live in a state of constant fear, unrest and dread.

"We hold that the stationing of said guards along the public highways, and public places is a menace to the general welfare of the State. That such action on the part of the companies in maintaining such guards is detrimental to the best interests of society and an outrage against the honor and dignity of the State of West Virginia. (Loud applause)

"As citizens interested in the public weal and general welfare, and believing that law and order, and peace, should ever abide, that the spirit of brotherly love and justice and freedom should everywhere exist, we must tender our petition that you would bring to bear all the powers of your office as Chief Executive of this State, for the purpose of disarming said guards and restoring to the citizens of said valley all the rights guaranteed by the Constitution of the United States and said State.

"In duty bound, in behalf of the miners of the State of West Virginia."

I want to say with all due respect to the Governor, I want to say to you that the Governor will not, cannot do anything, for this reason: The Governor was placed in this building by Scott and Elkins and he don't dare oppose them.[73] (Loud applause) Therefore, you are asking the Governor of the State to do something that he cannot do without betraying the class he belongs to. (Loud applause)

I remember the governor in a state, when Grover Cleveland was

194

perched in the White House — Grover Cleveland said he would send the Federal troops out, and the Governor of that state said, "Will you? If you do I will meet your Federal troops with the state troops, and we will have it out." Old Grover never sent the troops — he took back water. (Applause, and cries of "Yes he did.")[74]

You see, my friends, how quickly the Governor sent his militia when the coal operators got scared to death. (Applause)

I have no objection to the militia. I would always prefer the militia, but there was no need in this county for the militia — none whatever. They were law-abiding people, and the women and children. They were held up on the highways, caught in their homes and pulled out like rats and beaten up, some of them. I said, "If there is no one else in the State of West Virginia to protest, I will protest." (Loud applause, and cries of: "Yes, she will, 'Mother' will.")

The womanhood of this State shall not be oppressed and beaten and abused by a lot of contemptible, damnable bloodhounds, hired by the operators. They wouldn't keep their dogs where they keep you fellows. You know that. They have a good place for their dogs and a slave to take care of them. The mine owners' wives will take the dogs up, and say, "I love you, deah" (trying to imitate by tone of voice).

Now, my friends, the day for petting dogs is done; the day for raising children to a nobler manhood and better womanhood is here. (Applause and cries of "Amen! Amen!")

You have suffered, I know you have suffered. I was with you nearly three years in this State. I went to jail, went to the Federal courts — but I never took any back water. I still unfurl the red flag of industrial freedom, no tyrant's face shall you know, and I call you today into that freedom, long perch on the bosom — (interrupted by applause) — I am back again to find you, my friends, in a state of industrial peonage, after ten years absence I find you in a state of industrial peonage.

The Superintendent at Acme — I went up there, and they said we were unlawful — we had an unlawful mob along. Well, I will tell you the truth, we took a couple of guns, because we knew we were going to meet some thugs, and by jimminy — (interrupted by applause) — we will prepare for the job, just like Lincoln and Washington did. We took lessons from them, and we are here to prepare for the job.

Well, when I came out on the public road the Superintendent — you know the poor salary slave — he came out and told me that there were Notary Publics there and a squire — one had a peg leg — and the balance had pegs in their skulls. (Applause)

They forbid me speaking on the highway, and said that if I didn't discontinue I would be arrested. Well, I want to tell you one thing, I don't run into jail, but when the blood-hounds undertake to put me in jail I will go there. I have gone there. I would have had the little peg-leg Squire arrest me only I knew this meeting was going to be pulled off today to let the world know what was going on in West Virginia.

When I get through with them, by the Eternal God they will be glad to let me alone.

I am not afraid of jails. We build the jails, and when we get ready we will put *them* behind the bars. That may happen very soon — things happen overnight.

Now, brothers, not in all the history of the labor movement have I got such an inspiration as I have got from you here today. Your banners are history, they will go down to the future ages, to the children unborn, to tell them the slave has risen, children must be free.

The labor movement was not originated by man. The labor movement, my friends, was a command from God Almighty. He commanded the prophets thousands of years ago to go down and redeem the Israelites that were in bondage, and he organized the men into a union and went to work. And they said, "The masters have made us gather straw, they have been more cruel than they were before. What are we going to do?" The prophet said, "A voice from heaven has come to get you together." They got together and the prophet led them out of the land of bondage and robbery and plunder into the land of freedom. And when the army of the pirates followed them the Dead Sea opened and swallowed them up, and for the first time the workers were free.[75]

And so it is. That can well be applied to the State of West Virginia. When I left Cabin Creek ten years ago to go to another terrific battlefield, every man on Cabin Creek was organized — every single miner. The mine owners and the miners were getting along harmoniously, they had an understanding and were carrying it out. But they had some traitors who made a deal with the mine owners and the organization was driven out of Cabin Creek. There were no better miners in the whole State of West Virginia than on Cabin Creek, and no better operators, in those days. You got along together. They were trying to make it happy and comfortable for you, but the demon came and tore the organization to pieces, and you are at war today.

I hope, my friends, that you and the mine owners will put aside the breach and get together before I leave the State. But I want to say make no settlement until they sign up that every bloody murderer of a guard has got to go. (Loud applause)

This is done, my friends, beneath the flag our fathers fought and bled for, and we don't intend to surrender our liberty. (Applause)

I have a document issued eighteen years ago, telling how they must handle the labor movement — pat them on the back, make them believe that they were your devoted friends. I hold the document, taken from their statement in Washington. It plainly states, "We have got to crucify them but we have got to do it cunningly." And they have been doing it cunningly. But I want to say in answer to your statements, that you are dealing with a different class of workers today than eighteen years ago. We have begun education, we have educated the workers, and you can't enslave them. They will come again, and you will either take to the ocean and get out of the nation and leave us alone, or you will settle right with us. (Loud applause)

It is different now, my friends. It was Mark Hanna[76] who said some years ago — the shrewdest politician America ever had — he said, "I want to tell you that before 1912 the Republican and Democratic parties will be about to get their death blow."

Never in the history of the United States was there such an upheaval as there is today. The politicians are cutting each other's throats, eating each other up, they are for the offices. Teddy, the monkey-chaser, had a meeting in Chicago, he was blowing his skull off his carcass about race suicide. God Almighty, bring him down the C&O and he will never say another word about race suicide. The whole population seems to be made up of "kids." Every woman has three babies in her arms and nine on the floor. So you will see there is no danger of race suicide. When he sees this he will keep his mouth shut on that.

See the condition we are in today. There is a revolution. There is an editorial in one of the papers in your own state showing how little they have done for the workers, that the workers are awakening. The literature is being circulated among them. I myself have circulated millions and millions of pieces of literature in this country and awakened the workers. On the trains they say, "Oh, Mother, you gave me a book and that woke me up." As long as you woke up right it is all right. He says, "I have woke up right." Then if you woke up right, you are my children.

Oh, you men of wealth, Oh, you preachers, you are going over to China and sending money over there for Jesus. For God's sake keep it at home, we need it. Let me tell you, them fellows are owned body and soul by the ruling class, and they would rather take a year in hell with Elkins than ninety-nine in heaven. (Loud applause) Do you find a minister against the guards?

(Cries from the audience: "They are traitors, moral cowards.")

He will preach about Jesus, but not about the guards. When we were crossing the bridge at Washington, the blood-hounds were at the company store. These bloodhounds might have thrown me into the river, and I wouldn't have known it. The men were hollering, "Police! Police!" I said, "What is the matter with you?" They said, "Oh, God, murder! Murder!" Another one came out and his feet never touched the sidewalk.

My boys came running to me and said, "Oh Mother, they are killing the boys." The traction car turned the corner. I said, "Call them boys here." Then they went, they thought I had an army with me. Then I picked up a boy streaming with blood where the hounds had beat him.

You are to blame, you have voted for the whole gang of commercial pirates every time you get a chance to free yourselves.

It is time to clean them up.

(Cries of: "She is right, she is right!")

If this nation is to march onward and upward the day of change is here.

I have been reading of the *Titanic*[77] when she went down. Did you read of her? The big guns wanted to save themselves, and the fellows that were guiding below took up a club and said we will save our people. And then the papers came out and said those millionaires tried to save the women. Oh, Lord, why don't they give up their millions if they want to save the women and children? Why do they rob them of home, why do they rob millions of women to fill the hellholes of capitalism?

I realize, I remember what they did to me — the Guggenheims — I remember what the Guggenheim bloodhounds did to me, one night in Colorado. They went to the hotel after we had organized the slaves. I took the four o'clock train for the southern fields, and the bloodhounds, the chief of police, and the whole gang of commercial bloodhounds came up to the hotel and went to the register to find my room, and the hotel keeper said that I had left at four o'clock. We had a meeting that night. They took a fellow and drove him down the street barefooted and put him on the train and told him to never come back. And we are very civilized! They don't do that in Russia, it is in America.

They took me and put me in jail — I had the smallpox[78] — I had the Helen Gould smallpox covering me all over. And at four o'clock in the morning they came and the blood-hounds — Helen Gould's blood-hounds — and they bound four hundred miners in Colorado, for gold, and threw their widows and orphans out on the highways in the snow. When I was fighting the battle with those wretches they put me into a pen which you built, a pest house, it was burned down before morning, it wasn't worth fifty cents. We went down by a store, and the storekeeper said, "God, Almighty, put us down in the cellar and they won't know us, put the dirty clothes on us — when them dirty clothes found out that there was such a lot of rotten carcasses under them, the dirty clothes turned over." (Applause and laughter)

If your sheriff had done his duty as a citizen of this state and according to his oath, he would have disarmed the guards and then there would have been no more trouble.

(Cries of: "That is right, that is right.")

Just make me Governor for one month. I won't ask for a sheriff or policeman, and I will do business, and there won't a guard stay in the State of West Virginia. (Applause.) The mine owners won't take sixty-nine thousand pounds of coal in dockage off of you fellows. Sixty-nine thousand pounds of coal they docked you for, and a few pounds of slate, and then they give to Jesus on Sunday.

They give your missionary women a couple of hundred dollars and rob you under pretense of giving to Jesus. Jesus never sees a penny of it, and never heard of it. They use it for the women to get a jag on and then go and hollow for Jesus.

I wish I was God Almighty, I would throw down something some night from heaven, and get rid of the whole blood-sucking bunch. (Laughter and applause)

I want to show you here that the average wages you fellows get in this country is $500 a year. Before you get a thing to eat there is $20 taken out a month, which leaves about $24 a month.

Then you go to the "pluck-me" stores and want to get something to eat for your wife, and you are off that day, and the child comes back and says, "There is four dollars coming to me." The child says, "They said there was nothing coming to you." And the child goes back crying, without a mouthful of anything to eat. The father goes to the "pluck-me" store and says to the manager, "There is four dollars coming to me," and the manager says "Oh, no, we have kept that for rent!" "You charge six dollars a month, and there are only three days gone." "Well, he says, it is a rule that two-thirds of the rent is to be kept if there is only a day."

That is honesty! Do you wonder these women starve? Do you wonder at this uprising? And you fellows have stood it entirely too long. It is time now to put a stop to it. *We will give the Governor until tomorrow night to take them guards out of Cabin Creek.* (Very loud applause, and cries of: "And no longer.")

Here on the steps of the capital of West Virginia, I say that if the Governor won't make them go then we will make them go. (Loud applause, and cries of: "That we will;" "Only one more day;" "The guards have got to go.")

We have come to the chief executive, we have asked him and he couldn't do anything. (Laughter)

The prosecuting attorney is of the same type — another fellow belonging to the ruling class. (Applause, and murmurings in the crowd)

Hush up, there, hush up, hush up.

I want to tell you that the Governor will get until tomorrow night, Friday night, to get rid of his blood-hounds, and if they are not gone we will get rid of them. (Loud applause)

Aye men, aye men, inside of this building — Aye, women! — come with me and see the horrible pictures, see the horrible condition the ruling class has put these women in. Aye, they destroy women. Look at those little children, the rising generation, yes look at the little ones, yes look at the women assaulted. Some one said that that place ought to be drained up there. The mine owner's home is drained; the superintendent's home is drained. But I want to ask you, when a man works ten or eleven hours in the foul gas of the mine day after day if he is in condition to come out and drain.

(Cries of: "Not on your life, no.")

I have worked, boys, I have worked with you for years. I have seen the suffering children, and in order to be convinced I went into the mines on the night shift and day shift and helped the poor wretches to load coal at times. We lay down at noon and we took our lunches, and we talked our wrongs over, we gathered together at night and asked "How will we remedy things?" We organized secretly, and after awhile held public meetings. We got our people together in those organized states. Today the mine owners and the miners come together. They meet each other and shake hands, and have no more war in those states, and the working men are becoming more intelligent. And I am one of those, my friends, I don't care about your woman suffrage and the temperance brigade or any other of your class associations, I want women of the coming day to discuss and find out the cause of child crucifixion, that is what I want to find out. I have worked in the factories of Georgia and Alabama, and these blood-hounds were tearing the hands off of children and working them fourteen hours a day until I fought for them. They made them put up every Saturday money for missionary work in China. I know what I am talking about. I am not talking at hap-hazard, I have the goods. Go down, men of today, who rob and exploit, go down into hell and look at the ruins you have put there, look at the jails, We pay six million dollars a year to chain men like demons in a bastile — and we call ourselves civilized! Six million dollars a year we pay for jails, and nothing for education.

I have been in jail more than once, and I expect to go again. If you are too cowardly to fight, I will fight. You ought to be ashamed of yourselves, actually to the Lord you ought, just to see one old woman who is not afraid of all of the blood-hounds. How scared those villians are when one woman eighty years old, with her head grey, can come in and scare hell out of the whole bunch. (Laughter) We didn't scare them? The mine owners run down the street like a mad dog today. They ask who started this thing? I started it, I did it, and I am not afraid to tell you if you are here, and I will start more before I leave West Virginia. I started this mass-meeting today, I had these banners written, and don't accuse anybody else of the job (Loud applause)

It is freedom or death, and your children will be free. We are not going to leave a slave class to the coming generation, and I want to say to you that the next generation will not charge us for what we have done, they will charge and condemn us for what we have left undone. (Cries of: "That is right.")

You have got your bastile. Yes, we have no fears of them at all. I was put out at twelve o'clock at night, and landed with five cents in my pocket — by seven bayonets in the State of Colorado. The Governor told me — he is a corporation rat, you know — he told me never to come back.[79] A man is a fool, if he is a governor, to tell a woman not to do a thing. (Loud applause, and cries of: "Tell them again"; "Tell them about it.")

I went back next day and I have been back since the fight, and he hasn't bothered me. He has learned it won't do to tamper with women of the right metal. You have a few cats (mocking) — they are not women, they are what you call ladies. There is a difference between women and ladies. The modern parasites made ladies, but God Almighty made women.

(Applause and cries of: "Tell us one more.")

Now, my boys, you are mine, we have fought together, we have hungered together, we have marched together, but I can see victory in the heavens for you. I can see the hand above you guiding and inspiring you to move onward and upward. No white flag — we cannot raise it, we must not raise it. We must redeem the world.

Go into our factories, see how the conditions are there, see how women are bound up for the merciless money pirates, see how many of the poor wretches go to work with crippled bodies. I talked with a mother who had her small children working. She said to me, "Mother, they are not of age, but I had to say they were, I had to tell them they were of age, so they would get a chance to help me to get something to eat." She said after they were there a little while, "I have saved forty dollars, the first I ever saw, I put that into a cow and we had some milk for the little ones." In all the years her husband had put in the earth digging out wealth, he never got a glimpse of forty dollars until he had to take his infant boys, that ought to go to school, and sacrifice them.

If there was no other reason, that should stimulate every man and woman to fight this damnable system of commercial pirates — (cries of: "Right, right") — that alone should do it, my friends.

Is there a committee here? I want to take a committee of the well-fed fellows and well-dressed fellows, I want to present this to the Governor. Be very polite. Don't get on your knees. Get off your knees and stand up. None of these fellows are better than you, they are only flesh and blood — that is the truth.

(Committee formed around "Mother" and start into the Capitol building.)

These fellows all want to go and see the king.

(Laughter)

I will give the press a copy of this resolution and this petition, that was given to the Governor.

Now, my boys, guard rule and tyranny will have to go, there must be an end. I am going up Cabin Creek. I am going to hold meetings there. I am going to claim the right of an American citizen. I was on this earth before these operators were. I was in this country before these operators. I have been seventy-four years under this flag. I have got the right to talk. I have seen its onward march. I have seen the growth of oppression. And I want to say to you, my friends, I am going to claim my right as a citizen of this nation. I won't violate the law, I will not kill anybody or starve anybody, but I will talk unsparingly of all the corporation blood-hounds we can bring to jail. (Laughter)

I have no apologies to offer. I have seen your children murdered, I have seen you blown to death in the mines and there was no redress. A fellow in Colorado says, "Why don't you prop the mines?" The operator said, "Oh, hell, Dagoes are cheaper than props." Every miner is a Dago with the blood-sucking pirates, and they are cheaper than props. Because if they kill a hundred of you, well it was your fault. There must be a mine inspector kept there.

The night before the little Johnson boys were killed, the mine inspector — John Laing is a mine owner — he wouldn't inspect them — the mine inspector went there and said the mines are propped securely. The next morning the little Johnston children went to work, and when they were found their hands were clasped in their dinner buckets with two biscuits.

You work for Laing day after day. He is mine inspector. But he wouldn't be if I had anything to say about it. He would take a back seat.

(At this point "Mother" quoted a poem written by Rudyard Kipling addressed to the crowned heads of Europe.)[80]

I want to say to you mine owners, if you are here, I know you will go home and say we have been false to our homes, to our country, let us shake hands with these miners. Let us have no strike. You will have as much when you die, you will have as much rotten meat on your carcass for the rats to eat. (Loud applause)

Now boys, be good and come to the meeting Sunday at Montgomery, there will be no mines to be closed up that day. I want to say to you that these mine owners have contracts, and don't close the mines every day, let us get together and have concerted action.

(At this point "Mother" began to shake hands with the audience.)

Good bye boys. Don't bring them down, because the corporation is here and you will lose your jobs tomorrow.

When the strike is won I will — — — for you, and then you can get a jag on. I will get something better than beer for you.

I want to say — I forgot — I intended to pay a tribute to Major Elliott. Of course he has got to take orders. It is the sheriffs and the governor that I am opposed to. I want to say that never in my life did I meet a more perfect gentleman than Major Elliott. He arrested me in Clarkesburg, but he was a gentleman in every sense of the word. He didn't want to put me in jail, but he wanted me to go to the hotel and stay until my trial came up. But I prefer boarding with Uncle Sam when he wants me to.

I want to say to you that you need not be afraid of Major Elliott. I know that he will do the best he can with you, and I know, I believe in my own heart that he will tell those troops not to fire on you, and I want to tell you, Mr. Operator, you can't buy him to do it. Of course he is a public officer. As such he has got to obey orders from above, but he won't obey the mine owners. (Applause)

Before I leave you, I want to say to you there isn't a nation on earth but what brings out the troops when capitalism wants them, to murder you.

In France, the government is supposed to be atheistic, when the telegraphers went on strike the government brought the troops out to shoot the workers back.

In Germany, which is a Protestant nation, they called on the troops to shoot the workers down when they struck.

In Spain, which is a Catholic country, they called out the troops to shoot you back.[81]

Then here in America out comes the troops.

Don't you believe it is time to stop it? Don't you know you have the same government as when the immortal Lincoln was in Washington? He didn't bring out the troops to shoot you. With machinery you have changed the whole industrial world, you have changed literature, the pulpit in the teaching of religion. Your public press today is run in the interest of the ruling classes. These editors have got to do it. Don't blame the editor. I blame the pirates behind. The poor editors are like you, slaves, and you are slaves.

Nobody can change this but you. The other classes will never change it. The ministers will never change it. They will tell you to go up to Jesus, and Jesus will tell you to get back and fight.

I have been in the mines twenty-five years ago on the Monongahelia River. I went in on the night shift and the day shift. I went to study the conditions and to get posted. You were working long hours then. I talked with you in the mines and got you together, told you what you were facing. I worked on the night shift and the day shift, I put the literature in your hands. I lay on the floor with your baby children. Today we are four hundred thousand strong, marching on to liberty, marching on to freedom. We are the United Mine Workers of America today numbering four hundred thousand.[82] Then you worked 12 or 14 hours. We brought it down to 10, then to 8. Your stores ran and worked their help until 10 o'clock at night. The merchants said if you closed up they couldn't make any money. We brought it down, and you haven't got a merchant who will give up the business on account of making no money. You are now working 10 hours — (from the crowd: "Nine hours").

This is 4 hours too much. We are going to keep on and are going to make it 6 hours. When I came in you were working 11 hours and 15 sometimes. I fought these fellows. They gave you 9 hours. You are as much to blame as the mine owners, because you didn't stick to your organization. If you were true to your organization true to your manhood, you would not have to bother with the guards.

A fellow said the other day — Saturday — we are going to have a convention in Charleston to talk politics. I want to say that the man who is not true to the economical part of his life is not true to his political. The labor movement has two wings. She has the economic wing and the political wing. When you are organized thoroughly on the economic you can march on and make demands of the other fellows what you want.

Boys, I want to say to you, obey the law. Let me say to the Governor, and let me say to the mine owners, let me say to all people, that I will guarantee there will be no destruction of property.

In the first place, that is our property. It is inside where our jobs are. We have every reason to protect it. In the mines is where our jobs are. We are not out to destroy property. We are out to preserve and protect property, and I will tell you why. We are going to get more wages, and we are going to stop the docking system. Put that down. Your day for docking is done. Stop it. If they don't stop it we will. (Cries of: "Good, good.")

We'll take care of the property. There will be no property destroyed. (Cries of: "Not a bit.")

Not a bit, and if you want your property protected these miners will protect it for you, and they won't need a gun.

(Cries of: "It is our interest to do so.")

We will protect it, at the risk of our lives. I know the miners, I have marched with ten thousand, twenty thousand, and destroyed no property. We had twenty thousand miners in Pennsylvania, but destroyed no property.

They used to do that years ago, but after we have educated them they saw that violence was not the idea. We stopped it. We organized. We brought them to school once again. I will tell you why we are not going to destroy your property, Mr. Governor. Because one of these days we are going to take over the mines. (Loud applause)

That is what we are going to do. We are going to take over those mines.

The government has a mine in North Dakota. It works eight hours, not a minute more. There are no guards, no police, no militia. The men make a hundred and twenty-five dollars a month, and there is never any trouble at that mine. Uncle Sam is running the job, and he is a pretty good mine inspector.

(Cries of: "Tell it, mamma, I can't.")

There used to be, when I was in Illinois before, a bunch of these black brutes down at Arbuckle, and we had them organize. There was a fellow whose name was "Sy." We have them in the miners' union, as well as in the mines. I asked them whether they were grafting in the union — they got ten dollars apiece each month, twenty dollars in all. I went down and when they came up reading the financial statement and all those ten dollars were read, I said, "What is the ten dollars going for?" They told me. I said, "Get out of camp, I have no use for grafters."

We have them in the union. They have learned the lesson from the mine owners. There was a good old darkey there, and said, "Oh," said

Sy, "I done talked to the Lord for a week, and the Lord jest come and whispered in my ear last night, and said, 'Sy, Sy, Sy, I have done had a talk with "Mother" about that graft.' Come down tomorrow night, I said, O, Lord Jesus, don't fail to let 'Mother' come," — and I went. He said Jesus didn't lie. "Jesus said 'Mother' come here sure, she take care of that money, and wouldn't let them fellows get it for nothing." At once the fellows said Amen.

So we have to put a stop to the graft. We have a lot of grafters too. It is a disease. We have learned the game from the fellows above.

I want you to listen a moment. I want the business men to listen. You business men are up against it. There is a great revolution going on in the industrial world. The Standard Oil Company owns eighty-six great department [copy missing in original]

Now wait until I read this:

"The miners and workmen in mass-meeting assembled, believing in law and order and peace should reign in every civilized community, call the attention of honest citizens of the State of West Virginia to the fact that a force of armed guards of men belong to the reckless class, the criminal and lawless class, have no respect for the rights of their fellow men, who have been employed in the coal fields of Kanawha and the New River valley. These lawless and criminals beat up her citizens on the public high-ways, a menace to the traveling public."

(Comments) If you are molested you have a right to sue the railroad.

"They insult our wives, our daughters, arrest honest citizens in lawful discharge of their duties, without process of law; they carry on a course of conduct which is calculated to bring about warfare and disturb the peace.

"We earnestly insist that the recent trouble on Paint Creek Valley was brought about by the armed criminals against whose depredations we could get no relief from the courts."

(Comments) I will explain the courts to you directly, and I hope the judge is here. He belongs to the corporations if he is here.

(From the audience: "You bet your life he does.")

"We can earnestly and sincerely call upon the State administration, men in public life throughout the State, all good citizens, to co-operate with us, to use their influence by enforcing the law, by forcing such guards to disarm themselves and leave the territory where they are now stationed. We believe their presence there will lead to further riot and bloodshed and murder and general disturbing of the peace, a condition to be deplored by all law abiding citizens.

"We hereby promise and pledge our support and co-operation with Major C. D. Elliott, who is in charge of the State militia, in the interest of law and order, at the same time insist that law and order cannot be restored until the armed guards are discharged.

"We pledge ourselves to abide by the law, doing everything within our power to cause our sympathizers to do likewise, upon the condition that said guards and bloodhounds are disarmed and removed from the State.

"We condemn the action of the Circuit Judge of this county for leaving the bench at the time of threatened impending danger, at a time when there existed a condition that brought fear and unrest to the members of our families, to our neighbors and friends. We submitted our cause to said court in which the action of said armed guards was clearly set forth, through and by our attorneys, and an injunction and restraining order was asked for, and said restraining order was denied by the judge. We hold that the recent out-break and riot was due to the fact that said judge refused to grant a proper restraining order against said guards under the condition set forth in the bill and proof filed in support thereof.

"Resolved that a copy of this resolution be forwarded and transmitted to the Honorable William E. Glasscock — "

(Comments) What on God's earth did you give him this title for? Did he have any honor when he sent Gatling guns to shoot you? Quit saying "Honor" to those fellows. When I was in the court of Judge Jackson, he said, "When you are addressing the court you have to say 'Your Honor'." I said, "Who is the court?" I said, "Is the old man on the bench with the long beard the court?" He said, "Yes." I said, "How can I know he has any honor?"

— and a copy to Major C. D. Elliott.

(Comments) I will bet you if Major Elliott disarms those guards the miners will sit down. But I want to tell you operators that by the Gods you will have to settle with us. We are no slaves, no peons, and we are not going to submit to you. If you want peons, go down to Nicaragua and get them.[83]

(Continuing) Be good boys, don't drink. I will be down tonight, and we will have a meeting Sunday evening at four o'clock. Then we will decide what steps we are going to take.

The Governor is sick now don't bother with him, poor fellow.

(From the audience: "He is sick in the head.")

He was at the Republican Convention in Chicago, and had a pain in his back.

There is a man in this audience, he has a big hat on, and he will now speak to you.

(Calls for J. W. Brown, Socialist organizer, who came and got up on the dray and proceeded to make a speech).

*[Typewritten Copy in West Virginia Collection, "Coal Strikes,"
West Virginia University, Morgantown, West Virginia.
Also published in U.S. Congress, Senate, Subcommittee on
Education and Labor, Conditions in the Paint Creek District,
West Virginia, 63rd Congress, 1st Session, 1914, pp. 2262-81.]*

Speech to striking coal miners, Court House square, Charleston, West Virginia, September 6, 1912

This great gathering that is here tonight signals there is a disease in the State that must be wiped out. The people have suffered from that disease patiently; they have borne insults, oppression, outrages; they appealed to their chief executive, they appealed to the courts, they appealed to the attorney general, and in every case they were turned down. They were ignored. The people must not be listened to, the corporations must get a hearing.

When we were on the Capitol grounds the last time you came here, you had a petition to the Governor for a peaceful remedy and solution of this condition. The mine owners, the bankers, the plunderers of the State went in on the side door and got a hearing, and you didn't. (Loud applause)

Now, then, they offer to get a commission, suggested by the mine owners. The miners submitted a list of names to be selected from, and the mine owners said "We will have no commission." Then when they found out that Congress, the Federal Government, was going to come down and examine your damnable peonage system, then they were ready for the commission. (Applause)

Then they got together — the cunning brains of the operators got together. What kind of a commission have they got? A bishop — a sky pilot, working for Jesus; a lawyer, and a member of the State Militia, from Fayette *City*. In the name of God, what do any of those men know about your troubles up on Cabin Creek, and Paint Creek? Do you see the direct insult offered by your officials to your intelligence? They look upon you as a lot of enemies instead of those who do the work. If they wanted to be fair they would have selected three miners, three operators and two citizens — (Cries of: "Right, right.") — and would have said, "Now, go to work and bring in an impartial decision." But they went up on Cabin Creek — I wouldn't have made those fellows walk in the water, but they made me. Because they knew I have something to tell you, and all Hell and all the governors on the earth couldn't keep me from telling it. (Loud applause)

I want to put it up to the citizens, up to every honest man in this audience — let me ask you here, have your public officials any thought for the citizens of this State, or their condition?

(Cries of: "No, no, no.") Now, then, go with me up those creeks, and see the bloodhounds of the mine owners, approved of by your public officials. See them insulting women, see them coming up the track. I went up there and they followed me like hounds. But some day I will follow them. When I see them go to Hell, I will get the coal and pile it up on them. (Loud applause)

I look at the little children born under such a horrible condition. I look at the little children that were thrown out here —

(At this moment an automobile came down Kanawha Street and turned around and went back, but in turning made considerable noise which attracted some attention and interrupted the speaker, who said, "Don't bother about that automobile.")

Now, then, let me ask you. When the miners — a miner that they have robbed him of one leg in the mines and never paid him a penny for it — when he entered a protest, they went into his house not quite a week ago, and threw out his whole earthly belongings, and he and his wife and six children slept on the roadside all night. Now, you can't contradict that. Suppose we had taken a mine owner and his wife and children and threw them out on the road and made them sleep all night, the papers would be howling "anarchy."

(Cries of: "Right," and loud applause.)

When you held a meeting the other day down here at Cedar Grove the *Mail* said that evening that you were drunk. I want to say to the *Mail*, it was a lie of the blackest dye. (Loud applause) There was never in the State of West Virginia a more orderly, well-behaved body of men than those miners that were assembled at Cedar Grove. The militia were there to see that we were sober, and we were sober before they came, and we were sober when they went away. The *Mail* never told you, when the mine owners and their gang of corporation pirates met at the Hotel Ruffner and filled their rotten stomachs with champagne and made you pay the bills. (Loud applause)

Now, then, the State of West Virginia is the only state in the union — I have spoken in every state in this union, and in every city, I have spoken. When I got on the train at Charleston last Sunday morning to go up to — — —(The speaker tried to remember the name of the place but could not) — that has been clamoring for me since I came into the field — the militia at Pratt got instructions to jump on the train and go to Deepwater and find instructions there. They got on the train and went up and got instructions, and followed me up. They got an Irish — — — when I was taking coffee, to watch me, for fear I would slip away from them. The rat that stood there wasn't worth noticing, because a man won't do those things.

Well, when I got off the train at Lively, I understood those men had to walk fourteen miles in the hot sun to keep me from talking. I want to tell you something. The mine owners nor Glasscock, haven't got enough militia in the State of West Virginia to keep me from talking. (Loud applause)

When I found those men I looked them over. I found out they were working men. If they had been some of the big guns, you bet your life I would make them walk. I would make the fat get off their rotten carcasses. But when I surveyed those boys I said, "Boys, I want to tell you, this is a fourteen miles walk, it is a bad, rough road, and to keep you from walking that distance in the baking hot sun I will refrain from going." They said the boys can go, the men can go, but an old woman

208

with her head white eighty years old can scare hell out of the whole state, and she can't go. (Loud applause)

Shame on your manhood! If these operators were true, and if they were not thieves, they would not be afraid of anybody. (Cries of: "No.")

But when they plunder from these miners, these children, my fellow citizens, countrymen, thrown out on the highways and mothers insulted — do you think that they will be good citizens when they grow up? I don't. The revenge and resentment will be buried there if they grow into manhood, it will develop, they will kill, they will murder to get even with those who robbed them. I want you to stop that. I don't want it to go on. Your Governor may, but I don't. I want the children to have the best of influence, I want the children to have good schooling, I want women to know nothing but what is good, I want to leave to this nation a nobler manhood and greater womanhood. Can I do it? No, I can't, boys, with the administration you have got, I can't do it.

(Cries of: "We'll change that.")

I can do it if you men and women will stand together, find out the seat of the disease and pull it up by the roots.

(Cries of: "Yes," "yes," "yes.")

Take possession of that State House, that ground is yours. (Someone interrupted, and the speaker said: "Shut your mouth.")

You built that state house, didn't you? You pay the public officials, don't you? You paid for that ground, didn't you? (Cries of: "Yes," "yes.")

Then, who does it belong to? Then did the militia chase you off? You have been hypnotized. The trouble has been that they wanted the slave system to continue. They have had a glass for you and your wives and children to look into. They have you hypnotized. They want the ministers to tell you when you die you will have a bed in heaven. The blamed chambermaids might be on strike and we wouldn't get a chance to get a bed. (Loud applause)

Now, then, I will go to the tents and when those poor women — I have seen those little children — my heart bled for them — and I thought, "Oh, how brutish the corporations must be! God Almighty, go down and look at those conditions! Go see those miners!" They tell you about how much — they have a list of questions up here, "How much do the unions do to train the miners to clean the yards?" Did you ever know of such a damned, silly insulting question? (Loud applause)

I want to ask those fellows that put that down, "How do you suppose, when we have to fight you, we have got any time about yards?" You have got the yards. We clean them for you and you don't thank us for it. Your wife lives in style. Look down at those houses there on the river front. She dresses with the blood of children. She buys a dog and calls it "Dear little poodle, I love you." And you stand for it! And you stand for it! And you are a lot of dirty cowards, I want to tell you the truth about it. You are a lot of cowards, and you haven't got enough marrow in your backbone to grease two black cats' tails. If you were men with a bit of revolutionary blood in you, you wouldn't stand for the Baldwin guards, would you?

(Cries of: "No." "No." "No.")

No, you wouldn't. Or Glasscock either. When they saw you were going to clean up the guards they got the militia down and they don't allow President Cairns, of the Miners, to go up Cabin Creek. They don't allow Mr. Diamond to go up. But I want to ask you if the militia does allow the mine owners to take transportation up there? They do!

(Cries of: "No transportation.")

You know as much about it as a dog does about his daddy. (Loud applause)

I have been under martial law before, I have been in states where martial law was, but it was never carried to that extreme. We were at least allowed to go and visit our people. Here in West Virginia you can't go. You can't hold a meeting. I want to say to you that the right of free speech will be carried on if they hire all the militia in the state to murder us. We won't surrender that right. We will hold meetings. We will hold peaceful, law-abiding meetings. We will hold them all along. I have here a book, if I had the light to read it, one of the most damnable documents that those mine owners are sending out for the miners to sign.

I have got letters here from the slaves on the Norfolk and Western, "For God's sake, 'Mother', come up and do something for us." I have got letters from the Fairmont region, "Oh, 'Mother', for God's sake, come and do something for us." I have them from New River, "For God's sake, come and do something for us, and help us."

Isn't there something wrong? Say, boys, stop it. For ages and ages they have kept the lash on you. I could see it the day I went to Kaymoor. The poor devils were scared to death. I had to tell them to come with me. They were afraid of the blood-hounds. And while I talked the blood-hounds sat there. They made me wade the creek.

Now, every citizen will admit that when you rent a house the landlord has a right to give you a passageway to go to that house. You have a right to invite who you please to your table, haven't you? The bloodhounds came along and you have got to get out.

Now, then, is that something that the State must boast of? Is that something that you citizens will endorse?

(Cries of: "No," "No.")

Very good, then. They will come to you on election day. I will tell you when you can carry a bayonet and they can't meddle with you. You can carry a bayonet on November 5th, and you can go to the ballot box and put a bayonet in there and *stick it to their very heart.* (Loud applause)

Then they can have no militia.

(Cries of: "Won't they steal the ballots?")

They will not steal it if you do your duty. I would like to see the corporation blood-hounds steal my ballot if I had one. I would clean them up. He would go to the machine shop for repairs, and he wouldn't come out in a hurry when I got through with him. (Loud applause)

You fellows with the corporation hump on your backs, I hope you will.

Now, I want to say this: Ten or twelve years ago when I came in here, you had to work eleven or twelve hours, didn't you?

(Cries of: "That is right.")

They made you load coal for any price they wanted. We brought on a fight and got twice that for loading coal. We reduced the hours to nine. Up there on Paint Creek and Cabin Creek you obeyed the laws at that time. You had a good union at that time, but you have done in industrial unions as they do elsewhere, you elect the man that wants the glory instead of the man that will work for you. I am going to put a stop to that. I want to tell you we are going to organize West Virginia. I am going to stay in here until you have good officers. And you will have no officer that will get a detective from the sheriff to go up Paint Creek with him. By the gods you won't.

I don't want an escort that murders my brothers on Piney and Stanaford Mountain.[84] I don't want an escort to go with me. And you elect them to office, those contemptible murderous blood-hounds. I am protesting. I am speaking against the insults, I want to tell you that. I don't do anything behind anybody's back. What I do I will do openly, straight above board. I have knocked down your officers before, and I will knock them down again. They will play no double game when I am around. I have just as bitter feeling toward them as toward the Baldwin guards.

Another thing, when you elect a committee, elect men that can go to the superintendent and talk like men.

Another thing, I want you to do, boys. You have got a contract with the Kanawha companies, and I am responsible for closing those mines these days. I want to say to you, go back peacefully, law-abiding, leave drink alone. When we have won this battle we will all get a "jag."

Go back to work. Those men have their contracts made outside, and they are losing them. We have been upsetting their deal. I want to deal fair with every man. There are some good operators, some good men, but their hands are tied. We must not bust them up in business, as long as they are going to give us a hand and help us — we will help them. Go back like men and go to work. One operator said, "Mother, I have had to throw away six contracts." I don't like that. I am not very fond of the mine owners as a rule, but there is a sense of justice everywhere. I want you to help the men that have stood by us — stand by them.

I will be in here until the next officers are elected. I am going through the whole district and I will pick the men and I will openly advocate them. If they are not the fellows I want I will throw them down just the same as I would a Baldwin guard.

I am going to say to the police, the militia, the Adjutant General, and to everyone in this audience, that we will carry on this fight, we will make war in the State until the Baldwins are removed.

(Loud applause, and cries of: "Right you are.")

Vote for Tincher for Sheriff, I say this to all of you.

Another thing I want to say, there is a rumor gone out that you miners tore up the C & O track. I knew it is not right, but it has gone out that way. I know who tore the track up. But the papers all through the country put it on the miners — the whole gang of thieves, all the other papers in the country, outside of the *Labor Argus*. I want you to guard the C & O tracks and trains everywhere. The young men on the C & O are our men, and they are working to help us, and I want you to protect their lives. Don't meddle with the track, take care of it, and if you catch sight of a Baldwin blood-hound put a bullet through his rotten carcass.

(Loud applause)

Now, I want to tell you boys, we will not bother the C & O Road.

I want to say another thing. There is another man who travels the C & O Road, I asked him some time ago to go up to Huntington. He has been going to speakings. He went up. I was going down that evening, and all the coaches were full, and I was worn out. The express manager as well as this brother and I went into the Pullman Car and took a seat and sat down and talked the whole way. No, he did not go watching me. I invited him, but I wouldn't invite the blood-hounds to go up to Rayford with me, or Eskdale. His name was Cochran.

The Sheriff offered me an insult that I am going to resent. (Cries of: "Tell him about it.")

I don't allow any of those blood-hounds to watch me as I travel.

He travels up there, and I have known him for twelve years.

He is a pretty good fellow.

But the other blood-hound used to be up on the C & O and on New River trailing me like a dog. Somebody told me up on the creek who it was.

Boys, this fight is going on. I may have to call on you inside of two weeks again to make another move. Then I will get the police with me, I will have them all educated by that time. (Loud applause)

Now, I want to say, my friends, I have only one journey to go through this life; you have only one journey to go through this life; let us all do the best we can for humanity, for mankind while we are here.

That is my mission, to do what I can to raise mankind to break his chains. The miners are close to me. The steel workers are. I go among them all. One time when I took up the Mexican question, I went to Congress to save some lives; I had never seen them in my life, but they appealed to me and said, "It is up to you, 'Mother,' to save our lives." I went up to carry the matter to Congress. I came up before the big committee. They were Dalzell, Congressmen, representing the Steel Trust — he was chairman of that big committee; Smith, representing the Southern Pacific Railroad, was a member of that committee; Champ Clark also was a member of that committee. Dalzell said to me, "Mother Jones, where do you live?" I said, "In the United States, Sir." "What part of the United States?" said he. I said, "Wherever the workers are fighting the robbers, there am I."[85] (Loud applause) "Sometimes I am in Arizona fighting the Southern Pacific blood-sucking pirates and thieves," said I. "Sometimes, I am up on the Steel Range, fighting those murderers and plunderers, sometimes I am in Pennsylvania fighting the robbers and murderers and blood-suckers there, and by the Eternal God we will clean you up and put you out of business."

Now, my brothers, don't violate the law. Let them see that you are law-abiding.

Now, the *Mail* said that I was going to speak tonight. Yes, I did. The *Mail* said it supposed I was going to ridicule the Governor, and the Salvation Army. I never ridicule. Never in my life. I never will. I criticise the Governor, but do not ridicule him.

Another thing I do to my people, I show them how the Salvation Army came into existence. It was a necessity for capitalism. When it developed machinery, capitalism began to develop, an oligarchy of Wall Street began to reach out, and it had to have a Salvation Army to work on the workers' brains and keep them contented. I am a student of those things. I find out the cause that produces things. I am not fighting the Salvation Army. I do at times show how the Salvation Army, the church, and every other institution becomes commercialized in the age in which we live. I do not ridicule them. They are in a way to do good work. I do not approve of them for I know they are capitalistic in their makeup.

When the *Mail* or any other paper says I ridicule them I want to state it is false. I always show up to the workers how they are hypnotized, and I don't care whether it is the Salvation Army or the church or the Bishop on this Commission, or not.

The selection of this Commission was the three wings of capitalism. There is no wing of the workers on that Commission. From the questions they ask it is a plain truth that they understand nothing of your disease or trouble, and have never made it a study.

Now, then, my brothers, I am not going to be muzzled by the *Mail*. I have been assassinated by the slimy pig before, but it never made me retreat. I have measured steel in the middle of the night with the blood-hounds, but it never made me give up the red flag. I tell them we are in the fight to a finish.

Now, my brothers, I want you all to return home, peacefully, law-abiding. Go home. I don't mind you taking a drink, I know you need it. I don't belong to the temperance brigade at all. As long as liquor is manufactured it is going to be sold for profit. When you take the profit out of it, just as you have out of the postage stamps, then you don't need any temperance howlers. It will be made pure, and we will drink it pure. So the temperance brigade will keep in the background. If we want a drink we will take it, and we are not going to offer any apology for it.

Be good, "Mother" is going to stay with you. I am going to Colorado. There was a sheriff in the county, and the mine owners asked for the troops, and the sheriff said, "You can send no troops, no militia into the county I have charge of. The men elected me." He was the sheriff, and he did not allow the Governor to send the troops in there. There was no tyranny in that county. Once and awhile we licked a scab, we wanted to put brains in him, he had none. That sheriff is going to run for Secretary of State, and I am going out to sweep the state with him. I will put him into office, if it is the last thing I do. I want to put in all the officers, and we have got to put out the fellows who stand with the robbing class, and we have got to put them out of business, we have got to make an honest nation. You can't be honest today. A girl goes to school to church and prays to Jesus. One Monday she acts like the devil when she sells to you. The whole machinery of capitalism is rotten to the core. This meeting tonight indicates a milestone of progress of the miners and workers of the State of West Virginia. I will be with you, and the Baldwin guards will go. You will not be serfs, you will march, march, march on from milestone to milestone of human freedom, you will rise like men in the new day and slavery will get its death blow. It has got to die. Good night. (Applause)

[Typewritten Copy in West Virginia Collection, "Coal Strikes,"
West Virginia University, Morgantown, West Virginia.
Extracts also published in U.S. Congress, Senate, Subcommittee
on Education and Labor, Conditions in the Paint Creek District,
West Virginia, 63rd Congress, 1st Session, 1914, p. 2281.]

Speech to striking coal miners
on the lawn of the Y.M.C.A., Charleston, West Virginia,
September 21, 1912

I want to say to those children, they will be free; they will not be serfs. We have entered West Virginia — I have — and a hundred thousand miners have pledged their support to me, "If you need us, 'Mother' we will be there." Five thousand men last Sunday night said, "We are ready, 'Mother', when you call on us."

The revolution is here. We can tie up every wheel, every railroad in the State, when we want to do it. Tyranny, robbery and oppression of the people must go. The children must be educated. The childhood will rise to a grander woman and grander man in happy homes and happy families — then we will need no saloons. We will need no saloons, nor any of your prohibition. As long as you rob us, of course we drink. The poison food you give us needs some other narcotic to knock the poison out of it. They charge you $2.40 for a bushel of potatoes in the "pluck-me" store. Ten pounds of slate in 9700 pounds of coal and you are docked — then they go and "give for Jesus." How charming, "Mr. — — — is, he give us $500."

Let us, my friends, stand up like men. I have worked for the best interests of the working people for seventy-five years. I don't need any one to protect me. I protect myself. I don't break the law. Nobody molests me, except John Laing. John is the only dog in West Virginia that attacks a woman. He is the only fellow that would do that. I am not afraid of John Laing. I would give him a punch in the stomach and knock him over the railroad. I don't know who punched him — he lost his pistol. I put my hand on him and told him to go home to his mother. I gave him a punch in the stomach, and he fell over the railroad track and lost his pistol. He didn't know he lost it until he reached home.

He said, "You are disturbing *my miners*." My slaves! Scabs! Dogs!

Boys, I want to say here, don't go near the saloon today. You need the money to buy bread. When we win this fight then we will make pure liquor. We will go to Washington — we will go to see Taft, because Wilson and the Bull Moose[86] will be out of business. We will make Congress take over the liquor question, and make them make pure liquor. It will be like the postage stamps. We will need it for our stomachs. These fellows that are howling to make it "dry" — we will make it devilish wet — we are going to hand it all over to Uncle Sam. We won't put the brewers out of business, we will make Uncle Sam put them all to work, and reduce the hours of labor to six. The operators said, "God, Almighty, what are you talking about? Six hours!" Then we will go home to the children, and nurse and feed them. We will take the children out in the sunshine — (Cries of: "We will own the land") — and bring happiness into our homes. And then you will not want to drink. We will have a violin and music in every home, and the children will dance. Shame! Forever shame, on the men and women in the state of West Virginia, that stand for such a picture as we have here today — (probably referring to the children that marched in the parade) — Shame! When the history is written, what will it be, my friends, when the history of this crime, starvation and murder of the innocents, so they can fill the operators' pockets, and build dog kennels for the workers. Is it right? Will it ever be right?

Now, I understand Mr. White[87] is going to speak at the court house. He will have something to tell you.

This strike ain't going to end until we get a check-weighman on the tipple. That is the law. It is on the statute books — that your coal will be weighed.

The last legislature of Colorado passed a check-weighman law bill, to pay for the check-weighman. The check-weighman was selected by the miners. When I was in Nevada and Utah and in Idaho, I got letter after letter from those poor slaves. These letters would begin: "Mother, God Almighty, you ought to see how they are helping us. The first one had 900 pounds more in it than I ever got before." Another fellow said, "I had 1200 pounds more." Another said, "My car weighs almost twice as much as it ever had done." When the law went into effect, how their weight increased! Even now those fellows are begging me "When are you coming back, Mother?" "We are ready to strike the blow." They will never rob us again.

You miners here have stood for it, you have starved your children, starved yourselves, you have lived in dog-kennels — they wouldn't build one for their dogs as bad as yours. You have lived in them and permitted them to rob you, and then got the militia for the robbers. You can get all the militia in the state we will fight it to the finish — if the men don't fight the women will. They won't stand for it.

Be good boys, don't drink. Subscribe for the *Labor Argus*.[88] If I was sentenced sixteen months to jail, and these guys found it out I would be in jail longer. I don't worry about it. I am down at the Fleetwood whenever they want to put me in jail for violation of the law, come along for me, come. There is coming a day when I will take the whole bunch of you and put you in jail. (Applause)

[Typewritten copies of all five speeches are in West Virginia Mining Investigation Commission (A & M 2036), West Virginia and Regional History Collection, West Virginia University Library.
I wish to thank Professor Paul Nyden for calling my attention to the existence of copies of the five speeches in the archives of the West Virginia University Library.]

Notes

1. H. E. West, "Civil War in West Virginia Coal Mines," *Survey* 30 (April 5, 1913): 45-47; Stuart Seely Sprague, "Unionization Struggles in Paint Creek and Cabin Creeks, 1912-1913," *West Virginia History,* April, 1977, p. 188.

2. 33 West Virginia 179, 188; Hoyt N. Wheeler, "Mountaineer Mine Wars: An Analysis of the West Virginia Mine Wars of 1912-1913 and 1920-1921," *Business History Review* 50 (Spring, 1976): 70.

3. Quoted in Philip S. Foner, *History of the Labor Movement in the United States,* vol. 5, New York, 1980, p. 183.

4. Walter B. Palmer, "An Account of the Strike of Bituminous Miners in the Kanawha Valley of West Virginia, April, 1912 to March, 1913," pp. 2-3, typed ms., Records of the Department of Labor, file 16/103, National Archives, Washington, D.C.

5. U.S. Coal Commission, *Report in Senate Doc. 195,* vol. I, p. 168.

6. Thomas Edward Posey, "The Labor Movement in West Virginia, 1900-1948," unpublished Ph.D. thesis, University of Wisconsin, Madison, 1948, p. 25.

7. Report of Industrial Commission, vol. XII, pp. 38, 74-76; United Mine Workers of America, *Minutes of 13th Annual Convention, 1902,* p. 41.

8. New York *Tribune,* June 12, 25, 27, August 29, 1902; Charleston (West Virginia) *Gazette,* June 7, 1902; United Mine Workers of America, *Minutes of the 14th Annual Convention, 1903,* pp. 38-42; Charles Bierne Crawford, "The Mine Workers on Cabin Creek and Paint Creek, West Virginia in 1912-1913," unpublished M.A. thesis, University of Kentucky, 1939, pp. 17-18.

9. Charles Philips Anson, "A History of the Labor Movement in West Virginia," unpublished Ph.D. thesis, University of North Carolina, 1940, p. 117.

10. *Ibid.,* pp. 118-20; *Proceeding of the Twenty-Third Convention, United Mine Workers of America, 1912,* vol. I, p. 922; Palmer, *op. cit.,* appendix.

11. Howard B. Lee, *Bloodletting in Appalachia,* Morgantown, 1969, p. 17.

12. *United Mine Workers Journal,* June 27, 1912, p. 7.

13. Lee, *op. cit.,* p. 18.

14. Palmer, *op cit.,* p. 7.

15. U.S. Coal Commission *Report in Sen. Doc. 195,* vol. I, p. 169.

16. Palmer, *op. cit.,* p. 7; *United Mine Workers Journal,* December 26, 1912, p. 2; Ralph A. Chaplin, "Violence in West Virginia," *International Socialist Review* 13 (April, 1913): 729-35.

17. Frederick Allan Barkey, "The Socialist Party in West Virginia from 1890 to 1920: A Study in Working Class Radicalism," unpublished Ph.D. thesis, University of Pittsburgh, 1971, p. 110; Lee, *op. cit.,* p. 20.

18. Lee, *op. cit.,* pp. 21-22.

19. Foner, *op. cit.,* p. 185; *Autobiography of Mother Jones,* p. 149; Featherling, *op. cit.,* pp. 85-86.

20. Fred Mooney, *Struggle in the Coal Fields,* edited by James W. Hess, Morgantown, West Virginia, 1967, pp. 27-28; Barkey, *op. cit.,* p. 111; *United Mine Workers Journal,* July 4, 1912, p. 8. For a more critical view of the incident with the gunmen, *see* Featherling, *op. cit.,* pp. 89-90.

21. New York *Call,* July 27, 1912; Evelyn L.C. Harris and Frank J. Krebs, *From Humble Beginnings: West Virginia State Federation of Labor, 1903-1957,* Charleston, West Virginia, 1960, pp. 72-78.

22. Charleston *Gazette,* August 5, 1912; Charles Bierne Crawford, "The Mine Workers in Cabin Creek and Paint Creek, West Virginia, in 1912-1913," unpublished M.A. thesis, University of Kentucky, 1939, p. 38.

23. Ralph Chaplin, *Wobbly: The Rough-and-Tumble Story of an American Radical,* Chicago, 1948, p. 120.

24. Lawrence R. Lynch, "The West Virginia Strike," *Political Science Quarterly,* December, 1914, p. 645.

25. Mooney, *op. cit.,* p. 20.

26. *Ibid.,* pp. 30-31.

27. *United Mine Workers Journal,* January 23, 1913, p. 2.

28. New York *Call,* February 11, 1913; *Senate Report 321,* 63rd Congress, 2d Session, I, p. 946,

29. *New York Times,* February 10-11, 1913.

30. *Ibid.,* February 12-14, 1913; Virginia Lee, "Political and Civil Liberties During Certain Periods of Emergency in West Virginia," unpublished M.A. thesis, Marshall College, Huntington, West Virginia, 1942, pp. 269-72; Robert S. Rankin, *When Law Fails,* Durham, North Carolina, 1939, p. 85.

31. Richard D. Lunt, *Law and Order vs. the Miners: West Virginia, 1907-1933,* Hamden, Connecticut, 1979, p. 35.

32. Mother Jones to W. B. Wilson, February, 1913, Records of Department of Labor, CC: 20 16 /13, and Mother Jones to Senator Borah, February, 1913, *ibid.*, both printed below pp. 588-89.

33. Pratt, *op cit.*, appendix; Foner, *op. cit.*, vol. 5, pp. 191-192; *New York Times*, March 11, 1913.

34. Mother Jones to My dear friend, Military Bastile, Pratt, West Virginia, April 5, 1913, *ibid.*, and printed below p. 592; Foner, *op. cit.*, vol. 5, p. 192; Palmer, *op. cit.*, p. 22.

35. Carolyn Karr, "A Political Biography of Henry Hatfield," *West Virginia History*, October, 1966, p. 146.

36. *Appeal to Reason*, March 29, 1913, p. 1; April 26, 1913, p. 1.

37. *Autobiography of Mother Jones*, p. 162; Joseph Leeds, "The Miners Called Her Mother," *Masses & Mainstream*, March, 1958, p. 47; *Congressional Record*, vol. 50, part 2, May 9, 1913, p. 1403.

38. *See* John Francis Raffaele, "Mary Harris Jones and the United Mine Workers of America," unpublished M.A. thesis, Catholic University of America, p. 59; *New York Times*, May 28, 1913.

39. *Huntington Socialist and Labor Star*, May 12, 1913. The poem was later published in the *International Socialist Review* 14 (June, 1914): 322.

40. Quoted in Peter C. Michelson, "Mother Jones," *Delineator*, May, 1915, p. 8.

41. Quoted in George S. McGovern and Leonard F. Guttridge, *The Great Coalfield War*, Boston, 1972, p. 137.

42. U.S. Congress, Senate, Subcommittee of the Committee on Education and Labor, *Investigation of Paint Creek Coal Fields of West Virginia*, Senate report 321, 63d Congress, 2nd Session, 1913-14; *Conditions in the Paint Creek District, West Virginia*, 63d Congress, 1st Session, 1914.

The report of the subcommittee of the Committee on Education and Labor blamed the violence in West Virginia on the refusal of the operators to recognize the miners' union and on the equally strong determination of the miners to organize the mines. Two of the five senators on the subcommittee, in separate reports, suggested government ownership of the mines in order to solve permanently the labor-capital conflict. The report also criticized the appointment of a military commission to try civilians. (*Investigation of Paint Creek Coal Fields of West Virginia*, pp. 1-21.)

43. The proposed contract's terms were a nine-hour workday, the right to select a checkweighman, semi-monthly pay, and no discrimination against union miners. The operators and UMW officials accepted the compromise settlement, but the union leaders, as David A. Corbin points out, "apparently feared opposition from rank-and-file miners, for, instead of submitting the proposed contract to a referendum, as was usual in contracts involving wage disputes, they called a convention of selected miners' delegates to vote in the settlement terms." Socialist delegates led the opposition to the proposed settlement, but after three days ratified the contract.

As opposition to the proposed settlement mounted among the miners, Governor Hatfield took steps to suppress all dissent. The *Huntington Socialist and Labor Star* was visited by a mob of militiamen and deputies after it voiced opposition to the settlement; its offices and plant were wrecked, its type scattered over a wide area, and its staff arrested. In this repressive atmosphere, it was not really possible to voice further opposition to the settlement.

The National Committee of the Socialist Party selected Eugene V. Debs, Victor Berger, and Adolph Germer, to go to America's "Little Russia" to investigate conditions there. In its report, submitted to the National Committee of the Socialist Party on May 26, 1913, the committee exonerated Hatfield from much of the criticism directed at him in the Socialist press and by Mother Jones, and urged a "better understanding . . . between the United Mine Workers and the Socialist Party. . . ."

The report was bitterly criticized by Socialists in West Virginia for having "whitewashed" Governor Hatfield, an opinion Mother Jones shared. Debs charged his critics, especially the West Virginia Socialists, with seeking to undermine the United Mine Workers in order to open the door for the IWW to move into West Virginia and take over the organization of the miners. While Mother Jones was not enamored of the IWW, she rejected Debs's charge. In fact, the whole episode caused Mother Jones to turn both against Debs and the Socialist Party of America, and as we shall see, she "long remembered Debs and the party's handling of the affair." (Barkey, *op. cit.*, pp. 136-46; David A. Corbin, "Betrayal in the West Virginia Coal Fields: Eugene V. Debs and the Socialist Party of America 1912-1941," *Journal of American History* 64 (March, 1978): 987-1009; Foner, *op. cit.*, vol. 5, pp. 193-95.)

For a vigorous defense of the role played by Governor Hatfield in the strike, *see* Richard D. Lunt, *Law and Order vs. the Miners: West Virginia, 1907-1933* (Hamden, Connecticut, 1979), pp. 32-36.

44. Peter Gottlieb, Associate Curator, West Virginia and Regional History Collections, West Virginia University Library, to present writer, August 10, 1981.

45. With the change of the political complexion of the House of Representatives in 1910, the long reign of Speaker Cannon was ended. He was replaced by Champ Clark of Missouri, who was regarded to be a friend of organized labor. The new chairman of the labor committee was William B. Wilson, former secretary of the United Mine Workers, while three other trade unionists were also assigned to that body. For the first time in labor's memory, the committee reported speedily and favorably to the House proposals curtailing the application of the Sherman act to unions and the use of injunctions in labor disputes. By the time the 62nd Congress had completed its session on March 3, 1913, more legislation in which labor was interested had been enacted than during any previous Congress. The major setback was in the area of legislation exempting labor organizations from prosecution under the Sherman Anti-Trust Act. A bill to accomplish this was passed by both houses of Congress, but it was vetoed by President Taft, and though the House passed the bill over Taft's veto, before it could come up in the Senate, the 62nd Congress had expired.

46. The reference is to Governor John K. Tener of Pennsylvania.

47. The events described took place during the Arnot strike. *See* pp. 405-07.

48. *See above* p. 132. The person quoted is Francisco Madero.

49. The Panama Canal across the Isthmus of Panama was constructed after the Republic of Panama, organized in a revolt against Colombia with the assistance of U.S. naval forces dispatched by President Theodore Roosevelt, signed a treaty with the United States, granting the U.S. the right to build a canal. Construction was begun in 1904 and opened to traffic in 1914. It was officially declared open in 1920.

50. The reference, of course, is to President Theodore Roosevelt.

51. The Mayor was the reformer Seth Low. For the incident referred to, *see* pp. 103, 438-39.

52. Rumors that Secret Service agents were following Mother Jones and her "Industrial Army" of children were widespread. When the child marchers, led by Mother Jones, arrived at Oyster Bay, the Secret Service would not allow them through the gates.

53. When former President and Chief Justice William Howard Taft died on March 8, 1930, Mother Jones praised his courage in meeting her and helping her in the battle she was waging on behalf of Mexican revolutionaries imprisoned in the United States.

54. Andrew Carnegie (1835-1919), industrialist, who rose from poverty to head the Carnegie Steel Company. He was opposed to trade unions, but was active in several reform measures including anti-imperialism and peace.

55. Carnegie sold out to United States Steel in 1901 for $250 million.

56. After selling his concern, Carnegie turned to a career of philanthropy, endowing, among other projects, the "Carnegie libraries."

57. The reference is to the Homestead strike of 1892 during which Carnegie was in Scotland, but instructed Henry C. Frick, manager of the Carnegie works near Pittsburgh, on the Monongahela River, to break the union. Frick incited a strike and then requisitioned several hundred strikebreakers, through the Pinkerton Detective Agency. These were brought up the river on barges. A gun battle between strikers and strikebreakers resulted in seven dead. The strike was broken.

58. The Dick Military Act of 1903, authored by John Dick of Ohio, made the National Guard an integral part of the nation's military while maintaining its connection with the states. The legislation provided for the appropriation by the United States government of equipment, instruction and instructors, arms, and money for the support of the state militia. Immediately after the law went into effect, Congress appropriated $2 million to equip the National Guard with the latest weapons, and until 1916, the national government thereafter spent $5 million on the National Guard. (*Army and Navy Journal*, 52 (April, 1916): 1090.)

59. Rudyard Kipling (1865-1936), British author, famous as a story teller and for his verses, *The Jungle Book,* being among his most popular works. Kipling was a leading proimperialist writer.

60. The Civic Federation actually started in Chicago but it was transferred in 1900 to New York City.

61. A derisive name for the company store.

62. Walter Deal's speech is published in U.S. Congress, Senate, Subcommittee on Education and Labor, *Conditions in the Paint Creek District, West Virginia,* 63d Congress, 1st Session, 1914, pp. 2275-80. It dealt mainly with the guard system in West Virginia which Deal called "a disgrace to the Constitution of the United States and a disgrace to the State of West Virginia."

63. The reference is to Anne Morgan, J. P. Morgan's daughter.

64. In the original typewritten copy the pages skip from 6 to 10.

65. Peonage, used as a synonym for conditions of labor close to slavery, is a form of servitude where workers are so completely in debt to their employers as to have little hope of emerging into independence.

66. The feast of Belshazzar described in the Old Testament featured the warning of future doom in the handwriting on the wall of the words, "Mene, Mene, Tekel." Belshazzar was a Babylonian general of the 6th century B.C.

67. The Salvation Army, an evangelist organization established by General William Booth in England, was introduced into the United States in 1880.

68. *See* pp. 465-68 for the article Mother Jones wrote on the girls who worked in the Milwaukee breweries.

69. Mother Jones is referring to Jesus of Nazareth.

70. Helen Gould was the daughter of Robber Baron capitalist millionaire Jay Gould.

71. Victor Hugo (1802-1885), French poet and novelist, extremely popular among workers and progressive people all over the world.

72. In the publication of the speech by the Senate committee investigating the West Virginia strike, before Mother Jones's speech is printed, the following appears:

(Crowd of probably three or four hundred.)

Banners:

"Nero fiddled while Rome burned. That is what the governor of West Virginia is doing.

"Mountaineers are always free. Out of the State with the Baldwin murderers."

"No Russia for us. To hell with the guard system."

"Gaujot, king of the Baldwin murderers, leave the State or we'll hang your rotten carcass to a telegraph pole." (*op. cit.,* p. 2262.)

73. Thomas Scott and Stephen Benton Elkins were industrialists who exercised great influence in West Virginia railroads, mines, and politics. Elkins, who founded Elkins, West Virginia, was U.S. Senator from West Virginia from 1895 to 1911.

74. The audience was correct. Even though Governor John Peter Altgeld of Illinois objected to the sending of federal troops to crush the Pullman strike, insisting that there was no need for troops, President Cleveland sent them into Illinois over his objections.

75. The story related here is, of course, that of Moses leading the Children of Israel out of Egypt.

76. Mark Hanna (1837-1904), Ohio businessman and political leader who became boss of the Republican Party, helped place William McKinley in the White House, became United States Senator (1897-1904), and the first president of the National Civic Federation.

77. The unsinkable *Titanic* hit an iceberg and sank on its maiden voyage, April 15, 1912, with the loss of 1,513 lives.

78. Mother Jones is referring to the time in Trinidad, Colorado, when she was informed on April 17, 1904, that she had been exposed to smallpox, and was placed under quarantine.

79. *See above* pp. 110, 557.

80. *See above* pp. 172-73.

81. The incidents Mother Jones referred to occurred in these countries in 1910-1911. In France the troops were also called out to break the strike of railroad workers. Mother Jones strangely did not include England where the troops were called out in the great railway strike in August 1911.

82. Mother Jones exaggerated the membership of the United Mine Workers.

83. Peonage was especially identified with labor conditions in Central and South America.

84. *See* pp. 157,159.

85. *See* pp. 369-70.

86. The Bull Moose Party was the popular name for the Progressive Party of 1912, derived from Theodore Roosevelt's response to queries about his health,

at the time he arrived in Chicago to receive the party's presidential nomination: "I feel as fit as a Bull Moose."

87. John P. White, president of the United Mine Workers.

88. *Labor Argus* was the organ of the West Virginia State Federation of Labor.

I Want to Give the Nation A More Highly Developed Citizenship

Speech at Carnegie Hall, New York City, May 27, 1913

On May 27, 1913, the New York Call, *Socialist Party daily organ, announced on its first page:*

What is expected to be one of the most memorable meetings in the history of this city will be held tonight in Carnegie Hall when Mother Jones, the veteran labor agitator and "angel of the miners" will tell the story of the great strike of the coal diggers of West Virginia and the suspension of the Constitution and the inauguration of a reign of terror in that State at the behest of the mine owners and allied capitalist interests.

Mother Jones, who will speak under the auspices of the Masses,[1] *a satirical illustrated monthly published here, will come to the meeting almost directly from a military prison in West Virginia. After about three months of confinement, the aged woman was liberated about two weeks ago. . . .*

Mother Jones had spoken in Pittsburgh on May 19, 1913, and she reminded her audience of steel workers and miners that when she went into West Virginia, she was warned she would be killed. But instead, "I didn't come out on a stretcher. I raised hell."[2] She arrived in New York City on May 24, and was met at Pennsylvania Station by Anna Sloan, who was to escort her to her hotel. Sloan, however, knew Mother Jones only by reputation, and approached the first old lady she saw, asking her if she was Mother Jones. "I am Mother Reid," was the reply, "but I'd be proud to be Mother Jones."[3]

"An eighty-one-year-old labor agitator . . . was the central figure at a mass meeting that filled Carnegie Hall last night," declared the New York Times *of May 28, 1913. The headline in the* Times *read, "Mother Jones Stirs Crowd," and its report noted that the meeting was chaired by Max Eastman, Socialist editor of the* Masses, *and that two other speakers shared the platform with Mother Jones: Joshua Wanhope, a*

New York Socialist, and Charles Edward Russell, muckraker, Socialist writer, and Socialist Party candidate for mayor of New York City. "In a box in the balcony," the Times further noted, "under a banner of the Women's Trade Union League, sat 'Big Bill' Haywood."[4]

The Times observed that the meeting marked a coming together of Socialists of the right and center (represented by Wanhope and Russell) and IWW leaders. These groups had been heretofore hostile to each other, but events in West Virginia convinced leading Socialists that the working class "could rely on moral suasion or the awakening of sympathy no longer, and must be turned into 'an army of fighters' imbued with 'the spirit of revolution.'" Thus it noted that Wanhope, a representative of the moderate and conservative forces in the Socialist Party, had struck a new note in his Carnegie Hall speech:

We are past the point where we can teach morality to boa constrictors and ethics to hyenas. We are here to get the power to destroy the power they wield. There is hope for the laboring class so long as they are in it, as was shown in West Virginia, men who, seeing that it is a case of killing or being killed, are willing to take guns and do a share of the killing.[5]

Wanhope was followed by Mother Jones. But before introducing her to the audience, Eastman asked the audience to rise in welcoming her. "Scarcely had her name left his lips," the New York Call reported, "then the audience burst into shouting, stamping, and handclapping. Several women surged down the aisles toward the stage and threw kisses to the aged agitator and flowers at her feet."[6] After Mother Jones had spoken, a collection was taken up and $267.80 contributed. "It was intended for the striking miners. Mother Jones announced the miners would take care of the miners and said the collection could go to the Paterson silk strikers."[7]

In the Justice Department Records at the National Archives, there is a document entitled "West Va. Resolutions." It reads:

NOW THEREFORE, it is UNANIMOUSLY RESOLVED by this large and representative assemblage gathered together to honor "Mother" Mary Jones at Carnegie Hall, composed of members of the following organizations, parties, trades and industries, to wit: The New York Socialist Party; the Central Federated Union, representing the Garment Workers, Painters, Carpenters, Typographical workers, and all other trades; The Womens' Trade Union; the Young Peoples' Socialist Federation; the New York Daily "Call"; the Jewish Daily Forward; the Volkszeitung; The Masses Magazine; the Woman Voter, and others.

First: That the President of the United States be, and he is hereby requested, to take immediately whatever steps may be in his power and influence to further and advance the purpose of the resolution introduced into the United States Senate by the Hon. John W. Kearns (sic), Senator from Indiana, calling for a comprehensive and fearless investigation of the strike conditions in West Virginia;

Second: That the said resolution has the hearty endorsement of this assembly, consisting of more than 5,000 representative citizens, who demand, in the name *of humanity and liberty, the immediate carrying out the purpose of the said resolution.*[8]

I hope you do not believe that, as Comrade Wanhope has said, that the miners of West Virginia simply decided casually "to take guns and do a share of the killing." They got guns only when it became clear that the authorities, acting on behalf of their masters (the mine operators and other capitalists) would not accede to the just and peaceful requests of the miners.

I organized a meeting at which a committee was chosen to go to Charleston to present a petition to the Governor asking him to remove the Baldwin gunmen from the mine territory. We went, several thousand miners and myself, to Charleston, and met on the grounds in front of the State Capitol. The Governor came out and heard the petition read. To the committee which was to see him I said, "When you go in there, don't get down on your knees and don't say your honor." You know so few of these people have any honor.

The petition was unavailing. The guards were not removed. The men came back to Charleston, and held another meeting on the river bank. Then they went and bought up every gun in Charleston. They had appealed to the constituted authorities for protection, but they had failed, and they decided to fight for themselves — not because they favored violence but because they had no other choice.

Meanwhile, encouraged by the indifference of the Governor, the thugs began a veritable reign of terror. The war was then begun. Some guards were killed by miners in self protection, and the militia came. A short period of peace followed, and the militia was withdrawn. This was the signal for the agents of the mine owners to intensify the war against the workers. Men, women, and children were evicted from their homes; miners were shot down in cold blood, and the reign of terror grew even more terrible. When I protested the barbarism of the capitalists and their henchmen, I was deprived of all the rights of an American citizen and imprisoned in a military bastile for three months.

I am told that if I return to West Virginia, I will be again arrested, this time for having criticized the authorities of "The Little Russia in America" during my speech in Pittsburgh. Governor Hatfield will not arrest me. He doesn't understand the forces underlying the great economic conflict in West Virginia, and he is owned body and soul by the mining, railroad, oil and other capitalist interests of the State of which he is the chief executive. But he does understand that public opinion has been aroused, and that he has to make concessions to it.

I am in favor of using the ballot, and in all my career I have never advocated violence. What I want to do is to give the nation a more highly developed citizenship. You can't do this with the conditions that prevail in West Virginia. Why, they spent $500,000 on the militia in strikes while they closed down a large number of schoolhouses. Many of the children who were despoiled of their education will never again be back in school.

West Virginia is on trial before the bar of the nation. The military arrests and the courtmartial to which I and others were forced to undergo in West Virginia was the first move ever made by the ruling class to have the working class tried by military and not civil courts. It is up to the American workers to make sure that it is the last.

What galled me most about my confinement at the military prison at Pratt, West Virginia, was the knowledge that a bunch of corporation lickspittles had the right to confine me. But I must be frank and tell you that the second thing that galled me was the silence of many here tonight who should have shouted out against the injustice. I would still be in jail if Senator Kern had not introduced his resolution calling for an investigation of conditions in West Virginia. No thanks, then, to you that I am here today.

Cowards! Moral cowards! If you had only risen to your feet like men and said, "We don't allow military despotism in America! Stop it!" A lot of moral cowards you are. Not a word of protest did we get out of you, but instead you sat idly by and let these things be.

[New York Times, *May 28, 1913; New York* Call, *May 28, 1913.]*

Notes

1. The *Masses*, a Socialist monthly magazine, was organized by a group of New York radical intellectuals who were members of the "Youth Movement," and included Max Eastman, John Reed, and Randolph Bourne. Although it published fiction and verse as well as political commentary, its art was the most famous of its contributions. Among its art contributors were Art Young, Robert Minor, and Boardman Robinson. The magazine's opposition to American entrance into World War I led to its suspension, and soon after, Eastman began to issue *The Liberator*, which continued until 1924. In 1926 the *New Masses* began to appear.

2. Fetherling, *op. cit.*, p. 101.

3. New York *Call*, May 27, 1913.

4. *New York Times*, May 28, 1913.

Haywood recalled being at the meeting at Carnegie Hall to hear Mother Jones when he himself spoke at Carnegie Hall on April 19, 1914, in opposition to the United States' invasion of Mexico. In proposing to the audience the idea of a general strike in the event the United States went to war with Mexico, Haywood declared: "We will do this in memory of a good woman who stood here in Carnegie Hall with me a year ago. She was over 80 years old. But she was on her way to jail. We mine workers called her 'Mother.' We were interested in Mother Jones, and we appealed to President Wilson on her behalf. He forgot us. He could have let her out of jail, where she was put in defiance of all her legal rights." (*New York Times*, April 20, 1914.) Actually, Mother Jones had just gotten out of jail in West Virginia when she spoke at Carnegie Hall.

5. *New York Times*, May 28, 1913.

6. New York *Call*, May 28, 1913.

7. *Ibid.* The Paterson strike was led by the I.W.W. For a discussion of the strike, *see* Philip S. Foner, *History of the Labor Movement in the United States*, New York, 1965, vol. 4, pp. 351-72.

8. Unidentified document entitled "West Va. Resolutions," Justice Department Records, National Archives.

Rise Up and Strike!

Speech at special convention of District Fifteen, United Mine Workers of America, held in Trinidad, Colorado, September 16, 1913

On April 22, 1914, in the quiet of the afternoon, a telephone lineman was making his way through the ruins of a tent colony in southern Colorado. He lifted an iron cot covering a pit under one of the tents and found the blackened, swollen bodies of eleven children and two women. The news was flashed to the world, and the tragedy was given a name: the "Ludlow Massacre." All told, twenty-one persons, including the eleven children, lost their lives in one of the most shameful episodes in all of American history.[1]

The tragedy was the central event in a 14-month strike of members of the United Mine Workers of America against the management of the Colorado Fuel & Iron Company, which took a toll of sixty-six lives. It was a battle against conditions which today seem to belong to the Middle Ages, but which were typical of many industrial communities in America on the eve of World War I. But in none did the conditions more resemble those of medieval feudalism than in the Rockefeller-dominated coal fields of southern Colorado.

In 1902, John D. Rockefeller, Sr., bought control of the Colorado Fuel & Iron Company and the Victor Fuel Company, the two major producers in the southern fields, and made them part of Rockefeller's industrial empire. Colorado Fuel & Iron produced 40 percent of the coal dug in Colorado and dominated coal and iron production activities in the Southwest. In 1911, Rockefeller, Sr. turned over his interest in the corporation, which amounted to 40 percent of the stock, to his son, John D. Rockefeller, Jr., who made major policy decisions from his office at 26 Broadway in New York City. John R. Lawson, the most important leader of the 1913-1914 strike, in testimony before the Commission on

Industrial Relations, characterized the absentee owner, Rockefeller, as "invested with what is virtually the power of life and death over 12,000 men and their families, for the isolated nature of the coal industry lends itself to absolutism unknown in other activities. . . ."[2]

The situation was made even worse by the fact that both J. F. Wellborn, president of Colorado Fuel & Iron and E. M. Bowers, its superintendent, maintained their offices in Denver, two hundred miles from the mines. Responsibility for the mining area fell to E. H. Weitzel, whose office was in Pueblo, fifty miles north of the area.

Colorado Fuel & Iron owned twenty-seven mining camps, including all the land in these camps, the houses, the saloons, the schools, the churches and other buildings located within the camp environs, and the huts in which the miners lived and for which they paid exorbitant rents. A miner could be summarily evicted, since he had signed a lease agreeing that it could be terminated on three days' notice, and that he and his family could be immediately dispossessed. As a result, if a miner aroused the company's anger, this could bring about not only the loss of his job, but eviction from his home as well.

No words can adequately describe the contrast between the wild beauty of the Colorado countryside and the unspeakable squalor of these mining camps. The miners' huts, which were usually shared by several families, were made up of clapboard walls and thin-planked floors, with leaking roofs, sagging doors, broken windows, and old newspapers nailed to the walls to keep out the cold. Some families, particularly the black families, were forced to live in tiny cubicles not much larger than chicken coops.[3]

Within sight of the huts were the coke ovens, the mine tipple, and the breaker house, with thick clouds of soot clogging the air and settling on the ground, effectively strangling any shoots of grass or flowers that tried to keep alive. Wriggling along the canyon walls, behind the huts, was a sluggish creek, dirty-yellow and laden with the slag of the mine and the refuse of the camps. Alongside the creek the children played, barefoot, ragged, and often hungry.

The miners received their wages, such as they were, in company scrip, which was discounted when converted into cash; they traded in company stores, where they paid excessively high prices. They received treatment from a company doctor, whose fees were deducted from their wages whether they were sick or well. They worked in mines which were notorious for their lack of safety precautions and in a state which had a grim record of fatal accidents. In 1912, the year preceding the strike, the rate of fatal accidents for the entire nation was 3.15 for each million tons of coal mined, while in Colorado the rate was 11.86. The high accident rate in the Colorado mines was aggravated by the absence of any workman's compensation law in the state. The surviving widow and the children of a mine accident victim were left to wage a relentless struggle against poverty.[4]

Each mining camp was a feudal domain, with the company acting as lord and master. It had a marshal, a law enforcement officer paid by the company. Teachers were chosen and paid by the company. Company officials were appointed as election judges. Company-dominated coroners and judges prevented injured employees from collecting damages. Company guards — brutal thugs armed with machine guns and rifles loaded with explosive bullets — would not admit any "suspicious" stranger into the camp and would not permit any miner to leave. It was not difficult to imagine the conditions of the miners — the serfs — in such a community. Most of them were immigrants representing twenty-one nationality groups — Greeks, Italians, Croatians, Russians, Serbs, Montenegrins, Bulgarians, Poles, etc. — all equally held in contempt by the operators and their agents.[5]

On paper, Colorado had an excellent code of laws for the protection of workers. But in reality the will of the operator was the law. The operators prohibited the miners from appointing their own coal checkweighmen with the result that they were robbed of from 400 to 800 pounds in each ton; they paid their workers in company-printed scrip instead of legal currency, so that the average daily wage of $1.60 had a purchasing power of about one dollar; they worked the miners for more than eight hours a day; they prohibited them from patronizing stores of their own choice and compelled them to buy at company stores, where prices were often twice as high as elsewhere; they forced the miners to vote as the foreman directed — all in open defiance of the law. The truth is that neither state, county, nor federal law counted for much in the feudal domain dominated by the Colorado Fuel & Iron Company. Reverend Atkinson of Colorado reported the following exchange in an interview with Colorado Governor Elias Ammons:

Rev. Atkinson: Have you constitutional law and government in Colorado?
Gov. Ammons: Not a bit in those counties where the coal mines are located.
Rev. Atkinson: Do you mean to say that in large sections of your state there is no constitutional liberty?
Gov. Ammons: Absolutely none.[6]

In 1914, a report of the Commission on Industrial Relations stated: "Not only the government in these counties (Huerfano and Las Animas, coal counties), but of the state has been brought under their domination and forced to do the company's bidding, and the same companies have even flaunted the will of the nation as expressed by the President of the United States." Little wonder, then, that one student of the 1913-1914 Colorado strike describes it "not so much as a struggle for higher wages or other tangible advantages as a revolt against a political, economic, and social despotism."[7]

As we have seen the massive strike intervention of the state on the side of the coal companies in southern Colorado broke the strike of 1904, and *in October, it was called off.[8] Between 1904 and 1913, not a single change took place to improve the conditions of the miners. Indeed, many of the strikers of 1913 had been brought in the area as strikebreakers in the previous walkout. Yet so grim were both their working and living conditions that they, in turn, became the strikers a decade later.*

After secretely organizing a recruiting campaign for two years, the United Mine Workers sent Vice-President Frank J. Hayes, John McLennon, president of District No. 15, and John Lawson, executive board member, to Colorado. A policy-making committee was established, and in an effort to stave off a strike, attempts were made to get Governor Ammons to arrange a conference with the mine operators. These failed, as did an attempt by the Department of Labor to mediate the dispute. Early in September 1913, acting on a request from the UMW for assistance in mediating the dispute, Secretary of Labor William B. Wilson appointed Ethelbert Stewart as mediator. Before going to Colorado, Stewart first went to New York City to enlist the aid of John D. Rockefeller, Jr., but he could not even get in to see him. Instead, he was told by a member of Rockefeller's staff that any decision with regard to the policy of the Colorado Fuel & Iron Company would be made in Colorado and that the New York office would not interfere.[9]

On September 15, 1913, at Trinidad, Colorado, 250 delegates from the state's mining camps, opened their convention, singing:

> *We will win the fight today, boys,*
> *We'll win the fight today,*
> *Shouting the battle cry of union;*
> *We will rally from the coal mines,*
> *Shouting the battle-cry of union.*
> Chorus:
> *The union forever, hurrah boys, hurrah!*
> *Down with the Baldwins, up with the law;*
> *For we're coming Colorado, we're coming all the way,*
> *Shouting the battle cry of union.[10]*

Fed up with Colorado Fuel & Iron's refusal even to meet with union representatives, the miners demanded action, and they listened with rapt attention to Mother Jones, who had just arrived in Colorado from Michigan where she had joined the parades of the copper strikers, members of the Western Federation of Miners, as they picketed the Calumet & Hecla Mining Company.[11] In her hour-long speech, Mother Jones stirred the miners' spirit of revolt, and the convention voted unanimously to strike on September 23 for union recognition; a ten percent increase in wage scales; the eight-hour day; pay for "dead work" (timbering, removing fall, handling impurities, etc.); checkweighmen in all mines to be elected by the miners; free choice of stores, boarding houses, and doctors; enforcement of the Colorado mining laws; and "abolition of the notorious guard system which has prevailed in the mining camps of Colorado for many years." As in the case of the 1903 strike, nearly all of the demands were already on the statute books of Colorado but had been ignored by the company.[12]

I want to say a few words regarding that telegram.[13] Insofar as the public has had some ten years to protest against the horrible conditions that exist here, they have failed to take up the question that arises today in the nation, that is, industrial democracy. Realizing that it fails to demand better conditions, strike I know is the last resort. I do not advocate strikes and have prevented many of them throughout the country. It has been ten years since you have awakened to the fact that outrageous insults are being heaped on humanity in Colorado.

What would the coal in the mines be worth if you did not work to take it out? The reporter for the Pittsburgh paper was speaking to the manager of the Colorado Fuel & Iron Company mines some time ago and asked why greater care was given the mules than the men, and the manager very humanely replied, "A miner is cheaper than a mule to a coal company." That is on record in the Pittsburgh Survey of Pittsburgh, Pennsylvania.[14] It was from that I took it; he said they were only Dagoes. What a statement that is to be made by any human being. I want to say they are not Dagoes, because when a man comes to this country and the immigration commissioner passes him through, he is immediately an American citizen. He is no longer a Dago, nor a Scotchman nor an Irishman; he is immediately an American citizen, supposed to learn our laws and comply with them. It is strange anyone should be called a Dago in our day. They used to do that long ago when the boss would go to the Irishman and say "Pat give me $10.00; I heard those Welsh Rabbies say they would clean you up." Pat would say, "Sure I'll give you $10.00." Then he would go over to the Welshman and say, "Those Irish called you Welsh Rabbies, put up $15.00." The Welshman would. Don't you see their plan was to divide the working class. History tells us of a man who lived two thousand years ago. He was a slave at that time and he was bought and brought to a strange land, then sold to someone else and ran away. When he was brought to court for what he had done, they said to him, "Who are you stranger?" "I am a man. I am interested in anything that affects my class," was the reply of this slave. "I am devoted to my class." I wish to God I could permeate every worker in the State of Colorado with the same pride that filled this slave so many years ago. Whatever affected his people affected him, so my boys let it be with you. One brother said he got fair pay. I want to ask you what he calls a fair pay for the miners. You produce about $10.00 a day. You get one-tenth of it. The other fellow gets the balance of it. Do you call that a square deal?[15] I want to assure you my friend it is not. We have suffered here too long. We tried before to demand our rights, but the miners were beaten up, so were other men who came to lend a hand. They were beaten up on the trains; they had no protection whatever.

One morning about that time I had to leave for one of the other camps. I happened to sleep a little late and missed the train. I saw a boy beaten right here in Trinidad just as the train pulled out. There was no redress for it.

The time is ripe for you to stand like men. If the operators don't come to time, we will. This thing of standing for slavery in this country is going to come to an end. We are not going to raise the coming generation to be highwaymen. We are going to raise them to be intelligent, law-abiding citizens. We will take a hand in making the laws.

The governor can stop a strike any time. If I were governor I would stop a strike by simply saying, "These men have a grievance and demand redress from you. Come and discuss these questions with the miners on the fair soil of America like intelligent, law-abiding citizens. If you refuse I will close up your mines. I will have the state operate mines for the benefit of the nation." It is not right for public officials to bring in scabs and gunmen into any state. I am directly opposed to it myself, but if it is a question of strike or you go into slavery, then I say strike until the last one of us drop into our graves.

I went into the city of Charleston, West Virginia. I knew those boys since they were little trapper boys. One night the minutemen forced them and their wives and little babes out of the camp. They marched twelve miles before they found shelter. That was on the fair soil of America. If it was Russia we would rise in arms against it.

I have been in strikes of one kind or another. I have seldom been out of a strike for years, therefore I knew what to expect and told the boys to stand loyally together and be true to each other. I then said these boys must be saved if it costs me my life, so without waiting to consult the advice of the miners' officials, I took the 8:30 o'clock train and went to Paint Creek. There I found men, women and children turned out of their homes by the Baldwin-Felts thugs. Then I said: "I will not leave the state until the Baldwin-Felts thugs leave." We appealed to the marshal and other deputy officials, but they refused to give us any help. By this time I was thoroughly disgusted and said to some of the boys, "Tell the people I want them in Charleston Thursday afternoon. I will attend to their expenses, we are able to pay them. Charter trains if you have to." Three thousand of our men assembled in the city that day. We had our demands printed on banners and with them we marched to the State House grounds. They were ours, we had a right to take possession. I walked into the State House and asked for a platform. They brought it out and I got on it. We learned a lesson there with many others, that was, if the workers would only wake up to the fact that if they solidify their forces, they can get anything they want. I urged a petition from the governor and told him we appealed to the sheriff and other officers and being turned out everywhere we at last came to the chief executive of the State for redress. We told him we lived in America where our fathers fought for freedom. We lived in the Union, therefore, we had a right to unite our forces. We demanded that privilege. We asked the governor to banish the Baldwin-Felts guards because I knew when we cleaned them out everything would come with it. I said, "We will give the governor until 8:00 o'clock tomorrow night; if he does nothing by that time we will. I believe we have our rights as American citizens as much as the president or governor has. We propose to observe those." The governor and the state officials stood behind me. I appointed a committee and said, "Take this document to the governor's office, present it to him yourselves and don't go on your knees; we have no kings in America. Stand erect on both feet with your head erect as citizens of this country and don't say 'Your honor,'" very few have honor. They don't know what it is. Returning they said, "The governor will do nothing for us; he will make no response to this document." They asked why and I said, "Because the political machine that nominated him have control of him." The governor stood there with hat in hand and did not say a word. He had the opportunity of making himself the greatest man in the United States by saying, "Mother Jones is most unfair, the machine did not nominate me, the people did." But he did not say a word; he knew I was right. After the meeting the men saw they were to have no protection and declared they would protect themselves; so they bought every gun in Charleston. They did no underhand business there, they simply brought their guns and ammunition to their camps to fight back, and it did not let up until an extra session of the legislature was called. I appealed to the people of the state to demand an extra session of the legislature because there was a threatened revolution. The undercurrent was so great in this country they feared a great national outbreak of the people and consented to an extra session of the legislature to discuss the questions. It was time to do something when women and children were beaten by guards. The man that will not protect himself against a Baldwin-Felts guard has no right on the soil of America. We have a right to protect our women and children.

The fight was still on when I went to Cabin Creek. There was a stone wall built there eight or nine years ago and no organizer dared go beyond that wall or he would come out on a stretcher or a cripple. Two young lads came to me and said, "Mother will you do something for us?" They were trapper boys, the coming men with the spark of humanity in them. They said, "Mother we are in a difficult position. Up in Cabin Creek no one dares to come near us or they will be shot. We have no organization, would you come?" "I certainly will," I replied. "But," he said, "If you go they might shoot you." "Let them shoot," said I, "I would rather be shot fighting for you than live in any palace in America. We will get past that wall."

We held a wonderful meeting that day. If there had been a Victor

Hugo there with a pen he could have paralyzed the world with it. It never will be produced as it really was. The men came over the mountain with their toes out of their shoes and their stomachs empty. Fifteen hundred men of every description gathered there. Even the Baldwin-Felts thugs came. When I had talked to them one hour and a half I said they looked up as much as to say "Ah! God, is there a grain of hope for us?" Others would look at the ground, very likely thinking, "All hope is dead." Ah! It was an historical meeting boys. Oh! yes, it was historical and it will go down in history some say. When I was about to close that meeting I said, "Boys let Mother tell you one thing. Freedom is not dead, she is only gently resting. She is sleeping quietly waiting only for you to call." The voices of those fifteen hundred men rang out with, "Ah! Mother we will try to be true. Will you organize us into the United Mine Workers of America?" They lost all fear and humanity and came to the front. They arose as one man. When I organized them I said, "Put on your mining clothes tomorrow, don't say a word about this; don't speak of it in the mines. Take your pick and continue to dig out the wealth. Be good and don't make any noise about it." They were discharged of course. The strike came and I had to go to them. On the way I met an armed gang of guards with the miners. I walked over to one who was the captain of these bloodhounds and put my hand on the muzzle of that gun. I stood there and addressed the miners with my hand on the gun. Never in all my history did I see anything like it. That fellow thirsted for man's blood; he actually thirsted to see the blood of those miners. "Don't you dare to let a bullet out of that," said I, "I don't have trouble where I am; I don't stand for it." The gang got afraid. At another time when I stopped on the road to address a meeting, a big Greek got behind a tree and said, "come away or they will shoot you," but I stood up and held my meeting there. Soon an officer came to me and said, "Mother Jones I can't let you talk there any more." I answered, "I am on the public highway. It belongs to me. I have a share of stock there. I have a right to talk here." They stood there with their guns in their pockets. They did not shoot a bullet.

Don't be afraid boys; fear is the greatest curse we have. I never was anywhere yet that I feared anybody. I do what I think is right and when I die I will render an account of it. These miners have suffered, but it will have to come to an end my boys. If your operators do not give to you that which is fair, then I say strike, but let the strike be the very last move you make. Don't put it off either. The time is ripe now. If they don't come to time we will lay down the tools. We will go home. We will be quiet and good. We will tell the people "Hands off; this is our strike. We are able to look after our own business." We have waited a long time boys; I wanted to come here sooner, but I have been busy, and now I will tell the Baldwin-Felts guards I shall stay here and we will win just as we did in West Virginia. We drew the attention of the whole world. The whole civilized world centered her eyes on West

Virginia and why? Because we attended to business. We didn't allow any weaklings among us. If I saw a drunker organizer in the camp I ordered him out immediately and I will do the same here. If they think more of their stomachs than they do of your cause, they must go. The boys know I get after them. But we have good men in our ranks, thank God; we have men at the head of the United Mine Workers of America that I am proud of. If I were to leave you tomorrow I would feel that I had left men at the helm that you need not be afraid of.

The operators of the northern coal fields will have to come to time and New Mexico operators will have to come to time. You would have won when you struck before, but when I went to Louisville and asked you not to call off the strike, you were like a lot of lapdogs, afraid.[16] I told you then it was your fight and you had to win it. There is a man there who can prove to you that if you took my advice then there would be no strike in northern Colorado today. I know something about strikes. I didn't go into them yesterday. You have been trained by your masters to be dependent when there is a crisis on. Now you see we enter the bull pens, you fill the jails. I was carried eighty-four miles and landed in jail by a United States marshal in the night because I was talking to a miners' meeting. The next morning I was brought to court and the judge said to me, "Did you read my injunction? Did you understand that the injunction told you not to look at the miners?" "As long as the Judge who is higher than you leaves me sight, I will look at anything I want to," said I. The old judge died soon after that and the injunction died with him. At another time when in the courtroom the judge said to me, "When you are addressing the court you must say 'Your Honor.'" "I don't know whether he has any or not," said I. He turned me loose on my good behavior in a short time.[17]

Someone said to me, "You don't believe in charity work Mother." No I don't believe in charity; it is a vice. I wish there was never a charitable institution in the world. I would destroy them all if I had my way. We need the upbuilding of justice to mankind; we don't need your charity, all we need is an opportunity to live like men and women in this country.

Young men let me say to you, keep away from the saloon, the pool room, the gambling den. There is nothing for you in them. Develop your brain and heart by serving humanity and reading human history. Be true to your fellow man and stand loyally to the cause of the worker. No power on earth can dissolve us and we will get what we want if we are loyal. If you go ahead and do right victory is yours. The United Mine Workers of America will never leave the state of Colorado until the banner of industrial freedom floats over every mine in the state. It is up to you my boys to gain victory. I will be with you and your officers will be with you. I know these boys. I have worked with them. I have watched them. If they were not deserving of all I say, I would be the first one to condemn them. You need never distrust them.

Stand together and don't surrender this time. You will not be asked to do so by your officers. They will sell the coats on their backs first. I know them. I never knew them to quit. They did a lot for the fight in West Virginia. They have never yet told me what to do except they say, "Mother, why don't you take a rest?" My answer is, "When I organize Colorado and Alabama, then you can tell me to rest if you want to, but not until."[18]

I want you to pledge yourselves in this convention to stand as one solid army against the foes of human labor. Think of the thousands who are killed every year and there is no redress for it. We will fight until the mines are made secure and human life valued more than props. Look things in the face. Don't fear a governor; don't fear anybody. You pay the governor; he has a right to protect you. You are the biggest part of the population in the state. You create its wealth, so I say let the fight go on; if nobody else will keep on, I will.

[Proceedings. Special Convention of District Fifteen. United Mine Workers of America Held in Trinidad, Colorado, September 16, 1913, pp. 16-21. Typewritten copy in Western History Department, Denver Public Library.]
I wish to thank Lois McClean of Beckley, West Virginia for furnishing me with a copy of Mother Jones's speech.

Notes

1. New York *Tribune*, April 21, 29, May 10, 1914.
2. 64th Cong., 1st Sess., Doc. 415, Senate Commission on Industrial Relations, *Final Report and Testimony*, vol. VIII, Washington, D.C., 1915. p. 8006. Hereinafter cited as *Report of the Commission on Industrial Relations*.
3. *The Survey* 33 (December 5, 1914): 246.
4. U.S. Bureau of Mines, "Coal-Mine Fatalities in the United States, 1870-1914," *Bulletin No. 115*, p. 159; *Report of Commission on Industrial Relations*, p. 6435; Eugene O. Porter, "The Colorado Strike of 1913 — An Interpretation," *The Historian* 35 (November, 1973): 14-15.
5. *Report of Commission on Industrial Relations*, pp. 8022-23.
6. *Harper's Magazine*, May 23, 1914, p. 11.
7. *Report of Commission on Industrial Relations*, p. 8417; Samuel Yellen, *American Labor Struggles*, New York, 1956, p. 115.
8. *See* pp. 37-39, 104-10 and George G. Suggs, Jr., "The Colorado Miners' Strike, 1903-1904: A Prelude to Ludlow," *Journal of the West*, 12 (1973): 36-52.
9. *Report of the Commission on Industrial Relations*, p. 8417; Porter, *op. cit.*, p. 3.
10. *United Mine Workers Journal*, September 25, 1913.
11. Foner, *op. cit.*, vol. 5, p. 217.
12. *Ibid.*, p. 201.
13. The telegram, signed by E. L. Doyle, Secretary, District 15, UMW, was addressed to Governor Elias Ammons of Colorado who had asked the miners

not to strike. It went in part: "The coal operators have ignored all our invitations to settle our differences peacefully in a joint conference. Our people have been exploited and enslaved for years. We now demand justice, and we can never secure it without the union. When the operators refuse to meet us there is no way to settle our grievances peacefully, which we would like to do.

"We suggest you appeal to the operators as well as the miners. The operators can avert a strike if they want to. We have tried without success. It is time for the press to protest against the brutal tyranny and oppression existing in Colorado coal mines." (*Proceedings. Special Convention of District Fifteen . . .* , p. 16.)

14. The Pittsburgh Survey, conducted by the Russell Sage Foundation, provided firsthand information on working conditions in the city's mills and factories. Among the volumes published by the Pittsburgh Survey were: Margaret F. Byington, *Homestead: Households of a Mill Town* (New York, 1910); Crystal Eastman, *Work Accidents and the Law* (New York, 1910); John A. Fitch, *The Steelworkers* (New York, 1911).

15. The term "square deal" had been popularized by Theodore Roosevelt as representing his program as president. He intended, he declared on assuming the presidency, neither to harass industry nor to pamper it, but to carry out the law.

16. *See above* pp. 37-39, 104-10.

17. The reference is to Judge Jackson at Parkersville, West Virginia in 1902. *See above* pp. 78-99.

18. This sentence appeared differently in newspaper reports of Mother Jones's speech which published the following excerpt: "Rise up and strike. If you are too cowardly to fight, there are enough women in this country to come in and beat it out of you. If it is slavery or strike, why I say strike, until the last one of you drop into your graves. Strike and stay with it as we did in West Virginia. We are going to stay here in southern Colorado until the banner of industrial freedom floats over every coal mine. We are going to stand together and never surrender. When I get Colorado and Alabama organized, I will ask God to take me to my rest. I am going to force the operators to concede that human life is to be regarded above property life." (Denver *Express,* September 17, 1913.)

You Are Less Free Than the Negroes Were Before the Civil War!

Speech to striking coal miners, Walsenburg, Colorado,
October 27, 1913

Even before the Colorado miners walked out, the operators ordered them out of the company houses into a bitter mountain winter. The

UMW leased land just outside the company property, brought in tents from West Virginia, and set up tent colonies in Ludlow, Suffield, Forbes, Berwind, Starkville, La Veta, and seven other sites. On September 23, a scene of epic proportions was enacted in the coal mine district of southern Colorado. Between eleven and thirteen thousand miners — about 90 percent of the workers in the mines — gathered up their belongings and moved with their families to the hastily improvised tent colonies.[1]

The miners' wives and children tried to keep warm that winter, in temperatures as low as forty to fifty degrees below zero, by shoveling out from under four- to six-foot snowfalls, while their men fought a bloody war against strikebreakers, company guards, and Baldwin-Felts agency detectives sworn in as deputy sheriffs. The Baldwin-Felts agency brought in a special automobile, with a Gatling gun mounted on top, which became known as the "Death Special." Its sides armored, it roamed the countryside with several rifle-carrying detectives in the front seat, attacking the tent colonies indiscriminately. On October 5, the operators shipped four machine guns into the strike zones. The miners threw up breastworks and dug pits under the tents to protect the women and children.

The machine guns were not just for show. A machine gun fired into women and children being evacuated from the Forbes tent camp. One miner was killed, a small boy was hit nine times but survived, and a young girl was shot in the face. On October 24, 1913, mine guards, wearing deputy sheriff badges as usual, fired into a group of strikers in Walsenberg and killed four of them.[2]

Throughout all this, Mother Jones was a dynamo of activity, holding meetings and demonstrations to mobilize strike support and to still the fears of those who were intimidated by the violence of the operators and their agents. A typical example of her speeches during this period is the brief exhortation she delivered to strikers at Walsenburg, a few days after the bloody attack of October 24, 1913.

You men, you great, strong men have been enslaved for years. You have allowed a few men to boss you, to starve you, to abuse your women and children, to deny you education, to make peons of you, lower and less free than the Negroes were before the Civil War. What is the matter with you? Are you afraid? Do you fear your pitiful little bosses? Are you great, strong men, with so much latent power in you, afraid of your masters or the Baldwin-Felts thugs hired by your masters? I can't believe it. I can't believe you are so cowardly, and I tell you this, if you are, you are not fit to have women live with you.

[Barron B. Beshoar, Out of the Depths: The Story of John R. Lawson, A Labor Leader, *Denver, 1958, p. 65.]*

To Be in Prison Is No Disgrace

Appeal from cellar cell, Huerfano County Courthouse, Walsenburg, Colorado, March 31, 1914

On October 26, 1913, Governor Ammons called the state militia into the strike areas with orders to permit neither union intimidation of those willing to work nor the importation of strikebreakers. The militia arrived in Ludlow on October 31, and received a warm welcome from the miners. Within a few weeks, however, the feeling toward the troops changed. For one thing, under pressure from the coal interests, Ammons rescinded the second part of the militia's charge, and ordered the militia to become the protective agent for the escort of the scabs into the mines. Actually, the thousand or so soldiers under the command of Brig. Gen. John Chase, a long-time hater of trade unions, were literally strikebreaking agents of the Colorado Fuel & Iron Company. The company paid their salaries and the soldiers were quartered in company buildings and furnished with supplies by the company. Soon, the militia began recruiting mine guards to replace men released on the basis of hardship and business needs. The mine guards were in the favored position of receiving three dollars a day from the operators in addition to their one dollar as militiamen, both salaries paid by Colorado Fuel & Iron.[1]

During these developments, Mother Jones left Colorado for Washington, hoping to arouse sentiment in the nation's capitol for a federal inquiry into the Colorado strike. When she returned to Colorado, she was immediately deported by the militia. But, with the help of sympathetic trainmen, she was able to attend a special convention of the Colorado State Federation of Labor on December 16, 1913. The delegates went on record in favor of a statewide general strike if called by the union leaders, and requested that Governor Ammons remove General Chase and also transfer military prisoners to the civil courts.[2]

Led by Mother Jones and Louis Tikas, Greek-American Trinidad strike leader, 2,000 delegates and other unionists marched to the state capitol and met with Governor Ammons. He denied that the troops were guilty of misconduct, but suggested the delegates appoint a committee to investigate and report back to him. They did, and a committee of four union men and Professor James H. Brewster of the University of Colorado was appointed.[3]

After the state labor convention, UMW President John P. White asked Mother Jones to go to El Paso, Texas, to see if she could help halt the importation of Mexican strikebreakers into Colorado. Mother Jones discovered that American troops were escorting the scabs across the border, and she crossed over into Mexico and discussed the problem with Pancho Villa. With Villa's assistance and the aid of an interpreter he furnished her, she addressed meetings of Mexican workers, and, as she later wrote, "got my story over the border. I did everything in my power to prevent strikebreakers from going into the Rockefeller mines."[4]

After her return to Colorado from El Paso, Texas in January 1914, Mother Jones was in and out of prison so frequently that she had few opportunities for formal speeches. But she was not silent. Her first imprisonment came soon after she announced while still in El Paso that she was returning to the Colorado coal fields. "She will be jailed immediately if she comes to Trinidad," General Chase told reporters when he heard the news. "I am not going to give her a chance to make any more speeches here. She is dangerous because she inflames the minds of the strikers." To which Mother Jones replied: "Tell Genl. Chase that Mother Jones is going to Trinidad in a day or two and that he'd better play his strongest cards — the militia's guns — against her. He had better go back to his mother and get a nursing bottle. He'll do better there than making war on an 82-year-old woman in a state where women vote."[5]

Mother Jones went to Trinidad. Chase had her arrested on January 4, 1914, placed on a Denver-bound train under military escort which was authorized to get her and keep her out of the coal fields. As the train passed through Walsenberg, a large number of union men, carrying an American flag, were at the depot, and standing under her car window during the train's brief stop, they sang:

> The union forever, hurrah; boys, hurrah!
> Down with the milita, up with the law,
> For we're coming Colorado, we're coming all the way,
> Shouting the battle cry of union.

Mother Jones watched through the car window, and tapped with her fingers to show her appreciation.[6]

Unable because she was still guarded to speak before the Denver Trades and Labor Assembly, Mother Jones did manage to tell a delegation from the body: "I serve notice on the governor that this state doesn't belong to him — it belongs to the nation and I own a share of stock in it. Ammons or Chase either one can shoot me, but I will talk from the grave."[7]

Although under orders to leave the state, Mother Jones stayed with friends in Denver for several days, bought $500 worth of shoes at wholesale prices for the strikers and their families, and made preparations to return to Trinidad. When she found that detectives had been stationed in Denver's Union Station to make certain she did not take a train south again, she made her way by a circuitous route into the railroad yards and a friendly Pullman porter made up a berth for her. Once in bed, she told the black worker: "Just tell the conductor that Mother Jones wants to get off this train in the morning on the outskirts of Trinidad." The porter burst into a huge smile, and assured her the message would be delivered.[8]

Early the next morning the Colorado & Southern train came to an unscheduled stop just outside Trinidad, and Mother Jones stepped off and started walking briskly down the cinder-covered right-of-way. As one report of the incident put it:

At the station in Trinidad, milita watched every passenger alight. When the train had gone, they went back to the Colombian Hotel to report that dangerous old Mother Jones was not among the arrivals. Mother Jones spent three hours in a hotel across the street from the milita headquarters before the military learned of her presence.[9]

Soon a squad of soldiers, led by General Chase, were in front of Mother Jones's hotel door. General Chase offered her the chance to avoid prison by leaving Trinidad immediately. "Nothing doing, General," came the reply. "I am free, white and a bit over 21. This is a free country and I've got a right to go where I damned please." She was then placed under military confinement, on Governor Ammon's order, and taken to Mt. San Rafael Hospital, run by the Sisters of Charity, on the eastern outskirts of Trinidad. Five guards were assigned to a 24-hour watch over her, and she was refused permission to receive newspapers or books. In addition, her mail was returned to the sender opened, or was destroyed. She could see no one except the union attorney who filed a petition for a writ of habeas corpus with Las Animas District Court. But Judge A. W. McHendrie, "an undisguised friend of the companies," denied the request on the ground that martial law prevailed in the section.[10]

Nine hundred enraged Fremont county miners informed Governor Ammons if he refused to liberate Mother Jones they would march to Las Animas county to do the job themselves. A hundred women invaded the Columbian Hotel, brushed the guards aside, and surrounding General Chase, vainly demanded her release. Then, on January 23, 1914, the women of Las Animas county organized a demonstration and parade on behalf of Mother Jones. After much difficulty, parade permission was obtained from General Chase, and the long line of one thousand women and children, dressed in their shabby clothes, marched into Trinidad. At their head was an Italian woman carrying an American flag. Dozens of paraders carried banners reading, "God Bless Mother Jones," and "We're for Mother Jones."

A troop of cavalry, led personally by General Chase, intercepted the marchers, and when the marchers refused to disperse, and he accidentally fell off his horse, the infuriated General Chase gave the order, "Ride down the women."

Spurs sank home and the cavalry mounts plunged forward with snorts. Sabres flashed in the bright sunlight. Laughter (at General Chase's accident) turned to screams of terror. The women began to run back. Mrs. Maggie Hammons was slashed across the forehead with a sabre; Mrs. George Gibson's ear was almost severed from her head. Mrs. Thomas Braley threw up her hands in front of her face and they were gashed by a sword.

A cavalryman leaned from his horse and struck Mrs. James Lanigan with the flat of his sabre, knocking her to the ground, Another soldier leaned from his saddle and smashed 10-year-old Robert Arguello in the face with his fist. Pandemonium resulted. The paraders beat a disorderly retreat. Mrs. R. Verna, who had been marching in the parade with an American flag, was pursued by a cavalryman who tore the flag from her grasp and knocked her down with his horse.

General Chase, mounted again, was yelling like a mad man. A thousand women and children scurried for safety.[11]

Little wonder George P. McGovern and Leonard F. Guttridge conclude: "Never was there a more complete abdication of civil authority in peacetime to a military commander so temperamentally ill-suited for the sensitive particulars of a labor dispute."[12]

Meeting in national convention, the United Mine Workers received the horrified report of the attack on the women and children in Trinidad, voted unanimously to condemn the troops, and unanimously decided to send a telegram to Mother Jones expressing "love and admiration for your gallant stand for humanity," and demanding her immediate release. "Be of good cheer and rest assured that justice will yet triumph in corporation-owned Colorado," the message concluded.[13]

The union attorney now sought Mother Jones's release through a writ of habeas corpus from the Colorado Supreme Court in which the point was made

That on the 4th day of January, 1914, this petitioner, who is an aged woman — to wit, of the age of eighty-two years — went to Trinidad, in said county, on a lawful and peaceful mission, and, while there, was unarmed, and was guilty of no crime, wrong-doing, or illegality of any kind. Yet the said Chase, in pur-

241

suance of his said claim of military right, wantonly and wilfully caused a body of his soldiers to seize and imprison her, and, after detaining her as a prisoner for some time, he caused said soldiers to deport her from said county. That, although the courts of Las Animas County were, at the time, open and transacting business, and able and willing to commit to jail and punish anyone guilty of wrong-doing, the said Chase, knowing that this petitioner was guiltless of wrong, refused to carry her before any court, but forcibly sent her out of the county. That on the 12th day of January, petitioner again went to the city of Trinidad on a peaceable and lawful mission, and, upon arriving at said city, she was at once seized by a file of soldiers, acting under orders of said Chase, and she has ever since been detained, and is now unlawfully deprived of her liberty, and kept in close and solitary confinement by said Chase. . . . [14]

Arguments for the writ of habeas corpus were set for March 16. The day before that Mother Jones was released, having spent nine weeks in confinement. She was again put on a train for Denver. (The UMW immediately charged that her release was timed to forestall a ruling in her favor by the Supreme Court.) In any case, she was soon back in prison. Upon arriving in Denver, she told reporters she would be back in Trinidad before the end of the week. "I fully expect to be arrested and returned to prison when I reach the strike zone, but no governor or president can make me abandon my constitutional rights as a citizen to go where I please. So long as I live I shall refuse to submit to military despotism. If they do not arrest me at once I shall go ahead caring for the strikers' women and children and encouraging the men to resist tyranny and robbery by the coal operators."[15]

Immediately news of this statement reached Trinidad than General Chase dispatched a militia officer to board the train with Mother Jones, and arrest her as she approached Walsenburg. At 5:30 a.m., as the train neared Walsenburg, the officer ordered Mother Jones to leave with him. As she descended the officer asked Mother Jones, "Will you take my arm, Madam?" "No, I won't," retorted his prisoner. "You can take my suitcase."[16]

Under specific orders from Governor Ammons, who, like General Chase, had become paranoid on the subject of Mother Jones,[17] but without a specific charge, she was placed in a cell in the cellar of the Huerfano County Courthouse in Walsenburg, where she remained without due process, although the courts remained open. "The arrest of Mother Jones at Walsenburg," declared Professor James H. Brewster of the University of Colorado, "without a warrant, without any suspicion of crime, was one of the greatest outrages upon civilized American jurisprudence that has been perpetrated." And the committee which he headed, to investigate the strike and report its findings to Governor Ammons, asked in its report:

Has it come to this, that men so fear the truth that they must unlawfully imprison and silence this woman of eighty-two years?[18]

They could imprison, but they could not "silence" her. To be sure, during her 26 days in the rat-infested cellar, Mother Jones could not make speeches. But she did manage to smuggle out an open letter to the American people which was read at numerous meetings as a speech by the imprisoned labor organizer. In prefacing her "speech" which he read at a Socialist rally, Eugene V. Debs described it as the voice of a woman who was "the flaming incarnation of the world's proletarian revolt against capitalism's bloody misrule."[19]

"And why is 'Mother' thrown in jail again?" asked a writer in the International Socialist Review. *He answered: "Because she dared to live up to her white locks and her great heart — dared to live up to all that the name 'Mother' stands for and do battle for the men in the mines."[20]*

I want to say to the public that I am an American citizen. I have never broken a law in my life, and I claim the right of an American citizen to go where I please so long as I do not violate the law. The courts of Las Animas and Huerfano are open and unobstructed in the transaction of business, yet Governor Ammons and his Peabody appointee, General Chase, refuse to carry me before any court, and refuse to make any charge against me. I ask the press to let the Nation know of my treatment, and to say to my friends, whom, thank God, number by the thousands, throughout the United States and Mexico, that not even my incarceration in a damp underground dungeon will make me give up the fight in which I am engaged for liberty and for the rights of the working people. Of course, I long to be out of prison. To be shut from the sunlight is not pleasant but John Bunyan,[21] John Brown[22] and others were kept in jail quite a while, and I shall stand firm. To be in prison is no disgrace.

In all my strike experiences I have seen no horrors equal to those perpetuated by General Chase and his corps of Baldwin Feltz detectives that are no(w) enlisted in the militia. My God — when is it to stop? I have only to close my eyes to see the hot tears of the orphans and the widows of working men, and hear the mourning of the broken hearts, and the wailing of the funeral dirge, while the cringing politicians, whose sworn duty is to protect the lives and liberty of the people, crawl subserviently before the National burglars of Wall Street who are today plundering and devastating the state of Colorado economically, financially, politically, and morally.

Let the nations know, and especially let my friend General Francisco Villa know,[23] that the great United States of America, which is demanding of him that he release the traitors that he has placed in custody, is now holding Mother Jones incommunicado in an underground cell, surrounded with sewer rats, tin soldiers, and other vermin.

[Judith Elaine Mikeal, "Mother Jones: The Labor Movement's

Impious Joan of Arc," unpublished M.A. thesis, University of North Carolina, 1965, pp. 115-16; Barron B. Beshoar, Out of the Depths: The Story of John R. Lawson: A Labor Leader, Denver, 1958, pp. 159-60.]

Notes

1. Foner, *History of the Labor Movement in the United States,* vol. 5, pp. 202-03; *Report of the Commission on Industrial Relations,* pp. 6675-78; *Report on the Colorado Strike Investigation,* pp. 30-32.

2. *Denver Post,* December 17-18, 1913.

3. Barron B. Beshoar, *Out of the Depths: The Story of John R. Lawson: A Labor Leader,* Denver, 1958, p. 115. In 1981, on the occasion of the 67th anniversary of the "Ludlow Massacre," the Denver Area Labor Federation reissued *Out of the Depths.*

4. *Autobiography of Mother Jones,* p. 197; Featherling, *op. cit.,* p. 117.

5. Beshoar, *op. cit.,* p. 128.

6. *Ibid.*

7. Featherling, *op. cit.,* p. 118.

8. Beshoar, *op. cit.,* pp. 129-30.

9. *Ibid.,* p. 130.

10. McGovern and Guttridge, *op. cit.,* p. 189.

11. Beshoar, *op. cit.,* pp. 131-33; *Report of the Colorado Strike Investigation,* pp. 22-23.

12. McGovern and Guttridge, *op. cit.,* p. 171.

13. *New York Times,* January 21, 1914.

14. *In the Supreme Court of the State of Colorado. In Re to Mary Jones, Application for Original Writ of Habeas Corpus.* Horace N. Hawkins, Attorney for Petitioner. Copy in Department of Archives and Manuscripts, Catholic University of America, Washington, D.C.

15. *New York Times,* March 17, 1914.

16. *Ibid.,* March 24, 1914.

17. McGovern and Guttridge point out that when Senator Helen King Robinson called on Governor Ammons, she "found the governor all cordiality until she brought up the subject [of Mother Jones] at which he became agitated and launched into old stories of Mother Jones's past 'immorality.'" (*op. cit.,* p. 191.) "Perhaps," they conclude, "he had reached the point where rational discussion over how best to contain Mother Jones lay beyond him." (*ibid.*)

18. *Report of the Colorado Strike Investigation,* pp. 30-32; Colorado State Federation of Labor, *Militarism in Colorado,* Denver, 1914.

19. *Miners' Magazine,* March 26, 1914, p. 1.

20. Tom J. Lewis in *International Socialist Review* 14 (May, 1914): 685-86. Lewis was angered because many miners all over the country continued to dig coal, producing profits for Mother Jones's jailors. "Whenever the mine boys have been in despair, or engaged in a desperate struggle, they have called for Mother Jones and they have never called in vain. Word that she was on the way to assist in times of strike has always brought a thrill of joy and hope to every miner," he wrote, and went on to urge miners everywhere to "throw down their tools and MARCH ON TO THE JAIL WHERE she is incarcerated and set her

free with their own strong hands."

21. John Bunyan (1628-1688), British minister and preacher, author of the celebrated *The Pilgrim's Progress,* who was imprisoned for twelve years for holding religious beliefs not in conformity with those of the Church of England.

22. John Brown (1800-1859) was for a brief time in prison while awaiting execution for having led a small band of white and Negro followers to Harpers Ferry in Virginia, where they seized the federal armory and tried unsuccessfully to organize an insurrection which would end slavery. Although he failed, John Brown helped to precipitate the Civil War and bring an end to slavery.

23. The mention of Villa is to the Mexican revolutionary's offer to President Wilson to release Luis Terrazas, a wealthy landowner, if the President would "show the same regard for humanity toward one of your own citizens, a woman past eighty years, who is being illegally deprived of her liberty . . . I refer to Mother Jones." (*Appeal to Reason,* March 21, 1914.)

Labor's Memorial Day

Speech at Seattle, Washington, May 30, 1914

After twenty-six days in Huerfano County jail Mother Jones left Colorado. She was not in the state on April 20, 1914, when the militiamen attacked the tent colony at Ludlow, reduced the area to a shambles, and brought death to thirty-two persons, including two mothers and eleven children who were either shot or burned to death. "The soldiers and mine guards," an eyewitness reported, "tried to kill everybody; anything they saw move, even a dog, they shot at." Had it not been for the rescue efforts of Louis Tikas, a Greek strike leader in charge of the Ludlow tent colony, the Ludlow horror might have been even worse. Throughout the day, he and Pearl Jolly, the wife of a striker, moved from tent to tent, pulling the women and children out of their cellars and ordering them to move among the arroyos to the Black Hills, some two miles east of the colony. Tragically, Tikas himself died in the rescue efforts. Seized by the militiamen, he was attacked by the labor-hating, burly Lieutenant Kenneth E. Linderfelt, who seized his army rifle by the barrel and brought the stock crashing down on the head of the defenseless prisoner with such force that the stock of the heavy gun was broken. Muttering that he had ruined a good rifle, Linderfelt turned and walked away. Three rifle bullets tore into Tikas's back, killing him. The terse report of the incident by the military board simply stated: "Lt. K. E. Linderfelt swung his Springfield rifle, breaking the head of the prisoner, Tikas."

On Tuesday morning, April 21, the sun shone down on a pitiful scene. The Ludlow tent colony, which had for seven months been the homes of the striking miners and their families, was now a miserable shambles. Here and there, an iron bedstead, a stove, a child's toy, and bits of broken pottery and glass marked the former site of a tent. It was then that a telephone lineman, going through the ruins, lifted a twisted iron cot that covered one of the larger pits and discovered the bodies of two young mothers and eleven children, ranging in age from three months to nine years. The coroner's jury which investigated the cause of the burning of the tent colony concluded that the cause of the deaths was "fire started by militiamen . . . or mine guards, or both. . . . "

"The number of fatalities at Ludlow may never be known for certain," concludes George P. McGovern in his study of the strike. But it is likely that thirty-two persons were either shot or burned to death. After a farcical trial, Linderfelt and others connected with the outrages were found guilty and "punished" by trifling changes in their eligibility for promotion.[1]

The story of the "Ludlow Massacre" was headlined in the press all over the country. Some papers tried to shift the blame from the company and its hired gunmen to the miners. But the Denver Express *put the blame where it belonged: "Mothers and daughters were crucified at Ludlow on the cross of human liberty. Their crucifixion was effected by the operators' paid gunmen. . . . These dead will go down in history as the hero victims of the burnt offering laid on the altar of [the] Great God Greed."[2]*

On May 27, 1914, responding to a suggestion by the local Socialist Party, the Seattle Central Labor Council voted to set aside May 31, 1914, as a Memorial Day for martyrs of the cause of labor. The event was to feature a parade of all the trade unions of Seattle, and be climaxed by an open-air mass meeting at the corner of Third and Blanchard Street. On May 28, 1914, the Seattle Daily Times *reported that "'Mother' Mary Jones, the noted coal strike leader and others prominent in the labor movement will speak." Mother Jones would also lead the parade, riding in an automobile, which would be followed by "1,000 or more coal miners who are coming to Seattle to attend the mass meeting." After the miners would come the various labor organizations of the city, and then other sympathetic organizations. The parade would be divided into three sections, each containing a float symbolic of the mass meeting. Since the Labor Memorial Day parade and mass meeting had been stimulated by the "Ludlow Massacre," it was only natural that the arrangements committee would invite the miners to head the procession.*

Mother Jones arrived in Seattle on May 29 to be greeted by a delegation of about 1,000 trade unionists, headed by Martin J. Flyzik, of the United Mine Workers of Seattle. (Flyzik had first met Mother Jones more than twenty years before when he had been working in a Pennsylvania mine.) Jones registered at the Baden Hotel. Under the column labeled "From where," she signed "U.S." Asked if she had any particular city or place which she called home, she replied:

I call home anywhere there is a good scrap on and where I can render help to the boys. While here Seattle is my home, for I have come across the continent at your invitation — an invitation to start a worthy movement. Memorial services for the heroes of labor who have fought and died for the cause is a fine thing, and I am certainly glad to see Seattle take this step. Cities throughout the country will follow in your footsteps.[3]

On May 31, 1914, the Seattle Post-Intelligencer *reported:*

Their banners and emblems draped in mourning, and each wearing a tag bearing a picture of Mother Jones, noted labor leader, who was the guest of honor and speaker of the day, in their coat lapels, thousands of members of organized and unorganized labor turned out yesterday in a monster parade and mass meeting to memorialize their fellow workers who have died in fighting industrial battles. It was the first observance of its kind ever held in the United States, and the huge success which it met prompted those in charge of the project to stamp it an annual affair. . . .

The appearance of Mother Jones, familiarly called "the most devout friend of labor," was the feature of the program. The aged labor leader addressed two large open air meetings at Third Avenue and Blanchard.

That same day, the Seattle Daily Times *noted that "of course the central figure of the parade was 'Mother' Mary Jones, the noted coal strike leader who was the orator of the day. She rode in an auto with six children and A. Hutcheson, secretary of the joint committee . . . and was cheered early and often along the line."*

Both papers agreed that the parade was a huge demonstration, with the Post-Intelligencer *reporting that "more persons marched yesterday than at any of the previous Labor Day demonstrations in Seattle."[4] The procession was featured by its simplicity, and no banners or signs which did not relate to the occasion were permitted, "it being the aim of the committee to make the affair strictly a memorial observance."[5] Three flower-decorated floats were in the procession, one dedicated to the memory of "The Children of Calumet," the second to the memory of "The Women and Children of Ludlow," and the third to "The Heroes of Labor Who Have Lost Their Lives in Industrial Battles."[6]*

Before she was introduced to deliver the main address, a poem in honor of Mother Jones was read by Edward Bance Cooke. The poem had already appeared in the Seattle Union Record, *official organ of the Central Labor Council which (together with the local Socialist Party) sponsored Labor's Memorial Day. The poem went:*

Mother Jones, at eighty-two,
I toss my hat for you,
    Mother Jones.

Your old body holds the spirit
Of the freedom we inherit.
Was our Declaration signed
To be spat on and maligned
By some epauletted hind?
Is our Constitution void
When a corporate power's annoyed?
Is our history a lie
To forget, or to deny?
Mother Jones, at eighty-two,
We forget it — but not YOU,
  Mother Jones.

Mother Jones, at eighty-two,
What they tell me may be true,
  Mother Jones.
For your manners may be crude
And your tongue at times imbued
With a twang the world calls rude.
Mother Jones, at eighty-two,
Are they never rude — to you,
  Mother Jones?

Mother Jones, at eighty-two,
I would rather fare with you,
  Mother Jones.
Fare with you, succeed or fail,
Win the fight, or win the jail,
Than with officers, gold-laced,
Than with judges, snugly placed,
History will yet acclaim
Yours the honor, their the shame.
Theirs? Nay, ours!
We free men pause,
We desert the holy cause
Of the LAW against the laws;
Leaving all the fight to you.
Heroine — at eighty-two!
  Mother Jones![7]

The following account of Mother Jones's speeches at Labor's First Memorial Day is based on reports in the Seattle Post-Intelligencer, *the Seattle* Daily Times, *and the Seattle* Union Record.

"During the Civil War the emancipation of the slaves in the South was brought in as one of the leading measures. Today there is another war on — a great war with a bunch of high-class burglars and looters, and the measure of this conflict is the emancipation of the mine workers and the nationalization of the mines. Why should we permit a bunch of burglars to own the mines? Nature did not put that mineral in the bottom of the earth for them. It was put there for the use of all the people."

Mother Jones then painted a vividly pathetic picture of the firing on the tent colony at Ludlow, where the charred bodies of several children, women and men were discovered after the smoke had died away.

"This happened right here in America," emphasized the aged labor leader, "not in Russia or in Mexico, but right here under the American flag.

"The peculiar thing about it all is that the public in general has not been aroused to a very noticeable extent. It seems that the public has to be struck by a cyclone before it will come to the realization of the actual state of affairs.

"While I was down in Washington not very long ago, a Congressman asked me if I told the mine workers to buy guns. I replied that I certainly had told my boys to arm themselves and to do it in a hurry. And I am still appealing to mine workers and other workers all over the United States to arm themselves and be prepared to protect their families and their property. I would not be a fit woman to live in America if I did not tell my boys to be men and not cowards."

"Get together, is my message to labor. The worker who has a label on him is not true to the working class. I was a member of the old Knights of Labor, and went into the American Federation of Labor when the Knights disbanded, and I will live and die in the Federation, for it represents 2,500,000 workers.[8]

"I have been a Socialist for more than twenty-nine years, but I am not one of those who believe that individual freedom is going to drop down from the clouds — while we sleep. The fight can be won, and will be won, but the struggle will be long and education, agitation and class solidarity all must play a part in it. I have no patience with those idealists and visionaries who preach fine spun theories and cry down everybody but themselves.[9] Let us keep our feet on the ground."

[Seattle Post-Intelligencer, *May 31, June 1, 1914; Seattle* Daily Times, *May 31, June 1, 1914; Seattle* Union Record, *June 6, 1914.]*

Notes

1. Alvin R. Sunseri, "The Ludlow Massacre: A Study in the Mis-employment of the National Guard," *American Chronicle*, January, 1972, pp. 23-28; Monica Eklund, "The Massacre at Ludlow," *Southeast Economy and Society* 4 (Fall, 1978): 26-32; Foner, *op. cit.*, vol. 5, pp. 204-07; George P. McGovern, "The Colorado Strike, 1913-1914," unpublished Ph.D. thesis, University of Illinois, 1953, p. 282.

2. *New York Times*, April 21, 1913; Denver *Express*, April 22, 1914.

3. Seattle *Post-Intelligencer*, May 31, 1914. This is part of an interview with Mother Jones which appears below, p. 512. Unfortunately, the Labor Memorial Day idea was not picked up by labor organizations in other cities. Nor was

it continued even in Seattle.

4. Seattle *Post-Intelligencer*, May 31, 1914. Later, Mother Jones told a reporter for the Vancouver *Daily Province* of British Columbia that "Between 6000 and 8000 labor unionists" marched in the parade, and 20,000 attended the mass meeting afterwards. (June 11, 1914.)

5. Seattle *Post Intelligencer,* May 31, 1914.

6. According to the account in the Seattle *Daily Times*, the third float was dedicated to "All the Heroes of Organized Labor." (May 31, 1914.) The float dedicated to "The Children of Calumet" was honoring the memory of the sixty-two children who died during the fire alarm at the Italian Hall in Red Jacket, Michigan. This occurred in the midst of the Christmas party, 1913, given for the children of the striking copper miners, members of the Western Federation of Miners. Eleven adults also died. There actually was no fire, but it was never determined who it was that cried out the alarm or why he had done so. (*See* Philip S. Foner, *History of the Labor Movement in the United States*, New York, 1980, vol. 5, pp. 220-22.)

According to the Seattle *Union Record* of May 16, 1914, the purpose of the affair was to serve as a "memorial services . . . in commemoration of the martyrs who recently met death at the hands of murderous militia and gunmen in the Colorado strike zone." Evidently the event was broadened to include the other labor martyrs as well.

7. Seattle *Union Record*, May 23, 1914.

8. A.F. of L. membership had dropped to 1,482,872 in 1909 from 1,586,885 the previous year, but beginning with 1910 it resumed its upward advance, reaching 1,761,835 in 1911 and over two million in 1914. (Leo Wolman, *Ebb and Flow in Trade Unionism*, New York, 1936, p. 16.) Although she did not say so specifically, the audience understood that Mother Jones was comparing the A.F. of L. membership with that of the I.W.W. which was only 11,365 in 1914. (Foner, *History of the Labor Movement* vol. 4, p. 462.)

9. This was another oblique attack on the I.W.W.

Not an Industrial War, But a Civil War

Speech at Labor Temple, Vancouver, British Columbia,
Canada, June 10, 1914

On June 3, 1914, Mother Jones spoke in Everett, Washington,[1] at the People's Theatre. (Rain cancelled plans of the trade unions to hold a parade in her honor and to have the meeting held in the open air in the City Park.) The Everett Herald *reported the theater proved "all too small to accommodate the hundreds who wanted to see and hear the well-known woman."[2] Most of her speech dealt with her recent experi-*

ences in the Colorado coal strike. "Her voice seldom rose above a calm pitch, though occasionally when the scenes she described were of unusual order, the old lady's tones rang shrilly through the theater as she told of the deeds of 'armed murderers,' as she termed the militias," commented the reporter for the Herald.[3] In the course of her speech, Mother Jones referred to Rockefeller's office on Broadway in New York City as the "seat of government, the real working head of the nation which some people supposed to be located in Washington, D.C."[4] She then noted:

The Rockefellers and others of the plutocrats were the men really responsible for the horrors of West Virginia, Calumet and Colorado, while the government and soldiers who enforce their laws are more to be pitied than blamed. No gunman or soldier ever lived who had not had a mother, and the mothers of the future must do a better job of educating their boys so they do not grow up to be soldiers or company gunmen.

Not all of the militia in Colorado or in other states where I have fought were inhuman. In fact, I met some real nice boys among them, and they told me that they saw how they had been misled. But the gunmen are the hounds of the system.[5]

Returning to Seattle, Mother Jones made preparations to leave for Victoria, British Columbia, Nanaimo, and other areas in Vancouver Island where she was to speak on behalf of United Mine Workers members engaged in a bitter strike.

On August 12, 1913, coal miners at Nanaimo in British Columbia, Canada, members of the United Mine Workers, went out on strike. Instantly the militia was sent to the Nanaimo district, and soon a large number of the miners were arrested and imprisoned. The Miners' Liberation League proposed the calling of a general strike to force the release of the imprisoned miners, and when the British Columbia Federation of Labor referred the proposal for a general strike to its members, they approved it by a five-to-two margin. However, nothing was done to implement the resolution. On March 23, 1914, Justice Morrison at New Westminster handed down sentences upon a long list of miners held in prison. While many were allowed out on suspended sentences, a number of the most militant strikers were sentenced to six months to four years in prison.[6]

Just as Mother Jones was about to board the Canadian Pacific steamer Princess Charlotte at Seattle for the trip to Victoria, she was stopped at the gangplank by Canadian immigration officers and forbidden to enter Canada. She was told that instructions had been received from the chief of the provincial police of British Columbia to keep her out on the ground that she "would be a disturbing element."[7]

Mother Jones remained in Seattle while Frank Farrington, western representative of the United Mine Workers, wired William B. Wilson, Secretary of Labor, in Washington asking that his department insist that Mother Jones "be accorded every right she is entitled to as an

American citizen."[8]

However, Mother Jones did not let others speak for her on this latest deprivation of her rights. "I am past 80 years and have never been charged with a crime," she told Seattle reporters, "and so I cannot understand why I am prevented from entering a friendly nation. I never quarrel and I believe in law and order, and I do not blame the man who stopped me, for he had his order from higher up. It is merely carrying out a policy that means 'You shall not educate my slaves,' but it is a mistaken view and is bound to fall finally. I had been invited to go to British Columbia and did not know that I was committing any wrong in accepting the invitation of the mine workers there." She would wait another day, and if no word came from Washington, she would leave for the nation's capital "where I will carry on my own fight to find out why I am barred from Canada, and I will find out, even if I have to go before the senate."[9]

The trip was not necessary. Mother Jones left instead for Victoria on June 5, and was delayed at the immigration entrance while Robert Foster, secretary of the United Mine Workers at Nanaimo, telephoned provincial authorities for her clearance. In twenty-five minutes word came that Mother Jones was to be allowed to enter Canada. "It don't pay to fight a woman," Mother Jones told a reporter for the Victoria Daily Times.

The news that Mother Jones had been allowed to enter Canada was featured on the front page of every paper in British Columbia. The Daily Province of Vancouver also commented editorially that it was "a victory for free speech," and pointed out that before such tactics could be "in any measure successful," the Canadian authorities

would have to prevent the publication of papers and magazines, severely censor the means of communication, deny the right of public meeting or private assembly and generally put back the clock of civilization. That such a state of affairs is not a freak of imagination that nowhere existed as a possibility, South Africa, Colorado and a number of other places much nearer home bear witness.[11]

After breakfast at the Dominion Hotel in Victoria, where she was met by A. Watchman and A. S. Wells, president and secretary respectively of the B.C. Federation of Labor, and George Pettigrew of Ladysmith, she left for Ladysmith where she spoke to the striking miners and sympathizers. That same night she spoke to the striking miners at Nanaimo, and several days later addressed "a large and mixed audience" in the Vancouver Labor Temple under the auspices of the British Columbia Federation of Labor and the Vancouver Trades and Labor Council. She then returned to Victoria en route to the United States, and delivered her farewell address in British Columbia at the First Baptist building.[12]

In her speech at Victoria, Jones began by declaring that Oliver Goldsmith must have had the western continent in mind when he wrote,

"Ill fares the land."

> For at no time had so much wealth been produced by the workers and at no
> time had it been taken from them so boldly or rapaciously as at present. The real
> question of the hour is the ownership by the people of the tools of production.

The local reporter added that *"it was to be inferred from her address
that she would accomplish this, if control of legislatures by the workers
cannot be obtained, by guns and bayonets and a general strike."*[13]

Mother Jones's speech in Victoria was the most important address
she delivered during her stay in British Columbia. It was covered by all
of the local papers and even by some in other cities. The Vancouver
Daily Province *reported:*

> The large hall which has a seating capacity of about 600, was packed to the
> doors, scores of auditors finding places on the platform and others standing
> along the sides of the room. Practically every class of society was represented,
> drawn by the fame of the woman Demosthenes of the American labor movement.
> Fully half of the audience were women.[14]

The Canadian Annual Review *for 1914, a government publication,
described Mother Jones as "a female anarchistic orator from the
States," and merely reported that in her Vancouver speech, "she denounced religion and clergymen and dealt with the Militia in such
terms as this: 'If the capitalists rob us to buy guns for their hired assassins we will have to buy guns ourselves.'"*[15] *However, as the following
account of the speech, drawn from reports in the Vancouver* Daily Province *and the* BC Federationist, *official organ of the British Columbia
labor movement, makes clear, there was much more to the address.*

Mr. W. E. Walker, president of the Trades and Labor Council, presided, and Mr. George Pettigrew, international organizer of the United
Mine Workers, introduced "Mother" Jones in a brief address in which
he said that she had addressed six very successful meetings on Vancouver Island.

Her address sparkled both with humor and pathos. "The authorities
in Colorado gave me a trial by jury because I demanded it," she said.
"The boys too were brought from the bastile to stand trial. There were
lawyers from Charlestown but not one of them was required because a
drumhead jury had been selected, but the strikers made it perfectly
hot for them. The trial was a lesson of human brutality. My boys were
taken to prison, and the women and children cried and screamed to see
them." She telephoned[16] to Senator Kearns at Washington. "I send
you a message of the groans and tears of the women and children. Will
you relieve them?" Under the lounge in her prison cell were a couple
of beer bottles. She put the message in one of them. A messenger carried the bottles down the river for three miles, and so the message was

telegraphed. The authorities are at sea yet as to how the message got to Washington in spite of the gunmen and detectives. Judge Gough practically has been dead forty years so far as having any knowledge of human affairs is concerned. As soon as agitators appear they are branded as dangerous to the welfare of the community. There was peace in Palestine until Jesus arrived. There was peace in Egypt until Moses became a disturber. Just because "Old Mother Jones" became a disturber in the mining camps the great military organization became active. When she went into Virginia, the governor of that state, who was a progressive and belonged to the Bull Moose party,[17] used his power to crush the miners who had been robbed and plundered for twenty years. Ten years previous men were brought from Greece and Italy, and were placed in a state of peonage and became virtual slaves of the mine owners. Even the merchants and others became moral cowards under the iron hands of their masters.

She received fifty or one hundred letters from her boys — the miners — when a convention was called and the most horrible tales were told of sorrows and hardships suffered by the miners, who organized and gave the owners ten days to sign a new scale. The miners got tents and put all their belongings into them. Then they procured 28 wagons and all left the state. The men and women walked, the children being carried. "Good God, Mother, we're so glad to get away," they said. Everything they had on earth they took along with them. The gunmen, with their machine guns were prepared to slaughter them on the spot. A man in overalls told Mother Jones that the authorities were going to murder the men in Trinidad. She went out there and got trenches dug to put the women and children in. The sheriff notified the governor that they did not want any gunmen. But they came, and at Forbes a man, with his arms folded, was shot down in cold blood, likewise a little boy. The government was too busy in caucus to take notice of such doings. Three gunmen tried to break through the lines. "Yes, strikes are dangerous, but they are good things to settle these disturbances," said the speaker. She went to El Paso and spent an hour or two with General Villa in order to break up the strike.[18] A meeting was held and no Mexicans went to Trinidad. She was there three hours before being discovered and was kept in prison nine weeks. "Won't you go to Denver?" she was asked by the officer of the law. She said No. Habeas corpus proceedings were instituted and she became free. Again she was arrested and kept in a cell for 25 days where sewer rats abounded in plenty. She described in vivid terms the awful happenings at Ludlow. "The nation was aroused, but it must pay the bill. These people who died there did not die in vain. The fight will go on and on until the people will be free. This is in the civilized state of Colorado. There is no state on the continent more corrupt politically."[19]

Mrs. Jones referred in sarcastic terms to the instructions that were at first issued to exclude her from Canada as a dangerous character.

"Do I look very dangerous?" she queried. "An 82-year-old woman dangerous!" she scornfully added. "However, I am glad that they consider me in that light for it shows that my efforts have not been in vain."

Tracing the rise and fall of the nations since the remote ages, the speaker declared that during the past eighty years more wealth had been created than in centuries of ancient civilizations. With this great progression in industrial life a new class had arisen — "wage slaves." She predicted a great political upheaval. During the past eighteen months conflicts had occurred that had shaken the entire fabric of the American nation, and the Senate of the United States had had to take official cognizance of the serious troubles that had arisen through calling out the military to quell strikes. She paraphrased Jefferson's famous quotation: "Eternal vigilance is the price of liberty," to emphasize her point.

"Mother" Jones indulged in frequent gibes at the expense of Christianity and the ministers and others engaged in religious teachings.

"If the capitalists rob us to buy guns for their hired assassins," she remarked in the course of one of her bitter tirades against the military system, "we will have to buy guns ourselves!"

While describing the incidents of one of the strikes in West Virginia, she said that on one occasion she had advised "her boys" to spend their money on the purchase of firearms instead of at the bar.

The "wage slavery" question was going to be decided early in the present century, she declared. "It is the women who are responsible for the 'murders' committed by the militia," she argued. "When our women wake up and quit being sentimental parasites, we shall begin to accomplish things. It is in the home where the child is nursed, where character is formed, and where everything depends upon the early training, that the true work of reform can be done. I say shame upon the women for their apathy, their indifference and for allowing the wives and children of men striking for their rights to be roasted alive as they have been during recent strikes in Colorado.

"That was not an industrial war," she said referring to the Colorado conflicts. "It was a civil war. For the first time in the history of trades unionism in America the various organizations, among them some of the most conservative branches of industry, talked of buying arms and donated sums for that purpose.[20] But it is not guns that we need in the fight — but brains. We will use the pen, not the sword; the head, not the arm. We will put men in the Legislature who will protect our rights as citizens."

Among the many incidents regarding the military she related that on one occasion she walked up to the muzzles of a machine gun which had been trained upon herself and some of "her boys" and dared the man in charge to fire it.

She touched but lightly upon the Nanaimo situation, merely stating that similar tactics to those adopted in the States had been employed to cope with the strike on Vancouver Island, and expressing sympathy with the men involved. She urged the cooperation of all members of unions and spoke of the powerful weapon within the grasp of organized labor by calling a general strike of all trades.[21]

"You have to fight the same battle in British Columbia," she said. "Clasp hands, help the striking miners, join forces, read, study and think."

The millionaires, individually and collectively, were scored mercilessly. Mrs. Jones told of the method adopted to enforce labor's demands in South Africa. She said that when the representatives of one of the unions wished to have an agreement signed not long ago they covered the "boss" with their revolvers after he had first refused to accede to their demand, and then made him publicly announce that he had agreed to their terms.

[British Columbia Federationist, *Vancouver, June 12, 1914;*
Vancouver Daily Province, *June 11, 1914.]*

Notes

1. Two years later, Everett, a lumber-company-dominated city, was the scene of the bitter I.W.W. free speech fight culminating in the Everett Massacre. (*See* Foner, *op. cit.,* vol. 4, pp. 518-48, and Philip S. Foner, *"Fellow Workers and Friends": IWW Free Speech Fights As Told by Participants,* Westport, Conn., 1981, pp. 224-38.

2. Everett *Daily Herald,* June 5, 1914.

3. *Ibid.*

4. *Ibid.*

5. *Ibid.*

6. *The Labour Gazette,* Ottawa, July 1914, pp. 44-45; Carlos A. A. Schwantes, *Radical Heritage: Labor, Socialism, in Washington and British Columbia, 1885-1917,* Vancouver, 1979, pp. 203-04.

7. Seattle *Daily Times,* June 6, 1914.

8. Seattle *Post-Intelligencer,* June 6, 1914.

9. Seattle *Daily Times,* June 6, 1914; Seattle *Post-Intelligencer,* June 6, 1914.

10. Victoria *Daily Times,* June 6, 1914.

11. Vancouver *Daily Province,* June 11, 1914.

12. *Ibid.,* June 10, 11, 1914.

13. Victoria *Daily Times,* June 11, 1914.

14. Vancouver *Daily Province,* June 11, 1914.

15. *The Canadian Annual Review of Public Affairs,* 1914, p. 689.

16. The word should have been "telegraphed."

17. The reference is to Governor William E. Glasscock of West Virginia (not Virginia) who was associated with the Progressive Party. The popular name for the party, "Bull Moose," was derived from Theodore Roosevelt's response to queries about his health, at the time he arrived in Chicago to receive the

party's nomination for president in 1912: "I feel as good as a Bull Moose."

18. The point Mother Jones was making was that she met with Pancho Villa to obtain his help in preventing Mexicans from being used as strikebreakers against the striking miners in Colorado.

19. Here the account of the speech in the *British Columbia Federationist* ends, and the rest appeared in the Victoria *Daily Provincial*. It is interesting that both accounts do not at all overlap, and the one in the *Federationist* omits any reference to the church or to workers arming themselves. The headlines in the report of the speech in the *Federationist* reads: "The 'Mother' Jones At The Labor Temple. Venerable Lady Receives An Ovation from the Audience. In a Graphic Address She Told the Story of the Miners." The headlines in the *Daily Provincial* read: "Labor Temple Was Jammed to Hear Mother Jones. Addresses All Classes of Society for Over Two Hours. Some Applaud, Some Gasp at Her Criticism of Present Day Conditions. Tells Why She is Still "Fighting" in Her Eighty-third Year. Briefly Refers to Vancouver Island Strike — Uphold the Miners."

I am indebted to Fred Longley, Assistant Librarian, Department of Labour, Ottawa, Canada, for furnishing me with a copy of the *British Columbia Federationist* containing the account of Mother Jones' speech, as well as some of the other material related to her visit to Canada in 1914. I am also indebted to the staff of the University of Victoria library for their cooperation in enabling me to use copies of the Victoria and Vancouver papers in the library.

20. For evidence that Mother Jones's analysis is correct, *see* Foner, *op. cit.*, vol. 5, pp. 207-08.

21. The strike of the coal miners ended without recognition, but with acknowledgment of the workers' right to belong to a union. Unfortunately, the employers soon reneged on the agreement, and "blacklisting and discrimination were the net result of the two-year struggle for many workers. In the minds of many workers, however, the idea of a general strike had only been tabled for the duration of the war, and not abandoed." (Schwantes, *op. cit.*, p. 204.)

A Plea for a Strike Settlement

Speech at United Mine Workers of America convention, Trinidad, Colorado September 15, 1914

Early in September 1914, President Woodrow Wilson, who had previously sent federal troops to the strike area, submitted to both sides proposals to end the strike which called for the operators and miners to pledge themselves to a three-year truce based on six conditions which included: (1) the mine labor laws of the state be strictly enforced; (2) the restoration of work to all striking miners who had not been found guilty of violating the law; (3) prohibition of intimidation of either union or nonunion workers; (4) abolition of the mine guards; (5) prohibition of picketing and parading; and (5) no suspension of work pending the investigation of any matter in dispute.[1]

On September 15, 1914, 125 delegates met a Leadville, Colorado to consider Wilson's three-year "truce" plan for industrial peace in Colorado. Mother Jones urged acceptance of the plan in a speech to the delegates.

One year ago today I told you boys it was necessary to strike to obtain your rights under Colorado laws and free yourselves from industrial oppression. None could have fought the battle for liberty more bravely.

Industrial oppression must die. The time has come when to accomplish those results, the sword must disappear. The pen must take its place. We must read, study, think. We are the bulwark of the nation. We have it within our power to rid this country of industrial tyranny, but we must be calm and deliberate to do so.

We have in Washington today another Lincoln. He does not rush into things haphazardly. He has submitted you this proposition for a truce after long and calm deliberation. We must consider it in the same manner it was prepared, not with any great rush, but carefully weighing every point and every interpretation.

The president of the United States, when he found you could not settle your difficulties, sent the federal troops here to defend you, and now if you don't accept this proposition what more can he do? John D. Rockefeller owns the resources of a nation, but one man arises against the power and says to the miners of Colorado, "I will be with you if you are fair."

[Denver Express, September 16, 1914.]

Notes

1. Billie Barnes Jensen, "Woodrow Wilson's Intervention in the Coal Strike of 1914," *Labor History* 15 (Winter, 1974): 62-77; Foner, *op. cit.,* vol. 5, pp. 210-11.

An Appeal for the Striking Miners

Speech at convention of American Federation of Labor, Philadelphia,
November 13, 1914

*Following Mother Jones's appeal for support of President Wilson's
strike settlement plan, the UMW delegates at Trinidad voted to endorse
the proposals. However, the operators accepted only three of the proposals, rejecting two out of hand (2 and 3), and accepting the remaining
one only if modified. The result was that the strike continued.*

*In October 1914, Mother Jones had an audience with President Wil-
son who knew that she had endorsed his strike settlement proposals and
had urged the miners to accept them.[1] Mother Jones explained to the
chief executive that the state officials in Colorado were unable to deal
with the situation there. She urged Wilson to close the mines if the
operators still refused to accept the settlement he had proposed. After
Wilson replied that he was doubtful of his authority to close the mines,
thereby causing the* New York Times *to remind him editorially that
Theodore Roosevelt had no doubt on that score in 1902,[2] Mother Jones
left the White House, and soon was in Philadelphia where the American
Federation of Labor was meeting in convention. She urged the delegates
"in an extended speech" in November to use their influence to get Wilson
to speed up a resolution of the Colorado conflict. In the same speech, she
pleaded for immediate assistance to the hard-pressed miners in both
Colorado and Michigan, noting that it made no difference whether they
were members of the United Mine Workers or the Western Federation of
Miners. Indeed, she deplored internal union strife, jurisdictional disputes, and dissension in the ranks of organized labor, and in a none too
veiled thrust at the I.W.W., condemned dual unionism and urged "all
the organizations to remain loyal to the American Federation of
Labor. . . . "*

*Unfortunately, Mother Jones's "extended speech" does not appear in
full in the official proceedings of the convention. Only a summary was
published which appears below. This is followed by the only account of
the speech in the contemporary press, which was published in the*
Philadelphia Press *the next day. The indictment of John D. Rockefeller,
Jr. in connection with the Ludlow massacre and for his refusal to accept
President Wilson's strike settlement proposal, as quoted in the* Press,
*may have so alarmed the A.F. of L. leaders that they decided to sum-
marize Mother Jones's speech rather than quote her exact words. Fortunately, in the process, they eliminated a foolish statement by Mother
Jones indicting women as being responsible for any "brutal act committed by a man. . . . "*

Vice-President Duncan:[3] Anticipating that you are agreeable, I
have just instructed Delegate Hayes, of the Mine Workers, to escort

Mother Jones to the platform, as I see she is in the hall.

President Gompers in the chair.

Mother Jones was escorted to the platform by Delegate Hayes, vice-president of the United Mine Workers. President Gompers[4] introduced Mother Jones to the convention.

In an extended speech Mother Jones referred to strikes in various parts of the country that had been conducted by the United Mine Workers and the Western Federation of Miners in the past two years. She described in detail the conditions that had existed in West Virginia prior to the strike, the benefit that had come to the miners through that strike and the subsequent investigation by the government.

Mother Jones spoke at length of the strike in Colorado, of the conditions under which the miners lived and worked, of the brutality of state militia and mine guards after the calling of the strike, the murder of striking miners and the shooting and burning of women and children in the camps.[5] She spoke in bitter condemnation of the action of the Rockefeller interests in their treatment of organized labor and their defiance of law and government.

Mother Jones made an eloquent plea for harmony and cooperation on the part of the workers. She deplored internal strife, jurisdiction disputes, and secession in the ranks of the organizations. She urged all the organizations to remain loyal to the American Federation of Labor, and regretted that dual organizations had sprung up in any part of the country.[6]

In closing Mother Jones urged that the convention assist the Western Federation of Miners financially to help defend men who were in prison in Calumet, Mich., awaiting trial on conspiracy charges,[7] and stated that there were other men belonging to the coal miners' organization in Colorado who were in need of similar help. She asked that the convention take action urging President Wilson to hasten the work of mediation in the Colorado strike.

President Gompers, for himself and in behalf of the convention, thanked Mother Jones for her address and for her presence in the convention.

[Proceedings, *AFL Convention, 1914, p. 310*]

Mother Jones' Speech

Horticultural Hall yesterday was the scene of the most remarkable demonstration of a convention which has been replete with demonstrations. "Mother" Jones, "the angel of the miners," who has been the storm center of every strike into which her "boys" have been precipitated for the last two decades made a blood and thunder speech that moved the delegates to tears and inspired an almost continuous acclamation.

Eighty-three years old, this small white-haired woman with a bit of a brogue, threw a power, an eloquence and a stirring appeal into her speech unequaled by any of the men who have addressed the convention.

She came unannounced from the coal fields of Colorado. When Gompers said she was in the rear of the hall, everyone turned and as "Mother" came up the center aisle on the arm of Frank Hayes, vice-president of the United Mine Workers of America, each row of delegates she passed stood upon its feet until the entire convention was standing and as she reached the platform a thunder of applause broke.

She reviewed the history of the Colorado, West Virginia, and Michigan strikes and "the burning of the children and women at Ludlow." She said: "I could mediate in five days, the investigation has already taken a committee seven months.[8]

"I would tell Rockefeller that he had insulted every citizen in the United States by his treatment of the president's proposal to settle the Colorado strike. I would give him five days to settle and then the United States flag would fly over the mines and the people would own them.

"I would say to Rockefeller," she screamed, "If you are president of the United States we are ready to make war with you. Come on. If I could send the screams of the burning children to Washington and let the president hear them I wonder if that would make him move.

"Are you building palaces on the quivering heap of their bodies? Don't you hear the voices of the children crying who were shot in the trenches by the uniformed murderers and then the oil of John Rockefeller thrown over them to burn them to a crisp?"

Demand Aid

"Mother" Jones demanded aid for the men who were indicted in connection with the strike in Michigan and in Colorado.

"Those men in jail," she said, "are the foremost fighters of labor. We cannot permit the Shaws, of Boston, to put our men behind the bars. We will win in Colorado and when I have cleaned the State up I am going out to organize the steel workers.

"I have heard that women are taking a part in the affairs of the nation. What did they do about this? I tell you there is no brutal act committed by a man, but there is a woman more or less responsible for it. If women would put in more time planting the human spirit in the breasts of the young we should not have so many savages as we have today."

The speaker said that when she refused to leave Colorado on the order of General Chase, she was thrown into a cellar and spent twenty-six days and nights fighting rats with a beer bottle that had nothing in it.

She charged that Rockefeller had an army of gunmen who were shipped from one part of the country to another as the necessity arose.

Mother Jones told of her interview with Villa. "I had a talk with him," she said. "He's a fine boy. I had $65 that some one gave me for a present and I offered it to him.

"Villa," I said to him, "I want you to come over into our country to kill off some of those people who have crucified women and children — you're needed."

"I'll come," Villa said, "as soon as I am through with these murderers and crucifiers here."

[Philadelphia Press, *November 14, 1914.*]

Notes

1. On September 19, 1914, Edward Keating had forwarded to President Wilson a clipping from the *Denver Express* containing the speech of Mother Jones to the delegates at Trinidad, Colorado, and urged the President to read "the remarks of 'Mother' Jones. . . . " (Arthur S. Link, editor, *The Papers of Woodrow Wilson,* Princeton, N.J., 1979, vol. XXXI (Sept. 6-Dec. 31, 1914), p. 557.

2. In its editorial, the *New York Times* commented: "Once there was a president who said that he was prepared to settle a coal strike by taking the mines and operating them by a major general. The army is not now commanded by that sort of president." (October 20, 1914.)

3. James Duncan, international secretary and treasurer of the Granite Cutters' Association, was an AFL vice-president and member of the Executive Council.

4. Samuel Gompers (1850-1924), a founder and long-time president of the American Federation of Labor; headed the AFL from 1886 to 1924 with the exception of one year, 1895, and was also editor of the *American Federationist,* its official journal.

5. The most widely publicized of these attacks was, of course, the "Ludlow massacre" in April 1914.

6. In an attack on dual unionism, William Z. Foster, with whom Mother Jones was to work closely in the steel strike of 1919, had left the I.W.W. and organized the Syndicalist League of North America to mobilize the militants to fight inside the American Federation of Labor for a progressive trade union policy.

7. Over 600 strikers, members of the Western Federation of Miners, were arrested during the 1913 copper strike against the Calumet & Hecla company in Michigan. One of those arrested and imprisoned for assaulting scabs, and found guilty of assault and battery, was Annie Clemenc, a militant wife of a Croatian copper miner. (*See* Foner, *History of the Labor Movement in the United States,* vol. 5, pp. 215-18.)

8. There were two investigations of the strike in Colorado. One was U.S. Congress, House, Subcommittee of the Committee on Mines and Mining, *Con-*

ditions in the *Coal Mines of Colorado*, 2 vols., 63rd Congress, 2nd Session, 1914. The other was U.S. Commission on Industrial Relations, *Final Report and Testimony,* vol. 11, Senate Doc. 415, 64th Congress, 1st Session, 1916. For Mother Jones's testimony at both of these investigations, *see* pp. 375-447.

You Can't Fool My Boys, Mr. Rockefeller

Speech at Cooper Union, New York City, January 28, 1915

At the conclusion of a meeting protesting the Ludlow massacre in Carnegie Hall, New York City, Upton Sinclair organized a demonstration in front of the Rockefeller office at 26 Broadway. Wearing bands of black crepe to symbolize the deaths of the Ludlow victims, he and four women began to walk silently back and forth in front of the Rockefeller headquarters. When the group was arrested and jailed for this "disturbance," Mrs. Sinclair and others continued the "mourning picket line."[1]

Nine months later, Mother Jones was also at 26 Broadway, but she was there at Rockefeller's invitation. On January 26, 1915, John D. Rockefeller, Jr. testified for the second day before the U.S. Commission on Industrial Relations.[2] Mother Jones was among the crowd of spectators in the New York City Council chambers to hear his testimony. When he saw her in the audience, Rockefeller came over to her. "I wish you would come to my office and tell me what you know of the Colorado situation," he said. "Well, that's nice of you," replied Mother Jones. "I've always said you could never know what those hirelings out there were doing. I liked the way you testified yesterday, and I can see how easy it is to misjudge you."[3]

The previous day Rockefeller had testified that he had not visited Colorado for ten years, and had relied completely for information about the labor situation on the word of the officials of the Colorado Fuel & Iron Company. He was not opposed to trade unionism, Rockefeller added, but only to violent disputes. He was for free speech, against corporate control of elections, and some other practices of the company he owned in Colorado. He refused, however, either to support or condemn that company's labor measures on the ground that his knowledge of the firm was sketchy.

Mother Jones, taken in by his testimony, was only too willing to educate the multi-millionaire. "When I have a good motherly talk with him I believe I can help him take another view of the situation among the miners out West," she told a crowd of astonished and skeptical repor-

ters.[4]

The talk came the next day, January 27, 1915, at 26 Broadway, after which Mother Jones again voiced enthusiasm for Rockefeller. "I misjudged the young man sadly," she declared. "I called him a high-class burglar. I told him so this afternoon. I said, 'Mr. Rockefeller, my name for you has been 'the high-class burglar.' He laughed and I must say he took it good-naturedly. But I know him better now, and after talking with me he knows more about his father's mines in Colorado, too." She continued:

I said: "Mr. Rockefeller, the people in those mining camps should have the right to trade at any store they want to patronize. They have the right to schools run by the state. The company should pay them in cash, not scrip and leave them free to spend it where they like.

"I think you are right," Rockefeller told me.[5]

But Mother Jones soon woke up to the facts of life which she, perhaps more than anyone else, should have known. For one thing, Upton Sinclair wired her: "We are sure you will not let yourself be overcome by the sweet odor of the American beauty rose." More important, when Rockefeller was questioned at the hearings of the Commission on Industrial Relations by its chairman, Frank P. Walsh, Rockefeller's facade of upholding democratic principles and of being so far removed from the events in Colorado, began to crumble. Having examined the correspondence between the coal company officials and the Rockefeller office in New York, Walsh introduced concrete evidence that Rockefeller had fully supported the refusal of the company to negotiate with the union. It was clear from the correspondence that both the company in Colorado and Rockefeller insisted upon the unconditional surrender of the United Mine Workers. Furthermore, when asked by Walsh if he should not inquire as to the responsibility of company officials for the Ludlow tragedy, Rockefeller replied: "Well, I think so long as I am undertaking to do things that I think should be done I shall have to reserve the right to do them in the ways that seem to me best." Asked by Walsh if he did not feel moral responsibility for the violence, in view of the fact that the militia in the Ludlow killings were paid from company funds, Rockefeller answered: "I should have felt greater responsibility for the officers of the company if they had not used all means in their power to protect life and property."[6] Unable to restrain his anger at this indifference to the inhuman slaughter at Ludlow, Walsh burst out: "You close your eyes to the crime at Ludlow and the evidence at the inquest. You sit back in your office in New York and say 'I uphold the executives.'"[7]

A further blow to Mother Jones's faith, without however totally destroying it, came when the monopoly capitalist unveiled the Rockefeller Employee Representation Plan, worked out by McKenzie King, later premier of Canada. The plan, modeled on the company union set up in

1911 on the Philadelphia transit lines, provided that the men at each mine should elect at least two representatives to serve for a period of one year. These men were to meet annually with an equal number of company officials, and at these sessions, they were given the right to discuss grievances or other matters of interest, without, of course, the right to do anything about them if they were not redressed.[8]

"A sham and a fraud," Mother Jones told a New York City audience in blasting the Rockefeller plan. "You can't fool my boys," she added, "they know that this kind of scheme is a hypocritical and dishonest practice." When it came to company unions, not even Rockefeller could fool Mother Jones.[9]

Mother Jones's speech (or excerpts from it) was widely published, and the Socialist New York Call *which printed it in full, commented enthusiastically that Mother Jones had "blasted the high-priced Rockefeller whitewash plan and put the oil king's picture back in its proper frame."*

On Wednesday Mother Jones met and talked with Rockefeller. It is believed, with the belief backed by excellent evidence, that this meeting was planned and engineered from the Rockefeller end by Ivy Lee, Rockefeller's press agent, and that its purpose was to bring the young monarch out of the grill before the United States Commission on Industrial Relations with flying colors. Instead of coming through a hammered and cornered plutocrat, he was to come through as a bighearted friend of the common folks.

The capitalist press swallowed the story by the yard. Mother Jones was quoted by the column. So was Rockefeller. It was love to the finish, and the class struggle was all off. But Mother Jones doesn't let any one get away with things for very long. She read what had been printed. She read it again. She boiled and she wondered and she expostulated. . . . Mother Jones came back. At 85 she is a fighter every minute. She is never out of training. The capitalist class doesn't give her a chance to get out of training. And so last night she took all of the pretty polish off the neat little frameup.[10]

This, however, went too far. For Mother Jones never did lose her faith in Rockefeller, and given the Rockefeller penchant for hiring gunmen to indiscriminately shoot down workers who protested against inhuman conditions and sought to unionize to improve them — a practice the Rockefellers demonstrated in Bayonne, New Jersey in 1915-1916 as well as in Colorado[11] — it seems in retrospect to have been a curiously naive belief for a woman of Mother Jones's vast experience in the class struggle to hope that John D., Jr. would change by learning the true conditions in his Colorado mines.

Mr. Rockefeller is a very pleasant young man. He assured me that he is anxious to help the workers in their struggle for a chance to live as free men and women, and we are going to give him every chance in the world to show that he means it.

Good intentions are all right as paving blocks, but what we want is performance — and we want it now. I don't believe Mr. Rockefeller understands the needs and aspirations of the working people yet. If he did understand, and if he is sincere, he would realize that the new scheme for meeting his men in Colorado is a sham and a fraud.

He is letting the workers elect one representative at each mine, and these delegates meet with the company officials in Denver. They have no organization behind them. They are absolutely powerless to enforce any just demand. They have no treasury. The operators could put over anything they pleased, and if the men tried to resist by the only means in their power — a strike — they would be starved out in a week.

So far Mr. Rockefeller has given only lip service to democracy in industry. His new plan in Colorado masquerades as a basis for collective bargaining. It is the shadow, not the substance. You can't fool my boys. They know that this kind of a scheme is a hypocritical and dishonest practice. I don't believe Mr. Rockefeller understands this, because he says he believes in unions and collective bargaining and democracy in industry.

I urge Mr. Rockefeller to go out to Colorado as quickly possible to see things for himself and make alterations in a condition, which have kept the miners in as bad a position as if they were in Russia and not in America. I want him to go out to Colorado while the ashes of Ludlow are still hot. There is no use of him going out next summer or next fall. Now is the time, while people are thinking about it.

I am sure that Mr. Rockefeller will not be willing to take the credit for being a liberal and enlightened and humane man without making good on his promise. He can't eat his cake and have it, too. So far his company has not given up an atom of its arbitrary power. It is up to Mr. Rockefeller to prove that he is not trying to win favor with the public by putting out a few fine-sounding phrases.

The United Mine Workers is the only organization of coal miners in America. Mr. Rockefeller's employes will need its help if they are to enjoy the rights that he says they ought to have.

I am going to wait and see what happens. I like what Mr. Rockefeller says, and I hope he means it. It looks as though he had opened his eyes and that the great strike, with all its suffering, had not been in vain.

Mr. Rockefeller is a pleasant-spoken young man. He says he wants to help my boys in Colorado. This is what I want him to do. I want him to do now what he has always had a chance to do.

For ten years the C.F. & I. and the rest of them have starved and hammered down my boys out there. They have lived like dogs. The companies haven't only underpaid them, but they have taken away the little they got through company stores, and company saloons. My boys and their families have had no more rights in Colorado than animals. The company was against them; when they tried to help themselves they were blacklisted and beaten or shot down, and nobody back here in the East knew or cared. It was worse than what I read about Russia. That is what I want to stop. I want to have people know about it. I want to have young Mr. Rockefeller go out now and see for himself.

Nothing is settled out there. The strike's over and unionism was ground under the heel of tyranny, ground down in the mud.[12]

I believe in democracy. I want my boys to be good Americans. I am against violence. I hate bloodshed. In the strike they shot down in cold blood thirty of my boys and their wives and children. And what is the result? The murderers have been whitewashed and freed, and now the companies have had 200 of my boys indicted for murder. I want young Mr. Rockefeller to see this and understand it.[13]

I'm not going out to Colorado with him. Why, they'd mob us at every depot. They would think that I was bringing him with me for protection. I don't need any protection.

[New York Times, *January 29, 1915; New York* Call, *January 29, 1915; undated, unidentified newspaper clipping, Mother Harris Jones Papers, Department of Archives and Manuscripts, Catholic University of America, Washington, D.C.]*

Notes

1. *New York Times,* April 29, 30, 1914.

2. Rockefeller had previously testified before the House Mines and Mining Committee as had Mother Jones, who followed him to the witness stand, as she did before the Commission on Industrial Relations in May 1915. For her testimony before these committees, *see below* pp. 375-447.

3. *New York Times,* January 27, 1915.

4. Adams, *op. cit.,* pp. 162-64.

5. "Mother Jones and Mr. Rockefeller," *Outlook,* February 10, 1915, p. 302.

6. *New York Times,* January 29, 1915.

7. *Ibid.,* Jan. 26, 28, May 21, 26, 1915; *Report of Industrial Commission,* pp. 7763-89.

8. Foner, *op. cit.,* vol. 5, pp. 162-63.

9. *New Republic* 1 (November 17, 1914): 203; *The Survey,* October 6, 1917.

10. New York *Call,* January 29, 1915.

11. Several workers were brutally murdered by Rockefeller gunmen and the Bayonne police during the 1915-1916 strikes at the Standard Oil Company refinery in Bayonne, New Jersey.

12. A special convention of the UMW in Denver called the strike off on December 10, 1914. After fifteen months, the strike had been crushed by a combination of guns, bayonets, and hunger. At least sixty-two men, women, and children had been killed. Not one militiaman or mine guard had been indicted for murder. (Foner, *op. cit.,* vol. 5, pp. 210-11.)

13. Rockefeller did come to Colorado in 1915, but he did so only to inaugurate his company union plan. It was a plan, George P. West, who studied the Colorado strike for the U.S. Commission on Industrial Relations, concluded, that was devised not for the benefit of the workers, "but for the purpose of

ameliorating or removing the unfavorable criticism of Mr. Rockefeller which had arisen throughout the country following the rejection of President Wilson's plan of settlement." It offered the workers only the illusion of collective bargaining, and embodied "none of the principles of effectual collective bargaining and instead is a hypocritical pretense of granting what is in reality withheld." (63rd Cong., 3rd Sess., *House Document 136*, Washington, D.C., 1915, *Report on the Colorado Strike Investigation*, p. 35.)

Thank God, I Have Lived to be a Grandmother in Agitation!

Speech at convention of United Mine Workers of America,
Indianapolis, January 20, 1916

Although technically the Colorado strike was lost by the United Mine Workers, the union itself showed a new spirit of life during the same period, and the 1916 convention, meeting at Indianapolis on January 18 to February 1, 1916, could boast that 150,000 miners had joined its ranks since the 1914 gathering.[1] But the convention also revealed that the internal conflict between union militants and the bureaucrats at the top of the national organization and a number of the districts, who were mainly interested in moderation and using the union treasury to enrich themselves, was mounting in intensity. Indeed, Mother Jones herself had come under attack by moderate UMW leaders during the Colorado strike who charged that while whe might be very useful in the early stages of a strike in arousing and inspiring the men, she was an obstacle in the latter stage because she did not know the meaning of compromise.[2] In fact, however, she had been in favor of President Wilson's plan of settlement, and had urged the special convention on September 15, 1914, to accept the president's proposed settlement. She went even further, praising Wilson as the first real "statesman" in the White House "since the days of the immortal Jefferson and Lincoln," and praised him for having sent the federal troops to Colorado "to defend you." But while she was influential in influencing the special convention to accept the proposed settlement, there were those in the UMW who felt that Mother Jones's effusive support of Wilson's plan and praise for the president convinced the coal operators that the union could not long hold out and encouraged them to stand pat.[3]

None of this fazed Mother Jones in the least. She came to the 1916 convention with a record of continuous activity on behalf of hosts of workers all over the country, and even in Canada. She had spoken in Kansas City, Chicago, Columbus, Cleveland, and Washington in behalf of John R. Lawson, the UMW Colorado leader framed on a murder charge and sentenced to life imprisonment at hard labor. The account of the "Lawson Public Protest Mass Meeting," held under the auspices of the Chicago Federation of Labor at the Garrick Theatre, July 11, 1915, and chaired by President John Fitzpatrick, reported:

Mother Jones gripped the hearts of the audience. There were dimmed eyes when she told the story of Ludlow, of how eleven babies with their mothers were roasted alive in a pit into which they had been driven by machine guns.[4]

"You men are cowards to permit to exist a condition by which such atrocities can be committed. You are moral cowards all of you.

"Awaken! Fight! Not among yourselves, as you now do, but against the common enemy, who is pressing you to earth and offering you as a sacrifice to the god, Gold.

"You have the power. Set out to right conditions and you can. But there must be solidarity of action and unity of purpose. Do not grovel at the feet of Gold, but arise like men to crush the men and systems whose deeds cause crimes like those of Ludlow and Calumet."[5]

Then, as we have seen, she spoke at the "Labor Memorial Meeting" in Seattle, and crossed over into British Columbia to assist miners on strike in neighboring Canada. But only after a dispute with Canadian immigration authorities who tried to keep her out of the strike zone. After intervention by the Labor and State Departments in Washington, she was allowed to pass into Canada, and addressed strike meetings in Victoria.[6]

The miners were not the only ones she had helped in their struggles. On her way to testify before the Commission on Industrial Relations in May 1915 she had stopped off in Roosevelt, New Jersey, to help striking workers at the Williams and Clark chemical plant. Two days before, a pair of strikers had been shot and killed by plant guards, and a county prosecutor's investigation revealed they were shot in the back and when not on company property. Addressing the 900 strikers, Mother Jones advised them to hold out "to the last ditch," but to remain calm and not use guns regardless of the provocation. "Stick to your husbands," she told the wives of the strikers at a special gathering. "Don't let them go back as scabs. Help them stand firm, and above all, keep them away from the saloons."[7]

Her work with women, however, was not confined to strikers' wives. She took special pride in her activities on behalf of women workers in the needle trades. Early in February 1915 she spoke before 7,000 New York City members of the ILGWU's Ladies' Waist and Dress Makers' Union, and endorsed their criticisms of the "Protocol of Peace" under which they were operating since 1910 and which the workers complained the employers were freely violating.[8] "I would rather raise hell *in this country than anywhere else on earth," she told them as she aroused the workers to "great enthusiasm." "I have just fought through a sixteen months strike in Colorado and it ended in our forcing John D. Rockefeller to admit that we were right. I have been up against armed mercenaries in labor troubles all over the country, but this old woman with a hatpin has scared them. I can go into any city of the country and no mayor or governor can stop me as long as I pay my fare."*[9]

The New York waist and dress makers loved it, and so too did the striking Chicago waist and dress makers who were being arrested and jailed when she told them: "It's an honor to go to jail when your cause is just." Her arrival, called "explosive" by the Chicago press, helped the city's dress and white goods workers win their first victory — a reduction in hours to 50 a week, union recognition, higher pay, and an arbitration plan.[10]

A few weeks later, she was back in Chicago, this time to help 25,000 clothing workers, members of the newly-organized Amalgamated Clothing Workers of America, on strike since September 29, 1915. The police had responded in classic Chicago style — escorting strikebreakers through the picket lines by brute force. Riding through the picket lines on horseback, they arrested the strikers, most of them women, at the slightest provocation, jamming fifteen to twenty of them into patrol wagons designed to hold less than ten. By the end of the day, many women bore bruises delivered by the officers' clubs.[11]

As the strike dragged on into October and the manufacturers refused to arbitrate, Mother Jones rushed to the scene to add her voice to the calls for arbitration. But the manufacturers held firm, and in a dramatic gesture, Mother Jones called on Secretary of Labor William B. Wilson, her former associate in the United Mine Workers, to enter the strike. "Send at once to investigate clothing strike," she wired on October 18. "It's fierce, girls getting 8 cents an hour as slaves. Signed, Mother." Secretary Wilson replied that he had an observer on the scene but did not feel it was wise to interfere while the City Council was investigating working and sanitary conditions in the city's sweatshops and clothing factories. Mother Jones then led a parade of women strikers and sympathizers through the streets of Chicago, hoping to dramatize the strikers' cause and bring additional pressure on the manufacturers. As usual, she came under attack from the conservative press as an "outside agitator" who was stirring up the peaceful, law-abiding clothing workers of Chicago. But the strikers appreciated Mother Jones's assistance, especially since their allegiance to the A.F. of L. prevented both the Chicago Federation of Labor and the Women's Trade Union League from offering any concrete aid to members of the Amalgamated Clothing Workers, a pariah in the eyes of the A.F. of L. bureaucracy.[12] *But just as Mother Jones had refused to allow criticism in the UMW of her assisting the Western Federation of Miners to keep her from helping the copper strikers in Michigan, she paid no attention to those in the min-*

ers' union who were opposed to her aiding a union like the Amalgamated, an outlaw organization to A.F. of L. bureaucrats who favored the corrupt, ineffective United Garment Workers.[13] In fact, Mother Jones was especially proud of her work in Chicago, and she answered her critics in her speech to the 1916 UMW convention:

> When it comes to a fight for my class I don't care if they are revolters or not. I am going to be with them when they are fighting the common enemy; then when the fight with the other fellow is over I will fight to make them come back into their bona fide organization. Girls worked in Chicago for eight cents an hour. In the strike the police got ten dollars for every girl they beat up. We are going to stop that.

The convention was called to order at 1:30 p.m., Saturday, January 29th, Secretary Green[14] in the chair.

A handsome azalia plant, covered with blossoms, was placed upon President White's desk, bearing a card which stated that three delegates from the Hocking district of Ohio presented it with their best wishes.

Secretary Green — I was vain enough to think this flower was for me when I first took the chair. However, I find it is for a more worthy man. The card says it has been presented by three delegates from the Hocking Valley of Ohio to President John P. White.[15] The chairman of the constitution committee thought it was for him, but he was mistaken. President White will not be here for a little while and, with your permission, we will pause for just a few minutes in our regular order to hear from Mother Jones. She is planning to leave soon and wants to say something to the boys before she leaves.

Mother Jones — Boys, I have looked over this convention from the platform, and I want to give expression to the feeling that in this gathering are men of the most highly developed brains this country can produce. You have come from the picks, but you are developing, and I want to say to you to keep on.

Now I want to call your attention to a few things. Away back in the old Roman age, two hundred years after the world's greatest agitator was murdered by the ruling class, there arose in Carthage a tremendous agitation among the oppressed, the exploited, those who had borne the burden for ages. The Romans began to be disturbed and thought they would go down to Carthage and capture those who were responsible for the agitation. They went down. All they captured in those days they retained as slaves or sold into slavery. Among the group that was captured was one youth. The Roman judge asked, "Who are you?" The youth said, "I am a member of the human family." "Why do you agitate?" asked the judge. "Because I belong to that class that has been crushed, robbed, and murdered and maligned in all the ages, and I want to break the chains of my class."

I wish I could convey that spirit to everybody in this audience today. If I could we would have another story to tell when we come here for the next convention. That is the spirit that should possess us all — that we belong to the class that has borne the burdens of nations, that has been starved intellectually, physically, and otherwise. But we are breaking the chains. Everywhere I go I see the sentiment growing.

I was in Youngstown, Ohio, two months ago. I spoke in Niles and other places. I am going back next week. They have asked me to come. When I saw the horrible condition of those slaves in the steel mills, when I saw the shacks they lived in, when I saw them up against those furnaces for twelve hours a day, when I saw them going home weary and broken, I thought, "Some day, not in the far distant future, there will come another John Brown and he will tear this nation from end to end if this thing does not stop." Those men were worn and weary and tired. The first thing they did after coming out of the mills was to go to a saloon and get a drink to brace them up to go home.

But I am glad to say we are making progress. When those men struck I was not at all surprised. Here is what one of the officers says: "Just what caused it I have been unable to determine, but from what I have been told I fear it has been caused by the armed guards on the bridge. Had these guards been kept within the limit of the mill property I doubt if there would have been any trouble with the workers. Witnesses told me the guards on the bridge fired the first shots, that aroused the fury of the mob and there was no holding them in check. I do not look for any further outbreak unless an attempt is made to operate the mills with strike breakers."

It is the gunmen that start the trouble. They started the trouble in West Virginia, in Calumet, and they started it in Idaho, Colorado, and everywhere. If this government does not take steps to protect the people then the people will have to protect themselves against gunmen. In Colorado the strike was not on a month when they began. I was in Aguilar and got a telephone call to go to Ludlow. Lawson happened to be there. I hunted him up and said: "There is some trouble in Ludlow; let us go there." We got into an automobile and I told the driver to move as fast as the roads would allow. When we got to Ludlow we found the men were without weapons, they were bewildered, they were not able to defend themselves. The gunmen were there on the track shooting at the tents where the women were. There were about half a dozen guns in the camp and Lawson started to take them away. I said, "Lawson, you leave those guns with the boys so they can protect themselves. If the law does not protect us we must protect ourselves."

There was a law and order crowd out there, there was a law and order crowd in West Virginia and in the Calumet region. Now let me make this statement to you newspaper men. Down all the pages of human history law and order has destroyed every nation that has gone down never to rise again, because law and order were in the hands of

272

the fellows who violated every law of right and justice. I have been in strikes for many years, I was in strikes before many of you were born, and I know what they are. We are always the victims of the brutality of the other class.

In my experience Colorado was no worse than West Virginia. They did not make me wade the creek in Colorado, but in West Virginia the gunmen made me wade a creek up to my hips to keep me from going to a meeting. The corporation dogs were on the track. The representative of the Baltimore *Sun* was with me. He started to go on the track and the dogs said, "She cannot come with you." The newspaper man said it was an outrage to make me wade the creek. Then one of them said, "I don't care a damn! Only for her there wouldn't be any trouble here." I am going to tell you right here — and you newspaper man with the white head put it down — that as long as there is an industrial slave in America and I am alive I am going to raise a row.

They didn't do half as bad in Colorado as they did in West Virginia, and I am here to prove it. In West Virginia they ran the "death special" up the creek, shot the men and women and the crowd on board said, "Run the train back until we give them another bout." Yes, they roasted the babies in Calumet on Christmas eve, they roasted a few in Ludlow. They roasted seventy-five in Calumet on Christmas eve.[16] They shot seven working men in the streets. They shot them in West Virginia. Now I am going to tell you that if you men had any blood in you, if you would have stopped fighting each other, mustered your forces and organized they would not have dared to shoot anybody. As long as you come here to the convention and blow off steam that has been gathering for two years, instead of coming here to do business for the future you will not gain much.

There is a fellow up in New York; I saw him one day and he said, "I am inventing something, a wonderful thing. I am sure you will take stock in it." "Sure I will," I said, "if it amounts to anything. What is it?" He said, "It is a skull scraping machine," and I don't know of anything more useful than that; if we could get our skulls scraped until they were clean we would come here and do business.

In West Virginia I went up Cabin Creek. There were thirty men on the track. We were going to a meeting. The gunmen were huddled together and the machine gun was turned on the boys. The boys did not have a pistol, they did not have a stick to defend themselves with. These gunmen were thirsting for the blood of men who had not injured them. I jumped out of the buggy I was in. The boys said, "For God's sake, Mother, don't go up there! They will kill you!" I said, "I couldn't die a more glorious death than defending your rights." I went up and put my hand on the machine gun and said to those corporation bloodhounds, "You can't shoot a bullet out of that," and one fellow who was thirsting for human blood said, "Take your hand off that gun." I said, "No sir. My class makes those guns and I have a right to put my hand on this one. You have got mothers, wives, and daughters. I don't want to hear their groans and see their tears. My boys, too, have mothers, wives, and children; I don't want to hear their groans or see their tears. They are not fighting you, they are fighting the class that is robbing them. Don't you want to give this nation a better citizenship, morally, physically, and intellectually?"[17]

One man stood behind a tree with a gun. I said, "You come out in the open." I went down and took him from behind the tree. He had his finger on the trigger of the gun. I took him by the back of the neck and said, "You come here." After that I went up and held my meeting. The supe came along and said, "Mother Jones, you cannot talk." I said, "For God's sake, did you ever see a woman that couldn't talk?" I talked for an hour. The supe didn't want to stop me, but the fellow who owned him was on the track and he wanted it done. I didn't want to be too hard on the supe and I said, "I am here on the road and I have a share in it. I have been told I could walk on the road." He said, "You are a little bit on the company's property." For about an hour and a half I talked and fooled the poor supe. I don't know whether he lost his job or not.

Some of you who come here don't know what we have to do who are in the trenches. We are trying to fight our battle peacefully, but it is a question if we can. The past has never been peaceful, it is a question if the future is going to be; but we are moving on, we are using brains instead of weapons, we are organizing, we are getting together. The children in Calumet, the children in Colorado, the men in West Virginia, did not die in vain. When I was going to Washington to try to get Congress to make an investigation in Colorado I got a telegram from Dawson, N. M., saying, "Come down, Mother; we want to join the boys in Colorado." Time and again I got that message, but I concluded it was best to bring peace if we could, but the very night I was leaving for Washington I was told that 285 men were blown into eternity in the Dawson mine. The mine belonged to the Philip Dodge crowd that are now fighting the miners in Morenci. Those boys in that mine and those babies in Colorado, Calumet, and West Virginia did not die in vain; they gave up their lives on the alter of human freedom and in the future men will stop and ponder and wonder at these sad days of old when we roasted babies on the alter of God-cursed gold.

It was not the Rockefellers that did it, it was not the Shaws, it was the working men of this nation; they are responsible for the death of those children. If you were not cowards you would be organized, you would pay your dues, you would carry on the campaign of education that would bring peace to the nation. If an assessment is put on some of you say, "I don't want to pay it; I pay my dues and I am not going to pay any more." Why you poor, measly, half-starved wretch, do you know what the men and women did who tramped the highways and byways to make it possible for you to have the means to pay the assessment with? I know if you don't.

Now some guy down the road will say, "What does Mother know about mining, anyway?" Don't I know about mining? Don't I? I worked on the night shift and the day shift in Pennsylvania from Pittsburgh to Brownsville. There isn't a mine that was open in those days that I didn't go on the night shift and the day shift, and I know what you have to go through. Then some fellow says, "I don't think we ought to have a woman on the pay roll." What do you think of that, Secretary Green? The man who asked that never read a thing in his life, he never even did a bit of thinking. The most valuable person on the staff of President Lincoln was a woman. She gathered more correct information for him and delivered it than all the men he had,[18] and I want to make the statement here that if you had twenty women in Europe they could stop that war. Twenty women with a consciousness of what war means to the children yet to come could stop that war. Don't you think they have as much sense in Europe as you have? They are all grown fellows who are fighting each other, and if they think it is better to go out and fight for the king than for humanity, for civilization, why, let the guys do it and let us fight at home to preserve this country.[19]

If I were president of the United States I would put a pipe line along the Atlantic seacoast; I would take one thousand trained men and put them there and say, "Now you do business." And you don't need an army to pay from twelve to twenty thousand dollars a year to the fellow with straps on his shoulders who goes strutting along like a peacock. You are the fellows who pay all the bills. Why, you ought to see those fellows who were in Colorado and West Virginia. And then the president is talking about preparedness — with a gang of sewer rats like that! Why, they couldn't prepare to clean the hall here, that gang couldn't!

One morning they took me off the train at Walsenburg. I had my fare paid to Trinidad, forty-five miles beyond. One fellow said, "You will have to get up." "What is the matter," said I, "are we in Trinidad?" "No, we are getting near Walsenburg." "I have a ticket to Trinidad." "It don't make any difference, you have to get off the train, we are the militia." I got off the train and there were the guns. I asked where they were going to take me and they said to the basement of the courthouse. I asked if there was a chimney there. They said, "Why? Do you want a fireplace?" The fellow who said that had a strap on his shoulder and a belt of bullets around his stomach. I said I wasn't particular about a fire but I wanted a chimney. "What do you want a chimney for?" "Because I have a trained pigeon and he goes to Washington every week and comes back and brings me all the news." "Did he come every week you were in Trinidad?" "Yes, every night." "And they never found it out?" "No," said I.

Just imagine a nation putting a belt of bullets around the stomach of a thing like that! He had a gun hanging by his side, a couple of pistols and he was sent out to shoot working men. Now just imagine what you are up against when you meet a thing like that! Another fellow in Trinidad told me: "My mother is in the insane asylum in Pueblo, and they fined me thirty dollars because I slept ten minutes too long and did not get out here on duty to watch you." "Why didn't you sleep all night, you fool?" said I. That is the type of man that is in the army, the navy and the militia.

I have been arrested five times by the militia and you have never had to hire a lawyer to defend me; I defended myself every time and I made them turn me loose.[20] Neither Secretary Green, Secretary Perry, nor Secretary Wilson ever received a bill from me for my services. I have sent in expense accounts, but I have never yet sent a bill for services to the labor movement. The secretary sends it to me, but I don't know yet what he pays, I am not financier enough. As I told Rockefeller, "If you gave me your institution, I would wreck it tomorrow; it would not last a month after I was in. All I want money for is to use it to lick the other fellow." I am not going to take any money to the grave; I didn't bring any here, and I don't want to go up to God Almighty as a high-class burglar.

There have been some tragic things taking place. Belk is acquitted in Colorado and Zancanelli is kept in jail. Ulich was in jail ten months. I was there three months. I presume I would still be in jail in West Virginia if Senator Kern had not taken the matter up.[21] I want to say to you that every working man in the nation owes a debt to Senator Kern. It was he who brought my case on the floor of the Senate when Goff — the corporation tool — said, "We had peace until they came in there, these foreigners." Well, we are not foreigners when we are creating the wealth and allowing them to rob us, we are good American citizens then; but when we protest against their robbery we are foreigners immediately. Goff said the biggest agitator in the country, the grandmother of all agitators, was old Mother Jones. Thank God I have lived to be a grandmother in agitation! I hope I will live to be a great-grand-mother in agitation!

You have made more progress in government, boys, in the last three years than you had made in 125 years prior to that. We have got more recognition in the last three years than in all that time. The secretary of labor, who is a member of the president's cabinet, was in Pennsylvania when the strike at Arnot took place.[22] That was before the anthracite strike. I was sent for and went there. The men were going to work next morning. I addressed a meeting that afternoon. Nobody went to work next morning, but I was thrown out of the hotel at eleven o'clock at night — I was an undesirable citizen. I went up the mountain. I saw a light and kept crawling up until I got there. When I got to the house a man there said, "Did they put you out of the hotel?" I said, "Yes, but I will put them out before I get through with them."

The president of District No. 2 worked day and night and gave all he had to that strike. One night I sat in W. B. Wilson's house. He was there with his feet bare. About eleven o'clock at night we were talking about a move I was going to make when a knock came on the door. Wilson opened it. I left the room. Three men came in, sat down, and discussed the strike. One of them said, "Say, Wilson, we can make it twenty or twenty-five thousand dollars if you go away and let this fight fall to pieces. You can take the old woman with you." Wilson never told that, but I heard it. He got up with his voice quivering and said, "Gentlemen, if you have come here to accept the hospitality of my home it is yours, every inch of it; if you have come here to get me to betray my fellow men and my own family, there is the door." Next morning we had black coffee and bread for breakfast but we made the fight and won. If they have had a fight since I have never heard of it. Now, that man is the secretary of labor, and you knife him and say everything about him, yet he went barefoot, tired, and weary and he did not get a Taft stomach on him when he was out organizing.

You stood here and attacked this man — President White. Now I want to make this statement before I close. I have worked under all your administrations. There is Flyzik back there. He comes here from the state of Washington. He was a kid when he walked fifteen miles over the mountains with me in Pennsylvania to meet the militia. The officers of the organization were sleeping in Hazelton when that army of women with Flyzik and a bunch of the other boys met on Track 13 in the middle of the night and brought out 5,000 men. You gave a ten-thousand-dollar house to the chief executive, but you never gave a dollar to those women, and they didn't own a shingle on the houses they lived in.

This administration has had more fights on his hands, more to go up against than any administration you have had since you were organized. The officers have had to stand more abuse — and I know the whole of them but I am not under obligations to any of them — than the officers of any previous administration. I am not under obligations to any of them. I don't allow one of them to pay for a meal for me. Do you know why? Because I want my hands clean, and if they don't fill the bill I want to go after them with clean hands and tell you all about it. We have got to be true to each other.

I made many trips from Colorado to see President White. I made many trips from West Virginia that nobody knew anything in the world about, because I wanted him to be familiar with everything that was going on. A man who has had Nova Scotia, Westmoreland, the Southwest, Vancouver, West Virginia, Colorado, and Ohio on his hands has not had much peace — I want to tell you that! I have watched these strikes with a great deal of care and I know how the people in this administration have acted. I am not in the habit of defending people who do not deserve it.

Here is a headline in a paper: "Forty armored strike-breaking cars gift of steel magnate to the State." The gasoline castles, Gary, and the rest of them have donated forty armored autos in answer to these warnings, so that the gunmen can go in safety and attack you in your strikes. And you had better line up because I don't care what political party you have in Washington, you must have an organized economic army on the industrial field. If you have that you can make Washington, Indiana, and every other state come to time. Get into your unions, pay your dues like men, and don't be grunting and saying, "By God, here is another assessment!" The other fellows sit back and laugh when you do that; they say, "We have them going now, we have got them divided."

Years ago I went to the coke ovens in Pennsylvania where they worked the men twelve and fourteen hours a day. I walked eighteen miles to get into the cotton mills to expose the infamies of your charity brigade, your foreign missions and other hypocritical movements of the capitalists who were murdering the children in the mills. A lawyer sent me five dollars. He sent it by one of the boys for the work I did in the mills. They were taking the hands of those children in the mills with their machinery. I took eighty of them to Philadelphia with me and showed them to the ministers and every one else in order to stir up the nation to the crime it was committing. We walked all the way to Oyster Bay from Philadelphia to see the man who was president of the United States at that time, to try to get Congress to pass a bill to stop that slaughter of the children in the mills, mines, and factories, and he would not see us. He is a brave guy when he wants to take a gun and go out and fight other grown people, but when those children went to him he could not see them. But we did not stop, and out of that fight we made has come this child labor bill that is before Congress. One paper called me a horrible woman for taking the children out. Why, the kids had the time of their lives. Everybody fed them. We got into the Oriental Hotel where the Wall Street people eat, and there was steak and quail on toast — the first time I ever ate quail on toast. We had the finest feast we ever struck. The young ones all went back strong and well, but they had to go into the mills again. However, Pennsylvania has passed a law that keeps them out.[23]

I never in my life asked President White for a favor. I wouldn't take it from him if he wanted to give it to me. I want to say to you here that you have the hardest-worked president, vice-president, and secretary you have ever had in your history. You talk a great deal about young John D. Young John D. is not to blame; you are to blame. They couldn't keep you from organizing in Colorado if you were men enough. I had a conversation of two hours and twenty minutes with John D.[24] I found him one of the most unassuming men. Young John D. never said "I cawn't," and I shawn't"; he talked simple like we do, and that is more than some people in the labor movement do. If you line up and demand your rights in a logical way Colorado will be the best organized state in the union, and John D. Rockefeller will help you to organize it.

I am going to Youngstown. I didn't ask Mr. White whether or not I could go — I am going anyhow. I went to the garment workers in Chicago. Somebody said afterwards, "Did Mr. White tell you to get away?" I said, "No, sir, he didn't; and if he had I would not have done it." Nobody owns me. When it comes to a fight for my class I don't care if they are revolters or not I am going to be with them when they are fighting the common enemy; then when the fight with the other fellow is over I will fight to make them come back into their bona fide organization. Girls worked in Chicago for eight cents an hour. In the strike the police got ten dollars for every girl they beat up. We are going to stop that.

I will be 85 years old next May, and I am as well able to fight as I was forty years ago. Don't bother about politics; keep close to the economic struggle; don't allow politicians to interfere with your business. Let them attend to their own business and we will attend to ours. Don't let the ministers bother you, we know the Lord Jesus Christ as well as they do. They don't let us go into their church conferences and they have no right to come into ours. I said to a man in New York, "Keep your hands off; this is our fight. I don't want any freedom that comes from the other class; I want the freedom I have fought for and bought myself and then I will keep it."

Our men in West Virginia were beaten up, and when I was in Washington and they asked me if I told the miners to buy guns I said, "Yes, I did; I told them to buy guns because an armed people have never yet been conquered." When the governor of West Virginia sent to Boomer to get the guns he sent a doctor — a political lickspittle. They let him bill the meeting and pay for the hall rent. I went down and took possession of it and said, "Boys, have you got any guns?" "Yes, Mother, sure." "Did you pay for them?" "Sure, we paid for them." "Then the guns are yours. Don't you give those guns to Dr. Montgomery, to the governor, to anybody else who comes after them. Keep them at home and if any gunmen come there to invade your homes do business." That is the way to do business, isn't it, Mr. Newspaper Man? Lawson gave the guns to the military when they came in. You bet your life I wouldn't have given them up!

I am going into the Fairmount region to organize the miners there; I am going up the Norfolk and Western, and I am going to take big, long Tom Haggerty along. And I want the very best organizers there are in the United States, the very best men you have, and I am going to pick them myself. We are going to turn over West Virginia thoroughly organized, and then, if I am spared I am going down to Alabama. If I am not alive I will be up with God Almighty and I am going to tell him to fix me up so that I can go down and raise hell with them anyway. An old mine owner in West Virginia said, "Why don't you die?" I said, "God Almighty wants me to live long enough to raise hell with you and make a man out of you instead of a thief."

Now, boys, be good. Stand by your officers and when the day comes they are not worthy of your confidence and support I will be the first to come to the front and tell you. Go home with a new heart, with new resolutions, with the hope of a new day for the children who will come after you. John Brown committed murder in his day; the courts of the country condemned him and he was hung. He was a criminal in the eyes of the court and in the eyes of many of the nation; but he was a hero in the eyes of God. He started the war on chattel slavery. We have got to carry on the war on industrial slavery.

Boys, look back the stairway of years, look back over our fights. I remember our fights in Chicago when we hadn't a penny, when no organizer was paid, when we had to tramp six miles to attend a meeting, and we did it cheerfully. I look back on those grand days when the men who fought so well paved the way for the movement you have today. Many of those men are in their graves. Martin Irons is one of those who was persecuted. I went to see his grave after he had been dead nineteen years. It was in Brownsville, Texas. When I got off the train I asked the agent if Martin Irons was buried there. He said he was. I got a butcher named Williams to go to the grave with me.

Martin Irons was a hero, but he was maligned, vilified, and persecuted.[25] He gave up his life that you might be here today. His grave was by a fence, overgrown with weeds and neglected. It was marked by a broken shovel. When he was Master Workman of the Iron Mountain Division he was called from Kansas City to St. Louis. The strike call was written up. When he was being shown to his room by the bell boy they said, "Come this way to this room." He went back with them to a room they had rented, they put a pistol to his head and said, "You sign this strike call or we will kill you." He signed the strike call. The secretary and treasurer were Pinkertons.

When Martin Irons left Kansas City I had five dollars. I wanted to give him three. He wouldn't take it. He said, "Mother, they have taken my home, killed my wife, they have ruined me, they have taken everything!" I said, "No, Martin, they have left you your manhood, and that is worth all the wealth in the world." So that day when I knelt at his grave in Brownsville I remembered these things. Humanity had forgotten him, but there was a mocking bird singing over his grave. I wrote the matter up. The boys in Mount Olive, Illinois, said they would give me a grave for him. I intended to raise his body and bring him up with the martyred dead in Mount Olive, but the State Federation of Missouri took the matter in hand and sent a tombstone there. If I live long enough I will bring Martin Irons' body and that tombstone to Mount Olive and bury him with his co-workers. When he was on the rock pile in Memphis, Powderly[26] sent him fifteen dollars to pay his fine. You boys have no idea of what we went through in those days. I look back over the long struggle, the dark hours, the suffering, and I know it was not in vain. I see the sun breaking through the clouds.

When I come back from Youngstown I will go to Colorado. The gunmen are there but they won't touch me. I am not a bit afraid of them. I am going into all the mining camps, Mr. White, whether you agree with me or not, that belong to John D. Rockefeller and I am going to organize the men into the United Mine Workers of America, no matter who is with it or against it.

At the conclusion of the address Delegate Gori, District 12, moved that a rising vote of thanks be tendered Mother Jones. The motion was seconded and carried unanimously.

*[Minutes of Convention, United Mine Workers of America,
1916, pp. 956-68.]*

Notes

1. Joseph G. Rayback, *A History of American Labor*, New York, 1963, p. 258.
2. See *New York Times*, October 24, 1914.
3. George S. McGovern, "The Colorado Mine War, 1913-14," unpublished PhD., Northwestern University, 1954, p. 343.
4. Today, on the site of the "Ludlow Massacre," there stands a monument erected by the United Mine Workers. Annually, thousands of union-conscious motorists turn off the main highway between Trinidad and Pueblo to look at this shrine. On the monument is the inscription: "In memory of the men, women, and children who lost their lives in freedom's cause at Ludlow, Colorado, April 20, 1914."
5. "Lawson Public Protest Meeting," printed report of proceedings, John Fitzpatrick Papers, Chicago Historical Society.
6. *Autobiography of Mother Jones*, pp. 195-99.
7. *New York Times*, January 22, May 22, 1915.
8. The "Protocol of Peace" ending the nine-weeks' "Great Revolt" of the New York cloakmakers (July to September 1910) won for the workers a 50-hour week, bonus pay for overtime, ten legal holidays, free electric power, installation for machines, no home work, weekly pay in cash, not checks, limitations on overtime, a joint board of sanitary control to help clean up filthy shops, a committee of grievances and compulsory arbitration, with no strike or lockout permitted before arbitration, and price settlements to be made in each shop by negotiation. The settlement had tremendously important implications for unskilled women workers, since the agreement covered the wages and conditions of every worker in the trade, from the unskilled tailors to the finishers. Despite these important gains, however, the settlement was a disappointment to many strikers, and a large number of the rank and file disapproved of it. One reason was that instead of the closed shop, there was "the preferential union shop." Furthermore, unlike the usual collective bargaining agreement, the protocol had no time limit; it could run indefinitely but could be terminated by either side at will. (Hyman Berman, "Era of the Protocol: A Chapter in the History of the International Ladies' Garment Workers' Union, 1910-1916," unpublished Ph.D. thesis, pp. 48-153; Foner, *Women and the Labor Movement:*

From Colonial Times to the Eve of World War I, pp. 349-50, 387-88.)

9. *New York Times*, February 7, 1915.

10. Wilfred Carsel, *A History of the Chicago Ladies' Garment Workers Union*, Chicago, 1940, pp. 89-91.

11. Lee Wolman, et. al., *The Clothing Workers of Chicago, 1910-1922*, Chicago, 1922, pp. 99-100; Foner; *Women and the Labor Movement*, p. 381.

12. Mary "Mother" Jones to Secretary W. B. Wilson, October 18, 1915; Wilson to Jones, October, 1915, Conciliation Service, file 313,121, National Archives, Washington, D.C.; Sidney Hillman to Joseph Schlessberg, October 22, 24, 1915, Amalgamated Clothing Workers files; Matthew Josephson, *Sidney Hillman, Statesman of American Labor*, New York, 1952, pp. 126-28; Melech Epstein, *Jewish Labor in the U.S.A., An Industrial, Political, and Cultural History of the Jewish Labor Movement*, New York, 1950-1953, vol. 2, p. 252; Foner, *Women and the Labor Movement*, p. 382.

13. For the factors which led to the split in the United Garment Workers' Union and the formation of the Amalgamated Clothing Workers of America, in December 1914, see Foner, *Women and the Labor Movement*, pp. 375-77, and Foner, *op. cit.*, vol. 5, pp. 260-65.

The A.F. of L. leadership, antagonized by the militancy and socialist ideology of the new union, set out to attempt to destroy it in its infancy, and threatened with expulsion any affiliate which recognized or assisted the Amalgamated.

14. William Green (1873-1952), born in Ohio and apprenticed in a coal mine at the age of sixteen, was elected secretary of his local when he was only eighteen. At twenty-seven, he was president of the Ohio subdistrict of the UMW, and at thirty-three, president of the Ohio district organization. Green was UMW national secretary-treasurer from 1912-1924, when he succeeded Samuel Gompers to the A.F. of L. presidency after Gompers's death. He remained president until his death on November 21, 1952. Although he was long associated with an industrial union (UMW), Green was a champion of craft unionism in the A.F. of L.

15. John P. White had been re-elected president in 1915 after a bitter campaign in which he was unsuccessfully challenged by John H. Walker, marked by the issuance by John L. Lewis, a White supporter, of forged telegrams in which Walker was supposed to appeal to employers for financial support in the race against White. (Melvyn Dubofsky and Warren Van Tyne, *John L. Lewis: A Biography*, New York, 1977, p. 31.)

16. During the copper miners' strike in Michigan in 1913, the Women's Auxiliary of the Western Federation of Miners at Calumet planned a strikers' children's Christmas party. The Italian Hall in Red Jacket was obtained for the party. On the afternoon of December 24, seven to eight hundred people, including several hundred children, filled the second floor of the Italian Hall. Lunch was followed by the Christmas party. One by one, the children met Santa Claus, and each received a gift. Just as the party was about to break up, someone rushed into the hall and yelled "Fire! Fire! Fire!"

Panic ensued, and in a matter of seconds, the narrow staircase was jammed with children and adults, pushing, shoving, and screaming. People stumbled and fell, and soon the narrow stairway was jammed with bodies. Firemen, alerted by an alarm, rushed to the scene and began pulling children off the top of the pile. When it was over, sixty-five children and eleven adults were dead. There had been no fire. But it was never determined by either the coroner's jury or a later congressional investigating committee who it was that had cried out the tragic words or why he had done so. (Foner, *op. cit.*, vol. 5, pp. 220-21.)

17. For a different version of this incident, *see* pp. 156-57.

18. The reference is to Anna Ella Carroll (1815-1893) who was alleged to be the adviser of President Lincoln in the Civil War. It is claimed that Carroll was responsible for the successful union strategy of the early western campaigns and for numerous other decisions of high policy.

19. World War I broke out in Europe in August, 1914. Unfortunately, as we shall see, Mother Jones did not adhere to this stand that the war was pointless for the working class.

20. Actually, the union lawyer, as we have seen, did seek a habeas corpus writ for Mother Jones when she was imprisoned under martial law in Colorado.

21. Senator John W. Kern of Indiana was instrumental in freeing Mother Jones from the West Virginia prison. (*See* pp. 225, 276, 283). Mother Jones aided Kern's campaign for re-election in 1916.

22. The reference is to William B. Wilson. For the Arnot strike, *see* pp. 405-7.

23. For the "March of the Children," *see* p. 100-5, 213. Jones is correct in her estimate, for the march was probably instrumental in the passage of child labor legislation in Pennsylvania, and had an effect on child labor legislation in other states, especially New York and New Jersey. (Featherling, *op. cit.*, p. 57.)

24. *See above* pp. 57, 263-64.

25. Martin Irons, chairman of the executive board of District Assembly 101, Knights of Labor, was the leader of the second Gould Railroad strike in the spring of 1886. His militant strategy and tactics frightened the top leadership of the Knights, and Terence V. Powderly (1849-1924), Grand Master Workman of the Knights of Labor, decided to intervene. A conflict developed between Irons and Powderly as the former saw the K. of L. leader as selling out the strikers in a deal with Jay Gould. In the end, the strike was lost, and most of the strikers were discharged and blacklisted on the railroads. Martin Irons himself was blacklisted in every industry, and deprived of any opportunity to make a living as a worker. Misfortune hounded Iron's steps. His wife died during the strike and his furniture was seized for debts. He attempted to earn a living as a lecturer, but failed. During his last years he was reduced to keeping a lunch counter in a small basement saloon in Missouri. But he remained a class-conscious, militant Socialist throughout these years of bitter privation. (See *Writings and Speeches of Eugene V. Debs*, New York, 1948, p. 42.)

Irons died in 1900 but his memory was kept alive by the workers of Missouri when, in 1910, under the auspices of the Missouri State Federation of Labor, they erected a monument above his grave paying tribute to him as a "Fearless Champion of Industrial Freedom." (Foner, *op. cit.,* vol. 2, p. 86.)

26. Although Mother Jones performed a great service in calling attention to Martin Irons's story, and in hailing him as "a hero," it is very likely that Irons turned over in his grave at her praise for Powderly. But then Terence V. Powderly could do no wrong in Mother Jones's eyes, and it must be conceded that in his attitude to her, he displayed an attitude of deep appreciation for her contributions to the labor movement.

You Women Must Organize if You Want Your Men to Earn a Decent Living Wage!

Speech on behalf of striking street car workers,
El Paso, Texas, August 16, 1916

On August 16, 1916, the El Paso (Texas) Herald *published the following item under the heading: "'MOTHER' JONES ARRIVES TO SPEAK IN CLEVELAND SQUARE": "'Mother' Jones will speak this evening in Cleveland square and will discuss local and national labor conditions. She arrived Wedensday afternoon from Bisbee[1] having been in Arizona to attend the State Federation of Labor meeting. . . . A union band will play from 7 until 8 o'clock when the speaking will start." Mother Jones also spoke on her experiences in West Virginia and Colorado and insisted that labor would not submit to a military despotism. The* El Paso Herald *headlined her speech "'MOTHER' JONES ROASTS MILITIA: SAYS THEY ARE 'LITTLE KIDS',"* and its subhead read: *"Woman Labor Agitator Makes Fiery Speech at Cleveland Square; Declares Diamonds of Street Car Officials' Wives 'Blood of Little Children;' Says She Wants to Die on the Firing Line." Unfortunately, the* Herald *did not publish the entire speech, but excerpts from the account follow.*

"Don't be afraid that the militia ever will shoot me. I don't know of a more joyous death than in fighting the battles of you laboring men."

"I'm not afraid of the militia; most of them are only little 'kids'."

"A hundred years ago employers enslaved men by owning their bodies. Today they enslave them by controlling the sources from which they get their bread."

"The nearer you get to Jesus, the safer you are."

"We laboring people are not going to submit to a military despotism."

"If this thing goes on there will be another Bunker Hill[2] in your city within a year."

"You working people make the bullets and bayonets with which you are killed when you strike."

"The destiny of this nation lies in its women. No nation can grow greater than its women."

"Why do you city officials allow these hired gunmen here?"

These are some of the "Punches" delivered by "Mother" Jones in a speech at Cleveland Square Wednesday night on the El Paso street car strike. Meantime a crowd of 3000 people cheered, jeered, groaned, or listened in impressed silence. A drizzling rain that threatened to burst at any moment into a thunder storm was ignored by the big gathering of laboring men, soldiers, well-to-do residents of the neighborhood, women, girls, and children.

Before "Mother" Jones was given a chance to speak, the crowd endorsed a resolution by the Central Labor union condemning the El Paso Electric Railway company and petitioning the mayor and city council to suspend the ordinances regulating jitney busses until there is a settlement of the present strike.

Has Snow White Hair.

The El Paso municipal band furnished music for the occasion and "Mother" Jones was escorted to the speaker's stand by a committee consisting of Wm. J. Moran, Ponder S. Carter, W. E. Lunsford, Lee Pollard, and others. "Mother" Jones, a small woman who, with her snow white hair and spectacles, exemplifies her cognomen, received an ovation as she approached the platform. Many in the big crowd were deceived by "Mother" Jones's years and her small stature, for she proved a dynamic "spellbinder" with a voice that carried to the outermost listener. She herself declared she is 84 years old, but she looks a dozen years younger.

Wm. J. Moran acted as master of ceremonies, introducing both Ponder S. Carter and "Mother" Jones.

Clubwomen, churches, the missionary movement, the militia, the United States senate, the nation's court system, "the stupidity of the working men," "the indolence" of their wives, the "piracy of the rich high class burglars," and the city officials all came in for stinging lashes from "Mother" Jones's sharp tongue.

"Take Out Electric Meters."

"If 4000 of you labor men and sympathizers with the street car strikers would take the electric meters out of your homes and use candles for a while you'd soon bring the pirates to time," she said. "But your wives won't let you. Shame on them! They would rather sell their babies into bondage than do without the comforts of electric lighted homes.

"You women must organize if you want your men to earn a decent living wage. It is up to you. Think of your babies and their future. The employers have unions, pretty good ones, too. And they stand together like all high class thieves.

21 Cents An Hour

"You street car men pay 50 cents for the privilege of sitting in a room and waiting for the privilege of being called out to work. No slaves ever had to do that. Would any of you city officials work for 21 cents an hour? No, not one of you. Then why do you expect the street car men to work for such a wage?

"While the wives of you street car men are wondering where the next meal is coming from, the wives of your masters are strutting about with their dresses cut to here. ("Mother" Jones indicated a point near her waist line) and their hands loaded with diamonds. These diamonds are the blood of your little children whom they have robbed and starved.

Belongs on Firing Line.

"I tell you it is the women who must organize to help the men. We want no Sunday school people. We want practical men and women. I do not belong in the church or the parlor or the clubroom. I belong on the firing line. At the same time, I do not believe in murder or violence. The day of brute force and violence has passed. We must get what we want by other means.

"The avenues by which we make our bread are taken away from us and then we go to China and we tell the Chinese what fine Christians we are. Every state is calling for an extra penitentiary. We have Christianity on one side and robbery and thievery on the other.

Guest of the State.

"You fellows fill the jails. There would be no jails but for us. The other fellows don't know how to build them. I have been arrested as many times as you have. I had the men in uniforms take care of me. I wasn't like you, a guest of the city; I was a guest of the state.

"I went to the strike in West Virginia. They sent the militia with me. I am not afraid of the militia; most of them are only little 'kids.' One of the most pathetic sights I have ever seen in my life was when I trained my boys up there near the militia camp. I took them over to the church in face of the militiaman. The nearer you get to Jesus, the safer you are. The state paid $600,000 to the militia to crush those miners, but they did not do it.

Sentenced To Penitentiary.

"I was sentenced to five years in the penitentiary there. For five weeks I was the only military prisoner. Their scheme was to get rid of the best men by putting them in prison.

"I want to ask why you allowed the gunmen and scabs to come here. You yourselves patronize the 'scabs.' You will have a union card in your pocket and a scab hat on your head. Why don't you look to see if the things you buy from your merchants have the union label?"

286

Compliments President.

"Mother" Jones gave a striking picture of the scenes at Ludlow, Colo., during the coal miners strike and described the shooting down of the men by the militia. She complimented President Wilson, but said she hoped Senator Borah, of Idaho, would be president some day because of the stand he has taken toward labor.

[El Paso Herald, August 17, 1916. I wish to thank Itoko McNully, Library Assistant, Southwest Section, El Paso Public Library for furnishing me with copies of clippings from the El Paso Herald containing notices of and excerpts from Mother Jones's speech. A clipping from the Herald but unnamed and undated with the excerpts from the speech, is in the Mother Mary Harris Jones Papers, Department of Archives and Manuscripts, Catholic University of America, Washington, D.C.]

Notes

1. For Mother Jones's activities in Arizona, see pp. 370-71, 474-77, 511.
2. The Battle of Bunker Hill, the first major engagement of the American Revolution, occurred on the morning of June 17, 1775 in Boston. While the British troops were able after three charges to capture the hill, they lost 1,054 killed while the American loss was 449.

You Ought to Be Out Raising Hell!

Speeches to New York City striking carmen and their wives, October 4, 6, 1916

After the 1916 UMW convention, Mother Jones left on a wide-ranging speaking tour across the country which found her addressing rallies of strikers in different cities. Space limitations make it impossible to describe all of the labor disputes of 1916 in which she was involved, but one in particular is worthy of discussion because of the screaming headlines it provoked, such as the one in the New York Times: "CAR RIOT STARTED BY 'MOTHER' JONES."[1]

A more sober version was the headline on the front page of the

Socialist New York Call *which read: "Mother Jones in Fiery Speech To Traction Strikers Says Women Can Help in Fight."[2] However, regardless of the headlines, the speech Mother Jones delivered to the wives of the striking carmen had an electric effect. In a story copied by papers all over the country, the* New York Times *reporter wrote:*

Two hundred women, wives, and relatives of striking carmen, heard "Mother" Jones, the aged labor agitator, deliver an inflammatory speech against the traction officials of the city yesterday afternoon, and then attacked one of the surface cars of the New York Railway Company.

The fight which followed exceeded any outbreak the police had had to deal with since the strike began. Many of the women carried babies and were accompanied by children, but they left these on the sidewalk while they attempted to tear the car apart. They hurled paving blocks through the windows, and when the police interfered the women attacked them with their fists, finger nails, bricks, and other missiles.

Subdued after thousands of onlookers had been attracted by the fight, six of the women were arrested, but not before they and many others had been clubbed and roughly handled. One powerfully built woman fought so viciously after the arrival of police reserves that it took four patrolmen to carry her, fighting every inch of the way, to a patrol wagon. Three women were arrested on charges of having assisted the women in the disturbance. . . .[3]

The 1916 strike was the most successful bid for union recognition and improvements in the most outrageous working conditions the major transit companies of New York City and Westchester had faced in twenty years. On July 22, 1916, the Amalgamated Association of Street and Electrical Railway Employees of America, had ordered a strike on the surface lines of Yonkers, Mount Vernon, and New Rochelle, after management had refused to arbitrate. The strike on these lines, owned and operated by the Third Avenue system, rapidly spread to all the surface lines in Manhattan, Bronx, Queens, and Richmond. Following a tenuous truce, hurriedly mediated by Mayor John P. Mitchell of New York, and Oscar S. Straus, chairman of the Public Service Commission, First District, the strike broke out again because of the attempt made by the management of the Interborough subway and surface cars, to institute a company union. As an added strategem, the company instituted a "yellow dog" contract which prohibited an employee from participating in union activity to improve his wages and working conditions — the lowest and worst in the entire country. Those who refused to sign the "yellow dog" contract were dismissed. In the meantime, the work of gathering strikebreakers began with feverish haste.

Enraged by these developments, over the opposition of the Amalgamated leadership, the carmen struck again. The strikebreakers were immediately brought in to run the cars, with police protection. Thugs and gunmen manned the cars in New York City.[4]

Mother Jones arrived on October 3, the same day the strikebreakers began to operate in full force, partly replacing the 11,000 carmen who had struck. The following day she was brought to Mozart Hall at Eighty-sixth street and Second Avenue where hundreds of wives of the strikers were waiting to hear her. Mother Jones was escorted by William H. Fitzgerald, Amalgamated general organizer and the strike leader, and by Melinda Scott and Margaret Hinchey, of the Women's Trade Union League.[5] Her speech, recreated from excerpts in the New York Times, *New York* Tribune, *New York* World, *and New York* Herald, *is followed by one she delivered the following day to the striking car workers at Harlem River Casino.*

I know something of what life is like for street car workers. I have talked to men who work on the cars from one end of the country to the next, and I know how terribly exploited they are. But none are more exploited than the carmen in this, the leading city of the United States. You know and I know that your husbands have to work seven days a week with no provisions for days off; that their basic work day consists of ten hour time actually spent on a car run, but that it frequently takes 15 hours of working time to receive their ten hours pay. No provision exists for any overtime pay. It is not unusual, as you know, for your husbands to spend upwards of 80 hours a week on the cars. The car runs are frequently not consecutive but are split by three-or-four hour breaks. When do your husbands have time for you and your children? The church and the press are worried about families breaking up, but when the workers go on strike to have the time to keep their families together, these same lackeys of the employers denounce them for doing so. And on top of this, the wages your husbands bring home for the longest work week of any car workers in the country are the lowest earned by men in this trade anywhere.

So is it any wonder they are on strike? A few months ago I told the wives of the car strikers in El Paso, Texas to raise hell. I want to say the same thing today. Women can win this strike just as they won it in El Paso. If necessary I will organize a hundred thousand women out of town and bring them to New York City to lick the cops and the scabs. You can't beat the women.

But it should not be necessary.

But it should not be necessary to do this. You, the wives of the strikers, ought to be out raising hell. This is the fighting age. Put on your fighting clothes. America was not discovered by Columbus for that bunch of bloodsucking leeches who are now living off of us. You are too sentimental.

[New York Times, *New York* Tribune, *New York* World, *New York* Herald, *October 5, 1916.*]

I'm not afraid of Police Commissioner Woods or God Almighty. We build the jails and we are not afraid to go into them. I'll raise as much hell in jail as I would out of it.

They say I started the riot. Well, I'm not going to say whether I did or not. Anyway, I'm not going to make any apology. If the police are organized to shed our blood we are going to organize to shed the other side's blood.

Tell the mayor and your councilmen and the police commissioner that if they want to hang me, let them hang me, but when I am on the scaffold I'll cry, "Freedom for the working classes!" and when I meet God Almighty I'll have him damn them.

The strikebreakers are rats, I'd know what to do, if they came and took bread from my mouth.

Organized labor has not yet learned the lesson of lining up its women. The plutocrats have learned it. They give their women suffrage, prohibition, and other fads to keep their minds busy. Labor must get the women thinking of getting bread and other necessities. Let the working women realize what they can do, and they will join with the men, and industrial troubles will soon be over.[6]

[New York Times, *New York* Call, *October 7, 1916.*]

Notes

1. *New York Times*, October 5, 1916.
2. New York *Call*, October 7, 1916.
3. *New York Times*, October 6, 1916.
4. Samuel Weitzman, "The New York Transit Strike of 1916," unpublished M.A. thesis, February, 1952, pp. 3-23; Melvyn Dubofsky, *When Workers Organize: New York City in the Progressive Era*, Amherst, Mass., 1962, pp. 88-126; Philip S. Foner, *History of the Labor Movement in the United States,* New York, 1982, vol. 6, pp. 65-102.

The strikers' demands included a ten-hour working day to be concluded within twelve consecutive hours; overtime to be paid at the rate of time and a half; and the right of workers to be represented by the Amalgamated.

5. *New York Times*, October 6, 1916.
6. The dismissal of woman's suffrage in this instance is particularly strange in view of the fact that the Women's Trade Union League which supported the strike and helped the wives of the strikers fought for both "bread and other necessities" and suffrage. (*See* Foner, *Women and the American Labor Movement*, pp. 482-83.)

Despite the militancy of both the carmen and their wives, the strike was lost. One of the reasons was the failure of the New York City unions to support a move for a general strike on behalf of the car strikers. (Dubofsky, *op. cit.*, pp. 126-38.)

Let Us Have a Strike — A Strike to Strike the Kaiser off the Throne

Speech delivered at 1918 United Mine Workers convention

In her speech to the 1916 UMW convention, Mother Jones told the delegates that the women of Europe could stop the war that had enveloped the continent and was threatening to drag the United States into the conflagration. "Twenty women with a consciousness of what war means to the children yet to come could stop that war," she cried. As for the United States, it should have nothing to do with the slaughter in Europe. "They are all grown fellows who are fighting each other, and if they think it is better to go out and fight for the king than for humanity, for civilization, why let the guys do it and let us fight at home to preserve this country."[1]

A little over two years later, Mother Jones again addressed a national UMW convention, but this time the United States was itself at war. Congress, at the request of President Wilson, had declared war against the Central Powers (Germany and her allies) on April 6, 1917. Mother Jones, however, no longer spoke of the war as a conflict in the interests of kings, but as a war on behalf of humanity, and she told the delegates:

We are in a war today, the nation is facing a crisis and you must not look at it with indifference. . . . Don't think this war will end tomorrow, not at all. And if we are going to have freedom for the workers we have got to stand behind the nation in this fight to the last man. There may be those who want peace. I don't want peace on any terms, I am not willing to take it or concede it. Perhaps I was as much opposed to war as any one in the nation, but when we get into a fight I am one of those who intend to clean hell out of the other fellow, and we have got to clean the kaiser up. Now, mind you, I don't mean the German people, I mean the kaiser, the dictator; I mean the grafter, the burglar, the thief, the murderer — the men of that type will have to be cleaned up.[2]

Mother Jones, of course, was not the only person in the American labor movement to change from opposition to all-out support of the war.[3] Indeed, she was not even the only one in the United Mine Workers to undergo such a change. John P. White, president of the UMW, refused to participate in the trade union conference held in Washington, D.C. at A.F. of L. headquarters where Samuel Gompers obtained a unanimous adoption of a resolution in support of the war should the Wilson administration call for it. In a letter to Gompers, dated March 3, 1917, White noted that he saw "no humanitarian issue in the present war," and "little sentiment among the working people in favor of this terrible war." But as soon as Congress declared war, White rallied the

*United Mine Workers behind the war effort, proudly became a perma-
nent member of the wartime Federal Fuel Board and labor adviser to
fuel administrator Harry A. Garfield, promptly resigning his UMW
presidency.[4]*

*Still better than any of the others, Mother Jones should have known
that the war would injure and not advance the cause of the working
class, and she had seen enough Kaisers in the United States' industrial
feudalism to realize that the German Kaiser could do little to make conditions worse for those in the feudal domains of West Virginia and Colorado. Certainly she should have known how the conflict in Europe was
being used as a device to suppress the labor movement in the United
States. A month before the trial of Tom Mooney and Warren K. Billings
on the false charge that they had thrown a bomb into a Preparedness
Day parade in San Francisco on July 22, 1916, killing nine and
wounding forty, Mooney had asked Mother Jones to help.[5] She replied:
"I feel you boys have been victims in this diabolical crime and innocent
from the beginning, I will do everything that I can to help you. . . . I
am yours in the struggle for a nobler civilization."[6]*

*Mother Jones was active in the Mooney protest movement, but, while
both were socialists, she did not share his opposition to America's entrance into the war. In fact, she showed no interest in the stand the
Socialist Party took at its emergency convention at St. Louis, Missouri,
April 7, 1917, the day after the American declaration of war against
Germany. After heated debate, the majority of the 193 assembled delegates adopted a report which declared the party's "unalterable opposition to the war just declared by the government of the United States."
The convention noted that American intervention "into the European
war was instigated by the predatory capitalists," and branded the declaration by President Wilson and Congress as "a crime against the
people of the United States and against the nations of the world." Finally, the Socialist Party pledged "continuous, active, and public opposition to the war, through demonstrations, mass petitions, and all other
means within our power."[7]*

*Not only did Mother Jones not play any role in the Socialist Party's
antiwar activities, she threw her influence against the leading party
champion of opposition to the war. In 1916 when Eugene V. Debs was
running for Congress in Indiana on an antiwar platform, Mother Jones
went to the state and campaigned for John Kern, the Democratic senator and ignored Debs.[8] Whether, as contemporaries and historians have
claimed, she was being used by the A.F. of L. and the Democratic Party
to embarrass and defeat Debs,[9] or whether, as seems to be clear from the
correspondence between her and Margaret Prevy (included below), [10]
her experiences with Debs and the Socialist Party in the Paint Creek —
Coal Creek strike of 1912-1913 in West Virginia, and a belief they had
betrayed the strikers, turned her against the party and its leaders, can
be debated.[11] But the fact remains that Mother Jones became a suppor-*

ter of the war drive, spearheaded by the very men who were leaders of Wall Street, the men who ran the National Civic Federation — the men whom she had long accused of being the real enemies of the American working class.

In her Autobiography, Mother Jones has only one reference to World War I. It reads:

During the war the working people were made to believe they amounted to something. Gompers, the president of the American Federation of Labor, conferred with copper kings and lumber kings and coal kings, speaking for the organized workers. Up and down the land the workers heard the word "democracy." They were asked to work for it. To give their wages for it. To give their lives for it. They were told that their labor, their money, their flesh were the bulwarks against tyranny and autocracy.[12]

She goes on to make it clear that the workers were fooled and betrayed. What she does not mention is that she was one of those who had sold the war to the American workers.[13] Her speech to the 1918 UMW convention is an excellent example of her salesmanship.

Yet here, as in almost everything she did, Mother Jones was not free of contradictions. In her speech to the convention, she urged the miners to dig coal for the war and indicated that the only strike that should be contemplated was a strike against the German Kaiser. Yet she herself was being roundly condemned by the coal operators for having imperiled the war program in the coal fields. George Wolfe, manager of the Winding Gulf Colliery in Raleigh County, West Virginia, informed the owner that the "Old Hag," as he called Mother Jones was stirring up the workers:

Mother Jones is with us again and held a meeting at Sophia yesterday afternoon in which she urged all to meet her tonight and organize, then strike. She states that the Operators are receiving six ($6) dollars per ton for their coal and the pitiful 20% raise is a mere bagatele, when by organizing and striking they could receive so much more. In your communications with the National Defense Council,[14] it might be well to call their attention to this, as it does not look well for greater output of coal to have such characters going around the country. The Old Hag has announced that she will invade the sacred precincts of Winding Gulf on the 5th day of May.[15]

Clearly, the fact that the official labor movement, including the United Mine Workers, had pledged not to strike during the war, did not influence Mother Jones, devoted though she was to the support of the nation's war effort.[16]

When Mother Jones appeared before the West Virginia State Federation of Labor Convention in the spring of 1918 to support the government's third Liberty Bond drive and asked the delegates to "back the president with bonds," she at least added that the wealth of the *capitalists ought to be conscripted along with the bodies of the working men![17]*

President Hayes:[18] I feel that the convention is very anxious to hear the distinguished visitor who has just come on the platform. She is a pioneer in our movement, a woman who has been with us for many years and has helped in all the great strikes that have occurred for years past. She needs no introduction to this convention of the United Mine Workers of America. I am now going to present the grandmother of the movement, a young lady of eighty-seven, Mother Jones.

Address of Mother Jones.

I want to say, boys, that I am glad I have lived to see this gathering of the miners in this country in this hall today. Years ago no one ever dreamt that this great mass of producers would meet in the capital of a great state. I am not going to throw any bouquets at you — I am not given to that at all. I did not expect to speak in this convention. I came here more to look it over until the officers of West Virginia came back. For the first time in the history of West Virginia we have good officers; that is, we have honest, clean, sober men. They don't make any crooked deals with the high class burglars — and if I catch one of them doing it I will see that he is hung so he will not make another.

I want to call your attention, as I have often done, to a few illustrations of what is taking place the world over today. History tells us that away back in the days of the Roman Empire they were gathering in the blood of men who produced the wealth, just as they have been doing up to this time. Back in that time the Roman lords said, "Let us go down to Carthage and stop the agitation there." They went down and all they arrested at that time they sold into slavery or held them. They do pretty much the same today, for the courts put you in jail, which is worse than any slavery. The Roman courts said to one young man, "Why do you carry on this agitation? Don't you know it is dangerous?" The young man said, "No, I didn't know it is dangerous, but I will tell you why I carry it on. I belong to a class that has been robbed, plundered, murdered, maligned, vilified, jailed, persecuted all down the ages, and because I belong to that class I feel it is my duty to awaken that class to their condition. The earth was not made for a few, but for all God's people." I wish I could imbue every man in this hall today with the same spirit that had possession of that pagan slave. Mind you, he was not a modern Christian, he was a pagan slave, but he was teaching Christ's doctrine to his brothers.

We are in a war today, the nation is facing a crisis and you must not look at it with indifference. Never in the history of the American nation has the government assumed such a responsibility as it has on its shoulders now. Don't think this war will end tomorrow, not at all. And if we are going to have freedom for the workers we have got to stand behind the nation in this fight to the last man. There may be those who want peace. I don't want peace on any terms, I am not willing to take it or concede it. Perhaps I was as much opposed to war as any one in the nation, but when we get into a fight I am one of those who intend to clean hell out of the other fellow, and we have got to clean the kaiser up. Now, mind you, I don't mean the German people, I mean the kaiser, the dictator; I mean the grafter, the burglar, the thief, the murderer — the men of that type will have to be cleaned up.

I heard you talking about the responsibility for the shortage of coal. There is no shortage of coal. The miners of this country are willing to dig coal day and night if the nation needs it. But there is a shortage of common sense in making the other fellow give up the cars. The miners are willing to dig Sunday, Monday, or any other day, but they can't get the cars. Without anybody knowing anything about it I took a trip from Charleston to Cincinnati. I got an old sunbonnet, put it on and went into every yard. I looked over the yards and saw cars by the hundreds laid away instead of being given to the miners. The miners in Cabin Creek worked only six hours in one week, and in Paint Creek not an hour. And then somebody will come forward and blame the miners! Let me tell you the miner is the best citizen there is in America. The miners in the Fairmount region haven't had cars, and the shortage of coal cannot be blamed on them. I counted sixty cars of coal this morning as I came along and they were all sidetracked. Why are engines not taken from other roads and attached to those cars to take them where they are needed? You cannot do business up in Washington, you have got to do it out through the country. Sitting down blowing off steam in Washington won't settle the question; you have got to have some people out to do the work. Not the fellow working for a dollar a year. That kind of gentleman don't know anything about it. Pick men from among the coal miners who understand the situation and they will furnish the coal. The president has taken over the railroads.[19] Well, then, let us have cars. But cut out the watered stock, because if we own the railroads we are not going to stand for watered stock. They have been robbing us long enough and we will attend to that later on — we are not going to bother with it now.

Every miner in West Virginia is perfectly willing to work day and night if the government needs him. The miners cannot produce the coal if you don't give them the cars to dump it into. The trouble lies with the railroads. What we must do is to settle down to one thing — no more strikes in the mines, not a single strike. Let us keep at one strike, a strike to strike the kaiser off the throne. Let us settle little grievances without conflicts, because the nation is in no condition to deal with those things today. Never in our history has the president had such things to contend with. Not Washington, nor Lincoln, not a president who ever sat in the presidential chair has gone up against it like the man who is there today. I am not in the habit of paying tribute to public officials as a rule, but I will say that the first time in your history you have been recognized as good citizens of the United States has been by the present chief executive of the nation. When he wrote to you he at least recognized that you are the bone and sinew of this nation, for without you the nation would perish. So I say I pay my respects to President Wilson. He took a stand that no president ever did before. He offered a proposition for the settlement of the Colorado strike when it looked very dangerous for the nation.[20] I don't believe even President Wilson realized how dangerous it was, but he sent out a proposition and the miners accepted it. You have been a little free from strikes since, but not from internal agitation and conflict. Now, boys, I want to tell you we have got to stop and bury all internal bickering[21] and rise like men to meet the danger to our nation. This is no time to fight to see who will be officers. You know when there is wrong there is no one in your ranks who will fight it more openly than I will, but I feel this is a time to give an example to workers all over the world.

I congragulate you on this magnificent convention. Talking to a mine owner today we discussed a few questions. He said, "I want to show you what organization does. In 1902 we had a convention of miners in West Virginia. In 1918 we had another. I stood in that convention and surveyed the men who were there representing some 30,000 members. As I looked at them I saw the change that had come about. The men in the convention this year got down to business, discussed vital questions; there was no conflict, each brought out his views, he got a hearing and then all agreed finally. That is the outcome of organization, education, and agitation. They were not drinking; they were attending to business."

I was in that convention and we didn't have any temperance cats howling around there; we didn't need them. The men had learned self-respect since they got shorter hours, did away with the pluck-me stores and got their pay in Uncle Sam's money instead of corporation scrip. They did not have to buy Armour's rotten beef from the company store. At one time I was staying at a miner's home after holding a meeting in 1901 with the enslaved army that was in the mines at that time. The mother got up in the morning and opened a can of Armour's choice roast beef. She started to put it in the buckets of the boys and found three fingers in the can under a layer of beef. Farther down she found part of a hand. I got it and took it away with me. We were going to have a meeting in the opera house in Montgomery the next day. I showed the men what they had to pay for in the pluck-me store. It was Armour's choice roast beef, mind you, and three fingers of the worker had been chopped off. They don't have to do that now. If they got a can of that sort of stuff they would hit the pencil pusher over the head with it, but in 1901 they had to take it or they were blacklisted. They are not blacklisted now, they have an organization behind them.

Another thing they have now is schools for the children. That convention in Charleston last week taught me one great lesson. There were men there from along the Kanawha River that were in bondage fifteen years ago. Often I had to go around in those days to hold a meeting with them in the dead of night. Now I can go in the daytime in all but a few places. We cannot do that in the Pocahontas field yet, but we are going in there one of these days, and I tell you when we do there'll be hell let loose. We want them to understand we are going out. America is fighting for democracy abroad and we are going to fight at home, so that when we lick the fellows abroad we will have here at home a nation with laws that will not be set aside by the Supreme Court.[22] When that day comes the Supreme Court will not be telling you you are criminals. The Supreme Court doesn't know what it is to suffer. In Washington, where four or five of them were discussing the great issues of the day, an old fossilized fellow who had been dead forty years before he was born said, "You know that the miners and the workers spend their money in saloons." I let him shoot off his hot air a while and said, "How much of your money did they ever spend? How much of their money did you spend? You spend a lot of it, because you have a stomach four miles long and two miles wide. If the miners do take a drink once in a while they need it. They have to go into the mines and work in water day after day and watch the roof for fear it will come down on them, watch for poisonous gases, and in West Virginia in some places they have to spend fourteen hours a day, or did some years ago. You know nothing about these things. You have been living off the life blood of your fellow-man and you have no conception of what he has to contend with."

To go back to the war. We will stay with Uncle Sam. He is the best uncle you ever struck. There is no other uncle in the world like Uncle Sam, and the convention must express its deep appreciation of President Wilson, who is the first president that ever sat in the executive chair of the nation who recognized this body of workers. It isn't anything but what he should have done, but he is the first one that did it, and for that reason I want to pay my respects to him. If we are going to have any difficulties let us go to the national government and put our case before them before any strike is called. Let us dig the coal and let us demand that we get cars to fill with coal. You know there is a game being played because Uncle Sam has taken over the roads. The pirates are onto the game and they are trying to embarrass the government. I will tell you what we will do. We will line up an army in West Virginia, capture the cars, get the engineers and firemen to run them down to the mines, load them and run them to Washington and New York.

You have a young president here; he is very young yet, but I want to tell you something. I want you to stand behind President Hayes and help him, and don't harass him any more than you can help. Let us stand together as one man behind him. There never was an hour in the history of organized labor when it was so essential for us to bury the hatchet, stand together and fight this battle of the nation to a finish as now. And when we have won, if they don't give us a square deal we will fight then. I want you to stand behind your president and do everything you can. He is young now, but before he gets through he will grow old. You have got a secretary who is one of the most able men in America in the industries. I have been watching him carefully. I watch them all and I know them all from A to Z.

I was traveling all night and I was fussing all day yesterday. A fellow asked me if I didn't think it was time for me to die, and I said "No, I have a contract to clean hell out of you fellows and I cannot go until I have helped civilize you." Now, be good boys and let us make this fight of our nation a fight to the finish. Show the world there is one grand body of men in America that stands loyally for the flag. You must understand that the men who watered the clay for seven long years with their blood, with blistered feet, weary backs and throbbing heads, they did it in order to hand down to you the noblest emblem ever handed down during all the generations of man as an evidence of their belief in social justice and industrial freedom. Their memory is dear to me. Every star in that flag was bought with the blood of men who believed in freedom, industrial freedom, particularly. Now it is up to us to carry on the work. Organize, organize, organize.

There is a system of industrial feudalism in the state of West Virginia but before another year ends the backbone of that damnable system will be broken and men will rise beneath those stars and stripes as they should rise, free for the first time. We propose to put the infamous gunmen there out of business. We will make them find other occupations. You are robbed and plundered to pay these gunmen that are hired to keep you in industrial slavery. If it takes every man of the 500,000 miners in this country to march into West Virginia we propose to drive out that feudal system that survives there. It is an outrage and an insult to that flag. They may as well prepare for business, for we are going to do it. The president of the Winding Gulf gang said in Washington, "Don't you know that Mother Jones swears?" I was asked, "Do you swear, Mother Jones?" I said, "You don't think I'm hypocrite enough to pray when I'm talking to those thieves!"

Now line up and stand with the government. No matter who says no, you fellows, every man of you, stand together, and when the fight is over across the water, if we have any kaisers at home we will line up. We will have the guns and our boys will be drilled. We will do business then and we will not ask to borrow money to buy guns. We will have the guns Uncle Sam paid for and we will use them on the pirates and put a stop to slavery. We will give the children of the future a chance to grow. We will teach the people of all the world what that flag stands for and we will not be betrayed by the workers. Let us pledge ourselves in this convention to stand beside the president until the battle is won. I would advise every one to join the Home Guards. Some one would ask why I recommend that. I recommend it because when they call out their army to crush the workers and destroy the future of the nation we will have the guns and we will turn them on the common enemy, not the workers. You have a chance today that has never come in the history of this country before and I want you to take advantage of it.

I had an appeal made to me that touched me more than anything has in years. A company of boys were going abroad from Bentley, West Virginia. The mother of one of the boys fainted. Her boy, with tears in his eyes, gazed at her. In spite of that the last thing he said was, "Mother, keep up the union until we come back and then we will all be one." There never was a grander appeal made by men who had been in slavery and bondage and had just accepted their chance. When they made that appeal I got a new light. I saw those boys going over the ocean to fight the battle for freedom, and they said, "Keep the boys together until we return and then we will all be one." So I say to you, boys, keep up the education and the agitation.

I know there may be some who will find a little fault with what I am going to say, but let me make this appeal to you: Instead of going to poolrooms and playing poker with mine owners or with any one else, get a book and read and study and prepare yourselves for the future. When you have an idle time, when you feel your brain is rested, get food out of some economic work by some master mind. When you play poker with a mine owner and you win money from him it is a bribe and he gives it to you for that purpose. I know some of you will condemn me, but I am onto the game. Stay at home and bring up your children to be good citizens. Your wives and children are the best companions and home is the best place in the world.

I want to say to you, President Hayes, if you send any organizers into the field where I am and they play poker games, if you don't take them out I will lick them and put them out. I complained about one and you took him out. The fellow lost $35 playing poker one night and I lodged a complaint against him. He wouldn't lose that money, it would go in on the pay roll and you would pay it. Now, I am warning you, and I want to tell you, Mr. Hayes, if you send any leeches and bloodsuckers into West Virginia we will send them out. We won't put up with them. We have got good men; there is no organization in the country that has as good men as the miners have, but they seldom get on the pay roll. Those men have got to work if they come into the field where I am or I will put them out.

A motion was made to print the speech made by Mother Jones.

President Hayes: That will be done without a motion. I have known Mother Jones for a number of years, I have worked with her in various fields, and she has always had the respect of the international organization. For seven years she worked under my direction as an organizer and the only orders I ever gave her was to go where she pleased. She always did that and she always said what she pleased. She is a free lance in this movement and I think the "young president" will profit by her suggestion.

So far as the organizing staff is concerned, it compares favorably with any other organizing staff in the country. I don't think Mother Jones intended to reflect upon the many good men on the organizing staff. If there is any man among the organizers who is not honest and who does not perform his duties, he goes off that staff. In the case she referred to the man went off the staff immediately when she reported it to me. I want to make that clear so that there will be no misunderstanding in the minds of the delegates to this convention as to where I stand upon the question she brought to your attention. I appreciate the splendid work Mother Jones has performed in the interest of this movement. She has rendered valiant service and in behalf of the delegates I desire to thank her for her address this afternoon.

Mother Jones: I worked under President White from the time he became president until he resigned and never at any time did he tell me what to do or where to go. There was only one time in the whole history when he said to me, "Mother, would you go into West Virginia and see if you can straighten out the boys?" I went in, but that is the only time he ever said a word to me in all the years I worked under him. I want now to express my appreciation for the kindly and courteous manner in which he treated me. If other presidents who preceded him had done the same the miners would not have been required to spend the amount of money they did in organizing some of the states and fewer lives would have been lost. We have harmony in West Virginia and we are certainly indebted to President White for that.

[Minutes of the Convention, United Mine Workers of America, 1918, pp. 359-67.]

Notes

1. *See* p. 275.
2. *See* p. 291.
3. At first Samuel Gompers, a prime example of this shift, denounced the war in Europe as "condemnable from every viewpoint," and stated his opposition to all efforts to prepare for national defense as maneuvers to involve the United States in the war. But by late 1915, Gompers had made a complete about-face, become an ardent champion of preparedness, and an enthusiastic supporter of American entrance in the war. (See Simeon Larson, *Labor and Foreign Policy: Gompers, the AFL, and the First World War, 1914-1918*, Rutherford, N.J., 1975, pp. 17-25; Bernard Mandel, *Samuel Gompers*, Yellow

Springs, Ohio, 1963, pp. 211-35; Marc Karson, *American Labor Unions and Politics, 1900-1918*, Carbondale, Ill., 1958, pp. 92-100.)

4. Lewis L. Lorwin, *The American Federation of Labor*, Washington, D.C., 1933, p. 145; Leonard Philip Krivy, "American Organized Labor and the First World War, 1917-1918: A History of Labor Problems and the Development of a Government War Labor Problem," unpublished Ph.D. thesis, New York University, 1965, pp. 20-28.

5. In the spring of 1916, Tom Mooney and his wife, Reena, led a bitter and unsuccessful fight to organize the car men of San Francisco. As President Wilson's mediation commission later reported, the utilities decided to "get" the Mooneys, and they were joined by the employers of San Francisco who were determined to maintain the open shop. Warren K. Billings was another young labor leader. Mother Jones had known Mooney even before the Preparedness Day frameup. In December 1915 Mooney had written to her, asking her to come to California to help the International Workers Defense League, of which he was the secretary, to help the three-year-old organization to pay off the debts incurred in acquitting Mooney of a charge of illegal possession of explosives. (The League was organized to help radicals in court, publicizing their cases, raising funds, and hiring attorneys. Local leagues were formed for specific cases, and the San Francisco league, of which Mooney was secretary, helped to raise support for Mother Jones during her imprisonments in West Virginia and Colorado. (Richard H. Frost, *The Mooney Case*, Stanford, Cal., 1968, pp. 30-42. There is a good deal of material about the League in the Thomas J. Mooney Papers, Bancroft Library, University of California, Berkeley.)

6. Tom Mooney to Mother Jones, Nov. 25, 1916; Mother Jones to Tom Mooney, Dec. 15, 1916, Mother Jones Papers, Department of Archives and Manuscripts, Catholic University of America, Washington, D.C. For the complete text of Mother Jones's letter, *see below* pp. 613-15 and for other correspondence dealing with the Mooney case, pp. 616-17, 622-23.

Mooney was sentenced to death and Billings to life imprisonment, but a series of labor protests in St. Petersburg, Russia, led by the recently-returned-to-Russia V. I. Lenin, played an important role in persuading President Wilson to commute Mooney's sentence of execution to life imprisonment. Despite ever-mounting evidence of their innocence and a continuing struggle for their release, in which Mother Jones participated, Mooney and Billings languished in prison for twenty more years. Both were finally pardoned by Culbert L. Olson, a progressive governor of California, for a crime they had never committed.

7. Alexander Trachtenberg, *The American Socialists and the War: A Documentary History of the Socialist Party Toward War and Militarism Since the Outbreak of the Great War*, New York, 1917, pp. 38-43.

8. After the United States entered the war, Debs continued his opposition to the war and he was arrested and imprisoned in federal prison, found guilty of violating the Espionage Acts passed in 1917 and 1918. Many other Socialists were also imprisoned during the war under the Espionage Act, including Kate Richards O'Hare, a leading woman in the Socialist Party, as were scores of leaders and members of the I.W.W. (*See* William Preston, Jr., *Aliens and Dissenters: Federal Suppression of Radicals, 1903-1933*, Cambridge, Mass., 1961, pp. 50-63; H. C. Peterson and Gilbert C. Fite, *Opponents of War, 1917-1918*, Madison, Wis., 1957, pp. 53-63; Philip S. Foner, *Women and the American Labor Movement: From World War I to the Present*, New York, 1980, pp. 38, 45.)

There is no evidence to indicate that Mother Jones ever protested the imprisonments or joined in any movement urging their release from prison.

9. Ray Ginger, *The Bending Cross: A Biography of Eugene Victor Debs*, New Brunswick, N.J., 1949, pp. 354-55.

10. *See* pp. 612-13.

11. *See above* pp. 218-19. Lorwin, (*op, cit.*, pp. 1006-07) believes that the experiences in West Virginia turned Mother Jones against the Socialist Party and Debs.

12. *Autobiography of Mother Jones*, p. 209.

13. Even after the war when she repeatedly pointed out how the capitalists had profited from the war and the workers had gained little, she kept referring, in speeches to strikers, to World War I as "your war." "The war — your war — has made the steel lords, richer than the emperors of old Rome," she told steel strikers in 1919. (*Ibid.* p. 222.)

14. The Council of National Defense was created by President Wilson in the summer of 1916. It was the first official step taken by the United States towards industrial preparedness for war. Samuel Gompers was later appointed as one of the seven members of the Advisory Commission of the Council of National Defense, and made chairman of the Committee on Labor.

15. George Wolfe, manager of Winding Gulf Colliery, to Justus Collins, president of Winding Gulf Coal Co., April 30, 1917, Justus Collins Papers, West Virginia University Library, West Virginia University, Morgantown, West Virginia.

16. Keith Dix, "Mother Jones," *People's Appalachia 1* (June-July, 1970): 9.

17. Frederick Allan Barkey, "The Socialist Party in West Virginia from 1898 to 1920: A Study in Working Class Radicalism," unpublished Ph.D. thesis, University of Pittsburgh, 1971, pp. 205-06.

18. Under the UMW constitution, if the president died or resigned, the vice-president automatically succeeded to the highest office and held it until the next scheduled election. Upon White's resignation to take a position with the federal government on the Fuel Administration Board, Hayes became president. Addicted to alcohol, he proved to be an ineffective union leader.

18. On December 28, 1917, in order to prevent the occurrence of strikes on the railroads during the war, and to make it possible to use them more efficiently for war-making purposes, all of the important railroads of the nation were placed under the control of the federal government. The telephone and telegraph system followed on July 31, 1918.

19. The government also took over the telephone and telegraph.

20. Hayes had hardly become president when he was attacked by district leaders in Illinois, Washington, and Kansas, who were out to succeed him as president.

21. The reference is to the fact that the Supreme Court had practically wiped out labor's victory in the Clayton Anti-Trust Act, passed during the first Wilson administration, which Gompers hailed as "Labor's Magna Carta" because it seemingly outlawed injunctions in labor disputes. But as early as 1917, in the Duplex Printing Press Company case, the court, in granting an injunction to the company, argued that "the emphasis placed on the 'lawful' and 'lawfully,' 'peaceful' and 'peacefully' . . . (in Section 20 of the Clayton Act) strongly rebutted a legislative intent to confer a general immunity for conduct violative of the Anti-Trust laws." In the same year, the Supreme Court decided in favor of the Hitchman Coal Company against the United Mine Workers, and the majority decision gave legal sanction to the "yellow dog" contract. This was followed

by a widespread use of this anti-labor contract, despite the existence of the Clayton Act, until it was declared unenforceable by the Norris-LaGuardia Act in 1932. (Foner, *op. cit.*, vol. 5, pp. 140-41.)

22. In the spring of 1918, Mother Jones announced that for the first time she was "urging working men and women to buy government (war) bonds." (James Weinstein, *The Decline of Socialism in America*, New York, 1967, pp. 164-65.) Then when she rode at the head of a win-the-war parade in Charleston, West Virginia, with the mayor and county sheriff at her side, and followed by a mile-long procession of union miners, the *United Mine Workers Journal* noted "What a Difference," and editorially contrasted the new attitude toward UMW leaders with the "old days of the Paint Creek Strike — not so long ago . . . when Mother Jones tried to help the coal miners" and "was thrown into jail and guarded by mine-owned militia." (Quoted in David Alan Corbin, *Life, Work, and Rebellion in the Coal Fields: The Southern West Virginia Miners 1880-1922*, Urbana, Illinois, 1981, p. 181.)

If You Want to See Brutal Autocracy, Come With Me to the Steel Centers

Speeches at United Mine Workers of America convention,
Cleveland, Ohio, September 9, 1919

When Mother Jones mentioned in her Autobiography *that workers believed during the war that they would enjoy real "democracy" when victory came, but were disillusioned after the armistice, she cited one example — the steel industry. There were, of course, others. There had been much talk throughout the war years about "industrial democracy," and to many workers, this had meant at the very least, that the principles and policies established by the War Labor Board would be retained, and that "collective bargaining" under which labor might meet business on an equal footing would become a permanent feature of labor-capital relations.[1] The War Labor Board's endorsement of collective bargaining and union standards, and the government's policy of filling its contracts with union labor had contributed to the rapid growth of the A.F. of L. Between January 1917 and January 1919 its membership rose by a million to more than 3½ million. In 1918 alone, the federation increased its size by 19.6 percent.[2]*

Within three months of the armistice, the American economy entered a recession brought about by the transition from war to peacetime production. When normal production resumed, employers were determined to operate without unions and with much lower wages than they had granted to workers under government pressure and as a patriotic gesture to win the war. They made it clear that what they really had in mind for labor all along was the "open shop," and that if workers had to be represented at all, they should be represented by company unions.[3]

The Wilson administration also showed no interest in helping labor to maintain its wartime gains. The emergency war labor adjustment agencies, especially the War Labor Board, were scrapped and, after having built up labor's hopes with assurances that "wartime sacrifices" would be amply repaid in peacetime, the government proceeded to shed any responsibility it had assumed toward the American workers.[4]

All this, it must be remembered, was occurring at a time when the world was undergoing a revolutionary upsurge. In November 1917 the Bolsheviks gained power in Russia, establishing the first socialist state in world history, and touching off rebellions in Germany and Hungary. In Italy workers seized factories, while in Great Britain, the Labour party, which had replaced the Liberals as the nation's second party, proclaimed its program for a postwar socialist order.[5]

In the United States, too, workers were on the march. The year 1919 was one of the most militant in American labor history. During these twelve months, 3,630 strikes were called, a number never before reached and not to be exceeded until 1946, and 4,160,000 workers were involved, representing about 22 percent of the entire work force. The Literary Digest called it a year characterized by "an epidemic of strikes," and the Outlook lamented: "Everywhere strikes . . . The strike fever is in the air. . . . The situation changes kaleidoscopically. The disease that has struck our industrial systems breaks out in one place as it subsides in another; one strike is scarcely over when another one begins."[6]

The year began with a general strike in Seattle where for five days in February, the city's workers paralyzed local industry and services except for those of a life and death nature, and before 1919 was over, the strike wave included a wide variety of working people from telephone operators to steelworkers and coal miners. In Boston, early in September, even the city's Irish police force walked off the job. Later that month, the largest strike of the early twentieth century occurred as 360,000 iron- and steelworkers left work in the first mass strike to affect that giant industry.

The steel strike was the only one in which Mother Jones was involved in 1919, and turned out to be the last major strike of her long career. While she was on the Pacific Coast mobilizing support for Tom Mooney and raising funds for the defense campaign,[7] she learned that a National Organizing Committee for Organizing Iron and Steel Workers had been established by the A.F. of L., that John Fitzpatrick[8] and William Z. Foster[9] were its leaders, and that the committee was planning to launch an organizing campaign to bring the unorganized steelworkers into the labor movement, and win for them an eight-hour day in place of the existing twelve-hour day, one day off during the week, instead of the existing seven-day week (with a twenty-four-hour shift on Sunday), union recognition, and an end to autocracy in the company towns. Mother Jones respected both Fitzpatrick and Foster as able and honest labor leaders, and she decided to proceed at once to Pittsburgh, and lend her experience and voice to the campaign to organize the steel industry.[10]

When she arrived in the steel city, she met at once with William Z. Foster. Foster explained that the National Organizing Committee was an awkward and cumbersome vehicle through which to conduct an effective organizing drive since it consisted of a coalition of twenty-four separate craft unions, each retaining its own jurisdiction and autonomy, but that in order to obtain A.F. of L. backing for the organizing drive both he and Fitzpatrick had had to accept this method. Apart from this, the steelworkers were not easy to organize; most of them were immigrants and spoke very little English. They had been hired for that very reason, Foster continued, for immigrants were easier to control than native Americans, and would work for lower wages since they had little choice. In addition, the steel towns had been "closed" to union organizers, and every effort to unionize steel since the disastrous defeat at Homestead in 1892 had ended in failure except for the victory of the I.W.W. at the Pressed Steel Car Company in Pittsburgh in 1909, and that had not lasted long. Already the companies had influenced local judges to issue injunctions prohibiting meetings and speeches of any kind — even on street corners and empty lots. Committee organizers were working in spite of the injunctions, and as a result, at any given time, half of them were in jail.

Mother Jones had gone through all of this before in West Virginia, Colorado, and other company towns, and she informed Foster she was leaving immediately. For the next two weeks, she traveled up and down the Monongahela River, speaking to thousands of steelworkers in dozens of towns. Two items in the Pittsburgh Post, the first on August 18, and the second on August 27, 1919, tell something of her activities:

3,000 CHEER "MOTHER" JONES ON SOUTHSIDE

Steel Workers Crowd Hall at Organization Meeting.

More than 3,000 Southside iron and steel workers crowded the Falcon hall on South Eighteenth street last night, in a meeting held for the purpose of organizing the employes of the Southside steel mills. There was no disorder and four patrolmen detailed from the South Thirteenth street police station had no trouble handling the crowd.

"Mother" Jones, the principal speaker of the evening, was applauded lustily when she made her appearance at the hall, accompanied by J. G. Brown, general organizer of the American Federation of Labor, and John Weirencki, local organizer, who were the other speakers.

In her address, "Mother" Jones derided the "spotters" who she said, were in at-

tendance at the meeting. She told of her experiences at the miners' strike in Fairmont, W. Va., a year ago and of being jailed for her utterances. . . .

Weirencki addressed the meeting which was attended largely by foreigners, in their native tongue, urging the men to join the American Federation of Labor. It was announced that permanent headquarters will be opened by the organization committee of the American Federation of Labor at South Eighteenth street.

MOTHER JONES FREED: THREE ARE FINED

Following a hearing before Burgest P. H. McGuire in the Homestead police station last night, "Mother" Jones, a worker for the American Federation of Labor, who with three others was arrested last Wednesday, while speaking from an automobile to a gathering of iron and steel workers in Fifth Avenue, Homestead, was discharged. J. G. Brown of Seattle, Wash., and J. L. Boghan of Chicago, organizers for the Federation, were each fined $1 for holding the meeting without a permit. . . .

On September 8, Mother Jones temporarily halted her organizing to attend the UMW convention in Cleveland, and was called upon by Acting President John L. Lewis[12] to address the delegates. Her speeches were almost entirely devoted to the steel organizing campaign, and she urged the delegates to throw their full weight behind the drive.

The chair will ask the delegates who are seated on either side of Mother Jones to escort her to the platform.

The entire delegation arose and applauded as Mother Jones was escorted to the platform.

Acting President Lewis: This is one great assemblage of men where Mother Jones needs no introduction. She comes today from somewhere, I know not where, but from wherever she hails we know she has been on an errand of assistance and mercy to the down-trodden toilers, and she merely stops for a moment to come into her own union, there to greet her own boys. Her life has been devoted to the cause for which she has given her years and her wisdom and her ability. She has come to be loved by every man who has ever attended our conventions and by all the mine workers of the United States. We claim her as our own.

ADDRESS OF MOTHER JONES.

I didn't come into the convention this afternoon to speak, but they took me by surprise — like the police did. I am not going to take up much of your time. There has been too much time spent in oratory. For the last four weeks I have been with the steel workers. If you want to see brutal autocracy, come with me to the steel centers and I will show it to you. The world does not dream of the conditions that exist there.

Eighteen years ago I talked to the men of Youngstown and they said to me: "What are we going to do, Mother?" "I don't know what you are going to do unless you get together," I told them. The steel company, with its usual methods of bribery, gave them stock at eighty dollars a share. In a few months it dropped to thirty dollars, although they could not strike. They had them by the throat. A few of them struck, but they had to go back beaten. If there is any body of men in the United States that require your thought and consideration it is the steel workers. I was in Monessen last Sunday and 18,000 men came to a meeting. Some of them were worn out, some had hopes for another day. Some had their backs bent with the burden of years and the whip of the master. But they all came believing there was a new message for them.

One chap said to them: "You know we are going to have a strike. Now you must be peaceful, we must have peace." Imagine what a statement to make to men who were going on strike! I wonder if Washington was peaceful when he was cleaning hell out of King George's men. I wonder if Lincoln was peaceful. I wonder if President Wilson was. And then this gentleman gets up and tells us we must be peaceful! When he sat down I said: "I want to take issue with you" — an old fossilized thing that hadn't worked for twenty years, but he drew his salary — "I want to tell you we're not going to have peace, we're going to have hell! Strikes are not peace. We are striking for bread, for justice, for what belongs to us."[13]

The speaker who preceded me referred to Mr. Gary. The boys wrote and asked Mr. Gary to give them a hearing. He refused. Then the president of the United States wrote and asked him for a hearing and he refused again.[14]

Mr. Chairman, I would like to be president of the United States for one month. If I had been president and Mr. Gary had said, "Nothing doing!" I would have sent two United States marshals up with a pair of handcuffs, have him brought to Washington and said: "Now, there is something doing!" Going on your knees to a bunch of robbers and begging will do no good. When any pirate insults the president of the United States he insults the whole nation.

The men of Monessen were told by the mayor on the first of April that they could not speak, but we talked anyhow. When I addressed the meeting I said: "Mr. Mayor, I will give you a lesson it may be well for you to follow. When I was a rather young woman, down on the Mississippi River, where there were no railroads to carry passengers in that direction, they used to go on the steamers. The freight was carried in those steamers and the ones that got in first got the most freight. One particular steamer was making an effort to get in first. A lot of steam was coming out of the steamer and the captain thought he would lose the race. He told a darkey to sit on the valve. He did. After a while he said, "Massa, this thing's getting too hot." "Never mind, keep your seat." After a while the darkey said, "This is getting too hot,

307

sure." "No matter, I want to get into port." The darkey stayed a while longer and said, "Massa, if you don't let that steam out it will blow hell out of all of us." What happened? In a few minutes the steam blew the captain and all of them into the Mississippi River. "Mr. Mayor, let them blow off their steam. You are a great deal safer if they do that, and so is the nation." These men in public office who want to stop free speech are creating more Bolshevism and I.W.W.ism than any other institutions you have got. I said to the 8,000 men in that meeting: "How many of you are going to come into this strike?" They all put up their hands and gave three cheers for Uncle Sam. The Sunday before we went to Duquesne. The secretary of the steel workers was arrested. Another man got up to speak and he was pulled off. And then, of course, I had to step in — it wouldn't go unless I said something. I got up and all I got a chance to say was: "Men, stand like the men of '76!" when two big, burly policemen got me by the shoulders. "What's the matter?" said I: "Come and we will show you." "All right," said I. I went along. I have been in bull pens and locked up before, but this was the first time I was ever behind iron bars.

Then the lap dogs of the Gary crowd came there and one of them said: "Now, Mother Jones, I want to tell you something." I had my nose out between the bars looking at him. He said: "With your experience you ought to do a wonderful lot of good; you should not be agitating." "Why?" I asked. "Because," he said, "you could do better work." "I thought this was a very good work." "Oh, no," he said. "Stop a minute," I said. "Right here in and around Pittsburgh today a million people went on their knees and paid a tribute to the man who agitated nineteen hundred years ago in Palestine; and not only that, but they arose and sang songs of gratitude to Him."

Another lap dog of the steel trust said: "Oh, but He wasn't an agitator." "Why the hell did you hang him for then?" said I. He had no reply to make to that. Then he said that the people there were all foreigners. "That is the very reason we want to organize them," I told him. "We want them to understand what American institutions stand for, and if they do not understand the language they can not understand the institutions."

"But they are all contented," he told me. "Then they are very dangerous citizens," said I, "because an American citizen is never contented; he sees a civilization beyond, and beyond that he is going to aim at and go after. We are going to organize them all anyhow, and you can jail us all you want to. We build the jails. Now when we get brains enough we will put you in jail."

In Homestead the labor men were allowed to speak for the first time in 28 years.[15] We were arrested the first day. When I got up to speak I was taken. Eight or ten thousand labor men followed me to the jail. They all marched there. When we went into the jail they remained outside. One fellow began to cry and said: "What for you take Mudder

Jones?" and they took him by the neck and shoved him behind the bars. That is all he did or said. We put up a bond of $15 each. We were to come for trial the next day, but the burgess didn't appear. They postponed the trail on account of the mob that appeared outside. When they got me in jail the police themselves got scared to death. One of our men said: "Mother can handle those men." He was told, "No, nobody can handle them." "Yes, she can; let her get out." I went out and said: "Boys, we live in America! Let us give three cheers for Uncle Sam and go home and let the companies go to hell!" And they did. Everybody went home, but they went down the street cheering. There was no trouble, nobody was hurt — they were law-abiding. They blew off steam and went home.

In Duquesne they took forty men. One man came out of a restaurant and asked what the trouble was. They got him by the back of the neck and put him behind the iron bars. He was kept there from two o'clock Monday afternoon until ten o'clock Sunday morning without a bite to eat or even a drink of water. That was the only crime the man had committed. Is there any kaiser who is more vicious than that? Do you think it is time for us to line up, man to man, and clean out those kaisers at home?

The steel workers have taken a strike vote and decided to strike. You men must stand behind them. Never mind what anybody says, that strike will come off next Monday. The miners and all the other working men of the nation must stand with them in that strike, because it is the crucial test of the labor movement of America. You are the basic industry. They didn't win the war with generals, and the President didn't win the war. They could have sent all the soldiers abroad, but if you hadn't dug the coal to furnish the materials to fight with, what could they have done? You miners at home won the war digging coal. You have been able to clean up the kaisers abroad, now join with us and clean up the kaisers at home.

Gary gave a banquet to the newspaper men in New York. I happened to be in New York at that time. During the dinner they discussed the labor movement, and some newspaper man said: "Well, you know there is a great deal of discontent." Gary said: "I will tell you what we can do — we can give them a cup of rice and that will quiet them." I want to tell Judge Gary to be careful or he may have to eat the rice himself before this thing is over. That is what was said to the people in France before the revolution, when they were starving, and the people didn't take rice; they did away with the divine right of kings, and we are going to do away with the divine right of these rulers who rob and plunder the people.

A woman was murdered in Pennsylvania the other day (Mrs. Fannie Sellens).[16] You fellows didn't amount to a row of pins! You ought to have lined up fifty thousand men and women and gone there and cleaned up that gang that murdered that woman in cold blood. You haven't got any manhood in you! You want Congress to investigate. How very thoughtful you are! They got Congress to investigate for you. Not on your life! Why didn't you do as we did in West Virginia? We do business down there.

A Delegate: "Our officers have told us to keep out of politics. I advise them to go into politics."

Mother Jones: Oh, shut up with your rotten politics! We have got things more serious than politics.

I went up Stanford Mountain and talked to a boy up there. He said: "Mother, when you find us you will find us always together." That very night up went the mine owners' gunmen and shot that man while he slept. One man lay dead over there, another over here — two as loyal men as ever lived — and the blood streamed down on each side. Even in death they were together. The shacks were riddled and those people had been murdered while they slept. Ten days afterward I went up the mountain again, and out in the field I saw a mother with her baby kneeling over the grave of one of those men. When she saw me the baby said: "Oh, Mother Jones, won't you bring my daddy back? Won't you bring him back and let me kiss him?" When the history of these struggles is written by those who saw them at first hand it will not be a eulogy of officers, it will be a history of the crimes the workers have stood for, and hundreds in the days to come will stand aghast as they read.

I want you to stand by the steel workers. The call has gone out and I don't think it will come back.[17] I know what I am talking about. I don't live in the parlor, I am not a Sunday school teacher, I am right down in the trenches and I see the horrors. I remember one awful night when that man came to see me (pointing to President Keeney, of District 17) at one o'clock in the morning. It was in 1912. He came to me with tears in his eyes and said nobody would come to them. He asked if I would come.

I was thinking it was time to break in there anyhow, so I said I would go. He said, "But they might kill you." I said I was not afraid, that I could meet no more glorious death than fighting those thieves and robbers. We went up that morning with a company of militia. Of course, the governors always have to send the bayonets when labor is going to pull anything off. In the face of the gunmen, the bayonets and their employer, in the face of a whole gang of operators those men asked me if I would organize them. I asked if I organized them would they stay in the organization. They all said "Yes." Then old "Peggy" Dwyer, who has only one leg, wheeled around on that and said: "Yes, we will stay," and they made good.

In West Virginia you have over 50,000 miners organized, and before another year you will have over 80,000. If you send a fellow in there that don't suit us, Mr. Lewis, we will ship him out. That is the way we do business. I put up many a scheme to get rid of the leeches, and there are a few more of them I will get after before I get through. I remember when that boy there (President Keeney) was a little fellow. I gave him a book one Sunday and said to him and a few more: "Go up under the trees and read. Leave the pool room alone. Read and study and find out how to help your fellow miners." And he did it.

I will probably go back to the steel strike tomorrow. I told the boys I would be back for a big meeting Thursday night. Yesterday I wrote the attorney general in Washington and told him: "This thing won't go and it is the duty of the government to stop it. The people will not submit to this tyranny and oppression." I also sent an article to the Washington *Times*, because that is at the seat of government, it is where the congressmen and senators are. I called attention to these cheap office holders, these pie counter politicians who have no interest in the nation.[18] We have. You children will be the future population of the country, and it is your duty to stand together in this great battle that is coming. And when we get through America will be here for the Americans and not for the cheap, rotten royalty of Europe. We are Americans.

When President Keeney had the army up on New River the governor telegraphed to General Wood for the United States troops. That is the first thing they ask for when you are concerned; but they didn't ask for the United States troops to bring Gary down to Washington. Oh, no! that is another thing! Did you ever see one of those fellows beat up by a policemen? You bet your life you didn't! Did you ever see one of those fellows build a jail or make a club to use on you? No, you build the jails and make the clubs and they use them on you. It is only the working man that gets clubbed. He finds the stuff to make the guns and the clubs, he hires the policemen — the other fellow does — puts the club and the gun in his hands and he goes out and gets you. Did you ever see a man with five million dollars in the penitentiary? No, of course not. Then why don't you build a jail and a have a court that will put them in and put you out?

A rising vote of thanks was tendered Mother Jones for her presence in the convention and for her inspiring address. . . .

ADDRESS OF MOTHER JONES

Now, boys, I have got to go; I am called away. I don't know whether it will ever be my privilege to attend another of your conventions. The battle of ages is on; we have got to fight it and it has got to be won. In an hour or so I will leave for the steel strike in Pittsburgh. I have no doubt the bonds of those poor steel workers will be broken before we end. It has been a long struggle, but it is going to come to an end.

Now, I am going to say a few words to you, and I want you to pay attention to what I say. Don't forget the men and women who gave up their lives for this movement in Utah, Colorado, West Virginia, and

311

Pennsylvania. This movement was founded on the blood of men who tramped the weary pathway at night, often hungry and cold, to carry the message of a better day to you. Some of you remember the awful day at McCray's School House, when you walked forty miles, hungry and worn out, to attend that meeting. The fact of your meeting here today is due to the work of those men who are in their graves.

I remember one terrific strike on the Iron Mountain. There was no American Federation of Labor in those days. The organization wasn't very strong and men had very little money. When they were about to call the strike I said to one of the men: "I don't know whether it is safe or not; I question whether some of those aristocratic organizations will respond." He was called by telegraph from Kansas City to St. Louis. When he registered at the hotel he was being taken to his room when two men said: "Come this way." He went. They locked him in a room, put the strike call in his hand, and with two pistols at his head told him to sign it. He had to do it. The men were the secretary and treasurer of that organization, both detectives.

The strike went on, and of course it was lost. However, I think no strike is ever completely lost. We give the other fellows a fight and let them know we can come back. I met Martin Irons when he was going away with a little parcel under his arm.[19] I asked him where he was going and he said: "God knows! I don't. They have taken my wife, my home, my health — they have broken my heart. They have taken all I have — I don't know where I am going." "No, they haven't," I said. "They have left you the greatest gift God ever gave to man, they have left you an honest name and that beats all the wealth of the world."

I never saw Martin Irons again, but one day I got off the train at Bruceville, Texas, and asked the agent to take me to the cemetery where Martin Irons was buried. He took me to the grave of that warrior who paved the way for you. His only tombstone was the half of a broken shovel. I said: "This has ever been the fate of the heroes of the world." In Memphis he was arrested as a vagrant. T. V. Powderly sent fifteen dollars to pay his fine and got him off. I wrote the matter up and showed how he was deserted by those he tried to save. You have done that all the way down and through history. He did more than any man I know. He was maligned and persecuted. I wrote about his neglected grave and the State Federation of Missouri put a monument over his grave. I made arrangements with the miners of Illinois to give him a grave and raise money for a monument. I may do that before I die, for I don't like to have him down there alone.

There are men lying in their graves today that marched through blinding snow storms, they slept in section houses, they got something to eat from section men. They went barefooted to pave the way for you to meet here today, and, boys, I know that every insidious method is going to be used to wreck the organization they founded. You make mistakes, we all do. We were born hungry, the brain was starved. We had to work and let the other fellow live off us. Now I beg of you for the sake of your children, for the sake of the revolution that is on, I beg of you for the sake of the heroes that are going to break into the war Monday for a better civilization, to bury the hatchet and come together, regardless of what may happen. Let the enemy see that we are a solidified army and ready for the war if they want it.

I have got sore myself at times, but you all know you haven't an officer I will not get after if I am convinced he is a traitor, and if he is I will get him down or die. There is more than one of them I got down. Now I am asking you to come together. Mr. Lewis, get those boys up here and make them shake hands, and you shake hands with them. Be friends.[20]

Acting President Lewis: They are all friends of mine, Mother.

Mother Jones: Help your president to win the battle. Illinois was one state the powers that be were afraid of. Are you going to betray the boys that gave up their lives at Virden for this organization? No, I know you won't. Bury the hatchet. Your conventions are getting too big and cost too much money. The money comes out of your pockets and when you need it, instead of giving it to hotels, the railroads and the pool rooms, save that money and raise hell with the powers that are on our backs. We need every dollar we can get to clean the other fellow up, because we are on the war path now. I have a picture here that was taken in New York. It is of Gary and Schwab, the two gentlemen that dictate to the government. We are going to move, and we are going to dictate to those two high class burglars.

Now, bury the hatchet, every one of you. Shake hands with your president and secretary and say that you will be friends from now on. I wouldn't have your job for a million dollars, Mr. Lewis. I learned ten months ago that a tremendous fund had been raised to destroy the United Mine Workers from within. They cannot succeed from the outside, but they are playing the game from within. I want you to get up and tell those pirates that they cannot destroy this organization, for it is founded on too solid a foundation and it is going on until we win.

A rising vote of thanks was tendered Mother Jones for her presence in the convention and for her inspiring address.

[Proceedings of the Twenty-Seventh Consecutive and Fourth Biennial Convention of the United Mine Workers of America held at Cleveland, Ohio, September 9, 1919, pp. 536-43, 616-18.]

Notes

1. C. J. Hendley, "The Effect of the World War on American Labor," *Labor Age*, March, 1926, p. 22.

2. *American Federationist* 25 (December, 1918): 1097.

3. *Proceedings*, AFL Convention, 1919, p. 303; Theresa Wolfson and Abraham Weiss, *Industrial Unionism in the United States*, New York, 1937, p. 21.

4. *New Republic* 13 (July 30, 1919): 405.

5. *New York Times*, June 12, 1919.

6. Florence Peterson, *Strikes in the U.S., 1880-1936*, Department of Labor, Bulletin No. 61, Washington, D.C., 1938, table 18, p. 39; *Literary Digest*, October 25, 1919, p. 11; *Outlook* 119 (October 29, 1919): 224.

7. Featherling, *op. cit.*, p. 155.

8. John Fitzpatrick was a close friend of Mother Jones.

9. William Z. Foster (1881-1961), was born in Taunton, Massachusetts, but moved to Philadelphia with his family as a child, and was forced by poverty to work at the age of ten. He traveled about the country becoming acquainted with workers in different industries, supported William Jennings Bryan in 1896, became a Socialist, and while covering the Spokane Free Speech Fight for the Seattle *Workingman's Paper*, a Socialist weekly, was jailed and on his release, joined the I.W.W. Foster left the I.W.W. under the influence of syndicalism and the principles of "boring-from-within," and became a member of the Brotherhood of Railroad Carmen, A.F. of L., and founder and leader of the Syndicalist League of North America. A successful organizing campaign in the Chicago stockyards led to his being appointed secretary of the A.F. of L.'s National Committee to Organize Iron and Steel Workers, of which Samuel Gompers was chairman. After the steel strike, he went to the Soviet Union and in 1922 joined the Communist Party. Foster rose to the position of party general secretary and Commununist presidential secretary in 1924, 1928, and 1932.

10. *Autobiography of Mother Jones*, pp. 209-11.

11. William Z. Foster, *The Great Steel Strike and Its Lessons*, New York, 1920, pp. 64-69.

12. John L. Lewis had been elected vice-president of the UMW in 1918 when he ran on the ticket with Frank Hayes, the successful presidential candidate. In the spring of 1919 Hayes traveled to Europe on a joint A.F. of L.-UMW mission to discuss postwar reconstruction with European labor leaders, leaving Lewis in the United States to serve as the UMW's acting president. After his return to the United States in midsummer 1919, his alcoholism worse, Hayes proved unable physically to administer the union, and Lewis continued to run the UMW officially.

13. *See* Jones, *Autobiography*, p. 214.

14. Judge Elbert Gary, a corporation lawyer, ran the United States Steel Corporation for J. P. Morgan. He refused to deal with any representatives of labor organizations not controlled by the company, and even when President Wilson personally urged him to meet the steelworkers' representatives, he refused.

15. That is since the defeat at Homestead in 1892. For Mother Jones in Homestead, *see* David Brody, *Labor in Crisis: the Steel Strike of 1919*, Philadelphia, 1965, pp. 93-94; *Autobiography of Mother Jones*, pp. 212-213, 218.

16. Fannie Sellins was killed on August 26, 1919, a month before the steel strike actually began. The victim was a long-time organizer of the miners, who was lent to the strike committee by the United Mine Workers. She was originally an organizer in the garment trades in St. Louis, concentrating on unionizing women garment workers. She began work for the United Mine Workers during a 1913 strike against the West Virginia–Pittsburgh Coal Company in

West Virginia, helping the wives and children of the strikers who had been evicted and lived in tent colonies. "My job," she recalled, "was to distribute clothing and food to starving women and babies, to assist poverty stricken mothers and bring children into the world, and to minister to the sick and close the eyes of the dying." Arrested for violating an injunction she was chastized by the judge, who warned her "not to emulate Mother Jones." But she proceeded to do exactly that, telling a meeting of strikers and sympathizers: "I am free and I have a right to walk or talk any place in this country as long as I obey the law. I have done nothing wrong. The only wrong they can say I have done is to take shoes to the little children in Colliers who need shoes. And when I think of their little bare feet, blue with the cruel blasts of winter, it makes me determined that if it be wrong to put shoes upon those little feet, then I will continue to do wrong as long as I have hands and feet to crawl to Colliers." (Lunt, *op. cit.*, pp. 37-42.)

Sentenced to jail with other UMW organizers, Sellins appealed for a presidential pardon which President Wilson, after having postponed the imprisonment for sixty days, finally granted. Sellins returned to organizing work. Before she was killed, she organized three huge U.S. Steel mills and two independent company plants. She was murdered outside the mill yard of the Allegheny Steel Company in West Natona, Pennsylvania, where she was organizing the workers. On August 26, when she approached the company yards, she saw gunmen beating Joseph Strzelecki, an old worker, with their guns. When she begged the gunmen to stop, a company official knocked her down. She tried to drag herself to the gate of a friend's house nearby. The *New Majority*, organ of the Chicago Federation of Labor, took up the tragic story:

" 'Kill the — — !' shouted the gunmen.

"An auto truck hurried to the scene. The body of the old miner (Strzelecki) was thrown in. Mrs. Sellins was dragged by the heels to the back of the truck and a deputy took a cudgel and crushed her skull before the eyes of a throng of men, women, and children, who stood powerless before the armed men."

In announcing the slaying, the Pittsburgh *Daily Dispatch* reported on August 27, 1919: "Mrs. Sellins was known throughout the country as an organizer, having assisted the mine workers' union in many campaigns for new members. She formerly resided in St. Louis, Mo. She leaves one son and three daughters. . . . She was secretary of the Allegheny Valley Trades Council."

William Z. Foster later wrote: "The guilty men were named in the newspapers and from a hundred platforms. Yet no one was ever punished for the crime." (*op. cit.*, p. 16.)

On August 26, 1938, the anniversary of her tragic death, a monument was erected by District No. 5, United Mine Workers of America, with this tribute to Fannie Sellins:

"Faithful ever to the cause of Labor,
All of us deeply regret the fate you met.
Nobly you fought the fight against greed and gain,
Never flinching with your efforts when the bullets came.
Immortal to miners shall ever be thy name
Embellished in their hearts the sacrifice you made."

(*United Mine Workers Journal*, September 15, 1938; *Daily Worker*, September 18, 1938.)

17. Although President Wilson requested the National Committee to post-

pone a strike until the national industrial conference he and Labor Secretary William B. Wilson had set for October 6 and though Gompers favored yielding to the president's request, the strike committee decided to go ahead.

18. An examination of the Washington *Times* for these weeks reveals no letter from Mother Jones.

19. *See* pp. 280, 265-66, 613.

20. For the bitter internal conflict developing in the UMW, *see* pp. 348-49.

I'm a Bolshevist from the Bottom of My Feet to the Top of My Head

Speech to steel strikers and their wives, Turner Hall,
Gary, Indiana, October 23, 1919

On September 22, 1919, 279,000 steelworkers responded to the strike call. Within the next few days, the number reached 300,000; at the peak of the strike, as many as 350,000 workers were off the job. The strike continued until January 8, 1920, when the National Committee announced:

The steel corporations with the active assistance of the press, the courts, the federal troops, state police, and many public officials have denied steel workers their rights of free speech, free assemblage, and the right to organize, and by this arbitrary and ruthless misuse of power have brought about a condition which compelled the national committee . . . to vote today that the active strike phase is now at an end.

The strike was defeated by a combination of factors — principally the refusal of employers to negotiate, police and military brutality toward the strikers, with wholesale arrests of workers, the fragmented, craft-like approach taken by the A.F. of L. to organize the steelworkers over Foster's objections, the ability of employers to exploit ethnic and racial divisions among workers, the refusal of the craft unions to permit blacks to join the strike, and the anti-radical hysteria stirred up by the government's "red scare" and "red raids" of 1919, including the widespread publicity given by the press to the Department of Justice's charge that the strike leaders aimed to turn the strike into a Communist revolution.[1]

In 1920 the Interchurch World Movement published a report on its investigation of the steel strike of 1919. The report stressed the fact that the civil liberties of the steelworkers had been destroyed during the strike: "Men were arrested without warrants, imprisoned without legal process, magistrates' verdicts rendered frankly on the basis of whether the strikers would go back to work or not." There were twenty-two victims of an unprecedented antilabor brutality, shot or beaten to death by police or company gunmen.[2]

William Z. Foster was critical of a number of the AFL leaders during the strike, accusing them of having sabotaged the struggle by withholding funds and opposing the organizers' radical politics. But for Mother Jones he had only words of praise. "Mother Jones," he wrote in his study, The Great Strike and Its Lessons, "lent great assistance to the steelworkers, dauntlessly going to jail and meeting the hardships and dangers of the work in a manner that would do credit to one half her age."[3] She was indeed a veritable dynamo of activity on behalf of the strikers, travelling to steel towns in Pennsylvania, Illinois, and Indiana, searching out places where she could meet and talk to the strikers. It was not easy. "If I were to stop and talk to a woman on the street about her child," she wrote, "the Cossacks would come charging down upon us, and we would have to run for our lives. If I were to talk to a man in the streets of Braddock we would be arrested for unlawful assembly."[4]

But she managed to make herself heard, speaking to strikers wherever a hall could be hired. Of all her speeches during this great struggle, the one which received the widest publicity was the one she delivered in Gary, Indiana on October 23, 1919, in an auditorium surrounded by federal troops who had been sent to Gary to maintain order.[5] Inside the hall were strikers and their wives but around the wall stood groups of armed soldiers. But as the following account of her speech compiled from reports in the New York Times and Chicago Tribune makes abundantly clear, Mother Jones was not intimidated.

Making the first public appeal for violence since the steel strike started in the Calumet region and declaring herself a Bolshevik, Mother Jones stirred to enthusiasm some twelve hundred strikers and their wives in Turner Hall, Gary, Ind., today following the refusal of the authorities to permit her to speak in East Side Park.

"So this is Gary," said Mother Jones, who was cheered for five minutes.

"Well, we're going to change the name and we're going to take over the steel works and we're going to run them for Uncle Sam. It's the damned gang of robbers and their political thieves that will start the American revolution and it won't stop until every last one of them is gone.

"We are to see whether Pennsylvania, whether Indiana, whether Illinois belong to Kaiser Gary or Uncle Sam. If Gary's got it, we are going to take it away from him and give it back to Uncle Sam. When we are ready we can scare and starve and lick the whole gang. Your boys went over to Europe. They were told to clean up the Kaiser. Well, they did it. And now you and your boys are going to clean up the Kaisers at home. Even if they have to do it with a leg off and an arm gone, and eyes out.

"Our Kaisers sit up and smoke seventy-five cent cigars and have lackeys with knee pants bring them champagne while you starve, while you grow old at forty, stoking their furnaces. You pull in your belts while they banquet. They have stomachs two miles long and two miles wide and you fill them. Our Kaisers have stomachs of steel and hearts of steel and tears of steel for the 'poor Belgians.'

"If Gary wants to work twelve hours a day let him go in the blooming mills and work. What we want is a little leisure, time for music, playgrounds, a decent home, books, and the things that make life worth while.

"Steel stock has gone up. Steel profits are enormous. Steel dividends are making men rich over night. The war — your war — has made the steel lords richer than the emperors of old Rome. And their profits are not from steel alone but from your bodies with their innumerable burns; their profits are your early old age, your swollen feet, your wearied muscles. You go without warm winter clothes that Gary and his gang may go to Florida to warm their blood. You puddle steel twelve hours a day! Your children play in the muck of mud puddles while the children of the Forty Thieves take their French and dancing lessons, and have their fingernails manicured!

"I'll be 90 years old the first of May, but by God if I have to, I'll take ninety guns and shoot hell out of 'em. For every scab on the mills there is a woman that reared him. Women, the destiny of the workingman is in your hands. Clear hell of every damned scab you can lay hold on. We'll hang the bloodhounds to the telegraph poles. Go out and picket."

Mother Jones then lectured the soldiers on guard in the hall. "You went abroad to clean up the Kaiser," she said, "and the bones of 60,000 of your buddies lie bleaching on the battlefields of France. My God, ain't you men enough to come over and help us get the Kaisers at home? We'll have an army as big as yours and you'll be with us and we'll lick hell out of 'em. We'll give Gary, Morgan, and the gang of bloodsuckers a free pass to hell or heaven."[6]

"God Almighty never made a man that could stop a woman from talking," she continued. "You can arrest me, but I'll be free. I can raise more hell in jail than out. If Bolshevist is what I understand it to be, then I'm a Bolshevist from the bottom of my feet to the top of my head.[7] All the world's history never produced a more brutal and savage time than this and Mr. Soldier, I'm ready to prove my statement that we've got to change or this nation will perish. This is the century of the worker.

"All through human history man has been telling and dreaming to this day. Christ was the world's greatest agitator, but I defy any one to tell me Christianity reigns. A lot of hypocrites are trying to hypnotize us to get down on our knees to the robbers. For Christ's sake be men and women."

[New York Times, *October 24, 1919*
Chicago Tribune, *October 24, 1919.*]

Notes

1. William Z. Foster, *The Great Steel Strike and Its Lessons*, New York, 1920, pp. 75-90; Brody, *op. cit.*, pp. 164-85; *New York Times*, January 4, 1920; *New Majority*, January 17, 1920.

2. Philip C. Ensley, "The Interchurch World Movement and the Steel Strike of 1919," *Labor History* 13 (Spring, 1972): 224-26.

3. Foster, *op. cit.*, p. 53. Strangely, in his autobiography *From Bryan to Stalin*, New York, 1937, Foster makes no mention of Mother Jones in the 28 pages he devotes to the steel campaign.

4. *Autobiography of Mother Jones*, pp. 215-16.

5. The federal troops were sent to Gary after fighting broke out between strikers and Negro strikebreakers imported by the steel operators. (John Fitzpatrick to Samuel Gompers, Chicago, March 30, 1920, AFL Correspondence.) Failure to allow Negroes to join the ranks of the strikers encouraged strikebreaking on their part and was listed by Foster as one of the most important lessons organized labor must learn from the steel strike.

6. In her *Autobiography* Mother Jones makes the point that the soldiers who had fought the Kaiser "fought the American workingman when he protested an autocracy beyond the dream of the Kaiser. Had these same soldiers helped the steel workers, we could have given Gary, Morgan, and his gang a free pass to hell." (p. 226)

7. Mother Jones used almost the identical words of Eugene V. Debs who on the anniversary of the Bolshevik revolution issued a statement from federal prison in Atlanta declaring his support for the Soviet Union and asserting: "I am a Bolshevik from the bottom of my feet to the top of my head." (Philip S. Foner, *The Bolshevik Revolution: Its Impact on American Radicals, Liberals, and Labor*, New York, 1967, p. 83.)

I Urge the Unity of Working People Everywhere Regardless of Political Philosophy

Speech at the Third Congress, Pan-American Federation of Labor, Mexico City, January 13, 1921

After the defeat of the steel strike, Mother Jones took a well-earned rest in California, following which she was off again on a round of activities. During this period she discussed many issues in her speeches to workers including the woman's suffrage and prohibition amendments (both of which, we have seen, she opposed), but her two main themes were support for the Soviet Union and unity in the labor and radical movements. In her speech in Gary, Indiana, during the steel strike, she had declared herself "a Bolshevist from the bottom of my feet to the top of my head," and she was not indifferent to the campaign under way to destroy the infant Bolshevik Soviet Union by military intervention and an economic blockade.[1] She relates in her Autobiography *an incident during the steel strike which reveals her support for the movement to defend the Soviet Union:*

As I was about to step down from the little platform [in Mingo, Pennsylvania] I saw the crowd in one part of the hall milling around. Some one was trying to pass out leaflets and an organizer was trying to stop him. I heard the organizer say, "No sir, that's all right but you can't do it here! What do you want to get us in fer!"

The fellow who had the leaflets insisted on distributing them. I pushed my way over to where the disturbance was.

"Lad," said I, "let me see one of those leaflets."

"It's about Russia, Mother," said the organizer, "and you know we can't have that!"

I took a leaflet. It asked the assistance of everyone in getting the government to lift the blockade against Russia, as hundreds of thousands of women and little children were starving for food, and thousands were dying for want of medicine and hospital necessities.

"What is the matter with these leaflets?" I asked the organizer.

"Nothing, Mother, only if we allow them to be distributed the story will go out that the strike is engineered from Moscow. We can't mix issues. I'm afraid to let these dodgers circulate." "Women and children blockaded and starving! Men, women and children dying for lack of hospital necessities! This strike will not be won by turning a deaf ear to suffering wherever it occurs. There's only one thing to be afraid of . . . of not being a man!"[2]

A New York Times *headline of January 10, 1921, read: "'Mother' Jones Commends Soviets." The story was a special dispatch to the* Times *from Mexico City and quoted from a statement Mother Jones had given the Mexican press upon her arrival in that country to attend the*

Third Congress of the Pan-American Federation of Labor.[3] The Times's *report continued:* " 'Mother' Jones said that she considered Soviet rule in Russia good, but expected better things to grow out of that movement. She remarked that she thought Soviet rule possible in the United States in the future."[4] *In her* Autobiography *she added that in her address to the congress, she told the delegates:* "Soviet Russia . . . had dared to challenge the old order, had handed the earth over to those who toiled upon it, and the capitalists of the world were quaking in their scab-made shoes."[5] *Actually, the report of her speech in the official proceedings of the congress contains no specific reference to the Soviet Union,[6] but has Mother Jones declaring that she believed that Bolshevism was not a new principle, but "the soul of unrest," an unrest as old as the existence of opposing classes.*

The main theme Mother Jones stressed at the congress was the need for unity among labor and radical groups. "Stop this thing of throwing stones at each other; it is a horrible disease today in the labor movement. . . . As long as you permit the capitalists to keep you divided, calling each other names and poisoning each other, you are going to make no progress," *she cried. She spoke emotionally of a growing solidarity among the world's workers and of her happiness to have lived long enough to see her economic faith affirmed.* "It is a great age; it is a great time to live in. Some people call us Bolshevik," *she said,* "some call us IWWs some call us Reds. Well, what of it!" "If we are Red," *she continued,* "then Jefferson was Red, and a whole lot of those people that have turned the world upside down were Red." *There was worldwide labor unrest, she pointed out,* "because the world's workers have produced the enormous wealth of the world, and others have taken it."

To buttress her plea for labor unity, Mother Jones introduced a resolution urging the congress to go on record in support of members of the I.W.W. who were at that time in prison in the United States on the spurious charge of having violated the Espionage Act. Although Gompers had previously urged the Pan-American Federation of Labor not to take such a stand, this time his position was rejected and the congress adopted the resolution.[7] Perhaps to assuage the A.F. of L.'s president's feelings, Mother Jones urged all in the ranks of the labor and radical movement to cooperate with the A.F. of L. and to "shake hands with Mr. Gompers." *She pointed to the Pan-American Federation of Labor as an example of the right kind of unity, and predicted that if such unity existed on a wide scale, the workers* "will conquer the common foe of humanity. We are going to take over the industry. We are going to take the money from the robbers. . . ."

It is possible that there were many in the American and Mexican labor and radical movements who felt that Mother Jones went too far in her evaluation of the Pan-American Federation of Labor (PAFL). Indeed, she does not seem to have realized that one of the motivating forces behind the formation of the PAFL was the growing influence of radical

321

unionism (especially the I.W.W. and revolutionary syndicalism) in Mexico in particular and Latin America in general. Another was the broad offensive of the Wilson administration, and in particular by Secretary of the Treasury William G. McAdoo, to promote trade and exports to Latin America. The opening of the Panama Canal in 1914 facilitated this program, and the start of hostilities in Europe the same year, added a sense of urgency to the drive for control of Latin American markets by the United States as ties with Europe were weakened and cut. McAdoo's call for a Pan-American Financial Conference, and the resulting meeting in Washington in May 1915 signified the execution of the plans.

Gompers, anxious to have the A.F. of L. involved in U.S. expansionism in Latin America, petitioned for labor representation at the conference. But he was rebuffed. His response, made at the 1915 A.F. of L. convention was to organize Latin American labor under A.F. of L. leadership — without any interference by the government. This action paved the way for the formation of the PAFL.

In the meantime, Mexican labor split into two clearly defined factions. At the congress of Mexican labor in 1917, the pro-syndicalist, I.W.W. elements broke with the conservative, business unionists. The latter group, led by Luis N. Morenes, formed the Regional Confederation of Mexican Workers (Confederación Regional Obrera Mexicana — CROM). This was the group with which the A.F. of L. allied and with which it ultimately worked in the formation of the Pan-American Federation of Labor.

Although A.F. of L. leaders, especially Gompers, were champions of non-governmental interference with trade unions, they turned to the government of the United States to help in the formation and the continued existence of the PAFL. The Wilson administration, eager to incorporate unions in the U.S. and Latin America in both the war effort and the advancement of American imperialism in Latin America, was eager to cooperate. The PAFL was approved by the Wilson administration and funds were allocated to it in a surreptitious manner in order to avoid publicity either in the United States or Latin America. The Committee on Public Information, the war propaganda agency headed by George Creel, received the money, and distributed it to the American Alliance for Labor and Democracy, set up by the A.F. of L. to promote its war objectives and oppose antiwar groups. That organization then passed the money on to the Pan-American Federation of Labor. Beginning with a government contribution of $50,000, several hundred thousand dollars went from the U.S. government to the PAFL.

The Pan-American Federation of Labor was not formally established until November 1918 but an interim group, the Pan-American Federation of Labor Conference Committee functioned as the organization between 1916 and 1918, and it was this group's congress that Mother Jones addressed. Little did she know that the organization which she *believed had been given the mission of achieving "a new civilization of industrial freedom," was secretly cooperating with representatives of American imperialism and the government of the United States both to maintain the status quo in Latin America and open the door for further penetration of U.S. imperialism.[8]*

Delegate Tobin (presiding): At this time it gives me great pleasure to present to this congress one of the noblest characters that we have in the great masses of the workers in the United States. This woman for half a century has struggled amongst the working classes to make the world brighter and better for those who are suffering. She has devoted her life to the cause of the workers, making sacrifices that are almost impossible to explain. She is well-known in every section of our country and in every district in which she visits she brings with her a ray of light and hope. I feel it a very proud privilege and a distinct honor to introduce to you Mother Jones, of the United Mine Workers of the United States.

Address of Mother Jones

Mr. Chairman and fellow workers: The speaker said he was presenting Mother Jones, of the Mine Workers. It is true I have given most of my time to the miners' organization, but I don't belong to any individual organization or creed; I belong to the workers wherever they are in slavery, regardless of what their trade or craft may be. I want to say this is something I did not expect was coming to my life while here below — the privilege of speaking and attending a congress where all the elements representing the opportunities of the Western Hemisphere are here to discuss in this meeting the breaking of the chains and bringing in the light that would never darken the world again. We are today passing through a crisis. Many people say it was the war, but let me say to you, my friends, while the war was tragic, it has done a most wonderful work for the world. Bear this in mind, it has awakened the workers in every corner of the earth. From every corner today forces are moving and touching the human heart to all the shores of the world waters, my friends, and if you only read the news and take up the papers, you can see the pulse beating.

It is a great age; it is a great time to live in. Some people call us Bolsheviks, some call us IWW's, some call us Reds. Well, what of it! If we are Red, then Jefferson was Red, and a whole lot of those people that have turned the world upsidedown were Red. Do you know what? What is the distinction? What is socialism? What is Bolshevism? What is IWW? Why, my friends, it is the soul of the unrest that is back of all these movements. Who can satisfy a hungry stomach with a small bite of food? You have got to have the food before the stomach gets satisfied. You can't satisfy the people today with what they had two or four years ago. They are thinking. Professors wonder what is the matter. Newspapers wonder what is the matter. The churches wonder what is the matter. They are all coming to save us, every one coming along. They have got a dose of medicine for us. Don't you understand what is the matter today? The man up in the tower, watching the clouds rumbling all over, knows that before there is a crash of thunder there are clouds everywhere, and so it is today, my friends. There is unrest everywhere, and it is not only in the United States, but all over the Western Continent — it has reached everywhere. The reason is because the world's workers have produced the enormous wealth of the world, and others have taken it; therefore, when the war was over, soldiers began to ask what was this war for, and why did we give up our wives and join the army. There is discontent everywhere, no matter where you go.

The truth is reaching the hearts of the workers the world over, and we are in that age; we are in that day; as the shepherds were back in Jerusalem, when they were guiding the sheep along to care for them and see that they were fed. We are doing the same, we are developing the brain and the heart of the workers and we are feeding them, my friends, on a logical line; we are not feeding them with stars rotating up in the sky, but with logic of today, and you have got to realize one thing — that we are never going back to the conditions we have left behind. We are in a new age when new conditions face us, and all these things we have got, we are going to keep. Now let me say to you, I know what is your inheritance. I have made a study of all those things.

One time I thought this thing was going too slow for me, and again it was going too fast. I have seen children murdered on the altar of gold. I used to get discontented. We licked the high-class burglars, and the boys wanted to give me something, and I asked them to give me a horse and buggy and a good harness and I would go out and circulate the literature among the farmers, and the boys got a horse, an old blind horse. They got him very cheap and I got my horse harnessed, loaded up with food and got a friend to go with me, and we went through the country and circulated literature, and I thought we were going to save the world over night. Then we moved in another way, and so I got my crowd with me. We realize this, my friends, that you have got to educate the workers in the economic field.

Let me say this to you: There is no army of churches, no foreign home missions; there are no welfare workers; YMCAs; no Salvation Armies, that have done the Christian teaching for the betterment of the nations and of humanity that the trade union movement has done. It has had the enemies of capitalism on every side, but it has moved on regardless. It has faced the jails, it has been subjected to calumny and slander, but it has moved onward and upward and forward. Do not divide your forces. Bring in new blood and get together. Get together on the economic field. Now we have courts in America and they put us in jail, but we get out again and they can't muzzle us, and we keep on talking and go on educating. We are not afraid of courts. The courts are what we make them, and when we get advanced enough we will tell Mr. Judge to take a back seat. But we haven't got that far yet, and this delegation is having a mighty mission to fulfill. We have got to bear this in mind. Why, all the world is centered on this congress, from all over the world they are looking at us here today.

Now, why am I in Mexico? I have perhaps to explain to you I was here when President Madero was elected and a very prominent Mexican in New York who had to leave his country came to talk matters over with me for two hours. He said, "I wish you would come to Mexico." I took it up with the president of the Miners, I got one of the metal miners and one of the coal miners to come with me, and we came down here. We spent some time at the Palace. We spent a couple of hours with President Madero, and I want to make a statement here; I never in all my life came in contact with a more noble human character than I consider President Madero to have been. I sat over two long hours with him, and he said to me, "Mother: Come to Mexico; organize the miners; put them in the miners' union." But I said, "Mr. President, if I come down and do what I can at Cananea, the big American interests in all those mines will arrest me and put me in jail." President Madero said: "If they do I will come down and make them take you out."[10]

Now this is the situation today, my friends, and you are marching on. No man living would ever have thought four years ago that you in Mexico would be where you are today. You are beginning to pave the way for a stable government of the people, and I want to ask you to do all you can to render all the faithful assistance you can to the noble men you have got in office now. I have studied them all, my friends, and there will not be an invasion. I want to tell you that now there will be no invasion, that Mexico will be yours. This congress will stop that invasion, if it does nothing else, and the oil trust nor none of those will come to capture this nation.[11] I know that; I know what I am talking about, so it is up to you to stand like men; go on with the message, from this congress to your people. I want to tell you something: Stop this thing of throwing stones at each other; it is a horrible disease today in the labor movement. The capitalists are doing their noble work, as they look at it. They are poisoning one against the other. Now the world was not made in a day. Mr. Tobin, Mr. Gompers, nor Mr. Nobody else has not got the making of this thing. It is the workers themselves, and when the workers solidify the world will rise, my friends. As long as you permit the capitalists to keep you divided, calling each other names and poisoning each other, you are going to make no progress. Cut out this nonsense; get down to business and move along with the army. Now we have got a state over in West Virginia, the most remarkable state in the union, that does some remarkable fighting. We use the force of law wherever we can, but if we are forced to use the law of force, if the other fellow makes us, we do; we don't offer any apologies for doing it. We all have a gun, and we know how to use it; we don't do anything with it unless we are called on to do so. We are moving on, and we have better homes for our children, better playgrounds, and we have time to educate and agitate.

We are united against a common enemy. Now we must stop all this ramble, every day going along, every day battling wherever we are as we go along. We are moving, my friends, and are going to keep that battle on and we can say to you miners of Mexico and the miners of the United States: "Unite!" I speak so much about the miners, because mining is the basic industry and the miners are the federated army in the labor movement of America. I have learned them, and for that reason I remain with them. Again I am going to tell you, no good is coming from uplift. It is not coming from the top, it is coming here coming from below. It is doing this all over the world, and so you got this start two years ago. It has been traveling slowly around the world, and now it has reached the Western Hemisphere. It is the cause of human freedom, and we are prepared to enter the gate when that gate opens and the sun shines in that day that is coming.

There are many ideas brought in by capitalism to fool the workers. Capitalism knows the game thoroughly, for it has the time and the means to build the machine, and we don't. Now, I have gone over the country, I have been down here in Mexico and up in Canada and over in Europe and as for taking back water, the guns of capitalism can't make me do it. I fight for your children, and your women are to blame for lots of wrongs. I am going to be honest with you. If you raise a child properly we would have no murders and we would not have to resent war, because nobody would go to war. There would be more time in the home to develop the coming generations, plant the human feeling in their breast and show them their duty. If they spend their time in clubs, suffragette, and welfare work, we will be our own welfare workers. We want the right of happy homes. We want a noble mankind, a great womankind; that is what we are after.

The American Federation of Labor can do more to advance the nations, to plant Christianity in the bosom of mankind than all the churches and all your institutions. I have had some experience, men and women; I don't think there is anyone else that had to go through more than I have. I know that this institution of the American Federation of Labor is the one institution that is leading the nations upward and onward to the final goal. This may be my last visit to Mexico.[12] My days are closing in. I want to say to you, young men, there is a mighty task to perform. The world never before had such a mission for you as it has now. It has granted that opening for you to enter a new civilization that will make the millions and thousands happier. I stand here pleading with you as one of you to stand together on the solid ground for industrial freedom for yourself. You are here for a purpose. You are here to make your home better. And in the days to come when you have departed the loved ones left behind will come over your grave and with the birds above they will sing that beautiful song: "He did well; he did his work for us; because of what he did we are here to kiss the ground he is in." Oh, men, the stories I could tell you and this convention gives me new life. There is sitting behind me a young man (Fred Mooney, of West Virginia) who was nothing but a child when I first saw him. He spent fourteen years in the subterranean caverns of earth for twenty-five cents from his master for fourteen hours a day in the darkness. He dug the wealth and he sent it out. Today he is the secretary of nearly 70,000 miners. I schooled them; I educated them; I used to give them Bolshevist literature long ago; yes, I used to give them Bolshevist literature. We didn't call it that then. I didn't name it for you.

My friends, you are here to unlock the doors to the coming age. I knew that poor man sitting there before me when he went barefoot in West Virginia many years ago. I have known Mr. Tobin many long years. I have known this man here (James Lord) with the red head, since he was a kid. I have hammered him often. I know them all, but I want to say to you here that you could not get better, truer men than they are. I want you to shake hands and when you adjourn this mighty convention, the greatest event in history, I don't think in all the ages of time there ever was a gathering as important as this. It will go down in the ages of history. Unite your forces, stand shoulder to shoulder. Come up here and shake hands with Mr. Gompers. Shake hands with the boys. We are going on; we are going on for a better world; we are going to carry the message to Central and South America. We are going to carry the message that will conquer the common foe of humanity. We are going to take over the industry. We are going to take the money from the robbers that have robbed; yes, we are going to do business. I am trying to speak clearly. We have got the greatest, finest organization, but the robbers are trying to get the wealth, and we want to help you stand together. Some men have been thinking that my days are counted. I have more fight in me than ten years ago. You, South Americans, particularly, stand together now solidly. I am coming down to South America some day. Keep your heads level and build your organizations. Stand together, let nothing divide you, and make every part of this hemisphere a fit place for men and women and children to live in.

[Report of the Proceedings of the Third Congress of the Pan-American Federation of Labor, Held in Mexico January 10th to 18th, inclusive 1921, pp. 72-76. Copy in Mother Mary Harris Jones Papers, Department of Archives and Manuscripts, Catholic University of America, Washington, D.C.]

327

Notes

1. For the intervention and blockade and the opposition to it in the United States, *see* Foner, *The Bolshevik Revolution*, pp. 32-38.

2. *Autobiography of Mother Jones*, pp. 222-23.

3. Mother Jones was invited to attend the congress by Alvaro Obregón, who became president of Mexico just a few weeks before the congress met. Fred Mooney, a leader of District 17 UMW, accompanied Mother Jones to Mexico City, and his account of the trip is filled with dramatic incidents of the welcome Mother Jones received from the Mexican working class and trade unions of all persuasions.

4. For Mother Jones's view that the Soviet system could not automatically be transferred to the United States, *see* pp. 477-78.

5. *Autobiography of Mother Jones*, pp. 238-39.

6. Mother Jones, however, said much the same thing in her statement to the press in Mexico City.

7. Sinclair Snow, *The Pan-American Federation of Labor*, Durham, North Carolina, pp. 112-13.

8. *Ibid.*, pp. 5-71.

9. Daniel J. Tobin, a conservative craft unionist, was president of the International Brotherhood of Teamsters from 1907 until 1952.

10. *See* pp. 132, 166.

11. Paragraph 4 of Article 27 of the Mexican Constitution adopted early in 1917 provided that ownership of lands and waters within the national territory "is vested originally in the Nation." Fearing this was an opening wedge leading to nationalization, American oil companies, led by the Standard Oil Company, demanded action from the U.S. government to undo the constitutional provision. As Mexico's documentary account puts it: "The campaign against the new constitution, which crystallized the aspirations and hopes of the Mexican people, was at once begun in the United States, and especially by the Standard Oil Company," (*Mexico's Oil. A Compilation of Official Documents in the Conflict of Economic Order in the Petroleum Industry, with an Introduction Summarizing Its Causes and Consequences*, Mexico City, 1940, p. xxiii). Although Mother Jones's confidence was justified in the sense that there was no formal intervention by the United States to force repeal of the constitutional provision in his message to the Mexican Congress, September 1919, President Carranza devoted a large part of the document to "outrages" by United States troops, including four invasions of Mexican soil, numerous assaults against individual Mexicans, and abuses of the rights of Mexico by American warships. (*Papers Relating to the Foreign Relations of the United States*, Washington, D.C., 1919, vol. 2, pp. 644-45.)

12. It was not. Mother Jones returned to Mexico in April and stayed more than two months. For her correspondence from Mexico, *see* pp. 649-54.

Background to West Virginia's Bloodiest Mine War

Speech at convention of United Mine Workers of America,
September 26, 1921

During World War I (1914-1918) there was a tremendous increase in the output of coal in the United States. The wartime activity in iron, steel, munitions, and shipping absorbed much of the increased coal production. An additional demand was created by the closed mines in the war-torn areas of Europe. In the United States there was a net increase of about 800 new mines each year. At the same time many old mines increased their capacity by the installation of new machinery. High prices and profits drew into the industry more operators, more mines, and more miners. The United Mine Workers of America grew in membership, reaching the figure of 400,000 by 1919.[1]

But despite these changes, in one section of the industry very little changed — bloody West Virginia. World War I brought great prosperity to the coal operators in West Virginia, especially in the Logan County mines. But the industrial peonage that had provoked the Cabin Creek–Paint Creek strike of 1912-13 still prevailed. Wages had not kept up by any means with the increase in the cost of living. Miners were still paid in scrip, good only at company stores. They still worked 10, 12, and 14 hours a day. Their villages were still policed by armed thugs recruited by the Baldwin-Felts strikebreaking agency, especially in Mingo, McDowell, and Mercer counties. In Logan County, Sheriff Don Chafin had replaced Baldwin-Felts men with his own army of deputies paid by the coal companies. Miners still lived in camps where the company-owned dwellings were, in the words of the U.S. Coal Commission, "old, unpainted board and batten houses — batten going or gone and board fast following, roofs broken, porches staggering, porches sagging, a riot of rubbish, and a medley of odors" were the main features.[2]

Organizers still took their lives in their hands in counties where employers still preferred to deal only with the Baldwin-Felts Detective Agency instead of the UMW. The "whole territory," Philip Murray, UMW vice-president, declared after a visit to West Virginia, "with thousands of inhabitants, is absolutely under the control of the operators. The individual is hopeless."[3] In the notorious Hitchman (1917) ruling, upholding the yellow-dog contract, the court added to that hopelessness.

Still in 1919, miners in Mingo County decided they had had enough, and they applied to the local UMW for a charter. When all who were identified as supporting the move were discharged and evicted from company houses, a bloody series of strikes followed in Logan, Mingo, McDowell, and Mercer counties. The mine operators immediately dis-

patched contingents of their private detectives armed to the teeth with revolvers and Winchesters to make war upon the new union members. This private army proceeded to ferret out all organizers and active members of the union, and to evict them and their families from the properties of the mining company. Union organizers were beaten up and thrown out of the district. While traveling by train through the strike area with her message of unionism, Mother Jones was warned by a friendly trainman that the guards were on the train looking for her. He offered her a hiding place in the baggage car and she quickly accepted the offer.[4]

In late August 1919, union miners in the Kanawha fields, enraged by these assaults, began a march over the mountains to Logan and Mingo counties where they hoped to shut down the nonunion mines and break the iron grip of Sheriff Don Chafin. While some returned home before they advanced very far, the bulk of the marchers, five thousand strong and most of them armed, crossed over into Boone County. Here they were confronted by Governor John J. Cromwell who threatened them with federal troops and treason charges if they crossed into Logan county. This had the desired effect; the marchers disbanded and were brought to Charleston by special trains. The governor boasted to the press that he had broken up "a deliberate plan to discard the work of Washington and Jefferson, of Madison, and Monroe, of Lincoln, of Cleveland, of Roosevelt and . . . substitute the ideas of Karl Marx, of Nicola [sic] Lenin and Leon Trotsky."[5]

Assisted by the governor, gunmen continued to raid union halls in the southern counties. One of the main targets was Matewan, on the Kentucky border. Matewan was known as "The Home of the Hatfields and McCoys." These two families had been shooting at each other for years. But unionism ended the bloody feud. The Hatfields and McCoys joined the UMW and were striking together when Albert Felts, head of the Baldwin-Felts detective agency, came to Matewan with eleven armed agents to evict miners who had joined the strike. Young Sid Hatfield, Matewan sheriff, a former miner, refused to do the evicting; hence the influx of gunmen. When the Baldwin-Felts gunmen appeared, Sheriff Hatfield deputized twelve men to defend the town. A McCoy was one of his men. A battle broke out between the miners and the gunmen. When it was over and the smoke cleared, three townsmen, including the mayor, and seven gunmen were dead. Among them were Albert and Lee Felts, the strikebreaking chiefs.

The "Matewan Massacre" of May 19, 1920, sparked further violence and during July and August, more than forty men died in Mingo County alone.[6]

Hatfield and other miners were charged with murder. "I entered one of the trials of the Matewan defenders," Art Shields, veteran labor reporter recalled, "in a little courtroom, where the judge sat with his back to the court and his feet on each side of the open door. All visitors, in-

cluding two U.S. Senators, were frisked from ankle to neck. But the real drama was the futile attempt of the coal trust to wrest a guilty verdict from the jury."[7]

After a two-month trial, Hatfield and other miners were acquitted of the Matewan murders for lack of evidence. But on August 1, 1921, Hatfield was assassinated by mine-guard deputies.[8]

The murder triggered a second march on Logan. "Sid Hatfield," Art Shields wrote, "was a popular hero, and men grabbed rifles all over the state. Volunteers from Ohio and Pennsylvania were among them. Many Negroes were marching. It was a sudden, spontaneous uprising. Coal trains were commandered. And several thousand men were deep in enemy territory when I arrived before Labor Day, 1921. Their objective was Logan City. This was the main anti-union stronghold. It was ruled by Sheriff Don Chafin, who was known as the 'millionaire gunman.' He had personally killed a dozen men, the New York World reported."

Logan County, which Don Chafin ruled has been described by Winthrop D. Lane as "a leer in the face of liberty, a feudal barony defended by soldiers of fortune in the pay of mine owners."[9]

Mother Jones was involved in the steel strike at the time of the first Logan march. But after the Hatfield assassination, she returned to West Virginia, and following a furious debate with UMW local officials who were afraid her proposal for a public meeting of miners would exacerbate the heated situation,[10] a meeting was held on the capitol grounds in Charleston. Here on August 7, 1921, Mother Jones assailed the recently-elected Governor Ephraim F. Morgan as a "tool of the goddamned coal operators."[11] On August 24, Mother Jones joined the marchers on the way to Logan at Marmet. Here perhaps the strangest event in Mother Jones's long career occurred.

It became clear at Marmet that the operators were not going to rely upon private gunmen and state militia to beat back the marchers. Their new ally was President Warren G. Harding in the White House. Brigadier General Harry Bandholtz arrived in Marmet and warned the miners they would face federal troops if they moved further, and that the White House had sent him to demand that they disband and return home. To the miners' astonishment, Mother Jones urged compliance with the order. And to their additional astonishment, she produced a telegram which she said came from the president and proceeded to read:

To the miners encamped at or near Marmet with the avowed intention of marching on Logan and Mingo counties. I request that you abandon your purpose and return to your homes and I assure you that my good offices will be used to forever eliminate the gunmen system from the state of West Virginia. Signed Warren G. Harding, President of this great republic.

The following day, the headline in the New York Times read: "Mother Jones Joins Armed Miners; Alleged Message Called Bogus."

C. F. Keeney, President of District 17, UMW, was reported as having informed the press that the telegram Mother Jones had read to the marchers "was bogus," that Mother Jones had refused to show him the telegram, and that a call to President Harding's secretary had disclosed the information "that no telegram had been sent."[12]

What seems to have happened in this bizarre episode is that Mother Jones had reached the conclusion that the march would end in tragedy for the armed miners and had joined the procession simply to try to turn them back. This she had done in response to a plea from Governor Ephraim F. Morgan who, having failed to persuade the miners to disband, had asked Mother Jones for assistance. "Certainly appreciate your offer of assistance," Morgan wired Mother Jones in Washington on August 29, 1921. It was evidently then that Mother Jones conceived of the idea of reading the marchers a telegram purporting to be from President Harding asking the men to return peacefully to their homes. When it was discovered that she had faked the telegram, the miners felt both angered and betrayed. Someone even produced and distributed a leaflet calling Mother Jones a "traitor."[13]

The march to Logan and Mingo counties continued. They never made it to Logan. For this time the federal troops were called to supplement local authorities, and 6,000 soldiers, assisted by twenty airplanes under the command of Brigadier General Billy Mitchell, were ready to prevent the union miners penetrating into the non-union country. For two days (September 2 and 3) the "Battle of Blair Mountain" raged as armed union miners fought the U.S. Army, the infant air force, and local deputy sheriffs and private gunmen. On September 4 the miners surrendered and were disarmed. Three deputies had been killed; forty local gunmen were wounded, and one of the six air service planes which crashed, killed four aviators. Union casualties were never made known.[14]

Five hundred men, including three UMW officials (all of whom were dismissed by President John L. Lewis) were indicted by a Logan County grand jury on charges of treason and murder. After a change of venue to Charleston, the trial began in the same courthouse where John Brown had been prosecuted for treason for his Harpers Ferry raid and found guilty. But in legal battles lasting over the next two years, most of the charges were dismissed or the defendants acquitted or paroled.[15] Although Mother Jones had rejected an appeal that she come to West Virginia and testify as a defense witness for some of the miners on trial, she did return in 1923 to ask Governor Ephraim F. Morgan to release those still-imprisoned miners who had families. Morgan agreed and the men returned to their families.[16]

They returned to the same conditions which had provoked the bloody uprisings. In 1928 a Senate sub-committee was investigating conditions in the coal industry. In the midst of the hearings the counsel for the West Virginia operators challenged the right of the committee to do

*any investigating whatsoever. Coal was a purely state matter, argued
the lawyer, and the Senate had no business sending out "fishing" committees. Whereupon the attorney for the United Mine Workers replied:*

*If anyone friendly to the union undertakes to enter the wilderness of industrial
autocracy existing in the smokeless coal fields of southern West Virginia, he
must run the gauntlet of injunctions, "yellow-dog" contracts, house leases, and
mine guards. If the United States Senate undertakes to enter in quest of information as a basis of contemplated legislation, it must run the gauntlet of alleged
constitutional barriers. If neither can enter, there is nothing left except to invoke
divine providence to roll back the waters of the Red Sea and let "God's people
go."[17]*

In Civil War in West Virginia, *Winthrop D. Lane describes an interview with an operator who said to him: "You may tell the union . . .
that when it sends its organizers in here, I'll get an army." "And I'll lead
it," echoed his mine superintendent. Lane also interviewed Frank Kenney, the local union president, who told him:*

*I'm a native West Virginian. There are others like me working in the mines
here. We don't propose to get out of the way when a lot of capitalists from New
York and London come down here and tell us to get off the earth. They played
that game on the American Indian. They gave him the end of the log to sit on and
then pushed him off that. We don't propose to be pushed off.*

*They say we shall not organize West Virginia. They are mistaken. If Frank
Kenney can't do it, someone will take his place who can. But West Virginia will
be organized and it will be organized completely.[18]*

*And West Virginia was organized! In 1932 the Norris-LaGuardia
Act became law. In addition to imposing limits on the judiciary in labor
disputes, the law forbade the yellow-dog contracts which served as the
foundation for the* Hitchman *(1917) and* Red Jacket *(1927) rulings,
both of which stemmed from West Virginia cases and played a major
role in the successful effort of coal operators to defeat the UMW in the
twenties. In 1933, armed with the National Industrial Recovery Act's
Section 7(a), the UMW surged into the coal fields to organize the miners
of West Virginia, and within a few years, Keeney's prophecy was fulfil-
led.*

Vice-President Murray: I understand that Mother Jones has just arrived in the convention and I am going to request Brother David
Fowler to escort her to the platform. It isn't necessary that I should introduce Mother Jones to you at this time; it isn't necessary that I
should eulogize the work she has performed for the coal diggers of
America, and I will simply present to the convention at this time our
good friend, Mother Jones.

Address of Mother Jones

Mr. Chairman and Delegates: I have been watching you from a distance, and you have been wasting a whole lot of time and money.[20] I want you to stop it.

All along the ages, away back in the dusty past, the miners started their revolt. It didn't come in this century, it came along in the cradle of the race when they were ground by superstition and wrong. Out of that they have moved onward and upward all the ages against all the courts, against all the guns, in every nation they have moved onward and upward to where they are today, and their effort has always been to get better homes for their children and for those who were to follow them.

I have just come up from West Virginia. I left Williamson last Friday and came into Charleston. I was doing a little business around there looking after things. We have never gotten down to the core of the trouble that exists there today. Newspapers have flashed it, magazines have contained articles, but they were by people who did not understand the background of the great struggle.

In 1900 I was sent into West Virginia; I went there and worked for a while, taking a survey of the situation. At that time men were working fourteen hours a day and they did not get their coal weighed. They weighed a ton coal with an aching back, dug it, loaded it and didn't know how much was in it. However, we have moved onward and today they get their checkweighman, they get paid in cash instead of in company money as they used to; but that wasn't brought around in an easy manner, it wasn't brought around arguing on the floor.

I walked nine miles one night with John H. Walker in the New River field after we had organized an army of slaves who were afraid to call their souls their own. We didn't dare sleep in a miner's house; if we did the family would be thrown out in the morning and would have no place to go. We walked nine miles before we got shelter. When we began to organize we had to pay the men's dues, they had no money.

At one time some of the organizers came down from Charleston, went up to New Hope and held a meeting. They had about fourteen people at the meeting. The next morning the conductor on the train told me the organizers went up on a train to Charleston. I told Walker to bill a meeting at New Hope for the next night and I would come up myself. He said we could not bill meetings unless the national told us to. I said: "I am the national now and I tell you to bill that meeting." He did.

When we got to the meeting there was a handful of miners there and the general manager, clerks, and all the pencil pushers they could get. I don't know but there were a few organizers for Jesus there, too. We talked but said nothing about organizing. Later that night a knock came on the door where I was staying and a bunch of boys were outside. They asked if I would organize them. I said I would. They told me they hadn't any money. Walker said the national was not in favor of organizing, they wanted us only to agitate. I said: "John, I am running the business here, not the national; they are up in Indianapolis and I am in New Hope. I am going to organize those fellows and if the national finds any fault with you, put it on me — I can fight the national as well as I can the company if they are not doing right."

Thirteen of them came into the house. John was there. I said: "Boys, each one of you make yourself an organizer, go at night and get your brothers together." I went away and two weeks later I was coming up Glen Jean to get the train and the boys met me. They said they could pay for their charter then because they had organized and over a thousand had come into the union. We went up the mountains again. I requested the national organizer go up there and bill a meeting for me. Walker had gone home. The organizer came down and I asked him if he had billed the meeting. He said he had not. I asked him: "What's the matter?" He said: "The superintendent chased me down." "Why didn't you chase him up? I asked. "Well," he said, "I didn't come over here to get killed." "Then why did you take the miners' money if you won't face the guns?"

I took a couple of young fellows and went up there. I don't care for these old fellows because they are worn out. I went up to Thayer on Saturday night and stayed there. The next morning I lined up ten or twelve trapper boys and we went up the mountain. We walked six miles. I sent the boys down to the town to tell the men to come up to the meeting. I told him to ask the general manager and superintendent to come up, that we wanted to see them, and they came. The men sat down and talked. The company set up one of their lap dogs, a colored fellow and he rode a horse. The boys tipped me off to who he was. I told him to come over too, and he did.

I made him sit down at my feet and said to him: "Now I want to put everything in your skull the superintendent wants and you take it home to him." He wanted to get away but I held him by the hair. We organized every single man there that afternoon and from that day on they remained organized. A couple of years ago I went up there and the superintendent asked me to come into his office and sit down. I think they got along nicely together. You have got to use judgment and diplomacy today. This is a diplomatic age politically, religiously, and industrially. You must use common sense and judgment.

I had to go again to one of Paddy Rand's mines. He lived in Danville, Ill. We had the place organized but the boss told me the fellows wouldn't take the jobs he gave them. There were four of them getting $10 a week. I went down one night and waited until the secretary made his report. I asked what the $10 was for. He said those fellows were on strike. I said: "But the mine is open everybody can get work. They can get work and are not going to get ten cents. You fellows can not rob the miners while I am around. You fellows go to work or I'll clean hell out of you!" We stopped that swindling and holdup, and those who didn't go to work got out.

When we began organizing in 1903 the battle royal began. The companies began to enlist gunmen. I went up the Standifer Mountain and held a meeting with the men. There wasn't a more law-abiding body of men in America than those men were. While they were on strike the court issued an injunction forbidding them to go near the mines. They didn't. I held a meeting that night, went away and next morning a deputy sheriff went up to arrest those men. He had a warrant for them. The boys said: "We have broken no law; we have violated no rules; you cannot arrest us." They notified him to get out of town and he went away. They sent for me and I went up. I asked why they didn't let him arrest the men. They said they hadn't done anything and I told them that was the reason they should have surrendered to the law.

That very night in 1903, the 25th day of February, those boys went to bed in their peaceful mining town. They had built their own school house and were sending their children to school. They were law-abiding citizens. While they slept in their peaceful homes bullets went through the walls and several of them were murdered in their beds. I went up next morning on an early train. The agent said they had trouble on Standifer Mountain, that he heard going over the wires news that some people were hurt. I turned in my ticket, went out and called a couple of the boys. We went up the mountain on the next train and found those men dead in their homes, lying on mattresses wet with their blood and the bullet holes through the walls.

I want to clear this thing up, for it has never been cleared up. I saw there a picture that will forever be a disgrace to American institutions. There were men who had been working fourteen hours a day, who had broken no law, murdered in their peaceful homes. Nobody was punished for those murders.

We then went into the Fairmount Field. One night while holding a meeting at New England I paid a fellow to go and circulate bills. We held a meeting on the sand lot. The United States marshal and the deputy marshal were there. When the meeting closed I went away. A little boy told me to get into a buggy and he would drive me to the interurban. When I was going over a dark bridge there were six or eight fellows at the company's store. One fellow asked me where I was going. I said I was going into Fairmount and asked him to take care of the slaves because if he didn't I would have to hunt a job for him next day.

Barney Rice, Joe Poggiani, and another fellow from Indiana were there. I was hoping the boys would come, because those fellows could throw me into the river and say I committed suicide. Barney Rice came out calling: "Police! Police!" I asked what was the matter and he said they were killing Joe, that he was alone in the dark bridge and he had broken no law. The interurban turned the corner and I told those fellows to hurry. I ran into the bridge and the fellows who had attacked Joe had run away. He had a deep cut in his head. I dragged Joe out and bound his head up with a piece of my underskirt. I asked the interurban men to hurry him into Fairmount and they did.[21]

Next day the boys came down to see Joe. There wasn't a detective or a gunman that didn't run out of the city that night. Every one of the cowards left. I had about 150 men at the hotel, and the general manager asked: "Mother, what can I do for the boys?" I said: "Send up a couple of drinks for the boys, because they need it." There wasn't a gunman stayed in town that night. Even the United States marshal got scared, but nobody was hurt except Joe.

That was the start of this thing. Later on I went into Wise County. Old Dad Haddow of Iowa was with me. The colored people gave us their church for the meeting. The gunmen told us we couldn't hold a meeting there and we went out and held it at the corner of two roads. I said: "Dad, have you a pistol?" He said he had and I told him he had better show it. I told him the law said if the pistol was exposed, even a little bit, he would be safe, but if he had it concealed he might be arrested. Those hounds got around Dad and nearly tore him to pieces. They took him to the office and those fellows came, the general manager with them, and said: "Mother Jones, what is the matter? I am astonished, really astonished! The idea of you going into the house of God with a pistol!" "Don't you know," I said, "that I know God never comes around a place like this — he stays a damned long way from a place like this."

The gunmen were there and I was arrested. The old man nearly scared to death. They fined him $25. He didn't want to pay it, he wanted to appeal, but I said we would pay it. I paid the $25. That evening one of the men who had been in the crowd came to me and said: "Mother Jones, I want to pay my respects to you for paying that $25 as quick as you did. The scheme was to lock you up and burn you in the coke ovens." And you women raised those brutes! It is horrible to think of.

We battled on and here and there we organized and got better conditions for the men. In 1902 a board member and your President, John L. Lewis, went up Kelly Creek. They chased him out. I was determined to organize that Creek. I went to the town at Eastbrook and in the morning went across by ferry, then walked six miles. The company was paying two deputies to keep me out but we got into the mining camp. I told a merchant my business and he said we could use a hall over his building. I rented that for four months. I took the men down and organized them that night. The company suspected there was something wrong and the next day discharged forty of the men. Then the drivers got restless and came out. I was determined to finish the job and on Sunday went through the camp with the boys marching. I told them to ask every fellow they saw sitting on the steps of the houses to be an American and come down. They came.

We told Jack Roan, the manager, who had come over from Columbus that day, to come out. He didn't come out. In front of the hotel were two fellows and one said: "I would like to have a rope and hang that old woman to a tree." Another one said: "And I would like to pull the rope." After the meeting the boys pointed those men out. I stood with my back to a tree and said: "You said you would like to hang the old woman. Here is the old woman and the tree, where is your rope?" They ran away because there were more than a thousand men at the place. Since that day there has been no strike and no disturbance, but there is one thing we failed to do — we did not educate them thoroughly, because bringing them into the union was only the kindergarten; we should have educated them after they came in but we failed to do that.

Those men are isolated, they see very little of the outside world. The company controls everything. There is a company doctor, a company picture show, a company minister, a company teacher — for generally the teacher is the superintendent's sister and the chairman of the school board is the general manager's wife. Conditions are not like they are in Illinois or Pennsylvania. It is a peculiar state of affairs and very few organizers who go in there understand the psychology of the people.

Now I will come to the Cabin Creek strike. A statement was made before the senatorial commission in Washington that the international called that strike. I think Mr. White was president. The international did not call that strike and had nothing to do with it. I was in Butte, Mont., and saw that the Paint Creek Colliery Company was not going to recognize the union. I said I would go and give them a fight. The international office didn't know I was going there at the time. I went up Paint Creek and held a meeting. There was some military man there. Then I went around Kanawha and through the creeks there. On July 6 I went up Cabin Creek. At Montgomery the boys came for me at 6 o'clock in the morning and asked if I would go with them.

I left that Creek thoroughly organized in 1903 and went west. For nine years no organizer had gone up that Creek without coming out on a stretcher. Someone went to the governor and told him I was going up there. That was a board member. He said a company of militia had better be sent there. The railroad men circulated the bills. When the miners came down they didn't know who was going to speak. They came over the mountains and their toes were out of their shoes. A man got up to speak and I landed him out of the wagon and told him I was running the job.

The militia, the mine manager, the general superintendent, and the gunmen were all there that day. When I was half through my speech they asked if I would organize them into the United Mine Workers. I told them: "I did organize you once and you betrayed the organization." "Mother," they said, "We will swear that if you organize us now

338

we will stick to the death." They didn't have a dollar to pay for their charter. I told them to go home and not mention the meeting to anyone, not even to their families, but put on their overalls in the morning and dig as many tons of coal as possible, and then the general manager could go to Kentucky and take a few tons of what they dug and give it to the foreign mission cats to take Jesus to China so he won't get on to what they are doing here.

The gunmen were driven out of there and there has been peace ever since. They were driven out of Paint Creek, where they had sent a death special with thirty deputy sheriffs on board. When they wanted that special car equipped to send up the mountain the painters at Huntington said they wouldn't paint it. The machinists said they wouldn't equip it. Some other men were asked to do it and they said: "We will talk about it tonight and ask the Lord" — they were Holy Rollers. Well, the Lord must have told them to do it because in the morning they equipped the train and later that armored car fired into the tents of the strikers.

Here are the machine guns that were turned on us (exhibiting a picture). I went up to speak to the boys and the guns were turned on them. I didn't see them until I got on the track. There were twenty-five of those gunmen who turned on those law-abiding citizens. I put my hands on the guns. One fellow told me to take my hands off the gun. I said: "No, sir; my class go into the bowels of the earth to get the material to make these guns and I have a right to examine them. What do you want?" He said: "We want to clean out those fellows, every damn one of them." I told him they were not doing anything wrong, that they were only trying to earn money for their wives and children. I told him if they shot one bullet out of that gun the creek would be red with blood and theirs would be the first to color it. They asked what I meant and I told them I had a lot of miners up above who were fully armed. There was nothing up the mountains but a few rabbits, but we scared hell out of them! We organized the men there. We have them solid to this day.

Those are the guns they sent across seven states to Colorado when the men there struck. The railroad men hauled them. Those are the guns that murdered the women and children at Ludlow, Colo. Here are the Baldwin thugs (showing several pictures). Here are some of the boys who were killed. Some young men joined the militia in Colorado, but when they found they were called out to turn their guns on the miners they went home. The mine owners said they would have to have an army. Here they are in this picture. They were not citizens of the state. The laws of Colorado said a man must be a citizen before he could put on the uniform; but these were the private armies of overlords and they kept committing crimes against the miners and their families until the horror of Ludlow shocked the country. Here is a picture of the children who were murdered.

After the horror took place at Ludlow Mr. Rockefeller asked me about it in New York. I said my suggestion would be for him to go out and look into conditions. He did and he was horrified at what he found out there. We drove those people out of Colorado — there are no Baldwin thugs here today.[22]

When we had the Matewan fight they came down to throw the people out of their houses without any warrant of law. Two of those men who shot the people in Matewan had been in Colorado. Your women had the ballot in Colorado for twenty-eight years; there was one in the Senate of that state, but they never raised their voice against this infamy. What good is the ballot if they don't use it?[23] They put the most infamous men in office, for they stood for the killing of those children. I put in twenty-six days in a cellar under the court-house, where they had me locked up, when a major came to me and said he would give me money to leave the state I told him he and the governor could go to hell. The major got a fine place later for being so docile.

This war is going to go on until you bring it up to Congress. There would have been a great many more murders, Mr. White knows, if he hadn't stood behind me and helped me. He gave me money often to go places; he never turned me down and he knows I always got results. Senator Kern spoke about these things on the floor of the Senate and a committee was appointed to come down. No man ever stood on the floor of the Senate in Washington who did more for the working class than Senator Kern of Indiana, but the workers turned him down when the next election came.[24]

A great deal more might have happened if Mr. White hadn't stood behind me in every move I made. Every one of our men was turned out and we never hired a lawyer. I don't believe in lawyers. I defy your bookkeepers to show one five-cent piece that was ever spent by me for a lawyer. I wouldn't allow it — I fight my own battles everytime. If we weren't so ready to hire lawyers and sky pilots we would do a great deal better than we are doing.

You are not going to settle this question in West Virginia. It will grow and grow and reach into other states unless you demand of Congress to do away with private armies. That system is eating the vitals out of the honor of the nation. The father of the family is robbed; the money he honestly earns is paid out by the overlords to these gunmen, and the children are raised up under the influence of murderers and robbers and thugs. Your churches don't do anything about it. Your temperance workers say you can not have a drink. Well, we will have all the drinks we want and not say a word to you about it. You can introduce resolutions from now until doomsday; you can go begging to Congress — nobody has any respect for a beggar; you can go to Congress and tell the congressmen you want this thing changed, that you want West Virginia put on the map of the United States.

The governor can not do it because he belongs with the interests.

The men in the state legislature can not do it because if they lose those jobs they can't get any others. You are to blame and nobody else. You have got the power to change it. Be men enough to arise and do it. West Virginia is coming back and things will be straightened out there.[25] I see the court has put on another injunction.

President Lewis: Just applied for it.

Mother Jones: Well, didn't they put one on you before? In Washington the telephone company wanted to extend their lines and they sent their men over into old Virginia. The men began digging a hole one morning near a farmer's place. The farmer asked what they were digging a hole for. They said it was to plant telephone poles. The farmer said: "This is my ground; who told you to plant those poles?" They said the telephone company paid them to do it.

"But this is my ground," said the farmer. "That doesn't make any difference, the telephone company is a trust and can get the ground when they want it." The farmer said: "You get out of here." They wouldn't go and the old fellow got a gun and told them they had better leave. They jumped over the fence and left. He warned them not to come back any more.

In two or three days the men came back. The old fellow looked them over and said: "Didn't I tell you not to come here?" "Yes," they said, "but this time we have got you. We have an order of the court and it gives us permission to plant these poles. You can not do anything about it. Read the order."

The farmer read the order, scratched his head for a minute, then went to the stable and unchained an animal he had in there. He led him out and said: "Sic 'em! sic 'em!" The bull went tearing down the road and over the fence went the telephone men. The old fellow went up his porch and began smoking. They asked him to chain the bull up. He said: "I haven't anything to do with the bull." They asked him again to call the bull off that they had an order of the court and they had read it to him. The old farmer said: "Yes, but why in the hell don't you read it to the bull?"

The day is gone in American history when judges can assume the role of lords above us. The pulse of the world is beating, my friends, as it never beat in human history. Not alone in America is it throbbing but the world over. Editors don't know. They sit in the office using a pencil and stabbing us in the back sometimes. Ministers don't know; statesmen don't know; professors in the universities don't know what is going on; but the pulse of the world is throbbing for the civilization that was started back in Jerusalem two thousand years ago. You can not crush a man today; you may put him in jail; you may fill your jails, but the fight will go on. You are living in an electric age. The current is touching the human heart of man, and never again will the system of slavery that has prevailed in the past and that we are driving out now come into the world.

I want to warn that judge today that it is best to bring conciliation to bear than to drive us apart. America will live on, and we are going to march and we are going to bring back the old times of Patrick Henry and Jefferson and Lincoln. It is up to you to stop wasting time on technicalities and get down to business and save this money you are spending. You are going to need it. Put away your prejudice and let us fight. I spoke Labor Day in District 2. Then I went down into Mexico and New Mexico. I got a paper there in which I saw that President Brophy of District 2 was doing business.[26] I wrote him a letter congratulating him. I am glad to know that District 2 has a good president, and, Brophy, I am with you. Whenever you want to raise hell with the other fellows, send for me!

I am going after this fellow (indicating Vice-President Murray) because he isn't doing business in Pittsburgh as he ought to. That used to be the old fighting ground. Vice-President Murray, you do business there.

And now I am going to say something to the women. The destiny of nations depends upon the women. No nation has ever grown beyond its women. Whatever corruption, whatever brutal, ugly instincts the man has he hasn't got from his mother. I have studied this for fifty years; I have studied every great man I have ever met and he has always had a great mother. Many times I walked fifteen miles to see a woman after I had met her son.

I want to say to John P. White before I close that I express appreciation of him for what he did for me when he was president. At no time did I go to him and explain to him what I wanted done but what he handed me money or endorsed what I had done, and we got results. I could have done a great deal more in West Virginia, but I think from all we can hear that we are going to go forward. Don't blame the governor of West Virginia. Don't be so ready to knife him. There are things no statesman can override. This is a dangerous time. Presidents and governors must move with care. There is no state in America that has better miners than West Virginia. Some of the noblest characters you have are there and you know it. They live up to the creeks and the speakers who appear before them do not always use their language or appeal to them. You must know the life of those men. There isn't another state in the Union like West Virginia, and the organizers that go out, Mr. Lewis, don't understand the game. I have gone to Mr. White time and again and have told him to take them out because they didn't fit into the situation. I don't believe in giving the miners' money to anyone who doesn't bring results.

I asked Mr. Lewis to send a man into Mingo to handle the finance. He mentioned one or two and then said: "What do you think of Fowler?" "He is just the man," I said, and he gave him to me and we got results. I am interested in the children and in those poor fellows who can't be reached except by the capitalists' papers that go in. That is all they know. You must educate them, and I want to say, Mr. Editor of the Journal, that you ought to cut out that picture "How to Dress." We know how to dress when we get the money to dress with. What you want to tell us is how to pull that money out of the other fellow.

Up in Princeton the men were asking for years for organization. We sent a boy up to bill the meeting but he didn't tell them who was going to speak. The boy had to run away the minute he circulated the bills or he would be killed. I went up with Mr. Houston, the attorney for the miners. We were told the meeting would be in the park three miles and a half away. I said we wouldn't hold it there, that we would start a riot out there, and then they would say: "Old Mother Jones went out in the park and started a riot." I said: "See if the city authorities won't give us a place in the town to meet." We got it and seven thousand men came there, largely railroad men, machinists and farmers. Seven cars of Baldwin-Felts thugs came down, loaded with whiskey and guns. There was no prohibition men there that day. Houston got up to speak and I saw that something was being plotted. I got up and spoke, but I hadn't talked more than ten minutes when they began to start the riot.

When I wound up my speech I said: "Mr. Baldwin-Felts guards, I am going to serve notice on you that I will take this thing up to Uncle Sam, explain the matter, and if Uncle Sam don't protect the children of the nation Old Mother Jones will. They won't be raised under the influence of murderers like you." The railroad men were afraid I would be killed and asked policemen to take me away. I told them I was not afraid of being killed, that I would rather die fighting than die in my bed. I want to say to you mothers to quit buying pistols for your children. Train them to something better than a pistol and a gun. Almost every child today has a toy pistol. You began training them to use a pistol while they were in the cradles and the welfare workers never raise their voices about it. The legislature should pass a law that no mother should buy a pistol for a child.

I am going back to West Virginia and I want to ask you, for God's sake, for the sake of the children, to stand up like men and work shoulder to shoulder. You are the basic industry of the world, you are the basic organization of labor. You and the railroad men get together. Meet with the railroad men and join hands, because the battle royal is ahead and you must get the railroad men with us so they will not haul scab coal, the gunmen, the militia, and the guns to shoot us.

I had two guns put to my head on Sunday. I took the matter up in Washington. The company telegraphed to New York for their lawyer to come down and watch me. I went to the War Department and from there to the Navy Department, then to the Fuel Department. The secretary there asked me what I would advise. I advised him to call both sides there and have him sit at the table. They came up. Dwyer, Ballantyne, and myself sat in the room. The officials went to vaudeville that Sunday night although they were going to meet the governor the next morning. You must discharge such men from office right away; you must do in the future as we have done in the past in West Virginia; we must act with the forces of law.

The miners' organization is the most law-abiding organization in the world. The miners are not law-breakers. They are honest, hard working men. They break no law until the gunmen get after them. You must go to Congress and demand that the murderers and the gunmen who help rob, degrade, and murder men, women, and children be punished. I am going to take the matter up with the president and put the whole history before him. I will tell him this question is up to him and to get Congress to protect the miners in West Virginia.

Another thing I want to set right. The international office never called the Cabin Creek strike. That statement was made and it was never corrected. I went up the Creek and if anybody is responsible I am the one and not the international. I didn't ask the men to strike. The company discharged the men and then the strike was on. Now I want you to hold public meetings and wake the public to what is going on. Not one of the writers who went into Mingo, Logan, or McDowell ever wrote the true story. That is why their scribbling has no effect on the public mind. If you show where the real evil lies and wake up the sleepy and indifferent public you will get those conditions changed.

Delegate Wilson, Local 2654, moved that the convention tender Mother Jones a rising vote of thanks for her visit to the convention and for her address.

The motion was adopted by unanimous rising vote.

Vice-President Murray: A roll-call has been determined and a sufficient number of delegates supported the demand. The delegates will be in order and all those who are standing will be seated. As soon as we can conveniently arrange to call the roll the members of the Credentials Committee will be here to do it. In the meantime Mother Jones desires to address the convention.

Address of Mother Jones

You know, boys, I cannot yell as loud as I used to. A group of men met in Louisville, Ky., and there were many of the Blues and the Grays. A short time before they had used the guns against each other. But they met and buried the guns and shook hands and said: "We have wiped out chattel slavery, but we are facing something darker, more dangerous, than chattel slavery. Now we must join together as one grand army to fight for industrial freedom and put a stop to slavery in the long years to come."

These men organized. That was before some of you were born. A few years before that they had been holding bayonets against each other, but they buried them, not to use them again. They organized and started out to carry the message of hope to their brothers. They had no money. In 1876, when the Union Pacific was bringing over Chinese to break the labor movement, the battle began there. They fought the battle, not with guns, but with intelligence. They made the government in Washington come out and put a stop to the Chinese coming in to invade the American labor movement.

I was all through those battles. I am now facing my closing hours of life. It hasn't been smooth sailing. There have been storms in the past for labor, and yet the real storm has not begun. I had a hand in that Chinese agitation; we kept it up and stopped the Chinese coming over. The Union Pacific had been bringing them over in hordes and using them to break the labor movement. This is not a yesterday's lesson with me.

I am now entering my ninety-third milestone. When you hold your next convention I may be moldering in the dust. Let me warn you now that the enemy is lined up and thoroughly prepared for battle. It must be with us as it was with the Blues and the Grays — we must shake hands and get together. I am going back to West Virginia. I am not going to give up the battle there, because I know it is the storm center of the labor movement. Let me warn you of what is coming. There are stormy days ahead of you. There are going to be hungry days for your children. We have some good boys in West Virginia and some good fighters, but we have got some damn snakes, too. Look after the snakes.

Now the time is here for us to get together. Stop your foolishness. This isn't a mob gathering. The whole world is looking at this convention. There is a sane way of doing business; don't let the world think we are a mob gathered here in Indianapolis. I am not going to say goodby when I leave. I am going to be with you until death closes my eyes. Nobody can put me out. That has been tried, but I put out those who tried it before I got through with them.

The brave and true die only once; the cowards and traitors die often, and they have got some horrible deaths at that. Be true to your organization. The wires are set to break you up. I know what I am talking about. I am not looking for any office. What will the world think of us when the newspapers send out the poison ivy? You know the newspaper fellows have got to put in something to keep their jobs.

Do you know how much money you are spending here? It isn't your money; it is the money of the children and the women. You are giving the money to the capitalists, the hotels, street cars, and pool rooms. You cannot give it to the beer rooms because you can't get a damn drop out of them. Now let us stop this foolishness that has been going on and go before the world as a sane people.

There are some fellows who don't want me to go back to West Virginia, but I am going anyway. One fellow said I couldn't do any more talking in West Virginia. Why, he's been dead for forty years and the world has run away from him! The world has been made for a long time, and the Lord has never yet made a man that has been able to stop a woman talking. The gunmen, the courts, the thugs, and the militia have tried to keep me from talking, and they couldn't do it. My days are getting short, but as long as life remains I will stay with you.

You are the fighting army of the working class of America. I plead with you to do your business rapidly, get through here, go home and go to work to earn some money. We are going to win the battle in West Virginia. As long as I am able to crawl I will be around there.

[Minutes of the Convention, United Mine Workers of America, 1921, pp. 727-41, 974-76]

Notes

1. Charles P. Anson, "A History of the Labor Movement in West Virginia," Unpublished Ph.D. thesis, University of North Carolina, 1940, pp. 124-25.

2. *Report of U.S. Coal Commission*, Part 3, Washington, D.C., 1925, p. 1431.

A more optimistic picture of conditions in West Virginia at the end of World War I is presented by Hoyt N. Wheeler, but his picture would hardly have been endorsed by the miners. (*See* Hoyt N. Wheeler, "Mountaineer Mine Wars: An Analysis of the West Virginia Mine Wars of 1912-1913 and 1920-1921," *Business History Review* 50 (Spring, 1976): 83-85.)

3. John M. Barb, "Strikes in the Southern West Virginia Coal Fields, 1919-1922," unpublished M.A. thesis, West Virginia University, 1949, p. 31.

4. *Ibid.*, pp. 42-50.

5. John J. Cornwell, *A Mountain Trail*, Philadelphia, 1939, pp. 59-60.

6. Evelyn L. K. Harris and Frank J. Krebs, *From Humble Beginnings: West Virginia State Federation of Labor, 1903-1957*, Charleston, West Virginia, 1960, pp. 152-53; Howard B. Lee, *Bloodletting in Appalachia*, Morgantown, W. Va., 1969, pp. 52-69.

7. *Daily World*, September 4, 1966.

8. Lee, *op. cit.*, pp. 69-71.

9. *Daily World*, September 4, 1966; Winthrop D. Lane, *Civil War in West Virginia*, New York, 1969, pp. 52-53.

10. C. Frank Kenney and Fred Mooney, District 17 officials, both argued with Mother Jones against her proposal. Later Mooney wrote that Mother Jones "became abusive, and going into the assembly room where 25 or 30 miners were congregated, she proceeded to read our pedigree in true Mother Jones style. She told them that 'Keeney and Mooney had lost their nerve; they are spineless and someone must protect these miners!'" (Mooney, *op. cit.*, p. 89.)

11. Charleston *Gazette*, August 8, 1921; Lee, *op. cit.*, p. 96; Mooney, *op. cit.*, p. 89; William R. Trail, "The History of the United Mine Workers in West Virginia, 1920-1945," unpublished M.A. thesis, New York University, 1958, pp. 22-24.

12. *New York Times*, August 25, 1921; Mooney, *op. cit.*, p. 89; Lee, *op. cit.*, p. 96.

13. Morgan to Mother Jones, August 29, 1921, telegram; Archives & Manuscripts Section, West Virginia Collection, West Virginia University Library;

Lunt, *op. cit.*, pp. 124-25. *See also* p. 673.

For another discussion of the incident, *see* Lois McLean, "Mother Jones in West Virginia," *Goldenseal* 4 (January-March, 1978): 21. McLean writes: "Mother Jones may not have had an actual telegram but she certainly had gotten the message that troops would be used against the miners." (*ibid.*) Thomas Lewis, former UMW national president who became executive secretary of the West Virginia's New River Coal Operators' Association, accused Mother Jones of having sold out the marchers for money from the operators, a tactic, he charges, she often practiced, and which the union knew "but used her anyhow." (Quoted in Featherling, *op. cit.*, p. 189.) Featherling dismisses this charge as well he should, and feels that at the age of ninety-one Mother Jones had little need for money. He takes the same position as that adopted later by Lois McLean, namely, that Mother Jones probably feared that if the march continued, the miners would be walking into a well-armed opposition led by federal troops. (*ibid.*)

Neither in her speech to the 1921 UMW convention nor in her *Autobiography* does Mother Jones refer to the Logan March, the "telegram" from President Harding, or anything else connected with her role in the incident.

David Alan Corbin insists that "too much . . . emphasis has been placed on the telegram." He takes the position that the miners of southern West Virginia were unwilling to follow Mother Jones's advice and abandon the march because they had lost faith in her effectiveness as an organizer, arguing that she had accomplished little despite twenty years in the state. He cites petitions and circulars "denouncing Jones and demanding that she be kept out of southern West Virginia." "It seems," Corbin concludes, "that the 'boys' had grown up and left their 'Mother.'" (David Alan Corbin, *Life, Work, and Rebellion in the Coal Fields: The Southern West Virginia Miners 1880-1922,* Urbana, Ill., 1981, p. 282.) Corbin, however, does not confront the issue of whether Mother Jones was correct in her fear that the miners would be slaughtered if they continued the march. According to Art Shields, who talked with Mother Jones at this time, she expressed great concern over the strength of the federal military forces who were being mobilized to confront the miners, and was worried that her "boys" would be walking into a trap if they continued the march. (Interview with Art Shields, October 23, 1982.)

14. Bart, *op. cit.*, pp. 109-12; Lee, *op. cit.*, pp. 98-100; Anson, *op. cit.*, pp. 232-35; Maurer Maurer and Calvin F. Senning, "Billy Mitchell, the Air Service and the Mingo War," *West Virginia History* 32 (October, 1968): 342-43.

15. Bart, *op. cit.*, pp. 110-13; McLean, *op. cit.*, p. 21. "He (Morgan) was the only West Virginia governor for whom Mother Jones had a kind word," McLean adds. (*ibid.*)

17. McCalister Coleman, *Men and Coal*, New York, 1943, p. 133.

18. Lane, *op. cit.*, pp. 87-88.

19. Philip Murray (1886-1952), the son of an Irish coal miner, Murray was born in Blantyre, Scotland. In 1902, already a full-fledged miner, he emigrated to the United States with his father. He worked in the mines near Pittsburgh, educated himself, and at the age of eighteen, having proved his militancy in a fist-fight with a weighman who tried to cheat him, was elected president of the UMW local. Forced out of his job, he devoted himself to the union and when John L. Lewis became acting president on Hayes's resignation in 1919, he appointed Murray as acting vice-president. In 1920, the same year Lewis was elected president, Murray was chosen vice-president, and he remained Lewis's

most loyal lieutenant for many years, succeeding him in 1940 as president of the Congress of Industrial Organizations (CIO) when Lewis resigned.

20. The reference was to the bitter battle between supporters of Alexander Howat, president of the Kansas district, and the administration machine headed by President John L. Lewis. "Except for a speech by 'Mother' Jones, 92-year-old organizer of the union, all debate today was devoted to the Kansas cases," the *New York Times* reported on September 27, 1922. For background to the issues involved, *see below* pp. 348-58.

21. *See above* pp. 49-51, 54, 78-100.

22. There was also no union except the company union. The battle of the miners, however, continued, and in 1928 another strike broke out at the Rockefeller-dominated Colorado Fuel & Iron Company, and this time the United Mine Workers was victorious. Later, the United Steel Workers of America organized the steel mines of Colorado Fuel & Iron.

23. This would seem to imply that woman suffrage was a useful weapon for the working class if only the right to vote was made use of.

24. Mother Jones campaigned for Kern's re-election in 1916, but he was defeated.

25. However, by October 26, 1922, the West Virginia strike was over, having been called off by the national UMW. The mines in West Virginia remained largely unorganized until the New Deal.

26. John Brophy, central Pennsylvania UMW leader, was a foe of John L. Lewis and participated in the rank-and-file movement against him. However, in later years he worked with Lewis in the CIO.

I Want to See More Alex Howats and I Want to Live Long Enough to Develop Them

Speech at United Mine Workers of America Convention, 1922

John L. Lewis was born in 1880 of a Welsh miner family in Lucas, Iowa, a coal-mining community. Between 1897 and 1901, Lewis worked as a farm hand and coal miner. He then left the family home to wander in the mountainous West from which he returned to Lucas late in 1905 to become a coal miner again. But he refused to settle into the life of a miner. He took over the management of the local theater. In 1907, he ran for mayor of Lucas, but lost. That same year he joined a grain and feed business which failed. He speculated in the grain market and lost. And he married "above him" to Myrta Bell, a physician's daughter.

In 1908 Lewis and his wife moved to Panama, Illinois, a coal-company town which had a strong local of the UMW, one of the ten largest in the state. They were followed by the rest of the Lewises. A year later, John's brother Thomas, became a police magistrate. In 1910, John became president of the union local. From that time on he never again entered the mines as a worker. He resigned the local post in 1911 to become special organizer for Samuel Gompers, president of the American Federation of Labor. He was succeeded as local union president by his brother, Thomas, who was at the same time manager of the coal mine which employed the union members.

The Lewis family, Melvyn Dubofsky and Warren Van Tyne make clear in their definitive biography of John L. Lewis, "enriched themselves at the expense of the union members." A later investigation "uncovered a pattern of corruption and embezzlement whereby Tom and Dennie as well as their father, Thomas H., maintained a dual set of books, issued illegal checks, and forged checks to double the expenditures approved by the local union."[1] John L. Lewis never criticized or disassociated himself from his brothers because of this.

In his quest for power in the labor movement, Lewis relied entirely on corruption. "Whenever possible," Dubofsky and Van Tyne point out, "Lewis used influence, voters, and power he controlled in the large union local to inveigle patronage appointments from UMW superiors rather than run for office and face a union electorate."[2] From the beginning he was involved in election fraud. From 1911 to 1918 he never ran for office. Yet his rise to power was phenomenal. In June 1915 UMW president White appointed Lewis as union statistician, undoubtedly in payment for his support. Lewis "engaged in electoral shenanigans worthy of the most cunning of big-city bosses." On July 15, 1917, White appointed Lewis as business manager of the United Mine Workers Journal, a powerful position from which he could influence the thinking of the union miners. A short time later White resigned as UMW president to join the Fuel Administration during the war administration, to be succeeded by Vice-president Frank J. Hayes, "an amiable, ineffectual dipsomaniac," who had no heart for the routine work connected with the job of chief executive. Hayes appointed Lewis as vice-president, but with the president continuously drunk, Lewis took over the union completely. On February 6, 1920, Hayes resigned and Lewis was confirmed by the UMW Executive Board as president. Thus Lewis had moved to the top of the UMW, presenting himself for endorsement by the membership only once![3]

As president Lewis began to live like a millionaire. His departure for a six-week vacation in Great Britain on the S. S. Celtic was reported in the society column of the New York Times. On his passport, he described himself, not as a labor leader, but as an executive. According to Dubofsky and Van Tyne:

. . . he followed his own rules of social etiquette religiously. He kept fellow officers of the UMW at a distance, practiced aloofness and acted in the union as a *king to his court. Lewis reserved his friendship for business executives, high public officials, and members of the hereditary American elite. They dined with the Lewises on a reciprocal basis, and he charmed them with well-told stories and stimulating conversation. The Herbert Hoovers, the Gardner Jacksons, the Harrimans, the Cyrus Chings, corporation executives in general — they were the type of people John L. Lewis cultivated.[4]*

Cusling's Survey, *a business newsletter, reported that Lewis was "one of the wisest small traders that ever takes a flyer in the stock market. His success . . . shows that he knows economics far better than nine out of ten coal operators. And he is making more money for himself today than are ninety-five out of a hundred operators."[5]*

Lewis's main concern as president was not to lead the miners to improve their miserable working and living conditions and reduce the fierce exploitation by the coal operators. Rather it was to increase the profits of the coal industry, even if it meant shrinking employment of miners, so long as he could reserve for himself control of a much smaller union. "Lewis," Dubofsky and Van Tyne point out, "personally preferred a total reorganization of the soft-coal industry. He and his economic adviser W. Jet Lauch, throughout the 1930s corresponded about and discussed privately their plans to stabilize the coal industry by consolidating production into fewer, more efficient units; restricting competition in marketing and pricing; and liberating the coal industry from the anti-trust laws."[6]

Lewis consolidated his power by fraud, bribery, and corruption. He took from the districts the right to elect their officers and appointed his henchmen as officials. He created an army of gunmen and gangsters. He ran union conventions as it suited himself. At the 1920 UMW convention, Lewis refused to recognize a motion from the floor, and when asked whether the convention was to be ruled by parliamentary law or not, he replied, "Yes, but before parliamentary law comes the law of reason." Soon Lewis discarded the "rule of reason," and recognized only those whom he wished to speak, closed the debate when he wished, had objectors forcibly thrown out, and in general disregarded the wishes of any number of protesting delegates however large. To those who objected, he thundered: "May the chair state that you may shout until you meet each other in hell and he will not change his ruling."[7]

The 1920 national convention put the finishing touches on his dictatorship when it gave him authority to expel union members, revoke charters of subdistricts and local unions, and set up his own organization in their place. This, as Spencer D. Pollard notes in his study of democracy in the government of the UMW, enabled Lewis to establish a tight, monolithic dictatorship.[8] But it could not eliminate resistance!

The seeds of resistance go back to the Washington Agreement of October 1917 adopted by the Federal Government acting through its Fuel Administration, the mine owners, and the miners' union to insure production of enough coal to win the war. The contract was to go into effect

April 1, 1918, and extend to the end of the war but not to exceed two years. In return for wage increases, the Washington Agreement stipulated that the miners would not go on strike for the duration of the war. A penalty clause provided for the automatic collection, by the operator, of one dollar for each day a miner was guilty of striking in violation of the agreement. The penalty clause provoked a bitter debate at the UMW 1918 convention, but the officers urged it be accepted because of the increase in wages that went with it. They insisted it was necessary for the good name of the organization, and they were able to put it across.[9]

Prices on commodities rose rapidly during 1918 and remained high in 1919. As a result the wage increase provided in the Washington Agreement was soon dissipated by the mounting cost of living. In June 1919 the War Fuel Administration, the agency through which the government had become a party to the Washington Agreement, went out of existence. The miners' resentment against the agreement grew rapidly as time went on after the Armistice without the war being officially declared ended. Since the war was over, the miners felt they should no longer be bound by the provisions of the Washington Agreement. On the other hand, the union officials, following John L. Lewis's views, were inclined to accept the operators' opinion that the war was not over. In the summer of 1919 the smoldering discontent erupted in a rash of wildcat strikes. The strikers were fined; the fine being deducted from their pay when the operators enforced the penalty in accord with the Washington Agreement. Infuriated, the miners struck again, this time against their officials as well as the operators. In District 12, Illinois, union officials admitted 25,000 miners were out, while the insurgent leaders claimed three times as many.[10]

Lewis asserted the suspension of work was "illegal," and warned the insurgents that such violations of the Washington Agreement would not be tolerated. When they persisted in fighting for their rights, they were expelled and their locals suspended. Nevertheless, when the UMW convention assembled in Cleveland in September 1919 Acting President Lewis, forced to act by the growing demand for the abrogation of the Washington Agreement from rank and file miners, agreed that the contract be terminated on November 1, and that the penalty clause be omitted from the new agreement. "President Lewis has picked up all the demands of the radicals whose champion he now appears to be," reported the Literary Digest. *"One is led to believe, however, that Lewis has not assumed this role but rather that it was thrust upon him."[11]*

The second outburst of opposition to Lewis' policies came as a result of his actions in ending the great coal strike of 1919. In spite of an injunction issued by Federal Judge A. B. Anderson of Indianapolis, at the request of Attorney General A. Mitchell Palmer, ordering the UMW officials to call off any strike, four hundred thousand miners, anthracite and bituminous workers, went on strike on November 1, 1919, for a 60 percent increase in pay, a six-hour day and a five-day week. Judge An-

derson issued the final injunction on November 8th, giving the union seventy-two hours in which to cancel the strike. President Lewis chose to capitulate. He made no attempt to resist the injunction, held no referendum, and did not even announce the terms under which the miners should go back to work. The terms, when finally disclosed, provided for an immediate wage increase of 14 percent, and left the disposition of all other questions to the judgment of a commission to be appointed by President Wilson. After holding extended hearings, the commission granted less than half the miners' demands. The coal diggers obtained a 27 percent wage increase, but the demand for a five-day week, six-hour day was ignored.[12]

Because of his retreat during the 1919 strike, Lewis faced strong opposition within the union. "Like a pusillanimous poltroon," wrote one critic, "he betrayed the rank and file, obeyed the injunction and cowered behind the skirts of 'Americanism.'"[13] (The last phrase related to Lewis's explanation in calling off the strike that "We are Americans." We can not fight the government.") John Walker, the Illinois UMW leader who was one of Mother Jones's closest friends, told her that Lewis's "surrendering and bowing in abject submission allowing the men to be driven into the mines like cattle, without a fight at all . . . makes the decent Mine Workers, who understand what it means, blush with shame."[14]

The opposition to Lewis included men who were motivated primarily by a desire to displace him as president, like Frank Farrington, the opportunistic leader in Illinois who eagerly carried out Lewis's orders suspending locals and expelling militant miners;[15] independents like John Brophy, who did not lift a voice in criticism of Lewis's role in the 1919 strike;[16] Socialists like Powers Hapgood, Communists like Pat Toohey and Tom Myerscough, who worked closely with non-Communist insurgents;[17] and mavericks like Alexander Howat.

Alexander Howat was the president of District 14, which comprised the state of Kansas. Prior to the war an internal scandal in the union grew out of charges that Howat, who had taken the offensive against the international officials, had accepted bribes from the operators. The affair "dragged through the courts with the Kansan suing his detractors and forming around his chunky person a perpetual opposition to the administration of the union." According to McAlister Coleman, the rank and file never questioned Howat's honesty or his militancy. "Nor did the diggers feel that in his right mind Alex would consciously sell out the union."[18]

In 1920 the Kansas legislature passed a law creating a Court of Industrial Relations designed to enforce compulsory arbitration and prevent strikes in labor disputes. Howat and other officials of District 14 refused to testify before the court, claiming the law creating it was unconstitutional. "We refuse to testify before this court, because we do not recognize the court," he declared publicly. Howat notified the miners the law would be ignored and opposed. Ninety percent of the Kansas miners walked out when Howat and other district officials were arrested and jailed for defiance of the Industrial Court law. Despite an injunction secured by the state authorities restraining the union leaders from ordering further walkouts, the strikes continued to spread.[19]

The coal operators' association in Kansas appealed to the international union to force the miners back to work in compliance with the contract. Lewis agreed with the mine owners, and refused to support Howat on the ground that the strikers were in violation of the contract between the union and the operators. He ordered the Kansas officials to put an end to the work stoppages. Lewis justified his action with the argument that he was acting in response from Kansas miners who wanted relief from Howat's "ruinous government." "The miners of Kansas," Lewis cried, "shall not be permitted to be sacrificed to the whims and caprices of a demagogue."[20] But a study of the dispute concludes that "Howat had wide support" not only in Kansas but throughout the entire union. In 1920 as the anti-administration candidate for vice-president, he had received 132, 416 votes against the administration candidates's 143,452.[21]

Howat defied Lewis's order to send the men back to the pits. The international president then appointed three members of his executive board to make "a thorough investigation of conditions" in Kansas. The committee studied the situation and since they were all Lewis's henchmen, not surprisingly, they presented a report sustaining Lewis's contention that the miners were on strike in violation of contract and recommended a resumption of work in compliance with the agreement with the operators. Howat was then ordered to appear before the international executive board. Nothing was said by Lewis and his executive board about the Kansas Industrial Court.[22]

The District 14 leader refused to obey the executive board's decree, and Lewis brought the matter before the UMW international convention in September 1921. Lewis asked the convention to sustain the international executive board's action. For almost a week the delegates debated the proposition. Howat's supporters contended that the adoption of Lewis's recommendation would be taking sides with the operators against the miners. Although Illinois, Indiana, and Kansas voted for Howat, the Lewis machine was able to overwhelm their votes and the administration's recommendation was adopted by a final vote of 2,753 to 1,781.[23]

While the Kansas miners, supported by the Illinois district, continued in a state of rebellion against the international officers, Lewis proceeded to liquidate his adversary. On October 12, 1921, he suspended the Kansas district's charter, ousted Howat and other district officials and named "provisional" officers to reorganize the unit. A month later the miners who continued the strike were expelled from the union by Lewis's order. New local unions were organized to replace those whose charters had been revoked. The local union to which Howat belonged was one of those that lost its charter, and the international officials held that Howat was therefore no longer a member of the United Mine Workers.[24]

At the 1922 international union convention, Howat and one hundred and twenty-five of his suspended followers came to the gathering. The Kansan forced his way onto the platform and demanded that his appeal from the action of the international officials be heard. Lewis interrupted him and declared he was not entitled to any consideration as he was not a delegate nor even a member of the union. The president insisted that the convention consider only wage matters and ruled that Howat's appeal to the delegates to consider reinstating the deposed Kansas officials and locals was out of order. When a storm of protest broke out, Lewis permitted a debate on whether Howat could appeal to the convention from the ruling of the chair.

The convention was in wild disorder while the case was being discussed. When the chair called for a rising vote, the Howat supporters won. Administration forces, however, were then successful in obtaining a roll-call vote, and Lewis's ruling was sustained by a narrow margin amid stormy scenes verging on rioting.[25]

Lewis had succeeded in purging one of his most powerful critics. Several months later the international executive board restored autonomy to District 14 where the membership was now composed only of those miners who had remained loyal to the international officials.[26]

It was in a futile effort on Howat's behalf that Mother Jones made her farewell speech to a United Mine Workers Convention. She had traveled to Kansas to organize and speak in support of Howat, and had assisted in getting the Kansas leader out of jail long enough to attend the UMW convention in February 1922. It was during the vote on whether to allow Howat a hearing on his expulsion, that suddenly Mother Jones interrupted the proceedings, "She did not ask permission to speak but walked quietly up to the front of the stage and held up her hand," wrote a correspondent. "Absolute quiet prevailed as she remonstrated with 'her boys.' She begged her beloved coal diggers to save the Kansas miners' union, to quit fighting among themselves." After she had concluded, he added:

The crowd seemed to have gone mad as they cheered this wonderful old soldier of theirs that had been in the front line of every battle in the miners' union. It was with difficulty that order was obtained, the call of the roll continued.[27]

Mother Jones lived to see the Lewis dictatorship consolidated in the union she had helped build as one local after another was placed under presidential trusteeship, giving Lewis control of the entire organization. She also lived to see UMW membership drop from 600,000 in the mid-1920's to between 60,000 and 150,000 in 1928.[28] She did not, however, live to see the union rebuild its forces and membership during the early

*New Deal, with West Virginia finally organized. She did not live either
to see John L. Lewis shift his ground and call at the October 1935 A.F.
of L. convention for it to organize industrial unions in the mass production industries. After the convention, Lewis joined with leaders of ten
other A.F. of L. unions to form the Committee for Industrial Organization (CIO) to promote industrial unionism within the A.F. of L. Most
unfortunate of all Mother Jones did not live to see John L. Lewis become
a hero of the entire American working class as president of the independent CIO and play a crucial role in the most dynamic chapter in the history of the American labor movement.*

At this point Mother Jones proceeded to the stage and requested the
delegates to remain quiet while she addressed them, as follows:

Mother Jones: Boys, do you know that the whole world has got its
eyes on this convention?

A Delegate: And on Howat, too.

Mother Jones: Everywhere the electric current touches it is notifying the world what you are doing here today. Don't you know your
money is being wasted?

A large number of delegates shouted, "Yes."

Mother Jones: The children at home need the money to feed them.
Have you no consideration for the men who laid the foundation of this
great organization that the whole industrial world looks to you for a
lesson? Do you know that you are able to assemble in this convention
on the bones of the men who marched miles in the dead of night to get
you together to bring more sunshine to your children and to the children of the nation? And then you are wasting time here.

A Delegate: It has been done by the officers.

Mother Jones: What can the officers do? Didn't you elect them? I
want you to muzzle up now.

I came to this convention because of the headlines in the papers. I
thought I would come here and look after you and see that you behave
yourselves. You must realize, my friends, that we are facing a crisis in
the industrial organizations of the world; you must realize that the
enemy who has been fighting from the outside is now boring from
within. You must wake up to the fact that all of us make mistakes at
times, but there is a way for us to remedy those mistakes. Let us do it
quietly, sanely, and in a business-like way. You should not come to
this convention to howl and hoot. Your officers deserve some consideration.

I don't endorse a wrong at any time. You haven't an officer in the
country in any labor organization that I won't get up and raise hell
with if he is not true to you. I don't get myself under obligations to any
officer· I keep my hands clean and can fight any of them and do fight
them and will fight them again if necessary. You came here to this
convention to outline your coming contract and you are wasting all

this time. You are putting a weapon right into the hands of the enemy to hit us with when the time for a settlement comes.

I was down in the state of Kansas recently. I was in Kansas twenty-five years ago. I drove through the coal fields with an old horse and wagon. That was the beginning of the organization in that state. I happened to be in Omaha when the boys came to me and said they would strike, but if they did they would be blacklisted. They asked me to come out there. I went out to Kansas and held a meeting that night in an old barn. The whole thing was closed up in the morning; there wasn't an engineer or anyone else working, and in five days we won the strike.

The boys wanted to give me some money but I told them I didn't want the money, but I wanted an old horse. The horse I had in mind was blind, but his two ears were open. So they got the horse and wagon for me and I piled the wagon with literature and went through Kansas and Missouri. There weren't many organized miners there at the time, but we got the men together and held meetings in the schoolrooms.

Now I have been in Kansas again. When I took this last trip to Kansas no individual asked me to go. The miners of Kansas telegraphed me to come to them if I was able to move. I want to make the statement now that whenever the miners call for me in any part of the country and I am able to go to them, God Almighty won't keep me from going. I studied the Kansas affair very carefully. In the first meeting I held I told them I came down principally to get Alex Howat out of jail. And I got him out, didn't I? You bet your life I did!

I have known Alex Howat for twenty years, and while I have not always agreed with Alex, I want to make this statement to the audience and to the world: That my desire is to have a million Alex Howats in the nation to fight the battles of the workers. He has fought for his men and he has fought that damnable law that the governor of Kansas put on the statute books to enslave the workers. He fought it nobly and he is willing to go to death for it, and because he did it he was put in jail and denounced. If Alex Howat never did anything else he called attention of the nation to that slave law.

The New York *World*, in an editorial, denounced the Kansas Industrial Court Law. Men in the United States Senate said it wouldn't work. If the men of Pennsylvania had done the same thing that Alex Howat did in Kansas when the damnable Hessian law was brought over by Gruin of Philadelphia, and put on the statute books of Pennsylvania, we wouldn't have it now everywhere. At the first meeting I held in Kansas there were United States marshals, the sheriff, and the mine inspectors. In that meeting I made this statement: That whenever I went to Washington on the B. & O. Railroad I got off at Harper's Ferry. I would ask the conductor to wait three minutes and I would tell him what I wanted. The conductor said he would always wait. My object in getting off was to pay my respects at the grave of a man from Kansas to whom a monument has been erected in Harper's Ferry.

John Brown didn't come from Maine, he came from Kansas.[29] It was John Brown of Kansas that was fighting against chattel slavery. I have never heard of a monument being built to the judge or the jury that condemned him to death; they are unknown; but there is a monument to John Brown at Harper's Ferry and I never go to Washington on the B. & O. Road that I do not get off and pay my respects to that monument. In the years to come there will be another monument built to the memory of a man from Kansas, and that will be built to the memory of Alex Howat.

I received a letter from one of those women in Kansas who took part in that march. I want to read it to the delegates.

Ringo, Kansas, February, 13, 1922

To the Delegates of the Convention:

Dear Fellow Workers: As a voice from the toilers, from the loyal women of District 14, Kansas, we, the mothers, wives and daughters of loyal union men are depending upon you in the convention as a body of experienced union working men to judge the wrong that has been done us here in Kansas, a wrong which no court can try to settle, but a wrong which can be justified by you when you sit in the convention today. We depend upon you as friends, men and judges to consider the future of Kansas, and, in fact, in the whole of the United Mine Workers.

We call to you, not for money, but for justice; not in behalf of our district president, Alex Howat, and Vice-President August Dorchy, whom we in Kansas feel there was never two nobler men than they are, who have stood for a principle such as the United Mine Workers stand for. Men have fought for it, and while fighting for that principle today in behalf of that principle, we, the women of Kansas, ask your attention and ask you to try our case as a jury of the United Mine Workers of America to decide upon a verdict that will save our organization that is on the verge of being destroyed by a few traitors within our organization.

Men, think well, as upon you depends much of the future of the organization, even the lives of the women and children.

There is an appeal to every honest, thinking man, coming from the mothers of Kansas, and I want to say to you men here that those women will go down in history when the men who were guarded by guns in the scab hotel will be damned by the world.

I had a hand in laying the foundation of this organization in Kansas and I am not going to see it perish. It is going to stand as a monument to the workers of the nation. Now, boys, settle it, and stop this howling like a lot of fiends. Do business like men and then come here and meet your officers. Be good to them when they come, Mr. Lewis. Come to your board and to your own offices and settle this question. Now settle down to business today.

357

I didn't feel very well able to come here, but I wanted to talk to you, I wanted you to let the world see that you are thinking men, that your organization is dear to you, that the future of this country depends upon what you do in this convention. Stop all this noise. When we are through and we cannot get what we are entitled to we will go out and raise hell all over the nation. I don't feel very much like talking today, but here is one woman who, if I stand alone, I will stand behind Alex Howat for the fighting qualities he has and for the manhood he has shown.

When this gathering is over you fellows get together. Come before your board and do business there. Don't be giving those fellows (pointing to the newspaper reporters) a lot of stuff to help the bloodsuckers and pirates of Wall Street. They will get a lot of stuff like they had when the Structural Iron Workers were in trouble.[30] I am going to go before the board with you, and they have got to treat you right, because if they don't I will get after them. Now, be good boys. I left this convention yesterday almost broken-hearted. Four railroad men came to me on the street and said: "Mother, what is the matter with the miners? How could they take the vote they did against those Kansas men?" Don't you see that everybody is watching us? We haven't enough good fighters. I want to see more Alex Howats and I want to live long enough to develop them.

[Minutes of the Convention, United Mine Workers of America, 1922, *pp. 84-88.*]

Notes

1. Dubofsky and Van Tyne, *op. cit.*, p. 23.

2. *Ibid.*, p. 24.

3. John Hutchinson, "John L. Lewis: To the Presidency of the UMWA," *Labor History* 19 (Spring, 1978): 213.

4. Dubofsky and Van Tyne, *op. cit.*, p. 98.

5. *Ibid.*, p. 150.

6. *Ibid.*, p. 106.

7. *Proceedings*, UMWA Convention, 1920, p. 29; McAlister Coleman, *Men and Coal*, New York, 1943, p. 126.

8. Spencer D. Pollard, "Some Problems of Democracy in the Government of Labor Unions, with Special Reference to the United Mine Workers of America and the United Automobile Workers of America," unpublished Ph.D. thesis, Harvard University, 1940, pp. 30-61.

9. James A. Wechsler, *Labor Baron*, New York, 1944, pp. 45-46; Marion D. Savage, *Industrial Unionism in America*, New York, 1922, p. 96.

10. *United Mine Workers Journal*, February 1, April 1, June 15, August 1, September 1, 15, 1919; Sylvia Kopald, *Rebellion in Labor Unions*, New York, 1924, pp. 5, 18, 62, 89-91, 117-19; Selig Perlman, and Philip Taft, *History of Labor in the United States,* New York, 1935, vol. 4, pp. 435, 470.

11. "How the Wheels Go Round in the Miners' Union," *Literary Digest*, November 22, 1919, p. 59.

12. Perlman and Taft, *op. cit.*, p. 471; *United Mine Workers Journal*, September 15, November 1, 15, December 15, 1919, April 1, 1920; Coleman, *op. cit.*, p. 98; *Proceedings*, UMWA Convention, 1920, pp. 44, 156-57.

For a labored defense of Lewis's role in the 1919 strike, *see* Dubofsky and Van Tyne, *op. cit.*, pp. 60-61.

13. Eric Haas, *John L. Lewis Exposed*, New York, 1937, p. 32.

14. John H. Laslett, *Labor and the Left: A Study of Socialist and Radical Influences in the American Labor Movement, 1881-1924*, New York, 1970, p. 224.

15. Kopald, *op. cit.*, pp. 89-91.

16. There is still no good study of the Communist opposition to Lewis. See as a starter "Bankrupt Leadership in the Miners," *Labor Herald*, July, 1923, p. 28; Tom Myerscough, *The Name is Lewis — John L. Czar of the U.M.W.A.*, n.p., n.d.; David M. Schneider, *The Workers (Communist) Party and American Trade Unions*, Baltimore, 1928, pp. 30-49.

18. Coleman, *op. cit.*, p. 88.

19. *New York Times*, April 20, 1920; *United Mine Workers Journal*, August 15, 1920.

20. *New York Times*, August 5, 1920.

21. Stanley Joshua Jacobs, "Opposition to John L. Lewis Within the United Mine Workers," unpublished M.A. thesis, University of California, Berkeley, 1949, p. 64.

22. *United Mine Workers Journal*, August 15, February 15, June 1, September 1, 1921; *New York Times*, August 16, 1921.

23. *United Mine Workers Journal*, October 1, 1921; *New York Times*, September 29, 1921.

24. *United Mine Workers Journal*, October 15, December 1, 1921.

25. *Ibid.*, March 1, November 1, 1922; New York Times, February 16, 1922.

26. *United Mine Workers Journal*, November 1, 1922.

27. Undated, unnamed clipping headed "Mother Jones for Howat at Meeting," Mother Mary Harris Jones Papers, Department of Archives and Manuscripts, Catholic University of America, Washington, D.C.

Mother Jones called John L. Lewis "an empty piece of human slime." (John H. Keiser, "John H. Walker, Labor Leader from Illinois," in Donald F. Tingley, ed., *Essays in Illinois History*, Carbondale, Illinois, 1968, p. 149.

28. Saul Alinsky, *John L. Lewis; Unauthorized Biography*, New York, 1949, p. 61; *United Mine Workers Journal*, November 15, 1928.

29. During the Kansas-Nebraska conflict of the mid-1850s, John Brown went to Kansas with his sons to keep the territory free of slavery. It was while he was in Kansas that the notorious incident occurred involving the killing of five pro-slavery men at the Pottawatamie River in 1856.

30. The reference is to the dynamiting activities surrounding the International Association of Bridge and Structural Workers. The McNamara case of 1911 involved the indictment for murder of J. J. McNamara, secretary-treasurer of the union, and his brother J. B. McNamara for the bombing of the *Los Angeles Times* building which left twenty-one dead, the McNamara confession, and the arrests and federal trials of leaders and members of the union on charges of dynamiting and the convictions of 38 who were indicted. (See Foner, *op. cit.*, vol. 5, p. 31.)

My Old Eyes Can See the Coming
of Another Day

Speech at conference of National Farmer-Labor Party,
Chicago, July 3, 1923

*Well known though she was in Socialist, Communist, and labor party
circles, as an uncompromising champion of the workers, Mother
Jones's national reputation came mainly from activities in organizing
drives and strikes, especially, though by no means exclusively, among
the miners. Her political philosophy could be summed up as the need to
subordinate political to economic action. She did talk of the importance
of putting pressure on Congress and the state legislatures to obtain laws
needed to enable the workers to operate effectively on the economic front,
but she never viewed political action to be as important as trade union
action. On September 21, 1920 she wrote to Rhyne Walker, editor of the
New York Call; "We have a terrific fight in the southern end of the state
[West Virginia]. I don't pay very much attention to the political phase of
it. I know the future battle of it is going to be in the field of industry, and
this fellow has got to be educated to his power."* [1]

*Yet that same year she attended a convention of labor party suppor-
ters in Chicago, and three years later, she both attended and spoke at
the Farmer-Labor Party Congress. She knew, for one thing, that the increasing use of the injunction in strikes was smothering labor's
economic strength. John Fitzpatrick, the leading champion of a labor
and farmer-labor party in trade union circles, showed Mother Jones a
letter he had received from John P. Frey, editor of the* International
Molders' Journal. *Frey wrote: "It is folly to spend $50,000 or $100,000
in a strike . . . when a decision of the judge can overthrow all that the
strikers are able to accomplish." While Frey, a leading A.F. of L.
ideologist, was committed to the federation's political policy of "reward
your friend and punish your enemy," and continued to cling to non-partisan political action, Fitzpatrick had lost faith in the ability of labor to
solve the injunction problem through the two major parties, and he
urged Mother Jones to become more active in the emerging movement
for an independent party of labor.* [2]

*Although a Socialist of long-standing, Mother Jones, as we have
seen, and the Socialist Party had developed a distinct love-hate relationship. Yet the vision of a socialist state never dimmed. She welcomed the Russian Revolution as a manifestation of world-wide social
change and was convinced that the day might soon come when the
workers in the United States might accomplish what had been achieved
in Russia. A labor party was a logical step in that direction, and a logical development too of the great labor uprising of 1919. While she never
became a Communist, Mother Jones did have great respect for William*

Z. Foster, and the campaign Foster waged through the Trade Union Education League and the Workers' (Communist) Party for a Farmer-Labor Party added to the influence exerted by John Fitzpatrick in bringing Mother Jones to the 1923 conference.

In 1920 trade unionists who advocated a labor party amalgamated with progressive farmers' groups to organize the Farmer-Labor Party of the United States. The war in Europe had increased prices for farmers' products, and at the same time it had encouraged large-scale farming which gave the richer farmers a considerable control over transportation, elevators, and credits. The small farmers organized for self-protection through the National Non-Partisan League, organized by Arthur Townley in Minnesota in 1915. By 1918 the League had attained majority control in one and impressive minorities in six plains states. Conscious of their political strength, small farmers saw good reasons to unite with trade unionists who, in the face of weakening organizational power as a result of the postwar "Open Shop Drive," were turning increasingly to labor politics.[3]

In 1920 the Farmer-Labor Party nominated Parley P. Christensen for president of the United States, but was able to win no more than one percent of the presidential vote. The Farmer-Laborites then looked about for new allies, and thought they had found them in the Conference of Progressive Political Action (CPPA). The CPPA had been formed in late 1921 at a gathering called by William Johnston, the former socialist who headed the Machinists' Union. Socialists and Farmer-Labor Party supporters active in several states responded quickly to the call. So too did the Communists, but, over the objection of John Fitzpatrick and the Chicago Farmer-Laborites, they were rejected as delegates, and excluded from the conference. The advocates of a Farmer-Labor Party at the conference pointed to the depression of 1921 and the growing agrarian movements in the Midwest as necessitating the immediate formation of a Farmer-Labor Party under CPPA sponsorship. The Progressive Conference did not call for a third party, however, but issued a statement recommending that all groups at the conference support candidates sympathetic to labor in the 1922 elections. It also called another meeting for December 1922.[4]

The Farmer-Laborites believed that the railroad brotherhoods, the most powerful labor bloc in the country, would lead the way for a third party. When Congress voted to end wartime controls over the railroads and return them to full private ownership, the unions affected had responded angrily, and called, through the Plumb Plan, for nationalization of their industry. But increasingly the conservative brotherhood leaders had retreated from the Plumb Plan, and when the Farmer-Laborites at the second CPPA meeting got under way in Cleveland, they made it clear they would not support a third party. The Farmer-Labor Party delegates introduced a resolution endorsing independent political action, and proposing the immediate formation of a new national party.

But the brotherhood leaders refused to go beyond the "non-partisan political program" associated with the AFL, and since they had the majority of votes, they were able to defeat the resolution for a third party 64 to 52. With this, the Chicago Farmer-Laborites, headed by John Fitzpatrick, bolted and moved to form a new third party in 1923. The Socialists voted to remain in the CPPA, but the Communists decided to join the Chicago Farmer-Laborites in forming a Farmer-Labor Party. William Z. Foster, Communist leader, believed that the Fitzpatrick-Foster alliance which had operated during the stockyard and steel-mill organizing efforts, might be revived to further the cause of independent political action.[5]

After they left the CPPA, the Chicago Farmer-Laborites issued a call for a convention in Chicago on July 3, 1923, to take steps to form a Farmer-Labor Party immediately. Invitations went to all groups and individuals on the left as well as to many international unions. The Workers' (Communist) Party which had been excluded from the CPPA meetings, was invited to send delegates. A fervent champion of unity in radical and labor organizations, Mother Jones welcomed both the calling of the conference and the invitation to the Communists. Like the others who came to Chicago, she was under the impression that the purpose of the gathering was to launch a Farmer-Labor Party, and in addressing the delegates, she urged them to use their heads and organize a new political party of workers and farmers.

To her surprise it soon became evident that John Fitzpatrick and the Chicago Farmer-Laborites were more interested in breaking relations with the Communists than in the formation of a new party — even though they had specifically invited the Workers' Party to send delegates. When the Chicago Farmer-Laborites, headed by Fitzpatrick, demanded that the convention bar groups advocating violent overthrow of the government, an obvious device to exclude the Workers' Party delegates, Mother Jones was among the delegates who voted disapproval, defeating the resolution by a vote of 500 to 40. Thereupon Fitzpatrick's group walked out of the very convention they had called.

Two farmer-labor parties resulted from the unfortunate split — the Federated Farmer-Labor Party organized in Chicago and the national Farmer-Labor Party headed by Fitzpatrick. But neither party flourished, and within a year, both had passed from the scene.[6]

Although discouraged by the factionalism which had weakened the third party movement, Mother Jones had a new opportunity not long after the Farmer-Labor Party conference, and in the very city in which it was held, to see again the devastating impact upon labor of "government by injunction."

In the winter and spring of 1924, the International Ladies' Garment Workers' Union was involved in a general strike against the dress manufacturers of Chicago. The strike, launched on February 27, 1924, had as its aims a 10 percent wage increase, a forty-hour week, and collective bargaining in the industry. Ninety percent of the three thousand strikers were young women, and they put up a heroic fight.

The very day the strike began, Judge Dennis E. Sullivan issued a sweeping injunction against any form of picketing. Over five hundred women strikers were arrested for violating the injunction, and jail sentences of from fifteen to fifty days were handed out to ninety of them. Meanwhile, police and thugs freely attacked the women strikers.

At the end of the first week of the strike, Mother Jones, en route to California from New York, stopped off in Chicago long enough to speak to the "girl strikers." "This strike of yours is war. It is damned real war," she told them. "You girls are fighting and I want to tell you to keep on fighting. Don't care about police in and out of uniform. Don't care about jails, courts, or injunctions. Picket, strike, fight."

But the strike was weakened by injunctions and police interference, and in July, after 1,500 arrests, it ended in defeat.[7]

In her Autobiography, Mother Jones wrote in 1925 that she "rejoiced to see the formation of a third political party — a Farmer-Labor Party. Too long has labor been subservient to the old betrayers, politicians, and crooked labor leaders."[8] She says nothing, however, about her role in the presidential campaign of 1924, in which Robert M. LaFollette ran on the Progressive, Farmer-Labor Party ticket, with A.F. of L. endorsement. But the New York Times carried two interesting stories during the campaign. The first, on September 16, 1924, quoted at length Samuel Gompers' praise of Robert M. LaFollette, and noted that in commending the Progressive and Farmer-Labor presidential candidate to labor voters, Gompers said:

Labor's support of LaFollette is based on the fact that he has ever been willing to risk his political standing by advocating measures to make the government more responsive to the will and wishes of the people. Robert M. LaFollette has been a leader of leaders, a pathfinder in political progress, a fearless foe of greed and exploitations, and a champion of the rights of the people. . . .

On September 27, 1924, the Times headlined the news: "Coolidge Endorsed by 'Mother' Jones. She Tells the President That Prosperity Assures Him a Majority of Labor Votes." The story, a dispatch from Washington, read:

"Mother" Jones, the famous defender of the Miners' Union, called on President Coolidge today and assured him that a majority of union men will vote for him. She said that the American Federation of Labor cannot swing the vote of its member unions. The workers are satisfied with their present standard of living, she said, and, with prosperity prevailing throughout the country, have confidence in Mr. Coolidge.[9]

This, to put it mildly, must have startled miners and other workers who remembered Coolidge as the man who, as governor of Mas-

*sachusetts, had broken the Boston police strike in 1919, and who had
yet to experience the "prosperity" so apparent to Mother Jones.*

An ovation greeted "Mother" Jones. She told of the rise and passing
of the Greenback[10] and the Populist Parties.[11] Coming down to present gathering she declared it the most important since the Revolutionary War.

She told of the great industrial wars, at Homestead, Pa., in various
mining districts of West Virginia, in Colorado, and elsewhere. She told
the delegates that "You've got the ballot but you have never used it."
She referred to the old party politicians as "political sewer rates," ad-
ding that congress was made up of men who could blow off more steam
than a locomotive could carry in ten years.

Enthusiasm again swept the conference when she said: "Had all the
railroad unions been amalgamated the strike last year wouldn't have
lasted 24 hours."[12] She also made a scathing attack on those labor officials who betrayed the workers for $10,000 jobs, no doubt referring to
Grable, former president of the Railroad Maintenance of Waymen,
among others, who got lucrative jobs as a result of treason to the workers committed during the rail strike.

"Down in Johnstown, Pa., once," she said, "they asked me if I was a
red. I said yes! They asked me if I was a Bolshevik, and I said 'yes,'"
and more cheers broke spontaneously from the gathering.

"You must organize and use your heads," said "Mother" Jones. "You
have been letting bosses override you too long. You must clear out the
crooked labor leaders among yourselves.

"All you need to do is to unite politically and you can have a
thorough clean-up. You will be able to clean out the gunmen in the
coal fields, particularly in West Virginia. It is time to get back to the
spirit of the Revolutionary fathers.

"The producers, not the meek, shall inherit the earth. Not today
perhaps, nor tomorrow, but over the rim of years my old eyes can see
the coming of another day."

*[The Worker, July 14, 1923; New York Times, July 4, 1923;
Autobiography of Mother Jones, p. 238.]*[13]

Notes

1. Mother Jones to Rhyne Walker, September 21, 1920, Walker manuscripts, Manuscript Department, Lilly Library, Indiana University,
Bloomington, Indiana.

2. John P. Frey to John Fitzpatrick, July 9, 1917, John Fitzpatrick Papers,
Chicago Historical Society; John Howard Keiser, "John Fitzpatrick and Progressive Unionism, 1915-1925," unpublished Ph.D. thesis, Northwestern University, 1965, pp. 114-15.

3. *Autobiography of Mother Jones*, p. 238.

4. Nathan Fine, *Labor and Farmer Parties in the United States*, New York, 1932, pp. 367-68, 375; James H. Shideler, *Farm Crisis, 1919-1923*, Berkeley, California, 1957, pp. 58-87; *New Majority*, March 4, 1922.

5. William Z. Foster, *From Bryan to Stalin*, New York, 1937, pp. 176-77.

6. *The Worker*, July 14, 1923; *New Majority*, July 21, 1923; Foster, *op. cit.*, pp. 179-80; James Weinstein, *The Decline of Socialism in America 1912-1925*, New York, 1969, pp. 284-87.

Alexander Howat, anti-Lewis dissident leader in the United Mine Workers voted with Mother Jones against the resolution to exclude the Communists.

7. Philip S. Foner, *Women and the American Labor Movement: From World War I to the Present*, New York, 1980, pp. 162-63; Chicago *Tribune*, February 28, March 1, 2, 1924; Wilfred Carsel, *A History of the Chicago Ladies' Garment Workers Union*, Chicago, 1940, pp. 168-70.

8. *Autobiography of Mother Jones*, p. 238.

9. *New York Times*, September 27, 1924.

10. The Greenback Party was organized in 1876 with Peter Cooper as its presidential candidate. Its platform called for increased issuance of paper currency. It became the Greenback-Labor Party in 1878 with labor demands such as the eight-hour day, abolition of convict labor, etc., added to the original platform.

11. In 1890, farmers' representatives, meeting in Ocala, Florida, formulated a list of demands, which became the basis for a later platform, adopted at Omaha, Nebraska, following the formation of the People's (Populist) party. The Populists called for nationalization of railroads, a graduated income tax, postal savings banks, direct election of Senators, and other provisions, including free coinage of silver. The party attracted labor support and labor-populism emerged. In the presidential election of 1896, William Jennings Bryan, Democratic candidate, captured the Populist movement and it declined soon afterwards.

12. The railroad shop craft workers went on strike, with Brotherhood support, on July 1, 1922, to protest a decision of the U.S. Railroad Labor Board. The Board had approved drastic wage reductions requested by the roads, as well as the farming out of stock to contractors who hired non-union labor. The Board then voted that a strike was an illegal action against a government agency, a decision that enabled railroad companies to deny seniority rights to the strikers. The seniority issue then became a third major grievance of the workers. When leaders of the brotherhoods began to make separate agreements with the railroads, especially the Baltimore & Ohio, the strike was weakened and ultimately defeated. (Edward Berman, *Labor Disputes and the Presidents of the United States*, New York, 1924, pp. 226-46.)

13. The Chicago *Tribune* and the Chicago *Daily News* carried none of Mother Jones's remarks to the convention. The *New Majority* did feature a picture of Mother Jones at the convention on the first page of its issue of July 14, 1923 (strangely taken with John Fitzpatrick), and identified her as the "most photographed person" at the convention. But it did not report her speech. I am indebted to Professor David Roediger of Northwestern University for furnishing me with this information.

Power Lies in the Hands of Labor to Retain American Liberty

Mother Jones's last speech, spoken into the Movietone news camera
on her 100th birthday, May 1, 1930

In its report of Mother Jones's last speech, the New York Times *carried the following dispatch from Silver Springs, Maryland:*

Sitting under an apple tree surrounded by friends of labor who had
come to celebrate her 100th birthday, Mother Jones made as fiery a
speech today as she did thirty years ago when exhorting miners to
strike.

Her cheeks were pink with excitement. Labor leaders carried the
frail little old lady, dressed in her best black silk, to the front yard of
the Walter Burgess country home.

Her iron will had pulled her through weeks spent in bed that she
might live to see this day. Scores of telegrams received from labor
unions all over the country,[1] masses of flowers and a huge birthday
cake bearing 100 candles keyed her up for the ordeal of being the
centre of an admiring throng all day long.

Out on the lawn she faced the talking picture cameras, took a deep
breath and a drink of water, and began an impromptu speech which
brought loud applause and sent the near-by circling crows wheeling
back to the woods.

A dog enjoying a nap in the May sunshine jumped to his feet as the
white-haired labor leader said in a ringing voice:

"America was not founded on dollars but on the blood of the men who
gave their lives for your benefit. Power lies in the hands of labor to retain American liberty, but labor has not yet learned how to use it. A
wonderful power is in the hands of women, too, but they don't know
how to use it. Capitalists sidetrack the women into clubs and make
ladies of them. Nobody wants a lady, they want women. Ladies are
parlor parasites."

*[*New York Times, *May 2, 1930]*

Notes

1. "Most precious of all to Mother Jones," the *Times'* account added, "were
the telegrams which came pouring in from labor unions of horsehoers, garment
workers, tailors, grocery clerks, and many other trades expressing admiration
and gratitude for the work she had done."

TESTIMONY BEFORE CONGRESSIONAL COMMITTEES

Testimony Before Committee on Rules, House of Representatives on H. J. Res. 201 Providing for a Joint Committee to Investigate Alleged Persecutions of Mexican Citizens by the Government of Mexico, Washington, D.C., June 14, 1910

In 1909 and 1910 a rising tide of public condemnation, in which Mother Jones played a significant role, emerged in reaction to the severe harassment by the United States government of Mexicans in this country who were seeking the overthrow of the Díaz tyranny in their native land. Organizations and individuals condemned the aid the Mexican dictator was receiving from the Post Office Department, the Immigration Bureau of the Department of Commerce and Labor, the Department of Justice, the Department of State, and various state and territorial authorities in the hounding and persecution of these Mexican refugees from the Díaz dictatorship, the ability of paid agents of Díaz to operate freely in this country in cooperating with federal and state officials in this persecution, and the contrast between the American libertarian tradition and friendship for men and women battling oppression and the treatment of the Mexicans. Led by William B. Wilson, former United Mine Workers official in Pennsylvania and a friend of Mother Jones, a number of liberal congressmen demanded a Congressional investigation of the persecutions. After the House adopted Joint Resolution No. 201, introduced by Congressman Wilson, hearings were held in Washington between June 10 and 14, 1910, before the House Committee on Rules.

The hearings, with Congressman Wilson in the chair, heard the reading of a letter submitted by Samuel Gompers, president of the A.F. of L. (originally sent to President Theodore Roosevelt) condemning the Díaz dictatorship and the persecution by U.S. officials, in collaboration with the Mexican authorities, of Mexican opponents of the dictator. It heard John Kenneth Turner, author of Barbarous Mexico, *and John Murray, president of the Political Refugee Defense League, San Antonio, Texas, furnish in harrowing detail specific evidence of persecution of Mexicans in the United States, especially Ricardo Flores Magón and his followers, the Magonistas.*

Mother Jones was the final witness to testify after which the hearings concluded.

Mr. Wilson:[1] Mr. Chairman. I would like to have Mother Jones speak.

The Chairman: Mother Jones, please give the stenographer your name and residence.

STATEMENT OF MRS. MARY JONES

Mrs. Jones: My name is Mary Jones.

The Chairman: Please take a chair. Where do you live?

Mrs. Jones: I live in the United States, but I do not know exactly in what place, because I am always in the fight against oppression, and wherever a fight is going on I have to jump there, and sometimes I am in Washington, sometimes in Pennsylvania, sometimes in Arizona, sometimes in Texas, and sometimes up in Minnesota, so that really I have no particular residence.

The Chairman: No abiding place?

Mrs. Jones: No abiding place, but wherever a fight is on against wrong, I am always there. It is my pleasure to be in the fray.

Mr. Wilson: Mother Jones, you were down in Douglas, Ariz., I believe at the time of the arrest and kidnaping of Manuel Sarabia?[2]

Mrs. Jones: Yes.

Mr. Wilson: What do you know about that?

Mrs. Jones: I was in Arizona at that time. We had a strike on there with the Philip Dodge copper interest. The smelters, the men, or the slaves, rather, working in the smelters, had not been organized, and I went down there in Douglas to help organize those workers.

Mr. Wilson: Mrs. Jones, I suggest that you might be more comfortable if you were sitting down.

Mrs. Jones: I am so accustomed to standing when I am talking that I am uncomfortable when sitting down. That is too easy. [Laughter.]

Well, I was holding a meeting on the streets of Douglas one Sunday night for the workers that were in the smelters. An automobile was run out from the jail, from what I learned afterwards and this young Sarabia was thrown into it.

He screamed out, "They are taking my liberty," and then they choked him off. I do not know how many were in the automobile, but coming down from the meeting where the crowd had been all the evening and the streets were vacant otherwise, one of the workers came to me and said, "Oh, Mother, there has been something horrible going on at the jail," and he said, "Some man has been taken there and deprived of his liberty." I said, "I suppose it is somebody with a jag on," and did not think further of it at all. So we went to the hotel I was staying at, and we were discussing the meeting over with a dozen of these

370

poor unfortunate wretches in the smelters, and just then the editor of
El Industrio, whose paper has been suppressed since, came running
down very much excited and said, "Oh, Mother, they have kidnaped
our young revolutionist." Well, kidnaping seemed to be in the air just
about that time. The Idaho affair was on, and I just did not understand
at first what he meant. He was very excited, so I said, "Sit down a moment." There were perhaps six or seven of us sitting down there, and
he sat down, and I said, "Whom did they kidnap, did you say?" He said,
"Our young Mexican revolutionist." I said, "What for? How so?" He
said, "He worked on the paper here, and they threw him in jail this afternoon, and while you had a meeting in the crowd there they ran an
automobile out and took him away." I said, "Get as many items on that
as you can, and get a line on it, and immediately telegraph to the governor, and you boys find out all you can about that and telegraph it to
Washington. Do not stop a minute, because if you stop they will murder him." They are bloodthirsty out there. So they telegraphed the
governor and telegraphed to Washington before the morning.

The next day we met, and I went into the office of *El Industrio*,
thinking the matter over, and this gentleman, the editor of the paper,
came to me. He is also a Mexican, and he had lived in this country for
some time, and he was speaking of the horrors of the affair, and I said,
"That must be stopped. The idea of any bloodthirsty pirate on a throne
reaching across these lines and crushing under his feet the Constitution," I said, "which our forefathers fought and bled for." I said, "We
must get up a protest meeting and arouse the territory about it tonight." I said, "If this thing is allowed to go on, they are liable to come
and kidnap any of us."

So two deputies that were on duty, that were put on that evening,
said to me then — they just came in — "It was a horrible affair." And
they said, "We had instructions, Mother, not to give them any supper,
although he had the money to pay for it." And I said, "Well, we will attend to that tonight. We will have the meeting on the street." So we
had some issues of the *Examiner*, the Douglas *Examiner*, which was a
weekly. The other papers belonged to the Southern Pacific bunch and
the Copper Queen, and of course we could not get anything into them,
but we got hold of the Douglas *Examiner*, and we took several copies of
it and circulated them throughout the town, and got up a meeting that
night.

I spoke at the meeting, and I am not very choice, you know, when the
Constitution of the country is violated and the liberties of the people
are trampled on. I do not go into the classics of the language at all. I
am not praying at that time. [Laughter.] So I put the matter very
strong before the audience.

Then I had to leave Arizona and go up to the steel range in Minnesota, where a strike was going on. I had to go up there and fight the
steel robbers, and so of course I left the scene there, but I started the

ball rolling. Before I went away I went up to Phoenix to see the governor, who, I believed was of the American type of Patrick Henry and Lincoln and Jefferson, and I felt it my duty to go and see him. We have very few of that type of men in this age. The general run of them are after the fleshpots of Egypt instead of the rights of the people of the country. So I went up and paid my respects to the governor, and there I met Captain Wheeler, whom I had met before. Captain Wheeler had orders to go into Mexico and bring back young Sarabia, which he did.

Mr. Clark: Was he a soldier?

Mrs. Jones: Captain Wheeler was captain of the rangers, and a pretty fine fellow to be captain of the rangers. I never think men who head the army of a bloodthirsty pirate dressed up in uniform are very fine men, but he was an exception to that rule.

I left there then, but in 1908, immediately after the campaign. I learned from those men in jail at Los Angeles their condition.[3] They were without money, without aid, and I felt that they were just like Kosciuszko, Carl Schurz, Kossuth, and Garibaldi, and men of that kind, who received protection in our country from the tyrannical governments which they fled from, and I felt they were entitled to some protection, and that if they were without money, but were in the fight for liberty, a fight against the most bloody tyrant that has been produced, I would protect them; and so, although I was not in very good health, I went out and raised $4,000. I sent it West to get stenographers, hire attorneys, and bring witnesses to Tombstone, Arizona, where they were to be tried. I did not expect any great amount of mercy from the court at Tombstone, because Judge Doan is not a very humane man. People who are feasting and eating and drinking with those who own the fleshpots of Egypt are not generally very humane characters. But I still felt that probably through the efforts we were making, and the publicity we were giving it, they would not be turned over to be murdered, and if they could be saved from being murdered that would satisfy me, knowing that some day we would get them out of the clutches of the tyrant. And so they were tried and sentenced to eighteen days in Yuma. From there they were moved to the new prison.

Now, then, to finish my part of it. After I had raised that money and sent it west and they were tried and sentenced, there were four then in the penitentiary in Leavenworth. I went up to the penitentiary to see them, and saw the warden, and I went to see this Sylva, who was dying at that time, apparently. He was sick, and he appealed to me. To think that in an institution like that a patriot should perish and we should stand by and see him. So I immediately came to see the president[4] about him, and I put the matter before the president, and the president gave me a very nice audience, and he said, "Mother, if you will bring me the evidence, I will read it over." I went back to the penitentiary, got a notary public, got a man who spoke the language, and I took him up there, and I asked the warden to give me permission to speak with those prisoners, and the warden very graciously brought them in, and they sat there and I took the evidence. When they were about going out of the room I looked at these men and thought, how sad it is that our Constitution must be buried underfoot in the interest of the tyrant across the line. So I looked at the poor fellows, and I said, "Boys, be good boys and some day you will get out," and the warden turned and he said, "Mother, they are always good; they have never given us any trouble."

I came here and brought the documents to the president in Washington again, and the president said, "Mother Jones, I am very much afraid if I put the pardoning power in your hands there would not be anyone left in the penitentiaries." [Laughter.] I said, "Mr. President, if this nation devoted half the money and half the energy to give men an opportunity to get out of the penitentiaries — the men who are forced into them — we would not need any penitentiaries in this country."

Now, that was my part of it. I then went into Texas. We agitated the question there along the line and drew the attention of the people of Texas to the crimes of our officers. We pay, I believe, over $8,000,000 a year to hire secret service men. They must hold their jobs, and someone has got to be made a criminal in order that reports can be sent to the government.

Mr. Wilson: Mother Jones, do you know how long it was from the time Sarabia was kidnaped in Douglas, Arizona, until he was returned?

Mrs. Jones: Eight days. Captain Wheeler went to —— [5]

Mr. Clark: Mother Jones, who sent this captain down there, the governor of Arizona or the president of the United States? You do not know?

Mrs. Jones: That I did not inquire into, so long as they made an attempt to bring him back.

Mr. Clark: You do not know where they were keeping him?

Mrs. Jones: Yes; they were keeping him in the Hermosillo Penitentiary. I felt that it was our duty as citizens of the United States to look into these things. I do not think, gentlemen, that this country should run penitentiaries in the interest of the Mexican government. From all I can learn and from all I have seen along the line, and even in Mexico itself, I think the conditions are almost appalling and it ought to be investigated to the very end, no matter who has to suffer. I believe that justice should come first, and I believe that the blood that our forefathers spilled should not have been spilled in vain, and that these wretches who have some interest in human freedom and liberty should not be arrested, threatened, and hounded.

Now, the document that I brought to the president was evidence from Guerra that this secret-service man, Priestly, when he took him to the court, talked to him and told him, "You must swear so and so," and the wretch did not understand the English language and simply expressed what the secret-service man told him to. He made that statement, I think, in the presence of the warden of the federal penitentiary.

I have been interested in these cases from the humane point of view, and also from the patriotic point. I believe that this country is the cradle of liberty. My forefathers came here. I came here under the shelter of this flag, and when we say that we can not start an expedition to suppress these wrongs, we say something that is unjust and contrary to precedent. The Irish Fenians[6] started it in Canada and carried it into this country. All the money that supplied Parnell[7] in the effort to overthrow English rule in Ireland came from this country, and it is not long ago since $50,000 was sent from Boston over there to Ireland.

We have only sent to these men the little money we can collect; and, gentlemen, in the name of our heroes, in the name of those unborn, and in the name of those whose statues stand in Statuary Hall, I beg that this body of Representatives will probe down to this evil and protect these wretches from the tyranny and oppression of that bloody pirate.[8] I would like to get a chance at it. [Laughter.]

Mr. Wilson: I simply want to state, Mr. Chairman, that we have in our possession, or Mr. Turner and Mr. Murray have in their possession, a mass of additional evidence along the same line that has been presented. Out of deference to the wishes of the committee we have boiled it down as much as we could, and we feel that we have demonstrated the necessity of an investigation of the entire question.

(Thereupon, at 12:15 o'clock p.m., the hearings were concluded.)

[Hearings on H.J. Res. 201, Providing for a Joint Committee to Investigate Alleged Persecutions of Mexican Citizens by the Government of Mexico. Hearings held before the Committee on Rules, House of Representatives, June 10, 11, 13 and 14, 1910 (Washington, 1910, pp. 91-93).]

Notes

1. William Bauchop Wilson (1862-1934) was born in Scotland, and worked in the coal mines of Pennsylvania after he came to the United States in 1871. He rose to become president of the district union and an organizer of the United Mine Workers of America in 1890 when it was organized. Wilson served as secretary of the UMW from 1900 to 1908 and as a member of the House of Representatives from 1907 to 1913, being one of a group of "labor Congressmen." He was appointed by President Woodrow Wilson as the first Secretary of Labor when the Department was created in 1913, and remained Secretary until 1921.

2. *See* pp. 55, 121, 143-45, 460-61.

3. The men were Ricardo Flores Magón, Librado Rivera, and Antonio I.

Villareal. *See* pp. 55, 121, 133.

4. The president referred to was William Howard Taft.

5. Manuel Sarabia had been shanghaied from Douglas, Arizona, to Hermosillo, Sonora in Mexico. *See* pp. 55, 121, 143-45, 460-61.

6. Fenians (or Fenian Brotherhood) were an Irish-American revolutionary secret society, active especially in the years 1863-70. Founded in the United States in 1858 by John O'Mahony, the members bound themselves by an oath of "allegiance to the Irish Republic, now virtually established." Branches were established in all parts of the world.

7. Charles Parnell (1846-1891), Irish nationalist leader, who developed the weapon of boycotting to secure Irish independence. Parnell felt that while parliamentary methods were useless to achieve this goal, a parliamentary machine could be so handled as to obtain independence for Ireland from England.

Testimony before House of Representatives Subcommittee of the Committee on Mines and Mining Investigating Conditions in the Coal Mines of Colorado, Washington, D.C., April 23, 1914

Four years after Mother Jones testified before the House Rules Committee's investigation of "Alleged Persecutions of Mexican Citizens by the Government of Mexico," Mother Jones was again before a committee of Congress, this time the Subcommitee of the Committee on Mines and Mining in its investigation of the Colorado Coal strike. Mother Jones followed John D. Rockefeller, Jr. to the witness stand. In his testimony, Rockefeller had reaffirmed his opposition to unionism and his determination to pledge vast sums to retain the open shop. He also expressed unlimited confidence in the company officers in Colorado in the way they were dealing with the strike, and he posed as a champion of the real rights of the workers employed by his company. "I have been so greatly interested in the matter, and have such a warm sympathy for this very large number of men that work for us," he told the committee, "that I should be the last to surrender the liberty under which they have been working and the conditions which to them have been entirely satisfactory, to give us that liberty and accept dictation from those outside who have no interest in them or the company."[1] He admitted, however, that his knowledge of what conditions were like in Colorado was not based on any first-hand knowledge. He had not visited the coal camps in a decade; he had not even been to a board of directors meeting in ten years, although he was in charge of his father's properties in Colorado.[2]

Mother Jones covered a wide field in her testimony, vigorously supporting the union shop as against the open shop, and calling upon the president of the United States to order Rockefeller to settle the strike by recognizing the union and thus proving that the United States was not "a Rockefeller government." Confronted by members of the committee with statements she had made during the strike in West Virginia which they charged urged the strikers to acts of violence, she denied the charge and then commented: "That is not half as radical as Lincoln. I have heard him make a great deal more radical speech."

Present: Representatives Foster (chairman), Byrnes, Evans, Austin, and Sutherland.

Present also: Representatives Taylor of Colorado and Kindel.

TESTIMONY OF MRS. MARY JONES

(The witness was duly sworn by the chairman.)

The Chairman: Mrs. Jones, please give your name in full and your residence to the stenographer.

Mrs. Jones: Mary Jones. I am usually called "Mother" Jones for years.

Mr. Evans: Do you have any objection to telling your age?

Mrs. Jones: My age? Oh, no, indeed. I will be 82 the first of next May.

The Chairman: And your residence is where?

Mrs. Jones: Well, wherever there is a fight.

The Chairman: You do not have any permanent residence?

Mrs. Jones: I perhaps will tell you, Dr. Foster, as I did Chairman Dalzell during the Mexican refugees investigation.[3] When he wanted to know where I lived I told him wherever there was a fight going on against the robbers; sometimes up in the steel mills, sometimes in Pennsylvania, sometimes in West Virginia, sometimes out in Arizona, sometimes down on the border. I am not located anywhere.

The Chairman: Now, you have been in Colorado lately?

Mrs. Jones: Yes, sir.

The Chairman: When did you first go there? Do you remember?

Mrs Jones: The first strike —

The Chairman: I mean this last trouble.

Mrs. Jones: Oh, I went in September, I think it was. Well, it was the third day after Labor Day. I was in Texas — at Thurber, Texas, a mining town.

The Chairman: That was before the strike began?

Mrs. Jones: I went from there directly to Trinidad.

The Chairman: You were there, then, before the strike came on?

Mrs. Jones: Oh, yes; I was there before the convention was called.

Mr. Sutherland: Before it was called, you say?

Mrs. Jones: Yes — well, it was called, but before it assembled.

The Chairman: You were at the convention?

Mrs. Jones: Yes.

The Chairman: Have you visited these mining camps? Did you before the strike began?

Mrs. Jones: No.

The Chairman: You were not in them?

Mrs. Jones: I did 10 years ago, when I was there,[4] but this time I had not been out to the mining camps. After the convention adjourned I went into Denver to do some correspondence,[5] and then I came back to Trinidad. I was there before the strike broke out — two or three days — in Trinidad[6].

The Chairman: Now, you tell us from your experience there what you know with reference to this strike and any causes leading up to it.

Mrs. Jones: The causes leading up to it — they had grievances. Now, they told me that they had to dig 6,000 pounds of coal and would not get credit, perhaps, for but 2,000. Many of them told me that. And their wives told me the sad condition they were in. And then, you know, they are blacklisted; they did not dare speak of organizing or anything, or rebelling against it. There was no redress for that at all. It was brought out, the same complaint that you had in West Virginia, you know; only the conditions in Colorado were more brutal than they were in West Virginia. There is no question about that, from what they tell me.

The time the strike took place I went to Ludlow, and they had got the tents, and I went out to see that the women and children were properly cared for. And in going out — I think it is fourteen or fifteen miles — the mud there is very slippery, and they had twenty-eight wagons during that number of miles coming in, and it was pathetic to look at them. It was a rainy day, and the mothers had their babes in their arms. The horses did not seem able to carry all. And they were walking with little babes in their arms.

I spoke to two or three of them and said, "Why don't you wait until tomorrow?" And they said they were glad to get away to-day and they were going into Trinidad for shelter.

Well, I went up to the tents and the mattresses were all wet, and the little babes and the women slept on those mattresses the night before. There was one Italian there, and I said, "Joe, where did you sleep last night?" And he said, "I slept behind that old house over there, Mother." "Well," I said, "it was rainy," and he replied, "Well, roof he stuck out." "Didn't you get wet?" "Yes; but no like comforts anyway. No have tents nor nothing. Stayed there all night."

The women, they did not seem to regret it at all that they were out. It was the natural impulse, I suppose, of revolt, you know.

The Chairman: Now, tell us of some of your experiences in reference to the strike as you know about it there.

Mrs. Jones: Of course, I have been three months in a military bastile,[6] so I have not quite as much fire in me as I had. However, one day I went out to speak to those women and children, to take them some little things to eat —

The Chairman: Where is that?

Mrs Jones: To Ludlow, where I was about to go — no; I had been down to Aguilar, and I went down to the tents to talk to them, and I was telephoned for to come immediately to Ludlow. I had been to Ludlow and had gone from there to Aguilar, and I was telephoned for.

But they telephoned from Trinidad to me to go immediately to Ludlow, and I said, "There must be something wrong there," and I said to the automobile man, "You drive just as quick as you can, because I am afraid they have some trouble or they would not have telephoned me."

So I went down, and the guards were shooting from the track, from the C. & S. track, and the women were all excited, you know, and the children and the men —

The Chairman: Shooting where?

Mrs. Jones: Shooting from the tracks to the tents.

Mr. Evans: Do you know about what date that was?

Mrs. Jones: It was some time in the middle of October. I could not exactly tell the date, but it was some time in the middle of October, I think.

Of course, the women have a natural tendency, you know, to get nervous, and I tried to get the women into the tents. "Now," I said to the boys, "don't you do any firing at all. Keep away; don't return them the fire." They did not, but they went away from the tents, and I don't know what they did there; but there was nobody hurt, I think, that day. But those guards kept irritating them, and I said, "Don't bring on any trouble. These women and children are here. Don't start any trouble here."

And the boys said, "Are we going to let them shoot us down?" "No; I don't think they will do that," said I; "they are just trying to irritate you." So I got them all quieted down, and I went back to Trinidad. I got the women to promise me they would not go out of the tents that evening at all.

I went back to Trinidad, and there was not any more trouble there for some time; but one morning — I think it was somewhere about the 20th of October — I was sitting in my room writing a letter, and the door opened without knocking and a man said — he came in; he had his overalls on; he was a railroad man — he said, "My God, mother," said he — his arms were up, all excited — "they are going to clean up the miners," said he, "and the tents." I said, "Who is?" He said, "Oh, the gunmen, the gunmen, the gunmen," said he; "they are going to murder them all."

I ran out to the head of the stairs, and he got out on the street before

I could get to him again. I did not want to go after him in the street because it would attract attention, and maybe the man would lose his job, so I went back, dressed myself, and went down and got some of the boys.

I said, "I want to go to Ludlow and Aguilar, and I guess if we have time," I said, "I will go to Segundo today." So I did not tell them what I was going for, because circulating the news irritates and gets the people worked up unnecessarily. So I went out and saw one or two of the level-headed boys, and I said, "Boys, you had better dig some trenches and put your women into it, and children. There may be trouble," said I. "I don't know whether there is going to be, but there may be. Now, be careful and cool; sit up nights and watch; don't let your women get out and get excited."

Then I went down to Aguilar. I held a meeting at Aguilar. In the box to my right was a lot of little boys, about — oh, perhaps twelve of them — and I turned from the audience to the little boys and I said, "Boys, you see my old white head?" and they nodded. First they were embarrassed. They thought I was going to make them get out of the box and let the women get in, and they nodded. I said, "Well, I want to tell you something. Every hair there has grown white," said I, "while I have been taking the thorns out of the pathway so that you may have a chance to be a man and live a man. Will you keep away from the saloon?" said I, and they said, "Yes." I said, "This fight I am making is for you." And they jumped out of that box and just threw their arms about me, and the whole audience roared at the acts of the children. They caught my head, and one pulled the other away to kiss me.

The marshal of the town came and I said, "Marshal, I would like to see you privately, if I can; I have something to tell you." So we went into a room and the marshal — I said, "I understand that the gunmen are going to make an attack on some tent colony; I don't know which one, but I thought it was best to warn you to be prepared." He says, "Mother, I told that sheriff to keep those follows out of here. I telephoned to him and said not to let any more of those fellows come in here; if he did, I would have to keep them out because my people were quiet." "Well," I said, "that was a good move to make. Now," I said, "I don't know that they are going to make any attack on Aguilar, but I know the attack is going to be made on some tents."

So I went back to Ludlow again that day. I went down to the tents and spoke to the people there, and I went back to Ludlow and looked in there, and everything seemed quiet, and the boys seemed quiet, and I went back.

I had already made arrangements to bring the little children in from these tents, because they have not much pleasure in life, and I thought I would throw one day's joy into their lives anyhow. I had got a little money and I thought I would give them a little refreshments, and I got a band of music engaged and I thought I would parade them through the city of Trinidad to show the people, as much as anything else, these are the future citizens of our state and nation when we pass away. They will take our places and we must make life as bright as possible.

So I had the parade. I went to the C. & S. and they would not give me any cars, and I went to the Rio Grande and the man at the Rio Grande said I could have them, but as I was taking my supper he came in and he said, "Mother, I am sorry, but I have been notified from Pueblo that you can not get the cars; that they could not spare the cars." I said, "That is all right."

So I sent word to the tents: "When the C.& S. comes in in the morning put all the children on — as many as you can get on — and bring them in." And the same at the Rio Grande. Then I got the boys to help me to get wagons to send out to the tents where there was no railroads to come in at the hour of the parade.

And I had a parade. I think I had about 1,200 children, but they told me — the humane man told me they had counted and there was 1,500. That is a question, however, that is not of much importance.

I paraded them through the town, the band ahead of them, and when I came down by the Columbia Hotel I was going to take them there where they were going to have something to eat, and the band — I said, "Now, boys, you needn't stay any longer." Because they were all workingmen.

And just as I was going down somebody said, "The governor is in town,"[7] and I said, "Where is he?" And they said, "Why, he is down at the Santa Fe" — that hotel — the Cardenas. And I said, "Now, here is a chance for him to come out and address them and get these people with him." So I started down. I went after the band and I said, "Say, I want you to come back and go on down to the Santa Fe depot and by that hotel, you play there, and then we will go around it." So we went, but he didn't show up at all.

Then I came back by the post office, and coming back by the Columbia Hotel again I was taking the women and children on to the hall. Of course, in all such cases there is a lot of curiosity — people out to see what is going on. The streets were full of men and women, and when we passed the Coronado — the street to their hall is right a little cater-cornered from the street going to the C. & S. depot. And just as I was turning the corner somebody hollered, "For God's sake, Mother, come back."

I knew there was something, so I said, "Take these children and women on to the hall," and I turned back, and I saw the mob of men there, and I said to a fellow — he was all excited — "Run and get me a chair." And he brought the chair out, and I put my hands up, and I said, "Now, here, we have had the keys of the city of Trinidad today, and the people have given us the hospitality of the town. I want you everyone to stand — no gathering at all." I had a way of my own of talking to those fellows, you know, and they minded me. I said,

"Mother tells you to move on," and they move. Some began to move, and some did not. Somebody came up and said, "They won't go until you go." So I said, "Come on, everyone of you men here; clear the streets." So, immediately the street was cleared.

I went on down to the hall where the children were eating, and then I came back; and this humane man from Denver — his name is Lyone, I think — the humane man from Denver — I think he was one of the Felts men that I saw in West Virginia at the machine gun, one day up on Cabin Creek. He was standing sort of bewildered there; and I said, "I want to tell you something. Let this be the last time you undertake to incite a mob. Mobs are mighty dangerous things to tamper with. You are lucky your head is not in the street." "I realize it," he said — he nodded.

So I went away. I was tired, wornout anyhow, because I had been up nights. The excitement was so great, and I had just come from West Virginia and Michigan.

So I went away, and they disbanded. I didn't see the governor. The next day I concluded to come here to Washington to try to get a Federal investigation; and I didn't want to say anything about it, because they had threatened to arrest me a couple of times, and I thought, "I am not going to say anything about it for fear they will arrest me to stop me from going." So Frank Hays and Lawson,[8] I think, were the only two that knew it.

So I came here to Washington and saw Mr. Keating, and there was not very many Congressmen here, you know. I don't know whether I saw Senator Kern at that trip or not, but I saw the president.[9] I got Senator Lane to make an appointment with the president. The interview was just a few words, a few moments; and I said to the president, "That affair is a very serious thing, Mr. President, out in Colorado."

Mr. Sutherland: Do you remember the date of this, Mrs. Jones?

Mrs. Jones: I have not the date, but perhaps Senator Kern could set the date, or Senator Lane. He says, "Yes, I realize it." "Because," I said, "we never know what those things are going to lead to, and it is so essential for us to take precautions." He said, "Yes, I am quite interested and I would like to have a longer interview with you." And so I promised to come back the next week. I told him I was going to Boston that night — to leave for Boston that night. It was rather a rush day anyhow at the White House, I think. There seemed to be a great many people there.

But I didn't go back again; I went on out to Colorado. Well, they got the convention — they were going to call a state-wide strike. Well, I don't believe in those things. I am opposed to them.

The Chairman: Did you advise them against calling a state-wide strike?

Mrs. Jones: Yes; I advised the secretary. I don't believe in those things at all. There is a way of settling those things without creating a terrific turmoil. So I said to two or three parties, "Don't attempt such things. Don't tolerate it at all. Call a convention."

Mr. Sutherland: This was all before the convention?

Mrs. Jones: Before the convention. This all happened before the convention. I was watching that convention very closely — kept my eye on the delegates in the convention, and when the man got up to tell about digging his grave — and I tell you it was pathetic — it just made me tremble to think such a thing could be.

Mr. Evans: Madam, are you not mistaken about this being before the convention?

Mrs. Jones: What?

Mr. Evans: This incident you are now relating. That was long after the strike started, about the man digging his grave?

Mrs. Jones: That is what I am telling about.

Mr. Evans: But that was after the convention?

Mrs. Jones: No; that happened before the convention.

Mr. Evans: Then you are speaking of one convention and I am speaking about another. I am speaking about the convention that called the strike.[10]

Mrs. Jones: No; I am speaking of the federation — the convention that the State Federation of Labor called.

Mr. Sutherland: Where was that convention held?

Mrs. Jones: In Denver.

Mr. Sutherland: Yes; that man did go up there and testify.

Mr. Evans: Yes; you are right about that.

Mrs. Jones: There was not any incident like that in the first convention. They were only just telling their little grievances in that convention.

I got up on the platform and I said to the convention — I said, "This is horrible. I would suggest to the convention that they go in a body to the governor and ask him whether he is standing for the interest of the people or for 26 Broadway.[11] Now is the time," I said, "to put him up against it — whether the people and the honor of the state come first before the interest of 26 Broadway."

Well, they got up — I know how to handle those fellows. There is nothing ever happens when I make a move with them. Green, though, the national secretary of the miners[12] — he got scared to death. He said, "There is some of those fellows with their lips white." I said, "What of it? That don't make any difference." And he jumped up on the platform, and he blocked the whole thing.

Well, my object was this, that the governor would not have any time to organize his militia, that he would have to tell the truth right straight through to those delegates where he stood. That was the object I had in view. I was not afraid of anything happening, because in all my history of strikes nothing has ever happened where I have been with them personally. I can be traced from the first strike to the last, and I don't allow it. I don't stand for it at all.

So, then, Mr. White wanted me to go to El Paso, and I went down to El Paso, because they were bringing some Mexicans — strike breakers — and I went down to El Paso. I had been in El Paso two or three or four times before. I was there during the Mexican refugee cases before Díaz left Mexico.[13]

So I went down to El Paso and I looked the situation over, and I went over to Juarez, and I had a talk with General Villa and with his staff, and some of the staff came over to see me before I left, and I held a meeting in El Paso.

When I came back I rather expected what was happening. When I got off the Santa Fe train the captain of the militia ran and said, "There she comes." I looked at him for a moment, and he had four or five militiamen more with him. The porter put my little satchel down on the platform. They ran and took it up, and he says, "We want you." I said, "What's the matter? I am going to Denver." "Get back on the train." "I am not going on the Santa Fe," said I; "I am going on the C. & S." "Get in here," he said, "and get your ticket." "The ticket is not here," said I; "it is at the other depot."

Well, they were like a lot of mad fellows some way. I looked at them — I never lose my head in such times as that at all. I generally keep it pretty level.

So he took me into an automobile with some militia in it, and took me up to the Columbia Hotel. I said I would like to get a little breakfast, and I went into the restaurant and got a cup of coffee. Then I was taken upstairs to the mail-carriers' room and held there until the train came. Then I went downstairs to an automobile. There were bayonets at my back and one at my left and this captain that arrested me at my right, and another captain in front. I went down to the depot, and there was the cavalry and infantry. Oh, there was awful excitement there.

So I went in and got my ticket and went on the train. They sent three or four militiamen with me on the train — Captain Nichols, a very nice fellow. He said, "You are going right on to Denver?" I said, "Yes."

So, at the depot at Walsenburg the miners — some of them heard I was coming, and they came down. I didn't get off the train, because I thought I would not create any excitement. I just went to the window and shook my handkerchief at them and went back and sat down, and I went on into Denver.

A reporter for the *News* met me, and I was laughing about it, and he was laughing, too. Quite a number of our boys met me at the depot, and so I went back. I stayed in Denver a week, and I bought $500 worth of shoes. I had a $500 check sent to me, and I bought $500 worth of shoes at a wholesale house to go down and give to them, because in those cases you have got to be very careful that you give them to those who really need them. It creates a sort of spirit of envy, you know, and we have a great deal of the human hog in all portions of the human

383

race yet. So I thought I would go and find out really who most needed them, and I would send them as if somebody had sent a present to them, you know.

I got down to Trinidad and went into the hotel. I understood they had two detectives at the Oxford watching me. But I went there in a sleeper, got off at Trinidad, and walked right up. Nobody saw me that knew who I was. I didn't want to create any excitement. They would get their cavalry and their infantry and all the curiosity people would come out, and the newspapers have big headlines, and you would think we were all insane people the way things go on.

So, I got into the hotel and I was there three hours before they found out I was in town. So they had to communicate with Denver, because General Chase was in Denver with the governor,[14] and they came in — the militia did — and took me into an automobile. I said, "Did you come after me, boys?" I heard them coming through the hall. They laughed and said, "Yes." I said, "I have a few little duds here" — I had been combing my hair and I was jesting with them. I got into an automobile.

The whole street was covered with infantry and cavalry and everything. It was revolting to look out to think we are such insane people in the twentieth century. And I was taken to the hospital in Trinidad and locked in the room there, and there was five guards always on duty for nine weeks.

Mr. Sutherland: Five guards?

Mrs. Jones: Five militiamen.

The Chairman: Always on duty?

Mrs. Jones: Always on duty, sir. They came at 6 o'clock every evening and went off at 6 o'clock the next evening. There was one in front at the window and the others were in the hall. I never got a line, never got a newspaper, never had a book. I never saw a human being, only Mr. Hawkins; I think I saw him three times — Mr. Hawkins, the attorney.

The Chairman: They did not give you a book to read?

Mrs. Jones: Not a line of anything. No one was allowed, not even a guard, to speak to me; but the corporal used to come in to make a fire; he was very nice. The boys — I didn't ask them to do anything. I knew they had their instructions, and I didn't want them to overstep their orders, so I wouldn't ask them for anything.

Then, I didn't like the idea of the militia coming in with meals. And I had a feeling about it that perhaps they would put something in my meals — now, that is the truth; I am going to be honest to the committee — and I played sick so as to get the sister to come in.[15] I was sick anyhow because I was cut away from the air, and my head just bothered me to death. So I asked the colonel if the sister could bring me in my meals, and he said yes. I didn't like those militiamen coming in three times a day.

So the sister came up bringing me my meals, but she had orders not to speak, and I didn't ask her to. But Colonel Davis came to see me several times, and asked me if I would not go to Denver, and I said, "No; I will not go to Denver. I will go to Trinidad, and I will go to Denver when I want to; when I am turned loose." So he talked with me and went away and came back again. And he said, "Mother, aren't you ready to go to Denver?" I said, "Colonel, I want to tell you something. I have constitutional rights in this country. I have never in my life violated a law." And I said, "The governor can bring his militia, all he has got, and he can cut the flesh off my body inch by inch, and then if he has not got enough bayonets, he can send and get more and cut all my bones inch by inch, but I will not surrender constitutional rights to military despotism." So he went away again.

Then, I was nine weeks there. The next morning, Monday morning, he asked me once how did I leave the military prison in West Virginia, and I said, "Why, Captain Sherwood came one day to see me," and he said, "Mother Jones, the governor has telephoned to me to bring you up," and I said, "What does the governor want?" "I don't know," he said, "but he asked me to bring you to Charleston." "Well, I suppose I will have to obey," said I. "We just have forty minutes, Mother, so I will put on my civilian clothes." "Well," said I, "What am I going to do? I won't be presentable going with you, because I have had these things on three months." He said, "Never mind, Mother; I will feel highly honored to take you." So I went, and the governor turned me loose.

He came back again after that, and he said, on this Sunday, "Mother Jones," said he, "if the governor wants to see you in Denver, will you go and see him?" I said, "Yes. While I may not have very much respect for the governor, I have for the office he holds, and, of course, I shall go."

So there was not anything more said about it until he came back that evening, and he said, "You have just got eight minutes to get the train." "Well," I said, "I didn't know you were going this evening," and he said, "Yes." I was going to bed, and I dressed and got my things together, and the guards were all taken out of the hall. I was taken down the back way and put into the automobile, and rushed around from back streets and put onto the Santa Fe at a crossing. I went into the sleeper and went into Denver.

I didn't know I was turned loose when they took me to the hotel, but he made an appointment for me to go to see the governor at 9 o'clock. I said, "I want Hawkins to go with me." and I said, "I won't go to see the governor without my attorney." So he and General Chase consented, and I said, "Make the hour 10." So they went away and left me there. I didn't know I was turned free until Mr. Hawkins came. Hawkins said, "Is Mother Jones a prisoner yet?" and General Chase says, "No."

So I went up to see the governor, and I said to the governor, "Governor, you can examine for seventy-seven years the police records all over this nation from one end of it to another, and the counties where sheriffs have been, and you will never find my name there. There is not a policeman in the nation has ever meddled with me or touched me or undertook to arrest me. They have always protected me. And there is not a sheriff in the United States that has ever molested me. The only time," said I, "that I ever was in court was when I was taken into the Federal court in 1902, in Judge Jackson's court. The United States marshal arrested me, but he didn't want to put me in jail.[16] There were nine of us arrested. He said he had engaged a room at the hotel. I had refused to go to the hotel. So I went to jail with the other eight boys, and the jailer and his wife took care of me that night with them." I said, "That is the only time I was ever in court," said I, "was when I was in the Federal court in West Virginia for the violation of an injunction. But now it is the militia, the militia, the militia."

"Well," I said, "America passed the Declaration of Independence so that military despotism should not exist in America, which it had for hundreds of years in England. Now," I said, "the first invasion of that was down in Idaho during 1902." Then I said, "They have transmitted it during the Peabody administration to Colorado, then over to West Virginia, and back again here. Now," said I, "I am going to fight it to a finish. If I am a criminal," said I, "it is a strange thing my name is not on the police records."

Well," he said, "if anybody told me not to go anywhere, I would not go." Well, I didn't want to argue any more with him, so I went away. "I am going back to Trinidad," said I. He said, "Don't go to Trinidad." I said, "I am going there. Colorado belongs to the sisterhood of states, and when she was taken into the sisterhood of states I was a citizen of the state, and I have a share of stock in there." So I went down the next Sunday and the military took me off the train. In the morning — I had my fare paid, and my sleeper to Trinidad, and I was taken off the train.

The Chairman: Where?

Mrs. Jones: At Walsenburg.

The Chairman: What was done with you then?

Mrs. Jones: Put into the cellar.

The Chairman: The jail at Walsenburg?

Mrs. Jones: Yes; that is the jail.

The Chairman: How long were you there?

Mrs. Jones: Three weeks and three days.

The Chairman: Then what happened?

Mrs. Jones: The habeas corpus — I was going to have a hearing, I think, on a Saturday, and they turned me loose, I think, on Tuesday morning. The colonel came and said, "Mother, I have some good news for you. I don't know whether you will consider it good or not." I, of course, thought what it was immediately. He says, "The general has telephoned me to tell you that you are free; you can go where you please." "Well, I will go up to Trinidad." I said, "I don't like that way of doing business; it is too small entirely." He didn't say anything in reply to that, but the general says, "You can have transportation to any part of the state where you want to go." "I never take any favors from the enemy," said I. "I will transport myself."

The colonel — I think he did everything that a man could do that his office would permit him to do to make it pleasant there. He gave me newspapers and said, "You can have books or anything you want, Mother." And he gave me my mail.

The Chairman: That was at Walsenburg?

Mrs. Jones: That was at Walsenburg. I must give him credit for it. He was a man in every sense of the word. He didn't at all make it any more uncomfortable than he possibly could for me.

The Chairman: You were taken out of the jail at Walsenburg on Thursday morning and the question of habeas corpus was to come up on Saturday following?

Mrs. Jones: Yes. Here is the whole history of it, as far as I am able to go into it, Congressman Foster. Of course, I always look after those women and children, and I think if I had been in Colorado now and the governor had left my hands loose, this tragedy would not have taken place.

The Chairman: You think you could have prevented it?

Mrs. Jones: I could have prevented it. I prevented it in West Virginia and I have prevented it in the anthracite regions and other places. I don't approve of it. I believe in educating the workers — it may take us a few years. I believe in the brain instead of the muscle. I believe in the pen instead of the sword. I am not in favor of it in this age. I know I prevented a terrific outbreak in West Virginia, but I was arrested.

These miners are aggravated to death at times, and it takes some one who understands the psychology of this great movement we are in to take care of them when they are annoyed and starved and robbed and plundered and shot. We don't seem to understand this great question that confronts the nation today at all times.

The Chairman: Do you know anything about the living of those miners out in Colorado? Were you there before the strike occurred, or about the men at all? Do you know how they live?

Mrs. Jones: I was not very much through there.

The Chairman: So you really do not know?

Mrs. Jones: I know their living is horrible, because they have told me about it, but I have not visited them.

The Chairman: You have not visited them personally to see?

Mrs. Jones: No, not before the strike. You know, I was put out of there during the Peabody administration. They came into my room one night and took me out. I was getting ready to retire, and I was put out with seven bayonets that night, and landed down at the depot with 5 cents in my pocket. I had orders not to go back, but I went back the next morning. I went into Denver, and I wrote Governor Peabody a note and told him, "You don't own this State" —

The Chairman: What do you know about the purchase of guns and firearms by the miners out there?"

Mrs. Jones: I don't know anything about that. You see, I have been locked up for three months. I was here in Washington, and I went to New York and spoke, and I went to Massachusetts and spoke to get them to urge their Congressman for the investigation. I thought it would stop the strike as it did in West Virginia, in Massachusetts. That was my object in doing that. I came down there, and I sent them some shoes down to Walsenburg the day after I got out of jail. I think it was $100 worth. But I don't know a thing on earth about guns.

I am not in favor of guns anyhow, and in all my travels I never had anyone who carried a gun. I would tell them, "Have you got a gun? Yes or no? If you have got a gun, put it away. You can not go out with a gun." Because if they have a pistol with them, and any irritation takes place, the first thing they do is to use it. If they don't have it they can't use it. That is my principle about those things. I believe in peace, but, of course, there can be no peace — I don't believe in a despot, because a despot always resorts to perjury to protect his despotic acts. I am fighting that. That is what I am fighting.

Mr Sutherland: Did you ever see the report of your speech that you made at the convention at Trinidad, the convention at which the strike was called?[17]

Mrs. Jones: No; I didn't pay any attention to that.

Mr. Sutherland: Did you on that occasion urge them to strike, or to do violence of any kind?

Mrs. Jones: Never in the world. That is false.[18] If that statement was made, it is false. There was only one time, gentlemen, that ever I made that statement, and that was in the state of West Virginia. I made it on the capitol steps.[19] Three thousand miners had come to ask the governor to call an extra session of the legislature to do away with the Baldwin guards; that they did not believe in guns. I said, "The way to do this is to arouse public attention." And I myself sent for the 3,000 miners, and closed up the mines. They came up there peacefully, not a gun among them. I went into the statehouse and got a platform and came out, and I had the document already written, and I read it to the governor. He stood by my right, and the whole statehouse machine was there. There was 3,000 miners probably up there. The first banner they had was, "Nero fiddled while Rome burned." That is what the governor of West Virginia is doing.

I read those documents, and I said —

Mr. Sutherland: Which governor was that?

Mrs. Jones: Governor Glasscock,[20] not a bad man at all; a really good, so-called Christian man. But he didn't understand statesmanship, and he was a sickly man — nervous. He was not a malicious man, and he was not a bad man. There was a great deal said about him that was not so at all. I always have a kindly feeling for that man. He was a sickly man and unfitted for the position — under the strain — and I had a great deal of consideration for him.

He came out; he was standing there, and I said — when I read this it was requesting him to either call an extra session of the legislature or else to order the sheriff to do away with the Baldwin guards, and he immediately — I read it. I called the committee and I said, "Now, here, you take this thing and present it to the governor. Don't get on your knees," said I; "stand straight up under the flag, and don't say 'Your honor.' Just say, 'Mr. Governor,' and come back." They said, "Will we wait for an answer?" I said, "No."

So they came back, and I said to the audience, "Now, the governor won't pay any attention to you. Why? For this reason, that you did not nominate him. The biggest political crook in America," said I, "nominated Governor Glasscock — selected him — and that is Elkins."

The crowd said, "Then he ain't our governor." "No," I said, "but I think he will do what he can for you." The bankers said to put me out of the state. "No," he said, "she has not done anything." He said, "The civil authorities can do it." The civil authorities said, "She has violated no law; we can not do it." So they had a discussion about it. And after I had talked two hours I said to the men, "You will do something for me?" They said, "Yes." "Stay away from the saloons," said I. "Save your money and buy a gun." I said that jestingly; but they did buy guns. I said, "Don't give the money to the saloons."

Mr. Taylor of Colorado: Mrs. Jones, have you any suggestions to offer to the committee as to the conditions in Colorado now? What is your idea about it? That is what is affecting us and what we are thinking about very seriously.

Mrs. Jones: It is what affects me. I wish I was out there. Of course, I would be blamed for it.

If I was president of the United States I would notify that governor immediately to dispose of those gunmen. "You have not called an extra session of the legislature to pass a bill that gunmen may put on a military uniform. There are still constitutional rights in this state. You have to obey even if you are governor of a state. Now, immediately dispose of those gunmen."

Because, I tell you, gentlemen, and you realize it, for twenty-five or thirty years we have had government by injunction. We have not had government by legislature; we have had government by injunction by the courts. Naturally there was an undercurrent of revolts against the courts. You have a government by gunmen today in those states.

The Chairman: What do you mean now by "gunmen"?

Mrs. Jones: I mean these imported gunmen that are brought in. They are permitted to arm themselves with machine guns and use them on the workers, because the ruling class wants quick results. And if we are interested in the nation, in our honor, in the uplift of the children; if we do not want to fill penitentiaries and jails and make criminals, it is the duty of every statesman to appeal to the legislature to make laws to do away with those things.

Mr. Byrnes: Do you think it is a wrong public sentiment that is responsible for it?

Mrs. Jones: No. I tell you, the public pay very little attention to those things until they are aroused. You know the American public are the most indifferent people to freedom and liberty of any nation of the world. We have never had freedom; we have been told by our forefathers how we could get it.

Mr. Byrnes: Have the ministers of the gospel there urged those people to preserve law and order?

Mrs. Jones: I tell you the ministers of the gospel say very little themselves about those things. The people are getting indifferent about that, too.

Mr. Byrnes: They did not join you in your efforts, did they?

Mrs. Jones: Not that I know. I don't know any of them that did. They never came near me, I know.

Mr. Byrnes: Did you ever hear of them doing it?

Mrs. Jones: No; I did not.

Mr. Sutherland: Mother Jones have you ever advised them out there to stop the strike and get together and compromise their differences?

Mrs. Jones: No; I have not. Frank Hays and the leaders — they are all sober men. They are not men filled with passion at the head of the miners' organization today. There is no passion in those men. They are cool, level-headed men. They do not drink or carouse.[21] Their brain is always clear when they go to duty, and they have at all times advised those miners to peace. They have tried time and again to get a conference with the companies, the mine owners. They have never been able to do it. They are treated with contempt.

Mr. Sutherland: Were you out there when they had the conference, about the time Secretary Wilson was out there?

Mrs. Jones: Yes; I saw Secretary Wilson.[22] I have known Secretary Wilson for many years.

Mr. Sutherland: And he advised them, did he not, to accept the proposition that was then made about that time?

Mrs. Jones: I don't know about that. I was preparing at that time to go to — I think I was going to El Paso — going to San Antonio, to stop bringing the scabs. I don't remember. He may have done it, but I have no information of it.

I had a talk with Secretary Wilson at that time. I spent an hour with him at the hotel in Denver. We had known each other a great many years. I have been in conference with him in Pennsylvania, in his home, and during the great conflicts in Pennsylvania I have been there. He is a very cool, level-headed man — very. He has, to my knowledge, stopped a great many outbreaks that would have taken place if there had been more hot-headed character at the head of it.

Mr. Sutherland: Under the circumstances that exist in Colorado now, what do you advise as a means of settling this strike? I mean without saying it must all be done on one side or the other?

Mrs. Jones: Oh, there is always some fault on both sides. I am never one of those who think we are saints; not at all. There is always some fault. I believe in making concessions. We made concessions in West Virginia.

Mr. Taylor of Colorado: What else would you suggest, Mrs. Jones, aside from removing the gunmen?

Mrs. Jones: I think as soon as you have removed those gunmen you will have peace. And I think that the president could take a hand in this.

I want to tell you gentlemen something. I have not been in strikes a good many years. I have not been in the offices; I have been up against the guns. The great trouble with our statesmen today, they don't grasp the psychology of this thing. They are men entirely away from the working class. Now, you could avoid strikes to a very great extent if you would. It could be done. I know it can, but you see we go at it only in a sort of temporary way.

If I was chief executive of the nation, I would simply say to Mr. Rockefeller, "Now, here; get down. You have got to make concessions to those people. You have got to stop robbing them."[23] They have got a right to profits — I don't deny that — until such time as the people become sufficiently educated to take hold of the industries themselves. "The honor of this nation is at stake. It can not be sacrificed for you, Mr. Rockefeller. Now, here; come to time. Make concessions. Give those men the right to organize. Give them the right to have their coal weighed. Pay them every two weeks." And they have not many demands.

Mr. Taylor of Colorado: Suppose Mr. Rockefeller says that he declines to work the mines? Then what?

Mrs. Jones: Then I will say, "All right; we will work them."

Mr. Byrnes: Suppose he says this, that he is willing to grant every demand made by the miners except recognition of the union to the extent of making a contract with them? Do you think there would ever by any chance of settlement of the strike on that basis?

Mrs. Jones: I think maybe there would, although I will tell you something. My experience has been you can not enforce those concessions that are made unless you have an army behind you to enforce it.

Mr. Byrnes: Look at this present strike. Speaking from your long experience, if he will grant every demand that is asked by the miners except the recognition of the union, do you think that any influence could be brought to bear on the other side toward securing any concession that would settle this unfortunate strike?

Mrs. Jones: I tell you, you have very fair-minded men at the helm of the miners. They are not what you call radical, erratic men at all. They are men who know this thing from A to Z, and I am perfectly sure they will make some concessions. They will meet them halfway.

Mr. Byrnes: Now, this man says they will grant every demand with that exception. What would be your advice to the organization under those circumstances?

Mrs. Jones: Under those circumstances — I will tell you the truth about it; I would demand the organization. I would sacrifice other things. Other concessions I would sacrifice, but I would demand the right to organize. You have the right to go into the Knights of Pythias. The Catholics go into the Knights of Columbus. You go into the Masons, and nobody bothers you. So in the industrial field they want organization to protect them. Why not allow them to join that?

Mr. Byrnes: To go further, we asked him that — I think I did myself — whether he did not think so, and he said yes; he thought they had the right to organize. But he makes this point, that while he will grant their other demands, he will not make a contract with the organization which will preclude the possibility of any man other than a member of the organization working in his mines. That is the point they seem to make.

Now, is there any chance, do you think, of getting together? That is what every member of this committee would like to know.

Mrs. Jones: Yes; I understand what you are getting at. I don't think that they could, because it would involve strikes again. The organization — it would be revolting against the men, you know. I do not see why — on that ground — Mr. Rockefeller can refuse that.

Mr. Taylor of Colorado: I think his idea was, Mrs. Jones, that while it is true that other people have a right to join the Knights of Pythias and other organizations, and have a right to belong to a union, yet when you go to contract with people you do not contract with them as Knights of Pythias.

Mrs. Jones: We understand that.

Mr. Taylor of Colorado: And his idea was that the men had no right to compel them to contract with them as a federation of labor men; in bulk; that while they have a right to join the Knights of Columbus, yet we do not deal with them as Knights of Columbus. We do not contract with people in their union capacity, and when we hire a mason we do not say we won't hire a member of the Knights of Pythias.

Mrs. Jones: No; because they won't fight. He won't have any trouble with them. He can rob them if he wants to. I understand his object very well. That is just exactly like the steel industry. Now, I pleaded with them not to accept that, and today there is not a more horrible condition anywhere scarcely than you will find in the steel industry. They saw what was coming; the men were organized; and they went to work and they offered them the stock at $40 and brought it down to $35. I told them, "They will get you. That is a bait they are throwing at you."

There are a great many angles to these questions. If it were me, I should say, "No; the right to organize is ours; we are going to organize. And the right to demand how much we are going to get for our labor is ours. You demand how much you will get for the coal. You go into the market and make people pay you that price. Now, we have the same right that you have."

Mr. Byrnes: One of the members of the delegation from Colorado, I think it was, referring yesterday to the situation, stated that the State of Colorado had no money just at this time to pay its soldiers, and that this might be an excuse for not ordering the militia out.[24] Do you think it would help the situation at this time if they did order the militia back to that strike district?

Mrs. Jones: No. There was no need of the militia there at all. The militia — now, there was some very nice young men in the militia. There is no question about that at all. I am not one of those blind, prejudiced people.

They have not got any money since January. Now, I gave some of those young fellows that was on duty there nights — I gave them a little change. You know, they are young people. They wanted to go to the show, and I said, "Now, I have not got much money, boys, but I will give you some, and when I get up against it you will give it to me." And they said, "Yes." I said, "Here is some change for you to go to your show tonight." But the majority of those militiamen are brutal.

Mr. Byrnes: It would not do any good to send them back there? It would do harm?

Mrs. Jones: Not a bit. There was a time they came pretty near cleaning up the militia there. They were so outraged at that time, pulling their wives out — now, I want to say to you gentlemen here that the labor movement of this country is not going to stand for those insults to their women, and whenever a nation or a statesman tolerates the degradation or insulting of a woman that day that nation is going up against decay.

Mr. Byrnes: Secretary Dawes said in his telegram to us that if something is not done they will feel called upon to call for volunteers. Do you think that if they were to arm and go down there —

Mrs. Jones: They wanted to do it when I was in those bull pens — in that cellar. I am opposed to those things. The law is there; the courts are there. And I am one of those who wants to go through the courts — put them up against it.

Mr. Byrnes: Would you advise them not to do that?

Mrs. Jones: Certainly; I would advise them not to do that.

Mr. Byrnes: Someone was telling me that the miners were to meet tomorrow on the grounds of the capitol. In view of the fact that Secretary Dawes has had such a thing in mind, don't you think it would be well to advise him not to do that?

Mrs. Jones: I shall telegraph him today to stop that. Not only that, but I will go on the train and go right straight back. I would stop that business, because that starts rebellion. The public — that is, the working class — are all worked up during the mixup. You know, they came so rapidly in succession. That I would not stand for at all.

Mr. Byrnes: In order that you may not be misinformed by what I saw, I don't say he was going to do it, but "If something is not done we will feel compelled to call for volunteers."

Mrs. Jones: I think, of course, when it comes to the burning up of homes, and women and children in there, if there is a particle of humanity in us it arouses us; don't you know that?

Mr. Austin: Mrs. Jones, I have not been there; I have been compelled to be absent, but I am a member of the subcommittee that visited Colorado. What is your suggestion in the way of a remedy to stop the troubles in Colorado?

Mrs. Jones: There is only one suggestion. Just say, "Here, we will concede the right to you to organize."

Mr. Austin: How is that?

Mrs. Jones: "We will concede the right to you to organize." That will settle it.

Now, here, gentlemen, I am talking to thinking brains here. That governor — you see, there is an unfortunate phase in our age; we get time service in office instead of statesmen. It was so in Colorado, in Michigan; it was so to an extent in West Virginia. Now, there are men, as a rule, who have no grasp of the great economic revolution that is going on. Our forefathers forty years ago didn't dream of what was going to take place with us today. Neither did the men who framed the Constitution ever dream of those changes that were to take place. We jumped over night.

Now, that governor turned the militia in from that field last Thursday. He stood for uniforming these gunmen, making them militia without any calling of the legislature. He leaves his state in a turmoil, and he comes here about the conservation of trees. What about the conservation of the people of the state?

Mr. Byrnes: At the time he left —

Mrs. Jones: He left on Saturday.

Mr. Byrnes: Was there any fighting then?

Mrs. Jones: No; there was no fighting then.

Mr. Byrnes: When did it start?

Mrs. Jones: It started, I think, Tuesday.

Mr. Austin: Now, give us your remedy to prevent friction and bloodshed.

Mrs. Jones: I am glad you are coming to that, gentlemen, because it is a sad, sad picture for our state to be in. Now, here, immediately I would tell Rockefeller, "We are not going to have a Rockefeller government. Now, here, stop. These men are going to organize."

The workers of this country must be protected and kept from friction and bloodshed. The way to do it is their school. Many of them have never had a chance to go to school. Now, we have to allow them to get educated, and the way to do that is in their local unions.

Mr. Eyrnes: You would want the government to tell Rockefeller to sign a contract with the union?

Mrs. Jones: Immediately; no fooling about it.

Mr. Austin: Now, he has been before this committee stating his position, that he favors the open shop.

Mrs. Jones: I know he does, of course, because he can do all the robbing and stealing he wants to in the open shop.

Mr. Austin: Then you are not in favor of the open shop?

Mrs. Jones: I am not in favor of the open shop. I am in favor of it when the government owns the machinery of production.

Mr. Byrnes: They even went this far, that they have no objection to their own men organizing, and treating with them, but they object to their contracting with the national organization. You think there is no chance of settlement as long as they hold that view?

Mrs. Jones: I don't know. Perhaps there might be some concessions made.

Mr. Byrnes: They will do anything else, but they will not consent to treat with the national organization. They will allow their own men to organize; they will go that far, and treat with a committee from their own men. Would you advise them to make any settlement other than a recognition of the national organization?

Mrs. Jones: I will tell you. I have had a great deal of experience there, perhaps more experience than any officer in the union, and I have always found out that the men lost out in the end and you had to have another strike. You are liable to have a strike on the railroads. I get letters from parties: "For God's sake, we will soon need you, Mother" — you know, they have a way of writing to me — "we will soon need you; we are going to be up against it." Now, it is the duty of every man and woman who has any consideration for the people of the nation — just see how much money those fellows made in 1912, and see the starving wretches, and see the penitentiaries we are filling in order to make millionaires and decorate their wives with the blood of these children. Why, gentlemen, it will have to stop. [Exhibiting some pictures.] Now, here is a picture of the tents. Here is a picture of the home of the millionaire. Here is a picture of the money they made in one year alone.

Mr. Austin: What legislation do you think congress must pass that will meet the situation in Colorado, Michigan, West Virginia, and the other states?

Mrs. Jones: First, I would pass a bill that no corporation, no matter who they were or where they were, should ever think of such a thing as importing these murderers and bloodhounds, as I call them.

Mr. Austin: What do you think about the state passing an act to disarm everybody and prevent the carrying of arms of any kind?

Mrs. Jones: I am not opposed to that, because there might come a time — the Constitution permits the right to bear arms everywhere. I am opposed — now, any villain may go to your home —

Mr. Austin: Take the Colorado fight. The people have got intensely interested.

Mrs. Jones: Both sides are, you know.

Mr. Austin: Yes.

Mrs. Jones: The employees and the striking miners will arm themselves.

Mr. Austin: And go to killing?

Mrs. Jones: And the railroads will stop, because they are all excited about this. It is a spasmodic fever. Congress should send a telegram to the governor and to the miners, both. You see, these men are liable to tie up all the railroads. It may be the starting of a revolution in our country.

Mr. Sutherland: Mrs. Jones, do you think it would help the matter any to have regular soldiers out there who would have no partisanship as between the two sides, in order to keep the peace?

Mrs. Jones: No; I am opposed to regular soldiers. I am opposed to soldiers in any form.

Mr. Sutherland: But there is a condition there that apparently needs something on both sides.

Mrs. Jones: That can be settled very easily. I understand that situation perhaps as well as anyone in the country does. I could go down there to-morrow — if you would make that governor take his dogs of war away I could go down there to-morrow, and there won't be a shot fired from a single mining camp. Not one shot will be fired, gentlemen, from a single mining camp. I can handle those men. One thing that has aroused those men is putting me in those bull pens.

Mr. Byrnes: What sort of a place was it at Walsenburg?

Mrs. Jones: Oh, it was horrible. The only comfort I had in it at all was that the colonel was a man. He certainly was, and he did everything that his position would permit him to do.

Mr. Austin: What was his name?

Mrs. Jones: Verdickburg.

Mr. Austin: Really, how did they treat you there?

Mrs. Jones: As far as the treatment was concerned — I will tell you about the treatment. If you will consider five bayonets watching you day and night, no one to talk to you, and at your door when they opened your door to bring your meals in there was two bayonets outside the door — it was so blamed ridiculous I used to laugh at it. Here I was, an old woman —

Mr. Austin: Did they have guards inside of the hospital?

Mrs. Jones: Yes; one outside the door.

Mr. Byrnes: Was the purpose of the guards to prevent you from getting out or prevent other people from getting in and trying to get you out?

Mrs. Jones: I don't know what their object was.

Mr. Austin: Can the Colorado strike be settled without the recognition of the union, Mrs. Jones?

Mrs. Jones: I do not think it can. Now, Mr. Foster is from Illinois, and he remembers when there was terrific turmoil there. It was only when a lot of our men got killed that the mine owners came to time. Now, they have not had any conflicts in Illinois for seventeen years. Peace has been going on. They meet every year or two. They have their squabbles while they are adjusting their questions. When they meet, the miners want to get all they can out of the other fellow, but they settle, and they have a feast with each other after the thing is settled.

Mr. Byrnes: Now, you said that people made mistakes in the selection of officers, as in the case of Governor Glasscock and one or two others. What difference is there between the Peabody administration and that of Governor Glasscock?

Mrs. Jones: Peabody had a lot of backbone, and he came right straight out. I like an open enemy, and he came right straight out, and you knew how to fight him.

Mr. Austin: Mrs. Jones, in Colorado we found a very large percentage of those miners unnaturalized foreigners. Are they as peaceable and law-abiding and amenable to our laws as our own native Americans?

Mrs. Jones: More so. I want to tell you something, gentlemen. I have had more experience with those foreigners in the anthracite region. I met the militia — the crack team of Pennsylvania — at 3 o'clock in the morning. John Mitchell and all the organizers were sleeping in their beds. There were 5,000 men that had to be brought out if that strike was going to be won. But I gathered up the men and the women, and they were all foreigners, nearly. I marched down fifteen miles from the mountains that night with them. I met the militia between 3 and 4 o'clock in the morning. They were going to charge bayonets. I said, "Who are you going to charge bayonets on?" "On you people." "Why," said I, "Not at all. They are not fighting the state, the county, the nation, or anything else. We are after 5,000 of our brothers to get bread for our children. We want to give to the nation a more highly developed citizenship. You don't believe that?" "No, I don't." "Well, that is all I am for. I am going to take up these 5,000 villains." And then he woke up. The women had mops and brooms. They were mostly foreigners. There was not a human being hurt.[25]

Mr. Austin: Mrs. Jone, now, where there is a disagreement and they are unable to settle it, you do not believe in and do not advise violence.

Mrs. Jones: No, sir.

Mr. Austin: By striking miners?

Mrs. Jones: No sir.

Mr. Austin: Because your position on that occasion and speech of yours in West Virginia has been furnished in the Senate hearings.

Mrs. Jones: Certainly. They put all kinds of things in my speeches, and there is no question but what I do say some things. I will admit that I do under certain circumstances.

Mr. Byrnes: The speech I asked you about, Mrs. Jones, was submitted and agreed to by the counsel for the miners and the counsel for the operators by agreement, and inserted in the West Virginia strike hearings. I think Mr. Sutherland has already referred to it here today. A copy of your speech, I think, was reported to be from the State capitol steps.

Mrs. Jones: Oh, I will tell you about that. I did not do anything like that.

Mr. Byrnes: Did you ever read it?

Mrs. Jones: No; I never paid any attention. I do not do any underhand things. I am out to make things better. I have talked to the governor and I talked to the president of the United States.

Mr. Byrnes: You talked right from the shoulder.

Mrs. Jones: I talk right from the shoulder. I do not stand for violence or fight.

Mr. Byrnes: I have nothing further to ask Mrs. Jones.

Mrs. Jones: I think, gentlemen, that it behooves every man and woman to use their very best efforts to bring peace. These great revolts, of course, are a part of the great evolution that is going on in our great industries in the country, but if we are wise and just these things can be settled. That is my idea of those things — without bloodshed.

Mr. Byrnes: Some one told me there was a message from the counsel for the operatives or a request from the governor — did not get it from the governor — but said they were in danger of the miners taking the mine there, and wanted to know if you would not ask them to forward troops to be sent in there. You are opposed to Federal troops being sent in there?

Mrs. Jones: You do not need my experience in those things. You do not need troops at all. If the governor had come out that day, when that great meeting was in Trinidad and talked to the children and the people it would have been different. You can swing those people with you, do you not know?

Mr. Byrnes: You might. They give you credit with that, but do you think the governor could?

Mrs. Jones: Certainly he could.

Mr. Byrnes: Do you know of anybody who has done it but you?

Mrs. Jones: Oh, yes; I do.

Mr. Byrnes: Will you not do what you can now to induce them to produce order out there and stop this bloodshed?

Mrs. Jones: I can go back to Colorado tomorrow.

Mr. Byrnes: That would be too late. Can you telegraph?

Mrs. Jones: Telegraph?

The Chairman: Telegraph them, if you can, and stop this. You better send a telegram as soon as you get out of here, because it is an awful thing.

Mr. Byrnes: And stop that arming.

Mrs. Jones: If he takes the "dogs of war" away, I will go out there tonight and there will not be a human being hurt in Colorado.

Mr. Byrnes: The trouble is, when he took all away except one company, this riot seems to have occurred.

Mrs. Jones: They left these "gunmen" there with the machine gun. A machine gun should never be used anywhere but in civil war. I told Congressman Foster here today that I went up in West Virginia. There they had this machine gun. I had a group of miners. We were going to a mine. These fellows — the gunmen — turned that machine gun to murder every one of those men. I jumped out of the buggy, and the boys hollered, "Don't go, mother." I put my hand on that machine gun, and the fellow said, "it was thirsting for human blood" — thirsting for a chance to murder, to see the blood of humanity run. I said, "You don't put a bullet out of that." And had my hand on that machine gun. He said, "Take it off." I said, "I won't take it off. It is a new make of gun and I want to see if it is perfect." And one of these fellows was at the gun — there were thirteen of them — those "bloodhounds," as I term them, immediately quieted down. That whole creek would have been streamed with blood. And I just went up and held my meeting, and took my men up past them. Those guards have mothers and wives and sisters, and you do not want hot words.

Mr. Taylor of Colorado: Why was it, Mrs. Jones, that after the governor took away all the troops this thing broke out?

Mrs. Jones: Because these guards opened fire on these men; that is it.

Mr. Taylor of Colorado: Did the guards open fire on the men first?

Mrs. Jones: I do not know; I was not there, you know; but my feeling is that they have done it every time. I have been in strikes for years and years, from Arizona all the way down, all over the country. There has not been a big strike of any importance in the country that I have not been there. I know those people. I know how the whole thing is done. I love the nation's honor. I am opposed to those fellows training the rising youth to murder, to fill our penitentiaries.

Mr. Byrnes: Mrs. Jones, here are those West Virginia reports. Did you make a speech — I just want to ask you whether this is correct or not. The counsel for both sides put it into the record. Did you make a speech from the levee at Charles Town?

Mrs. Jones: Yes; I did, one night; oh, yes.

Mr. Byrnes: Did you say this —

Mrs. Jones: It was one afternoon.

Mr. Byrnes (reading):

Let me say to you, I don't want a single officer of the militia molested in any way. I am not going to say to you don't molest the operators. It is they who hire the dogs to shoot you. I am not asking you to do it; but if is going to oppress you, deal with him. I am not going to take backwater because I am here in the capital. No backwater for me. No man lives on the face of God's earth that is oppressing my class that I am afraid of.

Is that your speech?

Mrs. Jones: That I may have said; I do not know.

Mr. Byrnes: Also, do you remember saying this [reading]:

You have it inscribed on the steps of your capitol, "Mountaineers are free." God Almighty, men, go down through this nation and see the damnable, infamous condition that is there. In no nation of the world will you find such a condition. I look with horror when I see these conditions.

You gather up money to send to China to learn them to know more about Jesus. Jesus don't know any more about you than a dog does about his father.

I was in church one day when they raked in $1,600, and at the same time they were robbing the representatives of Jesus to feed them who robbed them. You build churches and give to the Salvation Army, and all the auxiliaries of capitalism and support them to hoodwink you.

But I want to say they will not be able to get an army in the United States big enough to crush us.

Do you remember saying that, or words to that effect?

Mrs. Jones: I do not know; I supposed I do say a great many things. We say a great many things when we are up in arms that we do not know about.

Mr. Byrnes: Let me ask you one more question. [Reading:]

Nero fiddled while Rome burned. That is what the governor of West Virginia is doing.

Mrs. Jones: That was on a banner. That governor — they said a great deal about him. I want to go to his home some day and speak there to vindicate him. He was not at all to blame. The man was sick, and he had two secretaries. They had more whisky in them than they had sense sometimes, and the man was not really to blame; but this fellow they have got now — I take the other fellow before I would him.

Mr. Byrnes: You would take the other fellow before you would him?

Mrs. Jones: Oh, yes.

Mr. Byrnes: Just wait one second. Who is the present governor?

Mrs. Jones: Oh, they took down all of my speeches that I made in West Virginia. They had a stenographer.[26] I have a faculty of saying to "put that down."

Mr. Byrnes: Tell them to take it down?

Mrs. Jones: I always talk to the reporters when I see them taking things down, you know. In these great conflicts we have do you not know that —

Mr. Byrnes: You have not read these speeches?

Mrs. Jones: Oh, no; I never bother reading any of them.

Mr. Byrnes: They give you credit with speaking —

Mrs. Jones: I am liable to go and make them same speeches.

Mr. Byrnes: They give you credit with saying [reading]:

Just make me governor for one month. I won't ask for a sheriff or a police-man, and I will do business, and there won't a guard stay in the state of West Virginia.

Mrs. Jones: That is true.

Mr. Byrnes (resuming reading):

The mine owners won't take 69,000 pounds of coal in dockage off you fellows. Sixty-nine thousand pounds of coal they docked you for, and a few pounds of slate, and then they give to Jesus on Sunday.

They give your missionary women a couple of hundred dollars and rob you under pretense of giving to Jesus. Jesus never sees a penny of it, and never heard of it. They use it for the women to get a jag on and then go and hollow for Jesus.

I wish I was God Almighty. I would throw down some night from heaven and get rid of the whole blood-sucking bunch.

Mrs. Jones: That is true; I guess I did say that. That is not half as radical as Lincoln. I have heard him make a great deal more radical speech.

The Chairman: Are there any other questions you want to ask Mother Jones? [After a pause.] I guess that is all, then. If there is anything you can do, Mrs. Jones, to stop the trouble out there I hope you will do it.

Mrs. Jones: Mr. Foster, I will do anything in the world. I will go right away from here and I will telegraph.

Mr. Taylor of Colorado: Telegraph those men to stop shooting, and tell them not to hold meetings on the capitol grounds and getting into riots.

Mrs. Jones: If I had been out there this thing would not have happened, but the governor would not let me stay among them. I do not stand for violence; I stand for education.

Mr. Byrnes: If you will telegraph them not to hold that meeting you will be doing something to help law and order.

Mrs. Jones: I plead with you gentlemen here, for the sake of the children — and they are to be the future citizens of this nation when we pass away. We leave them here. Are we going to leave them to fill the penitentiaries and the jails? I said to President Taft — he said to me, "Mother Jones, I am afraid if I put the pardoning power in your hands there would not be anybody left in the prisons;" and I made this reply to the President: "Mr. President, if you give me that $6,000,000,000 a year that you spend on prisons," I said, "and let me spend it on the people to keep them out of prisons, I do not think we will need many prisons."[27]

The Chairman: We are all trying to make conditions better.

Mrs. Jones: I know you are; I want to say to you, gentlemen, that my boys out there are very well satisfied with you — with the committee that went out there.

The Chairman: We tried to get both sides of the question.

Mrs. Jones: And when you can keep them that way they are all right.

(Whereupon, at 12:20 o'clock p.m., the subcommittee stood adjourned to meet at the call of the chairman.)

[U.S. Congress, House, Subcommittee of the Committee on Mines and Mining, Conditions in the Coal Mines of Colorado, 63rd Congress, 2nd Session, 1914, pp. 2917-2940.]

Notes

1. U.S. Congress, House, Subcommittee of the Committee on Mines and Mining, *Conditions in the Coal Mines of Colorado,* 63rd Congress, 2nd Session, 1914, p. 2874.

2. *Ibid.* p. 2850. Rockefeller's statement that he was fighting for the workingman's freedom to work for whom and on such terms as he pleases, "will not bear investigation," a House investigation of the Colorado strike declared later. "One must conclude he would rather spend the money of the company for guns, pay of detectives and mine guards, and starve the miners into submission." (U.S. Congress, House, Subcommittee of the Committee on Mines and Mining, *Report on the Colorado Strike Investigation,* House Doc. 1630, 63rd Congress, 3rd Session, 1915, pp. 42-43.

3. *See* p. 370.

4. *See* pp. 55, 412-17, 557.

5. The reference is to the letter she sent to Governor Peabody. *See* p. 557.

6. *See* p. 229.

7. Governor Elias Ammons.

8. John R. Lawson, United Mine Workers organizer during the Colorado strike.

9. President Woodrow Wilson. *See* p. 57.

10. This is the convention at which Mother Jones spoke calling upon the workers to strike. *See* pp. 226-36.

11. The office of the Rockefellers.

12. William Green, secretary-treasurer of the United Mine Workers.

13. *See* pp. 186, 239, 383.

14. Brigadier General John Chase.

15. The reference is to the Mt. San Rafael Hospital, run by the Sisters of Charity, on the outskirts of Trinidad.

16. *See* pp. 54, 78-82.

17. For the speech, *see* pp. 226-36.

18. It is not clear whether the objection is to the call to strike or to the violence, but very likely it is to the latter.

19. For the speech, *see* pp. 193-206.

20. Governor William E. Glasscock.

21. This certainly did not apply to Frank Hayes who was simply addicted to alcohol.

22. William B. Wilson.

23. Comments by Jones on Rockefeller, *see* pp. 251, 263-64, 270, 278, 339-40.

24. Mother Jones failed to point out that the Colorado Fuel & Iron Company paid the soldiers' salaries and quartered them in company buildings and furnished them with supplies. (Foner, *op. cit.*, vol. 5, p. 203.)

25. *See* pp. 405-7.

26. Not all of the speeches, such as those during the 1902 strike in West Virginia, taken down by stenographers for the companies, have been preserved. But for those during the 1913 strike, *see* pp. 152-222.

27. For a different version of what was said, *see* pp. 143-44, 156.

Testimony before the Commission on Industrial Relations, Created by the Act of Congress, August 23, 1912, Washington, D.C., May 13, 14, 1915

The result of a demand by a group of social workers after the bombing of the Los Angeles Times *building in 1911 and the imprisonment of the McNamara brothers for the "Crime of the Century," for an investigation of conditions in American industry, the Commission on Industrial Relations began its real work in December 1913 "to inquire into the general conditions of labor in the principal industries of the United States . . . to discover the underlying causes of dissatisfaction in the industrial setting and reports its conclusions thereon."[1] Three labor representatives, three management representatives, and three representatives of the public, all appointed by President Woodrow Wilson, made up the Commission. Frank P. Walsh, known for his work in labor activities in civil and social movements as well as for his work in labor arbitration in Missouri, was chosen as both a public representative and chairman of the commission.*

Probably the most widely publicized phase of the commission's investigation surrounded its inquiry into the Colorado coal mine strike of 1913-1914, especially the hearings at which John D. Rockefeller, Jr.,

testified. Mother Jones testified in May 1915 and was, the New York
Times *declared, "one of the most entertaining witnesses that could have
been brought before that body. Not a question interrupted her and she
proceeded in her quaint way without being tied down to geography or
continuity of events."*[2]

TESTIMONY OF MRS. MARY JONES

Chairman Walsh: What is your name?

Mother Jones: Mary Jones.

Chairman Walsh: Where do you reside?

Mother Jones: Well, I reside wherever there is a good fight against
wrong — all over the country.

Chairman Walsh: Do you claim a residence in any particular state?

Mother Jones: No. Wherever the workers are fighting the robbers I
go there.

Chairman Walsh: Now, it may seem unnecessary, but you are the
lady that is known to the country as "Mother Jones," are you?

Mother Jones: I suppose so, Mr. Walsh.

Chairman Walsh: I will go right to the cause of the inquiry. You
have listened to a great deal of it here, I notice.[3] It is the administration or the lack of administration of law in industrial disputes. So I am
going to ask you first, Mrs. Jones, were you in the Pittsburgh railroad
strike of 1877?

Mother Jones: Yes.

Chairman Walsh: At what point in the country were you, Mrs.
Jones?

Mother Jones: At Pittsburgh.

Chairman Walsh: I would like you to give your experience in that
strike, so far as the administration of the law or the conduct of the officials was concerned.

Mother Jones: Well, the strike began in Martinsburg, Ohio.[4] It
started with the Baltimore & Ohio Railroad employees, and it reached
down to Pittsburgh and east to Scranton. I was in New York. I came
down. I was a member of the Knights of Labor at that time, and some
of the boys met me and asked me to stay over with them, and I did. So
the traffic was stopped and a lawless element that had got into
Pittsburgh during the panic of 1873, they had gathered in from the
eastern part of the country and, of course, began to revolt and started
to rioting. The employees of the railroad and others went to the mayor
of the city and asked him if he would not swear them in as deputies to
preserve the property and have the law enforced. While this was going
on the sheriff of the county telegraphed to the governor, and the governor sent the militia.

Now, at that time I believe the troops went to Pittsburgh, but the
fight turned onto the Pennsylvania Railroad; it concentrated on the

404

Pennsylvania Railroad mostly, and some of the militia was quartered in the roundhouse. The business men of Pittsburgh, who for years had complained of discrimination by the railroad company against the city, were free in their expression of enmity against the company. Some of them connected with this committed acts of violence and actually participated in the riots that followed. Cars were set on fire and run down the tracks to the roundhouse, which was destroyed, together with over 100 locomotives belonging to the Pennsylvania Railroad Co. The feeling at that time of many workers and sympathizers was one of distrust, and in many instances amounted to hatred, because the corporations of that day were open and successful in passing antilabor legislation, tramp laws, and other legislation, which caused the workers to feel that they were being discriminated against. The corporations succeeded in the passing of the law which required that in case of a strike the train crew should bring in a locomotive to the starting place before the strike would begin. It was because of that legislation that so many locomotives were housed at Pittsburgh and became the prey to the flames by an outraged populace and not by the workers and not by strikers. I know most of the strikers; all had done everything they could to keep order. Not but what they felt the sting of the lash, the injustice that was done, but nevertheless they wanted to keep order and be steady because they felt that the railroad company had discriminated against them so much.[5] That is about as much as I remember of that. I haven't the notes. I have them laid away, Mr. Walsh, but I am over all the country, and I don't know where to lay hands on things.

Chairman Walsh: You made notes of all these strikes at the time?

Mother Jones: Mostly; I have made notes of them all.

Chairman Walsh: Were you in the anthracite strike in Pennsylvania in 1900.

Mother Jones: Yes.

Chairman Walsh: I wish you would give us whatever comment you have on that as to violence and administration of the law and the action of the authorities in it.

Mother Jones: I had been down in Arnot, Pennsylvania. We had a strike there for six months, but there were no deputies and no gunmen and no militia brought in there, and there was no violence. That is the home of the secretary of labor.[6]

During the whole six months, it was a nine months' strike, but it was six months after I went there; but the men were orderly and they themselves took care of the property. The superintendent and the officials of that company could come up four miles from Blossburg at any hour of the night they wanted to alone, and they were not afraid and had no reason to be. That strike was settled very peacefully. The Erie Co. conceded to the men most of what they asked for, and there was no violence during the whole nine months.

Then I went into Maryland. I was not in Maryland very long until I was sent for to come into the anthracite region.

Chairman Walsh: When was that, Mrs. Jones, in 1902?

Mother Jones: No; in 1900.

Chairman Walsh: Oh, yes.

Mother Jones: And in that — there were only 7,000 men organized out of 160,000, and I addressed the convention the day that I got in from Maryland and they called the strike right afterwards.[7] Well, of course, we had to go over all the district — three districts — to rally them together. There was no violence up in either Scranton or around Hazelton, and very little of it down in a town named Shamokin — scarcely any violence there, but the militia was brought in. First the company would guard the mines so that the men could not get out, or that we could not get near them; and if we billed a meeting, why the company would always attend the meeting and the men could not; it was the force of the company entirely that attended the meeting, and I concluded that these men had suffered long enough.

I want to say, Mr. Walsh, that I do not take any orders from any officials. I belong to a class who have been robbed, exploited, and plundered down through many long centuries, and because I belong to that class I have an instinct to go and help break the chains; and so I concluded some moves had to be made to bring the men all out; and I organized the men and women, the women particularly, and I made raids every night; we marched and pulled out those mines — the men. There was no violence. The sheriff in Hazelton was a very fine man. He understood the law, and he knew he could manage the affair without bringing the military there. But I went down to Panther Creek. There were 5,000 men there that could not be reached, and I knew they had to be got out in order to get more bread for the children that were coming, so one night, without saying anything to anyone, I gathered up 2,000 or 3,000 women, and naturally the men followed. That is their natural instinct — to know what we were going to do. We started. I had to go into the saloons and tell them to close up and not give any liquor to the boys. I knew the women did not go near the saloons; I was the only one that did. We marched, and about 2 or 3 o'clock in the morning we met the militia. There was a poor little sheriff, not to be condemned at all, but he was unable to grasp the thing, and he yelled like a mad dog in the night to send the guns to him, the governor. I did not know it, or I would have telegraphed the governor to keep the guns at home and there would be no trouble. Then we marched fifteen miles over the mountains from Hazelton to Panther Creek, and there we met the militia in the middle of the night. The militia did not know what kind of an army I had with me. He thought it was just a few strikers; he told us to go back. I told him that the American workingman never goes backward; we go forward, and we did not go out to go back; and he said he would charge bayonets. Well, he didn't do it anyway; but it took us three hours to go back two miles. I don't like to resist officers and create any trouble, but I saw he was a sort of Sunday-school fellow and there wasn't much to him, and I concluded to just pat him on the back a little, and I pulled out the 5,000 men.

Chairman Walsh: You mean by that that you induced the 5,000 men to go out on strike?

Mother Jones: Yes; I wanted them to win the fight. I had a large army with me and I wanted them all, and so I had to get these miners out, because they were furnishing the coal. I brought out the 5,000 men. We held up the street cars and did not hurt anybody, and the men — oh, once in a while when a boss wanted to jump over us we picked him up and threw him over the fence to his wife, and told her to take care of him. We did not hurt him, but we wanted him out of our way; so that thing continued until 10 o'clock in the morning; and we had the 5,000 men out and that ended it, and that part of the strike was ended peacefully.

The women had nothing but brooms and mops and they were very hungry, and the militia had ordered breakfast at some hotel and I told the women go in and eat their breakfast and let the state pay for it; and it was our breakfast anyhow. So they did. We ate the breakfast. We had more strength to get back.[8]

Mr. Mitchell, then president of the miners, did not know anything about these moves, but I saw him in the morning, and I told him I was up against the militia, and he was a little nervous. But I never get nervous when I face bayonets. I think they are human beings like all the rest of us, and I go in a fight and I am not afraid of bayonets when it comes to a struggle for our rights. One day I got my army together of little boys. I was training them for the future. And when we got everything straightened out the mines closed, and we went back to Hazelton, and Mr. Mitchell asked me what we had done. I told him nothing in the world — just pulled out the 5,000 men and told the militia to take a rest. The militia did not follow us, did not interfere with us otherwise at all. And they treated us with a great deal of courtesy, looking at it from their point of view.

At this time the winter was coming, and I knew that the people would need coal and that the strike would have to come somewhat to a climax. So in Lattimer — I happened to be in Tennessee when the twenty-three men happened to be shot in the back by the sheriff and the deputies.[9] I did not come east right away, because I had other work to do. I concluded I would have to take the matter up, and the general manager sent word that if I came in there I was going to get killed. Well, it does not make any difference to me when I die, if I am dying for a good cause. I concluded I would go in there, and the newspaper men, while I am always friendly to them, I know they have to make their living just as the balance have, they were in the habit of going to the barns to get buggies to take them out, and the barn fellow would tell ahead of time what I was doing. So this night I told the clerk at the hotel, "Don't notify the newspaper men that I am going out." In that evening I had got one man from each mining department; the others did not know that I had seen anyone but themselves, and I arranged with them to bring their army and meet me.

I got the women — I got about 1,500 women lined up, and we walked into Lattimer. It was dark, and we knocked at every door and told them there was no work to do; that they would have to rest. The general manager didn't know, neither did the sheriff, so they began telephoning. The manager and the sheriff came, and he said, "What are you going to do, Mother?" And I said, "I am going to close up this mine." And he said, "Are the women going to close it up?" And I said, "Yes; we are going to close it up." So the drivers came along to take the mules to the mines, and I had all of the women centered in front of the company's store, and we had 3,000 men down at the mines that the company or the sheriff or nobody knew anything about — they had come in on different roads — and I said, when he ordered the boys to take the mules to the drivers, that the mules would not scab, he had just as well leave them at home in the barns, because the mules remembered that Patrick Henry had passed a Declaration of Independence[10] and that the mules were conscious of that, and he had just as well make up his mind that those mines were going to be closed, and we had no pistols or guns, nothing but just our hands, because I don't believe in those instruments and I don't travel with any organizer who carries them. We closed up the mines. The reporters heard of it later in the morning and they came down, but we had our work done by the time they came, so we went back, went home; that really was the key to the situation; that settled the first anthracite strike.

The militia didn't commit any brutal acts, nor did they undertake to force us in any way. I must give Colonel O'Neal credit for that. He was the colonel of that militia; that was the crack Fourteenth of Pennsylvania, but it was not very crack that day, I assure you. We carried on our work and finished. That was the first anthracite strike in 1900, and at the close the men called a convention and the strike was called off, and I think Mark Hanna had something to do with settling it.[11] Then I was sent into West Virginia —

Chairman Walsh: That was in 1902?

Mother Jones: In 1900. The strike in Pennsylvania, I think, had closed in November; that strike, it didn't last very long, only six or seven weeks was all that it lasted, and the men got some concessions; not all they wanted, but they got some to satisfy them. There was no rioting; no bloodshed. The sheriff at Hazelton, Sheriff Harvey, was a very sensible, clear, level-headed man. He came to me that morning and asked me to take them home, and I said, "No; no one is going to get hurt." And he said, "They want me to call for the militia." And I said, "Don't obey them; there is no need for them," and there was no one hurt that morning.

I went into West Virginia; the organization sent me there. I surveyed the situation there. I was mostly in the Kenowa and Norfolk & Western, in the New River country, and I was also in the Fairmount region. I never in my life was arrested until I was arrested in the Fairmount region under a Federal injunction. I was arrested while I was speaking to a large crowd in Clarksburg, and some one sent me word that we were all under arrest, and I said to the audience, composed of a great deal of strikers, "Don't you undertake to surrender; I am under arrest, but you keep up the fight; it is a fight for more bread." The United States marshal, Elliott, he didn't come up to me; he sent one of the deputies to send one of our own men to tell me I was under arrest. I had never been in court before then in my life, and we were carried eighty-four miles, to Parkersburg, to prison, but the marshal sent his nephew with me. He sent five of the deputy marshals with the boys. There were nine of us altogether. The young man said to me, "Mother, my uncle told me to take you to the hotel; he has engaged a room there." I didn't say anything until I got off the train, and so when I got off the train the deputies were taking my boys that way and I was going this way, and I said, "Boy, we are going the wrong way." And he said, "Oh, no." And I said, "The boys are going the wrong way, then." And he said, "No; they are going to jail; you are going to the hotel." And I said, "If the boys go to jail, I go to jail, too." And so I turned around and went to jail.

The jailer and his wife were very nice and courteous to me; they didn't lock me up in a cell; they just took me in as a member of the family; but they locked my boys up; and then we were all taken into the Federal court and tried. The judge gave the boys from sixty to ninety days. I did think I was going to be hung, because in the close of that meeting we had I said to the audience, "We are all arrested, but you keep the strike up; don't pay any attention to that injunction machine in Parkersburg, he scabbed on his father." That was the federal judge.[14] I didn't know much about courts at that time; I had never been there; and so when I was taken into court the prosecuting attorney played that up very much, indeed. He said, "She even insulted your honor." And I didn't know where the insult came in, and he said, "She called you a scab." And the judge said, "Did you call me a scab, Mother Jones?" "I certainly did, Judge." He said, "Who did I scab on? How came you to say that?" "Why, when you ordered my arrest, it just struck me that when the immortal Lincoln — I made a point to read the newspapers — that when the president had sent the commission of appointment that he didn't distinguish senior or junior, that you bore the same initials that your father did, and he was away and you appointed yourself. You took the appointment, and you appointed yourself, and that was scabbing on your father, Judge." He said, "I never heard that before." I said, "I think if you will run up the files of the papers when the president appointed you that you will find it in the press of either Boston, Philadelphia, or New York, perhaps in all of them." And he said, "You must have a wonderful memory." And I said, "No; I did not, but I didn't have anything else to hit you with when you arrested me, and I thought I would hit you with that."

The prosecuting attorney recommended me to the mercy of the court. I don't want any mercy from any court. I don't do anything but what is my duty to do as a citizen of this nation, and I don't ask you for mercy. I am asking for justice, and not mercy, and I told the judge not to have any mercy on me. The prosecuting attorney said, "If I would leave the state"; "No; I won't leave the state." And so I was turned loose, but the boys were put in jail. There was one of our boys that was rather in poor health, Mr. Walsh. I want to show you the good points in men, if they are reached, no matter where they are or what position they are in; there is a human side, I believe, to all of them. That judge was looked upon as a terrible fellow by the whole labor world, and most of the other people, and this young man said to me, "I am sorry you are going, Mother." I said, "I am sorry, too, because I should have been put in jail with the boys, but the only one I feel sorry for is old Barney Rice; his wife is very frail, and he has some little children," and he said, "If you go out to see the judge, I think he would pardon Barney." And I said, "I don't think he would." And he said, "Yes; I think he would." I said, "All right, all he can do is to tell me to get out and not come back again"; and so I went out and saw the judge and pleaded with him, and he asked me to come to dinner. His wife was a kindly, good, Christian woman — that is, as Christianity is considered today, and as soon as the dinner was over, the judge came in and I said, "I came to see you about Barney Rice." And he said, "What is the matter?" And I said, "Barney is in awful poor health; I don't think you would have sentenced him to 60 days in jail if you knew the condition of his health." And he said, "What is the matter with him?" And I said, "He has heart disease." And he said, "Has he?" And I said, "Yes; I am afraid it is going to prove fatal. He has a very nervous wife, Judge, and she might collapse when she hears of this." And he said, "I don't want that." And I said, "I know you don't." He called up the jail and asked for Rice to come to the phone, and he came and he asked him how his heart was, and Barney didn't use very religious language to the judge over the phone; he didn't know he was a judge, but he used some classical French to him, and the judge said, "What is the matter with your heart?" And he said, "There is nothing the matter with my heart, it is that old judge." And he said, "Have you heart disease?" and he said, "No; I have not." And the judge repeated to me what he said and I said, "Judge, that man don't know his heart from his liver; I have been out with him, and I think you had better let him out." He called up the jail doctor, and I told this young man, I asked him if he knew that man and he said that he did; and I said, "You get hold of that doctor and have him examine that fellow's heart, and show that there is a disease of the arteries, and so forth; I want to get the man out." This young fellow did; he was a very close friend of the doctor's, and old Barney got out the next day.

The judge had very many fine qualities, and I have a very kindly feeling toward him, no matter what anybody else might say about him.

We had another judge in the New River country, Judge Keller. He issued an injunction that we should not feed the miners, and food that was bought in Cincinnati by the miners' representatives for the miners was switched down into Kentucky and kept there, and he arrested a lot of our men for violating his injunction. There is no injunction on earth that would keep me from feeding hungry people if I was rich enough to get it, because there is enough in the world for all. I was not arrested; that was the only time that I was ever arrested by the civil authorities in my life. I never was arrested by a policeman or sheriff; I have always had the militia, outside of the one time, to deal with.

Now, then, I am coming to that part of it — the strike of 1902 in West Virginia. There is a very sad, sad story to be told about that. They were pretty peaceful boys down there as a rule, and we kept them in line, and there was one mountain, Standford Mountain, and they had issued this injunction, that men could not look at the mines. That injunction was always issued on me, and the boys went one day to take a walk along the highway and came back and went home peacefully and quietly, interfering with nobody nor anything. They had never been in court in their lives, none of those boys; they were law-abiding, good men, living quietly up there in the mountains. The United States deputy marshal came in the next morning with a warrant for thirty-three of them. They were holding a meeting in their hall, quietly, and he read the warrant, and some said, "You can't arrest us; we have broken no law; we have hurt nobody; and you will have to leave the town." I think his brother was a company doctor, and they asked him to come, and he did come down and take him away. Anyhow, the next night they went up that mountain, and they shot seven men while they slept. There were about 100 of those gunmen and their deputies and these mine owners and their sons, and they went up that mountain, and while those men slept they shot them; they riddled their little shacks with bullets and wounded twenty-three as they were sleeping. I was going to a meeting the next morning, very early, and I was told what happened, and I went and called a couple of boys and told them that they had had some trouble on Standford Mountain, and let's go up. We went up, and the picture I shall never forget. The mattresses were all seeping with blood, and the bodies were lying there. It was sad, and I shudder at the picture, and the women were screaming, and the babies were running to me to call back their papas. It was a sad, sad picture. I knew those men had violated no law outside of walking

411

on the highway and that supposed injunction. They got a coroner, and he held an inquest over them. A few were arrested, but no one was ever convicted for the crime.

Five or six days after this I went back up that mountain; there was a grave out in the field, and a woman was over it and a little baby, and the little baby, when she saw me she screamed, and she said, "Oh, Mother Jones, come and pick up my papa!" And she was scraping the clay with her little, tender hands, and the wife was watering with her tears. That young man was as law-abiding a young man, I think, as you could find in the country. I don't think he ever thought of such thing, but he was shot while standing up on the mountains.

Now, these men did not realize what they were doing.

I left West Virginia; I was called for to go to Illinois for a meeting there, a memorial meeting over the mutilated bodies of the men that were killed in a battle in Illinois — 97[15] — and I was to speak on that day, and I went. On my way back — Secretary Wilson was secretary of the miners — and I stopped off at the office, and he said, "You will have to go right into Colorado at once. The governor has sent the labor commissioner here and a board member to see the board and convince them there that there should not be a strike called." I went into Colorado; I examined the situation; I went around the camps; and the men and women told me their sad stories. I called a meeting of the men that night, the officers, and I related to them that the metal miners were in revolt at that time, on a strike, and so we discussed the matter until morning. I was sent back to Indianapolis. I reported in Indianapolis that the fever was there, and at fever heat. The men were almost wild to come out, and I discussed it with three or four of the officers. So I was sent back immediately to Colorado, and I went back. The governor sent for me when he heard I was down at Trinidad, and he sent for me, and I came up to Denver.

Chairman Walsh: That was when, Mrs. Jones, in 1903?

Mother Jones: In 1903. That was the first strike. The governor sent for me, and I never go to see those officers alone; I generally take some of our officials with me when I go. I know them pretty well. He said, "Are you going to have a strike in the southern coal fields, Mother Jones?" I said, "I don't know, governor; that is up to you. If you can bring the conflicting parties together, I think we can ward off the strike, and both sides concede." He said, "I don't want a strike." "Neither do I, but we will strike rather than slavery." I said, "I suppose you are very anxious to know, Governor?" And he said, "Yes, I am; why do you think so?" And I said, "I suppose you want to get your militia ready to go out." He said that he had them already in another district in Colorado to open a mine. I was not aware that the state owned the mines. I thought they were private property, belonging to a combination of private individuals, and he said, "So they are, but we have to get the militia after that lawbreaking organization." "Who are you talking about, the Western Federation of Miners?" "Yes." And I said, "It is strange that they have become lawless and lawbreakers since you got in. They have developed this state and have their families here, and I think they would hardly become rioters at once." He said, "I won't discuss it." And I said, "What did you send for me for?" And he said, "I want to know if you are going to have a strike." And I said, "Yes, we are, and you had just as well know it now as any time."

And I went back, and the strike order went out. I went around holding meetings of the men, women, and children. We didn't have as large a tent colony then as afterwards. From the miners themselves there was little violence at that time, but the militia was brought in there. The sheriff came to me Saturday night and said, "Mother Jones, I heard the miners are going to organize and make a raid down on some camp" he told me about, and I said, "Sheriff, you are sheriff of the county, and you ought to know that these miners are not going to do anything of the kind. If they do, I would know it the first one." He said, "The governor has a representative here." "Of course, that is perfectly natural that he would have a representative here, but there is no need of the governor sending any troops here. You and your officers of the law here can take care of this situation. There has been no trouble that amounts to anything, and let me guarantee to you that if there is to be any trouble I will give you the first news. Is there any trouble in the county?" "Not that I know of," he said. And I said, "If there is, you get your buggy right out." It was 11 o'clock at night, but I says, "I will go with you to any part of the county, and I will guarantee to you that if there is any trouble we will stop it immediately." "There is none, Mother," he said. I said, "Very well, why don't you go home and to bed and don't bother about this?"

The militia came on Monday. They gambled all night. The representative of the C. F. & I. — I have forgotten his name — and the sheriff and his militiaman; one of them lost, I heard, $700, but that didn't bother me, because it didn't concern me how much it was; it was among themselves. However, Monday the militia came in, and we didn't know anything about it until I got a telephone message from Denver early in the morning, and they said they better watch yourself; and I said, "Let them come," and that afternoon the militia came in, and I told one of our officers that I had just got a telephone from Denver that they were mobilizing the militia, and that he had better see the boys and tell them to keep quiet, and he did, and the militia came. I went out to the camp several days, talking to the women and children, and Saturday evening I came in; I had been out all day. But before that we went out to a meeting, and coming back from that meeting I met a wagon loaded with guns that were going to Bowen, I think, and I said to the party with me, "There has been something doing; if those fellows belong to Bowen, they are the gunmen." and I think the superintendent was with them; I am not certain. But when we came back to Bowen a young woman came out screaming. She said, "Stop, oh, stop," and I said to the party with me, "I guess they are drinking in there; keep away, don't mix in it," and she pleaded and pleaded and pulled and pulled; she was an Italian; and so we finally went in. I went into the house, and old man Farley sat there with his head all tied up, and a young man named Rooney was lying in bed all covered with blood. You could have put your finger down through them. They had been at a meeting and were coming home when those fellows attacked them from ambush and almost beat them to death.

There was not very much violence during that strike until the militia came. Then one Saturday night I was going to bed when a knock came on the door, and I said, "Come in," and the militiaman opened the door and he said, "Come on"; and, of course, I had to go; there was the bayonets, and I said, "Just wait a moment, will you please, until I dress?" and so I went up to the militia headquarters, and the major asked me where I lived, and I told him I lived wherever there was a fight, and so he called the militia, seven of them, and told me to get my things, and I got a few little things I had, and there was such a hurry — there were seven militiamen, two at my back and two at each side and one in front of me — and they took me down the street and put me on the train and went with me to La Junta, Colorado, and left me at the depot at La Junta. I had only five cents in my pocket. And a railroad man came, and an Associated Press man, and he said, "Are you Mother Jones?" And I said, "yes," and he said, "I thought so, because I saw the militia going." And I followed the milita when I saw they were leaving me there, and I said, "I want to say to you fellows that there is not money enough in the United States Treasury to hire me to acknowledge I was the mother of one of you." They didn't say anything, and they went away. This Associated Press man and the railroad man came and asked me what I was going to do, and I said I didn't know, I didn't have time to decide. And I found out there was two of our men there, but the railroad man gave me money. They did not go back, but went to Indianapolis. I went back. I had orders not to come back, but no governor owns the state and no president owns the United States, and I happened to be in this country before any of them, and I had a share of stock in there, and I said I was going back the next morning, and I went back the next morning.

Well, I sent the governor a note, which was not a very polite one, either, because when I get worked up I am not a very polite character, Mr. Walsh.

Then I went down to the western slope, and came back after I held two or three meetings. I was going to speak at Glenwood Springs, and a railroad conductor told me that there was a company of militia coming, and I said, "Let them come"; and I held three meetings, and I went then to Helper, Utah. And I went to the hotel at midnight and got a room and the next morning I got my breakfast and went to the post office to find out when I got my mail, and I went to an Italian family and got a room in that house, and I took my things over there and didn't see anything more until the next day, when we were going to have a meeting. The next day was Sunday, and the miners all came up. There was a vacant lot in front of the house where I was staying, and the miners all came along and we were going to hold the meeting there, and the company doctor came and said, you know he didn't think it was right to hold the meeting, and the marshal said, "I don't think it is right for you to hold the meeting here, and I don't think you ought to do it." I said, "How far does your jurisdiction extend?" And he told me, and I said, "Well, we will go outside of your jurisdiction." And I took the miners and went two and a half miles down farther. I held the meeting. They had notified the railroad men not to come to my meeting, but the men all came, and I held the meeting and went back and went to my room. Quite a number of the boys came up town again, and I had not been in the room sixteen minutes until the company's doctor and the marshal came in and said, "You are quarantined, Mother Jones, for sixteen days," I said, "What is the matter?" And they said, "Why, you might have had the smallpox." Well, I said, "Maybe I have, but why don't you quarantine the whole train?" They said, "You know you mingle about a great deal." I never have an argument, because it don't do any good and it causes trouble, and I was afraid the men would get excited, and I said, "Boys, you go on down town." And he came along Monday and put a yellow flag on the door. "Smallpox in here." He brought me some books and magazines, and I put them in the stove, because I thought the poor little stove would do anything for his corporation and I put the books in the stove, and the next day, Tuesday, the secretary for the miners came and he was sitting there and I was discussing things with him what they should do, so along came this doctor, and he said, "My, my, my, didn't I tell you not to let anybody inside that gate?" And I said, "You did not; I am a patient, and if you want to keep anybody outside that gate you put a picket at the gate and keep people out; I am a patient and I am not going to do picket work also." And he took hold of this fellow and he got scared, and I said, "Mike, don't get scared, he is only going to inject something into you; don't get afraid; let him inject it."

And they took me down and I was put in the back of an old store. There was no violence, for these miners were as lawabiding as this audience is; there was not a single one of them doing anything, only just striking. They were singing a little down in their tents. I was in the back of an old store, and on Saturday night I learned that they were coming in Sunday morning and going to arrest all of the boys; so I sent for them and I said, "Have you got any guns?" And they said, "Yes." And I said, "You take them up and bury them under the range," because I thought if the boys that had their guns and those men came in suddenly there would be some trouble; and I said, "Boys, you go and bury your guns and you go back; I am going to stay up all night," and they said "No" and I said "Yes," and tomorrow we will talk things over.

At 4 o'clock in the morning the sheriff and forty-five deputies came up. I heard them whooping, and so I put my head out of the window and said, "What is the matter?" The sheriff was the first one, and he said, "We are going to arrest all these fellows." I said, "What have they done?" He said, "They are striking." I said, "They have a right to strike; this nation was founded on a strike, and they have the right to strike; and we have a right to strike; Washington struck against King George, and we will strike against King Gould." But they took them all; they were not allowed to put on their clothes, and they shook like aspen leaves. They took them up several miles and held them there until night and got a box car and took them down to Price.

After they were gone a woman came to me with her babe, weeping bitterly, and said, "You see my Johnnie?" I said, "Yes," and she said, "Let me tell you, Mother, this baby was born at 11 o'clock at night, and I got up in the morning and got breakfast for eleven men to go into the mines." And she was watering the baby with her tears. "Now," she said, "tell me what to do; they have got my John; they have got my house; we rented a little piece of land from the company, and I took in boarders and I put up a little house on it, and I want to give my children a chance; but now they have got my house, they have my health, and they have got my John, and what will I do?"

Now, I want to say to this commission and to this audience that are listening here, on the quivering heart and the aching breast and blasted hopes of this mother, and of thousands like her, Miss Gould and her class carries on her philanthropy in the Scofield mines, where 400 men were roasted to death; their bones are rotting out there, and their wives and children are carrying on life's struggle as best they can, and, my friends, we can have no civilization until such things are abolished.

That woman with her babe and four children was sad to look at, but she is only one of many thousands I know of in this terrific struggle for industrial freedom. It touches a human cord in most anyone. I brought that up before Mr. Rockefeller when I had the meeting with him. I feel that men in that position do not grasp these things as they are, nor do the people outside, nor do our officials who live in offices, nor do our nespaper men; it takes those who are down with them to see the horrors of this industrial tragedy that is going on in our nation today.

I then resigned from the miners for a while; there was other work I had to do, and I took up the Mexican refugee cases, they were going to shoot and murder the men, and I raised the money to save their lives. And I came back and the boys sent me to Colorado again.

A judge had sent fifteen of them to jail, and they were holding a big protest meeting, and I went there. As I said before, judges are human, like everyone else. I went to see my boys and then went to see the sheriff, and I asked the sheriff to let my boys out on the ground every day, and I said that if any of them went away they could arrest me and put me in their place. So the next morning he went up to the jail and let the boys all go out on the ground, and they could stay out until 10 o'clock every night; and then I went to see the judge himself and had a talk with him, and finally the boys got out of jail.

I then came back and was sent into Westmoreland County, where the strike was. There is where I came up with the constabulary — the mounted constabulary.

Commissioner Lennon: Was that the strike of about five years ago, Mother Jones?

Mother Jones: Yes.

Chairman Walsh: Of 1910?

Mother Jones: Yes. I went into that Westmoreland strike, and I did not have any conflict with the constabulary. The only time I came against them at all was when twelve or thirteen women were arrested one day and carried into a squire's office; and he, poor wretch, you could see he was a narrow creature; and I went with the women, and I told them to take their babes along. I said, "Wherever you go, take the children, they are yours"; and so the women took all their little ones and babes; and when the people gave their evidence about them, which did not amount to anything, the judge said he would fine them $30 apiece. I said to the women, "Tell him you are not going to pay it," and he said, "Then you will get thirty days in jail." I said, "Tell him all right, they will go to jail." And the women asked for some one who could take the babies, and I said, "No, God Almighty gave you the babies, and you keep them until they are taken away from you."

Two of the constabulary went with the women, and the women ran across some scabs on the way and they licked them, and I took care of the babies until they licked the scabs.

On the say to Greensburg the motorman wanted to stop the car, and I said, "You can't stop this car, it is contrary to law; you must obey the law until you get to the station." They said,, "These fellows want to get off," and I said, "You won't let us off, and you won't let them off."

Well, the women were singing all the way to Greensburg, and the two constabulary turned them over to the sheriff, and the sheriff said, "Mother Jones, I would rather you had brought me a hundred men than these women"; and I said, "I didn't bring them, the old squire sent them up; you hold him responsible." He said, "I don't know how to manage them"; and I said, "What did you get married for if you can't manage women; these women are peaceable, you can manage them." And they were sent up to the room, and I sent them food, and milk for the babies; and I said to the women, "You sing all night, sing all day if you want to, but sing all night and don't stop for anybody." And they didn't; they sang the whole night, and the people complained about the singing, and the women would not shut up, and the babies would not shut up, and nobody would shut up, and they turned them all out.

And then I went out West to do some work for the Harriman shopmen;[22] and while I was in Butte, Montana, one day I picked up a paper, and it said the Payne Creek Colliery Co. would not settle with the miners again, and renew its contract again. I said, "This means that every sort of organization is to be driven out"; and I said, "I will go into the fight and make it cost that company something before I get through." I telegraphed to San Francisco to cancel the dates with the officers of the shopmen, and took the train and went in. I went down to Payne Creek and a little boy came running to me and said, "Mother Jones, did you come to stay?" and I said, "Yes; I came to stay." The child was crying, and said, "Mother, do you know what they have done to me and my mamma?" I said, "No"; and he said, "They beat my mamma up, and they beat my little brothers and sisters, and beat me, and if I live to be a man I am going to kill twenty of them for that."

I went up and held a meeting with them and found out — got inside information; and the gunmen were all around, and some of the military in plain clothes in the meeting we had; and I went down the Kanawha River and held a meeting with the miners already organized.

One night two of the miners came to me at about 2 o'clock at night, at Montgomery, and they said, "We have been down to Charleston, and no one will go up Cabin Creek; will you come?" I said, "Yes." For nine years no organizer had dared to go up that creek, and if he did, he came out on a stretcher, or a corpse. The boys said, "They will kill you, Mother"; and I said, "It don't make any difference to me when I get killed; there is a duty to be performed, and I am going." I said, "Is it billed?" And they said, "No"; and I said, "I will attend to that," and the railroad men circulated the bills.

I went up on Tuesday, and the governor heard I was going and sent a company of the militia; and those men came down over those mountains, and their toes were out through their shoes; they walked twelve miles, some of them. They stood there and looked up as much as to say, "Have you brought us any message of hope?" I talked to them with the militia there, and the company's representatives, and I said, "Boys, freedom is not dead," and some poor wretch hollowed, "Where is she?" "She is gently sleeping, and when you call her she will awake." Those men screamed, and they said, "Will you organize us, Mother?" I said, "Yes." They said, "into what?" I said, "Into the mine workers," and I said, "If you get organized, will you stay organized? I left you all organized ten years ago when I went away," and they said, "We will, Mother." I took them over by the church; I don't go to church; I am waiting outside for the fellows in the church to come out and fight with me, and then I will go in. Outside of the church I stood up on a bench and organized the men, and I said for everyone to take out their mine clothes in the morning and to take their picks and shovels and dig coal, and I said, "Tomorrow you go to work and don't say anything about this meeting." And then I went home. And then they came after me again, and one day I was going to Red Warrior, and I had perhaps twenty men with me. There was not a stick among those men. One old darkey had a battered-up gun, he was carrying along for fun, and up above that tipple there was a machine gun with a company, and the machine gun was turned on the men.

I was in a buggy, and one or two ahead of the crowd, and they turned back; they got scared to death and turned back, and I jumped out of the buggy and ran up, and they said, "For God's sake, Mother, don't go up there," and I beckoned them to step back, and I went up and put my hand on the machine gun, and I said, "Boys, you can't send one bullet out of this gun." One of the men with his lips quivering — he was thirsty for blood — he said, "You take your hands off," and I said, "No; I won't take my hands off, and you won't shoot a bullet out of that gun," and my poor boys were trembling. They were in their shirt sleeves going home.

I was going to hold a meeting up there, and some one said, "What are those fellows up there for? Have they got guns?" I said, "No one has a gun. That old darkey had a battered one that wouldn't shoot a cat; he is just carrying it for fun." One gunman stood behind a tree with his sharpshooter, and I said, "You get out in the open and don't dare shoot a bullet out of that gun; you have yourselves mothers and wives and children probably, and I don't want to hear their groans; and I don't want to hear the groans of the mothers and wives and children of my boys; don't you hurt them." One of them said, "Why don't you stay up on the creek?" And I said, "I have something to do besides staying up on the creek." Then they came down like rats, and the whole army gathered there. I said, "Let us stop that, let my boys pass up to their homes, and let us have peace and not tears," and I shook hands with all of the gunmen. I said, "Let us have peace on this creek; you take care of the mines up there, and the boys won't trouble you."

Chairman Walsh: What year was that?

Mother Jones: That was in 1913. And then I went up soon after that — I was going up to Berwind, and there was a reporter from the Baltimore *Sun* with me that met me in the depot at Charleston, and he said to me, "Mother Jones, where are you going?" And I said, "I am going up to Cabin Creek." He said, "Can I go with you," and I said, "You certainly can go," and we went and we got off of the train and came down over the tipple; they didn't see us coming down, or they would have stopped us, but when we got by the company's store where there was a pathway, there was a creek, and the C. & O. Railroad here (indicating), and everybody walked on the road, and I started to go up on this side when a fellow hollered at me. "You get down," and the reporter said, "That creek is there; she will get all wet"; he said "I don't care a damn, she ought to be wet; if she wasn't here, there would be no trouble." He said, "You don't mean to say you are going to make her walk in that creek?" And he said, "Yes." No creek or anything else will bluff me; and I was pretty wet up to my hips, and the general manager and superintendent came, and I sat there and my dress was all wet, and I was dripping; and I came, and I was talking, and I threw it into them; I gave it to the general manager and everyone else; I don't say anything to the miners that I would not say to them. It is a fight for human freedom and liberty.

I held my meeting, but the road was only that wide (indicating), and if you step a foot east or west it was private property. One miner said to me to come up and get a cup of tea, and they said, "You can't go up." The man was paying rent for his home, but he couldn't give me a cup of tea. And the reporter for the Baltimore *American* came along, and I didn't get anything to eat or drink or get a chance to dry my clothes until I got to Charleston at 6 o'clock that evening.

I carried the fight on — I knew the boys would — only this is a spectacular age. They have no conception of freedom or justice; until it hits them they don't care. I thought, "I will make a move that will stir the state and draw the attention of the people to this"; and I went out, and at that time I got 3,000 or 4,000 miners and came up to the capitol with a banner which said, "Nero fiddled while Rome burned"; that is what the governor of West Virginia did. And we went into the statehouse grounds, and I read the document to the governor asking him to do away with the Baldwin guards; that this nation was not founded to be governed by gunmen; and I read the document on the steps of the statehouse to about 5,000 people. The governor was at my right, and I said that if the government would not do business that we would by 8 o'clock to-morrow night. So we sent the document in, and the governor still remained there, and they said, "We will wait, Mother, for him to answer"; and I said, "No; you go back."

Chairman Walsh: That was still in the strike of 1913?

Mother Jones: Yes. So I said to the crowd, "This governor is not going to do anything for you." Some one said, "Why?" I said, "Because the biggest political crook that ever cursed a nation elected him — Senator Elkins,"[12] and when he says "Bark," and he does it.

I talked for an hour and a half,[13] and there is an inscription on the steps of the capitol that mountaineers are always free, and I called attention to that inscription and I said, "Now, I want to state right here to this audience that we are going to make that good or we will tear up the inscription," and the governor stood there; and so when the meeting was over I went away. I was tired and worn out, for I had been preparing for that for some days; and some one got up and began to blow off a lot of locomotive hot air, and the boys came up to me to stop it, and I took him by the shoulder and told him to get down, and I got up and said, "This meeting stands adjourned until I need you again. And I want you to stay away from the saloons and save your money, because you will need it." Somebody in the audience hollowed, "Well, what will we do with it, Mother?" "Buy a gun," said I; and they bought the guns; they went to every store in town and bought the guns and put them on their shoulders and went off with them.

Well, I went to Washington to see if I could get an investigation, because I believe the longer those things go the more bitter both sides get; and I worked here for a day or two and came back, and the Bull Moose charged again up in Paint Creek in the night and shot the women and shot the men and shot their legs off, and so on the fifteenth, I think it was, there was a great deal of excitement down in Hansford, and I went down to see what the trouble was, and came back. Well, that night the militia came and arrested a lot of our men — over 200 of them — and I heard the boys on the Kanawha side of the river was lining up to protest against the arrests, and I was afraid there was going to be some trouble. I took the train and went down, and the boys was all at the station and each group began to catch me and said, "Come with me, Mother." "Where have you been," said I. "We have been holding a meeting." And so I went down to Boomer with them; and the conductor held the train, because they were appealing to me. And I went out and held the meeting that night, and I says, "Now, everybody goes home and tomorrow at 10 o'clock come up to Longacre, and there we will discuss it." And so tomorrow at 10 o'clock I was there, and the whole mob got there, and I talked with them, and I says, "Now, boys, you go, each union, and you elect a sober, good, clear-headed man. I want to take him up to the governor, so as to have a talk with the governor to stop arresting our men until we find out what they are being arrested for." Military arrested them. So they did come, and I took them into the church and instructed them what to do and what to say to the governor, and I paid their fare, because they didn't come in the meeting with any money, and I paid their fare up; and when we got up and got off the train — now, I suppose there were 500 persons can swear to my side of it, and how I got that committee and took them up to take them to the governor peacefully and quietly, because these men were getting enraged — there were a good many foreigners among them.

I knew if I kept them quiet for a day or two that they would cool off and nothing would happen until we would straighten things out. So I was arrested as soon as I got off the train and thrown into an automobile and carried down to the Robber's Roost, a hotel near the bridge, which I call the Robber's Roost, because the pirates used always to put up there. So there was no warrant that I saw, and so I was taken to the C. & O. train and put on the C. & O. train and carried down and handed over to the military twenty-five miles from where I was arrested.

And I was handed over to the military while the civil court was open.

Well, I was held there for three months, and they established a drumhead court and the court appointed two lawyers, and they came to see me, and they said that the court appointed them to defend me. I said, "Gentlemen, personally I have nothing in the world against you; but there is no lawyer in the United States that will defend me in that court." Well, some civilian lawyers came down, and they wanted to defend me — not to cost anything, and I said, "No, sir; there is no lawyer will ever go into that court to defend me." And so we were taken into court. I think we were five days there and some nights until 11 o'clock at night. There were about thirty of the men that consented to take a lawyer, but there were six or seven of us that would not have a lawyer to defend us, and we were sent over to the bull pen and the boys were held in their bull pen and I was held in mine, and we saw the military on each side of the bull pen day and night watching. And it was great fun for me. I used to see the poor kids dressed up in that uniform, and I wondered what their mothers thought of them; and I used to feel sorry for them, and I used to give them an apple once in a while. There was a break in the floor and they used to send things up to me out of the cellar; and I felt sorry for them because they were carrying guns to shoot people, and I used to give them an apple; and several nights the Bull Moose came down —

Commissioner Lennon:[14] (Interrupting). Explain what the "Bull Moose" means.

Mother Jones: The "Bull Moose?" The train the military used. And they came down several nights; and a party in it wanted me to go to Ohio; said my health would break down there. "Well, let it break. I have only one death to meet. I am going to Ohio." Well, the attorney general, I think it was, that came down, and I said to the attorney general, "Now, I want to make a statement right here. This thing has got to end. I want to tell the governor of the state that he can chain me to that tree outside there and he can get his dogs of war to riddle this body with bullets, but I will not surrender my constitutional rights to him. I happen to be one of the women who tramped the highways where the blood of the revolutionists watered it that I might have a trial by jury. The civil courts are open, and I demand that the law be enforced." And so I did not; we were tried, anyhow. We were kept in that bull pen, but I would not surrender.

And one day these boys were taken away from there, and I listened to their babies screaming on the depot when they were taken. I did not know where they were going. I was the lone person in that jail — in that military prison — for five weeks. The others were all taken away; they carried them to Clarksburg, but I was the lone person there, and the editor of the *San Francisco Bulletin* sent his wife across the continent to find out what was happening to me,[15] and she came up there and got hold of the whole information, and she went up to the United States Senate, and saw Senator Kern, and went to *Collier's Weekly*; the other magazines would not publish it, but *Collier's* did after it was tamed down. And she saw Senator Kern and it was discussed on the floor of the Senate, and some one going by threw a *Cincinnati Post* in and I picked it up and the first thing that attracted my attention was, "Wall Street telephoned Senator Kern to withdraw that resolution and they would make it an object for him." And it said that they did not telegraph nor send anyone nor write. They took the quickest way of reaching him. "Heavens," said I, "Those officials will never understand what that means to the industrial world." And I had no writing material, but there was a book there, and I thought I would send a note to Senator Kern; and then I thought, "Well, he won't pay any attention to that. They are tired of those things." And I got a telegram blank and made up a telegram, and this is what it stated:

Senator Kern, Washington, D.C.:
From out the military prison at Piat, West Virginia, I send to you the groans and heartbreaks and tears of men, women, and children, as I have heard them in this state, pleading with you in their behalf for the honor of the nation to push that investigation, and children yet unborn will rise and call you blessed.

And I had two bottles and I rang them together, and a fellow came down in the cellar, and he came, and I says, "You take that up as quick as you can to that telegraph office. Don't go to this one here, but go three miles up the road, and tell him to send that telegram to Washington for me"; and the fellow says, "This is fine stuff; tell Mother Jones it will be in Washington before you get home." And so I slept good that night, when I knew that telegram had gone to Washington, and I had bluffed the gang in Wall Street for once; and I had a good sleep. And the thing came up in the Senate, and old Judge Goff — he is not a bad fellow at all, but he has been dead for forty years and doesn't know it. The old judge had a telegram from the governor stating that I was not at all incarcerated; that I was in a very pleasant boarding house; and he went on about outside agitators, and who they were and what they were. Well, this nation was founded on agitation. The chattel slavery was abolished through agitation, and God grant the agitation keeps up until the last chain of slavery is broken. And he said, "That is old Mother Jones, and I want to tell you that if you listen to her as I did you will find out she will convince you." But I never convinced him; but he should never have been in the United States Senate at all. The old fellow was not a bad fellow, but he is dead and the world has run beyond him. Senator Kern pulled out his telegram and read, and the Senators in Washington told me that in fifty years nothing had every struck the Senate like that telegram. I says, "Well, thank God, something struck them; they needed a cyclone once in a while, and if the telegram stirred them up, so much the better." Then — I hope I am not tiring you, but there is a great deal of history connected with this, Mr. Walsh.

Chairman Walsh: Just go ahead. A little matter came up which I had to answer.

Mother Jones: So the governor sent for me the next day, and I was taken up to Charleston, and he told me that I could go to the hotel and he would see me tomorrow. Well, he did not see me tomorrow, or the next day, either; but I went up to Washington then and saw Senator Kern in the United States Senate, and I worked until we got an investigation. And now I want to show before I close this West Virginia affair — I came down that creek one day — that Cabin Creek — and when I got down to the foot of the creek there was a miner, a colored fellow, and they were hammering him — the colored fellow. I watched them; it was on the platform. They rushed into the station, and the whole mob went in, and I went in to see what was the matter, and when I went in there they had him up in the corner, and this poor fellow was hollering, and I felt sorry for him, and I went over and I pushed the whole mob away, and I says, "You come here." "Oh, Mother," he says, "you take me." I says, "What did you do?" He says, "I was after scabs," he says, "over in North Carolina." "Well, you deserved all you got; but I don't want your mother crying. Now, come out here, and I want you to go down to the C. & O. Come on and get out." Now, the military, in plain clothes, were in that depot, and they never interfered; so I took the fellow out and took care of him and took him away from the crowd, and the crowd dispersed, and I put him on the train, and I says to the conductor, "Here is money for that fellow's fare; take him away." So he did.

Now, this man, Nance, was going by on the platform, and a military officer in plain clothes went to arrest this Italian, and Nance says to him, "You can't arrest him," and he says, "Well, I am going to." "Well, you can't without a warrant." He says, "You get a warrant. I have no more respect for you than I have for a Baldwin thug." So Nance went away. Now, he came back ten days after that, and he was arrested by the military and tried in court, and got five years in the penitentiary; and that is all there was to that, because I was there, and I was the one that broke the thing up before it ended; and that was the only crime — the only charge — and they held a drumhead court and sentenced that man to five years in Moundsville.

Well, another day I came down, and here was a railroad man and another one of the Baldwin train men, and the man says, "Don't go up the creek; they are on a strike," to some scabs. So he says — this fellow says — "You can't stop him," and he says, "Well, I am going to," he says. "They are going to take the bread out of my brother's mouth"; and they were in a squabble, and I walked up to see what it was about. Now, there was a militiaman there in plain clothes, and I went up and I took hold of this man and I says, "That train man is right; he was put there to do his duty, so let him do it, and you come with me," and I took him away. Now, that man was arrested, and he got two years in Moundsville, and that was all there was to that; I want to say to this commission, I can go before the world and swear to it if I were dying the next moment. That was the sum total of the crimes, and he was put two years in Moundsville.

There were fifteen men for similar reasons put into Moundsville for from one to seven or ten years, I think; and so I concluded now we will make a job of this; these men are not guilty of any crime. And I started out and borrowed the money, and billed meetings, and came to Washington, and I had a large gathering in the armory that night in Washington, and we put the matter up; and the next morning the door of the penitentiary opened, and they signed their names, and every single one of them was let loose. They went up to Wheeling, and nobody knew but the administration that they were freed. After the meeting was held in Washington, and congressmen and senators were at that meeting, and when the matter was put up to them there the doors of the prison opened, and they were turned loose. Now, if that is law, I think there is something wrong.

Now, I am coming back to the Colorado situation, and that will wind up, I don't know how long it is going to wind up. But after I was turned loose in Charleston by the governor — now, mind, I was not taken into any civil court nor no charges brought against me, only one, and it was the stealing of a machine gun. Well, I don't know what I did with it, whether I hid it or what I did with it; but I was accused of stealing a machine gun. However, the machine gun was lost; that is true. It was an $1,800 machine gun, but I didn't steal it; I didn't happen to be around at that time. But I want to show you the rotteness of the thing; and then you wonder that men rebel, and won't work.

I went to Texas to speak on Labor Day. The general manager invited me as their guest — him and his wife both. I declined to go for this reason — that I never do go to persons in that position. I may have to fight them, and it would not be a very pleasant thing after I had taken their hospitality; and so I declined to go, and I said to the boys, "I prefer to go to a hotel." And we held a Labor Day meeting there, and I left that day and took the train and and came into Trinidad, and when I left the train the boys met me at the depot, and they said, "We are going to have a convention here." I did not know they were going to, because I was on the go all the time. "What for?" I said. The boys were all up in the air; they wanted to strike. "Well, can't you settle it without?" I said. "Well, we are going to try." So they sent propositions after propositions I learned, and the convention came and the strike was called. Now, I don't know whether you gentlemen in Colorado read the statements at that convention, but they were very deplorable and very condemnatory to me. The papers, because they all represented the C. F. & I., they had to write as they were dictated to, and they charged my speech up with calling the strike. Well, I don't care for that; I don't care what charges they make against me. So the strike came, and the tent colony was established. The day of the strike came on the twenty-fifth, I think it was, of September, 1913.

I went out of the colony because it was rainy and drizzly, and I wanted to see that the little children were cared for, if there were any there; and I went to carry some clothing to them. In that fourteen miles between Trinidad and the tent colony I met twenty-eight wagons; mothers with babies in their arms were walking. It was a cold, drizzling rain. I want to say to this commission that it was the earthly belongings of those people, it was their earthly savings that were in those wagons. There is not a second-hand man in the United States that would have given $30 for the contents of the twenty-eight wagons, yet it was all these people had. When I came to the tents, the mattresses were wet, and I said to the women, "You didn't sleep there all night?" "Yes; and the baby slept, too." And an Italian said — I said, "Joe, where did you sleep?" And he says, "Out on the ground." "Why, it was raining and the ground was wet." "Sure, mother," he said, "but I no like the company; like better than sleep in company house." Now, this was the sentiment, and nobody can understand this unless they live with those people. I know their lives, and it was on the blood of those people that we carry on our charity institutions and everything else. And that tent colony went on, and we fed them, and then the scabs were coming — there was a convention called in Denver — and I like to put fellows up against it, sometimes; and that convention was not a miners' convention; it was the state convention of the Federation of Labor. And we had an old man, that I had brought in from the camps, that they made him dig his own grave, the military did. They made him dig his own grave, and they stood over it telling him to dig two feet more. He was going to the post office, and they would not let him go. And he says, as he dug the grave, "Let me kiss my wife and babies." "Dig that grave; go on." That was the reply. So he dug the grave. So when this convention took place, I says, "Bring him in; let him tell it on the platform here." And so I had him put on the platform. And I got up, and I asked the convention to rise as a unit and to go up to the Statehouse and demand of that governor where he stood — whether for the honor of the state and the uplift of her children or for the interest of twenty-six Broadway[16] and make him tell it right there, because he won't have time to organize his machine, and he would have to tell the truth.

I had a number of mothers, also, with their babies, to put them up to him, and ask him if they were going to deprive those babies — we had star orators, but star orators they say never get frightened, but they do get scared when they get up against it. Those people are not going to hurt anybody; they were merely going after information that they had a right to get from the governor. The next day the governor had time for his machinery to get to work, and he had two secret-service men walking into the capital with him, and any time that I ha e to have a secret-service man escorting me I will get down, and out. If my own actions and honor don't protect me I won't ask any sleuth to do so.

Well, then, the scabbers were coming in from Mexico; I had been to Mexico a few years before that, down to see Madero and de la Barra and other men; and I was going to El Paso to stop the scabs coming in, and I went down. I was there a week and held some meetings[17] and I wanted to see the revolutionists and have a talk with them. The morning I came back was the fourth of January, 1914. When I got off of the train here was the bunch. I got off of the Santa Fe. They ran and said, "Here she comes," and I looked around. "Take her back." I said, "What is the matter?" "We have got you." "Here I am, take me, I am going to Denver." "Get on that train." "I am not going on that train." "Get in here and get your ticket." "They don't sell the C. & S. tickets in that office." He went and asked the telephone, and they said there would not be a train for an hour and a quarter yet, so I was put in an automobile and taken to the Columbia Hotel, and I was taken to a room. On the way to the room I said that I had not had any breakfast; I would like to have some breakfast. They said, "Take her in to breakfast," and I asked the captain who was escorting me, I said, "Who is going to pay for this?" And he said, "The state will pay for it." And I said, "All right, if the state pays for it I will get a good breakfast." I don't often have an opportunity to do that, but the state was paying for it and I got a good breakfast. I was taken to the room, and a half a dozen were there to take care of me. The train came and the automobile came, and with three bayonets, one at my back and one at my left, and this fellow that had arrested me was at my right and there were two others in front. When I got to the depot there were the cavalry and the infantry and the gunmen after one old woman eighty years old. I said, "You are awful brave fellows, your mothers ought to put you in a nursery and give you a nursing bottle for ten years."

I got on the train and the captain came along and said that he was going to Denver. I told him I was glad to have him. He came along and said, "Don't come back," and I said, "If I don't feel like it, I won't," and so I went on into Denver. While I was here in Washington I picked up a paper and saw where the governor would have me arrested if I came back, and I won't let any governor run a state that I have an interest in; I have one share of stock, and so I went back, and he put two detectives in the hotel to watch me. He put one at the gate watching the trains, and I thought that I would fix him right there, and I would let the world see that you are not such a wonderful governor after all. The militia was there, and a man, I think he called himself a humane man, I don't know whether he was taking care of dogs or human beings, but he came up Sunday and said, "Are you going down to Trinidad, Mother?" And I said, "Yes." And he said, "When?" And I said, "The last of the week." And he said, "I want to know because I want to go on the train with you." I told him I would be glad to have him, I knew he was a Baldwin rat, and I wanted to go along. He said, "Where are you going this afternoon?" And I said, "Trade and labor." And he said, "May I go with you?" And he escorted me up the street so no one would hurt me, and I said, "I told the boys that the governor said I could not go to Trinidad, but that he didn't own it; I had a share of stock in it, but that I was not going until the last of the week; that I had some matters coming from Washington." I went to my room, and the fellow went home contented; he said there were two other fellows in a house across the street in a room watching me.

I had my sleeper all bought on Saturday, and I got into the sleeper and went to sleep, and when the train pulled out I was asleep, and I told the conductor when he got there to stop the train before it got to the depot. He held up the train, and I got down and walked up the street, and into the hotel and sent out and got my breakfast, and was in the hotel three hours before they found out I was there. I sent for the boys, and they came up and I said to the boys that they were liable to arrest me, but don't you fellows make any fuss or move; just let them arrest me; don't say a word and make a move, and keep the boys all quiet and off of the streets, because you can not do that, because the curiosity of an animal is aroused whenever anything is going on. So I had my breakfast, and presently along came the troopers — tramp, tramp, tramp — after three hours. The governor had telephoned and telegraphed, "Arrest her at once," and the general said, "Get her," so they did. I said, "You come after me," and they said, "Yes." I said, "Wait until I get my few duds." I got into an automobile, with a bunch of guns and bayonets behind me and in front, and the poor fellow that was running the automobile was scared to death, but I told him to keep that machine going straight, that they wouldn't hurt him. There was 150 cavalry, 150 infantry, 150 horses with their heads poked at me, 150 gunmen of the Standard Oil Co., and the old woman, and I shook my hands to the boys good-by. I was taken to the hospital and put in a room, and I was kept there for nine weeks and didn't see a human being except Attorney Hawkins. But there was a thing that they called a colonel that came along once in a while and that wanted me to go to Denver. But I said, "No; I will stay here." He would come strutting about every now and then, and there were a lot of poor boys there. They had stationed three of the militiamen — three on the outside of the door and two in that room and one outside of the window. I couldn't eat. I didn't have much appetite locked up in a room, and so I have my food to the militia boys. They are good boys when you get at them right, and I gave my fruit to them to eat and got on the right side of those fellows, and they told me they had not gotten any money for several weeks, and I said, "I have five or six dollars. I will give it to you boys, and you can go to the show tonight." I gave it to them, and they went, and I got them with me, and they said, "I will tell you, Mother, we will never take up a gun again to shoot a worker," and I said, "That is what you should have done before."

Chairman Walsh: At this point, Mother Jones, we will stand adjourned until tomorrow morning.

Mother Jones: I have a good deal to tell you yet, Mr. Chairman.

Chairman Walsh: All right.

(Whereupon, the hour for adjournment having arrived, the commission here adjourned until Friday, May 14, 1915, at 10 a.m.)

Washington, D.C., Friday, May 14, 1915 -10 a.m.

Present: Chairman Walsh, Commissioners Garretson, Weinstock, Lennon, O'Connell, Aishton, and Harriman.

Chairman Walsh: Call Mrs. Jones, please.

TESTIMONY OF MRS. MARY JONES — Recalled

Chairman Walsh: I think last night when we adjourned, Mrs. Jones, you had just detailed your arrest in Colorado, and if you would, please I wish you would continue to put in the whole Colorado incident down to the end, so far as it has to do with you.

Mother Jones: I think I closed about where I was arrested.

Chairman Walsh: You were arrested at Trinidad?

Mother Jones: And taken to the Sisters of Mercy Hospital. They turned it into a prison, a portion of it, and I was incarcerated there with three military men, one in front of the door, and one at each side of the door, and one outside of the window, and the whole military camp across the way from the hospital, and then the headquarters of the military was in the next room to me. And I didn't see anyone for nine weeks that I was incarcerated there but my attorney —

Chairman Walsh: That was Mr. Hawkins, I believe?

Mother Jones: Mr. Hawkins and Mr. Clark, who represented him. He came once to see me to get me to sign some documents for writ of habeas corpus, and Major Boughton came with him; and I made some remarks with regard to they wouldn't get the writ of habeas corpus granted from the judge there. I knew very well they would not, because he represented the interests there, and I did not want our people to spend any money, because they had none to spend. So, however, they applied for the habeas corpus and it was not granted.

The superioress came and told me — I think the colonel got her to do so, thinking I would succumb and surrender — that it was turned down. I said, "All right," and she says "You ought to go to Denver." "I will go when I get ready; when my hands are free. I don't need any instructions or advice on that at all." And so she went away and I was kept there; I never got any mail, not a newspaper or a postal card or a single thing for nine long weeks that I was alone in that room. But the colonel used to come every once in a while to see me to see if I was getting ready to surrender, and I said, "Colonel, I will not surrender," or "captain" He says, "I am not a captain; you are pulling me down." I says, "What are you?" He says, "A colonel." He was a strutting jack to tell me what his title was, and so on. I says, "All right, sir." And so he went away and didn't come back for a day or two. And I never saw General Chase at all until the morning I was taken to Denver, at the close of the nine weeks, when they were going into the supreme court in Denver for writ of habeas corpus. He came to me on Sunday and he said, "Would you go up and see the governor if he wishes to see you?" I waited a moment and I said, "Well, yes; I will go up and see the governor if he wishes to see me. While I have no respect for the governor personally I have a great deal for the office he holds, and out of respect I hold for the office he holds I shall comply with his request." And so that is all I heard of it. And he came that evening eight minutes before the Santa Fe train was to go out, in an automobile, and said, "Are you ready?" "Why," I said, "No; I am just getting ready to retire." He says, "Get ready; they are going in eight minutes." He said, "Jump, jump, jump." Well, I had a little valise there, and I got it and I handed it out to the guard at the door to put the straps on it, and he took the valise and threw it out in the automobile, and they locked the guard up in his room and cleared the whole hall, and so I was taken down the back way — not the front way at all, but the back way — and was put into an automobile in the dark.

The automobile ran away. I had the fellow that was running it — he was running it down by the C. & S. road — to make a short cut to the Santa Fe; and he made him go around some dark alleys. I want to say, Mr. Walsh, it was the first time in my life that I made up my mind I was going to die; I concluded that they were going to kill me, and I was preparing to make a fight before I left. However, after a while we struck the Santa Fe train, pulled away, out entirely away from the depot. That was switched away from the depot, and I was put on. I got a little relief when I was up in the Pullman, and so I went to bed. There were two of the military officers there, this man colonel that used to come all of the time, and another one, a doctor, and we went into Denver. In the morning the general met me at the train. He introduced me to the general, and I didn't catch his first name, and I said to the colonel, "Who is that?" (he was in his civilian clothes), and he said, "It is General Chase." "Oh," I said, "that is General Chase?" "Yes. We will go to the Adams Hotel." "General, if you would, concede to me the right to go to the Oxford; I have been going there for years and know them all, and I don't care to go to the Adams." It was rather aristocratic and was out of my line, and I didn't care to go there, and so we went to the Oxford, and he said, "We will come after you at 9 o'clock to go to the governor." "I think you had better put it off until 10; I want Mr. Hawkins to go with me," and he said, "You don't need him; the governor will treat you courteous," and I said, "That is not the question involved; I want my attorney to go with me to the governor, and I won't go unless he says go," and he said "All right."

They went away and left me, and I immediately went to the phone and called Mr. Hawkins, and Mr. Hawkins was not yet out of bed, and he said, "Is this you, Mother?" and I said, "Yes; they brought me in, but I don't know what they are going to do with me." And he said, "Who is with you?" and I said, "Nobody." "What did they say?" he said. I said, "They said they were coming after me at 9 o'clock, but I got them to postpone it until 10 o'clock." Mr. Hawkins came down, and Mr. Lawson with him and I told him the whole story, and he said, "They have kidnapped you, Mother." I said, "I don't know what they have done." But he called the Adams Hotel and asked General Chase what they had done with me, and he said, "She is turned loose; she is free." But we went to see the governor. He says, "I didn't sent for you." And I said, "Your colonel said you did. Somebody must be telling something that is untrue, either you or him." Mr. Hawkins and he talked for a long time, and Mr. Lawson.

I said, "Governor, I will tell you something; you don't own this state, nor you don't own Trinidad. I have broken no law; I have never in my life been in a police court or district court, and I am going back to Trinidad." He said, "If anybody told me it was not the thing to do, I would not do it." "If Washington took that advice we would be under King George the Third; if Lincoln took it, Grant never would have gone to Gettysburg." I didn't tell him just when I was going, but some newspaper men came around and wrote the matter up. I stayed at the hotel for a few days, and I said to Mr. Hawkins, "I have no use for a despot in this country; it was not founded on despotism; and I am going back to Trinidad." And he said, "Do you feel able to, Mother?" And I said, "Yes; I feel able to." "Very well," said he; "when you get ready, you can go back."

I openly got my ticket and went to the train and into the sleeper, and Reno, the C.&F. detective was right across the berth from me. My ticket was registered for Trinidad, and my sleeper also. When I got to Walsenberg, before I got in there the military man called me. I let on I knew it was the military, but I didn't undress at all that night, and he said, "You have to get up." I said, "No; I am going to Trinidad." "But we want you." "Who are you?" "Oh, I am the military," he said. "Oh," I said, "all right; I will be with you." I got up and went into the dressing room and combed my hair back and came back. I was taken off of the train by the militia, and the train crew got a little excited; the engineer jumped down and came back and shook hands with me, and the conductor, and I said, "Boys, keep quiet; let this go." We started off with the military, Mr. Brown, an organizer of the United Mine Workers, who happened to be with me on that train. I said to this young fellow, "Where are you going to take me?" He said, "To jail." I said,

"Where is the jail?" "In the cellar under the courthouse." I said, "All right. Is there a fireplace in it or a chimney there?" And he said, "I don't know; do you want a fire?" "I am not so particular about the fire, as having the chimney." And he said "What do you want the chimney for, and not the fire?" And I said, "I will tell you about that; I have a pigeon that I have trained, and it goes to Washington, and there is a new wireless invention around its neck, and every week he comes back from Washington, gets on top of the chimney and unwinds that message and sends it down to me." He said, "Did he come when you were at the hospital?" And I said, "Yes; he came every week." And he said, "They never found it out?" I said, "No; I am telling you that now." Imagine an educated woman that raised a thing like that; imagine a state that put a belt full of bullets around his stomach; imagine the nation that stands for such insults to the intelligence of the people. And so I was put in the cellar.

It was cold, it was a horrible place, and they thought it would sicken me, but I concluded to stay in that cellar and fight them out. I had sewer rats that long every night to fight, and all I had was a beer bottle; I would get one rat, and another would run across the cellar at me. I fought the rats inside and out just alike. I was there twenty-six days, but one thing I have to say, the colonel that had charge of that, Colonel Berdiker, came to me that morning and said, "Mother, I have never been placed in a position as painful as this; won't you go to Denver?" I said, "No, Colonel, I will not." He said — my breakfast came in, two spoonsful of black coffee and some dry bread, and he said, "Don't eat that breakfast; I will send you some." He sent me my meals all the time I was there; at least, he got the miners to do it. He was very kind and did everything in the world that his officers would let him do; he had to obey orders, of course, but he was a man in every sense of the word. So I was there twenty-six days, and during the twenty-six days I never slept a night; I used to sleep some daytime. And the end of the twenty-six days the habeas corpus — the Supreme Court had notified the militia to deliver me in person to the Supreme Court, and they had to turn the militia loose before they could deliver me; before they could turn me loose. And so one morning the colonel said, "Mother, I have some good news for you; I don't know that you will consider it good news, but the general has just telephoned to me that you are free." I said, "No; I don't consider that good news; I consider it a very dirty, contemptible way of doing business, Colonel; it is not the method I admire at all in a person in the general's position." He said, "You can have transportation wherever you wish to go," and I said, "You tell the general I never have taken any favor from the enemies of my class and I shall accept none from him; I shall transport myself wherever I wish to go, and if I don't have the money to do so, I will walk." And so the colonel shook hands and went away, and the boys came and got my valise and I went to Denver.

Then my attorney knew, of course, the habeas corpus business was turned over, and they sent me to Washington, to Congress.

Now, I do not want to take up the time of the commission, because you are worn out, and there are a great many, many things said here that have no bearing whatever upon the discontent and unrest of the nation, and if the commission will just bear with me for a moment or two I shall read this. This is the Pennsylvania strike, and I shall turn this over to the commission. This is simply an outline of it. I shall get through just as quickly as I can, Mr. Walsh. [Reads:]

There is gradually creeping into the decisions of the courts a most dangerous doctrine to liberty, and that is that the militia, under the orders of a governor, may deprive people of their liberty at the will and pleasure of the governor. Such a doctrine has not existed in England for hundreds of years, and it was not supposed to have any foundation in law in the United States until within very recent years. In my judgment, this attempt on the part of some of the courts to sanction deprivations of liberty, if not checked, threatens not only the liberty of all the citizens but threatens the very existence of government itself. It is being recently held in a number of courts that where a strike exists the governor has power to imprison the strikers at his pleasure. We all know that the courts of the country would not stand for any such doctrine if a governor sought to imprison bankers, lawyers, clergymen, doctors, and merchants, and if the courts are going to hold that strikers can be imprisoned without any charge against them, when we know that the courts would not hold the same thing as to bankers, lawyers, clergymen, doctors, and merchants, there is the greatest danger of working people refusing to submit to such a government.

Magna Charta, that great charter of human liberty, which was adopted in 1215, was a protest against military encroachment. The king, with his soldiers, had imprisoned people to such an extent that it was necessary to declare in Magna Charta that no freeman should be seized or imprisoned or condemned or committed to prison except by the laws of the land.

In the fourteenth century, during the reign of Edward III, Parliament, for the still greater protection of the rights of our English forefathers, provided that the king should have no power to seize the citizen, and that no citizen could be arrested except by indictment or presentment in court.

Charles I attempted to deprive the people of England of this right, but he paid for it with his head. King George III attempted to force a condition of military rule on the American Colonies, and in 1774 Benjamin Franklin went to Great Britain and entered a protest in the name of the American people. The prime minister laughed in his face, and Lexington, Concord, and Bunker Hill was the answer to that laughter.

American history affords but four attempts to set aside the writ of habeas corpus and trial by jury, prior to 1899, and each case met with a severe rebuke from the law courts north and south alike.

Citing these cases as they appear in historical record, the first attempt was made in 1815 when Andrew Jackson, puffed up the military pride, declared himself the military despot of New Orleans. He arrested and imprisoned an editor, and refused to obey the writ of habeas corpus. The courts of Louisiana arrested General Jackson and forced him to pay a fine of $1,000.

In 1861 President Lincoln undertook to suspend the writ of habeas corpus, but the courts all over the North with great unanimity declared that President Lincoln could not exercise such despotic power. At the same time in the Southern States the military power was making the same claims as to their power that Mr. Lincoln was making in the North, but with clarion voice the courts of the South declared the same as did the courts of the North, that the military commanders had no such power.

The most conspicuous case in all American history is known as the Milligan case. In Indiana, about the close of the war, a military commission seized a civilian by the name of Milligan and condemned him to death because he sympathized with the South, and the president of the United States approved the death sentence, but the Supreme Court of the United States promptly held that no civilian, where the courts were open, could be tried or condemned by a military commission.

For thirty-four years after this no attempt was made to claim that a writ of habeas corpus did not have full force and effect in America; but in 1899 there was again a series of decisions against striking workingmen, which decisions exalt the militia above the civil authorities, and which decisions, in my judgment, if not checked, will result in the destruction, not only of liberty, but of government itself. The Idaho Supreme Court held in the case of Boyle, a striking miner, that the court would not inquire into the cause of his detention, but would allow the governor and his soldiers to work their will. The opinion states no authorities, and in no way attempts to review glorious decisions delivered in favor of liberty which had been rendered for over 100 years. The court simply refused the miner his release. This was followed by a somewhat similar decision in Pennsylvania in 1902, known as the Shortall case. Then came the Moyer decision in Colorado in 1904, where it was held by a divided court that the governor could hold Mr. Moyer in jail at his pleasure. Then came the West Virginia decisions of 1912, in which the West Virginia court held that strikers could be tried and sent to the penitentiary by military commission, and were sent to the penitentiary for terms ranging from two and a half to seven and a half years.

A perusal of the details of these cases just cited from 1899 to 1914 shows an ever-increasing encroachment with each succeeding case upon the civil rights and liberties of the people by the military power. In 1899 the writ of habeas corpus was first suspended in a case growing out of labor disputes; in 1904 it was no longer considered an offense by the Supreme Court of the United States for the governor of a state, acting as the commander in chief of the military forces, to imprison civilians and hold them indefinitely; in 1912 in West Virginia we find encroachment extending still farther. Here a definite "war zone" was established and proclaimed to be such by a declaration of martial law, yet the military power went outside of that prescribed "war zone," and placed under arrest civilians under warrants made out and returnable to the civil courts, and tried them before the military commission. That this military edict issued by the governor of the State of West Virginia in full:

State Capitol, Charleston, November 16, 1912.

General Orders, No. 23:

The following is published for the guidance of the military commission, organized under General Orders No. 22, of this office, dated November 16, 1912:

1. The military commission is substituted for the criminal courts of the district covered by the martial-law proclamation, and all offenses against the civil laws as they existed prior to the proclamation of November 15, 1912, shall be regarded as offenses under the military law and as a punishment therefore, the military commission can impose such sentences either lighter or heavier than those imposed under the civil law, as in their judgment the offender may merit.

2. Cognizances of offenses against the civil law as they existed prior to November 5, 1912, committed prior to the declaration of martial law and unpunished, will be taken by military commission.

3. Persons sentenced to imprisonment will be confined in the penitentiary at Moundsville, West Virginia.

By command of the governor.

C. D. Elliott,
Adjutant General

Passing from West Virginia in 1912 to Colorado in 1913 we see the military despot still advancing. Here the militia comes into the scene without even the excuse of a declaration of martial law, the civil courts are set aside, men and women are placed under arrest promiscuously and held indefinitely and incommunicado.

This militia, acting under orders from its commander in chief, has committed the most barbaric of crimes culminating in the destruction of the tent colony of Ludlow, the only home these poor wretches could ever boast of, and the massacre of the men, women, and children on April 20, 1914.

The perpetrators of these fiendish crimes were tried by a court-martial presided over by the very men who gave the orders to shoot down the citizens, and notwithstanding that these militiamen charged with the crime, confessed as to their individual acts, and in fact proudly boasted that they broke their rifles over the heads of their defenseless prisoners, yet they were exonerated by this military commission and given a clean bill of citizenship.

Contrast this case with the case of John R. Lawson;[18] Mr. Lawson is the international board member of the United Mine Workers of America and a citizen of Colorado. For years practically every law on the statute books of the state for the protection of life and limb, and the sanitation of mines, has been violated by the operators. Driven to desperation by the nonenforcement of the law, and the ceaseless, relentless oppression of the big corporations, the miners on September 23, 1913, went on strike.

No sooner had they gone on strike, in fact, for weeks before the strike was called, the operators were scouring the country for gunmen, whose profession is that of shooting the miners back into submission. They engaged the services of the notorious Baldwin-Felts strike-breaking agency. These people were brought into the state by the hundreds, bringing with them their artillery, including rapid-fire guns and armored automobiles, in violation of the law. The logical results followed. Men who have the courage to strike and pit their empty stomachs against modern corporate greed are not going to be shot down like dogs without a protest. A fight took place between the miners and the hired assassins of the operators, in which one of the hirelings was killed. Lawson was charged with the murder, tried before a jury that was "hand picked" to convict contrary to the laws of the state, and sentenced to life imprisonment by a corporation judge who was created for that purpose.

Last Monday I sat in this room and listened to a discussion between this commission and Mr. Gilbert Roe on the question of the existence of some mysterious thing which neither side made out to establish, namely, a condition of equality before the law as between capital and labor.

I want to go on record before this commission by saying that there is no such a thing as equality before the law in disputes arising between labor and capital. Before we can have equality before the law, labor must possess some rights that are recognized by law. Today the wageworkers of this country have no economic rights that are recognized by law.

Take the case of a man out of work. He had no right to a job. The law does not say that as a citizen he shall have a right to work and earn a living. As a rule, he lives about two weeks from the bread line. If he gets out of work, he is out of money and out of home. According to the law, he becomes a vagrant. If he begs, he is put in jail; if he steals, he is sent to the penitentiary; and if he attempts to commit suicide and is caught at it, he is sent to an insane asylum.

In Colorado they organized and went on strike. The operators, who own the courts of law, turned their hirelings loose on them, clothed in the majesty of the law. These hirelings plundered and murdered these strikers with impunity, as the testimony taken by this commission will prove, and what has the law done?

A grand jury indicted 150 miners, but the same grand jury found no indictments against the coal operators or any member of the Colorado Fuel & Iron Co., though the facts were established that these operators imported gunmen and machine guns, both in violation of the law, and that strikers were killed and even women and babies were suffocated in the fire at Ludlow. Rotten and one-sided as the law is in Colorado, it was still a question whether or not a conviction of the miners could be secured, but our modern industrial pirates never overlook a chance. During the last session of the legislature Senator Hoyden, an attorney for the Colorado Fuel & Iron Co., who represents in the legislature a district known as Kingdom of Standard Oil, introduced a bill to establish a new judgeship. The bill became a law, and one Granby Hillyer, another corporation attorney, who was engaged with Jessie E. Northcutt, the salaried attorney of the C.F.&I. to prosecute the miners, was elevated to the bench, and although outspoken in his prejudice against the miners, refused to vacate his seat and allow the case to be tried by an unbiased judge. During this trial it was brought out that John Lawson was not within twelve miles of where the fight took place between the miners and the Baldwin gunmen in which he is accused of killing one of the hirelings, yet the hand-picket jury of the Colorado Fuel & Iron Co., have found him guilty of murder in the first degree and sentenced him to imprisonment for life.

Referring again to the tendencies toward militarism, what, I ask, do all these recent decisions mean? The answer is perfectly clear and plain. The American people are just like their revolutionary and colonial forefathers. They would have the same hatred against military rule as existed in the days of '76 or '61, but the military rule that has existed since 1899 is military rule against one class of people, and one alone, namely, strikers, and hence the great body of American people outside of the workingmen have not felt the oppression and have not been aroused to the fury that is being aroused among the working classes. If former Governor Ammons in Colorado had treated a dozen lawyers, clergymen, doctors, bankers, and merchants the way he treated the miners in Las Animas and Huerfano Counties we know that a terrible storm of indignation would have been aroused that would have been identically the same state of feeling that existed among the colonists in 1776. The citizen of Great Britain was not oppressed by the military, and he looked with some indifference upon the struggle of his kinsman across the Atlantic to throw off military oppression. If a governor, who is the representative of capital can use the soldiers to put the workers in prison and keep them there, then a workingmen's governor may do the same thing to a capitalist. Every workingman feels that this would not be permitted by the courts. He knows it would not, and hence he is aroused to indignation against the courts permitting the governor to so act as against the worker.

It is this feeling which is rising throughout the United States, and which, in my judgment, if not checked, will result in terrible consequences. In my judgment, the working people will not stand for any such treatment at the hands of the courts, and it behooves the courts, if they do not want anarchists made out of workingmen to hark back to the principles of our forefathers, and to declare that the great writ of habeas corpus is now, as it was in ancient days, a sacred writ, and one that no governor and no military commander can refuse to obey. It behooves the courts to hold, just as did the courts in the days of Lincoln, that military power can not imprison men without a charge where the courts are open and unobstructed in the transaction of business. Unless we do get back to this principle, consequences, similar to those which have occurred throughout the history of all the past will result. Charles I was not the only king to lose his head because of an attempt to hold people by the use of soldiers and bayonets. Louis XVI and Marie Antoinette lost their throne and their heads because the crown claimed the right to imprison people at the pleasure of the crown.

I have only to add that in my own case, I was held in West Virginia for three months, in 1913, and Colorado in 1914 for three months more practically incommunicado, without the slightest charge being made against me and with the courts open and unobstructed in the transaction of business in the counties where I was confined. No one has dared to file any charge against me in court, or made any claim against me that in thought, word, or action I have done wrong.

I have this, I have Mr. Hawkins, I am not sufficiently educated and never had time enough to go down through history, but I requested Mr. Hawkins to help me to prepare that to use in my addresses to the people and awaken the American people to the dangers that were approaching us.

Before I close I would like to ask the permission of the commission, the Child Labor Federal Commission that is here, I am more or less responsible for it. I was called to the strike of the textile workers in Philadelphia.[19] I saw the little boys who had not seen their eleventh year with their hands off here [indicating]; their wrists, taken off from their wrists. I saw their fingers, and I saw those children maimed for life. I asked the reporters; I asked the children first, "Do you work in the mills?" "Yes," "How old are you?" "I am just a little over ten, Mother." And so it went with boys and girls.

I said to the reporters, "Why don't you publish this and make comment on it?" And they showed me the advertisements, and said that they would be only too willing to, but that they didn't dare. I concluded

I would have to wake up the people of this nation, and I went to work and organized some 6,000 or 7,000 children, many of them with their hands off. I telegraphed to the papers in New York to send me down reporters, feeling that the Philadelphia papers would not take any notice of it, and so the New York papers sent down the reporters. I had those children in Independence Park; the police didn't know that we were coming until we were down there. We had our banner, and I marched them to the business part of the city and the newspaper district. I had a table in front of the city hall. I put those children up there. There were 50,000 people at that meeting; the biggest gathering that ever assembled in Philadelphia in their history, they said. I showed them children with their hands off, a sacrifice on the altar of profit, giving to this nation maimed and useless citizens. I spoke to the ministers, and asked them if they were not carrying out Christ's doctrine, suffer little children to come unto me, they are all that is pure and holy, and you say, "Suffer the little ones to go into the slave pens, and we will grind them into profit." And that is what is done. They closed up; the New York papers and the Philadelphia papers got to fighting one another, and that was all I wanted when I can get those fellows to fight one another, I am all right. It was given publicity, and was discussed in the universities and colleges, and finally got quieted down, and I asked the parents to let me have the little boys, and they said, "Yes." I got seventy-five little boys; some with their fingers off and their hands off, and I said, "I am going to see the president and have a bill passed to prohibit the murder of children for profit." I was only going thirty miles, but the children were so happy, and the agitation was so great; they never had had the sunshine or the grass before, and now they were bathing in the rivers, and the people were feeding them.

They had their little tincups and knapsacks, and were marching, and were having the finest time they had ever had, and the newspapers were hammering me, and the priests and the ministers were hammering me, but I am alive yet. I am still here, hammering them, and so I marched them along until I got them in Jersey City.

I sent some one over to New York to ask the chief of police if he would give me protection for the children, and he was a military fellow, the commissioner, and the chief was away, and he said, "No; you can't come into New York." Well, I concluded I would show him whether I could or not, and I went over myself and asked him if he had any reason, and he said, "Yes"; but he would not give it to me. "Very well," I said, "I will take it to the mayor." And Low was mayor of New York at that time. He evidently knew I was coming, because the usher said that the mayor would see me directly. I said, "All right." In a few minutes the mayor came in, and I told him my business, and he said, "Mother Jones, I had to sustain the commissioner's decision." "Do you have to, mayor?" "Yes." And I said, "I don't see why New York pays an understrapper, if the other man does the business." He just kind of looked down and said nothing.

I said, "Mayor Low, have you a reason?" And he said, "Yes." "You won't object to giving it to me?" And he said, "No"; and I said, "Perhaps we can clear it up."

The reason was, I was not a citizen of New York, nor neither were those children. "Is that your chief reason?" He said, "Yes." "Well, I think I can clear that up, Mayor Low. I think we will straighten that out immediately. Sometime last summer there came over here a piece of royalty from Germany, and the United States voted $45,000 to fill that fellow's stomach for three weeks. And President Roosevelt hired a massage doctor to rub him down so he could get back. Was he a citizen of New York," I says. "No," he says, "he was not." "Did he ever create any wealth for this nation?" "Well, no," he said. And I says, "We did. Don't I have the same right to come in here that he had?" He says, "Yes." So I went in and I got my children all in, and we had a big meeting that night and the police took care of us, and the captain says, "Mother," he says, "you need never go to the chief or the mayor or to anybody else when you want to come in; you come to me and it will be all right."

So my children did have a meeting and we raised $3,000 or $4,000 or $5,000 for the strikers; and I took my children down and took them down to Boston Bay, and Boston came and took them children and showed them the elephants and everything; and they never had seen anything like it.

Now, the reporters were all going to Oyster Bay, and they blocked my job, and I wanted to see the president, so I telephoned Senator Platt[20] to give me assistant; and he said, "All right, Mother." And I went down. Well, you know this Oriental Hotel, and that is where the robbers of Wall Street go to roost through the summer. So I took the children and went down there, and I had my little band, and they had every place blockaded. You can't step on that sacred ground without there is an officer after you. And I went to a section man, and I says, "How am I going to get in to them fellows?" He says, "I don't know. You can't go in at the door?"

"Well, no; the thing is so guarded I can't get in." He says, "Well, I don't know, Mother." "Well, I want to go in with these children, and I want breakfast." And he says, "There is only one way to get in there, and that is through the saloon. And if the saloon keeper lets you in there, you can get in." "Do you know him?" "Yes," he said "I know him; yes." "Well," I says, "come on down with me, and I will get you a drink." And you can always buy an Irishman a drink. And so we went to the saloon and went in, and I says to the saloon keeper, I says, "Can I go in to see them pirates today with these children?" And he says, "Yes." And so I took the children and went in, and the children had a little band, and so they sang, "Hail, hail, the gang's all here." Well, that bunch all got up and ran away and went upstairs; the men and

439

women; and the hotel gave us our breakfast, and we all had good things, and the children had never had any such breakfast. The cook fixed it up. You know, he was a miner cook, and he fixed up everything; and the little ones went off happy.

Well, I went down to Oyster Bay, and the reporters didn't know where I was going, and I got in and didn't see no one of the secret-service men; and I thought I would go up and see President Roosevelt about having passed that bill; and when I got up to go there, he put secret-service men all the way from his house down to Oyster Bay to prevent the children coming up there. He had a lot of secret-service men watching an old woman and an army of children. You fellows do elect wonderful presidents. The best thing you can do is to put a woman in the next time, and she will do it.[21]

Well, that ends that now, and I will not take up any more time; but before I close I have got a letter here. I will have to look it over carefully. It relates to the murder of one of the deputies in Utah. The morning after they had arrested all the men these fellows came along, three of them, and I only had a stone to fasten my door, and I heard the footsteps coming, and I jumped to my feet, and this fellow opened the door and pushed the stone in, and he came in, and he put his gun under my jaw and his finger on the gun, and he says, "Now, if you don't tell me where I will get $3,000 of the miners' money I will blow your brains out." He was one of the sworn deputies that arrested the miners the day before. And I said, "Well, wait a while; I will tell you about these brains; let's talk that over first. You need not waste a lot of powder on these brains. If you blow my brains out yours and mine will not mix. So, save your powder." "Now, where is it? Give it to me. I don't want any talk; and," says he, "I won't have it." And I says, "There are one or two good fellows up in Indianapolis that have the money in the bank." And he says, "hasn't the secretary got any money?" And I says, "Yes; but he pays every bill with checks." "Haven't you got any money?" "Yes." "Get it out," he says. "I want it." So I took out 50 cents. That is all I had. And he says, "Is this all the money you have got?" "That is all I have here, and I am not going to give it to you." He says, "You won't give it to me?" I says, "No; I want it myself, because I have got the Gould smallpox, and when I get out I want to get a jag on and boil it out of my system, so I won't inoculate the nation." So the fellow finally went off. And he was killed afterwards for bank wrecking in Utah. Now, that is —

Chairman Walsh (Interrupting): Let me suggest, Mrs. Jones, that you submit that into the record.

Mother Jones: All right.

Chairman Walsh: I don't want to hurry you, but Mr. Weinstock[22] said he had a question.

Mother Jones: Well, all right, Mr. Weinstock; go to it now. But I want you to understand now, Mr. Weinstock, before you go to it, I am

440

not an educated woman; you are, and I am not.

(The matter referred to will be found among the exhibits printed at the end of this subject as "Jones Exhibit.")

Commissioner Weinstock: In your statement yesterday, among other things you told about the experiences you had, I think, in the vicinity of Greensburg.

Mother Jones: Yes, Pennsylvania.

Commissioner Weinstock: And there was some one with you on a street car or a railroad car, and you wanted to get off?

Mother Jones: A street car.

Commissioner Weinstock: And the conductor refused to let you off?

Mother Jones: No; you have that wrong, Mr. Weinstock. The conductor never refused to let me off; it was the women and the babies. The judge had sentenced them to 30 days in jail. I would not let them women leave their babies behind, so they got on the street car, and when we got to a station there were three or four scabs got on the car, and the women were going to jail, and they had a certain resentment against those scabs because they go in and take their bread.

Now, Mr. Weinstock, remember we strikers are striking for a better condition for all, whether they are union men and women or nonunion; they are all workers anyhow; but they make the fight and they raise the wages of the nonunion mother as well as the union one. We are in a conference you know.

So these women were a little irritated when they saw those scabs get on, and they gave me the babies, and I took the babies; I think I had four or five of them in my arms and another bunch of them around me, and they went and lampooned those scabs, and the scabs began to holler. There were two of the constabulary there, but they were nice boys and they didn't meddle; I think they were a little leery of what was going to happen; and I would not let the street car motorman stop to let those men off until he got to a regular station. They were hollering, "Stop the car," and the motorman got a little nervous, too, and I said, "Now, you don't stop that car; it is against the law, and you must obey the law."

Commissioner Weinstock: That is the point I wanted you to refresh my memory on. You called attention to the fact that they must obey and respect the law.

Mother Jones: Yes, the motorman; he had no right to stop the car there; it was an interurban car.

Commissioner Weinstock: I take it from that, Mother Jones, that you are an advocate of law and order and would insist on people obeying the law and respecting it?

Mother Jones: I certainly do, but when the law jumps all over my class and there is no law for my class, and it is only for the other fellow, then I want to educate my people so as to put my people on the bench. I don't know whether you are a lawyer or not?

Commissioner Weinstock: I am not, Mother Jones; I am glad of it. I am a plain, everyday business man.

Mother Jones: I am glad of it.

Commissioner Weinstock: From what you have explained, Mother Jones, it is evident that some explanation is needed. There appears in the record of the congressional committee a copy of which I have here, setting for a hearing before a subcommittee of the Committee on Mines and Mining of the House of Representatives, a statement attributed to you, which evidently is a mistake, and does you a grave injustice, and I think you should be afforded an opportunity at this hearing for the purposes of our record to correct it.

(This is entered here as Operators' Exhibit No. 105, "Address made by Mother Jones, delivered before the convention in Trinidad, Colo., on Tuesday the sixteenth day of September, 1913.")

Among other things you are alleged to have said, speaking, I think, of some labor trouble in West Virginia:

We told him we lived in America beneath the flag for which our fathers fought; that we lived in the United States, and we had a right and had a ground to fight on; and we asked the governor to abolish the Baldwin guards. That was the chief thing I was after, and I tell you the truth, because I knew when we cleaned them out other things would come with it.

So I said in the article we will give the governor until 8 o'clock tomorrow evening to get rid of the Baldwin guards, and if he don't do business we will do business. I called the committee, and I said, "Here, take this document and go into the governor's office and present it to him. Now, don't get on your knees; you don't need to get on your knees; we have no kings in America; stand on both feet, with your heads erect, and present that document to the governor." And they said, "Will we wait?" I said, "No, don't wait, and don't say, 'your honor,' said I, because few of those fellows have any honor and don't know what it is.

When we adjourned the meeting and saw we were not going to get any help, I said, "We will protect ourselves and buy every gun in Charleston." There was not a gun left in Charleston; and we did it openly, no underhanded business about it, for I don't believe in it at all. We simply got our guns and ammunition and walked down into the camps, and the fight began.

Now, as one who believes in law and order and obeying the law, there must be some mistake, or you were misquoted, and this is an opportunity for you to correct it.

Mother Jones: I am going to tell you about that. I made that speech, not in Trinidad, but on the steps of the statehouse in Charleston.[23] The strike was not on very long — three or four months, I think three months — and I did so, and the governor stood there, and the whole statehouse administration was there. When I said, "We demand of the governor to abolish the Baldwin guards," I did so; I don't deny it. I don't believe in any such brutal combination; they are a disgrace to our nation; they violate every law; they teach the coming children to be lawbreakers, brutes, and murderers, and for that I am strictly opposed to those armies. And I would say, Mr. Weinstock, that I would ask this government and ask this commission to demand of Congress that she pass a bill that the government take over all of those detective agencies and run them on an honorable basis.

I don't believe — I have had more experience with those people than any other one person in America and I have never seen one of them hurt. I could have had all those deputies and sheriffs murdered that morning down at Half Way, in Utah, if I had just said one word to those men the night before, but that would not settle the disease; the disease still remained. The disease lies in the private ownership of my bread, and one class of men can say how much I shall eat and how much my children shall eat. I stand for a better citizenship, and I stand for law and have stood for law, and in all my career it can be proven, the records of the courts, police, and county, and everywhere can be searched, and there has never been a charge against me; I am always in favor of obeying the law; but if the high-class burglar breaks the law and defies it, then I say we will have a law that will defend the nation and our people, for whenever a nation undertakes to crush her producers and to debase and dehumanize them, that nation is going over the breakers; it is the history of all nations down the stairway of time. In fifty years we have created more wealth than any other nation in the world has done in 700 years, and one group owns that wealth and the masses of people are impoverished.

I am for schools. I said to the governor of West Virginia, "If you had taken that $700,000 that you spent to crush my class, the miners, and put it into the schoolrooms of the state, and given to the nation a more highly developed citizenship, morally, physically, and mentally, it would have been more valuable to the Nation. I saw the schooldoors closed on the children, and for many of them never to open again. Many of them had to go out and struggle for bread, and many were made criminals and idiots, and if that money, that $700,000 that was put into the militia, to crush my class, had been put into the schoolrooms we would have had less use for law.

Commissioner Weinstock: There is no change to be made in that statement?

Mother Jones: No; that can stay. I will tell you how that came to be put into the record. They had a little two-by-four lawyer in Charleston, and he made up a job with the coal company's lawyer to run that in, so that he could get it on me, and the miners are paying him $7,500 a year for doing nothing, only incarcerating them, and I am going to put a stop to that thing.

Am I through? I am tired.

Commissioner Weinstock: You know the purposes that this commission is created for, Mother Jones — that is, that Congress expects this commission to come back to it with recommendations for remedial legislation. Now, if you were a member of the commission, Mother Jones, what would you recommend to Congress to remedy the condition that you complain of?

Mother Jones: I will tell you, as I stated before we got to discussing this question, you and I, I was not an educated woman; I belong to the classes. I should recommend to Congress that they should do away with all of these arms and detective agencies, because they create crime. They are criminals.

Commissioner Weinstock: That is, to do away with the gunmen?

Mother Jones: And these detective agencies; let the government run their agencies, and you will have less trouble, less crime, less penitentiary subjects, and you will have better manhood and better womanhood. I have a great deal to tell the commission, but it is unnecessary; but you see, Mr. Weinstock, we have spent years in the past, we are an infant in the history of nations yet, practically speaking. Now, we have spent our years following our birth inventing machinery, building railroads, telephones, telegraphs, and everything else, and we are reaching a stage where these inventions are taking the place of labor. There must be something done by the national government to relieve this discontent, because we have armies of unemployed. Last Sunday I addressed a large meeting down here in Pennsylvania. It was the glass industry, where a thousand men were employed. The machine came in and threw the whole thousand of skilled mechanics out — ten men are doing the work of 1,000, and it is so in many other industries.[24]

Now, Mr. Weinstock, we had a federal commission fifteen years ago. I think Mr. O'Connell remembers that. That commission went through this nation; it made some of the finest recommendations that could be made to Congress.[25] Those recommendations lie up in the archives of this nation, and I venture to say in the last fifteen years not twelve Congressmen have read them. Now, you see, you had an investigation in Colorado; one whole year passed away, and two days before Congress closed they brought that up on the floor of the House. They had an investigation in Michigan that they never brought up at all. What good are the investigations if the public don't know what is happening in the country? My advice, and I give it to the workers when I speak to them is, when you send a man to the Senate or Congress or to the legislature, when he comes home have a platform at the depot, and make that representative tell you what he has done for the best interests of the nation, and render an account of himself right then and there, and then you will not have so many congressmen fighting for bills for the protection of 26 Broadway and other institutions like that.

Am I through?

Commissioner Weinstock: Your recommendation, then, briefly, is this — I want to make sure that I understand it thoroughly — that the remedy for industrial unrest would be to wipe out the detective agencies?

Mother Jones: That is only one step. Now, I believe in taking over the mines, Mr. Weinstock. They are mineral, and no operator, no coal company on the face of the earth made that coal. It is a mineral; it belongs to the nation; and was there down the ages, and it belongs to every generation that comes along, and no set of men should be permitted to use that which is nature's. It should be given to all of nature's children in other nations.

Commissioner Weinstock: Then your remedy would be public ownership of the mines?

Mother Jones: All other industries, and then we can get the hours of labor down and put men to work. I also believe in the ownership of the transportation lines. I don't want to put you out of a job, Mr. Aishton.

Chairman Walsh: We thank you, Mrs. Jones; and you will be excused permanently.

Jones Exhibit

Sketch of life of C. L. Maxwell, better known as "Gunplay" Maxwell, outlaw, ex-convict, deputy sheriff, and mine guard for Utah Fuel Co. Killed at Price, Utah, August 25, 1909.

In June 1900, Maxwell and two of his gang held up and robbed the bank at Springville, Utah, killing the cashier. In the pursuit that followed one of the bank robbers was killed, and Maxwell and a companion named Warner were captured. They were sentenced to a term in prison at Salt Lake City.

Maxwell, being of good address and having a good education, soon gained the confidence and good will of the warden, who gave Maxwell unusual liberties.

On account of the liberties afforded him Maxwell had opportunities to communicate with other prisoners, and he planned to break jail and take a number of the most desperate ones with him, among them being Warner, his pal. The governor of Utah and the prison trustees had arranged to visit the prison on a tour of inspection, and Maxwell, knowing this, planned the break for that day. Now, here is where Maxwell's true character is shown. He went to the warden of the prison and told him that the prisoners were plotting to escape, and that his old pal, Warner, was the leader of the gang. After giving the warden the details of the plot as he had planned it, the warden concluded to let the plan go on, as if he was not aware of it, but he took extra precaution to prevent the plan from succeeding.

The governor and the board arrived as per their program, and when Warner and the others made their break for freedom they were promptly overpowered. Maxwell was brought before the governor, and for his loyalty and good conduct in exposing the plot he was pardoned. Maxwell then went to Helper, where he engaged in gambling, and being a bad man in general, in 1903 and 1904 he was hired by the Utah Fuel Co. as a mine guard and held a commission as a deputy sheriff for some time.

In 1907 he shot L. C. Reidel, a coal miner, at Helper. He was never prosecuted for this.

In 1906 Tom Kelter, a conductor on the Denver & Rio Grande Railroad, was elected sheriff of Carbon County, and he made up his mind to get rid of "Gunplay" Maxwell. Maxwell had organized a gang and was hanging around Helper. Sheriff Kelter learned of a plan of Maxwell's to rob the bank at Green River on July 9, and work on his counterplot began at once. He came to Salt Lake and engaged Ed Johnson as deputy, and also engaged John MacQuarrie, another deputy, of unquestioned courage and skill with a gun.

In his plan to rob the bank Maxwell had enlisted the aid of five men, four of whom were known to the officers.

The plans of Sheriff Kelter and his deputies to capture the gang were spoiled by an accomplice of Maxwell's now living in Green River, who warned Maxwell that a close watch was being kept, and that their plans were probably known.

Maxwell left for Ogden, where he remained with his second wife, Mrs. W. H. Seman, as she calls herself. Funds were apparently low, as Maxwell pawned the woman's jewels, on which he realized nearly $400, before starting for Carbon County again. This time he planned to hold up the paymaster of the Kenilworth mine.

On Saturday afternoon, when they paymaster rode through Spring Glen on his way to Kenilworth, he was accompanied by a strong guard under the leadership of MacQuarrie and Johnson. Maxwell and a partner were provided with horses and hidden behind a shack along the road near the water tank halfway to Kenilworth when the paymaster and his guards passed. They sized up the party and evidently concluded that it was too big for them, allowing the men to pass, believing they had not been seen. Maxwell's partner on this occasion was a heavy built man who is not known in the vicinity of Price.

About ten days ago C.E. Davies, who has been implicated with Maxwell in a number of "expeditions," and who was ordered to leave the country for his connection with Maxwell when the bandit shot L. C. Reidel at Helper two years ago, appeared at Price and began making inquiries concerning Sheriff Kelter and his "gunmen" deputies, naming MacQuarrie and Johnson. Davies remarked that he had heard that both MacQuarrie and Johnson were bad men with guns, but that Maxwell would be in Price on Thursday and make short work of Kelter and his gunmen.

On Monday morning, the day he met his death, Maxwell appeared in Price, saying he had walked in from a sheep camp. He immediately began to load up on Price whisky, telling what a bad man he was with a gun. To demonstrate his fierceness, he accosted two traveling men, and at the point of his revolver he compelled them to enter a saloon and buy drinks. Sheriff Kelter ordered his deputies to arrest Maxwell, and when the deputies approached him Maxwell said to Johnson: "You are the —— I'm after," at the same time pulling his gun.

Johnson and MacQuarrie fired at the same time, the balls from their guns entering Maxwell's breast and going clear through his body. The ball from Maxwell's gun went through the lapel of Johnson's coat. Men who were watching the affair from across the railroad track saw the dust fly from his coat and saw the tear in his back as the bullets passed through his body, and also the spatter of dust as the spent balls were embedded in the ground.

[64th Congress, Senate Document No. 415, Final Report and Testimony Submitted to Congress by the Commission on Industrial Relations Created by the Act of August 23, 1912, *Washington, 1916, vol. XI, pp. 10618-45, 10917-19.]*

Notes

1. The three labor members of the commission were conservative labor leaders — John B. Lennon and James O'Connell, A.F. of L. vice-presidents, and Austin Garretson of the Railroad Brotherhoods. Social workers and liberal intellectuals criticized President Wilson for having refused to appoint a representative of Socialist trade unions and/or the I.W.W. Gompers, however, insisted that only conservative labor be represented on the commission and his view won.

For the McNamara Case and the creation of the United States Commission on Industrial Relations, *see* Philip S. Foner, *History of the Labor Movement in the United States,* vol. 5, New York, 1980, pp. 7-31; Father John S. Smith, M.A., "Organized Labor in the Wilson Era, 1913-1921," unpublished Ph.D. thesis, Catholic University of America, 1962, pp. 36-42. For a summary of the commission's work and its recommendations, *see* Graham Adams, Jr., *Age of Industrial Violence 1910-15: Activities and Findings of the U.S. Commission on Industrial Relations,* New York, 1966.

2. *New York Times,* May 14, 1915.

3. Mother Jones sat in the audience during the testimony of several witnesses who testified on the Colorado strike, especially John D. Rockefeller, Jr.

4. The strike began in Martinsburg, West Virginia, July 16, 1877, and not Martinsburg, Ohio. Martinsburg was the center of extensive repair shops and terminus of one of the regular divisions of the Baltimore & Ohio Railroad. (*See* Philip S. Foner, *The Great Labor Uprising of 1877,* New York, 1977, pp. 33-35.)

5. Actually, many groups were involved in the crowd actions in Pittsburgh, although Mother Jones was correct in emphasizing the hatred for the railroads among businessmen. (*See* Foner, *Great Uprising,* 29-30, 50-64.)

6. The reference is to William B. Wilson.

7. *See above* pp. 77-78.

8. *See above* pp. 405-7.

9. The "Lattimer Massacre," one of the most cold-blooded crimes against the

working class in American labor history, occurred on September 10, 1897, during the great coal strike.

10. Patrick Henry (1736-1799) was a Virginia delegate to the Continental Congress in which he served from 1774 to 1776 and was one of the signers of the Declaration of Independence.

11. The coal strike of 1900 occurred in the midst of the presidential campaign of 1900, and Mark Hanna, Republican political boss as well as president of the National Civic Federation, played an important role in bringing about a settlement. See pp. 54, 83.

12. For Senator Elkins, see pp. 191, 221, 389.

13. For the speech referred to, see pp. 193-205.

14. John B. Lennon was president of the Journeymen Tailors' International Union and member of the A.F. of L. Executive Council.

15. The reference is to Cora (Mrs. Fremont) Older, wife of the editor of the *San Francisco Bulletin* and an important magazine writer in her own right. Older came to West Virginia in 1913 to investigate the grounds for the imprisonment of Mother Jones and forty-eight miners by the military. In articles in *Collier's* and the *Independent,* Older revealed that the military's provost marshal was also the Associated Press correspondent and was withholding news of Mother Jones's confinement and trial. (*See* Cora Older, "Answering a Question," *Collier's,* April 19, 1913, pp. 26-27, and "The Last Days of the Paint Creek Court Martial," *Independent,* May 15, 1913, pp. 184-87.)

16. 26 Broadway was the address of the Standard Oil Company and other Rockefeller interests and it was where John D. Rockefeller, Jr. had his office.

17. *See* pp. 239, 383.

18. Lawson was accused of murdering John Nimmo, one of the deputies paid by the companies and appointed by the sheriff. No effort was made to prove that Lawson had fired the fatal shot. He was sentenced to life imprisonment at hard labor, and after a nationwide protest movement, in which Mother Jones participated, his conviction was overturned on appeal. Commenting on his conviction, the Commission on Industrial Relations declared: "It is anarchism for profits and revenge, and it menaces the security and integrity of American institutions as they seldom have been menaced before." (63rd Cong., 3rd Sess., *House Document 136,* Washington, D.C., 1915, *Report on the Colorado Strike Investigation,* p. 22.)

19. *See above* pp. 100-5, 167, 213, 219, 438-39, for the incidents discussed in this and other paragraphs that follow.

20. Thomas Collier Platt (1833-1910), U.S. Congressman and Senator from New York who became a powerful Republican leader and known as "Boss" Platt. He was largely responsible for the election of Theodore Roosevelt as governor of New York in 1898.

21. Here again is an example of Mother Jones's contradictory views towards women's participation in politics.

22. Colonel Harris Weinstock was one of the three members of the public on the commission. A Californian, he had headed the investigation of the brutal treatment of I.W.W. free-speech fighters during the San Diego Free Speech Fight of 1912. Although he was critical of many of the I.W.W.'s general principles and specific practices, and particularly attacked its free-speech tactics, Weinstock vigorously condemned San Diego's police, and other officials, its press, and its leading citizens for brutal violations of the constitutional rights and civil liberties of the free-speech fighters. (*See* Philip S. Foner, *History of the*

Labor Movement in the United States, vol. 4, New York, 1965, pp. 199-200.)

23. *See* pp. 193-205 for the speech referred to.

24. The same year, 1915, the *International Molders' Journal* observed: "There is no body of skilled workmen today safe from one or other of these forces — the introduction of machinery and the standardization of tools, materials, products, and process, which make production possible on a larger scale, and the specialization of workmen — tending to deprive them of their unique craft knowledge and skill. Only what may termed frontier trades are dependent now on the all-around craftsman. These trades are likely at any time to be standardized and systematized and to fall under the influence of this double process of specialization." (51 (1915): 197-98.)

25. In 1901 the U.S. government published the *Report of the Industrial Commission on the Relations and Conditions of Capital and Labor Employed in Manufactures (including testimony taken up to November, 1900). See* especially volume VII. It is this investigation and report Mother Jones was referring to.

ARTICLES

Civilization in Southern Mills

The miners and railroad boys of Birmingham, Alabama, entertained me one evening some months ago with a graphic description of the conditions among the slaves of the Southern cotton mills. While I imagined that these must be something of a modern Siberia, I concluded that the boys were overdrawing the picture and made up my mind to see for myself the conditions described. Accordingly I got a job and mingled with the workers in the mill and in their homes. I found that children of six and seven years of age were dragged out of bed at half-past 4 in the morning when the task-master's whistle blew. They eat their scanty meal of black coffee and corn bread mixed with cotton-seed oil in place of butter, and then off trots the whole army of serfs, big and little. By 5:30 they are all behind the factory walls, where amid the whir of machinery they grind their young lives out of four-teen long hours each day. As one looks on this brood of helpless human souls one could almost hear their voices cry out, "Be still a moment, O you iron wheels of capitalistic greed, and let us hear each other's voices, and let us feel for a moment that this is not all of life."

We stopped at 12 for a scanty lunch and a half-hour's rest. At 12:30 we were at it again with never a stop until 7. Then a dreary march home, where we swallowed our scanty supper, talked for a few minutes of our misery and then dropped down upon a pallet of straw, to lie until the whistle should once more awaken us, summoning babes and all alike to another round of toil and misery.

I have seen mothers take their babes and slap cold water in their face to wake the poor little things. I have watched them all day long tending the dangerous machinery. I have seen their helpless limbs torn off, and then when they were disabled and of no more use to the master, thrown out to die. I must give the company credit for having hired a Sunday school teacher to tell the little things that "Jesus put it into the heart of Mr. — to build that factory so they would have work with which to earn a little money to enable them to put a nickel in the box for the poor little heathen Chinese babies."

The Rope Factory

I visited the factory in Tuscaloosa, Alabama, at 10 o'clock at night. The superintendent, not knowing my mission, gave me the entire freedom of the factory and I made good use of it. Standing by a siding that contained 155 spindles were two little girls. I asked a man standing near if the children were his, and he replied that they were. "How old are they?" I asked. "This one is nine, the other ten," he replied. "How many hours do they work?" "Twelve," was the answer. "How much do they get a night?" "We all three together get sixty cents. They get ten cents each and I forty."

I watched them as they left their slave pen in the morning and saw them gather their rags around their frail forms to hide them from the wintry blast. Half-fed, half-clothed, half-housed, they toil on, while the poodle dogs of their masters are petted and coddled and sleep on pillows of down, and the capitalistic judges jail the agitators that would dare to help these helpless ones to better their condition.

Gibson is another of those little sections of hell with which the South is covered. The weaving of gingham is the principal work. The town is owned by a banker who possesses both people and mills. One of his slaves told me she had received one dollar for her labor for one year. Every weekly pay day her employer gave her a dollar. On Monday she deposited that dollar in the "pluck-me" store to secure food enough to last until the next pay day, and so on week after week.

There was once a law on the statute books of Alabama prohibiting the employment of children under twelve years of age more than eight hours each day. The Gadston Company would not build their mill until they were promised that this law should be repealed.

When the repeal came up for the final reading I find by an examination of the records of the House that there were sixty members present. Of these, fifty-seven voted for the repeal and but three against. To the everlasting credit of young Manning, who was a member of that House, let it be stated that he both spoke and voted against the repeal.

I asked one member of the House why he voted to murder the children, and he replied that he did not think they could earn enough to support themselves if they only worked eight hours. These are the kind of tools the intelligent working men put in office.

The Phoenix mill in Georgia were considering the possibility of a cut in wages something over a year ago, but after making one attempt they reconsidered and started a savings bank instead. At the end of six months the board of directors met and found out that the poor wretches who were creating wealth for them were saving 10 percent of their wages. Whereupon they promptly cut them that 10 percent, and the result was the '96 strike.[1] I wonder how long the American people will remain silent under such conditions as these.

Almost every one of my shop mates in these mills was a victim of some disease or other. All are worked to the limit of existence. The weavers are expected to weave so many yards of cloth each working day. To come short of this estimate jeopardizes their job. The factory operator loses all energy either of body or of mind. The brain is so crushed as to be incapable of thinking, and one who mingles with these people soon discovers that their minds like their bodies are wrecked. Loss of sleep and loss of rest gives rise to abnormal appetites, indigestion, shrinkage of stature, bent backs, and aching hearts.

Such a factory system is one of torture and murder as dreadful as a long drawn-out Turkish massacre, and is a disgrace to any race or age. As the picture rises before me I shudder for the future of a nation that is building up a moneyed aristocracy out of the life-blood of the children of the proletariat. It seems as if our flag is a funeral bandage splotched with blood. The whole picture is one of the most horrible avarice, selfishness, and cruelty and is fraught with present horror and promise of future degeneration. The mother, over-worked and underfed, gives birth to tired and worn-out human beings.

I can see no way out save in a complete overthrow of the capitalistic system, and to me the father who casts a vote for the continuance of that system is as much of a murderer as if he took a pistol and shot his own children. But I see all around me signs of the dawning of the new day of socialism, and with my faithful comrades everywhere I will work and hope and pray for the coming of that better day.

Mother Jones

[International Socialist Review, *vol. I, March 1901, pp. 539-41.*]

Notes

1. Mother Jones may have meant 1898. The most important strike in the southern textile industry up to this time began on November 21, 1898, against all mills in Augusta, Georgia. The workers walked out to protest a wage reduction of from 25 to 40 percent, with "women who were making the smallest wages, cut the most." The employers countered with a lockout. In the end, strikebreakers, evictions of workers from company houses, and starvation defeated the Augusta strike. The strike leaders were not only refused work but blacklisted as well throughout the industry in the South. (Philip S. Foner. *Women and the American Labor Movement: From Colonial Times to the Eve of World War I,* New York, 1979, p. 248.)

2. Launched in 1900, the *International Socialist Review* became the organ of the militant, left-wing forces in the Socialist Party of America.

The Coal Miners of The Old Dominion

A few Sundays ago I attended church in a place called McDonald, on Loop Creek, in West Virginia. In the course of his sermon the preacher gave the following as a conversation that had recently taken place between him and a miner.

"I met a man last week," said the preacher, "who used to be a very good church member. When I asked him what he was doing at the present time he said that he was organizing his fellow craftsmen of the mines."

Then according to the preacher the following discussion took place:

"What is the object of such a union?" asked the preacher.

"To better our condition," replied the miner.

"But the miners are in a prosperous condition now."

"There is where we differ."

"Do you think you will succeed?"

"I am going to try."

Commenting on this conversation to his congregation the preacher said: "Now I question if such a man can meet with any success. If he were only a college graduate he might be able to teach these miners something and in this way give them light, but as the miners of this creek are in a prosperous condition at the present time I do not see what such a man can do for them."

Yet this man was professing to preach the doctrines of the Carpenter of Nazareth.

Let us compare his condition with that of the "prosperous" miners and perhaps we can see why he talked as he did.

At this same service he read his report for the previous six months. For his share of the wealth these miners had produced during the time he had received $847.67, of which $45 had been given for missionary purposes.

Besides receiving this money he had been frequently wined and dined by the mine operators and probably had a free pass on the railroad.

What had he done for the miners during this time. He had spoken to them twenty-six times, for which he received $32.41 a talk, and if they were all like the one I heard he was at no expense either in time, brains or money to prepare them.

During all this time the "prosperous" miners were working ten hours a day beneath the ground amid poisonous gases and crumbling rocks. If they were fortunate enough to be allowed to toil every working day throughout the year they would have received in return for 3,080 hours of most exhausting toil less than $400.

Jesus, whose doctrines this man claimed to be preaching, took twelve men from among the laborers of his time (no college graduates among them) and with them founded an organization that revolutionized the society amid which it rose. Just so in our day the organization of the workers must be the first step to the overthrow of capitalism.

Then my mind turns to the thousands of "trap boys," with no sunshine ever coming into their lives.[1] These children of the miners put in fourteen hours a day beneath the ground for sixty cents, keeping their lone watch in the tombs of the earth with never a human soul to speak to them. The only sign of life around them is when the mules come down with coal. Then as they open the trap doors to let the mules out a gush of cold air rushes in chilling their little bodies to the bone. Standing in the wet mud up to their knees there are times when they are almost frozen and when at last late at night they are permitted to come out into God's fresh air they are sometimes so exhausted that they have to be carried to the corporation shack they call a home.

The parents of these boys have known no other life than that of endless toil. Now those who have robbed and plundered the parents are beginning the same story with the present generation. These boys are sometimes not more than nine or ten years of age. Yet in the interests of distant bond and stockholders these babes must be imprisoned through the long, beautiful daylight in the dark and dismal caverns of the earth.

Savage cannibals at least put their victim out of his misery before beginning their terrible meal, but the cannibals of today feast their poodle dogs at the seashore upon the life blood of these helpless children of the mines. A portion of this blood-stained plunder goes to the support of educational incubators called universities, that hatch out just such ministerial fowls as the one referred to.

The very miner with whom this minister had been talking had been blacklisted up and down the creek for daring to ask for a chance to let his boy go to school instead of into the mines. This miner could have told the minister more about the great industrial tragedy in the midst of which he was living, in five minutes than all his college training had taught him

*　　*　　*

At the bidding of these same stock and bondholders, often living in a foreign land, the school houses of Virginia are closed to those who built them and to whom they belong by every right. The miners pay the taxes, build the school, and support the officers, but if they dare to even stand upon the school house steps a snip of a mine boss comes along with pistol in hand and orders them off. " — free speech," said one of them to me when I protested, "we do not need any free speech. You get off the earth." Not only the school rooms, but every church or public hall is locked against us. On every school board you will find at least one company clerk or mining boss, and it is the business of this henchman of the mine owners to see to it that the school buildings are not used for public meetings by the miners.

Yet these same school buildings are used by the operators for any kind of meeting they choose and any demoralizing, degrading show that comes along has free access to them, as well as all political meetings of the old capitalist parties. But when the labor agitator, or trade union organizer comes along trying to make it possible for the miner's children to go to school, the school houses are tightly closed.

*　　*　　*

In some of these camps the miners are forced to pay as much as $9 a barrel for flour, 14 cents a pound for sugar, 18 cents a pound for fat pork, and $8 to $10 a month rent for a company shack, the roof of which is so poor that when it rains the bed is moved from place to place in the attempt to find a dry spot. Many a miner works his whole life and never handles a cent of money. All he earns must be spent in the "Pluck me." Every miner has one dollar stopped for a company doctor. With 1,200 men working in a mine and a young doctor paid $300 a year, this means a nice little lump for the company. And this is the Divine system the preacher was defending.

*　　*　　*

In the closing hours of the baby year of the twentieth century I stood on the soil that gave birth to a Patrick Henry who could say, "Give me liberty or give me death," and a Jefferson, the truth of whose prophecy that the greatest tyranny and danger to American liberty would come from the judges on the bench, has been so often shown in these last few years. I had just left West Virginia with all its horrors, and as I was whirled along on the railroad I wondered if when I stood on the soil stained with the blood of so many Revolutionary heroes, I would once more really breathe the air of freedom.

Well, this is the first breath I received. I arrived in the northern part of Wise County, Virginia, over the L&N RR, to find a message waiting me from the superintendent of the mines saying that if I came down to the Dorcas mines to talk to the miners of his company he would shoot me. I told him to shoot away, and that I did not propose to be scared out by the growling of any English bulldog of capitalism.

Here is the oath which every miner is forced to take before he can go into a mine or get an opportunity to live.[2] (The name of the miner is omitted for obvious reasons.)

"I, John Brown, a Justice of the Peace, in and for the County of Wise and State of Virginia, do hereby certify that —— has this day personally appeared before and made statement on oath, that he would not in any way aid or abet the labor organization, known as the United Mine Workers of America, or any other labor organization calculated to bring about trouble between the Virginia Iron, Coal and Coke Company, and its employes, in or near the vicinity of

458

Tom's Creek, Wise Co., Virginia.

"Witness my hand and seal, this the 19th day of Dec., 1901.

— J. P.

Yet men who call themselves civilized will continue to vote for a system that breeds such slavery as this and will join in the cry of the mine owners, against letting "Mother Jones circulate that Socialist literature." For such people it is the worst of crimes to let these poor slaves know that any other state of things is possible.

This superintendent should remember that the shooting of John Brown did not stop the onward march of the Civil War and the emancipation of the blacks, and should know that the shooting of Mother Jones will never stop the onward march of the United Mine Workers toward the goal of emancipation of the white slaves from capitalistic oppression. The laborers will move onward in their work until every child has an opportunity to enjoy God's bright sunlight and until some Happy New Year shall bring to every toiler's home the joyful news of freedom from all masters.

"Mother" Jones

[International Socialist Review, vol. II, January 1902, pp. 575-78.]

Notes

1. For a discussion of the boys working in the mines, *see* pp. 92-93, 94.
2. The original of this document is on file at this office. — Editor, *International Socialist Review.*

Oh! Ye Lovers of Liberty!

Brothers and Comrades: From the bastile of capitalism in Los Angeles comes the cry of our brave brothers, calling on you to stand for freedom, right and justice.[1] I know and feel that the cries will not be in vain. You responded cheerfully to the needs of our comrades of the industrial revolution as they were voiced from Idaho,[2] and I know you will be none the less responsive now, in behalf of our Mexican comrades.

If ever there was a time in history when it was imperative that men and women should promptly rally to the banner of freedom and justice, that time is now. Before, it was the power of the state and the nation that the capitalists were using for the destruction of the working class.

Now, it is the United States government seconding the murderous despotism of Russia and the irresponsible dictatorship of Mexico. The fight has become international; yet it centers in the United States. If these foreign vultures of oppression win now, then our liberty goes.

For Diaz and American capitalism are partners, even as American capitalism and the Russian czar are partners. Pierpont Morgan goes to Russia and shakes hands with the czar; and now the czar comes to America demanding the surrender of political refugees. Mrs. Diaz, when visiting in Texas is entertained by members of the Copper Queen syndicate whose headquarters are at 95 John Street, New York, and Elihu Root, of New York,[3] is wined and dined by the tyrant dictator, Diaz, when in Mexico.

This tyrant, this fiend, beside whom King George was a gentleman and lover of the poor, has given to American capitalists concessions that are worth millions of dollars, and guarantees them peon labor that dare not ask higher wages under penalty of being shot for violating the law; and in return he asks that if political refugees escape to America, or if a Mexican dare to come to America and criticise him, they must be returned to him, that they may be shot.

Some sixty years ago the fugitive slave law was enacted, requiring slaves that escaped to free territory be returned to their masters. This was all in the United States of America. Yet the people refused to obey that law and arose in such a mighty protest that within ten years the institution of slavery was swept from the earth. Now we have the dictator of Mexico, and the czar of Russia, tyrants both, both foreigners, trying to enforce a fugitive slave law in the United States of America — a law infinitely more vile than that of the fifties — and the federal government lends its aid to the outrage. It is time that the people arose in all their sovereign power and said their say.

In 1906, two brave leaders of the strike of Cananea, Diegues and Caldrom, were sentenced to fifteen years in a dungeon by the sea.[4] A deserter from the American army, Kosterlitsky, waited with his troops across the border line for any strikers who might be handed over to him by agents of the Standard Oil company, and other reptile combinations. Already the prisons of Mexico are filled with men who were merely suspicioned of favoring the strikers, while the children of the victims are left to struggle and starve.

I happened to be in Douglas, Ariz., in August, 1907, when they kidnapped young Sarabia, threw him into an automobile, and, as he screamed for help, muzzled him, ran him across the line, and handed him over to the devourers of human flesh.[5] Kidnapping seems to be becoming very fashionable with the members of the American oligarchy of wealth.

In this connection I wish to say a good word for Governor Kibbie, who took quick action and had Sarabia brought back. He also would not furnish troops to the Copper Queen company during the strike at

Bisbee, Ariz. He had a clear view of the economic conflict, and understood that it was not labor that was riotous, but the minions of capitalism. During my stay in Arizone I also had the pleasure of meeting Captain Wheeler on several occasions, and believe he wants to do as nearly right as the powers that be will permit him. I must give him credit for the part he played in the strike at Bisbee. Yet, after doing full justice to all who deserve credit, the fact remains that the federal government is allied with the masters of the big corporations in trying to enforce international absolutism and to make slaves of the workers who shall be unable to escape their chains.

All honor to you, my brave comrades, Magon, Villarreal and Rivera, for the gallant fight you are making for human liberty. In days to come your names will be inscribed on the temple of liberty. When the wolves of capitalism shall have disappeared from the cities of our nation, when men shall be able to walk forth free without Oscar Lawlers and detectives dogging their footsteps, then the three Mexican comrades shall have their names written large as lovers of their race.

But let me ask you, Attorney Lawler, of Los Angeles, if you can reconcile your conscience to the crushing out of liberty and the human desire for justice. The class you represent has murdered and oppressed men, women and children in the interests of cursed greed. They have jailed the men who fed them; they have maligned us, villified us, buried us in dungeons, hung us on scaffolds, chopped us to pieces, nailed us to the cross of profits as they did the Laborer of Palestine nineteen centuries ago. Have you not, Attorney Lawler, of Los Angeles, nursed from your mother's breast the milk of human kindness: Will you stoop to stain your hands with the blood of these four brave lovers of liberty, by handing them over to that brutal dictator called Diaz?

Permit me, Attorney Lawler, of Los Angeles, to serve notice on you and your class that the working people of America are awake. You cannot make them slaves as are the peons of Mexico, slaves of the dictator whom you serve. Let me hand you the edict of the One you pretend to honor — "Thou shalt not kill."

We are serving notice on you. Your dungeons shall yet be turned into club rooms. We want peace, we want justice, we want that which is justly ours. By all that is good and holy we shall have them.

Men of America, women of America, rouse as you never roused before. Wipe from our jurisprudence the infamous fugitive slave law of this later day. Tear from our statute books the modern and most wicked Dred Scott decision[6] which makes of your government a hunter of the oppressed and persecuter of the helpless.

— 1908

[Leaflet in Department of State, NF, case 1741/104, National Archives.]

461

Notes

1. For the issue involved *see* pp. 55, 121, 133.
2. The reference is to the Haywood, Pettibone, Moyer trial of 1906.
3. Elihu Root (1845-1937), Wall Street lawyer associated with the House of Morgan who was U.S. Secretary of War (1899-1904) and Secretary of State (1905-1909). Mother Jones's leaflet was sent to Elihu Root by Willard Simm of Brokport, Maine, on January 22,1909, with the following comment: "Will you kindly give the enclosed clipping a careful reading and your immediate attention. As a citizen of these United States I protest against the giving up of the men named in this article to the tyrant Diaz to be shot or imprisoned. I also protest against those rusian subjects being given up whose only crime is their love of liberty." (Department of State, NF, case 1741/104, National Archives).
4. The Cananea strike of miners was one of the most important outbursts of protest against the policies of the Díaz dictatorship. The mines were owned by the American Colonel William Cornell Greene, and a major grievance of the Mexican miners was the labor practice which favored Americans over Mexicans, especially in housing and wages. The strike was broken by the Mexican army assisted by Rangers from Arizona.
5. *See above* pp. 55, 121, 143-44, 145, 370, 375.
6. The Dred Scott decision, handed down on March 6, 1857, by Chief Justice Roger B. Taney, declared the Missouri Compromise unconstitutionally forbade slavery above 36'30°, and hence Dred Scott was still a slave even though he had been taken into territory made free by the Missouri Compromise. The Supreme Court also advanced the idea that Negroes were not citizens of the United States and that all Negroes, free as well as slaves, had no rights whites had to uphold.

Save Our Heroic Mexican Comrades!

Address from Mother Jones
To the Socialists and Trade Unionists of America

From out of the bastile of capitalism in California and Arizona comes the appeal of our Mexican comrades and brothers, Magon, Villarreal, Rivera, and Sarabia, our Mexican comrades who have been bravely fighting for liberty in Mexico, are behind dungeon bars, the victims of the persecution of the Mexican dictator, aided and abetted by the hirelings of capitalism in the United States.

These valiant defenders of the people's rights are charged with having violated the neutrality laws of this country, a flimsy excuse for their incarceration. The real reason is they espoused the cause of their enslaved people and could not be bribed or intimidated to betray them.

Being driven from their own country by the hounds of the dictator, they went to St. Louis, where they organized the junta of the Mexican liberal party[1] and there began the publication of a paper exposing the whole diabolical conspiracy of the two governments to establish a system of mutual co-operation in the interest of the capitalist class by keeping the Mexican workers in a state of industrial peonage.[2]

The Standard Oil company, the Southern Pacific Railway company, the Philip (sic) Dodge Copper company and others heavily interested in the exploitation of Mexico all feared they would lose their grip if the liberal party should be allowed to rise in that country.

Let it be understood that Mexico today is an absolute despotism. Diaz rules with an iron hand, concealed in a glove of velvet. The heartless old hypocrite smiles his approval of James Creelman's characterization of him as a benevolent and fatherly old ruler.[3] He is fatherly to his subjects in the same sense that Nicholas is the "Little Father" of the wretches whose life-blood the vampire is sucking.

Diaz is surrounded by an army of spies who do his bidding without question. Criticism of his tyranny is treason, followed by imprisonment or death. Never was there a greater sham than the so-called "Republic" of Mexico. The "Republic" is merely an empty shell, a deception, a fraud, "a whited sepulchre filled with dead men's bones."

It is against this blood-stained despotism that our Mexican heroes, who have been lying in our jails these past fifteen months, have made their fight, and they have made it under circumstances which would have appalled and disheartened less resolute and unconquerable spirits.

There is not a doubt that Rockefeller, Morgan, Harriman and other Wall Street pirates are backing up the persecution of these Mexican patriots. They are the holders of Mexican bonds and the owners and exploiters of Mexican interests and they, of course, lend a ready hand to Diaz in keeping his hordes of peons in slavish subjection. Any uprising of the slaves would be a menace to the interests of our American capitalists and that is why the capitalist press is either silent while those outrages are being perpetrated or gives its influence to Diaz in crushing out the spirit of liberty among his subjects.

This crew of commercial pirates dictates to presidents, cabinets and congresses. The house of lords, known as the senate, consists of its special representatives. The courts are its private possession. Governors, legislators and other public officials are all under its domination. Alabama is a recent case in point where the governor proved himself the pliant tool of the plutocracy in crushing the famishing coal miners.

Morgan, the moving spirit among the capitalists and Taft the political instrument of that class, soon to be inaugurated president, were both the special guests of the monster who sits on the Russian throne at Petersburg and doubtless exchanged hearty congratulations upon the outlook.

Elihu Root, as secretary of state, was the special guest of Diaz, and it is easy to understand the mission of this foxy lawyer who got his start in the service of Boss Tweed, the notorious New York crook and boodler.

"Colonel" Green has sold out his mines in Mexico to the Standard Oil company.[4] An English and Canadian syndicate owns all the street car lines. The Philip (*sic*) Dodge copper syndicate of New York owns vast mining interests. The Southern Pacific has large railroad concessions and so have other companies of American capitalists, and *this is the milk of the cocoanut*. These capitalists would crush out the last vestige of Mexican liberty to keep in the graces of Diaz and protect their brigand interests which are rooted in a peonage as cruel and heartless as history records in the middle ages.

When it is understood that the wages of these peons, hundreds of thousands of them, is 15 to 25 cents a day for making gigantic fortunes for American, English and Mexican capitalists, it can be readily understood why the rising spirit of revolt is to be crushed and why Magon and his co-patriots are to be shot to death or buried alive in some hellish dungeon.

This is but a small part of the gruesome and revolting story of our Mexican comrades. They are fighting as brave a battle as men ever engaged in at any time in history. They are the people's champions and have risked their lives over and over again to serve the masses who look to them to lead their almost forlorn hope.

Can we be indifferent to the duty we owe these brave comrades of ours who are fighting for the same cause we are under far greater difficulties.

Comrades and fellow workers, let us all unite in a determined effort to rescue these patriots from their impending fate. There is no case against them. They are innocent of crime. They have violated no neutrality laws. Alll they have done is to rise in revolt against the despotism of Diaz and this is not only their right but their duty to do and for this they ought to be honored by every liberty-loving citizen of the American republic and especially by the organized workers who themselves know what it is to be persecuted for the sake of serving the masses in servitude.

You have saved Moyer and Haywood, you have saved Rudowitz,[5] and now you have got to save our heroic Mexican comrades! —

MOTHER JONES.

[Appeal to Reason, *February 20, 1909.*]

Notes

1. The *Partido Liberal Mexicano* or *magonista* movement, which Mother

Jones refers to, had its antecedents in the *Club Liberal "Ponciano Arriaga,"* which was founded in San Luis Potosi, Mexico, in 1899. The central Junta organized in St. Louis Missouri, was known formally as the *Junta Organizadores del Partido Liberal Mexicano.* By July 1906, the Junta had developed a party platform and revolutionary manifesto that called for the creation of secret clubs throughout Mexico and included a comprehensive social reform program. Ricardo Flores Magón was the leading figure in the movement.

2. The reference is to the newspaper *Regeneración*, which was founded in 1900 by Ricardo Flores Magón and his older brother Jesús. In 1902 *Regeneración* was suppressed by Díaz, but by the end of 1904, the Flores Magón brothers were publishing a new *Regeneración* from San Antonio, Texas. The paper was sent through the U.S. and Mexican mails to subscribers along the border and into the Mexican interior.

3. In March 1908, *Pearson's Magazine* featured an article by James Creelman entitled "President Diaz, Hero of the Americas." Creelman painted a picture of a man who was really interested in the welfare of Mexico.

4. The reference is to Colonel William Cornell Greene, the American capitalist from Arizona who owned the Cananea mines in Mexico.

5. Abraham Rudowitz was a Russian Jewish immigrant who was saved from extradition and execution in Russia. For the Moyer and Haywood case, *see* pp. 55, 118, 120.

Girl Slaves of the Milwaukee Breweries

It is the same old story, as pitiful as old, as true as pitiful.

When the whistle blows in the morning it calls the girl slaves of the bottle-washing department of the breweries to don their wet shoes and rags and hustle to the bastile to serve out their sentences. It is indeed true, they are *sentenced* to hard, brutal labor — labor that gives no cheer, brings no recompense. Condemned for life, to slave daily in the wash room in wet shoes and wet clothes, surrounded with foul-mouthed, brutal foremen, whose orders and language would not look well in print and would surely shock over-sensitive ears or delicate nerves! And their crime? Involuntary poverty. It is hereditary. They are no more to blame for it than is a horse for having the glanders. It is the accident of birth. This accident that throws them into surging, seething mass known as the working class is what forces them out of the cradle into servitude, to be willing(?) slaves of the mill, factory, department store, hell, or bottling shop in Milwaukee's colossal breweries; to create wealth for the brewery barons, that they may own palaces, theaters, automobiles, blooded stock, farms, banks, and Heaven knows what all, while the poor girls slave on all day in the vile smell of sour beer, lifting cases of empty and full bottles weighing from

100 to 150 pounds, in their wet shoes and rags, for God knows they cannot buy clothes on the miserable pittance doled out to them by their soulless master class. The conscienceless rich see no reason why the slave should not be content on the crust of bread for its share of all the wealth created. That these slaves of the dampness should contract rheumatism is a foregone conclusion. Rheumatism is one of the chronic ailments, and is closely followed by consumption. Consumption is well known to be only a disease of poverty. The Milwaukee law makers, of course, enacted an antispit ordinance to protect the public health, and the brewers contributed to the Red Cross Society to make war on the shadow of tuberculosis, and all the while the big capitalists are setting out incubators to hatch out germs enough among the poor workers to destroy the nation. Should one of these poor girl slaves spit on the sidewalk, it would cost her more than she can make in two weeks' work. Such is the *fine* system of the present-day affairs. The foreman even regulates the time that they may stay in the toilet room, and in the event of overstaying it gives the foreman an opportunity he seems to be looking for to indulge in indecent and foul language. Should the patient slave forget herself and take offense, it will cost her the job in that prison. And after all, bad as it is, it is all that she knows how to do. To deprive her of the job means less crusts and worse rags in "the land of the free and the home of the brave." Many of the girls have no home nor parents and are forced to feed and clothe and shelter themselves, and all this on an average of $3.00 per week. Ye Gods! What a horrible nightmare! What hope is there for decency when unscrupulous wealth may exploit its producers so shamelessly?

No matter how cold, how stormy, how inclement the weather, many of these poor girl slaves must walk from their shacks to their work, for their miserable stipend precludes any possibility of squeezing a street car ride out of it. And this is due our much-vaunted greatness. Is this civilization? If so, what, please, is barbarism?

As an illustration of what these poor girls must submit to, one about to become a mother told me with tears in her eyes that every other day a depraved specimen of mankind took delight in measuring her girth and passing such comments as befits such humorous(?) occasion.

While the wage paid is 75 to 85 cents a day, the poor slaves are not permitted to work more than three or four days a week, and the continual threat of idle days makes the slave much more tractable and submissive than would otherwise obtain. Often when their day's work is done they are put to washing off the tables and lunch room floors and the other odd jobs, for which there is not even the suggestion of compensation. Of course, abuse always follows power, and nowhere is it more in evidence than in this miserable treatment the brewers and their hirelings accord their girl slaves.

The foreman also uses his influence, through certain living mediums near at hand, to neutralize any effort having in view the organization of these poor helpless victims of an unholy and brutal profit system, and threats of discharge were made, should these girls attend my meetings.

One of these foremen actually carried a union card, but the writer of this article reported him to the union and had him deprived of it for using such foul language to the girls under him. I learned of him venting his spite by discharging several girls, and I went to the superintendent and told him the character of the foreman. On the strength of my charges, he was called to the office and when he was informed of the nature of the visit, he patted the superintendent familiarly on the back and whined out how loyal he was to the superintendent, the whole performance taking on the character of servile lickspittle. As he fawns on his superior, so he expects to play autocrat with his menials and exact the same cringing from them under him. Such is the petty boss who holds the living of the working-class girls in his hands.

The brewers themselves were always courteous when I called on them, but their underlings were not so tactful, evidently working under instructions. The only brewer who treated me rudely or denied me admittance was Mr. Blatz, who brusquely told me his feelings in the following words: "The Brewers' Association of Milwaukee met when you first came to town and decided not to permit these girls to organize." This Brewers' Association is a strong union of all the brewery plutocrats, composed of Schlitz, Pabst, Miller, and Blatz breweries, who are the principal employers of women. And this union met and decided as above stated, that these women should not be permitted to organize! I then told Mr. Blatz that he could not shut me out of the halls of legislation, that as soon as the legislature assembles I shall appear there and put these conditions on record and demand an investigation and the drafting of suitable laws to protect the womanhood of the state.

Organized labor and humanity demand protection for these helpless victims of insatiable greed, in the interest of the motherhood of our future state.

Will the people of this country at large, and the organized wage-workers in particular, tolerate and stand any longer for such conditions as existing in the bottling establishments of these Milwaukee breweries? I hope not! Therefore, I ask all fair-minded people to refrain from purchasing the product of these baron brewers until they will change things for the better for these poor girls working in their bottling establishments.

Exploited by the brewers! Insulted by the petty bosses! Deserted by the press, which completely ignored me and gave no helping hand to these poor girls' cause. Had they had a vote, however, their case would likely have attracted more attention from all sides.[1] Poor peons of the brewers! Neglected by all the Gods! Deserted by all mankind. The present shorn of all that makes life worth living, the future hopeless, without a comforting star or glimmer. What avails our boasted greatness built upon such human wreckage? What is civilization and progress to them? What "message" bears the holy brotherhood in the gorgeous temples of modern worship? What terrors has the over-investigated white-slave traffic for her? What a prolific recruiting station for the red light district! For after all, the white slave *eats, drinks,* and wears good clothing, and to the hopeless this means living, if it only lasts a minute. What has the beer slave to — the petty boss will make her job cost her virtue anyhow. This has come to be a price of a job everywhere nowadays. Is it any wonder the white-slave traffic abounds on all sides? No wonder the working class has lost all faith in Gods. Hell itself has no terrors worse than a term in industrial slavery. I will give these brewery lords of Milwaukee notice that my two months' investigation and efforts to organize, in spite of all obstacles placed in my way, will bear fruit, and the sooner they realize their duty the better it will be for themselves. Will they do it?

Think of it, fathers and mothers. Think of it, men and women. When it is asked of thee, "What hast thou done for the economic redemption of the sisters of thy brother Abel?" what will thy answer be?

Mother Jones

[Miners Magazine,[2] April 4, 1910, pp. 5-6.]

Notes

1. Here is another example of Mother Jones's affirmative attitude towards woman suffrage.
2. *Miners Magazine* was the official organ of the Western Federation of Miners.

Fashionable Society Scored

No nation can ever grow greater than its women. None ever has; none ever will. It is the women who decide the fate of a nation, and that has always been so, as history proves.

What tremendous power and responsibility, therefore rests with womankind. I wonder if they realize it. In the poorer classes I think they do, or are coming to, but the attitude of the rich is appalling.

I called the other day to see Mrs. J. Borden Harriman at the Colony

Club. While I sat in the reception room waiting to be received I watched the fashionable women come and go. Nearly all of them, if you asked them, would tell you proudly that they belonged to society. But if you asked them what society meant they could not answer you truthfully without covering themselves with shame.

I will tell you why they could not, or would not, answer. Because the word society, as applied to women of today, stands for idleness, fads, extravagance, and display of wealth.

The women I saw parade before me were "bluffs." They glanced at me languidly, because that in society is the correct way to look at anybody not of their own class.

They posed and strutted before me like the poor, ignorant geese that they are, and probably imagined that I was impressed. I was, but not in the way they intended. I realized that they were posing and strutting because they had nothing else to occupy their minds, and so I pitied them. My pity was not without censure, however, because in these times of suffering the idle rich woman who parades her finery before the hungry and poverty-stricken is a modern inquisitor turning the thumb-screws of envy and despair into the very vitals of those who are in reality her sisters.

The high ideals of womanhood can never be realized in Colony clubs. The mission of woman is to develop human hearts and minds along charitable and sympathetic lines. The canker worm that is gnawing at the vitals of our womanhood is the failure of the rich woman to fulfill her mission in life. We are society-mad, and the craze I am sorry to say it, but I realize that it is too true — is growing worse.

I look on Mrs. Harriman as an exceptional woman of her class,[1] but even she has only scratched the surface of things as they really are. In Mrs. Harriman I find a woman of force and character. She could be a great factor in the education of women of her own set. By that I mean she could educate them to a realization of their duty in life and help to turn them from their follies, vanities, and shame to putting their time toward helping their unfortunate sisters.[2]

Mrs. Harriman is groping and seeking the light, and with her ability to grasp great problems will do much toward bettering conditions wherever she may extend her work.

The hard part of Mrs. Harriman's task will be for her to overcome the effect of her environments, but she is very gifted and has an open mind, which is more than I can say for any others in her class that I have met.

As soon as every woman grasps the idea that every other woman is her sister, then we will begin to better conditions. For instance, I saw a girl in a store the other day ready to drop from weariness. Her fatigue was apparent, and yet I noticed a woman customer loaded down with expensive furs and jewels call on this girl to get down several heavy boxes of goods. Then, after glancing over them, she concluded she didn't want to buy anything. This rich woman wouldn't have asked her own sister to do that, but she didn't view the shop girl in that light. Oh no; she was "only a shop girl."

I spoke to this girl after the woman had left and found that she worked about twelve hours a day, and for one dollar a day. Out of this she had to buy her clothes, her lunch, and supply her carfare. What a life![3]

It is among the poor that you find that sisterly feeling I have spoken about, because the poor know what suffering is and means, and sympathize with others. You never see a well-dressed woman give up her seat in the subway to an old woman, do you? No, never; but I have often had a poor, tired shop girl rise with a smile and proffer me her seat because of my white hair.

Woman Who Doesn't Nurse Her Own Child is Wrong

The rich woman who has a maid to raise her child can't expect to get the right viewpoint of life. If they would raise their own babies, their hearts would open and their feelings would become human. And the effect on the child is just as bad.

A nurse can't give her mother's love to somebody else's child.

And while I am talking about children and mothers I want to say that if women are against war, they can do much to prevent it by changing their methods of bringing up children. Every woman should train her child to have a horror of war. Any woman who buys a toy gun or pistol for her child ought to be put in a sanitarium. When you see a child parading about in a cardboard suit of armor and a gayly colored helmet, carrying a gun, you can say to yourself that some mother is filling her child's mind with thoughts of murder, for that is what that uniform and gun represent. I don't believe in drilling men or children for murder, and whenever I see a man in uniform walking around with a belt full of bullets, I say to myself, "There goes a murderer."[4]

The power of women is limitless. Look at what they are doing for shattered Belgium.[5] A great work that, but why not do as much for their sisters over here. I didn't see the women rising en masse for their stricken sisters of Colorado, Calumet, and West Virginia during the mine strike riots, and God knows they needed help as much as the Belgians, and do yet.[6]

Let a woman put aside her vanities for the real things of life. It nauseates me to see your average city woman. She is always overdressed, and although she wears gloves she is careful to leave her right hand bared so that she can display her fingers crowded to their utmost with jewels. Whenever I see that sort of display, I think of the gems as representing the blood of some crucified child. The woman of today — the woman of the "upper classes," I mean — is a sad commentary on civilization, as we are pleased to call it.

Everywhere I go in a city I see this same display of jewelry. The women even go to church on Sunday with their fingers and breasts ablaze with diamonds. This includes the wives of ministers themselves. We never heard of Christ wearing diamonds.

When one starts to investigate conditions the result is appalling. We are supposed to be progressing, but a little study in comparisons seems to point the other way. For instance, it is a fact that although this country is in its infancy, and has gained in wealth more in fifty years than any other country has in 700 years, still we have more poverty in comparison with any of these old countries.[7]

No human being in this country ever ought to go hungry, and there's something radically wrong somewhere when our jails are continually overcrowded. An immense amount of good can be done with playgrounds and supplying other means to give the poor outdoor exercise. Healthy bodies go forward with healthy minds, and a man or woman, though poor, can smile and do more to overcome their condition if minds and bodies are kept in a normal state

I have always felt that no true state of civilization can ever be realized as long as we continue to have two classes of society. But there is a tremendous problem, and it will take a terrific amount of labor to remedy it. I think myself that we are bound to see a revolution here before these questions are straightened out. We were on the verge of it in the Colorado affair, and the reason we did not have it then was not due to the good judgment of public officials, but to that of labor officials who worked unceasingly to prevent it.[8]

Mother Mary Jones

[Miners Magazine, *April 1, 1915, pp. 1, 3.*]

Notes

1. Mrs. J. Bordman Harriman was a member of the United States Commission on Industrial Relations representing the public. In her autobiography the socialite turned social reformer called Mother Jones "the most significant woman in America though her life has been alien to everything comfortable American womanhood is supposed to stand for." (Florence Harriman, *From Pinafores to Politics,* New York, 1923, p. 143.) For a more critical view of Mrs. Harriman by Mother Jones, *see* pp. 127, 134, 143, 147.

2. Evidently Mother Jones did not pay much attention to the sisterhood developing between upper-class women and working-class women in the Women's Trade Union League of this period or regarded it as unimportant. She certainly knew that upper-class women in the League were helping their working-class sisters in a variety of ways, including joining their picket lines and, in some cases, even getting arrested and beaten by the police in strikes of working-class women. (*See* Foner, *Women and the American Labor Movement: From*

Colonial Times to the Eve of World War I, pp. 342-43, 484-87.)

3. In the Chicago Historical Society there are two versions of a poem written by Mother Jones and in her own handwriting dealing with shop girls. They are "Ballad of the Shop Girl" and "They Cry of the Shop Girl," and they read:

Ballad of the Shop girl

The wolf of poverty follows me
Through the dingy streets of Town
So close beside his shaggy hide
Might almost brush my Gown
And after him thrust the Wolves of Lust
for body and Soul have a scanty dole
from the pittance that I earn
and cold as the breath of the wind of death
are the Sad lessons that I learn
With a pitiful tinge of my weary feet
and a trap at every turn

I never may know Surcease from woe
but I know of fortunes frown

The Cry of the Shop girl

The Wolf of Poverty follows me on
Through the dingy streets of Town
So close beside that his shaggy hide
might almost brush my gown
and after thirst the wolves of lust
come eager to me down

And body & Soul have a Scanty dole and as the breath of the wind of death
are the lessons that I learn
with a pitfall dug for my weary feet
and a trap at every turn

And never a tempter is near at hand
to hire with a judas kiss and lead me away if lead I may
to the depths of the Black abyss
where in Serpen guise old Memories rise
and over the fallen kiss
I may never know Surcease from woe
but I know of fortunes frown
I am one of a Score of a thousand more
To be hired with a Judas kiss

I may never know Surcease from woe
but I know of fortunes frown

I am one of a Score of thousand more
who Toil in the cruel Town
and the wolf of lust & poverty

are waiting to drag us down

And the Christ that the Bible Teaches of,
for only men did die
or he else would heed in this dreadful week
my bitter disparing crye
and creeds alway for the heathen pray
and the Christian pass me bye

and many and fast the day which past

While early I work & late
and around my path for the aftermath
The Basilisk watchers wait
and civilisation bids me chose
the grave or a degraded fate

and I dread the of tomorrows dawn
and the weight of future years
My life is blurred by a hope deferred
and my heart is numb with fear
and my eyes that rise to the soulless skies
and ever with a womans tears

*(Four pages in handwriting of Mother Jones in Chicago
Historical Society — undated)*

4. As we have seen, when the United States declared war on Germany and her allies, Mother Jones changed her attitude on this issue.

5. The reference is to the work being conducted for Belgian War Relief after Belgium was attacked and overrun by the German army at the outset of World War I.

6. Mother Jones included women in the Women's Trade Union League in this indictment since they appeared to be interested only in labor struggles in which women alone were involved or were the majority of the workers.

7. In a book simply named *Poverty,* Robert Hunter revealed in 1904 that of the total population of eighty million some ten million lived in poverty, "under-fed, under-clothed, and poorly housed," with four million of them public paupers. In bringing his study up to date in 1914, Hunter concluded that conditions of poverty had not basically improved in a decade. (Quoted in Philip S. Foner, *History of the Labor Movement in the United States,* vol. 3, New York, 1955, p.14).

8. Mother Jones was probably referring to the tremendous outrage and anger aroused by the "Ludlow Massacre." As news of the tragedy spread, strikers in all parts of southern Colorado, joined by outraged laboring men and sympathizers, poured into the strike zone and struck back furiously against the wanton killings. The enraged strikers attacked company camps and mines throughout southern Colorado and even in the vicinity of Denver. Governor Ammons tried to stem the violence by ordering an additional six hundred militiamen to report to duty, but only about twenty-five percent of the men responded. At last, in desperation, the governor admitted the situation was beyond his control and asked President Wilson for Federal troops. On April 28,

1914, Wilson declared a state of national emergency in Colorado and directed that Federal troops proceed immediately to the strike area. (*Report on the Colorado Strike Investigation*, pp. 131-32; Billie Barnes Jensen, "Woodrow Wilson's Intervention in the Coal Strike of 1914," *Labor History* 15 (Winter, 1974): 62-77.)

Arizona in 1916

I went into Arizona in 1916 for the Western Federation of Miners,[1] to carry on a campaign of agitation and organization. Ed Crough, a very able organizer, was with me. It was there that I first met Governor Hunt of that state. There was a strike in Morrenci of the copper miners. The governor went down and told the sheriff to deputize forty miners, to watch the property, and to help him keep order, which he did. The governor himself appointed men on the county lines to keep out all scabs and gunmen. The result was that there were no crimes committed there, nor any disorder. Hunt walked in the pathway of Governor Tanner of Illinois in 1906 or 1907, when the Virden strike was on, and when the company undertook to import scabs. The governor ordered them to leave the state.[2] We haven't many governors of that type. The Copper Queen's Agent of 99 John Street, New York, would not have deported an army of miners from Bisbee, Arizona, and landed them out on the desert without food or water,[3] had Hunt been governor of Arizona at that time.[4] The strikes could be conducted much more peacefully than they are if governors undertook to establish justice, instead of resorting to force. I happened to be in Bisbee, Arizona some years before. I had there a large gathering of miners and other citizens there. I made a statement to the audience, asked the question why they should be afraid to organize, if they were real Americans they would get busy and organize, and with solid front tell the employers that they had organized into a union of their craft, and ask the company what objection they might have to it, and state that the American nation saw the necessity of the Union that each territory when she became state entered the Union. If our government sees the necessity of the Union, why should not the workers see the necessity of also entering the union of the workers to protect their interests against those of the exploiters of labor. They carried out my suggestion the next night and organized. Joe Cannon of Pennsylvania was then leading the miners of Bisbee, and no better leader could be had than he was. The company began to discharge men who joined the organiza-

474

tion. They sent into Texas for me to come back and I did. We carried on the fight, and had public meetings which were not interefered with by any officer. They were peaceful and educational. I went back there and remained for some weeks. That's where I first met Captain Wheeler of the State Rangers. He was at that time rather a broadminded man, but afterwards he fell under the influence of the Copper Queen, and became its pliant servant. There was no Governor Hunt in office at that time. The then governor was subservient to the orders of the Copper Queen. When once the workers become politically conscious and take political power into their own hands, there will be more Governor Hunts holding political office. I saw Governor Hunt one day pick up a poor wretch who had a knapsack on his back, and scarcely any shoes on his feet, and covered with dust. The governor stopped his car and asked the man where he was going. He told the governor, and he told him to get in the automobile. The man who was a miner declined saying that he was covered with dust and was not fit to get into the car. Nevertheless, the governor answered, "never mind the outside dirt, if your heart is clean." If America had more such men holding office, we'd have less friction than we now have. Unfortunately, however, when men become governors, they forget that they are just folks, and become autocrats and dictators.

Governor Hunt, after the "Work or Fight" law had been passed by the State Legislature, vetoed the same which he characterized as a "very obnoxious form of tyranny."

In connection with the strike at Bisbee, in 1917, the press throughout the country attributed the activities of the strikers to an influx of itinerants, IWWs and the like, and in some instances went so far as to charge that it was brought about at the instigation of the German government, then engaged in the World War, and that it was for this reason, or these reasons, that the good citizens of Bisbee banded themselves together and deported in freight cars some 1200 strikers, without food or water, and without the means of purchasing the same. The fact is that all of the men deported were residents of Bisbee, mostly strikers, and also some businessmen suspected of being in sympathy with the strikers, and a lawyer who defended them. The respected citizens who deported these men were the mine guards of the copper interests, who had the support and backing of petty county and city officials who got their position through the corporation interests. Governor Campbell of Arizona was necessarily the tool of the copper company, since he was indebted to the copper interests for his holding such office. Governor Hunt had been reelected to office. He had enforced the law for all alike, and by the votes of the people of Arizona was again chosen to hold that office. He had refused to permit alien armies of hired guards to perpetrate the will of the copper companies upon the workers in the mines at Clifton, Metcalf and Morrenci. Consequently the copper company set out to defeat him, but in spite of that he was chosen in the primaries and in the election which followed. Notwithstanding his being the choice of the majority of the voters in the state Hunt was counted out, and a present of the position was made to that tool of the copper interests Campbell. The miners in consequence could look for little aid from Governor Campbell.

The miners deported from Bisbee were guilty of no crime, and were accused of none. What they did, and what any others would do who had a spark of manhood in them, was to refuse to work under the oppressive conditions imposed upon them in Arizona mines. To make appeal to the governor of the state would be futile. He was there to carry out the instructions of the Dodge-Phelps syndicate, no matter how unjust, how criminal, how brutal. Not until the workers everywhere shall become politically conscious, not until they shall seize powere of the state and wield it in the interests of the working class, will there be any hope of working-class emancipation.

[Typed pages in Mother Jones Folders, John Fitzpatrick Papers, Chicago Historical Society — undated.]

Notes

1. This fragment of autobiographical experience by Mother Jones is in the Chicago Historical Society. In her *Autobiography*, Mother Jones writes about her visit to Arizona in 1913, but here she deals with another visit in 1916, and adds a number of details to her Arizona experiences, campaigning for Governor George Wiley Paul Hunt, which are not included in the *Autobiography*.

For the strike of the copper miners in Arizona, most of whom were Mexican-Americans, led by the Western Federation of Miners, *see* Philip S. Foner, *History of the Labor Movement in the United States* vol. 6, New York, 1982, p. 13-24.

2. For Virden strike and role of Governor Tanner, *see* pp. 55, 58, 107, 474, 511.

3. The Bisbee deportations of July 12, 1917, were the product of wartime vigilantism and the determination of the copper mine bosses to destroy the I.W.W. Some 1200 workmen, engaged in a strike led by the I.W.W. for better working conditions, were rounded up by the "Loyalty League" and deported to New Mexico, left in the desert without food and water, and informed that if they returned, they would be lynched.

4. Hunt was defeated by Thomas Campbell by 30 votes out of 55,000 cast. Campbell, a former mine owner, was seated by the state Supreme Court without pay until the outcome, which Hunt contested, could be settled. After serving about half of the two-year term, Campbell was deposed by the court who gave Hunt the majority of the 30 disputed votes. Hunt was not governor during the Bisbee deportations, but he charged that the cry of an "I.W.W. menace" was merely a camouflage by the mine operators to attempt to destroy all organized labor in the state. When he ran for a fourth term in 1918, Hunt was labeled by conservatives George "Wobbly" P. Hunt, and this time he was defeated. (*See* Alan V. Johnson, "Governor G.W.P. Hunt and Organized Labor," unpublished

M.A. thesis, University of Arizona, 1964.) For further discussion of the 1916 campaign, *see* p. 57.

The Russian Revolution and the United States

[. . . It is impossible,] for the physical transplantation to take place between Russians and Americans, so it seems to me to be equally difficult, if not impossible, for Americans to suddenly assume the state of political and social mind that has engaged the working classes of Russia since the overthrow of the Czar. American workingmen think as Americans, not as Russians, or Japanese, or Germans — indeed, American workers do not even think as English workers, and this is proven by the fact that in each of those countries there are labor unions, guilds, and political parties, each distinct from similar organizations in other lands and each adapted to the peculiar temperament of the people that desire to attract members, and also adapted to the industrial and political management of the country wherein they function.

This does not mean that I am criticizing the Russian workers for the manner in which they accomplished their revolution. I would be the last to aim a dart at them, and all that I am trying to point out is what seems to me to be an obvious truism: That the Russian way may not be the American way; and the German Socialists may feel that they are entitled to work out their own revolutionary principles along the lines of the German working class psychology.

We can give the Russian revolution and the Soviet government every possible support, morally, spiritually, and financially without surrendering our own identity as American Socialists and workers who have social and industrial problems peculiar to our national life and with which the average Russian in Russia is wholly unfamiliar.

Internationalism does not mean to me that any one country shall arrogate to itself the right to impose its nationalism upon all other countries, thus making them international. There is an international ideal that must be upheld, and that ideal embraces freedom for all mankind, regardless of race, sex, creed, or color. But it remains for the workers in each nation to achieve their revolutionary aims through their own efforts, and not by accepting without question or scrutiny the program of the one country which first saw liberty through the light of its people.

477

Russia could no more invoke its revolutionary methods and manners upon American workers with any degree of success than a single American family could force their peculiar traditions and mannerisms upon their neighbors. Any attempt so to do would only result in an open conflict which might possibly be aired in the police court.

I have gone into this subject from this angle because to me it is patent that by far the largest element of disagreement within our own ranks found source in the revolutionary inspiration furnished by the Russian revolution. Americans should not ignore the fact that this is America — and I cannot too often stress that geographical fact.

There is absolutely no certainty that the American workers would meet with success should they decide to abandon their own program of militant industrial and political unionism for that of Moscow; but there is a degree of certainty in the belief that they would get no hearing from the masses of American people. We cannot talk Russian temperament and psychology to American workers and voters and expect them to grasp its virtues in a twinkling, if at all. Nor would Russians lend a sympathetic ear to any American protagonist of political and industrial change if he sought to convert the Russian to the American plan.

The workers in the United States must come together some time if they would be saved from the jaws of the capitalist shark. Their unions now are flung apart about as far as they well can be and still be called unions, and in a political sense, the workers were never weaker than they are at this very moment.

The time was never better than right now for unity between the factions of the industrial and political movement of this country. Divided, the workers will gain nothing. United, the world and all its treasures are theirs.

Let us cease bickering and quarrelling, do the work that is necessary and within reach of our hand, and walk arm in arm toward Socialism.

[Section of unnamed, undated, unidentified article in Mother Mary Harris Jones Papers, Department of Archives and Manuscripts, Catholic University of America, Washington, D.C.]

INTERVIEWS

Mother Jones and a
Dozen Strike Agitators Arrested

Interview in jail, published in *Parkersburg (West Virginia) Sentinel,*
June 21, 1902[1]

A dozen strike agitators were arrested at Clarksburg on Friday afternoon about 3 o'clock and were brought to Parkersburg on the train
that arrived at 10:07 last night. The prisoners were taken to the
county jail.

The arrests were made by Marshal C.D. Elliott and deputies D.R.
Jackson, C.W. Law, and Chas. Hughes who have been in the
Clarksburg and Fairmont region for several weeks.

The prisoners are Mary Jones, alias "Mother" Jones, Thos. Hag-
gerty, Wm. Morgan, Bernard Rice, Peter Wilson, Wm. Blakeley,
George Barron, Andrew Lascavash, Albert Roppoke, Joe Reossky,
George Reossky, and Steve Tonike.

The prisoners were in charge of Deputy Marshals D.R. Jackson,
C.W. Law, G.A. Elliott, deputy sheriff John Long and Ormon Randolph.

Deputy Marshal Jackson in discussing the arrest said that the miners had rented a lot about forty yards from the buildings of the
Clarksburg Fuel Co. and were holding a meeting there which was addressed by several of those under arrest, the last speaker being Mother
Jones. These parties had worked their base of operations from the
Fairmont field to the Clarksburg region and were trying to incite the
miners that were still at work and get them to join the ranks of the
strikers. Mother Jones, it is stated, was unsparing of her denunciation
of the operators, the trusts, and capitalists, and severely criticised the
action of Judge Jackson. Marshal Elliott, as soon as the address was
concluded placed Mother Jones under arrest for a violation of the injunction of the U.S. Court. . . .

On the arrival here Marshal Jackson offered to secure quarters for
Mrs. Jones at a hotel, which offer she refused, giving her reasons that
she was a federal prisoner and would remain with the boys. She was
then given a room in the residence part of the jail.

Mother Jones was visited by a reporter at the jail this morning and
when asked as to what she had to say as to the arrest of herself and the
men she replied:

"Well, we are here to await the action of the United States court. We were arrested on our own ground which we had rented and which was entirely separate from the company's premises. We were holding a meeting which the authorities claim was a violation of the blanket injunction of 1897 which they claim holds good in this movement."

"This is a chivalric state, isn't it?" Mrs. Jones remarked. "I have been in all kinds of movements in all parts of the country in which labor and capital were interested and this is the first time anybody has tried to molest me. I am the first woman ever to be arrested under a federal injunction in a labor movement."

When asked why she did not accept the offer of Deputy Marshal Jackson to take her to a hotel her answer was, "I am a federal prisoner, the same as the boys, and consider myself no better than they are. Had they been taken to a hotel I would have wanted to go with them, but I expect to stand by the boys and will go with them even to the penitentiary if needs be. We expect to fight this matter to the highest court to see whether it is a case of one man rule or the people ruling." "Will the arrest of yourself and the boys affect the movement in any way?"

"No," she replied, "organizers from other states will take our places and the fight will be carried on just the same."

The question was asked how long she had been interested in labor movements. "Nearly all my life and I expect to continue to stay in the work the balance of my life as I cannot stand idly by and see the suffering of mothers and babies without making some effort to help improve the condition of affairs."

At this point Mother Jones was informed that her breakfast was ready and in taking leave of the reporter she said: "Young man, remember this fight is for the future of you young men; it is against the capitalists who are nothing more than robbers, or to use the aristocratic pronunciation, they are kleptomaniacs."

The arrests of the prisoners were not made under the blanket injunction of 1897 as stated by Mother Jones but under an injunction issued on Thursday by Judge Jackson upon the application of the Clarksburg Fuel Co.[2]

Notes

1. The sub-headings read: "For violating U.S. Court Injunction. Prisoners Brought Here and Lodged In Jail. And Will Answer For Contempt. The Agitators Were Arrested at Clarksburg." I wish to thank Ms. Ann R. Lorentz, Reference Librarian, Parkersburg and Wood County Public Library, Parkersburg, West Virginia, for furnishing me with a copy of the interview.

2. The injunction obtained from Judge John Jay Jackson in June 1902 contained, Edward M. Steel points out, "some unusual features." To obtain an injunction from a federal court, the claim would have to come from a nonresident of the state in order to maintain the principle of federal jurisdiction. Therefore,

the subterfuge was used of having the claim for the injunction come from J. H. Wheelwright, a Baltimore financier who held $60,000 in bonds of the Guaranty Trust Company of New York, "these bonds in turn were securities for the debt of the Fairmont Coal Company. On the grounds that Mother Jones . . . and other strike leaders . . . would irreparably damage the operations of the company and thereby prevent the payment of its obligations to the mortgagee, Wheelwright sought to prevent their agitating a strike, which was labeled as a conspiracy to injure the complainant. Second, an even more unusual feature of this injunction, was the blanket ban placed on all demonstrations, even on premises that were leased by the strikers." (Edward M. Steel, "Mother Jones in the Fairmont Field, 1902," *Journal of American History 57* [September, 1970]: 296.)

Mother Jones, the Noted Labor Organizer, Advances Her Theories on Strike Matters

Interview in *Parkersburg (West Virginia) Morning News,*
June 23, 1902[1]

While in conversation Sunday with a News reporter, "Mother" Jones, quoted as follows from "Ignatius Donnelly's Caesar's Column:"[2]

"The world, today, clamors for deeds not creeds; for bread, not dogma; for charity, not ceremony; for love, not intellect.

"Society divides itself into two hostile camps; no white flags pass from one to the other. They wait only for the drumbeat to summon them to armed conflict.

"The masses grow more intelligent as they grow more wretched; and more capable of cooperation as they become more desperate. The labor organizations of today would have been impossible fifty years ago. And what is to arrest the flow of effect from cause? What is to prevent the coming of the night if the earth continues to revolve on its axis? The fool may cry out: 'There is no night!' But the feet of the hours march unrelentingly toward the darkness.

"Believing, as I do, that I read the future aright, it would be criminal in me to remain silent. I plead for the higher and nobler thoughts in the souls of men; for wider love and ampler charity in their hearts; for a renewal of the bond of brotherhood between the classes; for a reign of justice on earth that shall obliterate the cruel hates and passions which now divide the world."

Mrs. Jones, after having furnished bond for her appearance at

United States court Tuesday, moved her quarters from a room in the county jail building to the Van Winkle hotel, where, she will remain until the trial of the agitators takes place. She does not seem to be troubled in the least about the outcome of the proceedings as she says she does not believe that either she or the men who were arrested showed any contempt by their actions after the injunction issued a short time ago by Judge Jackson was served.

Mother Jones is an attentive student of human nature. While a woman, she has those observant qualities that give her an opinion on any subject. She has made a life-study of the lives and ways of working men, especially of the miners.

She stated that the agitators, among whom she is considered a member of high standing, have never countenanced the brutality connected with some labor troubles in the past. It is her opinion that fighting does not gain for them the desired end, and that it won't be long until all troubles of the kind will be settled without compelling the men to overstep the boundaries of prudence.

"It should not be necessary at this civilized age for men to battle and cause the loss of life. The time is near when wars will not be the means of settling differences of either nations or men.

"It is a fact generally conceded that there are now two classes, each of which could work to the advantage of itself and to the other, but instead they cause agitations that grow and cause disturbances that are widely felt. To make those conditions different it is necessary for the working class to be educated to the realization of its standing, and not until that time comes will there be a proper feeling between the employers and the employees.

"In former years miners were considered a bad class. They came from different countries, and were of the kind that believed in settling all differences by force. Fighting was fun to them. They were not to be blamed for that, for they were educated to that point by those socially and officially their betters. Take for instance the troubles in Ireland years ago. The inhabitants of one county would fight those of the other until there was continual trouble. The same spirit was brought to this country, and, while the hardy miners could stand such hardship and rough treatment at the hands of their employers, they could not stand by and see themselves getting beaten for their wages. At that time it was almost an impossibility for them to get any redress, for organization was not thought of. The workers in one mine even would not stand together and demand consideration for their rights. They were enemies to each other, and were always unsuccessful in their attempts to better themselves. The permanent populace of the entire country saw the miners as a people who should not be deigned any attention whatever. They were rough and uncouth and in a manner, not considered as being the product of the Hand that made us all. That feeling is fast being lost, and well it may be. In a great part the miners are uneducated. They have never had the opportunities that have been afforded those in other walks of life. But, while they may not have refinement and learning, they have a sense of honor that may be envied by some other classes of people. They have begun to appreciate the beauties of life. They have begun to hold themselves in personal esteem, and are attempting to hide from the world the fact that they are untutored and have not the polish that would gain for them the esteem of the better classes.

"It won't be long until the working-men of the country will have the hand that controls affairs. That day is near, having been brought about partially by the state of commercial affairs. The trusts have done much to advance the masses. They are educators to which we should give great credit. While the masses are becoming educated they are rising, not only in their own estimation, but in that of the commercial oligarchists. They are rapidly coming out of the darkness in which they have previously existed. The natural trend of human affairs tends to their good and that to their uplifting.

"It is not intended that one man or a few of them can successfully control the destinies of men. It is a fact, though, that such is very nearly the state in which affairs now rest. These conditions cannot last, and many of us will live to see the day when the masses are in control. We who have studied the conditions see plainly the result, and feel that it is almost in reach at this time.

"Mother," Jones was asked what would be the result if the miners fail to succeed in gaining their ends in the present disturbance. She said: "If they were to lose today, the result would not hurt them. Truth crushed to earth shall rise again.[3] They have lost before, and have been strengthened at that. Every attempt they make is to their advantage, whether or not they fail in their purpose. Labor organization becomes stronger each day and will continue to until they are composed of such members that the destinies of the nation will be controlled by their action.

"The newspapers and even the clergy have misrepresented the facts in the miners' troubles that are now being experienced. It seems that the public in general has not learned to appreciate the true conditions. People continue to allow themselves to be mislead.

"It is necessary to only become acquainted with the conditions that surround the lives of the miners and their families to cause one to extend every sympathy, and if possible to lend assistance towards bringing about a change.

"In addressing crowds of these miners, how can I help being deeply appealed to? Many of them with pinched looks and ragged clothing compose the meetings. Each one of them has his eye open in hope that he will be given aid. Each heart contains that ray of hope that the miners will be bettered."

Mother Jones tells a story of a young man who was sent to follow in her steps and learn of her every action during the trouble between the miners and operators a short time ago. He had been hired by the mine owners and while he did not relish the position he did as he was directed. He attended every meeting which was held. Mother Jones soon learned of his activities and became acquainted with him. She said he was but about eighteen years of age, and of excellent parentage. He was not strong and could not well stand to follow her to the many places she went. He always registered at the hotels were she stopped. One day after she had covered more territory than usual, she found him in a very tired condition. She called him to her room and requested him to rest, saying that she would tell him of every movement so he could make his reports to headquarters. She said she appreciated the requirements of his duties and his physical condition, as well, and would report to him of her every movement when he was unable to be present at the meetings.

It was "Mother" Jones who gained a great victory for working children in Scranton some years ago.[4] She was successful in gaining for them the consideration rightly due them. She states that girls, some as young as eight or nine years, were required to work ten hours each day and many of them lived outside of the city and would have to walk three or four miles to and from their work.

She said the mothers of some of the children would go to the factory owners, and after making affidavit that her girl was thirteen years old, secure employment for her. If she be even less than ten years of age. . . .

Notes

1. The original headline read: "IF MINERS LOSE, THEY WILL GAIN IS VIEW OF 'MOTHER' JONES," followed by the sub-heading: "The Noted Labor Organizer Talks to Reporter and Advances Her Theories on Strike Matters." I wish to thank Ms. Ann R. Lorentz, Reference Librarian, Parkersburg and Wood County Public Library, Parkersburg, West Virginia, for furnishing me with a copy of the interview.

2. Ignatius Donnelly (1831-1901), a founder of Minnesota, who as a speaker and writer came to be known as the "tribune of the people." He served as lieutenant-governor of Minnesota and in Congress (1866-69), but became best known as a Populist, writing the preamble to the Populist Party platform of 1892. He was the author of many books, including the sensational novel *Caesar's Column: a story of the Twentieth Century,* published in 1891. The novel with its prediction of catastrophic times, sold over a million copies and became a bible of the populist movement.

3. This famous sentence originated with James Russell Lowell, the antislavery poet, but was used by many orators and writers and was often used in his speeches by Reverend Martin Luther King, Jr.

4. Mother Jones does not mention her work in Scranton in her *Autobiography.*

"Mother" Jones Will Lead Textile Child Workers Through Country to Win Sympathy. Army of 400 Boys and Girls in Living Appeal for Aid.

Interview in Philadelphia *North American,* July 7, 1903[1]

"Mother" Jones will lead a second "children's crusade" from this city (of Philadelphia) today. It will be composed of 400 striking juvenile textile workers and an equal number of adult strikers. It starts from the Kensington Labor Lyceum, Second Street, above Cambria, at 11 o'clock this morning.

The object of the "crusade" is to appeal to the people of the country to support the 75,000 textile strikers in their "demand" for a 55-hour-work-week. Sufficient money to support the strikers indefinitely is expected to come in as a result of taking the children throughout the country. So far as possible, parents will accompany their children.[2] Two members of the strikers' executive board and their wives will help in caring for the "crusaders."

"Mother" Jones, as commander-in-chief, has full charge of the campaign. After at first opposing it, the strike leaders have become convinced that it is an excellent plan to stir up the workers and the general public of the United States to lend a hand in the fight for shorter hours. "Mother" Jones spoke about the project to this reporter last night:

"I desire the textile strikers of Philadelphia to win their fight for shorter hours, so that more leisure may be obtained, especially for children and women.

"The herding of young children of both sexes in textile mills is the cause of great immorality.

"As the result of the competitive and the factory systems, the nation is being stunted, physically, morally, and mentally.

"I do not blame the manufacturers individually, but I do blame the community at large for making no effort to abolish these evils.

"The employment of children is doing more to fill prisons, insane asylums, almshouses, reformatories, slums, and gin shops than all the efforts of reformers are doing to improve society.

"I am going to rouse the Christian fathers and mothers of this country if there is human blood in their veins.

"If the manufacturers cannot afford to give their employees a living wage and shorter hours of work, then the system of making goods for profit is wrong and must give way to making goods for use.

"The sight of little children at work in mills when they ought to be at school or at play always rouses me. I found the conditions in this city

487

deplorable, and I resolved to do what I could to shorten the hours of toil of the striking textile workers so as to gain more liberty for the children and women. I led a parade of children through the city — the cradle of Liberty — but the citizens were not moved to pity by the object lesson.

"The curse of greed so pressed on their hearts that they could not pause to express their pity for future men and women who are being stunted mentally, morally, and physically, so that they cannot possibly become good citizens. I cannot believe that the public conscience is so callous that it will not respond. I am going out of Philadelphia to see if there are people with human blood in their veins.

"When I think of the present and future I fear for my country. The criminal classes keep increasing. Large sums of money are being poured out for almshouses, prisons, churches, souphouses, insane asylums, inebriates' homes, houses of refuge, reformatories, and schools for defectives, but they are only a drop in the bucket. The disease cannot be cured unless the cause is removed. Keen, unrestrained competition, rivalry for commercial supremacy, and lust for wealth tramples on humanity and feels no remorse.

"I am going to picture capitalism and caricature the money-mad. I am going to show Wall Street the flesh and blood from which it squeezes its wealth. I am going to show President Roosevelt the poor little things on which the boasted commercial greatness of our country is built. One single Philadelphia minister of Christ's Gospel has so much as touched on the textile strike in this city. I shall endeavor to arouse sleeping Christians to a sense of their duty towards the poor little ones.

"I have seen mothers in Philadelphia beating their children to make them go to work in the mills in this strike as strikebreakers, and I have seen foremen bodily throwing the children through the factory doors when the little tots were late. The herding together of boys and girls in the mills is the cause of the breeding of grossest immorality. The textile mills of Philadelphia are making slums and slum dwellers faster than reformers can unmake them.

"Understand me, I do not blame the manufacturers individually. They are, I repeat, victims of the competitive system. But I do blame society for allowing such evils to exist and to grow without an effort to destroy them. God help the nation if something is not done, for a day of reckoning will surely come and with it bloody revolution."

Notes

1. For discussion of the "Children's Crusade" *see* pp. 29, 41-42, 55, 100-3, 167, 201, 219.

2. The main purpose of the "crusade" was to call national attention and that of President Theodore Roosevelt to the plight of child labor and bring public support for legislation outlawing it.

Mother Jones Hits Out at the Courts
in Case of Mexican Artist[1]

Mother Jones, who goes ahead, fighting the battles of the downtrodden, turned up again in New York last night as a speaker. She joined with Gaylord Wilshire,[2] Joshua Wanhope,[3] and others at a meeting held in the Berkeley Theatre to protest against the conviction of Carlo de Fornaro, the caricaturist, who has been sentenced to one year's hard labor on the charge of libelling Rafael Reyes Espindola, an editor and politician of Mexico, in his book on Mexico published last year.[4]

Resolutions were adopted, protesting against the conviction, calling for repeal of the law under which the conviction was obtained, and asking that Gov. Hughes immediately pardon Mr. de Fornaro. Moreover, a collection was taken up to help fight the case in the courts, if that is found necessary.

Mother Jones, though she said last night that she was 74 years old,[5] is still marvelously vigorous, at least in speech. She said she had been spending a lot of her time of late down in the Southwest, where she had learned some horrible things about Mexican rule. She is going back there immediately, she declared. Assuming that the Berkeley Theatre was almost filled with spies of the Mexican and United States governments, she hurled defiances at them, and spoke more cruelly about Mexico and big Mexicans than Fornaro did in his book.

"In 1861 they used to say, 'All is quiet along the Potomac,'" she said. "Now the black press is saying that all is quiet along the Rio Grande.[6] But in 1861, while all that talk was going on, there was a glint of bayonets on both sides of the Potomac, and to-day United States officers are arresting all along the Rio Grande hundreds of Mexicans for no other crimes than that they have denounced the tyrannical Government in their own country."

"In Kansas to-day three young men are in prison for doing just exactly what Thomas Jefferson and Patrick Henry did for their country.[7] Our Judges and officers are doing scavenger work for the Mexican pirate. Let the Mexican bloodhounds here to-night take that to Taft if they want to."[8]

The aged woman shook her white head here and stamped her softly shod foot. She said that one day not long ago a young Mexican revolutionist she knew about in the Southwest was kidnapped from the jail in which he had been thrown after arrest on some trumped-up charge. He was hurried across the Mexican line in an automobile, she declared. She and some others went to work to save him, and after telegraphing to Washington and the State Government the young man was sent back by Mexico, tried and released.[9]

"We just happened to know about his case," said Mother Jones. "How many are there that we don't know about?"

Mother Jones lambasted the woman suffragettes. She had watched them in Colorado, she said, and they had done nothing worth while. They worked for the capitalists, she declared.

"What do you want to do here?" she cried out. "You want to go meowing around with Mrs. Belmont, like a lot of tabby cats.[10] If you were any good you'd have made the men do something here at the ballot by this time. Oh, I know, you come here and clap your hands until you get blisters on them, but you won't use your brains at the polls."

She then turned her fire on Justice Malone, who charged the jury in the Fornaro case. She had no doubt that he appeared at church the next day, she said. "But if you took the Ten Commandments before one of these Judges in court," she went on, he'd say, " 'The Commandments be hanged; they are not constitutional.' "

[New York Times, *November 29, 1909.*]

Notes

1. The sub-headline read: "They'd pronounce the Ten Commandments Unconstitutional, She Says. This at a Fornaro Meeting."

2. Gaylord Wilshire, a right-wing Socialist from California where he published *Wilshire's Magazine.*

3. Joshua Wanhope was a columnist on the Socialist New York *Call.*

4. Fornaro's book was entitled *The Real Mexico.*

5. According to her usual account, she was almost 80 years old.

6. By the "black press" she was referring to the reactionary papers, not the Negro press. In these papers, Porfirio Díaz, the bloody dictator of Mexico, was ruling a country of quiet, contented Mexicans.

7. For the Mexicans in Kansas federal prison, *see* pp. 55, 121, 133.

8. In his speech, Gaylord Wilshire "intimated that the conviction of Mr. Fornaro was due to President Taft's solicitude for the business welfare of his two brothers — H.W. Taft and Charles Taft, the former a lawyer in New York and the latter a ranch owner in Texas and Mexico. He declared that Charles Taft owned heavy interests in Mexico, that he needed the good-will of the Mexican Government, and that H.W. Taft had been employed in the case here against Fornaro." (*New York Times,* November 29, 1909.)

9. For the incident here mentioned, *see* pp. 55, 121, 143-44, 145.

10. The reference is to Mrs. O.P. Belmont, the wealthy New Yorker, who was active in the woman suffrage movement and aided the shirtwaist strikers. *See also* pp. 56, 136-38, 141.

My Mission on Earth

Interview in *Charleston (West Virginia) Gazette,* June 11, 1912

Last June, when "Mother Jones" traveled across the states from Butte, Montana, to aid the West Virginia miners in their fight, a reporter on the Charleston *Gazette* interviewed her. The following is quoted from this paper June 11th:

"Mother Jones . . . from the stump and through the press has shown a desire only to do something for the betterment of the great American laboring class. She is 80 years old. On the day of her arrival here she addressed a miners' mass meeting for an hour and a half — and unassisted she climbed a steep hill to the speakers' stand and made a stronger effort and a more telling address in every way than that of any of the others whose names appeared on the list of speakers, and most of whom were only half her years.

"Some people never get old, and Mother Jones is one who, no matter how long she be spared to her stormy career, will be gathered to her ancestors in the bosom of youth."

The reporter had heard a lot about the woman he was about to interview — and seen her pictured everywhere — had heard of her making fiery speeches in places where her life was in danger, and he expected to encounter a cyclone.

The reporter, however, was wrong.

What he really found was a kindly-faced woman of apparently 50 years — the only evidence of her four score years being an abundance of snow-white hair. She gave the reporter a kindly greeting — a greeting that reminded him at once of the name that had attached itself to the woman he had come to see — the name was that of "mother" — and the reporter knew whence the name had come.

"Mother" was right.

A few brief questions, and as many brief answers and the interview was over — for "Mother" Jones does not seek to be featured in the daily press.

"I am simply a social revolutionist," she said. "I believe in collective ownership of the means of wealth. At this time the natural commodities of this country are cornered in the hands of a few. The man who owns the means of wealth gets the major profit, and the worker, who produces the wealth from the means in the hands of the capitalist, takes what he can get. Sooner or later, and perhaps sooner than we think, evolution and revolution will have accomplished the overturning of the system under which we now live, and the worker will have gained his own. This change will come as the result of education. My life work has been to try to educate the worker to a sense of the wrongs he has had to suffer, and does suffer — and to stir up the oppressed to

491

a point of getting off their knees and demanding that which I believe to be rightfully theirs. When force is used to hinder the worker in his efforts to obtain the things which are his, he has the right to meet force with force. He has the right to strike for what is his due, and he has no right to be satisfied with less. The people want to do right, but they have been hoodwinked for ages. They are now awakening, and the day of their enfranchisement is near at hand."

That, in substance, is what Mother Jones had to say about her mission on earth. She bowed the reporter from the room. He had seen "Mother Jones."

[Charleston (West Virginia) Gazette, *June 11, 1912, reprinted in* International Socialist Review, *March, 1913, pp. 648-49.]*

"We've Got the Pirates on the Run"

Interview in the Brooklyn *Daily Eagle,* June 1, 1913[1]

"We've got the pirates on the run," said Mother Jones the other day, a few hours before she left New York to return to the mining districts of West Virginia. "I am going back. They may arrest me again if they want to, but I am going back to my boys."

And Mother Jones was happy. She had just been told that Congress had authorized a sweeping probe of conditions in West Virginia.[2] "We'll furnish them with all the evidence they want," she said. Mother Jones spent a day or two in New York, coming on from Washington where she furnished Senator Kern with "ammunition" to use in passing his resolution for an investigation. The last day she was here she gave up an afternoon to an *Eagle* interview, and told the reporter all about the present state of society.

Now that divine Sarah Bernhardt has left these shores for her beloved France, perhaps the most remarkable woman in America is the white-haired kindly-eyed old lady, known to 500,000 miners and three generations as Mother Jones. To a smaller number of mine operators, employers, and officials she is known as "the old woman," an agitator, and "trouble maker." She has been called a good many other names.

Aged 81, She Turns A State Topsy-Turvy

Any way you look at it, the indominable Mother Jones, at the age of

81, has just turned things upside down in West Virginia. Figuratively speaking, she has taken the civil and military authorities and mineowners of that sovereign state by the ears and started such a rumpus that the country is apt to have its attention centered upon West Virginia for many months to come.

"We've got our gatling guns going now," said Mother Jones. "The whole country is looking toward West Virginia. Things are going to be better down there from now on."

When reporters called[3] upon Mother Jones in New York — and there was a constant stream of writers at her hotel every day — they were told to wait in the public reception room. While they watched the elevator for the veteran labor leader, she bounced into the room from another direction, having scorned the "elevator contraption" and used the stairs, "just to keep young," as she explained.

"If these society butterflies would take a little exercise occasionally, there wouldn't be so many rich doctors," she said. "But come up to my room. We can be alone and say what we please."

By the time Mother Jones has ascended the stairs with the agility of a girl, it is easy to understand why newspaper correspondents, magazine writers, and other scribes who have been sent into the coal regions of West Virginia to describe the civil war that has prevailed in that state for over a year, have emerged, and taking their pens in hand have described — Mother Jones.

She is unique. Short of stature, with a slight limp in her walk, and with curly white hair and "specs," she resembles almost my grandmother who has lived a peaceful life in the bosom of a happy family. When she talks, you forget the happy grandmother simile. You think that grandmother is cross. Mother is very cross at the "pirates," as she calls the people in West Virginia. But through it all there is a wonderful tolerance and moderation. Her voice is a high falsetto, but not harsh. There is also the touch of the Irish, in brogue and oratorical flourish.

"What I mean by having our gatling guns going," said Mother Jones, "is that we have at least found an effective weapon against the oppressors. Sometimes the other fellow forgets that he can't go on forever mistreating workers. If we can't get the city or county or state to stop the abuse, we must go to the parent state — the nation. It is just as important that the nation protect its citizen in West Virginia as in Mexico, or anywhere else.

"I made three trips to Washington before the last administration closed and tried to get Congress to take up the investigation. I went first to the Department of Commerce and Labor, then to Mr. Henry, and the last time, I went to Senator LaFollette.[4] He said that it was so late that nothing could be done until the next session. But he promised to help. If there was any effort on the part of the mine operators to stop the investigation we fooled them, because they didn't know how we were working. All of this was before I was 'detained.' That is what Governor Hatfield called it. I wasn't under arrest, I wasn't in prison — I was 'detained.'

"They arrested me and kept me in a room, guarded day and night by three husky guards armed with rifles and revolvers, but I was merely being 'detained.' "

The comparison between Bernhardt and Mother Jones is not as irrelevant as might be supposed. Mother Jones is very dramatic. In talking about her boys and conditions in the mining districts, she rises and paces about the room like a tragedian. Her comedy effects are equally interesting, for Mother Jones has retained her sense of humor, and time after time she relieved a recital of sordid facts by a flash of wit, and the assertion, "I get a lot of fun out of it, too."

"It is not easy to understand conditions down there," said the Mother. "West Virginia is very different. Then, again, the average writer can't analyze the motives of the workers. They get facts, but they don't go beneath the surface and get the psychology of the labor movements. They are not of the workers. They do not live with them, work with them, and they can't understand without living with them.

"I have been living with the workers, fighting their battles ever since I can remember. I look after them. I have known most of the men on strike at Paint and Cabin creeks since they were boys. If their wives are sick, I look after them. I take care of the children, and give them food and clothes and money for candy, if it won't hurt them. I understand what the miners are up against and I understand how to handle them.

"West Virginia has been dominated by an invisible government for twenty years. In the state-wide strike many years ago, I went to West Virginia as an organizer. I was arrested for violating an injunction. Injunctions, in my opinion, are one-man laws. Naturally, the mineowners have no love for me. I don't mind that. With me it is class interest. It is a problem of economics.

"In 1904 I went west and spent my time in other sections where there was trouble. I came back to West Virginia on June 6. The miners of Paint Creek had been organized, but the operators refused to give them the Cleveland scale, and they went on strike. They were really locked out, and I went in there.

"The mineowners had brought in the Baldwin guards, which aroused a spirit of antipathy on the part of the miners. The men on Cabin Creek also went out, or rather, they had been locked out for attending meetings, for the Cabin Creek boys were unorganized. The Baldwin guards went in and threw them out of their doghouses, I call the homes, and the miners had to get tents. In some cases men, women, and children lived in the woods, sleeping under the stars, until we provided them with tents.

"We rented some ground near the mouth of the creek, and Eskdale became a tent town. It wasn't an ordinary strike. The miners were driven away from the mines, and lived in the woods in the best way that they could. There is no use to tell all the horrible things that the Baldwins did to the miners. One of the most brutal guards, and the man who is known all over West Virginia as the King Guard, was Ernest Gaujot. Mr. Michelson, who went down there for a magazine, told about Gaujot.[5]

"One of the miners, named Tony Sevilla, left his wife and children and went to Ohio to look for work. While he was gone, Gaujot and his men searched his house and beat and kicked his wife. When the men left and neighbors found Mrs. Sevilla, she was on her knees, making the sign of the cross. 'What has happened,' they asked. The Italian mother, pointing to her side, where Gaujot had kicked her, answered in broken English, 'I don't hear my baby calling me now.'

"The guards did all kinds of terrible things. They used dumdum bullets, which are prohibited by rules of modern warfare, and gatling guns. They assaulted men and women, and mistreated children. Union men and Socialists took their lives in their hands when they went into the sections. The miners, resentful of the Baldwins, decided to protect themselves and fight. They began to squabble, not with the state or county authorities, but with the guards. It kept getting hotter and the fighting more fierce, and the governor ordered out the militia and declared martial law.

"Governor Glasscock first ordered martial law. He was a good, religious man, and I felt sorry for him. He was not well. I knew he wasn't able to handle things. He let subordinates run the matter. You could tell, from the way it was bungled that some inexperienced persons were responsible for the direction of the militia. when the militia was called, the trouble was extended.

"Whole families were thrown out of their homes, and some of them spent four days and nights on the hillsides and cooked in the woods, before tents were provided. That was about the situation when I got there. The miners were up against it. Then 3,000 miners went to Charleston to see the governor. It was funny, some ways. There was an army of 3,000 miners come to see the governor. Then down the street came the mineowners, walking dignified and dressed up. The miners wanted the militia taken away. The mineowners wanted them to stay. And poor Governor Glasscock didn't know what to do. I didn't know what to do that day, either. I was sorry for him.

"The governor gave the miners no satisfaction. Then something happened. The 3,000 miners bought every gun there was for sale in Charleston. They bought carloads of them, with ammunition, and other things. The reason was that they had appealed to the governor, the courts, the sheriff, and from none of these had they got any satisfaction.

"The miners went back to the creeks and the fighting began. The miners cleaned up a few guards in short order. The militia got orders to disarm the miners and the guards. Now the militia is not composed of the best type of men. That is a fact. They began taking sides with the mineowners, and the miners didn't have much chance. They got excited. I saw that something had to be done.

"I called a meeting on the creek, and told the miners to come with us. We piled into a train and went to Boomer. They made some arrests, and I said: 'We'll adjourn and meet at Longacre tomorrow.' The next day they were all at Longacre. I said. 'Now let each local union elect a delegate. We want to send a delegation to the governor.' The delegates were elected and I took them into a church. I said, 'We will see the governor and see what can be done.'

"All this time the men were cooling down and we arranged to go to Charleston. There were only about a dozen of them. When we got to Charleston the fun began — "

Here Mother Jones got up and gave a vivid description of her experience. She laughed, and almost cried, and her acting of the different parts would make a splendid farce.

"We got to Charleston in the afternoon. The Legislature was in session. When we began piling off the train the town went crazy. They began to yell that the old woman had come to town with her army. Bells began to ring. The police alarm was sounded, and all the reserves in town were hustled out. Even the night force was hustled out, and policemen came running down the streets fastening their suspenders, and with their shoes unlaced.

"The Legislature was thrown into panic with the news, and some members got up and yelled to 'lock the doors,' and others shouted to have the old woman sent out of the state. All this excitement because an old woman had come up with a few miners to see the governor. A big policeman came up to me and said, 'You are under arrest.' I was arrested the first time on Lincoln's birthday, on the streets of Charleston, although I was held as a military prisoner.

Mother Jones Locked Up, Charged as Murder Accessory

"When I was arrested, says I, 'Well, what are you going to do with me?' The officer told me to follow him, and he took me to Robbers' Roost — that's what I call the hotel in Charleston where all the mineowners meet — I didn't want to go to the hotel. 'If I am under arrest, lock me in jail,' says I. But he took me to the hotel and by and by a justice of the peace came and issued a warrant for me. I was accused of being accessory to murder.

"But that is not the worst of it. The next thing they did was to put me on a train and send me back to Pratt, where they turned me over to the militia. I was a prisoner of war. When I got back, an officer said,

'Major Davis didn't know you were coming.' They put me in a front room of a cabin with armed guards at every corner. A family in the cottage supplied my meals.

"Meantime the militia had arrested the others. They were kept in boxcars and in other places. At Pratt the baggage room of the railroad station had been turned into a bullpen, and later they used the store as a prison. Big John Brown, the editor of the *Argus*, and the other boys were under arrest by that time. All of them fine fellows. They took the prisoners to Point Pleasant for a while, but the flood got them there and they were taken to Clarksburg and kept in jail.

"The drumhead court martial sat in Pratt. I objected to this kind of court and refused to recognize it while there were civil courts in session. Bond, the provost marshal was a big, overgrown fellow, every way but mentally. While I was in the bastile a lot of funny things happened. You would think I was the most dangerous person on earth.

Cleveland Newspaper Man Locked Up for Seeing Mother Jones

"Hollis, a Cleveland newspaper man, came there and talked to me and they put him under arrest for it. It was the most amusing thing you ever saw. Hollis had a kodak when they arrested him, and two armed guards took him to the bullpen between them. They were afraid of the kodak and held it like it was a bomb. As soon as the men in authority found out that a man from a big Cleveland paper had been arrested they wired to let him go, but when he came back to the bastile the guards wouldn't even let him look at me and hustled him off to the station to get him out of town.

"When Michelson, the magazine writer, and one of my boys tried to see me they told him I was being bothered by writers and didn't want to see him. General Elliott told him that he didn't like the newspaper men, and what they had written about the militia, and that he would put them in jail, no matter what paper they represented. 'I haven't seen your article,' said Elliott. 'If I had I might put you in jail.' 'All right,' said the boy. 'When I get back to civilization, I am going to tell the people about it.'

"Governor Hatfield was a physician, and should know better than to treat human beings as they were treated. Governor Glasscock had more excuse. He needed a physician. There wasn't any way of finding out where we stood down there. The findings of the court were all sent to the governor, and I don't know yet whether I was found guilty or not. But I was let out.

"After Senator Kern brought his resolution in the Senate I got more freedom. A new officer was put in charge. This was Captain Sherwood. He was in every sense a gentleman, and anything I can say or do for him I will. He was a real man, a fine specimen of manhood. He treated

497

me with every consideration. He took the guards away, and my mail wasn't interefered with anymore. He said: 'Mother, you can go about as you please, without a guard.'

Mother Jones Takes a Hand to Keep Things Moving

"When I took up the papers one day and read that certain influences in Wall Street had wired that the Kern resolution was to be withdrawn, I realized, for the safety of the nation, something must be done. The only hope any of us had was in the investigation, and the only hope for better conditions in the future rested in that resolution. I got a piece of paper and wrote to Senator Kern something like this:

" 'I have just passed my eighty-first milestone in this military prison. From out these walls I send you the heartaches and tears and sobs of broken men, women, and children, who plead with you not to let your resolution be defeated.' There was some more of it, all meant for Senator Kern personally, which I sent to Washington.

"The next day, when the matter came up in the Senate, he read my letter to the Senate. The next day Captain Sherwood came to me and said: 'Mother, the governor has just telegraphed me to bring you up to Charleston. Get ready. I will put on civilian clothes and accompany you.' I apologized for my appearance. I had worn the same clothes for three months, but he said it was an honor to go with me. We took the train and he delivered me over to the governor.

" 'Where do you live,' asked the governor.

" 'Wherever the fight for human liberty is hottest,' I said. He asked me if I wanted to see him, and we had a long talk. I told him that the state of West Virginia had spent $500,000 in the war on the miners that might better be spent on schools or in the welfare of the children of the miners who were living in the woods. I went to a hotel in Charleston and didn't see the governor any more. When I told him I was going out of town, he said it was all right.

"I came up to Washington then and helped Senator Kern. 'Montain Semper Liberi' is the motto of West Virginia. It means that mountaineers are always free, but the miners of West Virginia, who are mountaineers, are not free. They are mostly Americans, born and bred in the hills. Practically all of those at Paint and Cabin Creeks are native born. They are not naturally vicious, but will fight to defend themselves.

"There is always some poor devil, some half-starved fellow, who will take rash steps that he should not take, which give the mineowners an excuse for arming guards. The only way for workers to gain advantages in a situation like that in West Virginia is to keep their heads level. I am opposed to violence, and am always trying to show the men that the way to get relief is with the ballot.[6]

"During my trial I was accused of making inflammatory speeches.

This is part of the evidence: A mine superintendent was put on the stand. He was asked if he had heard me make any inflammatory speeches. 'Yes,' he said. 'She said the superintendent was a salary slave, while the miner was a wage slave. She said I was a two-by-four.' Inflammatory? A clerk also testified that I made inflammatory speeches. I had said that a clerk had to prop up his head with a pencil to make the mineowners think he was earning his pay. More inflammatory oratory?"

Mother Jones's Fighting Spirit Developed Years Ago

Mother Jones was born in Ireland. She came to Canada when an infant. Her first outbreak occurred in school when she was fourteen years old. The teacher made some slighting remark about the Irish, and she wanted to "lick" the teacher then and there. Since that time she has been almost constantly in the thick of some labor fight. She is a regular organizer of the United Mine Workers, but the organization has long ceased to give her orders. She goes where she pleases to go, and the miners pay her way. Her history is that of organized labor in this country.

"I remember in Chicago, long before trade unions were recognized or countenanced by the authorities," said Mother Jones, "we tried to hold meetings. One of the meeting places was in a loft, and all of us had to bring candles. One night a big Irish policeman nabbed us coming out. 'Go home,' says he, 'you've been plottin' agin the government. The government is good enough to ye. If ye come here agin, I'll break your heads.' Finally we found a room back of a saloon. Our meeting had gone on for some time and we were solemnly discussing resolutions, when the proprietor, a big, brawny fellow, came to door. 'Get out of here, the lot of you. You're drinking no beer at all,' says he.

"There is more freedom now, in most parts. People are more tolerant. There is a broader spirit of brotherhood. When I finished speaking at Carnegie Hall, the other night two Catholic priests and another preacher came up and shook hands. That couldn't have happened in years gone by. But we are up against a great economic problem. The revolution of machinery has produced a situation in the industrial world that is nearing a climax. There is trouble ahead. Things will get worse before they get better.

Statesmen Have No Grasp of Situation, Is Mother Jones's Opinion

"The most dangerous thing of all is that our so-called statesmen have so little grasp of it. They don't understand that the old order is passing. I am not a Socialist like the ordinary type, although socialism is inevitable. It is doing a wonderful work on the education side, and socialism is a matter of education and evolution. The Industrial Workers of the World are getting people that the unions would never get; but it is not right that the lives that have been sacrificed and the faithful work that has been done by the Federation of Labor should be discounted and trampled under foot. Industrial unionism is coming, but it is a matter of growth and cannot be forced. Great masses cannot be educated in a day.

"The IWW is spasmodic. Those who preach and talk as the leaders did the other day about wiping Paterson off the map are fanatics. The Federation of Labor has become systematized, and static, and the IWW is making a broader appeal, but strikes cannot be won without funds. To bring on a strike and go back licked by hunger is not progress for labor."

Mother Jones has a lot of ideas on conditions that should interest sociologists. Her grasp of affairs and alertness are simply amazing for a woman over eighty. She was early in the fight for the exclusion of Chinese coolies on the Pacific coast, and thinks we will soon have to settle the Japanese question decisively. "One of the most striking things to me," she says, "is the gradual dying out of the American type. In fifty years the changes in type have been almost beyond belief. The Japs are not the only Orientals to be feared. The Hindus will some day be a serious menace. They are coming in large numbers now, although little has been said about them."

Notes

1. The original headline read: "MOTHER JONES, 81, LEADS LABOR WAR IN WEST VIRGINIA," followed by sub-headings which read: "We've Got the Pirates on the Run," Is How Aged Fighter Describes Conditions. Tells of Miners' Battles. Locked Up and Tried by Military Law, Remarkable Woman Has Turned West Virginia Topsy Turvy." A mutilated copy of the interview is in Mother Mary Harris Jones Papers, Department of Archives and Manuscripts, Catholic University of America, Washington, D.C.

2. *See* pp. 160-61, 225.

3. Events proved this to be an overoptimistic prediction.

4. Robert M. LaFollette (1855-1925), Wisconsin political leader and reform governor and senator where from 1906 to 1925, he led the progressive forces. Opposed United States entry into World War I, ran unsuccessfully for president in 1924 as candidate of the Progessive, Farmer-Labor Party.

5. The reference is to Michelson's article, "Sweet Land of Liberty," *Everybody's Magazine*, May, 1913, pp. 615-28.

6. The emphasis on the ballot for men made Mother Jones's opposition to ballots for women particularly difficult to understand. She expressed this opposition at the same time in her interview with the *New York Times* which follows.

"Mother" Jones, Mild-Mannered, Talks Sociology

Interview in *New York Times*, June 1, 1913[1]

I believe no more in thug-statemanship than in thug-economics; either one will breed the other; they are brothers. I am neither Socialist nor Anarchist; I decry them both, and, naturally, in decrying them, I must decry their causes.

"Note this: The well-fed man will never knock down to steal his dinner.

"Note this, also: The violent employer and the violent employee both need curbing."

A white-haired old woman in a hotel room said these things and thus dazed me, for I had gone there with eyes ready for the blood-red flag.

Instead I got calm sociology, interspersed with humor which I shall not make an effort to transcribe because it would lose so much in telling; I had expected much incendiary talk in uncouth English and found an educated woman, careful of her speech and sentiments. If she had a red flag with her she kept it in her satchel with her comb and brush and powder puff. She has a powder puff. That, too, astonished me.

During the morning not a labor leader came to see her, but among her visitors were three semifamous writers for high-class periodicals, bent not on business, but wholly social calls; a woman author of importance; a widely celebrated woman student of the economic problems of the time.

Curiosity was not behind the visit of any one of these. All were a little more than friends, for all called her "mother" with affection. Indeed, the handsome, well-dressed, carefully spoken, hospitable, smiling, sympathetic, seventy-year-old woman who received them and myself was none other than that "Mother" Jones, widely heralded as the gray-haired virago of the West Virginia mines, the woman labor leader who was held a captive in what was called the "bull pen" on the theory that this was necessary for the safety of society.

I never saw her lead a strike: I have been told that she does so with force amounting to incendiarism. After two visits to her aggregating quite ten hours I should as much expect her to be violent as to see a matron at a charity ball spring into anarchistic action.

Which indicates that she is an extraordinary character. It is a fact that her name has held a state in terror, that the mineowners declare her as their strongest foe, that within the year the state of West Virginia has held her prisoner behind the shining steel of bayonets.

Only when we talked about the West Virginia situation did she show the slightest tendency to step down from her calmly judicial, somewhat scholarly attitude. She called some West Virginia capitalists rather mildly critical names; denounced the West Virgininan industrial system as a definite infamy; told sad stories of its women and its children victims, but even as she told of fighting and her willingness to fight, in certain circumstances, she declared that fighting is unnecessary and that the men and bosses ought to get together for the common good, each make some concessions, and go on about their business like calm, cooperating, reasonable human beings.

Her Views on the Future

There obviously is a "Mother" Jones other than this extraordinary and wholly unexpected one whom I met at the Union Square Hotel; but as long as this one was then so definitely in evidence and based the arguments which she set forth on an experience in the midst of labor turbulence undoubtedly unprecedented for a woman, what she says may be considered worth reading.

If she be, in truth, a Doctress Jekyll-Mrs. Hyde, she is as wonderful in her black silk, her carefully dressed, silvery hair, her silk stockings, and neat pumps, as Stevenson's male doublet is between the covers of his book.

"My husband died of yellow fever in the South," said she, "and the same disease made other widows by the tens of thousands. It is making no more widows, because we now have mastered it. The world is suffering, today, from an industrial yellow fever, not less fatal, but, I am certain, as preventable.

"We have applied to the economic disease which has distressed us all manner of remedies, all unintelligent. Students have delved widely, but wrongly in the main, in their search for causes. Each has devised his remedy; most remedies have failed because they did not touch the cause. Some remedies have succeeded; they got at the cause.

"I thoroughly believe that in the not far distant future an era of industrial peace is waiting; we shall overtake it. Real education is all we need to help us find it. I hate the Anarchist, be he in the mine breast with his pick against the coal or in the national bank with his hands upon the combination of the vault. There are many in both places; but they are growing fewer.

"We cannot be a law unto ourselves in this world. We must think of others, and the others, the majority, will ultimately make all law. The equality which is the ideal of this country, of course, is nearer now than ever, and such situations as that which now exists in West Virginia are the exceptions which unquestionably prove the rule. That is the sort of mediaevalism which is as abhorrent to the intelligent employer as it is to the suffering miner. The employers suffer from it, too; they are as unhappy as their men are. But they do not understand. It is an extraordinary spectacle.

"I have as little patience with the workingman who cries that all employers are hard-hearted wretches as I have with the employer who declares all workingmen to be mere brutes who must be managed or ground into the dust. For the dynamiter among labormen I have as little sympathy as for the mill owner who works children at his looms fourteen hours each day.

"Thousands of employers are feeling around for the way out of all this muddle; some of them are finding it and walking on it. If the workingmen were not as reasonable and progressive in most places the United States would be in poverty instead of riches. But, in order to be fair, we must remember this: The average employer has had a better chance than the average worker to learn economic wisdom.

"Some representatives of the employing class are wise today. 'Golden Rule' Jones, the present Mayor of Toledo, is a wise employer;[2] Gov. Waite of Colorado is a wise man;[3] Gov. Tanner of Illinois,[4] and Mayor Hunt of Cincinatti[5] have advanced and stand upon the ground of the enlightened. There are thousands of employers who are wise.

"There may be fewer in the mining regions than elsewhere; mining is a crude, rough business, shackled in tradition.

"But even the best of the employers have among them few who really are searching for the source of the disease. Not many of them definitely are on the trail of the mosquito; they are trying drugs instead of drainage as their cures. They won't cure, although it is a possibility that they may sometimes be valuable."

A Labor Slogan

"Search for the mosquito! That ought to be a slogan with investigators on both sides of the labor question. Personally I think the swamps it hides in are more frequently in the domain of the employers than in that of the employees, but what I think doesn't matter if we only find the insect's habitat and drain it dry, so that it will not breed future trouble

"Violence will never cure our labor troubles, injunctions will not cure them. Both are child's play. Advantages secured by them are surely temporary. If employers and employed will only settle down to deep effective thought, stop giving causes for strikes and striking without cause and think, think, think, we shall come out all right.

"We're going to come out all right.

"I don't believe in fighting in an economic battle any more than I believe in shotgun quarantine for yellow fever: you don't; nobody does. Yet we all are at it. It is silly. It's a sign that we are not yet civilized.

But mind you — I steadfastly maintain that there is quite as much of barbarism in the attitude of the employers, indeed more, far more, than in the attitude of working people.

"It's all tragic while it's silly. It brutalizes both sides, and this effect will last through generations. The spirit of implacable vengeance, which has been developed in employer and employed through all these years of labor strife, will bear its sad fruit in oncoming generations.

"The hopeful side is that the scientific investigation which will end in finding the mosquito and in identification of the swamps for drainage is already under way. We have uncovered the germ in some phases of the ailment; we have begun to drain some swamps. The child labor business was about the first triumph of science in this country's economic field. It was a startling triumph, and perhaps the pleasantest thing I have to think of is that it was through working for the mitigation of its horror that I found my entrance into the field of labor work.

"I was born in Canada, a good many years ago, and there I went to the Toronto public schools, passing through then into the high school and afterward into a convent school. I think they furnish a good brand of popular education, there in Canada; but they taught me in it some things which they probably did not have in mind. Among the details of my education was a hatred of injustice and a vast inquisitiveness.

"The hatred of injustice and the curiosity took me into the southern cotton mills. There I did my level best to learn the truth about conditions. I very carefully studied things at first hand, engaging myself as operative in mill after mill.

"The conditions which I found appalled me. Not only were the children workers practically enslaved, but this wage slavery extended to adults. It was the 'company store' system in its most aggravated form. It has been bad, at various times, in the coal regions. It never could be worse than it was there in those great southern mills.

"Today's advance over the conditions of eighteen or twenty years ago in southern mills is so extraordinary that my hope for what the next decade may bring about in general industry is great enough, perhaps, to be regarded by a less experienced and less optimistic student as a dream. Those horrors of the toiling infants and the weary mothers struggling for mere bread to keep the life within their bellies! The thraldom of the debt slaves!

"I did my modest best to help them all. I wrote extensively for many newspapers about the slavery of the little ones and helped, I hope, to arouse the early public sentiment against it. I did my best with the debt slaves. I remember actually helping one family to escape from a condition as intolerable as any Negro slavery which ever had existed in the same southern states.

"This family, consisting of a mother and three daughters, had at this company store run up a debt of $30 while the father had been lying in his final illness. I do not remember just how long this debt had been upon the books nor how much it amounted to at the time I took the thing in hand.

"The system was to dole out food and clothing in the smallest possible quantities, and charge rent at the largest figure, being careful to see to it that interest, food, clothing, and rent always aggregated just a little more, each month, than the total of the wages earned.

"The thraldom was complete. There was no hope of escape from it. Fourteen hours a day, seven days a week, for every member of that family, year in, year out, would never clear that debt away. I knew it, and they knew it; it angered me; it subdued them into spiritless and hopeless things, bowed by a weight of misery impossible to describe in words.

"I took a short cut out. I abducted the whole family. It was a real abduction, for they went almost against their will. They could not believe escape to be a possibility.

"I never shall forget that night. We started well after dark, of course, and even then the axles of the wagon were better greased than they had ever been before to stop the creaking of the hubs.

An Awful Journey

"I was already known to railroad men, who were anxious to serve me, and the station agent had arranged things so that a train which did not ordinarily stop at that station would that night pause to take us on.

"We drove along the miles of road, my charges shivering in fear, although the night was moist and hot, with all the qualms which might have thrilled us had we been a party of the antebellum abolitionists and escaping Negro slaves. Almost listening for the baying of bloodhounds, we reached the station, climbed furtively aboard the train, and started off. My charges all broke down then, quite hysterically. The strain had been so great!

"Now child labor and such episodes as that I have detailed are gradually disappearing; there is a sentiment against such laws as made it possible to hold a human being in debt thrall. The correction of these evils will be presently complete.

"In Pennsylvania, now, the labor of children under fourteen in mines and mills is forbidden, even though some parents fought against the law as bitterly as the mill and mine owners did. Ten years ago boys went to labor in the mines while they were still so little that their dinner buckets trailed upon the ground as they proceeded; now they are sent to school. In the fact that they are sent to school lies an argument for labor war in certain circumstances, for they never would have reached the school if the mine workers had not fought to get the right for them.

"But they are not the only gainers. I fancy that most mineowners who fought against child labor laws would now admit that Pennsylvania is getting not only more efficient labor, but better citizenship out of the workers in its mines and we must all admit that the better the citizenship becomes the better are industrial conditions, both for worker and for owner. The system which the mineowners so fiercely struggled to preserve was inefficient. It hurt both sides.

"I don't hate employers. What I hate is the cause of labor troubles. I hate no individual. There are those among the mineowners in West Virginia who deserve less hate than pity; they deserve more sympathy than I do, more sympathy than any of the striking miners do, for they are going to be beaten into doing right. The man forced into his righteousness is a sorry spectacle.

"How we have progressed! Railroad strikes were a terrific problem not more than ten years ago. Traffic was frequently tied up, and the business and the pleasure of the country paralysed. The militia was called out from time to time, and sometimes property was burned and trains were wrecked; occasionally strikers were shot down. We are getting saner now. We arbitrate our railroad difficulties.

"I believe still further sanity will come. Although I am no Socialist[6] I think that through labor troubles will come collective ownership of railways and that that will settle strikes on them forever. But whether it comes or does not, both sides gained when they became imbued with the idea that it was better to get together and talk things out in reason than it was to stand apart, hurling at one another bricks and epithets occasionally interspersed with bullets.

"In Illinois, not many years ago, strikes in the mining regions were almost continual. Again the get-together idea intervened, and there has not been a miners' strike in Illinois in fourteen years. Do you think the West Virginia problem is more difficult than any of the problems which came up in Illinois? I know it is not. But they have not got together yet down there. They will have to.

"What could be more tragic than the brutality of the injunction? Is it a wonder that some workingmen have begun to fear there is no justice in the courts? I think not. Well, the way to cure their fear is not to shoot them down, but to put justice in the courts. We have many courts with justices in them. Let's put justice into all of them.

"In West Virginia there are no state laws to check industrial despotism. For twenty years the situation which now is boiling over has been growing slowly hot there. A similar condition would not be tolerated in New York by either working men or workingmen's employers. You have grown beyond that here.

"It's nip and tuck. The employers' injunctions are as dangerous to civilization as the strikers' shotguns. The striker becomes violent, and the employer chooses another kind of violence. They're perhaps equally at fault. But who began it? Consider what occurred.

"When forty-five or fifty miners were taken to the drumhead court which was established, attorneys for the miners got a District Court to issue an injunction restraining the drumhead court. The drumhead court, consisting of appointees of certain corporations, went to Charleston and induced the judge to withdraw the injunction. Had he made it permanent instead, he would have been making history; but he did not. He missed the chance of being one of the greatest figures on the bench.

"Then fifty of us were tried by the drumhead court. I was held in the military prison, called the 'bull pen,' three months less five days. Others were detained three months and two weeks. We didn't suffer much; I was never really uncomfortable. But who gained anything?

"That's the point I'm trying to make. I am not railing against my imprisonment, but against the inefficiency of the system which so sillily imagined that to keep me there could do anybody any good. It accomplished absolutely nothing toward the solution of the trouble.

"To try to do that in that way was like an effort by a doctor who gives you a little morphine, when you ache, so that you won't feel the pain. The government of West Virginia gave a little morphine to the industrial situation. It did nothing toward the removal of the cause of the disorder which had brought about the ache.

"West Virginia shows the survival of conditions which existed elsewhere in the dark industrial ages of thirty years ago. It is very likely lucky for the country that I was locked up and that the others were locked up.

"It offered to the nation an object lesson of what most regions have grown out of, and perhaps thus stimulated thought which may take all of us a little further toward enlightenment. The next twenty years will carry us along a constantly ascending path into conditions even more conspicuously better than those which rule today, than the west Virginia conditions are now worse than those which rule elsewhere.

"The people of this country must learn to choose their leaders — political, industrial, and social — not because they are good fellows but because they are intelligent students of great questions. No job is too small to put a thinker into. The voters at labor union elections and corporate elections of directors, as well as voters at the polls in city, county, state, and national elections must try to find the men for every situation. When they get into the offices we will begin to hurry on the upward path. Politics, economics, and sociology should link arms.

"They are going to. Ten or fifteen years ago when some one spoke of the recall of judges the entire Nation rose in arms.[7] Today it is a common issue, and in some states it is a fact. It will presently be fact in others, and then will follow other great advances as sensational, as bitterly opposed at first and as generally adopted after they have been threshed out and perfected.

Investigation Is Progress

"The commission form of city government has penetrated the East as far as Jersey City.[8] That is a fine sign of the times. Imagine — Jersey City! It was once boss-ridden as few communities have ever been. The railroads absolutely owned it. But they did not profit by their ownership. Instead they killed the goose which laid the golden egg it represented. The goose was public confidence. Let any one kill public confidence, and that minute he is down and out, although he may not know it instantaneously.

"All the investigations which have swept the country, tending everywhere to uncover corruption which a few years ago would have been generally winked at and accepted as a political necessity, are fine signs. They mean progress.

"Here in New York City your police clean-up, even your taxi ordinance mean progress. Everything is marching toward the better. Labor troubles helped the march begin. Their terrors were not wasted if they started people thinking. The agitators who have agitated, though they may have been much criticised, even if they had been wholly in the wrong, and they were not, have usually served a splendid purpose, for they've made the people think.

"Why, I'm so great an optimist that some people may regard me as a dreamer. You didn't think that about Mother Jones, did you? It's true. I believe that strikes are going to stop, not because I think that capital will choke labor till it hasn't breath left for the effort of a strike, or because I think that labor will smash capital until it hasn't money left to fight with, but because I think intelligence will grow among employers and employed till, presently, we shall find strikes quite unnecessary. Nothing ever was so costly. War has not been. Strikes have, indeed, been war. We're going to save the money which we've wasted on industrial warfare.

"The Stock Exchange Investigation failed,[9] but it set a lot of people thinking right, and among them I've no doubt were many members of the Stock Exchange. Agitation pays.

"I am in no more sympathy with dynamite in the hands of labor leaders than I am with embezzlement as a practice among financiers. The capitalist who robs a bank is no worse than a labor agitator who blows up a mill.

"There are mineowners in West Virginia against whom we've been fighting, but who are not bad men. They're the victims of the circumstance that they are in an ill-developed industrial group. There are also bad mineowners — very bad ones.

"There are workers, there, who are innocent victims of the system which obtains, industrious men, anxious to be law-abiding and peace-loving. Don't you suppose that many of those men down there hate turbulence? The average human being only wants a quiet home, a well-

508

fed, comfortable family, so situated that its happiness is possible. There are also vicious workers.

"Neither side has a monopoly, either of vice or virtue. What is the use of shouting: 'They are perfect!' about anybody? The good men on both sides are good, the bad men bad. Out of their clash will come that working of the yeast which so fascinated the outrageous hero of Jack London's *Sea Wolf*[10] and humanity will feel the thrusting of its steady rise.

"I am not a suffragist. In no sense of the word am I in sympathy with woman's suffrage. In a long life of study of these questions I have learned that women are out of place in political work.[11] There already is a great responsibility upon women's shoulders — that of rearing rising generations.

"It has been in part their sad neglect of motherhood which has filled reform schools and which keeps the juvenile courts busy. If women had been really industrious in their natural field they might have warded off some horrors of the time. They can begin now to be more useful than they have been by studying these economic problems and helping toward industrial peace.

"The average working woman is unfitted for the ballot. She will rarely join an organization of the industry she works in. Give her the vote and she'll neglect it. Home training of the child should be her task, and it is the most beautiful of tasks. Solve the industrial problem and the men will earn enough so that women can remain home and learn it."[12]

What Neglectful Mothers Do

"Let the women stay at home and we shall have, when strikes come, better strikers; and we shall also have far better men for them to deal with. The rich neglect their sons as the poor do. In the prison inclosure recently I saw an old man going to the well each day for water. Behind marched a bayoneted militiaman. He was a weak and inoffensive old man; he was a strong young guardsman.

"I asked the young man what the old man had been arrested for. It transpired that he had failed to pay a fine of $10. He had not had the money. His offense had been not really criminal, but ethical. He had jeered at the militia.

"I asked the young man what he thought his mother (who was dead) would think if she could look at him as he marched back and forth, armed with a bayoneted gun, behind this old man who was not far from the grave and who had only jeered at the militia. I asked him pleasantly, but he laughed and hurried the old man.

"Now, that young militiaman is an example, no less than a riotous young striker is, of the rising generation for which neglectful mothers are responsible. The human being is the only animal which is neglected in its babyhood. The brute mother suckles and preserves her young at the cost of her own life, if need be. The human mother hires another, poorer woman for the job. Of course, the race must suffer for it.

"I have said that I hate violence; I favor drama. We must wake the sleepers somehow, and where blindness can be healed by shock we must provide the shock. Sometimes it hurts a little, but it helps the patient afterward, for lo! it makes him see. The Coxey Army's march to Washington was a great joke, but it helped mightily to bring about good roads.[13]

"And demonstrations are good things for labor in these learning days. They are good advertising, and the serious, progressive drama as well as comic opera needs advertising.

"I feel this: If labor would eliminate its violence and capital would eliminate injunctions, the battle would be practically over. We could then go sanely at arranging peace. Common sense, uninflamed, productive, could step in. But labor will be violent as long as capital swears out injunctions. Also, the first step toward peace must come from capital. It has more advantages. It must lead.

"The human being is most wonderful. We can do anything with him. If we would all agree to try to do the right thing with every human being over whom we are in power or over whom we have an influence!

"The capitalist and striker — both men are all right, only they are sick; they need a remedy; they have been mosquito bitten. Let's kill the virulent mosquito and then find and drain the swamp in which he breeds. That is the advice of Mother Jones. I'd rather wave a white flag with that lettered on it than to wave red flags. I'll fight when I am forced to and urge my boys to fight when they are forced to, but I wish we all might be quite reasonable and stop fighting. Fighting is a waste!"

Notes

1. The sub-heading read: "Incendiary Labor Leader Who Terrorized West Virginia Talks of Coming Industrial Peace, and Says She is Neither Socialist nor Anarchist." Excerpts from this interview also appeared in "The Indomitable Spirit of Mother Jones," *Current Opinion,* July 1913, pp. 19-20.

2. For an earlier different estimate of "Golden Rule" Jones, *see* pp. 90, 98, 100.

3. David H. Waite, governor of Colorado, aided the miners at Cripple Creek in winning their strike for the eight-hour day in the spring of 1894, and won the distinction among workers "of being the only governor in the United States who had ever called out the soldiers to protect the workers." Waite was elected on the Populist ticket.

4. For the part Gov. Tanner played in the Virden episode, *see* pp. 107, 474, 511.

5. Mayor Henry Hunt was Cincinnati's reform mayor, 1911-1913. His admin-

istration has been described as a "business administration" with a stress on the use of experts. His relationship to the local trade unions was better than most but still ambiguous.

6. *Current Opinion* put it this way: "Mother Jones is not swept off her feet by beautiful theories and utopian schemes. The Socialists claim her, but she doesn't claim them. She calls them sentimentalists. . . . Nevertheless, altho she doesn't seem to believe much in Socialists, she believes Socialism is inevitable." (*op. cit.,* p. 19.) It must be remembered that the interview came after a very bitter and disillusioning experience with Socialist leaders in the West Virginia coal strike. (*See* pp. 218-19.)

7. A tremendous battle developed over the inclusion of recall of judges in the constitution of Arizona when it sought to become a state in 1910-11, and as a result of conservative opposition in Congress and a veto by President Taft, the clause had to be deleted. However, as soon as Arizona did become a state, the clause calling for recall of judges was reinstated in its constitution. For the issue of recall of judges, *see* Foner, *op. cit.,* vol. 5, pp. 52-53.

8. The commission form of government, under which cities were administered by appointed commissioners, was part of the municipal reform movement and was viewed as a means of eliminating control of cities by the boss and machine operating in the interest of big business. Unfortunately, many commissioners proved just as capable of performing this work.

9. The Stock Exchange investigation occurred in 1907 in New York and was conducted for the state legislature by Charles Evans Hughes.

10. Jack London's *The Sea Wolf,* a novel published in 1904 with the theme of the struggle between man and nature, featured a captain who dominated his crew by sheer brute force.

11. For the completely opposite view expressed by Mother Jones, *see* pp. 26, 95, 97, 440, 448. This particular part of the *New York Times* was widely reprinted in papers and magazines opposed to woman suffrage.

12. This was a common refrain of male trade union leaders from the days of the National Trades' Union in the 1830s to the American Federation of Labor and was even echoed by male leaders of the I.W.W. *See* Foner, *Women and the American Labor Movement: From Colonial Times to the Eve of World War I,* 53-54, 455-57, 486-88.

13. Coxey's Army was the march of unemployed workers in the spring of 1894 to Washington, D.C. for relief from lack of jobs and starvation. The originator of the descent upon Washington was Jacob Sechler Coxey, a wealthy manufacturer of Massillon, Ohio, who formulated a plan under which the unemployed would be put to work on public work projects. He called for the federal government to issue $500 million in greenbacks to be expended for the employment of citizens on a huge nationwide road-building program. The marchers were dispersed by the police when they came to Washington.

She's 83; Full of Fight

Interview in Seattle *Post-Intelligencer*, May 30, 1914
by Roy Alden[1]

When seen at the hotel last night shortly after her arrival, Mother Jones was complaining good-humoredly about a Seattle chef installing too many toothpicks in a clubhouse sandwich she was munching. Mother Jones is 83, having recently celebrated a birthday, although she does not look it. She is short in stature, with gray hair, banked on the forehead by what may be termed a curling pompadour. Mother Jones speaks convincingly, pointing a significant finger when she utters a statement that she wishes to emphasize. Back of a pair of grandma glasses are a pair of interesting blue eyes, which sparkle as she talks.

On the subject of longevity, she observed:

"I'll tell you, son, it's the opportunity to fight that gives me long life. If I hadn't been engaged in fighting industrial battles I would have passed away long before this, but it is the spirit of the thing that fills me with vigor and energy. Why, do you know, I haven't got time to get sick."

Mother Jones says that the only effective solution of the situation in Colorado, in which she took an active part, is for the government to take over the mines.

"But I am not in favor of the government paying $10,000 for the mines," she continued. "I wouldn't sanction a move to give 10 cents for them. Nature did not put that coal there for a bunch of national looters and burglars to hold. I want the United States to simply take the mines over without making any compensation. Enough compensation has been paid already."

Mother Jones contends that the conflict between labor and capital will never end until the United States has taken over all industries, which she thinks will eventually result. Inauguration of the parcel post system, she said, is a step in this direction.

Notes

1. Mother Jones was in Seattle for Labor's First Memorial Day. *See above* pp. 57, 245-50.

Although an Octogenarian Is Still Active in the Cause of Labor

Interview in Vancouver *Daily Province* (British Columbia),
June 11, 1914[1]

The secret of longevity was disclosed by the labor organizer, Mrs. Mary Jones, or "Mother" Jones, as she is more familiarly known, in the course of an interview with a representative of *The Province* yesterday afternoon on her arrival from Victoria. "Mother" Jones is a keen-eyed, vigorous, motherly looking old lady, who in spite of her advanced years — she is in her 83rd year — shows few traces of the strenuous labor struggles in which she has been a moving spirit for the past 35 years.

"I attribute my good health and unimpaired facilities," she said in reply to a query, "to the life of activity which I have led. Many people retire from active life at the age of 50 and spend the rest of their years in peace and quietness. They allow their mental faculties to become dulled by not exercising them, and by not continuing to take an energetic interest in affairs.

"I was nearly fifty when I took up the business of agitating to improve labor conditions. My mind is kept constantly on the alert coping with difficulties, planning campaigns, organizing work along new lines and with striving to better present-day conditions. I have no time to think about getting old; besides I have a lot to accomplish yet.

"The average healthy individual," she continued, "could live to be a hundred easily if he or she would only follow out my precepts."

Long and Active Career.

Mrs. Jones is a wonderful woman — that fact is impelled to one's notice on first meeting her, and is strengthened after a few minutes conversation. She has been engaged in active propaganda and agitation on behalf of the labor unions since the Knights of Labor, the forerunner of the American Federation of Labor, was first organized. She referred to her early endeavors as "sowing the seed." Her husband was an iron moulder, and when the first move was made towards organizing, the labor forces of the United States, she became associated with the leaders, rapidly assuming the direction of affairs herself.

"The recent troubles in Colorado," Mrs. Jones declared, "are to be construed as another indication of the division that is in process between the classes and the industrial workers. The capitalists have the government on their side, the government has the military and the military have the bayonets with which to subdue strikers."

Calls Prisons "Bastiles"

She discussed the terms she had served in the military prisons, or "bastiles," as she preferred to call them, and the many labor fights in which she participated, turning from description of one industrial struggle to another and interpolating a remark here and there, to explain how she had stirred the President and Congress to action, by her appeals and maneuvres.

Mrs. Jones's principal object in visiting the Pacific coast for the first time was explained. In view of patriotic sentiment, inspired by consecrating a day each year to the memory of those who lost their lives on the field of battle, she said that organized labor had decided to adopt similar measures and on Memorial Day to pay tribute to those who had perished in industrial strife. Between 6,000 and 8,000 labor unionists marched in the first parade in Seattle a week ago last Saturday and 20,000, it is estimated, attended a mass meeting held afterwards.

Mr. George Pettigrew of Nanaimo, member of the international board of the United Mine Workers, accompanied "Mother" Jones from Victoria. In the course of her chat, she condemned the manner in which the Canadian immigration officer at Seattle had refused her permission to board the boat for Victoria and praised the Victoria inspector for his courteous treatment under similar conditions.[2] She declared that if the Canadian authorities had adhered to their first attitude of barring her from entering the Dominion she would have invoked the aid of the executive heads of the American Government to grant her the courtesies.

Notes

1. Mother Jones was in British Columbia to help striking Canadian coal miners. *See above* pp. 37, 51, 57, 251-57.
2. For the details of this incident, *see above* pp. 251-52.

Mother Jones Seeks Mine Peace in Colorado

Interview in New York *Tribune*, November 1914[1]

Proudly boasting she is champion octogenarian traveller in the United States, "Mother" Jones, leader of the striking miners, visited the *Tribune* office last night immediately before leaving for Philadelphia. Since January 1, "Mother" Jones has covered more than 70,000 miles, in spite of the fact that for a goodly part of the time she was detained as a prisoner in Colorado.

Two weeks ago she arrived in Washington from Colorado and was granted an audience with President Wilson, in regard to the situation in the Colorado coal fields.[2] Since then she has journied to Colorado and back East again. Tonight she will leave Philadelphia for Trinidad, Colorado, the centre of the strike zone.

"Mother" Jones is a sweet-faced, motherly looking, old lady, with sparse, snow-white locks. There is nothing to suggest that she is a fire-eater or agitator. She is somewhat under medium height and rather stout, and wears a widow's bonnet and a gown of rusty black.

"In spite of the work of the mediation commission appointed by the Department of Commerce and Labor at Washington last April," she said, "conditions remain unchanged in Colorado. Under the protection of the federal troops, nonunion labor has been imported, but as soon as the regulars are withdrawn there is likely to be trouble.

"The mine operators, headed by the Rockefeller interests, have refused to consider the terms of the settlement suggested by President Wilson.[3] The abolition of the company stores, the correction of the short-weight scales, the abandonment of assessments on the miners for the maintenance of schools on company property, and the discontinuance of company saloons — none of these reforms will be considered by the employers.

"It is significant that the men engaged in the present strike were originally imported as strike-breakers themselves ten years ago. Conditions became so intolerable that they were forced to unite in an effort to secure justice.

"The strikers are still living in tent colonies, and with the approach of winter the condition of their families becomes as pitiable as that of the refugees in poor, stricken Belgium. Meanwhile the regular troops are saving to the companies the cost of hired guards — an economy of some $2,000 a day.

"The state has arranged for the expenditure of $1,000,000 for the rehabilitation of the militia, which will take the place of the regular troops when the latter are withdrawn. If the personnel of men and officers in the militia is the same as last spring, however, we can expect to perpetrated then.

"The truth of the matter is that the coal operators own the courts and civil officers of Colorado, as well as the governor and the Legislature. My experience is typical."

"Mother" Jones said that the European war has aided the mine operators by distracting the attention of the public from the situation in Colorado.[4]

"My chief purpose in coming East," she said, "has been to call notice to the suffering wives and starving children of the Colorado strikers and to remind the citizens that the strike has not yet been settled. Public opinion can and should end it. These mine magnates should be brought into line. John D. Rockefeller should be made to feel the lash of public indignation."[5]

Notes

1. Undated clipping in Mother Mary Harris Jones Papers, Department of Archives and Manuscripts, Catholic University of America, Washington, D.C. The sub-headings read: "Does 70,000 Miles in Ten Months. Declares Operators will Never Listen to Reason and Must Be Made to Do So. Visits Tribune in Mission to End Coal Strike in Colorado."

2. On October 19, 1914, Mother Jones had an interview with President Woodrow Wilson on the Colorado strike. She urged the president to close the mines if the operators failed to accept his proposed settlement, and that he keep the federal troops in the state to ensure protection of the miners from the company-dominated militia. But Wilson rejected her suggestion voicing doubt that he had the authority to close the mines. The *New York Times* commented editorially the following day that President Theodore Roosevelt had threatened to take over and operate the mines in 1902 if the operators refused to settle, and added: "The army is not now commanded by that sort of President." (*New York Times*, October 20, 1914.) *See above* pp. 257-59 for the terms of President Wilson's proposed settlement.

4. The war in Europe began in August 1914.

5. For Mother Jones's comments on Rockefeller, *see* pp. 57, 263-64, 270, 278, 339-40.

Rockefeller Imposed Upon by His Agents, Says Mother Jones

A key example of the contradictory position Mother Jones took during this period is her uncritical comments on John D. Rockefeller, Jr. during his testimony before the Industrial Relations Commission and her bitter condemnation of almost every other spokesperson for industry who testified before the same commission. This is clearly illustrated in her interview with the Denver Express *shortly after she returned to Colorado from the East. In the same interview, Mother Jones indicated a critical attitude towards the pro-Belgian propaganda campaign sweeping the United States in the early months of World War I.*

When Andrew Carnegie testified before the Industrial Relations Commission in New York, he only aroused in Mother Jones, noted strike leader, a desire to throw a brick at him.

Returning here from the east, Mother Jones today told of some of her impressions of the noted witnesses appearing before the coimmission. Of John D. Rockefeller's, she said:

"I feel sorry for the old man. Wealth can't buy health. He's lost the latter and probably won't be permitted to enjoy the former long."

Eliot Should Be Dead.

This is what she said of President Emeritus Eliot, of Harvard:[1]
"Eliot should have died ten years ago. Then he might have made a name for himself. He's outgrown his usefulness. He told the commission that workers eat too much meat. I suppose he thinks that is one of the causes of industrial unrest."

John D. Rockefeller, jr., fared better than some of the rest.

Declaring that "the heart of John D. Rockefeller, jr., is in the right place," but that his action has been misdirected and knowledge of the true conditions of things kept from him by the men who manage his Colorado interests, Mother Jones defended the character of the son of the oil king by saying that she has never met, in all her travels and connection with men of power, a man of more unassuming nature.

Rockefeller Ignorant.

"He did not know what was going on out here until the recent investigations of the labor question were made in New York," she said.

"He didn't understand. He was born stifled in wealth. His mind has been moulded by professors who are thriving under the benefactions of his foundation and by those human vampires who are exploiting him. They manage his affairs while he, ignorant of the situation, is made the butt and target for all the wrongs of the country.

"The men whom he hires to do the work for him have not told him of the awful disasters, the horrible barbarism which occurred in Colorado. And why? Because it was to their interest to keep him from knowing. He never dreamed of it. They attended to his business, and he paid the penalty.

"Rockefeller is buried in wealth. He can't see, and the men whom he

517

hires for workers don't care for him, only for their jobs.

What of Carnegie Millions.

"The rich of the nation have been using brute power too long, and now the people are rising against it. Where did the Carnegie millions come from? Go to the graveyard at Homestead," and her strong voice broke with the earnestness of her thought.

"Ask the tombstones there, and they will rise in the ghostly light and say that it was the murder of the poor innocent mothers and children of Homestead that heaped up his millions.

"These are dangerous times for the country. The nation has long been up against an economic crisis,[2] and it is now facing the end of it. Conditions in Denver are pretty nearly the same as in New York, in proportion to the population of the two places. We have the cry for bread all about us, and yet the rich are contributing ship loads of necessities for the Belgians.

"What have we to do with the Belgians? For God's sake, let us take care of the home people who are facing starvation. Let us feed them, clothe them, educate them and make good citizens of them, before we turn our attention to places further distant."

Mother Jones will be in the city until Sunday. She will then go to the Southern coal fields.

[Denver Express, *February 18, 1915, and also in the Eugene V. Debs Scrapbooks, clipping, Tamiment Institute Library, New York University.]*

Notes

1. Charles William Eliot (1834-1926), president of Harvard and one of the most influential leaders in the educational activities in the country, was also widely hated in trade union circles for his public support of the open shop. In fact, his statement that the scab was the American hero was one of the most widely distributed pieces in the whole catalogue of open-shop propaganda. (*See New York Times*, Dec. 17, 1901.)

2. By the end of 1913-1914, an economic crisis was in full swing in the United States. It was to increase in intensity after August 1914, when the war broke out in Europe, severely disrupting American industry and causing food prices in the United States to skyrocket. The economic crisis reached its worst stage in the winter months of 1914-1915, when from 400,000 to 440,000 wage earners in New York City alone — 18 percent of the 2,455,000 wage earners in the city — were unemployed, to say nothing of those workers who were kept on part-time. According to surveys, unemployment was pretty much in the same proportion as in New York. It has been estimated that the total number of unemployed in the winter of 1914-1915 "reached as much as 4,000,000 and possibly higher." In addition, there were several million working only part-time.

(*See* John Graham Brooks, "The Challenge of Unemployment," *The Independent* 81 (March 15, 1915): 383-85.)

Mother Jones Demands 6-Hour Day

Interview in *Evansville (Illinois) Times*, September 4, 1916[1]

Eight-hour day! Huh!

Mother Jones, in Evansville Monday to speak at the Labor day picnic, thinks that six hours a day is enough.

(White-haired, she has, at 86, a complexion 16 might envy — rose and snow she is!)

"With modern machinery, all the work of the world could be done in six hours a day, she told a Press reporter. "The worker would have time to improve his mind and body.

"But the railroad brotherhoods have won a great victory.[2] Yet, they'd better look out for the Supreme Court! Some of the high class burglars may carry the eight-hour law to the Supreme Court and the Supreme Court may knock it out. This power to declare laws constitutional should be taken away from the Supreme Court. When congress says that a bill is a law, that should end it.

"Congress, in passing the eight-hour law for the railroad brotherhoods, has taught the workers that it could pass a law to give every worker in the country in every occupation an eight-hour day!"

Socialist, But She Wants Wilson

Mother Jones, famed as a socialist, was asked what she thought of the campaign.

"I think Wilson will be re-elected and I think he ought to be!" she said.[3] "I don't know of anyone we could put in the White House who would do better. Socialism is a long way off; I want something right now!

"Wilson went down to the capitol and told the congressmen that they MUST stop the child labor by which our rising generation was being ground into dollars![4]

"What other president did that? I myself got 80 children from the slave pens of Philadelphia — some of them with their hands cut off by the machinery! — and took them to Oyster Bay as an object lesson to President Roosevelt. But his secret service men kept me out and he never saw those children."

Won't Object to Wet Picnic

Mother Jones will have no quarrel with the Central Labor Union because they are selling beer at their picnic.

"No fanatics have a right to say what people shall eat or drink!" she said. "Other people have only a right to give us a chance to develop self-respect and self-control.

"I travel a good deal and I haven't found a dry state yet.

"Let the government manufacture all the liquor that is manufactured. Then it would be pure and its sale would not be forced upon anyone. Did you ever hear of anyone opening a corner emporium for the sale of two-cent stamps? No, indeed because there is no profit in the sale of two-cent stamps."

Notes

1. Clipping in Mother Mary Harris Jones Papers, Department of Archives and Manuscripts, Catholic University of America, Washington, D.C.

2. On August 29, 1916, President Wilson addressed Congress in person, in joint session, and appealed to the members to avert a total strike on the railroads by the enactment of an eight-hour law for railway transportation workers. The law was passed and signed by President Wilson on September 3, one day before the strike order became effective. The law, known as the Adamson Act, established the eight-hour day for train service employees effective January 1, 1917.

3. Woodrow Wilson ran for re-election in 1916 against Charles Evans Hughes, the Republican candidate. The Socialist Party nominated Allan Benson, former mayor of Milwaukee, as its presidential candidate.

4. At Wilson's urging Congress passed the Child Labor Act (also known as the Owen-Keatings Bill) early in 1916. It forbade interstate shipments of products made by child labor, but the law was declared unconstitutional by the Supreme Court.

I Am a Socialist, But I Admire What Wilson Has Done and Favor His Re-election

Interview in *Davenport (Iowa) News,* 1916[1]

"I am not a Democrat by philosophy. I am not of either Hughes' or Wilson's political faith. I am a Socialist.[2] But I admire Wilson for the things he has done. I am big and broad enough to see things squarely. And when any man or woman does something for humanity I say go to him and shake him by the hand and pat him on the back and say, 'I'm for you!' "

This was the statement made by "Mother" Jones, celebrated labor leader and lecturer, Saturday night.

She arrived in Davenport at 2 o'clock Saturday afternoon, from New York via Chicago. At 2 o'clock this afternoon she addresses a mass meeting of working men in the Moline theater, Moline. She was present for a short time at the Machinists' dance at the Coliseum Saturday night.

Stopping at St. James

Mother Jones received a Democrat representative in her room at the St. James hotel. She sat in a comfortable rocking chair by a south window, her figure silhouetted against the square of fading light.

As the reporter entered the room she rose easily and shook hands with him graciously. Her grip was firm. Her voice, slightly hoarse from many speeches, rasped a little as she talked. Yet it seemed but to emphasize her sentences the more.

As to Description

One rather hesitates to describe Mother Jones. She is not a large woman, though heavily-built. She was dressed simply in black. Her hair, silver-white, curled on top of her head and flung lingering tendrils around a face calm, kind, yet deeply-lined. Her chin, square and firm, pushed forward aggressively as she told of the indignities suffered by the toilers.

Started Work 40 Years Ago

"It's been 40 years since we first started this movement for an eight-hour working day," Mother Jones went on. "Franklin said that four hours was enough.[3] Of course, in the beginning, there wasn't as much noise made about this movement as there is now. There was no need to make all the fuss.

"Nowhere in human history will you find a time when the toilers produced as much as they do now. And nowhere in human history, likewise, will you find a time when the toilers were paid as little in proportion to what they produce.

"There is no reason why the United States should drift like ancient Rome. In the last 50 years there has been more money accumulated in the United States than there was in all the years of the existence of the ancient Greek and Roman empires. And those nations perished.

Criticizes Political Gathering

"Recently, in New York, there was held a banquet at which $15,000,000 was represented. Not one of the men present at that banquet ever produced one dollar's worth. All that they possess was taken away from the toilers.

"Before that, a train of women representing $1,000,000, went out campaigning for the politicians who attended the banquet.[4] They never went to Armour and said to him, 'You have many women working in your factories. They should be given a chance to rise. They are to be the future mothers of the land. Help them.'

Women's Condition Horrible

"You should see those women. They are paid $1.15 a day. Fifteen of them sleep in one room. After a certain time at their work their muscles become cramped and will only move a certain way. Those are the women who are producing the men and women of America.

"Yet the voice of these society women was never raised in protest. When one of the workers deviates from the straight and narrow path and goes down, there are 'homes' for her. And there she can stay with the brand of a fallen woman on her back forever.

"The society women are the fallen women! They are the ones who force women to fall.

"There's something wrong about it all. Something that must be remedied.

"A Race of Dollar Hogs"

"The United States has become the home of a race of dollar hogs.

"We have strikes and humanity is murdered by professional gunmen because the toilers ask for a little more money, a little more bread, a little more sunshine in their sordid lives. The dollar hogs are the murderers.

"The churches never protest against the wholesale murders. Take

Colorado for an example. The ministers never get up in their pulpits and preach for better things for the toilers.

But —

"But when the working men are strained to the limit and get out and raise h— , then out come the ministers hand-in-hand with the high-class burglars. Gunmen are hired to slaughter the workers and throw them into jail. The children are left alone to shift for themselves. The women toil along and 'go wrong.'

"America won't let her walls be stained with the blood of her people much longer.

"We demand an eight-hour law so that men and women can use their brains a little more instead of their muscles.

No Gunmen in Slavery Days

"No gunmen were ever hired in the days of chattel slavery.[5] Such a thing was unheard of in those times. Yet today they hire professional murderers to shoot the toilers down in cold blood and murder women and children. I have seen these things.

"This is a terrible indictment against the twentieth century in the United States of America.

Never Heard Before

"As I say, we fought for an even chance for 40 years. Yet never until four years ago did we get a hearing from the White House. Never until then did the executive of a nation come out of the White House and enter the senate and demand that the toilers be given an even break in the world.

"Wilson saved the country from a complete demoralization. If the railroad workers had gone out, it would only have been a very short time until the machinists and the boilermakers and all the rest of the workers would have followed.

"There is a continuous under-current — a seething spirit of unrest that occasionally bubbles up. This will cease when proper conditions are gained.

"And then besides, Wilson has done so many other things. Under his administration the country has been freer from want. He has fixed it for the farmers.

Kept Out of War

"He kept the country out of a war with Mexico.[6] That is something that I should have dreaded to have seen. It would have meant the murder of thousands of peons as well as the loyal boys of the army and national guard.

"It would have meant thousands of blighted homes, stricken mothers, deserted wives and fatherless children. It would have been a calamity."

And then, in softer tones, which took on a harsh note occasionally as she told of some of the indignities. Mother Jones told of some of the conditions she had seen in her many years of working for the organized labor interests of the country.

She is, without doubt, sincere in her views. She will make only a short stay in Davenport, leaving here this evening.

Notes

1. Undated clipping in Mother Mary Harris Jones Papers, Department of Archives and Manuscripts, Catholic University of America, Washington, D.C. The actual headline read: "LABOR LEADER SCORES HUGHES, BOOSTS WILSON," and the sub-headings went: " 'Mother' Jones, National Celebrity, in Davenport for Short Time. Decries Past Conditions. Says U.S. Home of Nation of 'Dollar Hogs' Holding Down Toilers."

2. Evidently Mother Jones had forgotten that three years before she denied being a Socialist (*See* p. 506).

3. In his section on the hours of labor in *Capital*, Karl Marx quotes Benjamin Franklin's stand with approval.

4. In 1916 the National American Woman Suffrage Association leaders announced that the suffragists would concentrate their efforts on a federal amendment. In the 1916 presidential campaign, the AFL supported Wilson for reelection, but since he refused to take a stand on woman suffrage, and since the Republican candidate, Charles Evans Hughes, took a "courageous stand for the federal amendment to enfranchise the women of America," most suffragists supported Hughes. A group of wealthy suffragists, including Margaret Dreier Robins of the Women's Trade Union League, hired a private train — the "Golden Special" — and toured the country making pro-suffrage and anti-Wilson speeches (Foner, *History of Women in the American Labor Movement: From World War I to the Present*, pp. 55-56).

5. Evidently Mother Jones did not know that armed slave patrols existed in the slave states before the Civil War with the objective of preventing slave insurrections and guarding against runaway slaves.

6. Although Wilson sent General Pershing with an expeditionary force into Mexico to capture Francisco (Pancho) Villa, a fruitless venture, he did not respond to pressure from United States owners of Mexican mines, led by William Randolph Hearst, who opposed the Mexican Revolution which began in 1910 and urged a declaration of war against Mexico. The slogan "He Kept Us Out of War" was used by Wilson campaigners in 1916, but it referred most often to the fact that he had, up to then at least, kept the United States out of the First World War.

Mother Jones Demands a New Trial
for Tom Mooney

Interview in *San Francisco Chronicle,* 1919[1]
BY ELENORE MEHERIN

Vindication for labor, justice for Thomas J. Mooney, and honor for the courts of the land.[2]

This is the three-fold purpose which today brought Mother Mary Jones, patriarch of the masses, to San Francisco to demand from Governor William D. Stephens a new trial of the Mooney case. Mother Jones came as the special representative of the Illinois Federation of Labor, whose 550,000 members voted unanimously to fight to the limit for a new hearing of the Preparedness parade bomb outrage.

Commutation of sentence, Mother Jones characterized as a cheap evasion. An immediate rehearing, not a pardon, is the demand which will be made on Governor Stephens. Every peaceable force in the state will be used to win victory in the fight. Should Governor Stephens refuse to use his influence, the matter will be brought directly to President Wilson. This is the decision reached by the Illinois Federation at its state convention, which closed last Saturday. Mother Jones is empowered to carry the contest to the highest tribunal in the nation.

Only Want Justice

"Pardon! We want no charity. We want justice! We will use every possible means within our power — if that fails, then we'll use other means."

Mother Jones is nearly 90 years old, but she stood up like one inspired, her face struck with intense emotion, her deep, resonant voice ringing with power. The memory of bitter struggles, of women shot down by machine guns in Colorado, of little children burned to death in capital's fight against strikers, trails like an echo in every vibrant tone.

"If Mooney is guilty, let him hang," her sharp gray eyes snapped emphatically. "The crime was terrible. It deserves the full penalty that the law allows. But prove the defendant guilty. That's what our courts are for. The American people are not going to stand by and see their courts made a laughing stock.

Labor Will Not Rest

"The laboring classes are not what they were twenty-five years ago. They will not cower down like grateful dogs to lick the hands of the master class. Labor will not rest under the damning disgrace which capital seeks to fasten upon it through the conviction of Mooney. We demand and shall win vindication. The Illinois Federation voted against strikes in all except the Mooney case.

"Commutation of sentence is a direct blow struck at the efficiency of our courts. What are these tribunals for if not to decide upon the merits of the evidence before them? Are they just to offer benches for professional loafers to sit upon?"

"And if Governor Stephens gives you no satisfaction?"

"Well, then, President Wilson will," Mother Jones answered with serene confidence.[3] "He will find some means to redeem the honor of the nation."

Most Treacherous of Ages

"This is the most treacherous and insidious age the world has ever known. The workers are passing through a bitter crisis, but they are awakened to its significance. The wretched, blighting miseries of starvation and oppression have been their teachers. They know and they are proclaiming their economic needs.

"Down the stairway of all the centuries the history of labor has never been written. The workers are born and struggle and die in the trenches. They are forgotten. Wall street grows fat on their blood and their flesh. But they are breaking free from the hypnotism which has kept them obedient."

Mother Jones was selected by the Illinois convention because of her profound knowledge of economic problems and because of her lifelong fight to win a just share of the profits for the producers of the world's wealth. It was she who interceded for the miners in the bitter Colorado feud. It was she who raised her voice against child labor and every oppression which robs and degrades the minds and bodies of the nation's little citizens.

World Calls Her Mother

For her services a devoted world family called her "Mother." In repose, she might be that quiet, gentle essence of the young grandmother of happy youngsters.

Until she spoke. And then she was the dynamic champion of oppressed multitudes. She was motherhood roused to frenzy against the oppressors of her children.

She is fulfilling her conception of woman's mission in the world.

"Women have stood by and allowed their children to be starved and crushed and they have not raised the sword to strike down these murderers who are sacrificing their little ones on the altar of dollars," Mother Jones said.

Mould Minds of Young

"No nation can be truly great, until its women turn their skill to moulding the minds and bodies of the young. Women have allowed themselves to be downtrodden. It is time for them to shake off this vicious heel, to stand up in their full stature and do the work that has been left for them.

"These clubgoers, these welfare workers, these uplifters — they are all collecting salaries off the evils which they are employed to decrease. They are lazy shirkers. They are dodgers and temporizers. Let them begin at the bottom where the dirt lies and sweep house from the corners out. Let them demand a decent world for their children. Let them build a new order instead of trying to patch up the decaying walls of the capitalistic edifice.

Task Up to Mothers

"That is the task for the nation's mothers. How many women rose as the custodians of law and order and defied the privileged few to outrage their courts?

"Did any? But the war, horrible as it has been, is bringing a better day. No one thinks as he did a few years ago. A bunch of highway robbers had the world by the throat and we should have gone down as Rome went centuries ago. Never again shall gold pollute the nation as it has in the past.

"In the mud of the trenches labor's eyes were opened. We shall prove with this Mooney case that no group of oppressors shall ever again blind them with the dirt of special privilege."[4]

Notes

1. Undated clipping, Mother Mary Harris Jones Papers, Catholic University of America. Since Governor Stephens commuted Mooney's sentence from execution to life imprisonment after an appeal to the United States Supreme Court failed in November 1918 and Mother Jones left the Coast to help in the steel strike of 1919, the interview probably occurred early in 1919.

2. For the background of the Mooney case and Mother Jones's role in the defense, *see* pp. 57, 292-93, 301, 304.

3. The confidence was unjustified. While President Wilson had urged Governor Stephens to commute the sentence to life imprisonment, he did not himself pardon Mooney or call call for a new trial.

4. Unfortunately, her experience in the 1919 steel strike showed that Mother Jones's confidence and optimism were not in keeping with the reality of domination of the government and press by big business.

"Madre Juanita" on Social Issues

Interview in *Excelsior* (Mexico City), January 10, 1921[1]
Translated from the Spanish by Roslyn Held Foner

Our information would not be complete if we had not also interviewed the elderly Mrs. Jones, who is accompanying the American delegates to the Pan-American Federation of Labor Congress, and whom the English-speaking workers affectionately call "Mother Jones," which the Spanish-speaking workers have translated into "Madre Juanita." The respectable Mrs. Jones, or "Madre Juanita," is a singular and highly interesting woman. In spite of her advanced age, she is absolutely in command of all her intellectual faculties, and gave examples of her astonishing memory. She is of extremely cultured and facile conceptions, and above all, gives proof of knowing the history of the world perfectly, and of being familiar with all the workers' movements which are developing in one or another part of the hemisphere.

When the first words had been exchanged with her, one is convinced that the name the workers had given her could not have been more appropriate. And we do not believe that there is a woman so identified with the sentiment of the classes who suffer, and who loves and helps them so lovingly and disinterestedly as she does. She wore an elegant dress of black velvet, with a jacket of the same color, with very beautiful lace also black, adorning her wrists and neck, with a few small purple decorations peeping out. Her completely white hair and her good-humored face, immediately inspired sympathy.

"Madre Juanita" had not come as a delegate,[2] but had been invited as an honored guest by high functionaries of the government,[3] and we know very specially that Señor General Villarreal, who greeted her affectionately at the station, made her his distinguished guest. And in addition , a group of ladies from Agrupación Central Femenil (Central Feminine Group) was charged with the responsibility of attending her.

Although the pleasant elderly lady had dedicated all her life especially to the plight of the miners, nevertheless, her activities and all her efforts have been placed in the service of the working class in general and of the unfortunates who were thrown into jail unjustly. She has traveled from one end of the United States to the other, solely to obtain the liberty of some poor worker who has unfortunately been incarcerated, and we know that she herself has experienced the cruelty of the prison cell on repeated occasions, solely because she has been considered an enemy of the present social system in existence throughout the world.[4]

In reality, the moment in which we were chatting with her in the "hall" of the Hotel St. Francis, gave us the idea that she is a woman of advanced and radical ideas. She believes in the destruction of the jails as an opprobium of civilizations. She believes that very soon politicians and statesmen will be shamed and eliminated. She believes that good customs and the duties of each individual should be cultivated by means of civic education and that the "garrote del gendarme" ("police club") or the threat of authority will not be necessary, that they no longer need to exist.

"Madre Juanita" gave us an extensive account of her activities as a worker, and the theories which she developed in the course of her work among the underdogs, to raise them in their moral level and to make them understand by means of special education, that they should love one another, as in a Biblical precept. And that in this world all should be loved, and there should be no hatred.

She told us that more than ten years ago, that is when she had hardly begun propagandist work in the south of the United States for the Mexican Revolution, she had occasion to help several Mexicans to obtain their freedom after having been imprisoned because of their propaganda work. Among the above Mexicans were the present Secretary of Agriculture and Development, General Antonio I. Villarreal,[5] who sometime ago, made a special visit to her in New York and to show his gratitude, gave her a gift of a gold watch which she still has. She also was able to help other Mexicans who had occupied high posts in the government which had followed in Mexico, including Señor Ricardo Flores Magón, although she was not able to get him out of jail because he was re-imprisoned. She informed us that Señor Flores Magón had to complete this year his eleven years of sentence in a Los Angeles jail.[6]

This is the second time that she has come to Mexico: the first time, she said, was when the government was that of De la Barra, whom she knew personally, as well as Señor Madero. She worked hard to obtain the friendship between that government and that of the United States, and always has eagerly pressed to get better relations between both peoples.

She told us also that she has been the personal friend of the last president,[7] and the highest functionaries in Washington esteemed her, listening to her always when she goes to advocate a just cause before them. She has even succeeded in selling these same functionaries the books on Bolshevism which have been translated into English,[8] the sale of which has been dedicated to rescuing men from jail who have unfortunately been prisoners. The funds were used to obtain and pay for the lawyers who defend them.

When we asked her what she thought of Bolshevism, she said that all social movements in the world were good, and that everything depended on the forms in which they were used by each person. She established the theory that since every individual had a different vision or point of view, it was natural that some should see Bolshevism as an anarchistic and destructive movement, and others should see it as the highest manifestation of the suffering classes.

She declared herself an enemy of "Prohibition,"[9] considering this law destructive of the liberty and will of men. "It is not with laws that we must banish vice, but with books and education. Then we shall see men hate drink instinctively." On this particular issue she explained to us that in her opinion, the worker who expends his energy in the factory or the mine, not being an intellectual, looks for liquor as one way of "occupying" his mind, as a means of recreation. And that the day in which we succeed in accustoming the worker to "occupy" his mind with healthy readings or more elevated ideas on the true conception of life, it will no longer be necessary for him to resort to liquor.

At times the lady was enthusiastic and her sentences, spoken with warmth and force, appeared to us as though she was addressing a large audience. It was difficult to follow all her ideas, although to be truthful, we must say that all her concepts were perfectly put together. So that we had the impression that we were dealing with a woman of rare talents, and, as we said in the beginning, with all her facilities, despite her advanced age.

Notes

1. I am indebted to Enrique Suárez Gaona and his wife Esther Schumacher, president and secretary respectively of ACEHSMO (World Association of Institutes for the Study of Labor History, centered in Mexico City) for furnishing me with copies of the Mexican papers covering the visit of Mother Jones to the Congress of the Pan-American Federation of Labor.

2. Among other Americans who attended the Congress, *Excelsior's* reporter also interviewed Samuel Gompers, A.F. of L. president. While most of Gompers's comments were generalities, two were of importance. For one thing, he made it clear that "in dealing with the workers' movement, helping those colleagues of the Latin American countries for their social and economic development, he wished to make help only those movements of a character which was purely labor in character, and that neither he nor the American Federation of Labor had any intention of associating with those groups which could be called intellectual, who unite themselves to workers of good faith." Secondly, when asked "if it were true that there existed serious difficulties between the A.F. of L., which he represents and the I.W.W., considered the most radical union, almost Bolshevik, of the United States," Gompers answered, that "the I.W.W. does not exist and therefore there cannot be difficulties." (*Excelsior*, January 10, 1921.)

3. For the story of the invitation and Mother Jones's speech at the Congress, *see* pp. 57, 326-28.

4. The exclusion of the Soviet Union in this report as a land in which that social system had been abolished was probably the work of the reporter for *Excelsior*.

5. *See* pp. 122, 130, 374, 461.

6. On January 4, 1904, Ricardo Flores Magón, at the age of thirty, left Mexico for the United States, never to return to Mexico alive. He spent the next nineteen years in the United States, more than half of them in prison. He was jailed in Missouri, in California, in Washington, and in Kansas, where he died at Leavenworth Penitentiary in 1922. Flores Magón's final arrest came on March 21, 1918, when he and his colleague Librado Rivera fell victim to the anti-radical Red Scare hysteria that swept the United States during the First World War. Convicted under the Espionage Act of obstructing the war effort, he received an appalling twenty-year sentence. (Rivera was given fifteen years plus the one-year term which had been deferred in 1916.) Flores Magón died at Leavenworth of a heart attack in the early hours of November 21, 1922.

Curiously, the reporter for *Excelsior* does not mention that Mother Jones broke with Flores Magón over strategy and tactics in relation to the Mexican Revolution. (*See above* pp. 529-35.)

7. The reference is to Woodrow Wilson.

8. This may have been a reference to the writings of V.I. Lenin which were translated into English during these years.

9. The Eighteenth Amendment to the Constitution (January 29, 1919) prohibited the manufacture, transportation, or sale of beverages, for intoxicating purposes. In 1933 the 21st Amendment repealed the prohibition amendment.

"Mother" Jones Fights for Sacco-Vanzetti[1]

Interview in Garfield Hospital, Washington, D.C.

WASHINGTON, Aug 24 — "They'll never dare kill them," declared an old, white-haired, partly deaf and almost sightless woman lying in a bed at Garfield Hospital here today.

She is "Mother" Jones, famous woman labor leader, now 98 years old and waiting for death. She was speaking of Sacco and Vanzetti.[2]

She does not know they were executed Tuesday.[3] She has not been told and will not be, for fear the shock might kill her. She thinks the men have won a reprieve.

"They'll never dare kill them," she repeated. "If they killed Sacco and Vanzetti, they would stir up the whole world. They would make 100 revolutionists where there is one today."

"Mother" Jones explained that it was all a "frameup."

"It's the judges," she boomed. "Our judges are too narrow-minded. Don't I know? They framed me right once. Quarantined me for smallpox, to get rid of me."[4]

"Mother" Jones, who was born in Ireland, taught school in Canada, lost her husband and four children in one week from yellow fever and for 60 years fought for what she called "downtrodden" laborers, raised a withered right hand to emphasize her remarks.

"You wait and see," she called to her departing visitor. "Sacco and Vanzetti never will go to the chair."

[Unidentified newspaper clipping, undated but undoubtedly August 25, 1927.]

Notes

1. The original heading for the article read: "'Mother' Jones Dying? Believes Sacco Alive."

2. Niccola Sacco and Bartolomeo Vanzetti, Italian-American anarchists, were arrested in 1921 and charged with the murder of two employees of a shoe factory in South Braintree more than a year before. In a trial featured by anti-radical and antiforeign hysteria, before Judge Webster Thayer, who openly expressed prejudice against the defendents, Sacco and Vanzetti were found guilty on purely circumstantial evidence and sentenced to electrocution. The Massachusetts supreme court and the U.S. Supreme Court refused to intervene, and an advisory committee appointed by the governor of Massachusetts refused to recommend commutation of sentence. Despite worldwide protests and nationwide demonstrations in the United States Sacco and Vanzetti were executed, victims of one of the worst frameups in American legal history.

3. Sacco and Vanzetti were executed on August 22, 1927.

4. For the incident referred to by Mother Jones, *see* p. 415, 531.

"Mother" Jones Urges Hoover Aid Strike of North Carolina Textile Workers

Interview in *Washington Times,* 1929[1]

The North Carolina textile workers will win their strike if they go about it in the right way.[2]

This is the belief of "Mother" Jones, aged heroine and ministering angel of a hundred labor battles who is dying in a little farmhouse seven miles west of Hyattsville, Md., from the infirmities of almost a century of harried existence. If she lives until May next she will be 100 years old.

"Mother" Jones is fighting her first losing battle — that against the grim reaper. She cannot leave her bed, but her heart is with the beleaguered Tarheel spinners. She believes if she could arise and take charge of the situation in North Carolina the strikers would win a speedy victory.

Experience Needed

"It takes experience to win a strike," she told a *Times* reporter today.

"The North Carolinians would have won their fight already," she said, "if the southern women had had experience in strikes and knew how to act in such a situation.

"To win a strike you have to keep your eyes on every point in order to watch the operators' moves.

"Those North Carolina girls are making a wonderful fight. There is no question about it.

"That's 'chivalrous' southern blood for you — jailing women. If the women in this nation would rise up and protest against such an inquisition the federal government would soon put a stop to it.

Budding Criminals

"When you starve mothers and children in their infancy, the brain of the coming generation fails to develop. Then you have criminals and imbeciles.

"You need more jails. Your court dockets are filled to overflowing with criminal cases.

"The women of the North Carolina mill sections deserve credit, and every woman in the United States should rise up in protest against the way the mill owners treat women in the Carolinas.

"Why hasn't President Hoover[3] taken some steps to stop those outrages?

"The North Carolina situation is a national disgrace and it is time for our federal government to step in when the honor of the nation is at stake.

Notes

1. Undated clipping Mother Mary Harris Jones Papers, Department of Archives and Manuscripts, Catholic University of America, Washington, D.C.

2. In 1929 over 350 mills in three southern states were closed by spontaneous strikes. The first began in March, in Elizabethton, Tennessee. That same month, strikes broke out in South Carolina, and workers in mill after mill — as many as ten thousand — walked out without benefit of any union. The leadership was assumed by independent, locally elected strike committees. Gastonia, North Carolina, was the scene of a strike that began in April and lasted for months, and the Marion, North Carolina, strike flared up in July. The largest and most bitterly fought of the strikes was in Gastonia where the newly-or-

ganized Communist National Textile Workers' Union led the strike. For a discussion of the strikes, *see* Foner, *Women and the American Labor Movement: From World War I to the Present,* pp. 225-43.

3. Herbert Hoover had been elected president in 1928 as the Republican candidate, defeating Alfred E. Smith, the Democratic candidate.

"We've Won Out!"

Mother Jones's Last Interview, in *Washington Post,*
December 1, 1930[1]
By Clara Louise John

"This Way to Mother Jones," read the guide posts along a well beaten country road 10 miles out of Washington. It is likely that they will soon be removed. In an upstairs room of the quiet farm house of Mr. and Mrs. Walter Burgess lies Mother Jones, "grand old woman of American Labor." With 100 years of strenuous life to her credit she is just about ready to start on the Great Adventure. Stricken to her bed last January from the sheer exhaustion of age, her physical energy has gradually ebbed away and now she no longer receives visitors.

"Mother" Mary Harris Jones passed her one hundredth birthday anniversary May 1, 1930. Until recently her mind was as active as ever. Only a few weeks ago we found her resting amid several big soft pillows, her head covered abundantly with snowy white hair. Mother Jones was particular about being "primped up." A warm and well preserved hand had stretched out in welcome from the folds of a blue bordered sheet. Her expression was a paradox of tenacity and tenderness. Her voice was strong and it took very little prompting to draw from her ardent expressions of her opinions about the things for which she had fought for the greater part of a century. "And we've won out!" she said, when she talked about the work that has always laid closest to her heart — the laws regulating child labor.

"Women can do so much if they only realize their power! The statement was detached and deep and she clung to the words in a way to make one feel that this is the torch she wanted to fling to other hands before letting slip her hold on life.

Summarizes Modern Condition

"Nobody takes a dollar to the grave!" she added, impressively, and then she launched into a fiery summary of her opinions about modern conditions. For even then Mother Jones was not thinking about death, but about the industrial problems of the machine age in relation to American labor. She recalled Aristotle's prediction that the time would come when an inanimate object would do the work of a dozen slaves.

"Today," she said, "modern methods of production have far outstripped the power of America to consume the product of labor. And now that we're into the machine age, neither the government nor the people are preparing for it. The only thing that can be done now is for the government to take hold and reduce the working hours. A five-day week and a six-hour day would mean work for everybody. But the people don't get the idea. Also, the president should sponsor more public works. Why doesn't he get about building that road to South America? I believe Borah would find work for everybody if he were president![2]

"Prohibition is one of the greatest afflictions that has been laid on the nation. They can't ram it down people's throats.

"I'm more radical than I ever was," she snapped, with a hint of her old-time energy. "I've had a lot of chance to think lately, and the more I think the more radical I get. The capitalists are still a bunch of high-class robbers and burglars, and I'm for anything that will keep them from impoverishing the people. And if the unemployment situation gets much worse men are going to do something about it. If they can't get work and fair wages they will change the system so they can.

"Now that we are in the machine age what should be done with all the leisure time?"

"People should study! Study!"

In Prison at 87

"How old were you the last time you were in prison?" The question sounded incongruous.

"Eighty-seven," she said, defiantly, after a moment's reflection. "They kept me in seven months."

She couldn't remember the number of times the Rockefellers had put her in jail, but her most outstanding encounter with them was in connection with the disgraceful Ludlow massacre in the Colorado mines in 1914. As might be expected, Mother Jones was on hand.[3] The guards sprayed the little tent colony of striking miners and killed 12 men and 21 women and children. She held the Rockefeller interests directly responsible for the slaughter. As a result of her agitations she was put behind the bars for nine weeks. As typifying cold capital the Rockefellers remained Mother Jones' pet hate, and she later disdained such things as invitations to dinner from them on account of her rigid principles.

Swearing, according to Mother Jones, is the poor man's prayer. And with her caustic tongue she has done a lot of her kind of "praying."

"I haven't been very discreet in my language," she confessed. "You've got to talk a language people can understand. The public is the sleepiest damn bunch you ever saw. You've got to wake them up! Then you get action!". . . .[4]

Mother Jones has been called the Angel of Mercy, who placed human rights above property rights.

"It feels fine to be 100 years old," Mother Jones confessed. "I wish I could live to be another hundred, just to see the changes. In another hundred years all the industries will be controlled by the people."

Saw Only Purposes

As you sat by the bed and talked to Mother Jones her Irish eyes seemed to burn with a fire born of the combustion of timid thought. You felt as though you could almost see through the world-old enigma of a soul imprisoned in a body for her spirit bleamed out as a thing apart and in your very presence you seemed to feel it defying not only obstacles, but time itself. It was as though she looked right out beyond all that has to do with places or the present, and saw only purposes.

And she's "won out!" More impressive, even, than the victories she has won is the crusading spirit of she who has had the courage to stand for a single purpose no matter what the odds. The whole house seemed to radiate her virile personality and one left its front door fairly intoxicated with courage, the courage to defy life's obstacles in the same way that Mother Jones has defied, not only her own, but obstacles confronting millions of the big human family.

Notes

1. An unnamed, undated clipping of the interview is in the Mother Mary Harris Jones Papers, Department of Archives and Manuscripts, Catholic University of America, Washington, D.C. The original headline read: "We've won Out!" and was followed by the subheading: "Thought Consoling to 'Mother' Jones, but She Says Labor Is Still Unprepared for Present Machine Age, Despite Many Victories."

2. William E. Borah (1865-1940), Senator from Idaho, 1907-1931, prosecutor in the Haywood, Pettibone, Moyer trial, but became a leader of the progressive Senators during the 1920s, advocating recognition of the Soviet Union by the United States and opposing the landing of U.S. Marines in Nicaragua, for which activities he was listed in *The Red Network* issued by Elizabeth Dilling in 1934.

3. Mother Jones was not in Colorado during the "Ludlow Massacre."

4. The omitted material dealt with Mother Jones's life and the celebration of her hundredth birthday on May 1, 1930. The interviewer quoted Mrs. Walter

Burgess who cared for Mother Jones during this period as saying:

"Before her 100th birthday 'Mother' had been right on her back for five months," explained Mrs. Burgess. "But she had told us that when her birthday came she would dress and celebrate. True to her word, on the morning of last May day she got up and dressed and went out and sat under the apple tree just as she had said she would do. The temporary recovery was psychological, for she hasn't been up again since. All day and until 8 that evening she received callers. Her first caller that morning came down the road at 7 o'clock, half hidden behind armfuls of lilacs. Her last one came at 11 p.m. One reporter came after she had gone to bed. He wanted her picture for his paper and rather than disappoint the poor fellow she insisted that she get out of bed and let him take it. 'Go ahead and shoot,' she said, 'if it will help you with your employer.'

Knew How to Talk

"There were 325 visitors here that day, yes, and we fed them all. 'Mother' always wants people to be fed. We had tubs, full of punch, dozens of homemade cakes, sandwiches, and, well, it was almost a barbacue!

Just before the movietone man had her perform for him, he tried to instruct her regarding what to say. 'What the h—— do you know about it?' she retorted, 'I was making speeches before you were born!'

"She was dressed in her best black silk, her cheeks were pink with excitement, she faced the cameras, took a deep breath and a drink of water and launched into a fiery, impromptu speech which brought loud applause. 'Power,' she told them, 'lies in the hands of labor to retain American liberty, but labor has not yet learned how to use the power. A wonderful power is in the hands of women, too, but they don't know how to use it. Capitalists side-track the women into clubs and make ladies of them. Nobody wants a lady. They want women! Ladies are parlor parasites!"

LETTERS

Mother Jones

To John P. Mitchell

friday Nov. the 30th 1900
Hazelton, PA

Pres. J. Mitchell
Indianapolis Ind

Comrade Mitchell[1]

I hasten to reply to your inquiries. first B. Jones told the blackest lie-without-one shadow of foundation unless it was that which he found in his hair brain — I consider James a dangerous man when he will Stoop to anything so base as to lie about his Brother to his Superior officers — Duffy is an honest Sober Straight forward fellow not a stereotyped orator but the kind of a Soul that we need in these dark days. James Said to me that Duffy might go to H — he be d — if he would take any orders from him — he Said he proposed to me every effort to down Duffy and he has I replied I regretted to See that Spirit — I thought we had come to the time when we Should put a side petty bickering and work for the good of all. I believe the organization is bigger than you or Duffy take your fight to the Street then come in and like men shake hands — his answer was that he would down Duffy with the organization.

He Said he had the Nomenation for V.P. for the A.F. of L. Board Member for Prest. of the District and an office to be general rostabout but he can get twenty five dollars a Month More than the U.M.W. give him I told him he ought to take it. I will Sum up the Whole Thing in these words — I consider James a very dangerous man in an organization there is no man whose charector he will not Stoop to blacken if he Stands in his way. The Sooner he is moved the better for all Concerned.

I have been up to Carbondale & bandling had fine meeting everything looks bright

You know you need never send any request to me.[2] I am ever ready to help our poor helpless people. Just say the word and I am off. Suffering Humanity needs our best efforts and we should not Spare ourselves particularly the Slaves of the caves need to be Saved.

Morkle's clerk went to Hinganon the other day ask the H to Sign a paper the H replied John Mitchell look after my bis we bring paper we Sign you me no Sign you mokle man for bis he no good for me me get John Mitchell look for me good no you[3] — Will leave for Virginia[4] Sun-

541

day or Thursday With best wishes for your health and Happiness I am fraternally your

Mother

The best Interest of the organization must be looked at first — last and always & I have watched Slosson closely find him a hard honest worker his people are true to him

A Pointer

James and Coins left Indianapolis to gather from Some things he droped keep your Eye open at the convention

I will forward some Matter to you to Night — but after reading return to Prest Duffy in McAdoo if you think best

Mother

[John P. Mitchell Papers, Department of Archives and Manuscripts, Catholic University of America, Washington, D.C.]

Notes

1. An ardent Socialist at this time, Mother Jones, like many Socialists, addressed their correspondents as "Dear Comrade." John Mitchell, United Mine Workers president, was, of course, not a Socialist.

2. Mitchell had asked Mother Jones to go to West Virginia and take charge of the organizing campaign the union was launching. She was to supervise the drive in the southern fields.

3. Mother Jones here appears to be writing in the English that Hungarian members of the United Mine Workers used. John Mitchell was very popular during these years with Slavic and Hungarian miners, as witness the song "Me Johnny Mitchell Man," the chorus of which went:

Me no 'fraid for nottin',
Me dey never schcare.
Sure me shtrike tomorra night,
Dat's de business, I don't care.
Right a-here me tellin' you —
Me no shcabby feller,
Good union citizen —
Johnny Mitchell man.

(Philip S. Foner, *American Labor Songs of the Nineteenth Century,* Urbana, Illinois, 1975, p. 211.)

4. Mother Jones set up headquarters in Montgomery, West Virginia.

To John P. Mitchell

To Prest John Mitchell
Scranton Pa

Dear Comrade

Just got your letter this Morning. — There was a fine Meeting here. Haskins was here poor boy he has his hands full — I gave them a few words about the Monument you proposed to our Martyred comrades in Lattermer[1] I turned the audience my way regret I could not go to other places that they wanted but I promised with your permission to come the 4th of July.

You have done just what you should have done. Now you will find out who has been the Traitor in the Trimmers camp. They will be brought to the front by this trial. While the traitors were laying traps to ruin the character of their officials they were not shrewed enough to cover up their tracks. Now they should be shown up to the Miners. You owe this to your children.

Let me say so long as you are the John Mitchell you are I'll be with you.[2] I will be in Scranton in a day or two I leave here to day but will stop in Pittsburg a day or so.

Take care of your health

Fraternally yours
Mother

[John P. Mitchell Papers, Department of Archives and Manuscripts, Catholic University of America, Washington, D.C.]

Notes

1. The reference is to the Lattimer Massacre of 1897. *See* pp. 407-9, 447.
2. The comment was prompted by John P. Mitchell's letter of April 1, 1901 in which he informed Mother Jones that groups around "the Scrantonian . . . have been making vacious (*sic*) attacks on me; and I have instituted legal proceedings against Mr. Little, charging him with criminal libel, and hope to be able to send him to prison. I know that many people think that I should pay no attention to such unscrupulous attacks; but I feel that I cannot permit anyone to question my honor, even if it costs me all the savings of my life time. While all who know him look upon him with distrust and suspicion, yet there are always those among the workers who are always ready to believe any false statements that are made against the officials of labor organizations. . . . While I have never asked anything from my craftsmen more than they agree to pay me, yet I do believe that I deserve to be respected by the anthracite miners." Mitchell asked Mother Jones to attend meetings in District No. 1, "and particularly in the vicinity of Scranton, and show this fellow up." (John P. Mitchell Pa-

pers, Department of Archives and Manuscripts, Catholic University of America, Washington, D.C.)

To John P. Mitchell

Sewell W. Virginia[1]
July the 31st 1901

for Prest Mitchell
Steveson Bldg
Indianapolis Ind

My dear Comrade Mitchell

For some reason which I cannot account for I have neglected writing you. You asked why I did not get to Lassalle. One reason I found when I got to St. Louis I could not make connections and return to Bellville, they had made their time long in May I did feel that it would be dealing fare with them — not to keep my word. Then the clay miners at the Brick yards were on a strike. They came in to St Louis and beged me to go out and help them — They had Music and flags and a big parade of men women and children. They won out in a few days after and I know that you would rather See those poor wretches win out than have me at Lassalle.

I regretted not having seen you when in Indianapolis but I presume Mr. Wilson told you the object of my visit — I regretted for find the condition of the Local in York as I did. Those boys promised me that they would abide by the decision of the National, they only wanted to be right — but they feel they have been unfairly dealt with. I think so. The fact that three locals from Macadoo made up the call for that convention to their charter looks to me rather suspicious and let me give you my honest judgment of the move the company are behind the Priest and has worked on Pres Duffy's religious Superstition. I told Pres. Duffy thing looked Suspicious and had to be handled with care. The women are taking a hand in it. If could have remained with them I think I could have healed up the breach. There no question in my mind but that it is a shrewd move of the Co. if that Local is broke up in a row it will Spread it has reached to Silver Brook the boys there came to me about it I wish I could see you before the Board meet. I am familiar with some things that has not been explained to you. . . .

We were up the Mountain to S. Caperton last night and came down the goat path after 12 o'clock. I had to Slide down Most of it.[2] My bones are all sore today. Boscome is sick after his trip and Ed Cahill says if they never come into the Union I wont go up there again but then we are going up next week again. One *Gen Manager* did not go with us he went to Charleston. The Ill. boys are good hard workers but they are beginning to realize this is not the smoothest field in the country to work in. I hope your little is better take good care of your own health.

Believe me always faithfully fraternally yours
Mother

[John P. Mitchell, Papers, Department of Archives and Manuscripts, Catholic University of America, Washington, D.C.]

Notes

1. Mother Jones moved to Sewell from Montgomery. Here she was joined by Illinois UMW miner, John H. Walker, who was later a president of Illinois District 12 and of the Illinois Federation of Labor.

2. These were not the only difficulties that had to be overcome in the organizing campaign. Many of the mining camps were remote and could only be reached by long walks through the woods and up mountains. John H. Walker later recalled that "on one occasion, when they were returning from a successful secret organizing meeting in the woods, one of the men spotted a large snake on the path. Mother Jones, without losing stride, just walked passed it, but the man behind her who was carrying her hat jumped so high in fright that he landed feet first on Mother's hat." (Lois McLean, "Mother Jones in West Virginia," *Goldenseal* 4 (January March, 1978).

To John P. Mitchell

Sewell West Virginia
Monday 12/2/01

My dear Mr Mitchell

I have hesitated to add to your already heavy burden. let me tell you I am not surprised West Virginia has not been organized.

I have well grounded Suspicions that Boskill is in the hands of our enemies. It would be to the best interest of the organization to move him at once, for several months without anyone knowing that I had any Suspicion nor do anyone know it now. I cannot go over the field here in this letter to you—I thought that good Motherly council might keep him on the right track but some *nature are rotten* to the core here is one.

We had a fine meeting yesterday John went to Aribucle this morning—he is one of Gods noble Boys.

I leave for Norton tomorrow with Some regrets as the work here needs me for another month then I could go way and stay. Keep up courage everything will be alright and Virginia will be with us the boys are responding nobbly.[1]

Sincerely fraternally yours in the Cause
Mother

*[John P. Mitchell Papers, Department of Archives and Manuscripts,
Catholic University of America, Washington, D.C.]*

Notes

1. After organizers had quietly worked the area for months, Mother Jones held public meetings that were bringing whole mining camps into the union.

To John P. Mitchell

Montgomery West Virginia
2.7.1902

My dear comrade

Owing to the frightful weather we have had I have very little of importance I have not been doing much for the last few days only getting nervous. There are so many calls from all quarters cannot reach them owing to the waters being up. My boys are doing good work. We meet every Monday morning and hold a council[1]—outline our work for the week so that each worker will know where to go and all know where the others are the first fellow who goes into a Saloon will be court marsheled and put in Irons for a week. We have no drinking every move must be strictly business all are in Harmony and there is Some pleasure in doing the work every night if we are near each other we gather in the general managers room thats me and disguss things in general change the program if we think best—we have a big mass meeting billed for next Sunday at Brooklis I expect to have a clash with John Lang. rest assured it will be the last one. We are going to organize that camp next Sunday. I have my crowed. There are some noble fellows in here.

Comrade Mitchell I am very surprised at the statment the Ill. boys made as to the amount of money it would take. If Ill. gives you $50,000 and leave you pick the men I will give you this State organized inside of a year[2] they had wheels in their heads—that is to say the least of it is poor policy. We give the enemy his weapon to Strike us with the operators say in the Statement of their own men they have in field.

Then some Board member said during the National convention that the output of Coal was *unlimited* So was the *Ignorance* of the *West Virginia Miners* that is an outrages Statement for any man to make whom those Miners are paying.[3] we are sent out to raise our craftsmen in the public mind and not lower them. If the author of that expression would look at home to my knowledge he would find as much Ignorance at his door as in West Virginia. Kiss the babies for me when you go home

Mother

[John P. Mitchell Papers, Department of Archives and Manuscripts, Catholic University of America, Washington, D.C.]

Notes

1. The group referred to were the organizers.

2. Three weeks later, she optimistically predicted: "I think I can give you this River (the Kanawha) organized by the 1st of May." (Mother Jones to John P. Mitchell, Feb. 27, 1902, John P. Mitchell Papers, Department of Archives and Manuscripts, Catholic University of America, Washington, D.C.)

3. It is clear from Mother Jones's letters that there were company men among the organizers.

To John P. Mitchell

Montgomery West Virginia
5-6 1902

My dear Comrade Mitchell

Pardon me for failing to carry out your instructions requesting me to write every week there has not been a Single night Since I Saw you in Indianapolis that I have not had a meeting. After I walk 8 or 10 miles and talk for 2 or 3 hours which I always do, I am a little nervous and have to rest up next day so as to be ready for my work at night. Then I know that some of the others write you all the time.

Well the cause is moving on.[1] Our people are responding like braves. I made a raid on Kelleys Creek one morning. Captured it they had a couple of Thugs watching me. I outwitted the pirates and got in took Clark Johnson and Ben Davis. These fellows were never in any move like this before and they hardly know what was going to drop. They are both good honest boys their heart in the work. After three weeks of hard work I feel Kelley Creek is ours. There has been more money spent last Summer to get this place and Cedar Grove organize without any response they are both in line now after I capture three or four Strong holds I can move to the Norfolk & Weston this place will Soon be in line.

Dont pay any attention to Such letters as Sewak Sends not that he does not mean alright—but it is a trick of the operators. Some of them are skoking and they dont know how to play their game poor innocent Wright from Indiana he is two tender hearted for these crooks he got wore out I told him to rest for a day.

This fellow Tinchure is no God Earth good and when they tell you that he could not get work it is false. I got the fellow work in three places he would not take it everything belonged to him blackeleged I do not trust him any fellow would Scheone as he did to Saddle himself on to his fellow man for support is not Safe he is an indiscreet talker has no knowledge of the movement he went to Mount Hope Local the other Night — called the men a narrow minded lot you told him to go to Leons Creek he never went Richard told him go to Paint Creek he never went — he went to fayette last week called a meeting the men turned out he never Showed up nor told any one else to go there the men came after me and told me how they were treated the Sooner this fellow is got rid of the Safer for all concerned, more so for the movement he is an office Hunter from the time he left the National Convention where he remainded longer than he Should untill the State Convention he did not work a day but going round the locals getting himself nominated for Vice President. he got defeated the men showing him that he had gaul than principle. I understand the Statement was made that his father lost his job because he harbered the organizers that is not true no organizer stoped at his fathers house they did not have to because there were boarding Houses and Hotels around there. None of us ever stops at a miners House We steer clear for we know they will have themselves discharged the next day thinking the organization will house them. These people in here must be made to know this their fight and that we have no nursery bottle for them. The Miners are finding falt with a black legs Son being carried when the Co bought his father to blackleg for a Suit of Clothes and the Women went in the Mines pulled him out I wont trust him I told Pres. Richards not to let him come on this River I wont work with anything I am Suspicious of their honesty this is a hour for this State those fellow working for their rotten Selves at the expense of the Human race. Will do thing we cannot *I am of the Candid opinion this fellow is not* Safe.

I have written a longer letter than I thought I would when I began. We have no meeting to night the Paed men are here so that is why I have time to night.

I find this boy Davis an honest earnest worker quite intelegent in time he will make a factor in the movement

I hope the anthracite trouble will be Settled without a Strike.[2] I know you must be Woren out. I often wish we could bear part of your heavy burden. I can only do my part here. When the Sun of emancipation begins to Shine for these poor wretches we can take our long looked for rest.

I have the Pa Be boys with me here they give me some good pointers one sent me a note Saturday about how the operators were going to head me that night their trick did not work. the boys came to the meeting and we took 22 new members last Sunday I had a mass meeting billed for Smothers Creek the bosses went round all day telling men not to come out. It was the largest meeting ever held there thats just how much they feared him I roasted the fellow before I closed.

John Boahen holds a meeting after mine I go back and hold another tears his argument all to pices. I Shone him for bringing out Such pauper Idiea he has quit. he gave up the job in disgust. I sent a comm. down to ask him who went to shoot P.W. to come to my meeting he Said he did not have Time I organized the Men that Sunday at green wood he sent a niger to watch me I took care of the n. while Ben read the obligar

take care of yourself

good bye
Mother

[John P. Mitchell Papers, Department of Archives and Manuscripts, Catholic University of America, Washington, D.C.]

Notes

1. A sufficient number of miners had been organized to enable the West Virginia UMW members to ask for a joint conference with the operators to establish a union scale, shorter hours, and improved working conditions. The operators ignored the invitation and a strike was called June 7, 1902.

2. On May 12, 1902, six days after this letter was written, 140,000 anthracite miners walked out in a temporary work suspension pending determination of the steps to be taken by the UMW convention scheduled to meet on May 15 at Hazleton, Pennsylvania. Although John Mitchell urged that a strike not be called, the convention voted overwhelmingly to continue the strike. In a letter to Mother Jones, May 10, 1902, Mitchell wrote: "I am of the opinion that this will be the fiercest struggle in which we have yet engaged. It will be a fight to the end, and our organization will either achieve a great triumph or it will be

completely annihilated." (John P. Mitchell Papers, Department of Archives and Manuscripts, Catholic University of America, Washington, D.C.)

To John P. Mitchell

Parkersbug, W. Va. (7-28-1902)[1]

Dear Comrade

Will write you Tomorrow have just been down to the jail to see the boys.[2] took them some *med* the jailor and the Marshal are both on my Strong and they let me take anything I want to the boys. I leave to night for Clarksburg where I shall do my full duty untill you call me out.

I think they have abandoned the idea of bring Sec Wilson here the marshal had a warent for him[3] and the Deputy was going after them the gang of pirates reconsidered the matter thought it was best not to bother anyt more

Take care of yourself for the cause needs you now more than ever—I hope you feel better than when you were in the West

Good bye God bless
Mother

The boys were laughing send you lots of love I got the best of the coal barrens[4]

I got a confidential Tip from a post nespaper man the Corporation and Some influential politicians were making a deal with T.L. to have me removed from will you more Tomorrow[5]

Mother
Noon friday 7-25-1902

[John P. Mitchell Papers, Department of Archives and Manuscripts, Catholic University of America, Washington, D.C.]

Notes

1. The West Virginia miners had joined the 1902 strike on June 7, and the union prepared an attack on the Fairmont Coal Company which "exercised almost monopolitic control of the production in an area of northern West Virginia," known as the Fairmont Field. Here the union had made almost no progress in contrast with its success in the southern fields. On May 10, 1902, John Mitchell transferred Mother Jones to Fairmont, writing: "I think the Fairmont

[field] would be the place in which you could do the most good, as the coal companies up there have evidently scared our boys, and of course, with good reason, as they have brutally beaten some of them. I dislike to ask you always to take the dangerous fields, but I know that you are willing. . . . " (John P. Mitchell to Mother Jones, May 10, 1902, John P. Mitchell Papers, Department of Archives and Manuscripts, Catholic University of America, Washington, D.C.) Mitchell's comment on the treatment of organizers was not exaggerated. "Organizers found it difficult to hire halls for meetings," Edward M. Steel notes, "were 'advised' to leave town, and even had trouble renting hotel rooms. Company detectives noted their every move." ("Mother Jones in the Fairmont Field, 1902," *Journal of American History* 57 (September, 1970): 291-92.)

After asking Mother Jones to go to the Fairmont field with all its dangers, Mitchell added: "I think, Mother, that it would be advisable for you not to exert yourself as much as you are doing, and you should take a rest now and then, so as to recuperate your strength. We cannot expect to do all the work ourselves, or see it done even in our lives, and I hope that you will not destroy your health and usefulness in the labor movement by over exertion." (Mitchell to Mother Jones, May 10, 1902, *op. cit.*)

2. Mother Jones is referring to the seven strike leaders who were in the Wood County jail for having, with Mother Jones, violated the injunction issued by Judge Jackson. Six had been sentenced to sixty days, and one, Haggerty, received an additional thirty days. Mother Jones had been let off by Judge Jackson with a warning. (*See* pp. 81-82).

3. The Parkersburg Daily News of July 25, 1902, reported: "Another rumor was in circulation that W. B. Wilson, secretary of the United Mine Workers, for whom an order of arrest was issued on Thursday, would not be disturbed or arrested, as it is the intention to ignore him unless he resorts to acts of violence."

4. Mother Jones may have been referring to the fact that she had not been imprisoned along with the other strike leaders.

5. T. L. Lewis, UMW vice-president from Ohio, was opposed to the strike in West Virginia, and he took over the strike leadership. Opposed to further demonstrations, he was anxious to get Mother Jones out of the area. Mother Jones went to the jail as a farewell visit to her boys, intervened on Barney Rice's behalf with Judge Jackson, entering a personal plea for clemency on the ground that he was ill, and departed for the anthracite field. (*Autobiography of Mother Jones*, pp. 52-55; Steel, *op. cit.*, p. 302.)

In August, she was back in the New River field, once again aiding the strike in West Virginia. At one meeting of strikers, someone opened fire on the audience listening to Mother Jones. A. D. Lavidner, a miner, "carried Mother Jones piggy-back across the creek and out of bullet range." Mother Jones left West Virginia again to speak and raise funds for the strikers and their families. In the end, however, the union miners were defeated by injunctions and the "Baldwin thugs." Mother Jones barely escaped alive. On one occasion, December 2, 1902, she narrowly escaped from a burning hotel in Montgomery. "The fire, of incendiary origin, had started in an adjoining room which had not been occupied for three days. This was the third fire within a few weeks at the hotel and it was suspected that Mother Jones' stopping there was the reason." (McLean, *op. cit.*, p. 18.)

To Henry Demarest Lloyd[1]

Montgomery West Virginia
4-19-1903

Mr. H D Lloyd
Chicago Ill

My dear Mr. Lloyed

I Send you by request of Mr. Mitchell Some clippings The thank you Judge is not correct. I did not thank him. he told me not to violate his Injunction I told him I would not violate the Law.[2] I was going out to continue the work for which I was arrested. If that violated his Injunction I feared it would be violated. he said I ought to Join Some Charity Organization I told him If I had my way I would Tear down every Charity Institution in the country to day build on their ruins the Temple of Justice My please was for Justice not Charity.

After two years of hard work the Miners have won a victory the operators of the Combine have met the miners in Joint Convention — little by little we are getting the poor Slaves awakened.

fraternally
Mother Jones

[Henry Demarest Lloyd Papers, State Historical Society of Wisconsin, Madison, Wisconsin.]

Notes

1. Henry Demarest Lloyd (1847-1903), liberal writer for the Chicago *Tribune* who became a Socialist. Lloyd wrote about the terrible conditions of miners in Hocking Valley, Illinois, and became famous for his *Wealth against Commonwealth* (1894), a classic expose of monopoly, concentrating on the Standard Oil Company.

2. The judge was John J. Jackson of Parkersburg, West Virginia. For the injunction, Mother Jones's arrest and the proceedings before Judge Jackson, *see* pp. 54, 78-82, 94, 99.

To Theodore Roosevelt

Elizabeth, New Jersey
July 15, 1903

President of the United States

Dear Sir:

Being citizens of the United States of America we, members of the textile industry, take the liberty of addressing this appeal to you.[1] As Chief Executive of the United States, you are in a sense our father and leader, and as such we look to you for advice and guidance. Perhaps the crime of child slavery has never been forcibly brought to your notice.

Yet, as father of us all, surely the smallest detail must be of interest to you. In Philadelphia, Pa., there are ninety thousand (90,000) textile workers who are on strike, asking for a reduction from 60 to 55 hours a week. With machinery, Mr. President, we believe that 48 hours is sufficient.

If the United State Senate had passed the eight-hour bill, this strike might not have occurred. We also ask that the children be taken from the industrial prisons of this nation and given their right of attending schools so that in years to come better citizens will be given to this republic.

These little children raked by cruel toil beneath the iron wheels of greed, are starving in this country which you have declared is in the height of prosperity — slaughtered, ten hours a day, every day in the week, every week in the month, every month in the year, that our manufacturing aristocracy may live to exploit more slaves as the years roll by.

We ask you, Mr. President, if our commercial greatness has not cost us too much by being built upon the quivering hearts of helpless children. We who know of these sufferings have taken up their cause and are now marching towards you in the hope that your tender heart will counsel with us to abolish this crime.

The manufacturers have threatened to starve these children and we seek to show that no child shall die of hunger at the will of any manufacturers in this fair land. The clergy, whose work this really is, are silent on the crime of ages, and so we appeal to you.

It is the hope that the words of Christ will be more clearly interpreted by you when he said "Suffer little children to come unto Me." Our destination is New York city, and after that Oyster Bay. As your children, may we hope to have the pleasure of an audience? We only ask that you advise us as to the best course.

In Philadelphia alone thousands of persons will wait upon your answer, while throughout the land, wherever there is organized labor, the people will anxiously await an expression of your sentiment towards suffering childhood.

On behalf of these people, we beg that you will reply and let us know whether we may expect an audience.

The reply should be addressed to "Mother Jones Crusaders" en route according to the daily papers. We are very respectfully yours.

MOTHER JONES, Chairman

Committee—Charles Sweeney, Edward A Klingersmith, Emanuel Hanson, Joseph Diamond.

[*Philadelphia* North American, *July 16, 1903.*][2]

Notes

1. For the background for the "March of the Children" and the reason for the letter to President Roosevelt, *see* pp. 100-5, 213.

In publishing the letter, the Philadelphia *North American*'s reporter, accompanying Mother Jones and her Crusaders, wrote: "With the increasing good luck of the 'army' so high has risen its hopes that 'Mother' Jones has positively called upon the President and lay before him the suffering entailed by the textile strike in Philadelphia. After a conference with her lieutenants action was taken which commits the 'army' to the long-discussed visit to Oyster Bay. The result is this letter, signed by 'Mother' Jones and the committee which was mailed to President Roosevelt." (Philadelphia *North American,* July 16, 1903.)

2. The Philadelphia *North American* assigned John Lopez to accompany the march, and he covered it from beginning to end.

The letter also appeared in the Trenton *Weekly State Gazette,* July 23, 1903, and is reprinted in C. K. McFarland, "Crusade for Child Laborers: 'Mother' Jones and the March of the Mill Children," *Pennsylvania History 38* (July, 1971): 292-93.

To Theodore Roosevelt

NEW YORK, July 30, 1903.

The Hon. Theodore Roosevelt, President U.S.A.

Your Excellency:

Twice before have I written to you requesting an audience that I might lay my mission before you and have your advice on a matter which bears upon the welfare of the whole nation.[1] I speak for the emancipation from mills and factories of the hundreds of thousands of young children who are yielding up their lives for the commercial supremacy of the nation. Failing to receive a reply to either of the letters, I yesterday went to Oyster Bay, taking with me three of these children that they might plead to you personally.

Secretary Barnes informed us that before we might hope for an interview, we must first lay the whole matter before you in a letter. He assured me of its delivery to you personally, and also that it would receive your attention.[2]

I have espoused the cause of the laboring class in general and of suffering childhood in particular. For what affects the child must ultimately affect the adult. It was for them that our march of principle was begun. We sought to bring the attention of the public upon these little ones, so that ultimately sentiment would be aroused and the children freed from the workshops and sent to school. I know of no question of to-day that demands greater attention from those who have at heart the perpetuation of the Republic.

The child of to-day is the man or woman of to-morrow, the one the citizen and the mother of still future citizens. I ask Mr. President, what kind of citizen will be the child who toils twelve hours a day, in an unsanitary atmosphere, stunted mentally and physically, and surrounded with immoral influences? Denied education, he cannot assume the true duties of citizenship, and enfeebled physically and mentally, he falls a ready victim to the perverting influences which the present economic conditions have created.

I grant you, Mr. President, that there are State laws which should regulate these matters, but results have proven that they are inadequate. In my little band are three boys, the oldest 11 years old, who have worked in mills a year or more without interference from the authorities. All efforts to bring about reform have failed.

I have been moved to this crusade. Mr. President, because of actual experience in the mills. I have seen little children without the first rudiments of education and no prospect of acquiring any. I have seen other children with hands, fingers and other parts of their tiny bodies mutilated because of their childish ignorance of machinery. I feel that no nation can be truly great while such conditions exist without attempted remedy.

It is to be hoped that our crusade will stir up a general sentiment in behalf of enslaved childhood, and secure and enforcement of present laws.

But that is not sufficient.

As this is not alone the question of the separate States, but of the whole Republic, we come to you as the chief representative of the nation.

I believe that Federal laws should be passed governing this evil and including a penalty for violation. Surely, Mr. President, if this is practicable—and I believe that you will agree that it is—you can advise me of the necessary steps to pursue.

I have with the three boys who have walked a hundred miles serving as living proof of what I say. You can see and talk with them, Mr. President, if you are interested. If you decide to see these children, I will bring them before you at any time you may set. Secretary Barnes has assured me of an early reply,[3] and this should be sent care of the Ashland Hotel, New York city.

Very respectfully yours,
MOTHER JONES.

[Philadelphia North American, July 31, 1903.]

Notes

1. All of Mother Jones's letters to President Roosevelt were published in the Philadelphia *North American,* but there were only two not three published. Since none of the letters are in the Theodore Roosevelt Papers in the Library of Congress, Manuscripts Division, there is no way of discovering the third letter, if one was actually sent.

2. It does not appear to have received the President's attention.

3. Roosevelt never responded to the letter, but B. F. Barnes, his acting secretary, wrote to Mother Jones from Oyster Bay, New York: "Dear Madam. I beg to acknowledge the receipt of your letter of the 30th ult. and to say that it has been brought to the President's attention.

"The President, as was shown by his action while Governor of New York, has the heartiest sympathy with every effort to prevent child labor in the factories and on this question no argument need be addressed to him, as his position has been announced again and again.

"Under the Constitution it is not at present seen how Congress has power to act in such a matter. It would seem that the States alone at present have the power to deal with the subject."

In publishing the letter the Philadelphia *North American*'s correspondent accompanying Mother Jones's "March," wrote: "The allusion to the President's sympathy as shown by his action while Governor of New York refers to an anti-child labor law which was passed under his administration. But that does not by any means satisfy the 'Mother.' She declares that labor has received as severe a blow in the face as though no letter had been received.

" 'The President did not grant the interview, and that was what we asked for,' she said. 'The letter drops us down, as they think, in a manner which disarms us. But I serve notice that the matter is not dropped here. If President Roosevelt was in such hearty sympathy with the child slaves while he was Governor of New York, what has worked such a change that he will refuse to see three boys who represent thousands of other children who are wearing out their lives in the mills." (Philadelphia *North American,* August 4, 1903.) Mother Jones showed her anger at the President by urging workers to pledge not to vote for the "monkey-chaser" in the 1904 presidential election. The reference to "monkey-chaser" was to Roosevelt's African hunting expedition.

To Governor James H. Peabody

Denver, Colorado, March 26, 1904

Governor James H. Peabody:

Mr. Governor, you notified your dogs of war to put me out of the state.[1] They complied with your instructions. I hold in my hand a letter that was handed to me by one of them, which says "under no circumstances return to this state." I wish to notify you, governor, that you don't own the state. When it was admitted to the sisterhood of states, my fathers gave me a share of stock in it; and that is all they gave you. The civil courts are open. If I break a law of state or nation it is the duty of the civil courts to deal with me. That is why my forefathers established those courts to keep dictators and tyrants such as you from interfering with civilians. I am right here in the capital, after being out nine or ten hours, four or five blocks from your office. I want to ask you, governor, what in Hell are you going to do about it?[2]

Mother Jones

[Autobiography of Mother Jones, *p. 103.*]

Notes

1. On March 25, 1904, Mother Jones was taken to the militia headquarters in Trinidad, Colorado because of her activities in aiding strikers at the Colorado Fuel and Iron Company and the Victor Fuel Company. There she was told she was to be deported, and on March 26, together with three other UMW organizers and sympathizers, put on a Santa Fe train for La Junta, Colorado, about 65 miles northeast of Trinidad. The deportees were told never to return, and in La Junta, still carrying the deportation paper, Mother Jones was aided by a friendly railroad conductor who put her aboard a train bound for Denver. When she reached the city, she took a hotel room and wrote Governor James H. Peabody, who had issued the deportation order, the letter.

2. The Goveror did nothing and in April, Mother Jones returned to Trinidad.

To John H. Walker[1]

Canton, Ill., 1-4-04 [05]

My dear John — for such you are to me:

Your very kind letter reached me this morning. No one could write that letter but a true comrade and no one could appreciate it as I do but a true and tried comrade.

John, I opposed a ring of fools that had charge of that strike in Colorado. I felt it my duty to do so.[2] I know that Mitchell would have to bear the brunt; they could retire and not be heard of again, but he would have to suffer the result. I *want to say right here,* I may never see him again, but one thing one thing certain, I will fight to death for him against any false assertion. I know the labor movement; I know the philosophy of the *monster capitalism.* Sometimes a man or woman are to be carried away by the glitter of the tinsel. I *for one shall be his defender.*

I resigned because I fought; some of the dirty ignoramuses that represented the national office were against me. I do not want to put John in a position where he would have to oppose them; his fight is hard enough. John Mitchell does not know everything those fellows did out there. I will fight the cause of the miners anyway, whether I am directly in their service or not. John Mitchell can always depend on me. I know whatever mistakes he has made, he is right at heart.[3]

So far as Debs[4] is concerned, I think he will take my word as quickly as anyone else in the United States. We have been close comrades on the battle ground for 14 long years. We can trust our lives in the *hands of each other.* I went up from Paris to see him; he had got up from a sick bed; I did not approach him upon anything but his health and the future of the workers' cause. Some of these curs were telling him what they were going to do at that convention. The D—— traitors did not *chirip.* It is impossible for me to break away from my engagements. You know the Socialist party has never in its history given me five cents. I am going out for the cause to wake the people up, and I can be more independent as I am. There is no man in the world that I will approach for a job. If John wants me he can send for me. I expect to go to N.Y. in April. I will call on him then, making only a friendly visit. I am not afraid of suffering. The boys of the W. F. of Miners will see that I am not hungry,[5] if the time ever comes; and what if it does?

John, I have been offered many good positions; indeed, I could be in Europe now if I wanted to. Let me tell you, John, you will always find me on the firing line with you.

I will write Debs to keep quiet until I have a chance to see him, and talk things over with him. We cannot afford to serve that dam Pittsburg gang so well.

Yes, John, I kow that poor Sam would give me the last cent he had. He is a man with a soul; every inch a man.

Tell Tom that I love him just as I always did; that I often wish that I could be with him over there. Poor Tom and were in many battles together. Regard to poor Noon and that clean, honest, soul, Flaherty; get him elected then I will have another friend on the Board. If I could see John and tell him about that old coward Ream and Bousfield, the only fellow the national had was Fairley. He came too late.

Good bye, John, I am always

Loyally,
Mother.

Write me 43 Walton Place, Chicago, Ill.

[Mother Mary Harris Jones Papers, Department of Archives and Manuscripts, Catholic University of America, Washington, D.C.]

Notes

1. John Hunter Walker (1872-1955), was born in Scotland and emigrated to the United States with his family at the age of nine. The Walkers settled in Braideood, Illinois where at an early age, John began working in the coal mines. After his father was blacklisted in Illinois because of his union activity, the family moved to the Oklahoma Indian Territory for a time, where John and his father worked in the mines. After membership in the Knights of Labor, John joined the newly formed United Mine Workers of America as an organizer. He rose to the presidency of District 12 of Illinois, the largest district in the union, a position he held from 1905 to 1913. In the latter year, he became president of the Illinois Federation of Labor. He was a member of the Socialist Party until 1916 when he was expelled for endorsing the re-election of President Woodrow Wilson in place of the Socialist candidate for president. After the U. S. entered World War I, Walker supported the war actively and served in several wartime government posts, for which he was bitterly criticized by Socialist and UMW leader Adolph Germer. After the war, Walker was active in the Farmer-Labor Party. An unsuccessful candidate several times for UMW president. Walker was at odds with the presidents of the UMW after John Mitchell, and particularly with John L. Lewis, whom he accused of collusion with the coal operators and of violating the union constitution. After he led an insurgent movement in Illinois, he was expelled from the union by Lewis in 1932. He was active in other union affairs until the 1950s. Throughout the twentieth century, he remained a close friend and correspondent of Mother Jones.

2. The reference is to Mother Jones's resignation from the UMW after the failure of the northern Colorado miners to continue their strike until the southern miners won their demands. *See* pp. 37-39, 104-110.

3. For the change in Jones's opinion of John P. Mitchell, *see* pp. 357, 407.
Mitchell's opinion of Mother Jones is set forth in an interesting correspondence in the summer of 1913. Edgar Marston of Blair & Co., New York City, wrote to Mitchell on July 30, 1913: "According to the enclosed, 'Mother' Jones has been invited to Thurber to spend the two days' celebration at Labor Day. I have not met 'Mother' Jones and my impressions of her are based on the newspaper reports of her addresses to miners, which, at times,have recalled to my mind Wardjohn. I hope 'Mother' Jones is not as anarchistic in her declarations. Necessarily 'Mother' Jones is ignorant of the spirit which predominates at Thurber, and I was thinking, if your relations are such, whether you might let

'Mother' Jones know that in talking to the miners at Thurber, it was not like addressing miners at a great many camps where there is a line drawn between capital and labor."

John P. Mitchell replied on July 31, 1913: "Replying to your favor of July 30th, I regret to say that I do not have a relationship with Mother Jones that would admit of my writing to her or communicating with her in any way. Years ago she was one of my staff of organizers, but for some reason she concluded that I was altogether too conservative, and she has in recent years denounced me in even stronger terms than she has used in denunciation of the 'capitalists.' Mother Jones is a most extraordinary woman. She is capable of delivering and sometimes does deliver most learned and scholarly addresses; at other times she becomes revolutionary and profane, and appeals only to the passions of her hearers. I am told that during the past few months she has undergone a change and is now in a conservative mood; how long this will last it is impossible to say." (American Federation of Labor Correspondence, Washington, D.C.)

4. Eugene Victor Debs (1855-1926), leader of the Socialist Party of America and its presidential candidate in 1900, 1904, 1908, 1912, and 1920. Founder of the American Railway Union in 1893, and leader of the Pullman Strike in 1894, Debs became a Socialist while in prison for violating the federal injunction in that strike. In 1912, he received 901,000 votes for president, and in 1920, though in prison for having opposed the participation of the United States in World War I, he received 919,000 votes for president. In 1905 Debs and Mother Jones worked together in the founding of the Industrial Workers of the World (I.W.W.), and both disagreed with the I.W.W. policies and left the organization. Mother Jones helped distribute Debs's pamphlet *Unionism and Socialism: A Plea for Both*, with its call for industrial unionism. *See* pp. 55, 109-11.

5. For Mother Jones's organizing work for the Western Federation of Miners, *see* pp. 112-15, 130-31, 412-13.

To William B. Wilson

Stensville, Montana 5-9-1905

My dear Comrade Wilson

Here I am out in the Mountans not on a pleasure but on duty waking up the Shonbuny Joint. I spoke in Butte last night under the auspices of the Smeltermen Union.[1] I had house packed Stage and all the boys did not know what to do for me.they gave me one hundred dollars and my fare to and from Chicago. they want me to remain out here till Summer and go in the Spring for a rest they would Pay the bills. I couuld not do that poor boys they earn their nickles to hard, if you could se [illegible].

I am glad Mrs W and the children are well I will be in the State of

N.Y. for three months this fall. I will make an effort to go and See them while East. I want to See Joe before I die. take care of him.

I spoke in Helena on Miners day the 13th of the Month Back to Butte for two more meetings then I go to Coakdale for the Coal Miners then I go East — I have So much to tell you when I see you the Time seems so Long I am young to go before I am to die. So that I just gaze on that face a reflex of the heart that has been true to the people. In looking over the field it looks as if you were going to have trouble next year. in fact it looks to me as if many crafts were in the threshold of industrial war. let it come we only can do what we can for them. We are permeating them with class conception of their real class interest trying to put the Spirit Solidarity in them let me warn you against that [illegible] member [illegible] he is no gods earth good for god or man. What cur will Stoop to lick the feet of those in powr for a Job I am going to See you Soon Love to Miss Mary Agnes your own goodself family Mother

[William B. Wilson Papers, Historical Society of Pennsylvania.]

Notes

1. For Mother Jones's work for the Western Federation of Miners during these years, *see* pp. 112-15, 130-31.

To William B. Wilson

New York, Oct. the 4th 1905[1]

My dear Comrade

I know you have not much time to read letters much less answer them. I regretted I did not See Agnes while in Indianapolis but I lost the address. I spent labor day at Montgomary the Boys would not me go before I spoke things are not wright in there but it's none of my affair now No wonder Some of them wanted to get rid of me there's a rotten cur that Iseman of Terre Haute I often wonder if we will ever be able to resque the poor wretches from the clutches of those Traitors in their own rank they only care for that Job that they hold as organizers.

Well I have tremendous meeting in N.Y. night after night I have to speak to thousand of People Some day they will overthrow the whole rotten Machine.

Now I want to ask you to do me a favor. Will you get that Phonograph packed up and sent to Chicago out of your way and all thos Pictures I have several invitation to go over to Europe from the comrades in France and England I am going South this winter to do Some work in the factories A gentleman in Europe will put up the money. My love to Sam life after all is worth living when we meet such Loyal Souls we feel there are Some grand Souls yet left out of the Struggle Comes the time and tried no matter what the filthy minds may say whose own Mothers were rotteen to the core I know that you and Sam believe me that a woman *pure and true* come what will you will both find me true to you. They have not injured me with people last night two thousand people wanted to carry me on their Shoulders! even if Mr Mitchell did have my Picture toren down from the Stand in Wilkesbarre[2] where the capitalist Henchman Bosefelt was going to Speak I gave Bosefelt H— about that Commission. Well so long as you and Sam and My own Dear Debs Stand I dont care for all the world fondly Loyally

Mother

Ship to 163 Randolph St Room 27 Chicago Illinois

[William B. Wilson Papers, Historical Society of Pennsylvania.]

Notes

1. The letter was written on the stationary of the Social Democratic Party, Local New York. For Mother Jones's work for the Socialists during this period, *see* pp. 156-57.
2. For the break between Mother Jones and John P. Mitchell, *see* pp. 37-39, 104-10.

To Terence V. Powderly[1]

Chicago, Ill.
May 9-1906.

T. V. Powderly
502 Quincy St., N.W.,
Washington, D.C.

My own Dear Comrade:

You no doubt wonder why you have not had a reply to your letter before this time. When I left you I went to Indianapolis spent a day or two there and proceeded to Danville, Ill., and was laid up for a month in the home of a Physicain friend and he patched me up for the work again.

Strange that I should have been thinking of you, and the work you did in the past, the day before and that day that I reached Chicago and found your letter awaiting me. Some how I felt that you would rebuke Gooding and their method. When I read your letter and read the clipping from the News Paper it brought tears to my eyes, and I thought of the days when we were together in battle, how they had accused you and maligned you, and how patiently you bore it all for the cause so dear to you.

I saw Darrow yesterday, he tells me he thinks it will be a long drawn out trial,[2] and it will need a great deal of finance to carry it on, and we must have it. He had a letter from Bolton Hall,[3] he gave him much incouragement and every guarantee of assistance. I wanted to go to Denver to have a long talk with the boys at the head of the Federation, but Darrow advised me not to go, for possibly there would be some charge trumped up against me and I would be put behind the bars out there, so I took his advice and will stay away, believing that I can do more good out of Jail than in it.

I must tell you something. Robert Hunter, the man who wrote "Poverty"[4] went to Washington to see the "Big Stick"[5] and the "Big Stick" said, "so you are the man who wrote "Poverty" are you?" Hunter said yes, and of coures Teddy did not like that because he had been swinging the circle in a Special Car telling all about the wonderful prosperity. He pased up and down the Cabinet Room, and said "every one of the Western Federation Of Miners ought to be hung, they are nothing but a gang of criminals" and then he said the "Beef Trust ought to be hung also." If I had been there I would have told him to go down to the Senate of the United States, and take a rope with him, and hang some of those commercial pirates.

I regretted to learn from your letter that you were not feeling well. Courage, Comrade, the day is dawning, as you say, and out of the darkness will come the light. The world needs more like you. Do not let any incident of the past distress you. You are the same honest T. V. Powderly of years ago, when the present labor lords were not heard of. You broke up the clay, and sowed the seed, and they are now reaping some of the harvest, and whatever comes or goes, whatever the dark day may be I shall always see you in the shadows of the past when you worked so faithfully, and patiently in labors cause.

Some day the unwritten history will be given to the children yet unborn, and it is possible that they will make pilgrimages to your grave and plant flowers there on. We live not for to-day, but for the ages yet to come, and the children yet unborn.

I expect some time soon to got to Washington and write up that book I promised you would be written.

Poor Douglas Wilson, go to see him some time, it will cheer him up.

I have always had a warm spot in my heart for him, he has been true to the cause. It is a sad sight for me to go to Washington and look upon that once magnificent frame, what a total wreck it is.

I expect to go to Oklahoma in a few weeks to do some work down there, and I would like to hear from you and above all keep cheerful and the future will be ours.

I have no words to express my appreciation for your rebuke to Gooding.

I am as ever yours faithfully and loyally for the Social Revilution.

Take care of yourself write a line to me know how Douglass feels send me that book we talked about if you can cheer up

Mother Jones

[Terence V. Powderly and Mother Jones Papers, Department of Archives and Manuscripts, Catholic University of America, Washington, D.C.]

Notes

1. Terence V. Powderly (1849-1924), leader of the Knights of Labor, was born in Carbondale, Pennsylvania, became a railroad worker at age thirteen, and served an apprenticeship in a machine shop. He joined the Machinists' and Blacksmiths' union in 1870 and became its president the following year. In 1874 he joined the Noble and Holy Order of the Knights of Labor, and in 1879 he achieved election to the highest office, Grand Master Workman. A moderate in his views, he was an inconsistent and troubled leader as the Order grew to enormous membership reaching over 750,000 in 1886. His policies helped in the Knights' rapid decline and he resigned from the Order in 1893, and as a reward for campaigning for President William McKinley, he was appointed U.S. Commissioner-General of Immigration in 1897. From 1897 to 1921, Powderly served as chief of the Division of Information of the Bureau of Immigration, and then held various other government posts until his death in Washington, D.C., June 24, 1924. A Catholic, Powderly was anxious to obtain the Pope's support while he was K. of L. leader.

The Powderlys (Terence V. and Emma) were very good friends of Mother Jones, and considering them as her family, she often stayed with them when she was not engaged in organizing or other labor activities.

2. Clarence Darrow (1857-1938), leading American lawyer on behalf of labor and radical causes, headed the defense counsel for Haywood, Pettibone, and Moyer. Darrow had defended Debs after the Pullman strike, and had been the attorney for the United Mine Workers before a Federal mediating board after the coal strike of 1902.

3. Bolton Hall (1854-1938), active follower of Henry George who, though a successful real-estate operator and businessman, was a vigorous critic of unfair taxation and of monopoly. Author of *Three Acres and Liberty*, published in 1907, which began a "back-to-the-land" movement.

4. Robert Hunter (1874-1942), social worker and Socialist whose book *Pov-*

erty, published in 1904, furnished Mother Jones and other Socialists with useful information on the extent of poverty in the United States.

5. The term applied to President Theodore Roosevelt after he made a speech in Chicago in which he advocated that the United States in foreign policy "Speak softly and carry a big stick." An illustration of the "Big Stick" policy was the taking of the Panama Canal by Roosevelt.

To Terence V. Powderly

Bisbee, Arizona,
May 24, 1907.

Mr. T. V. Powderly
Washington, D.C.

My dear Friend and Comrade:

For a long time I felt that I wanted to drop you a few lines and let you know that I am still alive, and fighting the common enemy as best I know how. I was in Washington last Fall and went there principally to se you, and spend a week or ten days getting notes on the old time fights, but after I arrived I found out that you had gone to Europe, a trip I considered you badly needed, after the long years of kicks and abuse you got from those who you had faithfully served; and though all the world may abuse you there will still be one, who will defend you. I know of the many dark battles you had to fight. You were rocking the cradle of the movement, you made it possible for others to march on. No doubt, with many of us you made blunders, but I know and feel that you did the best you knew how under the conditions with which you had to deal. It was the early stages of the training school for the future conflict. Last month I happened to be within a few miles of Bruceville; as the train was passing through there in the early morning, I stopped off and went out to see the pillow of clay on which the head of poor Martin Irons rested.[1] He sleepeth well, Jay Gould cannot waken him now.[2] His grave was marked by a piece of iron, it was his only tombstone.[3] It marked the spot where that brave warrior of labors battles rested. No tender hand seemed to care for it, but the wild flowers did not forget to plant their perfume around his grave. One thing struck me in the early morning, and that was that the birds had not forgotten that he was resting there, they had awakened from their slumbers, and were calling their mates to enjoy God's sunshine. They were not responding to the call of a trust whistle, only to the call of nature.

While awaiting for the train I called upon Dr. Harris, to my regret he was not home. I met his charming daughter, and left a message of deep appreciation from both you and me for the doctor for his kindness to Martin in his last hour.

I enclose you a few leaves from his grave, Knowing how deeply you will appreciate them, and how poor Martin would feel if he saw you press your lips to them.

Now Comrade let me congratulate you on the manly and fearless steps you have taken in defense of our brave boys in Idaho.[4] It is needless for me to say to you, that capitalism has no soul, nor no love for humanity or its sufferings, and those who take up the battle for the oppressed, must bear the penalty. How the spectacular performer in Washington has put his foot in it. The word "undesirable citizen" will go down in history.[5] He and his crew of pirates would no doubt give a great deal to undo that.

I hope you go out to see douglas Wilson. He needs your consoling words in his lonely condition, and his faithful wife needs some words of encouragement, I have always loved Douglas. He is a true brave fellow and the labor movement misses him from the field of battle. Tell him from me that I am going to write him a long letter some day in the near future, I would have done it before But I lost his address.

The enclosed circular, will tell you the same old story of the robber and the robbed.

Will you be home next Winter? There are some things of the past, over which I want to talk with you. I want to spend a week or ten days in Washington,

Beleive me ever faithfully yours in the cause of suffering humanity,

Mother Jones

If you can get me a copy of the government report of the Colo war do so I am told it is out of print

[Terence V. Powderly Papers, Department of Archives and Manuscripts, Catholic University of America, Washington, D.C.]

Notes

1. For the career of Martin Irons, *see* p. 280.

2. Jay Gould (1836-1892), with James Fisk and Daniel Drew, one of the leading Robber Barons in the post-Civil War period. Gould controlled the railroads in the Southwest on which the strike of Knights of Labor members was led by Martin Irons, but which ended in defeat and Irons's being blacklisted.

3. In 1910, under the auspices of the Missouri State Federation of Labor, a monument was erected above Martin Irons's grave paying tribute to him as a "Fearless Champion of Industrial Freedom."

4. The reference is to the frameup of William D. ("Big Bill") Haywood, Charles Moyer, and George F. Pettibone, leaders of the Western Federation of Miners, charged with the slaying of Frank Steunenberg, former governor of

Idaho. *See* pp. 55, 118, 120, 152, 464.

5. On the eve of the trial of the W. F. of M. leaders, President Theodore Roosevelt stated that Haywood and Moyers were "undesirable citizens." The President was condemned for attempting to mold public opinion against the defendants on the eve of a trial in which their lives were at stake.

To Thomas J. Morgan

E. St. Louis, December 30th, 1908.

My dear Comrade Morgan:[1]

I received your letter a day or so ago forwarded to me from Springfield. I appreciate very much the correction you made, only I thought it might have been well to have left the wife question out. I did not catch what you said about the Daily. The letter you sent me, that is the personal letter you sent me, I think it got in the fire with some other mail that I was destroying before I fully read it. I am afraid that Daly is going to involve us all in some trouble before we get thro' with it. Hoehn[2] thinks I had better not put that letter in the press owing to the criticism the enemies of the movement would make and the capital they might make out of it against the cause, but he says for me to send it to every national committeeman and every state secretary and all members of the executive board, also to the national office for the Bulletin. Let me have your opinion about it before I start out. I expect the bunch will move that I be thrown out of the party of course for exposing this graft,[3] but then I'll stand that, I'll still be a socialist. Now, I wrote to that King of ours about that $200 he owes me and I have received no reply. I am inclined to think that he wants some trouble, and if he does, I'll give him all he wants of it.

I am yours for the cause,
Mother Jones

[Thomas J. Morgan Collection, Illinois Historical Survey,
University of Illinois Library.]

Notes

1. Thomas J. Morgan, Chicago lawyer and leading spirit in that city's Socialist movement, had been an active figure (together with his wife Hannah Morgan) in the Socialist Labor Party, and continued his socialist activity in the Socialist Party of America.

2. Gustave Hoehn, formerly a leader of the Missouri branch of the Socialist Labor Party, was head of the Socialist Party local in St. Louis and editor of *St. Louis Labor* and an active figure in the Typographical Union.

3. Mother Jones is referring to her charge against J. Mahlon Barnes, which later precipitated a bitter battle in the Socialist Party. She accused Barnes, Socialist Party national secretary, of having borrowed $250 from her in 1905 and never repaying the loan. Barnes claimed he had repaid it the following year, but could not produce a receipt. For further discussion of this controversy, *see* pp. 578.

To Thomas J. Morgan

Hazleton, Pa Aug 1st 1910

Thomas H. Morgan
79 Dearborn St.
Chicago, Ill.

My Dear Comrade:

Your letter of July 16th at hand. Glad to hear from you and to find out that you and Frankel were in the lead in Chicago.

I am glad that Brower was elected to the National Committee.

I hope he will take no back water, and that he will fight that corrupt gang to a finish. Yes; Comrade we have nothing to loose but everything to gain for the slaves and our cause. I had a long talk with Stokes and Walling. Lemont I went to the Call office to see him but he had just left. I know him very well from Kansas city. He is a good fellow.

Comrade Morgan I have known you for almost thirty years in the fight I have never known you to flinch, although the bunch have tryed to blacken you everywhere through the country. If this movement is going to move onward for the benifit of the workers we must take our stand boldly and fearlessly with the working class. Not with the gang of self and notoriety seekers. Think of a movement called a working class movement that would not allow that Mexican question to come up in the Congress,[1] and the questions involved, the right of asylum, the right of free speech and free press. But we forced the U. S. Congress to take the matter up[2] and not the so called Socialist Congress that spend three days discussing the Immigration question,[3] the so called sex question that is not a class question.[4] I believe that it was the dam rottenness of that Congress that made me sick in Cincinnatti.

I am going o send you a copy of the hearing before the Committee of Congress in Washington so that you will get a grasp of the work I have been doing for the last two years. Comrade Morgan I brought that question up before Congress all alone.[5] No Socialist gave me aid. You see the dirty whelp must be guilty or he never would have made the slimy attack on me he did.[6] I am laying low for that fellow, and when I open up on him he will wish he had never known me.

The very fact that he made that attack on a woman of seventy six years who spent the best part of her days in the cause of humanity should condemn him in the estimation of every honest man and woman. I never drew a dollar from the movement. I have put many into it. The money I collected I can account for every dollar of it and when I get through with him he will wish he had never known me.

Comrade the more I get through the country the more rottenness I discover. And that bunch in the National office that can be owned by Hilqutt,[7] Berger,[8] Spargo[9] must be cleaned out of it, or the National office will be busted. And the Socialist movement will go by the board. If a Labor Party is ever started in this country. I am feeling the pulse as I go along and I want to tell you the sentiment of the people. Comrade Morgan you will agree with me that a party is rotten to the core that send a junketting party composed of eight members, not any of them of the working class to Copenhagen to represent the working mans movement.[10] We have five hundred of our brave comrades in the bastiles of Capitalism in Argentine,[11] pleading with us to do something for them. Instead of giving that money wrung from the blood of the working class back again to the commercial class; would it not have been better for us to have sent it to our comrades to fight the . . . with. Do you wonder that the old warriors in the movement are getting discouraged and giving up the battle in despair. It seems a horrible indictment against our movement. I feel sometimes as if something will happen to tear us to pieces. You could not have conveyed any better news to me than the fact that you and Frankel stood at the front of the helm in the vote. If we could only tour the State of Ill and turn it upside down we might be able to change Cook county.

I did not see you before I left Cihicago. But I through it in to Bental strong before I left there. If a change does not come and we don't put in class conscious men on office we are doomed. However I have confidence in the rank and file if we can awaken them.

Send the Provoker[12] to Charles P Gildea. 23 W Tamarack St. Hazleton Pa. He is one of our brave fighters and loyal to the end. He will help you in the fight and you can trust him. And also Alex' Dwyer; 8th & Alter Hazleton. Pa. I am holding big meetings here for the miners.

I have not quite got over my attack in Cincinnatti.

Write me again as soon as you can and beleive me always me as one of those who wants to be on the fore front of the battle for right even though I stand alone. Boland in Washington is a fine fellow. Clean to the core. Well we will see what will come out of the junketing tour. The boys will send you subscribtion for the Provoker. And get you as many more subscribtions in the right place as they can

I am Always your in the fight,
Mother Jones,

Notes

1. The reference is to the 1910 National Socialist Party Congress held in Chicago. (The gathering was called a "congress" instead of a "convention" because no candidates for political office were nominated.) Mother Jones was not the only one to criticize the Congress for failing to take a stand on the persecution of Mexican revolutionaries in the United States. William D. ("Big Bill") Haywood also criticized the Party leadership for not organizing aid for the Mexican revolutionaries. However, there is little doubt about American Socialist sympathy for the Mexican cause; many Socialists aided the Mexican revolution, and vigorously opposed American intervention against the Revolution once Díaz was overthrown. (*See* Diane K. Christopulos, "American Radicals and the Mexican Revolution, 1900-1925," Ph.D. dissertation, State University of New York at Binghamton, 1980, and Ivie E. Cadenhead, Jr., "The American Socialists and the Mexican Revolution of 1910," *Southwestern Social Science Quarterly* 43 (September, 1962): 95-113.)

2. *See* pp. 134, 369-75 for the Congressional investigation referred to.

3. The immigration question was discussed at the 1910 Socialist Party Congress for three days, after which a resolution, introduced by Morris Hillquit, New York Socialist leader, was adopted which placed the Party on record as favoring "all legislative measures tending to prevent the immigration of strike-breakers and contract laborers, and the mass organization of workers from foreign countries brought about by the employing class for the purpose of weakening of American labor, and of lowering the standard of life of American workers." (Socialist Party, *Proceedings of the First National Congress . . ., Chicago, May 5-21, 1910*. pp. 70-168.)

4. This is a revealing comment since it indicated that Mother Jones regarded such issues as woman's rights, including woman suffrage, as a "sex" not a "class" issue. In this attitude she stood in opposition to most women in the Socialist and labor movements. (*See* Philip S. Foner, *Women and the American Labor Movement; From Colonial Times to the Eve of World War I*, New York, 1979, pp. 270-74, 470-78.)

5. *See* p. 140.

6. The attack charged Mother Jones with seeking to obtain twice the money she had loaned J. Mahlon Barnes.

7. Morris Hillquit (1869-1933), Socialist lawyer and leader of the Party in New York. Hillquit was a leader of the moderate forces in the Party but closer to the Right Wing than to the Left Wing of the Party.

8. Victor L. Berger (1860-1929), Milwaukee Socialist leader of the Right Wing Socialists and editor of the *Social Democratic Herald*. Berger was the first Socialist to be elected to Congress, winning his seat in 1910.

9. John Spargo (1876-1962), English-born Socialist editor and author, associated with the moderate wing of the Party. Spargo had worked with Mother

Jones in the "Children's Crusade," and she made use of his book *The Bitter Cry of the Children,* published in 1906, in her campaign against child labor. But she was angered by Spargo's conservative views on most issues.

10. The reference is to the International Socialist Congress held in Copenhagen. It is interesting that at the Congress, Clara Zetkin, German Socialist Party leader, moved that the day of the demonstration of American working women (March 8, 1908) become an International Women's Day, and that March 8 each year be dedicated to fighting for equal rights for all women in all countries. Unlike Mother Jones, Clara Zetkin did not believe that equal rights for women was a "sex" and not a "class" question.

11. Union and Socialist activity in Argentina was very dangerous; it met with strong repression from the government. Mother Jones is referring to the imprisonment of hundreds of Socialists by the Argentinian government. (*See* Torcuato S. Di Tella, "Working Class Organization and Politics in Argentina," *Latin American Research Review* 16 (1981): 42-43.)

12. The *Provoker* was a weekly paper privately printed in Chicago by Thomas J. Morgan.

To Thomas J. Morgan

Hazleton. Pa. Sept. 9th 1910

Mr Thomas Morgan
Chicago. Ill.

Dear Comrade Morgan:

I have been apparently a little indifferent lately in not writing. That is no indication that I have not been just as deeply interested I have been doing some work along the line, talking about conditions. In going through the fileds from some of the Socialists I have concluded that there is a concerted movement on the quiet to blacken you or to kill any influence that the Provoker may have.

Whenever some of them are asked "Do you read the Provoker? edited by Tommy Morgan?" the first reply that comes—"God Dam Tommy Morgan. He wants to Morganize the movement". If you ask them "Do you know Tommy Morgan?" the reply will come "No I don't, but he wants to Morganize the movement."

If you tell them "that is strange" Morgan has been in the Socialist movement over twenty five years; he has never attempted to Morganize it; He has tryed to keep the movement under the control of the rank and file; Ask him Do you know that you have not send a working person to Europe to represent the American movement; they will tell you "No? they don't know that". And the fact of the matter is they don't know who went to Europe outside of Victor Berger and Luella Twin-ing, and Haywood. However I am picking out good comrades to have the Provoker sent to. Charley Gildea and I, have been talking it over among our selves as to how we can organize throughout the country and get the Paper enlarged and sent out.

Is it true that Simmons[1] has gone to Girard. I don't see any notice of it in the Appeal. I hope that Wayland[2] and Warren[3] wont be trapped into establishing another paper there. How very strange it is the selec-tin of delegates to Copenhagen should come entirely from those who are bleeding the movement and forcing there notoriety upon the com-rades.

I see now they are calling for funds to defray that junketting tour. to Europe. They have five hundred of our brothers in Argentine locked up. It seems to me if we understood Socialism instead of sending eight delegates to Europe we would send one and use the balance of the money to get our comrades in Argentine out of the clutches of the money power. That bunch of pleasure seekers who attended the Socialist Congress in Chicago did'nt consider it worth while to take up the Mexican question when it was the right of free speech, the right of free press the right of Asylum that was involved.

The United States Congress was forced to see the importance of it. The question was forced before the public which prevented the poor Mexicans refugees from being rearrested. I want to say that is as cold blooded a gang at the head of the Socialist movement as any gang of capitalist combination you can find. I want you to write to Charley Gildea 23 W Tamarack St. He is one of us and he understands what is going on. I notice you have had Germer from Illinois at a picnic in Chicago. He has been trained by Hunter and the gang.

The enclosed clipping is taken from the Hazleton Pa. Standard. You will note what I am doing.

Yours for the fight,
Mother

The enclosed letter you keep until I see you in Chicago.

[Thomas J. Morgan Collection, Illinois Historical Survey,
University of Illinois Library.]

Notes

1. The reference is to Algie M. Simons (1870-1950), a founder of the Socialist Party, and editor of Socialist journals. He was a moderate Socialist.

2. Julius A. Wayland, editor of the *Appeal to Reason.*

3. Fred Warren, assistant editor of the *Appeal to Reason,* who became editor after Wayland committed suicide in 1912.

To Thomas J. Morgan

Akron, O., Oct, 14, 1910.

Thomas J. Morgan,
Attorney-at-law,
Chicago. Ill.

Dear Comrade Morgan:

I have been trying to reach you with a letter for some weeks, but you know how hard it is for me to write and particularly to get someone to do the writing for me. Well, I see that the Committee has covered up the mess in the National Office,[1] but not for all time what a bunch of trimers we have at the helm of our movement I wish you could write and get some information from a comrade by the name of Slusser in Cleveland, O., he could give you some information about Mrs. Barnes and Lewis. He has gone West now and if there was any way that you could reach him, but I don't know how to put you on. I will inclose his card in this letter and he will tell you something that will startle the King. Keep on with the Provoker you can't imagine how it has disturbed the boyes in New York and what a force it is lining up for a house-cleaning. I took a trip up to Cleveland for the express purpose of feeling the pulse of the Comrades. I am doing work here now on that line. I am going to Canton, Sunday and will do my part down there to awaken comrades down there, if those fellows think we are not going to clean house they are very much mistaken and they don't know who they are delaing with I for one won't let up nor neither will anyone who understands the philosophy of the movement. We are not building a movement for free-lovers and job hunters. Just think of the bunch composing that N.E.C. establishing themselves as judge and jury and telling us they are the movement. You are going to get a number of subscribers from this place Mrs. Prevey[2] will gather them up here and forward them to you When you see Frankell give him my regards. What is Brower doing? Drop me a line to this place as soon as you can. I am,

Yours to the end in the cause that needs us all,
Mother Jones

[Thomas J. Morgan Collection Illinois Historical Survey,
University of Illinois Library.]

Notes

1. For several years the battle in the Socialist Party between the conservative and radical forces had centered around J. Mahlon Barnes, the national secretary, who had used his office to aid the conservatives. The battle against

573

Barnes reached its climax in the summer of 1910 when Chicago Socialist Thomas J. Morgan published a series of charges against Barnes in his privately printed weekly paper, *The Provoker*. Morgan had been retained by Mother Jones to compel Barnes to repay the $250 loan which she charged he had never returned but which he claimed to have repaid. In the process of forcing repayment, Morgan accused Barnes of dishonesty, incompetence, drunkenness, and practicing free love with national office employees. But the executive committee refused to place the matter before the National Committee, and did not act even after receiving a letter from a former employee of the national office substantiating Morgan's charges from personal experience.

Enraged by the failure of the executive committee to act, a number of locals passed resolutions calling for its resignation. As a result, the national committee capitulated and a National Committee investigating body was chosen to look into the charges against Barnes, including those brought by Mother Jones. The investigators, who included Oscar Ameringer, James H. Maurer, and Adolph Germer, found Mother Jones's charges to be "wholly without foundation," declared her allegation "was indeed a most frivolous one" which was "instigated maliciously" by attorney Thomas J. Morgan on Mother Jones's behalf to embarrass Barnes. The report as a whole held Barnes innocent of all misconduct. However, the executive committee refused to publish the testimony taken by the investigators. Instead, they obtained passage of a National Committee motion accepting the conclusions reached by the investigators. (*Socialist Party Official Bulletin*, Aug. 1910-Feb 1911, "Report of the Investigating Committee, Sub-Committee of the National Committee, February 28, 1911, *Socialist Party Official Bulletin*, February, 1911; Ira Kipnis, *The American Socialist Movement 1897-1912*, New York 1952 pp. 379-80.)

2. Marguerite Prevy of Akron, Ohio was a leading Socialist Party activist, at whose home many Party functionaries stayed while they were in the Ohio city. For correspondence between Prevy and Mother Jones, *see* pp. 612-13.

To Thomas J. Morgan

(Greensburgh,Pa)
(December 16,1910)

Dear Comrade Morgan:

I have been up to My Ears in a Strike of the miners here I have not had a moment to Spare 20 thousand men and women are here to be looked after I have not had a moment to Spare for the last Six weeks. I just got back after ten miles going and coming in a blizzard to a house away from civilization. I find the father down with Typhoid fever the Mother and Six children Shivring with cold no clothing not a thing to Eat. . . .

They know or care nothing for their Suffering. I have not Seen a

Socialist paper for weeks Nor do I hear anything from the Seat of War — it would not Surprise me if you did not hear of Congress from Milwakee Banqeting with Civic Federation next.

I have not been able to do anything for the Provoker here in this strike the people are not here. I am only Stiring them up on the Class war. It is a horrid picture of Capitalistic Brutality. . . . Negro. Salary graving Movement the Class Struggle is lost Sight of entirely. I never had any use for Beelyn his face to me does not indicate Strenght of Charector nor a depth of Sincerity. . . .

I see by the Bulleton that Goebel want to throw you and the provoker out I will be thrown out to he did not dare go that far let them play their game they will have to get down & out Now what ever you Say is the best course for me to pusue I will follow your advice . . . & the working class. . . .

I am quietly informed by parties in the Government Service that the Gove in Washing is gathering up notes about Wilshires money scheme If the prove them fradulent he will go up. there has been some notes taken from the provoker Send me the last 4 or 5 provokers I guess they turned the world up side down when they met in N.Y.

Loyally
Mother

Dec 16-1910
129 West 2nd Street
Greensburg Pa

[Thomas J. Morgan Collection, Illinois Historical Survey,
University of Illinois Library.]

To Thomas J. Morgan

Greensburgh, Pa.
Dec. 25-1910

Dear Comrade Morgan

Just came in from the camp of a lot of Strikers. Some of them in Tents. it is the Class War in its reality The poor little ones look as if the old world is hopeless for them The day is cold and I am cold with it The Scabs gave a dance last night There was a keg of Powder Somewhere round it went off and 25 of the wretches are in the Hospital as a result of an explosion — These industrial wars are fierece but as long as the profit System last lives will be cheap. . . . will come from that Board. Hilquit put him in there Lewis and Goebel Their job from Spargo Said they were not a debt collecting agency that I was a frivolous old women. They read the letter, Sent him. They could learn from that he never replied until I threatened to expose him they had Miss Flahertys evidence Browers and they said we were liers. It Seems to me I should ignore them I remember . . . they call on me I in time to giv her money to Spend I will not take the Money of the party. I am here in an industrial battle against the powers that oppress my class I have neither time nor Strength to waste with that bunch of Middle Class dictators

Yes I know what chose have done I guess the fellow in haverhill is not the only *victim* he has exploited that ex mayer of haverhill to a finish They will lick the feet of the fellow who will give them an easy. . . . don't think that I will flinch they can put me out of the party but out of the movement never count on me.

They have been doing thre dirty work their henchmen have been Danny Finny Morgan & Dam the *Pioneers* to Hell with old Mother Jones she's getting old We will make her Shut up She must go off and Die the capitalist don't think I am getting old they wish I was Well mercy me it is a little Lonely for me

always yours untill I rest in the far East
Mother

[Thomas J. Morgan Collection, Illinois Historical Survey,
University of Illinois Library.]

To Mrs. Conroy

Denver, Colo., Feb.5, 1911

My Dear Mrs. Conroy:

I arrived here on Wednesday night and was nearly worn out. I witnessed a big parade which was a protest against the courts. The gathering which followed was four miles long as they marched to the Capitol. I attended the meeting and addressed fully 12,000 people. It was a great day in the history of the labor movement in Colorado. I am very lonesome after my room and all of you — particularly after little Joe. I hope the strike will go on successfully in the Irvin field[1] and I know that I shall be anxious about its success. Tell John for me that I want him to quit reading novels and study a very important question

— that is — the economic questions that confront the day. I wish that you would do up all my things and send them to 802 Buckingham Place, Chicago, Ill., I hope some day to come back and see you all and I will always remember what a kind, nice home I had with you — I miss my room very much and I don't know when I will get another like it. Tell Mr. Conroy to take good care of his health and don't you overwork yourself.

I am, believe me always yours for
A Grander Civilization,
Mother Jones

Drop me a line to 605 Railroad Building, Denver, Colo.

[Pennsylvania Historical Collections,
The University Library, Pennsylvania State University]

Notes

1. Description of the protest, but no account of Jones's speech, appeared in *Rocky Mountain News*, February 2, 3, 1911.

To Thomas J. Morgan

Denver, Colorado, February 11, 1911.

Mr. Thos. J. Morgan,
79 Dearborn St., Chicago.

My dear comrade Morgan:
I received your letter this morning and have no words to express my appreciation of your efforts. I have just mailed your letter to Solomon and expect a return answer from him. I shall attend to the other letters to be forwarded to you at Chicago from this point. He took his attack from a statement that the Mine Owners made on me when I was here seven years ago and they put me out of the State by the bayonet.[1] He has to be shown up, and his colleagues with him, at any cost. You must have had a time at the investigation. His own statements would condemn him before any court in the country. Why did he undertake to pay you that money without a protest. Don't you know that no man would do such a thing, give up money without a protest. Don't you know that no man would do such a thing, give up money that he did not own without protesting and furnishing some proof that he had paid

it before.

I shall be in Chicago on the 22nd of this month. I had a telegram from Comrade Millard, of Cincinnati, telling me that all expenses would be paid. I concluded from his telegram that he is a pretty fair minded fellow. We had just as well fight this thing out now and clean up the rottenness in the movement. Let us take no back water, but go boldly to the front and either have a clean-cut movement or let us pull out from them. I have no fear of the result if we stand together and I believe we can and we will clean up the National Executive Committee and put them on record forever.[2] Now, I am not in a mood to write you a long letter just after reading yours. But you will please locate John P. Hopkins for me. I want to write him a letter for he has known me for thirty-eight years. I will close by saying,

Victory to our Cause,
Mother Jones

Notes

1. *See* pp. 110, 557.

2. In the end J. Mahlon Barnes was forced to resign after it was discovered that he had placed the mother of his illegitimate child on the party payroll and deducted two dollars weekly from her pay check as payment for a thirty-dollar loan he had made to her. The investigating committee termed this a "grave indiscretion," but on other charges against him, it refused to issue any public statement. (*Socialist Party Official Bulletin.* August, 1911.)

To William B. Wilson

Denver, Colorado, April 15, 1911.

Hon. W.B. Wilson,[1]
Washington, D.C.

My dear Mr. Wilson:

Permit me the pleasure of introducing to you one of New York's foremost citizens, Mr. Jos. T. Keily, and a very esteemed friend of mine. He has taken quite an interest in the persecution of the poor Mexicans.[2] Any service that you can render him, I shall more than appreciate and it will also be well rendered for the benefit of humanity. I am

Always yours,
Mother Jones

Notes

1. William B. Wilson, labor member of Congress, initiated the movement for a Congressional investigation of Mexican persecution.

The letter was not presented to Wilson until 1913, and was sent together with another letter dated February 18, 1913 which read:

"It appears from newspaper report that Mother Jones has been arrested with others, under martial law in the State of West Virginia.

"When I last saw her she was not over-well, and I fear that if subjected to any hardship her health might be seriously affected.

"Her life is too valuable to the cause of real humanity to be risked for any reason. Is there anything that you can do through your position, to aid her?

"The people whose oppressions she has been fighting have been able to keep practically all accurate information as to conditions out of the press. From what she told me when last here, the conditions in West Virginia are intolerable in the extreme and a disgrace to our civilization.

"Is it not possible for Congress to investigate these conditions and the reasons for a resort to martial law in West Virginia and the consequent suspension of the constitutional right of free speech and assembly.

"The enclosed letter of introduction was given me nearly two years ago in connection with Mexican matters, when I expected to visit Washington. It applies to the present matter peculiarly, for any service to Mother Jones is one for the ultimate benefit of humanity, hence I do not hesitate to use it.

"If I can co-operate with you in any way in her behalf, you can be assured in advance that my services are at your command.

> Sincerely and cordially yours,
> Joseph T. Keily.

"P.S. I have in my possession copy of the testimony taken before William E. Glasscock to inquire into conditions in the minding [*sic*] districts.

"This testimony conclusively shows by the testimony of the Government's own witness that the miners are denied the Constitutional right of proper assemblage and free speech.

"It requires but a slight study of the testimony before the Commission was using its position to make out a case against the miners."

(Record Group No. 174, Department of Labor, Chief Clerk's Files 16/13-H, National Archives. Joseph T. Keily was a member of the firm of Keily and Haviland, Attorneys and Counselors at Law, New York City.)

2. For Mother Jones's activities on behalf of "the poor Mexicans" persecuted in the United States, *see* pp. 55, 121, 143-45, 369-74, 460-61.

To Mr. Calero

To The Honorable Mr. Calero,
Secretary of Justice in the Republic of Mexico.

My dear Mr. Calero:

According to our agreement before I left Mexico in keeping with my promise I went immediately to Los Angeles and called on Flores Magon. Mr. Cannon whom you met in Mexico accompanied me. The editor of "Regeneracion" their organ, was present with one or two others. I approached the subject to them, by asking them if it would not be more logical for them to go into Mexico and carry on their agitation, there, as the Government permitted free, press, free ballots, and a free discussion of the issues of the day. They would not accept any proposition that Mr. Cannon or myself made to them. They charged everyone with being a traitor, but themselves. I stated to them that I had been down in Mexico, had met some of the public officials and I considered them very able statesmen. They replied to me that I was very much deceived in them. I said "You mistake the person you deal with. I have dealt with men in every avenue of life nearly; I can form an average estimate of a man's principles and honor when he makes a statement". We discussed the matter pro and con for an hour, but they believed only in direct action, the taking over of the lands. That seemed to be the question on which they based their contention. I made the statement to them that they could not take the land over by force and hold it, unless the law of a nation so permitted them. I thought it was much more advisable for them to go into Mexico, go into the Legislature, and make the laws to reclaim the lands legally and legitimately. I stated to them that I did not believe in force, as it was the last resort of intelligent people. But they stated they were already taking the land over and that it was only a question of time until Madero would be overthrown. I told them that I found Madero a very broad minded man, and that he would carry out the laws of justice a s far as he was able to. He said that already there was several states in revolt, but I said "You know in every nation that has had a Revolution it takes some time to settle down to a normal condition". It certainly will be so with Mexico, and if they would only act on reasonable lines I thought they would do a great deal of good for their people. After an hours discussion pro and con with Mr. Cannon myself and those men, I concluded it was useless to reason with them any further. We bid them good-bye and went away.

I then thought I would make another move. I took their Attorney, Mr. Harriman, who is now candidate for Mayor of Los Angeles, before I went he told me he was afraid we would be unseccessful but he said nevertheless, I would accompany you and explain things as clearly as

I can. On thursday, the 19th of October, I made my final visit there. Mr. Harriman puit it up to them in this way: "Now suppose the Mexican Government permits the Mexican working man to organize, and guarantees safety to the organizers. Would'nt it be better for you boys to go down into Mexico with a guarantee from the Government that you could carry on a legitimate educational agitation, than to remain here". Neither Mr. Harriman or myself could get them to accept any proposition that was made to them. In closing I said to them "Now, I want to say to you you have one of two alternatives, and I want to be honest with you. You cannot go into Mexico by force and take the lands, for the United States is a friendly nation to Mexico. They will not uphold any violation of International laws. There is one of two things before you. You will either go into Mexico, accept the proposition of the Government htat is given to you here today, or you will be arrested by the American Government and handed over to the Mexican Government. I am not prepared to say what will follow after that". And I said to them "if you are again rested the labor movement will take no hand in your defense. It has done everything honorable for you. It has delved down into its Treasury and defended you when you needed a friend". So I bid them farewell.

Mr. Harriman said to me after we left "I don't think I will continue as their lawyer, or have anything more to do with them".

Attorney Cleary of Bisbee Ariz., who defended them in Tombstone when they were brought from Los Angeles called on me while I was in Los Angeles, and I discussed the matter with him and told him my mission in Los Angeles. I stated to him that I had been to see those fellows but was unsuccessful in convincing them in their mistaken methods. I asked Mr. Cleary if they would go with me and see if he could influence them and shoe them the error of their ways. He said to me "I would not go near them", but after talking with him for a while he said "Well I'll consent to go with you, but" he said "I would not have anything legally to do with them again. They have no appreciation for those who sacrificed for them at the time they most needed friends.

I missed seeing him at the hour appointed, so I did not have the pleasure of his company.

I went around among the labor unions, their committees and officials. They do not entertain a very kindly feeling towards them. I exacted a promise from them that they would not in the future by any means permit the qualified labor unions of Los Angeles to render any aid to those men, for the reason, when men are granted the rights to agitate withing the border and under their own government, I don't consider that they have any rifht to come and do that agitation at long range, across the border under another Government. The officers of the labor unions agreed with me that I was perfectly correct. I learned that they receive considerable money from the Anarchists of Italy and Spain. How much truth there is in that I am not prepared to verify.

Now then Mr. Calero, so far as my promise to you goes, I have carried it out to the full extent of my hability, and in the future any services that I can honorably render to you in the interest of the oppressed class, I am ever and always at your service. Accept from me my deep appreciation of your courtesy to my conrades and myself while in Mexico. I shall always remember it with great pleasure. I shall sed a copy of this letter to President Madero. I understand that he had been a friend to them in their hour of need. I consider them one and all a combination of unreasonable fanatics, with no logic in their arguments and when people tell me that these fanatics are honest I cannot agree with them. Fanaticism has never won anything permanent for humanity's cause.

I am

Very Sincerely and Loyally yours,

Mother Jones

[Isidro Fabela, editor, Documentos Historicos
de la Revolución Mexicana, *volume 10 (Actividades
politicas y revolucionarios de los hermanos Flores Magón),
Mexico City, 1966, pp. 371-73.]*

To Flores Magón

Denver, Colo., Nov. 4, 1911

Mr. Flores Magon,
914 Boston St.,
Los Angeles, Cal.

Dear Sir:

In looking over the last two issues of your paper I find some misstatements as to my visit to yo and colleagues. I cannot conceive how you could so misrepresent the object of my visit. First you state "Not for sale", I believe that was the heading. I had nothing to buy you with or for. You stated, I had just come from President-Elect Madero with a proposition to you which you would not accept. It was not true. Mr. Madero never mentioned your name to me or any one else who was with me, whether he did not consider it worth mentioning or not I am not prepared to state. The Vice-President of the United Mine Workers, Mr. Frank Hays, Mr. Joe Cannon, representing the Metal Miners, accompanied me on my visit to President Madero. We found President Madero a gentleman in every sense of the word, a min with the most remarkable grasp of the economic struggle and the underlying causes. We discussed the matter after we left Mr. Madero and said to each other how remarkably well posted he was. It is not often that we find a man in his positio with so deep and clear a conception of the wrongs of the people and the causes that produce them. The only person who mentioned your name while I was in Mexico was your own brother, a gentleman in every sense of the word. He expressed his deep appreciation for the work done for you and your associates during the closing years of ex-President Diaz reign. He said "I will remember you through all the years of my life for saving the lives of my brothers".

You say I knew nothing but what Villareal told me, again your statement is false. I did not have the pleasure of meeting Villareal while I was in Mexico, which I much regretted.

You say "that I knew nothing of Mexico". I must have know something of the conditions in Mexico under which the people suffered or I could not go before the President of the United States nor could I have brought the matter up before Congress. You should have told me all this before I want to Washington with your case and not placed me in such an embarressing position before the President of the Nation and Congress.

Then again you attack the American Federation of Labor. You should have refused the $ 4,000 that they donated if they are what you represent them to be. You should have notified me not to accept a dollar from them or their colleagues to defend you. Many of those braves after voting me a hundred dollars, would say to me; "We have left our treasury in debt Mother, but go and save the lives of those poor fellows". The immigration commissioner is a member of the American Federation of Labor. When your colleagues were arrested under the immigration lawy and held for extradition, I went to San Antonio and held five meetings for your people there. I investigated the matter and immediately wrote to the Immigration Commissioner at Washington, and stated the cases to him. The United States Marshall was present at all the meetings. The victims were released.

I hope Mr. Magon, that this explanation will be satisfactor to you and convince you that the American Federation of Labor after paying all the bills, are not such a crimminal combination as you might suppose them to be. I hope this convinces you that my mission to Los Angeles was not at all in keeping with the statemant in your paper. Neither my colleagues or myself shall ever again insult you by taking any money from the American Federation of Labor to defend yóu if you should again get into the clutches of the law.

Y am, Sir

Mother Jones

[Isidro Fabela, editor, Documentos Historicos de la Revolución Mexicana, *volume 10 (Actividades*

politicas y revolucionarios de los hermanos Flores Magón),
Mexico City, 1966, pp. 380-82.]

Notes

1. These two letters of Mother Jones concern some of the most important issues of the Mexican Revolution. By a combination of corruption and terror, Porfirio Díaz won the general elections of July 1910. Francisco I. Madero, his defeated opponent, called on Mexicans to join him in an armed revolt. The revolt began on November 20, 1910, and by early May 1911, had won stunning victories. Díaz resigned and fled on May 25, 1911. A few months later, on the heels of a resounding triumph at the polls, Madero took the reins of political power into his hands.

Ricardo Flores Magón, however, refused to accept Madero's victory as a triumph for the Mexican people, charging him with being a tool of the rich Mexican capitalists and the wealthy investors in the United States who controlled so much of Mexico's land and natural resources. To achieve the "real revolution" in Mexico, Magón conceived the plan to seize Baja California and spread the revolution from the California peninsula throughout all of Mexico. He explained that Baja California would be the principal base of his operations to carry the "Social Revolution to all of Mexico and to all the world."

Many Socialists and radical labor leaders, including Mother Jones, refused to ally themselves with Flores Magón in completely rejecting Madero. Mother Jones, who visited Madero in October 1911, reported that his "heart seemed filled with the desire to relieve the suffering in his country," and that he even invited her to "come down and organize the workers and help them get back their land." On June 2, 1916, John Murray, who had by then become Samuel Gompers's adviser on Mexican affairs, wrote to the A.F.of L. president: "As you probably are aware, Frank J. Hayes, Joe Cannon of the Western Federation of Miners, and Mother Jones went to the City of Mexico in the time of President Madero, for the purpose of obtaining his consent to the organization of the mine workers of Mexico. Details of this conference in Mexico were given me by all of these three persons, and they said that President Madero expressed his entire willingness that not only the miners be organized in Mexico, but that all workers be organized in their various crafts. He told the delegation that he was particularly pleased to see them in Mexico on that errand. The interruption of this matter of course was caused by the death of Madero."

While it is true that Madero himself was an industrialist and landowner, as Ramón Eduardo Ruiz points out: "Madero was a humanitarian and progressive." He was shocked by the terrible conditions he found among Mexican industrial workers, and he acknowledged the right of workers to organize real labor unions. Even a number of leaders of his Liberal Party urged Ricardo Flores Magón to work with Madero, and several of them, including Enrique Flores Magón (Ricardo's own brother) broke with the Junta leader and left to join Madero.

But Ricardo Flores Magón remained adamant, and with the aid of some Socialists, the I.W.W. adventurers and mercenaries, plus a few Mexicans, Ricardo Flores Magón launched the revolutionary movement in Baja California. While the odd collection of North American Wobblies, Socialists, anarchists, adventurers, fortune-hunters and misfits of all sorts, fought with a small army of Mexicans, the leader, Ricardo Flores Magón, never took to the field, but remained practically in hiding in Los Angeles. In the end, the Baja California episode proved to be a disaster, with the remnants of the "army" being driven back into the United States by Mexican troops. The last episode of Flores Magón's "desert revolution," came in June 1912. Hoping to have a rapprochement with the *magonistas*, Madero sent Ricardo's brother Jesús, along with Juan Sarabia and Jose Maria Levya, both former PLM leaders, on a peace mission to invite Ricardo to return to Mexico and take a place in the revolutionary movement. But Ricardo Flores Magón refused to budge, and condemned his older brother and former friends as traitors. The mission failed. On June 4, 1912, the remaining Junta leaders were arrested by the U.S. government and jailed, with bail fixed for Ricardo Flores Magón at $5,000.

The Junta leaders were indicted on five counts of violating sections 37 and 10 of the U.S. criminal code, that is, "conspiracy to hire and retain the services of foreign people as soldiers." On June 22 the inevitable verdict of guilty was handed down. The rebels were sentenced to serve the maximum sentence — twenty-three months in prison — and were not released until January 19, 1914.

During these developments after the overthrow of the Díaz dictatorship and the assumption of power by Francisco Madero, Ricardo Flores Magón came under increasing criticism from Socialists in the United States for failing to return to Mexico and play a part in pushing the revolution forward. The most severe critics of Flores Magón were Mother Jones and Job Harriman. Mother Jones probably did more for the Mexican revolution and the Mexican refugees in the United States, including Flores Magón, than any other North American apart from John Kenneth Turner, and Job Harriman, California Socialist lawyer, who had defended the Junta members in previous federal trials.

In October 1911, Mother Jones and Job Harriman visited the Flores Magón brothers in Los Angeles. The two letters here were published following the meetings. Frustrated and angered by Ricardo Flores Magón's intransigence, following the meetings, Job Harriman told Mother Jones that he would not continue to be the lawyer for the PLM leaders "or have anything to do with them." Hence when these men were tried by the federal government in June 1912, Job Harriman refused to defend them, and they were defended by "a young and inexperienced lawyer who was unable to develop a convincing defense." As for Mother Jones, she felt so betrayed and frustrated by her dealings with Flores Magón and the PLM that she urged trade unions not to render any further aid to the Junta. She summed up her attitude in her letter to Calero, Madero's Secretary of Justice:

"I consider them one and all a combination of unreasonable fanatics, with no logic in their arguments, and when people tell me these fanatics are honest I cannot agre with them. Fanaticism has never won anything permanent for humanity's cause."

This must have sounded strange coming from one who had repeatedly been accused of fanaticism in the cause of labor and Socialism. But one must keep in mind that Mother Jones was also fanatical about the need to work inside mass organizations where the workers were assembled, and play a role in pushing such movement in a more progressive direction, rather than to isolate oneself with a "pure, revolutionary program," which reached only those who agreed with the revolutionists. The fact that Ricardo Flores Magón had the enthusiastic support of the I.W.W. did not impress Mother Jones. Although herself a charter member of the I.W.W., she had long since decided that the isolationist policies and anarchist tendencies within the Wobbly movement made it impossible for it to influence the mass of the American workers.

Eugene V. Debs agreed with Mother Jones in her criticism of Ricardo Flores Magón's views and policies. But he respected the *magonistas* for sponsoring a real revolution whereas Madero was "but a revised edition of Diaz." Announcing his belief that the forces represented by Flores Magón would still triumph, Debs called for their defense in their federal trial: "Personally I am not in agreement with all the plans and tactics of these leaders, but I am bound to admit their honesty, their sincerity, and their unselfish devotion to their enslaved people, and I am under obligation to fight for them against these fresh outrages perpetrated upon them by the hessian hirelings of American capitalism to the full extent of my power."

Debs, however, did agree with Mother Jones that the PLM leaders in the United States should help advance the Mexican revolution by working inside Mexico, and indicated approval of those *magonistas* who had joined Madero for this purpose. As he put it: "there is no road to successful revolution except through education and organization."

The above discussion is based on the following sources: Lowell L. Blaisdell, *The Desert Revolution: Baja California 1911*, Madison, Wisconsin, 1962; W. Dirk Raat, *Revoltosos: Mexico's Rebels in the United States, 1903-1923*, College Station, Texas, 1981; Alfonso Taracena, *La Verdadera revolución Mexicana, 1909-1911*, Mexico city, 1965; Isidro Fabelo, editor, *Documentos Historicos de la Revolución Mexicana*, Mexico City, 1966; Ramón Eduardo Ruiz, *Labor and the Ambivalent Revolutionaries: Mexico, 1911-1923*, Baltimore, 1976; John Murray to Samuel Gompers, June 8, 1916, Samuel Gompers Papers, State Historical Society of Wisconsin; Diana K. Christopulos, "American Radicals and the Mexican Revolution, 1900-1925," unpublished Ph.D. thesis, State Univ. of NY at Binghamton, 1980.

To Caro Lloyd[1]

Box 953, Charleston, W.VA.
Nov. 27, 1912

Miss Carrie Lloyd
New York City

My Dear Miss Lloyd:

Pardon me for not writing to you befor but I have had so much to do since I got back. I cannot give you any advice on coming down here just now owing to the fact that we have martial Law here including military desperatism, and I am afraid it would be only a wast of money on your side because you could not go into the strike field it is all we can do who are familiar with the field to get in there. I cannot express to you how deeply I appreciat the interest you have taken however if I were you I would try to make some arrangements with some magazines so that when the opertunity came you could avail your self of it to do good for the cause. That certainly was a tiresome night when we went to Brooklin, I hope to have the pleasur of meeting you in the near future.

Sincerely yours,
Mother Jones

[Henry Demarest Lloyd Papers, State Historical Society of Wisconsin.]

Notes

1. Caro Lloyd, a Wisconsin Socialist, was the sister of Henry Demarest Lloyd.

To William B. Wilson

[1913]

My dear Comrade Wilson

I just want to drop you a line about things here. I have had meetings every day they are good brave people, and if they were not this Strike would be lost long ago. of all the insulting tyrant that ever had authority this fellow Purcell beats them. We had a meeting of the field workers last Monday it was disgraceful he abused coursed every one he was the whole thing I have had nothing from any one but complaints from hour I landed to this, he has been putting in his licks about you I do not know where he heard it unless Pres M — mentioned it that you were a candidate for Congress last Sunday I was told of Some of his Sayings he went to See St. Claire last friday and gave it away that *our* funds were getting low but we were not *whiped yet* St. Clair Troubled refused any further concession he boast of getting a friendly invatation from the operators I have not time to write you all for I am going on this Train

I Saw a Telegram from McGuffin to one of the operators last Sunday

I went into the office to See one of the Telegraphers who is a warm friend of mine — Mc Cail is willing to Settle and I think had better take it

Since harry the money to Settle with his field hands he is with a car load of P — he is a beast

I wish I had time to write you this fellow is drunk half his time

fondly Mother

Send me Some Money

[William B. Wilson Papers, Historical Society of Pennsylvania.]

To William B. Wilson

1913 (Feb)

My Dear Mr. Wilson:

Here I am for the last week. They locked me in military prison the civil officers picked me on the streets of Charleston threw me in to an auto brought me 22 miles the Marshall Law prison the warrent was not signed by the Squire until after I was arrested anarchy if you can find anything like this in Mexico.[1]

Get this note to Senator Borah[2] type written and give to Senator Borah. Correct it where it needs they have over a hundred of our men in Military.

O the villains they shot a man dead while was taken his wife to the s(h)elter. She gave birth to a babe while they were burry him shot a woman through the leg talk about hostility women this beats anything that goes after they went to bed.

Have Senator Borah letter copy by Agnes they do not allow any one to speak to me.

When I get out I will give them H — /Mother/ I am just scribbling this to you.

[Record Group No.174, Department of Labor,
Chief Clerk's Files 16/13-H, National Archives.]

Notes

1. For the events leading up to Mother Jones's imprisonment, *see* pp. 152-58.

2. William E. Borah, Senator from Idaho.

To William E. Borah

Military Bastile,
Pratt, W. Va.

To the Honorable
Senator Borah,
U.S. Senate

Dear Sir:

Permit me to extend to you in behalf of the crushed and persecuted slaves of the coal mines of West Virginia my deep felt gratitude for your resolution demanding and investigation by the National Government.[1] The wretches have pleaded with the State to do something for them but in return they got the jails and bullets from the public officials.

I am in confinement now for a week at the age of 80 years. I am a military prisoner. This is just what the old monarchy did my grandparents 90 years ago in Ireland.

Senator, do what you can to relieve these wretches and the coming years will call you blessed.

Gratefully yours,
Mother Jones
Military Prison,
Pratt, West Virginia

*[Record Group No. 174, Department of Labor,
Chief Clerk's Files 16/13-H, National Archives.]*

Notes

1. Senator Borah's resolution was not adopted. It was the resolution later introduced by Senator Kern of Indiana which led to the federal investigation.

To Caro Lloyd

Pratt W. Va. — 17-3-1913
Military Bastile

My dear Miss Lloyd

Your very kind note reached me yesterday handed over by the representatives of the Spanish Inquisition — how deeply I appreciated your thoughfulness — Yes we are held for fighting against the most infamous system of peonage there is over a hundred of us up before the Most infamous court — since the fudel ages. I see that Michelson did not get his stuff in to the American[1] If it was anything against the workers any paper & magazine would be filled with falsehood.

And our Socialst papers are filled with thrash with what Vic Berger did in Congress[2] and he never did a thing only boodlBurge how little they realize what this Class War means they have 3 sqare meals thats about all they care.

here is the most far reaching thing that has ever taken place in this country if the people Stand for it, the death nel of human liberty have been sounded

I refused to recognize the court I so Stated to the military it was to but to me a species of Feudalism a part of the Spanish inquisition it was unAmerican a disgrace to our age they may chain me shoot me put in prison for life I will never go on record that for a moment I recognized.

I am scratching this off in a hurry it goes out underground I am watched on all sides of my room. My old pen scratching this off I am writing this blindly for I have to watch the window I'll take no back water for the Pirates will write you again

fondly
Mother Jones

[Henry Demarest Lloyd Papers, State Historical Society of Wisconsin, Madison, Wisconsin.]

Notes

1. M. Michelson's article, "Sweet Land of Liberty," a detailed exposure of industrial feudalism in West Virginia's mining communities and the bitter struggle of 1912-13, was published in *Everybody's Magazine*, May 1913.

2. Victor Berger was elected the first Socialist Congressman in 1910. It is interesting that Mother Jones did not smuggle out a letter to Congressman Berger asking him to call for a Congressional investigation of the situation in West Virginia, revealing how little faith she had in the Wisconsin Socialist. Berger, however, had sponsored a Congressional investigation of the Lawrence strike of 1912, despite his great dislike of the I.W.W. leadership of the strike.

To Caro Lloyd

(Apr. 4, 1913)
Pratt W. Va.
Military Bastile
In Prussianized America

My dear Miss Lloyd

Your beautiful letter reached me yesterday. It takes some time for a letter to reach me and the cooperation for me to read it I do not give them the Satisfaction of Seeing my mail if it is possible they wont get that satisfaction

I miss your dear Brother So much[1] with his master Pen how he would put the State of West Va on trial at Bar of the Nation I do not know what is matter with the Socialist papers[2] I do not expect much from the Call it has no grasp of these mighty conflicts We are up against a condition here that cannot grasp the situation Your beautiful letter brought me such an inspiration in this lonely Bastile I am writing this on my knees for the blood Houds ae watching every move when I know my

I will File I was tryed 4 weeks ago by the Drum Head Military Court I have not my Sentence yet do not know what the pirates will give me If I would sign a paper to leave the State they would Let me but I sign no paper accept no favors from Governor nor anyone else I'll die fighting the crew of Pirates

Long live the Industrial Revolution I have drawn the attention of the nation to their crimes & if I could tell you the things that disgrace the nation that have existed in this god cursed State it's a disgrace to any people & civilization You cannot expose only putting salve on the ulcer you must tear the ulcer open let the world see the root & what produced it When I am out I will go to see you

fondly yours in the fight for freedom
Mother Jones

[Henry Demarest Lloyd Papers, State Historical Society of Wisconsin, Madison, Wisconsin]

Notes

1. Henry Demarest Lloyd died in 1903.
2. Mother Jones's feeling that the Socialists were insufficiently active in protesting the treatment of miners and Party members in West Virginia emerged publicly in her speech at Carnegie Hall sponsored by *The Masses. See* pp. 222-25.

To William B. Wilson

Pratt West Vir
April 5th 1913
Military Bastile

My dear friend

Just going to drop you a line. on the 12 Feb they picked me up on the streets of the Capitol brought me down handed me over to the Military. I have been guarded day and night ever since by the Bayonots Not one moment have I been left alone. If a report-hopes to speak, through the window he is arrested & thrown into the bull Pen. 5 weeks ago they took me before a Drum-Head Military Court. I refused to recognize the right of that Court to try me stating that I had done or said nothing but what I had done or said all over this country would go on fighting for Liberty all my life. When they concluded the Judge Advocate their was not Sufficient evidence convict me on, but they have kept me hemed in. I have not been outside the gate in 8 weeks only when they took me to the court room. from close confinement I am Suffering with headachs. I know they would let me go if I would go out of the State but I will die before I give them that Satisfaction wont you write to this gov & tell him it does not speak very highly of America to hold a woman 80 years incarcerated with no charge against her and Senator Lafolete[1] to write to him with you I think after he gets a Letter from you he will act. this feller have been in about 5 weeks but he made no move to let me go. you know the mine owners are the Government they have Ten more of our boys in Clarksburg jail of all the black pirates that ever ruled a State they are here. Act just as soon as you get this Note. Sen Lafollette also I am insane for the want of air and exercise

Mother

[Record Group No. 174, Department of Labor, Chief Clerk's Files 16/13-H, National Archives.]

Notes

1. Robert M. LaFollette, Senator from Wisconsin.

To Mrs. Ryan Walker[1]

Pratt W. Va.
Military Bastile, Apr. 27, 1913.

Mrs. Walker
150 W. 104th St., N.Y.

My dear Mrs. Walker:

Your letter of the 19th reached me a few days ago. I was glad to hear from you and glad to know you at last thought I was still alive. This is a very serious situatin we have here and is not grapped by the outside world and God knows when it will be. I have been in here about eleven weeks. No word of protest has gone out from our dear Socialists. If Victor Berger or Hilford or any of those or any of their Jesuses[2] was in here what a howl would go up but there are 12 of us poor devils, eleven mean and myself, one of them the editor of the Socialist paper in Charleston, the other one of our speakers, John Brown with his wife and children left to perish outside.[3] We hear the cry of their little ones for their father, we hear the groans and sobs of his beautiful wife but the dear well fed socialists don't care for that. They can tell us what they are doing in the Balkan war or something of that kind, they are very much like the capitalists they will take as many miles across the ocean to see misery and overlook the horres of home.[4] I don't care much for myself because my carreer is nearly ended but I think of my brave boys who are incarcerated in Harrison Co. jail in Clarksburg and not a voice of protest raised in their behalf. They have been brave and true. They are now paying the penalty of what they have done but it matters not, this fight will go on and the workers themselves will have to take hold of the machinery and pick out the sky-pilots[5] and lawyers[6] and quit feeding them and giving them a job. I have been fighting this machine for years with scarcly any help.

I hope Ryan will be home soon, tell him I am still in the fight and the pirates can't shut me up even if I am in jail watched by the bloodhounds.

Mother Jones

*[Haldeman Mss. II, Manuscripts Department, Lilly Library,
Indiana University, Bloomington, Indiana.]*

Notes

1. Mrs. Ryan Walker was the wife of the editor of the New York *Call*.
2. This sentence was deleted in the *Appeal to Reason* of May 10, 1913 where it was published, having been forwarded by Mrs. Walker under the front-page

headline, "A Stirring Letter from Mother Jones." "Jesuses" probably refers to the Christian Socialists.

3. For an extract of Brown's letters to his wife from military prison, *see* p. 160.

4. This sentence was also omitted by the *Appeal to Reason* when it published Mother Jones's letter. The omission was probably carried out by Fred Warren, who became *Appeal* editor after J. A. Wayland committed suicide.

5. "Sky pilots" were ministers, who formed an important group in the Socialist Party.

6. Lawyers like Morris Hillquit were influential in Socialist Party leading circles.

To Caro Lloyd

Pratt, W. Va.
Military Bastile, April 27, 1913.

Cars Lloyd,
Nutley, N.J.

My dear Miss Lloyd,

Your two volumes of Mr. Lloyd's Bigraphy[1] came to me and was received with a great deal of pleasure. As I opened the package and saw what it contained, I, for a moment felt down hearted. I looked at Mr. Lloyd's beautiful picture, so natural, as I saw him the last time in Pa. I remember it so well the statement he made on the floor of the convention in 1896 at the Populist's convention when they nominated Bryan and were cheering. I said this looks like a complete sell out and he said to me in reply, "Mother, this is the last of the Populist movement, this is its funeral".[2] How true indeed was his statement, how far seeing was his vision. He seemed to grasp that the traitors had gotten hold of the movement and in that he was right. We have not since resurrected from that. I appreciate your kindly offer to me of coming to your quiet home to visit. I don't know that I could visit, there is so much to do for the cause and so little time to do it in and so very few who are willing to do. I don't know, dear comrade, what effect a letter from you would have upon this Gov.[3] He is strictly owned by the coal barons and I don't know whether he would pay any attention to it or not, however, it would do no harm to put it up to him. What we should do, is go after the socialists, if your brother was alive I would not be here now as he would long ago have taken steps to get me out. We miss him in more ways than one. We are short of such great characters.

594

I got a letter from the Trades Union Women in N.Y.[4] and of all the cold, sentimental documents that ever I read it was one of them, fortunately for me I have never mixed with them and I certainly shall not waste postage or paper in replying to them.

Now dear Comrade, I am still fighting away and perhaps I am doing just as much good within these prison walls as I would outside.

I think Leonard Abbott[5] sent me a clipping from the call. It was exceedingly thoughtful of you to put an article in. If they cannot grasp this great and mighty struggle, let them go by the waysie

Mother Jones

[Henry Demarest Lloyd Papers, State Historical Society of Wisconsin.]

Notes

1. *Henry Demarest Lloyd* by Caro Lloyd (2 volumes) was published in 1912 by G. P. Putnam's Sons, New York City.

2. For a discussion of the events at the 1896 Populist Party convention, *see* Philip S. Foner, *History of the Labor Movement in the United States,* New York, 1955, vol. 2, pp. 331-36.

3. Governor Henry D. Hatfield was inaugurated on March 4, 1913. For a different view of Governor Hatfield, *see* Richard D. Lunt, *Law and Order vs. The Miners: West Virginia, 1907-1933,* Hamden, Conn., 1979.

4. The Women's Trade Union League of New York. For the formation of the organization and its activities, *see* Philip S. Foner, *Women and the American Labor Movement: From Colonial Times to the Eve of World War I,* New York, 1979, pp. 301-71.

5. Leonard D. Abbott of New York was one of the leading figures in the Socialist Party, a member of the Board of Directors of the Rand School of Social Science, and a founder of the Intercollegiate Socialist Society.

To Terence V. Powderly

Military Bastile,
May 1st, 1913. Pratt, W. Va.

Mr. Terrence D. Powderly,
#502 N.W. Quincy St.,
Washington, D.C.

My dear Mr. Powederly:
I wrote you two letters but I have never had a line from one of them

and I know that it is not like you I think they have been held up by the Military sewer rats. I have been here 11 weeks, tried by a military drum-head court, kidnapped on the streets of Charleston and brought in to the martial law zone and handed over to the military and I refused to recognize the drum-head court and I have been held here with 11 others for 11 weeks and dont know what for. No sentence. I wrote to Wilson but he dont seem to do anything although he is a member of the cabinet.[1] There is 11 of us held prisoners but I am the only one in the Military camp. I know if you had received my letters or I would have received your there would have been something done long ago because you don't fool with things and don't make promises and not fulfill them. They have me held up for stealing a cannon from the coal company is one of the charges against me and the other is for making incendiary speeches. And of all the brutal gang ever you say, it is down here. No where in the country could you find more brutality than you do here. Men have been shot down in cold blood. The children have been starved to death, some of them. About four weeks ago they took 11 of the boys away from here. You should have heard the wails of their children and their wives. But it did not pierce the heart of a cold blooded pirates of the ruling class. The martial law is taken off here now and they are getting ready to move the militia. I don't know just exactly when they will get out but I suppose when they get out they will turn me loose.

If you write me, write to the Fleetwood Hotel Charleston and if I am here it will be forwarded to me.

I wish you would see Senator LaFollette. I know that he would write to this Governor at once and tell him if he don't take action that the Senate will, do you understand.

Give my love to Emma[2] and all at home. I can't write a very long letter because I am tired. I have been sick for some weeks.

Sincerely,
Mother Jones

[Terence V. Powderly Papers, Department of Archives and Manuscripts, Catholic University of America, Washington, D.C.]

Notes

1. William B. Wilson, Secretary of Labor under President Woodrow Wilson. In a letter of April 15, 1913, Wilson wrote to Mother Jones: "I am in receipt of your letter and have also seen several newspaper people who have succeeded in seeing you notwithstanding the objections of the military authorities. I regret that I am making but very slow progress in my efforts to handle the West Virginia strike situation. To begin with, the new Department (of Labor) has not as yet been furnished with any funds to handle its business. I expect that at an

early date the extra session of Congress will furnish some means to conduct the work of the Department, although it will likely be several months before it is on a proper working basis. In the meantime the resolution for the investigation of the strike situation has been reintroduced in the Senate by Senator Kern. I have brought the matter to the attention of the Cabinet, including a statement of the conditions under which the miners worked prior to the strike, the guard system that has been in existence, and the introduction of a system of court-martial in place of the regularly constituted courts which have not been impeded with the transaction of any business that might be brought before them. I have also taken the matter up with the Attorney General, and out of it hope to develop some method by which the natural, inherent and constitutional rights of the workers and their friends may be protected. My sympathies naturally go out to those who are downtrodden and oppressed, and I cannot conceive of any justification for the substitution of a court-martial in place of the regularly constituted trial courts. If the courts had been intimidated, coerced, threatened, or in any manner impeded in the trial of cases coming before them, I could have understood the reasoning that would lead up to the appointment of a military commission. That not having been the case, you may rest assured that I will continue to do all that I possibly can do to see that justice is secured."
[Record Group No. 174, Department of Labor, Chief Clerk's Files 16/13-H, National Archives]
    2. Emma Powderly, wife of Terence V. Powderly.

To Caro Lloyd

Military Bastile,
Pratt, W. Va., May 7th, 1913.

Miss Caro Lloyd,
Nutley, N.J.

My dear Miss Caro:
    Your letter reached me a few days ago but I was very sick with an abcess in the ear and was unable to reply. I certainly appreciate all the efforts you have been making. You seem to be the one woman in the U.S. that is taking hold of the question and doing what you could to force it into the public eye.
    I am still holding the fort in the prison although the great Governor says I am not in prison. I would like to know what he calls this place. I have been here three months incarcerated in one small room with a lounge to sleep on and no place to wash you face without going out on the porch and I am beginning to suffer with severe headaches which I am afraid will prove fatal one of these days. How brutal those men in

authority are. They never reverse the condition of others and wonder how they would feel if their wives or mothers were placed in the same condition. I know that the May Day celebration would not have touched this subject had it not been for you. You have indeed so much of your brother's nature in you that every letter you send me brings him so vividly to my mind. I looked upon him as one of the great men of the age but unfortunately he passed away a little too soon.

When my emancipation takes place you will be one of the first that I go to visit and to see. I got a letter from Mr. Northrop telling me that the single taxers had passed resolutions and I see your name among them. How strange it is indeed that you and he should be the two who are leading the battle in that location but it always takes some one to get the people started in any direction. I wont make this letter as long as I would like to for the reason that I have been suffering for several days with severe attacks of head ache and I presume it is from close confinement.

Write to me when you can as your letters are always an inspiration and I never read them but what they bring back the memory of your brother. I am

Always yours,
Mother Jones
Per M.D.

I have no time to waste with them nor do I think you have.

Sincerely,

[Henry Demarest Lloyd Papers, State Historical Society of Wisconsin.]

To Terence V. Powderly

Pratt W Va--6--3--1913
Military Bastile

My dear friend
You no doubt have heard of my arrest by the hounds of capitalism they have me in close confinement — there are two military guarding me day and night. No one is allowed to speak to me. the squashed all constitutional rights and handed me over to the military. here I am — the first thing I will do if I am turned loose will be to go up and see you.

Tomorrow at ten o clock we will be taken before the Military Court for trial.[1] They charge me and 3 national organizers besid the Editor of the Argus a local labor paper. neither one of us was in the marshall law zone they picked me up on the streets of Charleston — kidnaped me moved me with 2 others down the military camp. here I am now for 22 days! not allowed to speak to anyone or see anyone. Just think of it I have lived 80 years and never before charged with any crime. Now I am charged with stealing a cannon from the Military — inciting to riot — putting dinamite under track to blow up A.C.O. road — We were not there at all. Just think what the tools of the olagarchy can descend to. I know they are death on me for I have cost them hundreds of thousands of dollars.

They came to me yesterday wanted to get a Lawyer & witnesses I refused to get either. I said if I have brok the Law of the State or nation I do not want any Lawyer or Witnesses. One fellow Said I should be Drummed out of the State. I have a lot to tell you when I see you God spare me the Heart to fight them Love to my dear Emma tell her not to worry — I'll fight the Pirates forever

Mother

[Terence V. Powderly Papers, Department of Archives and Manuscripts, Catholic University of America, Washington, D.C.]

Notes

1. For the events of the trial, *see* p. 160.

To Eugene V. Debs[1]

Indianapolis, Ind., July 5, 1913.

Eugene V. Debs,
Terre Haute, Ind.

My Dear Comrade Debs:

I so much regretted that I did not see you when you were in West Virginia, but I had so much work to do in Washington, when the pirates left me out of the bull pen that I was unable to meet you. I have been so busy since I got out that I have not had time to write you a line, much as I wanted to.

I very much regret the sad incident that that fellow Simons and the Appeal. I expected nothing else when he went there. I think that Warren will learn when it is a little too late. I told him about Ricker and about Rogers, I told him about Shoaf.[2] You know that we are living in a peculiar economic age, and self interest comes to the front instead of principle or a cause. When I was going into West Virginia, to take up the battle of the poor slaves, I stoped off to see poor Wayland in Girard. He was not there but I saw Warren; Simons said he hoped I would get lost in West Virginia, and never return.[3] When a man is so cold and brutal as that there is nothing in him for a great cause. I have known Simons for some few years, and he has done just what I expected to the Appeal. But there is an unfortunate phase in our movement. that if you undertake to give people any warning they generally put you down as a knocker. I just read in the mojring paper which prompted me to write you that you took a girl home when the court said that you would have to either keep off the street or go down to the red light district, If that judge would not have exhibited his ignorance as he did the public might have more respect for him. If he would study the causes that bring those effects into society it would be far more to his credit as a member of the judiciary. That poor girl was a victim of a horrible system that is more brutal than the world has ever known, and God grants that we have more Eugene Debs, to protect such people from the depraved lions of capitalism.[4]

I am on my way to Washington, to work among the Senators, and explain to them the horrors of West Virginia. I shall be going through next month, to Texas, and I shall try to stop off at Terre Haute, and see you.

Give my regards to Mrs. Debs, to Theodore and his family.

I am, always yours in the great struggle for the race,

Mother Jones

[Eugene V. Debs Papers, Indiana State University Library,
Indiana State University, Terre Haute, Indiana.]

Notes

1. This appears to be the only letter of Mother Jones to Eugene V. Debs so far available. But there is a letter from Eugene V. Debs to Mother Jones, dated Jan. 28th, 1901, in which Debs refers to his "reading the papers and as usual find myself the victim of calumny. I have no complaint to make, but it does seem as if there should be a limit to such cruel outrages. The press dispatches spread the report broadcast that the statement was made on the floor of the convention that a Pennsylvania delegate collected money from starving miners for me and that I accepted it all. Of course the presumption is that a vast sum was paid me and that it was gouged from the lives of the famishing Miners. I can scarcely believe that such a villainous falsehood was uttered, and yet the effect with the general public is the same and I am once more freshly nailed to the cross. But I can stand it without a trace of resentment and if I can ever give a

hand to the Miners in any struggle, if that hand is not freely extended as it has always been in the past, it will be because it is paralyzed.

"You know without my telling you that I did not accept one dollar for my service from any one and that with the exception of a trifling part of my railroad fare, I paid all my own expenses besides. If any statement to the contrary is made it is maliciously false and in that case I desire you to ask the author of the statement how much money he gave me and if he names the amount, then challenge him to produce the receipt for it. . . .

"You have known me many years and you know if I would in any extremity take money from a striking, starving miner, I would first destroy myself. . . . That I am on all occasions made the target for calumny is simple evidence of the fact that the capitalist press is aware that I cannot be bribed or bullied and that therefore I must be undermined by slander. . . .

"Hail to Socialism, in which the miner can lift his bowed form from the earth and stand erect, a new being throbbing with immortal life."

(Original in William B. Wilson Papers, Historical Society of Pennsylvania; copy in Eugene V. Debs Papers, Indiana State University Library, Terre Haute, Indiana.)

2. Mother Jones is referring to the suicide of J. A. Wayland, publisher and editor of the *Appeal to Reason*. The editorship was taken over by Fred Warren, who was assisted by Algie M. Simons, Allan W. Ricker, Theodore Shoaf, and Louis W. Rogers, all active in the Socialist Party.

3. Simons hated Mother Jones for her persistent attacks on the moderate and right-wing elements in the Socialist Party Leadership.

4. For Mother Jones's changing view of Debs because of his role in the settlement of the strike in West Virginia, *see* pp. 218-19.

To Terence V. Powderly

Trinidad, Colo., Sept 20, 1913.

My Dear Mr. Powderly:

I just write you a few hurried lines. I was not able to get to Washington to the hearing. I had to go to Salt Lake to raise some money for the poor fellows in Michigan.[1]

What a proposition that sky-pilot made about putting the bible under our heads. How a man in his position could display such a lack of knowledge of the economic struggle, is more than I know. He has very little grasp of the affair in West Virginia, and cares less. He was fed and entertained by the exploiters of labor. When he went up Cabin Creek he was entertained by Charlie Caball, one of the biggest exploiters on Cabin Creek.[2] Charlie Caball brought four negroes, a couple of Italians, and a Slav that he had working, to tell the bishop how good they were treated and what fine money that made. But Chas. Caball did not tell the sky-pilot that he bought potatoes for 50 cts a bushel and sold them for $1.50 to his slaves, two hundred per cent profit. That is the christian doctrine of today. I almost broke down after I got back from Salt Lake. I have been wanting to write to you for some time, but when I get a moment I feel like I must rest. . . .

Mother

*[Terence V. Powderly Papers, Department of Archives and
Manuscripts, Catholic University of America, Washington, D.C.]*

Notes

1. The reference is to the strike of the copper miners, members of the Western Federation of Miners, occurring in Michigan.

2. Charles Cabell was the general manager of the Carbon Coal Company who later told Congressional investigators that the miners on Cabin Creek were peaceful and content until Mother Jones began holding her meetings. "After that time there was a great deal of unrest among our men, from that time on." (U.S. Congress, Senate. Subcommittee of the Committee on Education and Labor. *Conditions in the Paint Creek District, West Virginia,* 63d Congress, 1st Session, 1914, pp. 1443, 1450-52.)

To Terence V. Powderly

Denver, Colorado
March 22, 1914

Hon. T. V. Powderly
Washington D.C.

My own dear son:

I am just going to drop you a line or two so that you will know I did not forget you even in the military bastile.[1] Last Monday morning I closed five months and one week in the military bastiles of America out of ten months, so we can boast of our republic. In the last nine weeks which I spent in the military bull pen, I never got a line of a newspaper or a letter and the only human being, outside of the military, that I saw was my attorney Hawkins. He came three times during the nine weeks. The sisters permitted their religuous institution to be turned into a military prison.[2] I never saw more moral cowards in my life than those sisters were. It is a sais comment on a religious institu-

602

tion. They are simply owned body and soul by the Rockefeller interests. The priest would go by my window in the morning and take his hat off to the uniform muderer and not notice a poor wretch who was digging in the garden with his legs off.

How they have prostituted Christ's holy doctrine. Five big burly uniformed murderers with their guns on their shoulders and a belt of bullets around their stomachs and a saber hanging to their sides, came up every night at 6 o'clock to put in 24 hours watching an old woman 82 years of age. Four of those military were in the hall outside of my door and one outside of the window and the entire military was just a block away facing my window. The Sisters and priests stood for all that insult. My God how can he stand for the cold blooded hypocrisy of today. Men have no regard for human life. Right on the ground with that convent those uniformed murderers drilled every afternoon to learn how to become experts in the shedding of human blood. The military now is turned on to the working class and priests and presidents and ministers endorse the crime. Oh when the judgment day comes what a reckoning there will be. Tell Emma I have thought of her often in my lonely cell during the last weeks. As soon as this fight is over, I am going to Washington to write that book. It will be dedicated to your labor in the early days of the struggle. I would not undertake it, if it were not that I want to show some people up and vindicate the real hero of the labor movement. You and Martin Irons shall have the pleasure of seeing your name on the front page. The history of this thing, since I have been out here I cannot relate until I see you. I have so much to tell you, it would take pages and pages to relate the brutality. And the churches have stood for it all and endorsed it.

I leave again tonight for the field of battle. I suppose that just as soon as I get to Trinidad I will be arrested. They searched the train the night before last to see if I was on it. I presume they will do the same tonight so you can watch the papers. I wish you would get the Appeal to Reason of the 21st.[3] Villa, the revolutionary general in Mexico gave Wilson and the Democratic party a terrific slap.[4] Wilson ordered Villa to turn loose the wealthy Mexican who was held in Chihuahua and the Mexican said whenever you turn loose the 82-year-old woman that your military hold incommunicado I will comply with your request. She got protection in Mexico. No one would dare imprison that woman in Mexico but the brave soldiers of the American Revolution held her for nine long weeks.

I will have to close because I am getting a little nervous. Tell Emma to keep well until I see her. I guess the headlines of the papers will notify you what's happening down here.

I am always yours in the cause of freedom.

Mother

[John Hunter Walker Collection, 1911-1953, Illinois Historical Survey,

Notes

1. *See* pp. 238-45.
2. *See* p. 241.
3. Mother Jones is referring to the protests against her imprisonment in *Appeal to Reason*, the Socialist weekly published in Girard, Kansas.
4. *See* p. 245.

To Caro Lloyd

Washington D.C.
6-5-14

Mss C Lloyd

My Dear friend

Your kind letter reached me a week or two ago it had to wait a week or Ten days before I rec it. I have been driven to Death Since I came out of that Military Bastile[1] which apology I make for not expressing my appreciation of your kindness. I over worked but I have to keep at it. how much I would to be near you at Jimmes there are So few in life we can cling to in this Great Struggle

I droped your Post office order in Waterbury Con. one day last week will you notify the P.M. to Stop the Paymnt

I am going up to See you before I go west I never know when they will lock me up to Stay the Pirates are after me.

How much I would give to have a few hours with you I will be in New York in a few days again will be at the Madison Square Hotel

fondly
Mother Jones

[Henry Demarest Lloyd Papers, State Historical Society of Wisconsin, Madison, Wisconsin.]

Notes

1. Mother Jones is referring to her release from Huerfano County Jail in Colorado, following which she went to Massachusetts, New York, and

Washington. In the last city she attended hearings and testified before the House Mines and Mining Committee. *See* pp. 375-402.

To Caro Lloyd

July 21, 1914.

Miss Caro Lloyd,
Little Compton, R.I.

My Dear Miss Lloyd:

Your beautiful letter reached me in New York, and I immediately complied with your directions. I saw the post master last Saturday in New York. He said to ask you to get the post master at Nuttley, N.J. to issue an order payable to me in Denver, Colo. He said there was no danger of any one duplicating that order and said they could do nothing further about it in New York. It must come from Nuttley.

We had a beautiful meeting in New York on Friday night, the 17th.[1] I was wishing that you were there. I will enclose you one of the bills with this letter. Nothing would give me greater pleasure than to be with you for a day or two in the woods so we could talk things over. I met your dear nephew in Chicago. He urged me to go home with for that evening, but it was utterly impossible, much as I would love to have gone. You know I always feel when I am conversing with a member of the family that I am talking with Mr. Lloyd. He died many years too soon.

I shall write you from Denver soon, and hope it will not be long. Til we meet again.

Mother Jones

[Henry Demarest Lloyd Papers, State Historical Society of Wisconsin.]

Notes

1. *See* p. 225.

To Terence V. Powderly

Toltec Hotel, Trinidad
[1914]

Mr. Hughes, tell him I always think of him. See how that fellow Nugent falsified things about Keefe. What a terrible thing those judas's within our own ranks. That fellow Nugents was an organizer for the miners in West Virginia. He took their money and betrayed them. So did that fellow Kennedy. He was President of a District once and everything belonging to him scabed, and his whole rotten carcas inside is full of scabs. They are sending me all sorts of threats here. They have my skull drawn on a picture and two cross sticks under neath my jaw to tell me that if I do not quit they are going to get me. Well they have been a long time at it.

I would liked to have been at the hearing. I wish you let me know when the peonage question is coming up. I would like to go to Washington and hear that discussed, because I was the one who started the investigation in Washington.[1]

Well, give my love to them all, and save for yourself and Emma a great portion.

I am always yours, not for the revolution, but in it.

Mother Jones

[John Hunter Walker Collection, 1911-1953, Illinois Historical Survey,
University of Illinois Library.]

Notes

1. The reference is to the investigation by the House of Representatives' Subcommittee of the Committee on Mines and Mining into Conditions in the Coal Mines of Colorado. Mother Jones did testify before the Committee. *See* pp. 375-402.

To John H. Walker

Denver, Colo.
June 30, 1916.

Mr. John H. Walker, President
State Federation of Labor,

Springfield, Illinois.

My dear John:

Your letter of the 29th reached me a day or two ago when I arrived in Denver,[1] there is no one that I feel more glad to hear from than you, because I know when the sentiment is expressed it is meant.

I saw Frank P. Walsh yesterday, he says that he has exonerated Alec Howitt and the man from Oklahoma.[2] It was a glorious event as the knife was out in several quarters to stab Howitt. I was indeed glad to see the feeling that Walsh had about it, he felt as if it was the greatest victory that Labor has ever won.

Now, John so far as anyone writing to me, do you know that I have as keen an insight in discovering a trickster as anyone else and if anyone in Illinois had written to me about that meeting and wanted to know why I was not there, I would have immediately went to a notory public and taken an oath and made him swallow it. No one regretted my not appearing at the Decatur Meeting more than I did, but under the circumstances, John, there was very important work to be done in the West.[3] I also went to see the prisoners Caplin & Schmidt.[4] I found the boys looking well with good heart,

I also went up to see the boys in San Quintin. I saw Clancy, the McNamaras and Ryan.[5] I hated to leave, poor Ryan he stood by and when I looked back he stood there wiping his eyes. The warden extended a good deal of courtesy to me which I appreciated, so did the boys. I regretted more than anyone could have regretted, that I could not attend that meeting, but the circumstances that arose forced me to take the steps that I did. We must choose between the most important position for the Labor Movement always. It was nine o'clock Friday night when I got into Coffeyville, Kans., I had to drive 19 miles from the railroad station into Coffeyville. When I got on the platform I was still tired, John, but nevertheless I delivered the goods, and I had a packed audience from beginning to end. I had to leave next morning early, and it was Hell at both ends. They were after Moyer hot and heavy, but during my campaign, I changed the whole thing, I think the other side, the tools of the interests, got a blow they will not get over in a hurry. The Governor of the State extended all the courtesy that he could and I received a fine letter from him since I left.

John, would it be possible for you to be in Chicago next Sunday afternoon, I want to have a long, long talk with you alone, you know John, I would write to you so often, but when I get through with these campaigns I am kind of tired and I cannot do much writing and I cannot always have a stenographer near me. Take care of yourself becuase some of the rats have the knife out for you, but you have more friends than any man I know in the Labor Movement.[6] Here is a letter I am going to send you for Lord and I wish you would forward it to him, if I sent it to Washington it is generally there two or three weeks before he gets it, he should have some arrangements for having his mail forwarded, that thing of having mail laying in an office for weeks and weeks will not do for it might be that some important matter should be attended to immediately, and again, John, it does not register good business tactics.

I visited Frisco and the Building Trades there gave me a royal reseption. I addressed their meeting one night and got a very warm reseption from every member, and for the four days that I was in the City they devoted their time to giving me some enjoyment Never before in my life have I been treated with such warm feeling as they received me in Frisco, you know John I am usually hammered but the thing was so different with the boys in Los Angeles and Frisco that I could not help but feel it to the depth of my soul. There is one thing about it, John, that we sometimes find good men who are not corrupted. When I left Frisco I was feeling fine.

I will say goodbye and hope to see you in Chicago.

With all the warm regard and esteem I have for you,
Mother Jones

[John Hunter Walker Collection, 1911-1953, Illinois Historical Survey, University of Illinois Library.]

Notes

1. In his letter Walker informed Mother Jones of "an enormous meeting at Decatur on the 20th. . . . There was at least thirty thousand people at it. I never did see such a large turnout for a town as small as Decatur. They were all very much disappointed at your not being there. However, I explained that at the request of President Moyer and President White, who believed that you could do more than anyone else in the country in this particular matter; that you were in Arizona to do what you could to assist Governor Hunt, who do so much for the Western Federation of Miners, in the Clifton Morensa strike, and whom the Copper Mine Owners were trying to destroy for that very same reason, and it was because you felt you could do more good for the movement by doing that work, than addressing the meeting at Decatur, was the only reason for your not being there. . . .

"Personally, I am very sorry that you were not at that meeting. It was the greatest of its kind that I ever attended in a small town of 30,000, and I know that if you could have been there at that time; still I know how important it is after what he had done, for us to, if we can save Governor Hunt and even make him stronger so that not only he will be able to continue to do that kind og *[sic]* work and feel like doing it, but also for the effect it will have on men in public official positions everywhere in the country in the future.

"I hope too, Mother that you will actually acknowledge to yourself, that you are not as strong as a steam engine or a battle ship any more, and that you won't allow your love for the cause and your desire to work, let you injure your health.

"Take care of yourself; we need you, and you owe it to the labor movement as well as to yourself to stay with us as long as you can, which you can only do by taking care of yourself.

"With all the love in the world, I am."

(John Hunter Walker Collection, 1911–1953, Illinois Historical Survey, University of Illinois Library.)

Mother Jones had returned to Arizona to campaign for the reelection of Governor George Wiley Paul Hunt. The Arizona governor had been born in poverty, became a prospector, ferry boat operator, waiter, rancher, delivery boy, and banker. A member of the Arizona territorial legislature for eight terms, he presided as a Democrat over the constitutional convention when Arizona became a state in 1912. As the state's first governor, he won the applause of the labor movement for prohibiting the importation of professional strikebreakers and mine guards. As a result the 5,000 copper miners on strike in the Clifton district (most of them Mexican-Americans) were able to hold out for five months until they won a victory which gave them a wage increase of from 20 to 70 percent and an improved arbitration procedure, but no union recognition. Hunt's stand during the strike earned him the support of labor but the bitter hatred of the mine owners who initiated a movement to recall him.

Mother Jones was quoted in the Arizona press as having called Governor Hunt "the greatest governor that the country has ever produced," and when she arrived in Phoenix during an earlier visit to help reelect Hunt for a second time, he sent a car to meet her at the railroad station and a bouquet of flowers to her hotel. This prompted her to declare: "The governors of several states have sent their militia to meet me at the stations and they always brought a bouquet with them, but it was always a bouquet of bayonets. And if there was any inquiry about my health, it was always with the hope of finding me dead."

In 1916 when Governor Hunt was running for a third term, Mother Jones was asked by Charles Moyer, president of the Western Federation of Miners, and John H. White, president of the United Mine Workers of America, to help out in the campaign which she was more than happy to do. In the election, Thomas Campbell, a former mine owner, defeated Hunt by 30 votes out of 55,000 cast, and was seated by the state Supreme Court without pay until the outcome, which Hunt contested, could be settled. After serving about half of the two-year term, Campbell was deposed by the court who gave Hunt the majority of the 30 disputed votes.

(Alan V. Johnson, "Governor G.W.P. Hunt and Organized Labor," unpublished M.A. thesis, University of Arizona, 1964, pp. 5-17, 67-69, 76-85; unidentified newspaper clipping dated June 16, 1916, in Mother Mary Harris Jones Papers, Department of Archives and Manuscripts, Catholic University of America; Featherling, *op. cit.*, pp. 142-44; Philip S. Foner, *History of the Labor Movement in the United States*, vol. 6, New York, 1982, pp. 13-24.)

For an article by Mother Jones dealing with her visit to Arizona in 1916, *see* pp. 474-77.

2. Alexander Howat, president of Kansas District 14, had been accused of accepting bribes from the operators. For the battle between Howat and the machine led by John L. Lewis, *see* pp. 348-59.

3. The reference is to her campaigning for Governor Hunt.

4. David Caplan and Matthew Schmidt had been arrested in connection with the McNamara dynamiting and after trials which dragged into 1915, had been

found guilty and sentenced to years in prison.

5. The men mentioned were all imprisoned on the charge of dynamiting and had been associated with the International Association of Bridge and Structural Iron Workers. F.M. Ryan had been international union president.

To Edward Nockles

July 7, 1916.

Mr. Ed Nockles,
Sec'y Chicago Federation of Labor,
Chicago, Ils.

Dear Ed:

Am leaving for Washington and send my mail to the Atlantic Hotel, Washington, D.C. Sec'y Green, of the Miners, will go with us to Washington, so I think you had better write him an invitation. The more powerful the committee is the more effect it will have on the other side. I have to go to Atlanta, Ga., tomorrow but will be in Washington Monday. Have to go up to the prison there to do some work for the national office. Take care of yourself and give my regards to Olander and Fitzpatrick.[1]

Yours sincerely,

I looked for you at Hotel Mitel but you never showed up

Mother Jones

[John Hunter Walker Collection, 1911-1953, Illinois Historical Survey, University of Illinois Library.]

Notes

1. Ed Nockles, secretary of the Chicago Federation of Labor, sent the letter to John Fitzpatrick, Federation president, with the request that he "keep me posted where you are and be ready to leave for Washington." (John Hunter Walker Collection, 1911-1953, Illinois Historical Survey, University of Illinois Library.) The conference in Washington was to visit President Wilson and request he intervene on behalf of the men who were imprisoned during the dynamiting trials following the McNamara case.

To Edward Nockles

Washington, D.C.
July 20, 1916.

Mr. Edward Nockels,
166 Washington Street,
Chicago, Ill.,
Secretary, Chicago Federation of Labor.

Dear Ed:

I received your letter yesterday and your telegram the day before. I have made all arrangements with some very influential people in Washington to lend their hand. I am all ready paving the way. I have lost no time since I have been back from Atlanta. I think that we had best all stay at one hotel, so that we would be altogether, as there are some Senators and Congressmen who will want to see us and talk this thing over before we approach the President. I suggested that we ask for no parole, but a complete pardon and exoneration for the men, and influential persons that I spoke to agreed with me. They were glad to know that a few people were taking up the matter. If you get here on Tuesday then we can all meet and outline our policy collectively, so that there will be no blunders made. When we act we will have a clear understanding of what we wanted. Things are moving pretty well as I would like to see them. Of course I am not getting up in the air, Ed, because if I was knocked down I would feel it keenly, but I am very hopeful of the outcome of this move. I have been watching that strike in Illinois and was somewhat surprised of the Governor sending the troops there even at the request of a corporation sheriff.

Things will be so arranged here that you will not have to lose any time. If you get in at 1:30 Tuesday we will have the afternoon and the next day to work. We can arrange to have the President meet us on Wednesday.[1] You telegram to me the train that you leave on and I will meet you at the depot. Give my regards to Olander, Fitzpatrick. Pretty hot here Ed, and you will need all the summer clothes you can bring. I am loyally yours for a damn fine fight.

Mother Jones.

[John Hunter Walker Collection, 1911-1953, Illinois Historical Survey,
University of Illinois Library.]

Notes

1. The delegation met with President Wilson but nothing came of the meeting.

To Margaret Prevy

Mrs. Margaret Prevy,
140 High St.
Akron, Ohio.

My dear Mrs. Prevy:

Your letter reached me yesterday.[1] Permit me to say to you that whoever wrote you the falsehood should take a day off and learn to tell the truth. I went in to the mining districts of Indiana to have Senator Kerns returned to the Senate, because he saved me from serving five years in the state penitentiary of West Virginia with twenty-one of my fellows. I think the miners of this country owe him a debt that they should pay by returning him to the Senate. If we did not do it we would be ingrates. No political party in this nation ever paid me five cents. I was not there in the interest of any political party. I was sent there by the United Mine Workers to explain to the miners why they should return Senator Kerns. I had nothing to do with Debb's campaign.[2] I was not sent there by the National office to interfere with any party affairs. Senator Kerns befriended me on more occasions than one in Washington. I could always go to him in behalf of those who needed assistance.

The socialists in their whole lives never gave me a dollar. I have given them a good many. I know how they treated Miss Fleherty and others who served them in the days gone by. They are not runing my affairs and they don't own me and they had better learn to quit slandering people if they are going to revolutionize the nation. They had better revolutionize their own brains first. The democrats did not bring me there now would I go out for any political party. I went out for the labor organization that I am directly interested in. The political parties don't bother me very much. It is the individual. I have no apologies to offer to any member of the Socialist Party for any act of mine. If they would clean house they might have many more members. I have no earthly use for people who are forever digging up the actions of other people and overlooking their own. I hope this explanation will be satisfactory to you. The socialists of Terre Haute brought me there some eight or ten years ago. I had to pay my own railroad fare and pay my own expenses. If it was a Maywood Simons, or a Lana Morrow Lewis or people who had never been in the trenches nor ever in their lives fought one of labor's battles and the only interest they had was to bleed the wretches who were putting up the money, they would have been highly entertained and been paid generously, but whenever you go in the trenches and face the bayonets of the common enemy against the gang, they have nothing to say. I want to say here that I owe the socialists no apology, now will I offer one to them. I have seen enough of their treachery to those who have fought the battle and want to keep the party clean; but one of these days, Margaret Prevy, we are going to clean house and we will have a real revolutionary socialist movement and we will see that neither lawyers nor sky pilots are running our affairs.[3]

With love to Mr. Prevy and you, I remain ever one in the struggle for better days.

[Mother Mary Harris Jones Papers, Department of Archives and Manuscripts, Catholic University of America, Washington, D.C.]

Notes

1. Mrs. Marguerite Prevy, a pioneer Ohio Socialist who lived in Akron, had written on October 26, 1916: "Dear 'Mother Jones' We have been informed that you are campaigning for the Democrat Party in the 5th Indiana Dist. — the District from which the Socialists expect to elect Debs. I should be pleased to have you either *deny* or verify this report, I can hardly believe you would use what influence you have with the workers to defeat Comrade Debs for Congress." (Mother Mary Harris Jones Papers, Department of Archives and Manuscripts, Catholic University of America, Washington, D.C.)

2. For the reasons for the strained relations between Mother Jones and the Socialist Party, *see* pp. 225, 569-70, 572, 574-78.

3. This was a reflection of a fairly widespread criticism of the Socialist Party for being dominated by middle- and upper-class elements rather than by workers. (*See* Ira Kipnis, *The American Socialist Movement, 1897-1912,* New York, 1952, pp. 175-90.)

To Thomas J. Mooney

Washington, D.C.,
December 15th., 1916.

Mr. Tom Mooney,[1]
San Francisco, California,

My dear Mr. Mooney:
Your letter of the 25th ultimo reached me a week ago.[2] I have already got my hands full, but nevertheless I have been watching the trend of things in California. I realize that the enemies of society are

not on the working man's side, but on the side of those who rob the workers in the interests of dollars.

I am opposed to violence, because violence produces violence, and what is won today by violence will be lost to-morrow. We must ever and always appeal to reason, because society after all has made all the progress it has ever made, by anyalizing the situation carefully and bringing the matter before the public with reason on its side. Humanity as a whole is right, if they only learn the truth and the way out. The taking of human life has never settled any question. And the wrongs eventually revert back to those who commit them. I am not afraid to say that I probably, in the great industrial struggles that I have been in have prevented more blood shed than any other person in America. I felt in this case, as I read it, there was a hidden wire somewhere, that has not come to the surface. I cannot believe that the workers in California would resort to any crime of the kind. The people have a right to have a preparedness parade, if they wish, without being molested, or interfered with in any way. And we must be generous enough to concede to every citizen the rights we claim for ourselves. I feel that you boys have been the victims of this diabolical crime and are innocent from the beginning. I will do everything that I can do to help you. You refer to Mr. White, President, he will render you all the assistance that can be rendered in your defense. He is waiting for a meeting of the Executive Board to act, and never be afraid of him to act in a great cause. No man in America is more anxious to see justice administered than he is. So far as President Mahon of the Street Car Men, he has been up to his shoulders in struggles of his own craft. He has just returned from Europe, and had a terrific strike in New York;[3] and you must remember that these men have but one brain and the reponsibility of their craft is on their shoulders. Keep up courage for right and justice will finally prevail. I am going to Chicago on Sunday and I will ask them to take up your case. I dont think that they ought to be asked: I think that they ought to do it themselves. Give my best wishes to all the boys. You have got a good man in Robert Minor,[4] and no better man could go to the post George West. I am yours in the struggle for a nobler civilization.[5]

[Mother Mary Harris Jones Papers, Department of Archives and Manuscripts, Catholic University of America, Washington, D.C.]

Notes

1. Thomas J. Mooney, a molder by trade and a militant, radical labor leader in San Francisco, and Warren K. Billings, a member of the Boot and Shoe Workers' Union in that city, were the victims of a frameup resulting from the explosion of a bomb, July 22, 1916, during a Preparedness Parade in San Francisco, killing nine persons and wounding at least 40 more. The two were in-

dicted, charged with setting the bomb, even though a photograph showed Mooney a mile from the scene of the explosion at the time indicated, and evidence, too, that witnesses had been tampered with by the prosecution. At the time this letter was written both were in prison, Billings having been sentenced to life imprisonment, and Mooney about to be tried. In the trial he was sentenced to death. For further discussion of the case and Mother Jones's role in it, *see* pp. 292-93, 301, 304.

2. Mooney's letter, San Francisco, Ca., Nov. 25, 1916, was sent from County Jail No. 1, Cell No. 29, and began: "The last time I wrote you I was asking your aid to help dig some other fellow out of the Bosses Bastile." This was a reference to the time Mooney was secretary of the San Francisco branch of the International Workers' Defense League founded in 1913, and he had asked Mother Jones's help in the defense of David Caplan and Matthew Schmidt, arrested in connection with the McNamara dynamiting. Mooney's letter continued:

"This time it is to try to enlist your support moral, financial and economic to the end that I my wife and three others may again walk in free air, to fight in labors ranks once more." (In addition to Mooney and Billings, Rena Mooney, Mooney's wife, Edward D. Nolan, a leading member of the San Francisco machinists' union, and Israel Weinberg of the Jitney Bus Drivers' Union were arrested and charged with the preparedness crime.)

"We are all indicted on eight charges of murder, as a result of the bomb explosion that happened during the preparedness parade in this City on July 22, of this year.

"I might write at length on the details of this fight for your special benefit, but you know the struggle well enough. It is the same old story in this case. Though some try to make it a little different.

"This is one time that they have made the whole frameup out of the whole cloth, and apparently they intend to make it stick, or at least they did so far. One of or *(sic)* boys, Warren K. Billings, was convicted and sentenced to life imprisonment as a result.

"I am the next to be tried, Jan 3, 1917 is the date set for the battle to begin.

"We have been very fortunate in securing the services of the formost *(sic)* attorney of the Country Bourke Cockran to take up our case free of charge as a result of Frank P. Walsh, interceding for us in a measure.

"It will devolve on the defense to at least pay his personal as well as his court expenses which will be very high.

"Frank P. Walsh is also coming to the Coast to take up our cases, and Geo. West, Special Investigator, for the U.S. Industrial Relations Commission will soon start to write up the police conspiracy frame up for all of the labor papers as well as all others that will print what he will write. West arrived in town a few days ago.

"We are making a desperate effort to gain a new trial for Billings which all takes lots of money and the Defense is at this time depleted.

"I wrote John P. White Pres. of the United Mine Workers, about the cases and he never answered my letter. I asked him if he would send me a list of the names and addresses of the Secretary of the locals of the Mine Workers throughout the Country so we could give our cases the desired publicity and appeal for funds. I have not heard from him at all.

"Mother, I am enclosing to you some of the Publicity gotten out by myself also some put out by the Defense League. I hope you will find time to give what ever help your health and energy will permit you to when you read this stuff, I am sending you, as we sure need not only your help but the help of all others.

"I wish it were possible for you to come to the Coast to look over the situation and take up the platform in the larger Cities at advertised meetings as a forerunner to other work needed in order to insure success in our coming trials.

"I wish you would make an effort to get the United Mine Workers Local Union Secretary Directory, and if you have any influence with Adolph Germer, Sec'y of the Socialist Party at Chicago, to get from hi(m) if it is possible the list of the addresses of the Socialist Party locals in all parts of the Country. So they can be circularized by our publicity committee and at the same time an appeal for funds. I have been a member of the Party for the last nine years and an active member at that. I went thru the country on the Red Special with Debs.in 1908 and while on that trip I met Germer and Frank Hayes on the train while it was in the state of Illinoise [sic].

"The Socialist Party Here is not much, as they tried twice to help the corporation to send me to the prison in the way of putting me out of the party when I was in jail and charged with crime and the corporation was bending every effort to get me with the aid of two of the ablest lawyers as special prosecutors working with the Dist. Atty. and compelling the Sheriff who was such for 25 years in succession to sit at the Dist. Atty.'s table to aid in the selection of the Jury, that would convict. The only reason that I was not out of the Party was that I was a member of the Hungarinag Branch and they said if you put Mooney out, You will have to put the whole branch out.

"Debs has written an article about our case in the Rip Saw and the Melting Pot. The Appeal to Reason will carry a story about our case on Dec. 2, that will be this Sat.

"I have written to Pres. Mahon of the Street Carmens Union and he has not even answered my letter. One of the greatest reasons for my being in jail to day is the fact that I tried to organize the carmen of this city, and failed in my efort just one week before the bomb went off.

"I am enclosing you other matters of detail about my own as well as the general league publicity goten out in our behalf.

"I hope your health and tireless spirit will permit you to lend us a helping hand, for we sure need it. The defense treasury is at this writting depleated . . .

"I go to trial Jan. 3, and no money on hand to do many kinds of very necessary work. This is one time that Labor has all of the facts with it. We are absolutely innocent, of the crime or any Knowledge of it. Hoping to hear from You.

Fraternally and Sincerely Yours in Labors Fight.
Tom Mooney"

(Mother Mary Harris Jones Papers, Department of Archives and Manuscripts, Catholic University of America, Washington, D.C. There are no copies of this correspondence in the Thomas J. Mooney Papers, Bancroft Library, University of California, Berkeley.)

3. The reference is to the carmen's strike of 1916 in New York City and Westchester, and in which Mother Jones was a participant. *See* pp. 287-90.

4. Robert Minor, the radical cartoonist, was the chief publicity man for the International Workers' Defense League which had been revived to defend Mooney and Billings.

5. Mooney acknowledged Mother Jones's letter on December 28, 1916, writ-

ing in part on the stationery of the "Tom Mooney Molders Defense Commitee," and addressing it "Mother Jones. Any Where in the Country,": "Your most welcomed, and long looked for letter came to me the other day. It was in its self great encouragement to me and my codefendants. . . . Make an effort in every locality to get the different labor papers to take up the news of our trials and the case in general. Get all of the central Labor Bodies to endorse our fight. Fraternally and Sincerely Yours in Labors Fight. Tom Mooney. P.S. Have written John P. White, & Wm. Green with a hope that they will have the U.M.W. Executive Board do some thing at their next meeting in Jan." [Mother Mary Harris Jones Papers, Department of Archives and Manuscripts, Catholic University of America, Washington, D.C. This letter also is not present in the Thomas J. Mooney Papers, Bancroft Library, University of California, Berkeley.]

To John H. Walker

Charleston, W. Va.
[July, 1917][1]

Mr. John H. Walker,
801 Commercial St.
Danville, Ill.

Dear John:

I am going to write you a few lines, We had a convention here yesterday of the New River miners to accept an agreement that the distinguished officers made in Cincinnati. I mean the vice President and Johnie Lewis has become the general Jesus of the movement. Hayes made a speech.[2] I wish you could have heard that fellow. He has become what you call a self conceited empty brained dictator. In the conference in New York he struck the table with his empty fist and he told the operators that they had to come across that he had the goods on them. and he would get them before the Federal Goverment. And they told him to go to it that they had the goods on them and were very anziohs for him to make the brake. Just impagine men putting themselves in the position to take that water I don't know John what the futhure of this organization is going to be, but if they continue doing business as they have I doubt very much of its destiny And the other fellow, Lewis He represented John P. in the conference. There is nothing in that fellow but an empty piece of human slime. I get so disgusted sometimes that I feel like giving up the whole field. and going away off some where. If the organization ever gets into the hands of this fellow that is the end of the miners Zimmerman the board member from Ill.

is in here. and Valentine from Iowa. I think he is the best of the lot. F. J. gave the revalters the right to sit in the convention and President Keeney of the District forced them to get out at the point of the pistol and altho he was a big gun in his own estimation, the local officer carried the day. as for orarty and logic John, there is none in that individual, and is imposition on civilization to have the miners money paid in salary to such ablily. No wonder the operators get the best of them. If I was an operator I would sit back and laugh at the things that come across However, there are a few brave men here that will take the bull by the horn and do business regardless of who oppose them and who doesen't. That was a good meeting we had at Brazil, Only I am a little afraid they are going to loose that strike. John, the Sec'y of Central labor Hutchinson in Brazil, was a detective for seven years. He is a very smooth guy and the unsufiscated would fall for his philosophy. Would fall into his traps. I am alittle afraid of him, and if there is anyone in Brazil that you can trust, you better put them next to keeping an eye on him. He drops in Terra Haute quite offten and meets someone there. that he comunicates with when a man has once been in such organizations I am ever afterwards weary of them because a man with a principal will die before he will ever render service to a machine as rotten as the Detective agency. They are organized for no other purpose than to destroy the welfare of the human family. I don't know when I will see you again I am going to Henderson Kentucky for Labor day. I dont think I will be out of this state before them. There is so much to do and so few to do it. But you send my mail to Beckley, W. Va. and when you see Nockles and Fitz Patrick give them my best regards. They were not put on the defence committee. They were not the kind uncle Sam wanted I man uncle Same Gompus.[3] John, the whole labor movement is becoming an inactive institution. It is falling in to the mesh of interest. and welfare leaders are lending their hands to the game and the poor wretches are paying the bills. I look for the most despotic system of industrial slavery after the war the world had ever known. they are putting the breakes on us now, and paid officials are rendering them faithful service. Just see the committee they sent to Russia.[4] The slickest rottenest. Despirte on the soil of America. George E. Russell, the intelectual socialist,[5] and Duncan president of the granite workers. and ultra conservative. I am a little afraid that Loyd will get under their influence in Wasnington, We have not what I term a good watch dog in all of Washington to keep an eye on what these pirates are doing. I leave tomorrow for New River and expect to be up ther all summer Take good care of your self until I see you again. and give my love to them all at home.

Always yours,
Mother Jones

[John Hunter Walker Collection, 1911-1953, Illinois Historical Survey,

Notes

1. The letter is undated but the reply by John H. White is dated, July 12, 1917, so it was undoubtedly written early in July. Walker wrote in part: "I am returning letter which you left with Ed Nockels for me. It is to say the least, a deplorable state of affairs, and I sincerely hope that some means will be found of adjusting the matter on a decent basis, that will work out to the best interests of the organization. I would be willing to go to almost any extreme to accomplish this; it is pitiful that the present opportunity can not be taken advantage of, for the best interest of the men who work in the mines and their families" (John Hunter Walker Collection, 1911-1953, Illinois Historical Survey, University of Illinois Library). By the "present opportunity" was meant the period following entrance of the United States into the World War when prosperity for the coal operators appeared to give the union a chance to achieve many new gains for the miners.

2. When President John H. White resigned to join the Fuel Administration, he was succeeded to the presidency by Vice-President Frank J. Hayes who appointed John L. Lewis as vice-president. Since Hayes was usually drunk , Lewis took over the activities of the president.

3. Samuel Gompers, A.F. of L. president, was a member of the Council of National Defense, and could appoint labor representatives to a number of government wartime posts.

4. The reference is to the Root Commission to Russia, appointed by President Wilson following the first Russian Revolution in March 1917. Fearing that the new government, which had overthrown the Czar and was led by Alexander Kerensky, might lead Russia out of the war, Wilson appointed Elihu Root, Wall Street lawyer and financier and former Republican Secretary of State, as head of a commission to go to Russia to explore means of cooperation in the prosecution of the war. A Socialist, Charles Edwards Russell, and a labor leader, James Duncan, A.F. of L. first vice-president, were appointed to the Commission. Russell had broken with the Socialist Party in April 1917 to support U.S. entrance into World War I. (For the Root Commission to Russia, *see* Ronald Radosh, *American Labor and United States Foreign Policy*, New York, 1969, pp. 72-102.)

To John H. Walker

Fairmont W Va August 25-1918

My Dear John

I have been trying to See you but everytime you were gone. Just missed you by one day.

On my return from Colo you had just left for Penn. I had Some thing of Importance to tell you — John this organisation is in the hands of the Mine owners. When could I see you or where. I am going to Washington after Labor day I wish you be in Washington that week. Some time I am Sick at heart about the poor Devil[s] that are betrayed.[1]

This the rottenst age the world ever past thru in all history If I were to tell all I have seen in Colo my God it shake the

John I was in the Knights of Labor, when it was a million Strong.[2] It was wrecked in two years there was not half the rottens there is now

John if we are not in the Harness after the war we are in the worst State industrial Bondage.

If after this war Labor does not come into its own it will be due to the *Treachery* of its *Leaders*

Let me hear from you[3] I will be here untill the third then I leave for Washington write me Fairmont Hotel Fairmont Love & Loyalty Tell Carbine write me

Mother

[John Hunter Walker Collection, 1911-1953, Illinois Historical Survey, University of Illinois Library.]

Notes

1. Mother Jones is undoubtedly referring to the Washington Agreement signed by UMW top officials over the opposition of the rank-and-file. The Agreement raised wages during the war but also penalized the miners monetarily for unauthorized strikes. The penalty clause was deeply resented by the miners.

2. The Knights reached this membership or near it in the year 1886.

3. Walker replied on August 29, 1918, and wrote in part: "I know something about the situation down yonder, and like yourself, I fear for our organization in the future if it continues in the hands of the men who are deliberately betraying it to serve their own personal ends at this time. That condi[tion] is not alone true in West Va., Maryland, old Virginia, Sommerset County Pa., and I am almost sure as I am living, that it is also rue of the Coke regions in Pa., and in some of the places that are at least on the surface, organized.

"They are going to desperate extremes to prevent their defeat. At the same time, I really believe that it is going to be impossible for them to get away with it this time, because the miners everywhere are beginning to have an inkling of what the situation really is. This, coupled with the absolute inactivity, with the maudlin, idiocy, drunkenness and egotism of the one, the brazenness and domineering, blatant dishonesty, some cunning and intelligence, but no real ability in the other, it is having the effect that at least I am hopeful will enable us to root them out there in this coming election. . . .

"Anyhow when it is over, I will have the satisfaction of knowing that I did my damndest to straighten the thing out right, and if we don't make it right in this election then by God! the fight has only started. We will clean it out before we

get through and put our movement on an honest clean wholesome basis."
[John H. Walker to Mother Jones, August 29, 1918, John Hunter Walker Collection, 1911-1953, Illinois Historical Survey, University of Illinois Library.]
The reference to the "drunkenness . . . of the one" is to Frank Hayes, and to "the brazenness and domineering . . . in the other" is to John L. Lewis (although one might question the "no real ability"). In general, Walker's prediction, as we have seen above, was vastly overoptimistic. *See* pp. 348-59.

To Walter Wayland

Charleston, W. Va.
November 15th, 1918

Mr. Walter Wayland,[1]
Editor of the Appeal to Reason,
Girard, Kans.

My Dear Walter:

I have been for sometime wanting to write you to know how Julia and Edith are, I have had so much to do, that I have been unable to get around to that part. What has become of George Brewer[2] and Grace, I think they made a great mistake when they left the Appeal. I don't hear much of the party that they joined, it seems to me it went to pieces just as it rose. It certainly did not figure in the last campaign.

I hope that you will put some fire into the Appeal now that the War is over, the Appeal once was the best paper in this country, that is so far as the workers were concerned, but it has of recent years lost that fire, you must get a hold of some Editor who understands the reconstruction period for there is no doubt that there are stormy days ahead of us, and the Appeal can do more good than any other paper in the country if it is properly edited by men with the fight in them.

What has become of Copeland, I don't hear of him only that he went across the water, did he return? Even Copeland did not have the fire in him that was necessary to keep the Appeal going, that is to interesting readers, it was one of the papers that struck the angles in the right place.

I am going to the Illinois State Federation in a week or so, but you send those books here. I want Voitaire's Greates Work, *Candide*, you know he is a very great wrighter, he and Victor Hugo and Tom Payne wer my favors, when you father and myself used to set up at night and talk these over. Perhaps some day I will go down to Girard and see you again.

Give my love to the girls and to John tell them I love them just as I did in days of old.

Sincerely yours,
Mother Jones

PS I hope the coming year will be a prosperous one for the coming year.

[Haldeman mss. II, Manuscripts Department, Lilly Library Indiana University, Bloomington, Indiana.]

Notes

1. Walter Wayland was the son of Julius A. Wayland, founder of the Socialist weekly, *Appeal to Reason*. Julius A. Wayland committed suicide after a trumped-up charge of transporting a girl, formerly employed by the weekly, for immoral purposes across state lines thereby violating the Mann Act. His son succeeded to the editorship.

2. George D. Brewer was an editor of *Appeal to Reason* and publisher of *Worker's Chronicle* in Pittsburg, Kansas.

To Sara J. Dorr

San Francisco, Cal.,
Dec. 16, 1918.

Mrs. Sara J. Dorr, President,
Women's Christian Temperance Union,
3 City Hall Avenue,
San Francisco, Cal.

Dear Mrs. Dorr:

Permit me to extend to you the deep appreciation of Organized Labor the country over for the stand you have taken in behalf of justice. It is not a question of Thomas Mooney — the question goes further than Thomas Mooney. The great issue now before Organized labor and the thinking American people is the integrity of the courts. They are the bulwark of our institutions and their integrity must be preserved, for once the workers lose faith then all hope is blasted and no one can be responsible for the outcome.

It is the duty of every citizen to awaken to the fact that not alone is America interested but the eyes of the world are focused upon the courts of California and it is really up to her noble womanhood whether the terrible stain that is cast upon them in the Mooney case shall remain unchallenged.

The light is breaking. The maps of the world are being changed. A new world is in the making and our American woman can participate in that making. She can make it a safe and happy place for the generation yet to come to dwell in.

If thru our indifference, suspicion has been placed upon our courts then it is thru our vigilance and our spirit for love and freedom that we must transform them and surely the women of California will not let this issue die.

I shall convey to Organized Labor the world over that the women of San Francisco, particularly the members of the W.C.T.U.[1] are the first to demand a revolution in our courts and your action I am sure will awaken other women of our nation. It was the Dreyfus case in France that changed the spirit of the people and to you fair women of San Francisco all honor shall be due.

With deep appreciation for your good work, I remain

Sincerely yours,

[Mother Mary Harris Jones Papers, Department of Archives and Manuscripts, Catholic University of America, Washington, D.C.]

Notes

1. This is probably the first time Mother Jones praised a temperance organization.

To John H. Walker

San Francisco, Cal.,
Dec. 18, 1918.

John H. Walker, President,
Illinois State Federation of Labor,
Springfield, Ill.

My dear John:

I arrived here pretty tired but the train men were very good to me coming out and I got them all so interested that they wrote a vote of appreciation to Fremont Older, Editor, of the San Francisco Call.

I saw the Governor last Thursday.[1] I was accompanied by Mr. Scharrenberg so as to be safe and I don't know of any safer peson I could have taken with me. I didn't get any satisfaction out of him but he gave me a hearing any how but I have been keeping the newspapers busy since I came here. I will enclose you a number of the clippings.

How did things go in the election? I haven't heard a word out here any more than the papers carried that Frank Hayes won out by 60,000.[2] Its all right. Let him win. Things will shape themselves pretty soon.

I am going down to the oil fields to talk to those poor fellows on Sunday next. Then I shall leave for Los Angeles and from there I will go to Kansas City and try and see Howat and have a talk with him. Under no circumstances surrender an inch to those fellows. The fight is only begun, John.

I am visiting the unions at night to urge them to send a delegate to that Congress at Chicago on the 14th of next month. You have got to make that a success. Some of these pirates out here are getting a little alarmed. We want to give them a shaking up and let them know we are not asleep.

My regards to all the boys, and take good care of yourself. We will stand together till death. The brave and true die only once. Cowards and traitors die often and they have some horrible deaths at that.

I'll close up now because I have a lot to do this afternoon, I am

Yours,
Mother Jones

[John Hunter Walker Collection, 1911-1953, Illinois Historical Survey, University of Illinois Library.]

Notes

1. Labor protests against the death sentence imposed on Tom Mooney, which extended as far as Russia where they were led by V.I. Lenin, persuaded President Woodrow Wilson to intervene and urge that execution be suspended. Although the conviction was affirmed by the Supreme Court, continued protest, much of it organized by Fremont Older, progressive editor of the San Francisco *Call* and combined *Call-Bulletin*, who devoted much time and energy to have Mooney freed, and the findings of the Densmore investigation, resulted in the commutation of his sentence to life imprisonment by Governor Stephens.

Mother Jones then visited the Governor to obtain not merely a commutation but a full pardon and release of Mooney and Billings from prison. But Mooney and Billings remained prisoners, despite the conclusions by a succession of Federal investigations of their innocence.

2. Frank Hayes was elected president in the UMW 1918 election. John L. Lewis who ran with him was elected vice-president.

John H. Walker, who was defeated for the presidency by Hayes, wrote to Mother Jones on January 8, 1919: "It is just as you have said," and went on to indicate that the returns indicated a close final decision, but that "the chances are they will steal it by some means." [John H. Walker to Mother Jones, January 8, 1919, John Hunter Walker Collection, 1911-1953, Illinois Historical Survey, University of Illinois Library.] Melvyn Dubofsky and Warren Van Tine in their biography of John L. Lewis rather crudely describe John H. Walker as a "man consumed by his desire to obtain the union presidency and one unable to concede that he might lose a fair election, saw conspiracies everywhere." (*John L. Lewis: A Biography,* New York, 1977, p. 33.) Having already demonstrated that the UMW top officials, especially John L. Lewis, were prepared to use any methods to win an election, this comment makes little sense.

To John H. Walker

Los Angeles, Cal.
2759 Marengo St.,
Dec. 28, 1918

John H. Walker,
State Federation Office,
Springfield, Ills.

Dear John:

I received your telegram forwarded to me from San Francisco. It was not very plain owing to the transmission but it gave me to understand that you were elected presdient but I warn you now to keep close watch or they'll count you out as they did in the last election.[1]

You know, John, you're dealing with a terrific, powerful combination and the interests will do anythang and spend any amount of money to keep you from getting control of the United Mine Workes Organization. They know they can't play the game with you and when you do get in, I hope to God you'll have a house-cleaning. The leeches that those poor fellows have carried on their backs for years, if they themselves knew it and understood it, I'm inclined to thank they'd shake the nation and all thinking people would endorse them.

I read just a few days before where they said you we beat by sixty thousand. I knew, John, the statement was false, but the honest men who read it, regretted that you failed to take charge of the destinies of those poor hounded and deceived slaves. The pirates now will sit up and take notice and I slept good that night when I read that telegram.

I did not get the full meaning of it, I concluded that the victory was yours. There's a new day breaking for the Workers and you, no doubt, will help to bring the sunlight to the poor wretches who have been deceived, robbed, and plundered by their own people that they were paying.

I probably would have been back in Chicago by this time only the Oil Workers in Taft, held me up and after I spoke in Taft, they urged me to remain with them for a week or ten days and tour the Oil Fields so I concluded that I would comply with their desire. After all, John, it makes no matter where we do the good. They told me they'd pay my expenses. I told them that was not the question — the question was, could we bring them together into the organization and they said that if I toured their Oil Fields they knew that 95% of them would be in the Union. I am also working to get them to join the United Mine Workers, for their industry in reality is mining. They mine the oil while the subterranean miners mine the coal. It's a wonderful field, John. I think we must consolidate the workers and put an end to these jurisdictional disputes.

I will not be in Chicago for that Congress that's going to meet but the Densmore expose has stirred things up on the coast here.[2] They squashed all the endictments against Nolan. I could not get anything out of the Governor — more than that he said he as giving me a hearing. But Sharrenburg said that I said a great deal more to him than any man would dare to say — The Governor is a perfect tool of the interests — he has no love for the workers.[3]

I'll close by wishing you and all at home the happiest New Year and Prosperity to all around us.

Mother Jones

[John Hunter Walker Collection, 1911-1953, Illinois Historical Survey, University of Illinois Library.]

Notes

1. In July 1917 John H. Walker wrote to Mother Jones detailing the evidence which he declared indicated that votes "were cast illegally in the last International election" which resulted in his defeat for UMW president. "This is a rotten situation," he added, and concluded that "before our organization can be made much better, that kind of a condition has got to be eliminated, and without regard to who gets the position, provided they are honest and competent, every real friend of our union must do what they can to wipe out this situation, and put the organization on an honest basis." (John H. Walker to Mother Jones, July 19, 1917, John Hunter Walker Collection, 1911-1953, Illinois Historical Survey, University of Illinois Library.)

2. The Dunsmore investigation offered ample evidence of the crooked and illegal behavior of the prosecution in the Mooney-Billings Case.

3. Although Governor Stephens had commuted Mooney's sentence to life imprisonment, he refused Mother Jones's request that he and Billings be pardoned and released from prison. *See also* pp. 525-27.

To Edward Nockles

Telegram

January 14, 1919

To: Ed Knockels
166 Washington St.
Chicago, Illinois

To the delegates in Convention greeting.[1] May your resolutions be tempered with reason. Courts of our country must be exonerated. Convention must demand courts be cleansed of corporation judges. Place men on bench who will consider justice before dollars. Blot must be removed from courts. If the workers lose faith in courts then where are they to turn for justice.

MOTHER JONES

[Mother Mary Harris Jones Papers, Department of Archives and Manuscripts, Catholic University of America, Washington, D.C.]

Notes

1. The convention was for the purpose of organizing the Labor Party of Cook County and was sponsored by the Chicago Federation of Labor, headed by John Fitzpatrick and Edward Nockles. Later in the year the Labor Party of Illinois was launched at a conference of delegates of local unions.

To John H. Walker

Charleston, W. Va.
February 5, 1919

Mr. John H. Walker,
Springfield, Ill.

My Dear Mr. Walker:

Enclosed find my bill of expenses there is no charge for services outside of the real expense concurred in railroad fare and Hotel bill.

I learned a great deal since I came here and have a good deal to tell you that I can not write, I will be in Washington the last week in this month, perhaps something may bring you there. I see that Gem Lord has been notified by powers that be that his services is not needed any longer. I stopped off at the office and never in the History that I received with such courtesy, I couldn't tell myself what was up, but I know what they meant alright I cannot imagine that men who draw their salaries from the rank and file that stood for the things that I have learned since I came in here. However, someday there will be a reckoning, only I am afraid it will be a sad one for the rank and file.

I sent a satchel by parcel post when I was in Chicago, but they notified me that it was unmailable, I can't understand what objections they have to it, but I wrote to Knockles to get it and send it to me by express, but for fear he would not be in Chicago, you had better telephone to him. I can't write you anymore, so I will have to wait until I see you.

With good luck, I am

Yours sincerely,

Le asked me to go to Pitts to the Steel Workers they wanted me[1]
John its rotten

[John Hunter Walker Collection, 1911-1953, Illinois Historical Survey, University of Illinois Library.]

Notes

1. The reference is to the 1919 steel strike. *See* pp. 57, 303-15.

To Terence V. Powderly

Charleston, W. Va.
June 19, 1919

Mr. T.V. Powderly,
502 Quincy St, N.W.
Washington, D.C.

My Dear Friend:

I am just going to drop you a line to let you know that we are having awfully hot weather down here, I came back a week ago from Illinois, where I had some tremenduous meetings. Went to Ziegler, the mines belonged to Joe Lighter, eight years ago, when I went there they turned two machine guns on me, this time in on a special train and was met at the depot by the Mayor of Ziegler and a delegation there, and the Mayor is a Miner and I was their guest at his home that night, next morning I left and got the truck car and went to Christopher and there I got the Train for Sentralia, where I also had a tremenduous meeting. Then I came back to Fairmot, West Va., and had a parade of 14,000 miners, there were no sky-pilots or no politicians or nor pike counter hunter speakers of that day the speakers all were from the rank and file. Ex-Senator Watson gave them a park to meet in. Fifteen months ago if you would have gone in there in any mining camp in that district you would have been asked what your business was and put you out at the point of the gun even if your own brother would have been there, what a change has taken place, so we are making progress, but I had to leave there that night for Pittsburgh and from Pittsburgh I went back to Herin, Ill, then came into Chicago, and held three big meetings there with the cigar and Shoe wrkers, I have not had a moments rest until the last week, I have not been working very hard, so I am beginning to geather up my strength again. I see they are having a great convention up on the sea-shore. I don't know what the out come will be this week, but I am looking for some pretty hot times., but perhaps they will get weakning, I don't look on the labor movement of this country with very much enthusiasm for the people, they have not the men at the helm, and to tell you the truth going over the country as I do, if a revolution started tomorrow I don't know where they would get a leader, and I think the capitalist have got that down fine. however, we have to keep on pounding and hammering away.

I don't know when I will get to Washington, tell Mr. Powderly to take caer of himself this hot weather.

With best wishes to every body in the house, I am fondly,

Yours,
Mother

[*Terence V. Powderly and Mother Mary Harris Jones Papers, Department of Archives and Manuscripts, Catholic University of America, Washington, D.C.*]

To Ryan Walker

Charleston, W. Va.
December 12, 1919.

Mr. Rine Walker,
C/o New York Call,

Fourth Avenue,
New York, N.Y.

My Dear old friend Rhyne:
I wanted to see you while I was in New York and have a long talk
with you about old times. The last time I was in Kansas city I stopped
off a day or so with Snyders at their hotel, most all the old warriors are
gone or dead, you can't meet scarcely any of the old force. Plamer is
dead, Page is dead, Putnam is out in California. I had a letter from him
a year ago, and from what I learn I don't think he is the happiest man
in the world. What faithful loyal workers those men were in their
days, then Wayland is gone and the element that is in and around
Kansas city today so far as the revolutionary is concerned don't
amount to a row of pins. It looked at one time that we were going to
make wonderful progress, but it lookes to me as if that time has passed. When Wayland passed away another element got a hold of the pier,
and it hasen't amounted to a row of pins since.[1] I don't read it anymore.
The only papers I read now are something that I get from Australia or
from England. How much I would like to have an hour or two with you
and talk things over. You know Ryne, I am going all over the country,
and I don't tak up much with the vulchers, that have lead the movement for their own pockets. They can go on with a lot of star sentamen-
tal oratory, but that have never touches the core of thw workers pains,
it gives them a little soothing syrup but if the[2]

*[Walker Mss., Manuscripts Department, Lilly Library,
Indiana University, Bloomington, Indiana.]*

Notes

1. Mother Jones is referring to the *Appeal to Reason*, founded in Girard,
Kansas in 1895 by Julius A. Wayland and edited by Wayland until he committed suicide in 1912. Around 1900, when the *Appeal* had a circulation of 30,000,
Wayland began organizing his "salesman-soldiers." By 1912 over 60,000 readers had joined the subscription army, and the *Appeal's* circulation mushroomed
to 750,000 — larger than any other weekly periodical published in the United
States at that time, including the *Saturday Evening Post*. One of its agents,
Louis Klamroth, bicycled all over the Midwest, and over the years, sold over
100,000 subscriptions.
2. The letter is incomplete. In a letter to the present writer, July 16, 1981,
Saundra Taylor, Curator of Manuscripts, The University Library, Indiana University, writes: "We do not know the location of the missing portion."

To John H. Walker

Los Angeles, Cal.
Mar. 9, 1920.

John H. Walker,
801 Commercial St.,
Danville, Ills.

Dear John:

I regretted not to have been in Chicago when you got there but I was all in and had to get away. You know I had three months of awful hard work in the Pittsburg and I gave out[1] and I had such a desire to see you, John, before I left for there were so many things I wanted to talk to you about.

I have found out in New York that John L. has $500. worth of stock in the Casy-Adams Magazine. That John P. has $500. more and God knows how many more of them had their hands in it.[2] It's so rotten, John, that one hardly knows where to begin on.

I don't know what that convention did in Chicago with all of you people.[3] I had very little hope in the R. R. men's striking and I so said to them in the office in Chicago because there's so strike in 'em, John.[4] There's a great deal of begging from the Masters but the Railroad men are not fighters and they never have been to my knowledge. They don't even lend a hand to other men on the fight and raely ever do you hear of them donating any sum to any of our great conflicts. However, John, we've got to keep on the fight.

They made some vicious atttacks on Foster and if you read the Machinist's Journal you'll find even the enemy within making this attack.[5] John, I want to tell you something, I don't look with that hope for the Labor Movement that I did three years ago. The workers of this country are the most backward for action than any body of workers in any country in the world. Even China is ahead of us to-day.

The Ways and Means Railroad men may strike, but I doubt it. The fellow who gets fourteen thousand a year and expenses, will hardly take any chances.

In my opinion it is a very great mistake to pay those high salaries but we have nothing to say about it — they will have to go.

I wish I could have seen you before I left but I shall go down to Springfield when I go back to Chicago and see you if you won't come up to Chicago.

I wouldn't have much to do with that political movement if I were you. Keep your hands out of it. I don't think, John, it will have the effect that the boys thought it would. However, let us hope for the best.

I leave for Frisco, tomorrow night so send my mail to Box 95. San Francisco, Cal. The mettal workers there are on a strike and they have a very ugly situation. They revolted here and went into One Big Union

— they got sore at their officials and of course they had to pull out when they could not overthrow them. Instead of claning house inside, they went outside and weakened their forces.

I shall hold till I see you. I have a good deal to talk to you about, John.

The boys here did not speak any too well of Jim Lord's and that fellow davis' settlement in the Oil Field. It's a very weak instrument as I read it. Of course I didn't say anything because I thought it best not to.

Take care of yourself. I suppose you go into office the first of the monath and if you can, come up if I telegraph for you.

Love and regards for all those at home —

Sincerely yours,
Mother Jones

[John Hunter Walker Collection, 1911-1953, Illinois Historical Survey, University of Illinois Library.]

Notes

1. The reference to three months in Pittsburgh is to Mother Jones's work during the great steel strike of 1919. *See* pp. 57, 303-15, 527, 628.

In his reply, John H. Walker wrote: " . . . Ed told me what I knew before hand, that you were pretty much all in and you had to have a rest and you were going there to try and have a little breathing spell.

"I take it from your letter however, with reference to that fight that is on with the Metal Workers, that you are doing exactly what I said you would do, no matter how tired and worn out you were, if there as a strike on you would be in the middle of it as long as you lived." [John H. Walker to Mother Jones, March 16, 1920, John Hunter Walker Collection, 1911-1953, Illinois Historical Survey, University of Illinois Library.]

2. Mother Jones is referring to John L. Lewis and John P. Mitchell. John H. Walker replied to this information: "I am not surprised about that information that they all have an interest in the newspaper that the coal operators furnish them money, from under the guise of paying for advertising, when in reality it is paying them for betraying the Miners' Union and the labor movement, that was T. L. Lewis' method, and they are all part of the same arrangement." (*Ibid.*)

3. John H. Walker's comment on this point reads: "I was not at that Chicago Labor Party convention the last day, and up to that time they had acted fairly sensible. On the last day however, they fixed it so that the labor movement could not support them, which means that they acted in such a manner that there can be no help come for the labor movement from political sources, for sometime. The enemies of labor are going to be in all the positions of government, legislative, judicial and executive." (*Ibid.*)

4. John H. Walker's comment on this point is quite interesting: "With refer-

ence to the railroad men not striking, I think it is only fair to say that the spectacle of the national officers of the Miners' Union, the biggest organization in the country, with the reputation of being the best fighters in the country, surrendering and bowing in abject submission, allowing the men to be driven back into the mines like cattle, without a fight at all, not only demoralized them, but has taken the heart out of the whole of the rest of the movement. It will be sometime before they will recover again.

"That same action was responsible for encouraging the other side to pass the Esch-Cummins bill and to embolden all the Injunction Judges in the country into breaking more strikes, and by more vicious injunctions than ever before.

"It is a tragedy to think that an organization with members of the make-up of ours, who would be willing to fight until they died rather than be put in that position, if they could help themselves, being deliberately used in that manner to destroy the liberties of all the people, it makes the decent Mine Workers who understand what it means, blush with shame and hang their heads, and I hope they may get an opportunity to redeem themselves sometime in the near future, with the right kind of leadership.

"If they knew what was done to them and who did it, it would be "God help that bunch of traitors! They would do a good job for them." (*Ibid.*)

Walker is discussing the action of John L. Lewis in calling off the coal strike of 1919. *See* p. 352.

5. William Z. Foster was attacked in the *Machinists' Journal* as a former Syndicalist, Bolshevik, whose radical ideology was the main factor in the defeat of the 1919 steel strike.

To John H. Walker

Charleston, W. Va.
April 27, 1920.

Mr. Jno. H. Walker,
Springfield, Ill.

Dear John:

It looks as if I am never going to see you again. I did not hear from you all of the time I was in California, and you know I get lonesome when I do not hear from you personally. You and Ed Nockles are the two I look to.

These are stirring times John, and I don't know what the outcome is going to be. I am not as well and strong as I was when I saw you last, but however, I am still able to go out. I had a terrific meeting last night down at Kanawha city,[1] it is so pathetic to see those wretches, they are the common laborers and there has never been very much done for them. I had to amuse them John, as well as educate them, because giving them the dry stuff, they did not understand as so many of those organizers, do, you could have not got any response from them. Those who preceded me in speaking told them about paying their dues, joining the union and then they are wise guys get $50.00 for it. John, these organizers ought to be trained before they are sent out, but they do really more harm than good.[2]

They have a terrible time of it out on the coast they have a ship yard strike and the medal workers and they have a railroad strike, from mail I get from there, and the whole country seems to be torn to pieces.

We have not got any statesmen today that understand how to handle the situation, and I don't know John whether the labor party will bring the results the they boys hope for. I would give a great deal to see you and hope to be able to reach you some time in the near future. I expect to go up to Washington tomorrow or next day. Even Lord I don't hear from him any more.

I hope your wife and little one is alright and you try and get up a meeting there somewhere so I can go and address it and then have a long talk with you. I don't want to go to Chicago to expressly to meet you, I don't want to spend the money for that purpose.

I am not feeling as well John as I used to,[3] and I won't be able to do the work I have been. I hope you are going to have a successful year in your administration and that things will come out victorious for the workers.

Write to me when you get a chance, I am always devotedly yours,

Mother Jones

[John Hunter Walker Collection, 1911-1953, Illinois Historical Survey, University of Illinois Library.]

Notes

1. For Jones's work in West Virginia during this period, *see* pp. 54, 56, 156-222.

2. John H. Walker's comment on this read: "I can understand your situation in Kanawha, — that is about the same situation everywhere. If the organizers were only honest they would develop the knowledge and experience to do the job properly, but under the present administration in our union, I doubt very much that they would want an honest organizer or that they would permit one to work for them any length of time, if they felt safe to discharge them. It seems to be a worse situation now than it ever was." (John H. Walker to Mother Jones, May 4, 1920, John Hunter Walker Collection, 1911-1953, Illinois Historical Survey, University of Illinois Library.)

3. John H. Walker commented: "Nockels was showing me a telegram from Schmidty's sister in which she said that you were, while perhaps not as strong or rugged physically as you had been, still in pretty good health, I was pretty glad to hear of it." (*Ibid.*)

To John H. Walker

Charleston, W. Va.
June 18, 1920.

Mr. Jno. H. Walker,
120 So. 6th Street,
Springfield, Ill.

Dear John:

Every time I have gone in and around Chicago I have tried to see if I could get a line on you, but it is uterly impossible to do so, but when I was going to Southern Illinois to speak with you, I took sick on the train going into Washington, but was unable to keep my engagement, which I very much regretted.

I wish you would get one of those fellows to bill a meeting there some where, so I can get a chance to see you, sometime in July. I sold three hundred of the New Majority,[1] in the meetings I held in Illinois, but I got thirty dollars for them to help them out there is a great deal could be done John in that direction, if there was a system, but when we hold meetings and leave nothing with them to think about afterwards, it is almost useless work. You know the journals of today are not educational, I mean the Labor Journals. But the new Majority is a pretty good paper, in fact it is about the best one I know of, there is many things I want to discuss with you that I cannot write to you about.

I hope you are going to settle down in Springfield,[2] you know it is too much of a strain to be going in home in a hurry and in coming away in a hurry, you have no home life if you got no time with your family, and you are one of the fellows that are out most of the time. We having some hot times over in West Virginia, politically and industrially, I don't know what the future is going to be the laws that are made in the last four or five years in Washington have been sucidal to the labor movement, even tho their head-quarters of labor is there.

There is something wrong John somewhere, and I am afraid that Labor is going to pay the penalty dear and let me tell you that the labor organizations are up against all over this country. There is nothing in Utaugh ther is nothing in Mexico and the few they have in the northern coal field and in the western don't amount to much, ther is a terrible dissatisfaction there, they boys have time and again to come to me and beg me to come out there and stay with them, I was down in Louisville the first of April and O, My God! It was sad to hear those men complain about those National organizers, they said they were going to have a Policy meeting in Louisville and they were going to telegraph to attend it, you know John I could not do much if I did go, and it was useless to spend the money on railroads and there is so much to be done here and the poor devils need every penny of it, and the poor boys have a burden on their sholder here they are almost broke down and the fellows that come in from the National and there is only one here that can be relied on that is Old Batley.

The boys in Frisco were awfully good to me, I went out to St. Quinton to see Schmitty and the MacNamara,[3] the warden told me that is the Deputy Warden, that they had eighteen hundred and fifty-four prisons in that one prison along, and he said to me Mother Jones, do you see that door, every man that has gone in that door, and that is closed behind them in the last year has been a young man under thirty, some years under thirty. What an endicement John against us, there is something wrong in the whole social struggle.

We have 120,000 legal hold ups that is lawyers, and 132,000 men and women in behind the bars in the penetintery not speaking of the local jails, there is a terrible endicemtnt against our churchs and a terrible endicemtnt against the Rockefellers church fund. I get terribly discouraged at times but then again I feel the fight must go, and I can't give it up John, as long as I am able to go. I am not as well or as strong as I used to be, but I have just as great a desire to keep on fighting, and you must arrange a meetins soon so that I can see you. These poor officials here have all they can carry on their shoulders.

Take care of yourself and don't be carried away with that weakness of yours, doing a special favor for every fellow that want to work on your favor. The favor must be done for the million women and children and not for the individual. I don't care particular for Carbine billing meeting for me, I want to talk to you about it when I see you.

Well you give my love to the little ones at home and tell them some day I am coming down to visit, them, with best wishes and take care of your self for you are the one lone human being that I want to cling to until death. We have known and worked together John many long years in this desparate battle, and I hope to be near you somewhere when the last hour comes.

With best wishes and loyal devotion to you, I am,

yours sincerely,
Mother Jones

[John Hunter Walker Collection, 1911-1953, Illinois Historical Survey, University of Illinois Library.]

Notes

1. *New Majority* was the organ of the Chicago Federation of Labor and the most progressive labor paper in the country. It was extremely disliked by Samuel Gompers and other top A.F. of L. leaders. John Fitzpatrick played an important role in the founding and operation of the paper.

2. "We are moving from Danvile to Springfield," John H. Walker had written in his letter of May 4, 1920. In his reply to this letter, he wrote: "We moved

to Springfield but are living in a rented upstairs in a rather cramped condition. We expect however to get a place to ourselves as soon as possible and I think I will be settled for sometime. When we do have a place, I hope that you can make up your mind to come and stay with us." (John H. Walker to Mother Jones, June 25, 1920, John Hunter Walker Collection, 1911-1953, Illinois Historical Survey, University of Illinois Library.)

3. Matthew Schmidt and J. B. and J. J. McNamara were imprisoned at San Quentin prison.

To John H. Walker

Box 1332
Charleston, W. Va.
July 21, 1920.

Mr. John. H. Walker,
120 So. 6th St,
Springfield, Ill.

Dear John:

I was sadly dissapointed in Westville, for not meeting you. I thought surely you would show up at that meeting. I wanted to see you so much, there were so many things I wanted to talk to you about. You left Chicago the night that I got in, I got in on Thursday night.[1] What a geathering you had there of high-brows and know it all, who had no more conception of this death struggle that we are in than a lot of school children, I saw them geathered around of that Hotel lobby, I don't know John, I got all disgusted when I saw that geathering of high-brows, intelectual no-nothings.[2]

We are coming to a crisis anyhow, I see the railroad men are up against it. After waiting for sixteen months, they have got nothing hardly.[3] I am sick and tired of your meators, your whole system is eating up the vitals of the people, never in human history, will be pass through anything so treaterous as we are going through now.

I suppose the change will come and propably come faster than we realize, I would have given a great deal to see you John, because there are only a few of us that stand close together. I am going to Missourra for Labor day and if possible I'll go away a week ahead so as to see you on my way.

[John Hunter Walker Collection, 1911-1953, Illinois Historical Survey, University of Illinois Library.]

Notes

1. A national nominating convention of the American Labor Party met in Chicago on July 11, 1920. There were 500 delegates present, two-thirds of them from Illinois and Indiana. Max Hayes, an old trade union Socialist, was the national chairman, and John Fitzpatrick and John H. Walker, the former representing the Chicago Federation of Labor of which he was president and the latter the Illinois Federation of Labor, of which he was president, were the leaders. The Party was renamed the Farmer-Labor Party, and Parley Christensen of Utah and Max Hayes were nominated as presidential and vice-presidential candidates respectively,

2. John H. Walker replied: "There were a lot of the kind of people that you mention at that meeting in Chicago, — high-brow, intellectual know-nothings. Most of them were disappointed at its outcome. A considerable number of them have gone where they belong, over to the Republican-Democratic parties. It is a very difficult situation in our organization, the intricacies of the machinery within the movement which the big corporations have set up through which they can perpetuate their paid hirelings in high official positions of dominating power, by having them resign. When they get discredited, one of their puppets go into higher position through law or the constitution, or their puppets go into higher position through law or the constitution, from Vice to President; then have another one of the puppets appointed in their place, which enables them to use all of the powers, influences and machinery of the organization to do whatever they please.

"They corrupt and steal elections, and where they are not successful by that process they baldly trample the law under food and set the elections aside; they make agreements binding the membership without consulting the membership, in opposition to the membership's wishes, and then use the machinery of the organization and all of the power and influence of the corporations and political organizations that they are serving, added to the strength of the union to crucify anybody, member or officer that protests." [John H. Walker to Mother Jones, August 4, 1920, John Hunter Walker Collection, 1911-1953, Illinois Historical Survey, University of Illinois Library.] Walker himself was crucified for opposing John L. Lewis and his policies, which, in fact, the letter fairly well summarizes.

3. The Transportation Act of 1920 returned the railroads to their private owners and set up the Railroad Labor Board of nine members, three representing management, three the public, and three labor. The Board rendered a quick decision on wages on July 20, 1920, which granted a wage increase but not as great as the railroad workers had hoped to receive. The shop workers were granted a wage increase of 13 cents per hour.

To John H. Walker

Box 1332,
Charleston, W. Va.
Aug 17, 1920.

Mr. John. H. Walker, Pres,
State Federation of Labor,
E. & W. Bldg, 120 S. 6th St,
Springfield, Ill.

Dear John:

I received your letter yesterday, I was glad to hear from you. I send back check to you that you sent me, you had better hold it and take care of it, if I have it, it won't last two weeks until it is gone.[1]

I will be going to Missouri in a week or ten days, and I will then stop off at Springfield and see you, and have a talk with you. Things are pretty lively over here, we are doing business. I had a meeting at Princeton, West Va., yesterday the first labor meeting ever held there. It was only five miles from Bluefield, the head-quarters of the Baldwin Thugs. I must have had six or seven thousand people, there were seven wagon-loads of Baldwin Thugs at the meeting, but John, I licked Hell out of the whole crowd. I put a new life and a new spirit into the wretches, certainly it was taking my life in my hands, because I had to come back thirty-two miles, over rough lonely roads along the mountains, with only one man and he was a lawyer, and the Schaufer with me, everyone was afraid they would follow me and murder me, but we bluffed them and took the wrong road. It was near eleven o'clock when I got into Hinton, but after I crossed the river, I felt safe. I got into Charleston at four o'clock in the morning, had no sleep for twenty-eight hours. I had to go thirty-four miles over that rough road and back the same and then speak for one hour and a half to that tremenduous audence, but John, I sowed the seed anyhow, the voice of labor should not be raised there before, it was just as bad as homestead, but anybode else would have got killed.

Give my love to them all at home, I will let you know when I start for Springfield so you will be in town.

Sincerely yours,
Mother

[John Hunter Walker Collection, 1911-1953, Illinois Historical Survey,
University of Illinois Library.]

Notes

1. In his letter, John H. Walker wrote: "I am enclosing check for three

hundred dollars ($300.00). Sometime ago I needed this money very badly and took advantage of that occasion and took the matter up with Jim Lord of having him return that three hundred dollars if he could spare it at that time. He did so.

"I am able to get along without it now and am sending it to you, as I thought the other two hundred at any time, just drop me a note and I will see to it that you get it." [John H. Walker to Mother Jones, August 13, 1920, John Hunter Walker Collection, 1911-1953, Illinois Historical Survey, University of Illinois Library.]

To Theodore Debs

Box 1332.
Charleston, W. Va.
Aug 18, 1920.

Mr. Theodore Debs,
Terre Haute, Ind.

My dear Theodore:

I received your letter of the 16th. this morning. I must say that I was more than glad to hear from you. I have been thinking of you for several days, and I am going west in a few days and will stop off at Terre Haute and have talk with you about some things.

Poor Gene, he works on my nerves everytime that I turn my thoughts to Atlanta,[1] and I cannot conceive how they could keep a kindly soul like him locked up, he woulden't harm a little kitten.

I am worried to death sometime about a number of people that are going to jail and how cold blooded they are getting.[2] I will telegraph to you as soon as I arrange to go to Terre Haute, so you can met me.

With love to Mrs. Debs and your beautiful sweet girl, I remain,

Very sincerely yours,
Mother Jones

[Eugene V. Debs Papers, Indiana State University Library, Indiana State University, Terre Haute, Indiana.]

Notes

1. Indicted, tried, and convicted for violating the Espionage Act in opposing American entrance into World War I, Eugene V. Debs was first imprisoned in Moundsville prison in West Virginia, and then two months later in June 1919

was transferred to the Federal prison in Atlanta, Georgia. He remained in prison until he was pardoned by President Warren G. Harding on Christmas Day 1921.

2. Mother Jones is referring to the large number of I.W.W. leaders and members and antiwar Socialists in federal and state prisons, usually imprisoned for violating the Espionage Act or state Criminal Syndicalist laws.

To Ryan Walker

Charleston, W. Va.
Sept 21, 1920.

Mr. Rhyne Walker
New York Call,
New York City, N.Y.

My dear Ryan:

I received your letter sometime ago, owing to the pressure of work, I was unable to reply to it. I would have been glad to wrote you a few lines for Labor day, but the pressure was so hard, I could not find the time.

I see you are up against it in New York. The papers say that they are going to turn down the men that were elected by the people to the State Legislature.[1] If they can do away with those things, then farewell to Liberty in America, there is very little of it left anyhow.

I was in Kansis City on the 13th of this month I went up to see the Snyders, most all the old timers have gone from there, they are very few of them left, that is of the old warriours, one of the Snyders died in Oklahoma, very suddenly and the other brother is attending to their business in Kansis city, they are just as true and loyal as they ever were; but the movement there is practically dead. It is only a reminent of the old timers, are keeping it going and they are all going over to the Labor parrty.

Well there are stormy times anyhow, it is hard to tell what the future will bring forth. It looks as if that old spirit is dead in the people. They have no more street meetings in Kansis city, and I don't know that it will ever be reserected or not.

You know Ryan there were a great many sentementalist that got into our movement, and they are perretical educators, others got in and used it for what they gould get out of it for their pockets, and the wretch below had to bear the burden.

We have a terrific fight in the southern end of the state. I don't pay very much attention to the political phase of it. I know the future battle of it is is going to be in the field of industry, and this fellow has got to be educated to his power. University Profesors and the power orators have no grasp of this thing. A great many are using it for themselves.

I hope Mrs. Walker is well I don't know when I will get to New York. I have not been really well for the last two months, but perhaps some day I will try and see you

Give Mrs. Walker my best wishes, and tell her I hope to see her if I do get to New York.

You must come up and see me and spend an Hour with me I want to talk over old times with you. Write to me sometime and send me the Call, we don't get it here nowhere on the stand.

With best wishes to you and Mrs. Walker, I am,

Sincerely yours,
Mother Jones

[Walker, Mss., Manuscripts Department, Lilly Library, Indiana University, Bloomington, Indiana.]

Notes

1. Mother Jones was correct. Although elected to the state legislature, the Socialists were prevented from taking their seats. Those already in the legislature were expelled. It was part of the postwar Red Scare.

To Terence V. Powderly

Charleston, W. Va.
Dec 14, 1920.

Mr. T. V. Powderly,
Department of Labor,
Washington, D.C.

My dear Mr. Powderly:

The bearer of this letter, Mr. Fred Mooney,[1] Secretary-Treasurer of the United Mine Workers, District No. 17, I consider it quiet an honor and pleasure to be able to entroduce him to you, an vouch for his manhood.

Any favor that you can do for him, will be deeply appreciated. Try and get his pass-port, give him any service you can, and that service will be well rendered.

I don't know just exactly when I will leave for Mexico.[2] I'm feeling better that I have been for several days.

With deep appreciation, I remain,

Sincerely yours,
Mother Jones

[Archives & Manuscripts Section, West Virginia Collection, West Virginia Library.]

Notes

1. For Fred Mooney's work with Mother Jones, *see* pp. 42-43, 59, 156-57.
2. For Mother Jones's return to Mexico, *see* pp. 647-53.

To John H. Walker

Charleston, W. Va.
Dec 28, 1920.

Mr. John H. Walker, Pres,
The Illinois State Federation of Labor,
E. &. W. Bldg, 120 So 6th St,
Springfield, Ill.

Dear John:

I am dropping you a line or two. I haven't been well since I saw you, and I leave for Mexico city the first of the week with Secretary Mooney.[1] Perhaps the change of climate will be a benefit to me. You know there is so many of those revolutionist that I saved from being extradicted during the Deistz administration that are now a part of the Mexican government and they want me to come down there, so I am going to leave the first of the week.

I would like very much to see you before I go away but I cannot go by way of Chicago. I see they have won out out again in Indianapolis. Searles telegraphed the associated Press in Washington that they have won over whelimngly.[2]

I am not going to write much John.

With best wishes for a Happy New Year, and love to all at home, I am

Most sincerely yours,
Mother

E A Adams who is a member of Whites He told Hquiby that you won by 20,000. Votes over White Said he was Whites Manager. Safe organization when sick rotten Practices are resorted to and then boast about it

[John Hunter Walker Collection, 1911-1953, Illinois Historical Survey, University of Illinois Library.]

Notes

1. Mother Jones left Charleston, West Virginia on January 4, 1921, having been invited by Mexican President Alvaro Obregón to attend the third Congress of the Pan-American Federation of Labor in Mexico City. She was accompanied by F. Mooney, UMW Dist. 17 secretary-treasurer. *See* pp. 42-43, 327, 328.

2. Edward Searles was the editor of the *United Mine Workers' Journal*, having been handpicked for the post by John L. Lewis, and when Lewis ran for UMW president, Searles denied any space to his rivals. In commenting on Searles, John H. Walker wrote an indictment of the operation of the UMW under Lewis's leadership which is hair-raising:

"It is the most sordid narrative of robbery and betrayal of human beings that worked for a living, men, women and children, — injured men and the dead men and their widows and orphans that I have ever known anything about, and this is no hearsay Mother, you can go to Panama and get the sworn statements involving him and his family.

"Four of them were compelled to put back about a thousand dollars that they were caught with the goods on them so strong and conclusive that there was no escape for them, and that they were not entitled to. John Lewis' bosom friend and closest political associate and campaign manager William MacDonnell was proven as having been on the pay-roll of the company getting fifty dollars a month for betraying men who were injured in the mines, when their cases were settled under the law, at the same time he was posing as their representative and as an official of the local union.

"He also did the same thing for the widows and orphans. Collusion was also clearly obvious between them and the mine management, the management refusing to hire any one who opposed the gang and discharging any one opposing the gangsters in the Local Union who were robbing and looting the treasury and betraying the membership, injured men, widows and orphans. On the other hand the gang let the management refuse to hire anybody that he did not want to hire, and to discharge anybody for any or no reason at all, that he did not want to work there.

"They threatened and intimidated and beat up a number of men that opposed them in their machinations and more than one man was found dead the next morning who was seen in their company the night before, usually robbed. One man who confessed, had been forced into accepting the money and becoming one of them, because of his concen for his wife and nine children (he was the

644

only bread-winner and he did not have any money to leave town and he did not want to get beat up) he later was made Sub-District Secretary, but it preyed on his conscience so that he confessed, gave up his office as Sub-District Secretary-Treasurer and blasted his standing with the membership for life, rather than continue to be a party to it.

"It is horrible to think that such men get in powerful positions in the labor movement. The last year that John Lewis was one man committee man at this mine, there was over $81,000 checked off those men for local expenses. After this rottenness was exposed and the membership rose in arms John Lewis as International Vice-President, sent a National Organizer from the Anthracite fields at the expense of the International Organization for wages, hotel, railroad and other expenses, whose purpose (stated by himself under oath) was to electioneer, — to keep these traitors and thieves in office, and prevent the membership from putting them out.

"It is too horrible to describe or even contemplate. I sincerely hope that everybody who loves humanity and the movement, will take a chance on doing everything they can to clean this rottenness out of our union and to put clean, honest men in the official positions again. It is not only a cancer eating the heart out of our organization, but it is corrupting and diseasing and be-foulling the whole labor movement of our country, and spreading that same rotten influence over the whole world to the injury and disgrace of the whole human race and to the detriment of not only our generation, but future generations everywhere on earth.

"I hope you have a pleasant trip and that it benefits your health. I know it will give you a good deal of satisfaction to see those men again that you helped save their lives who are now working and fighting in the interest of humanity. The Lord keep you and spare you to humanity for many more years."
(John H. Walker to Mother Jones, December 21, 1920, John Hunter Walker Collection, 1911-1953, Illinois Historical Survey, University of Illinois Library.)

To John H. Walker

Box 1332,
Charleston, W. Va.
March 22, 1921.

Mr. John H. Walker, Pres,
State Federation of Labor,
Springfield, Ill.

Dear John:

I have been wanting to write to you for sometime, but I have been held up, I have not been very well. I got a letter from Ester sometime ago, and do you know for two or three days, I could not locate who it was, and all at once it dawned on me, I did not dream of her being in Indiana at school, but I wrote to her yesterday to let her know that I did not forget her. She is a very beautiful girl, that is she was a very beautiful child and no doubt raised by the mother that she had, she coulden't be anything else but a real democratic woman.

I am not well, John, but I am going west soon in sight of a couple of weeks and I want to stay a week with you down in Springfield, before I go to San Antonio, Texas, on my way to Mexico.[1] The boys won the fight here in Mingo,[2] they came out victorious yesterday, but it is an outrage to see the way of the courts of capitalism do business, and how they spend the Tax-payers money to carry on capitalist rot. I want to stay with you a few days; there is so much today to talk over about Mexico and other things that we don't have any time meeting each other and going away

Lord and Wallace will be here tomorrow night, to talk on the Kansas Court Law.[3] I don't think either one of these fellows can handle that question as it ought to be handled just now, owing to the fact that the Legislature is in session here, and no doubt they will attend the court to hear that lecture. You know it takes more powerful men than either one of those, with a deep personality to impress the people of today. Johnson was to come, but I don't know he left out. I see that Hearst is getting after Gompers, or rather Gompers is getting after Hearst. I think it was rather a mistake, John, for Gompers to open up the battle with Hearst, you know there isen't a more powerful newspaper man in the country than Hearst is, and Gompers can't hold his own within.[4]

Well, I read an article of Howat yesterday in one of the local papers and it was a very good explanation, he is a remarkable man he stood the fire for years, and it has not been all of the open enemy, a good deal came within the ranks of those who should have stood by him at all times and all hours. However, you know John, we have a whole lot of people in office that have a much deeper desire for the odor coming from the flesh-pot of capitalism than they have for their children desteny of the future of the nation. The labor movement will never be wrecked from out side, John, the wrecking force will be from within.

I have not had anytime to talk with you, but I am going down to tell Mrs. Walker that I want to stay four or five days with her, as I want to rest up. With best wishes, to you and all of yours, I am

Sincerely yours,
Mother

[John Hunter Walker Collection, 1911-1953, Illinois Historical Survey, University of Illinois Library.]

Notes

1. Mother Jones returned for a second visit to Mexico after the Pan-American Federation of Labor's Congress. Roberto Haberman, who represented Mexico's labor organization in the federation, wrote to her from Mexico City: "This is Good Friday, I think. It is good because of the fact that I am sure of conversing with you, and because I know that soon you will be with us again. . . .

"Have written a letter to Jim Lord trying to trace the five hundred dollars that (General) Villarreal sent you. You write to him too. It surely is funny that you did not get this money yet. Will also try to trace it through the banks.

"We are all expecting you down within a few weeks. Gen. Villarreal has a house ready for you, and a prettier place cannot be imagined. Also servants and an automobile. The only bad thing about all this is that you will have my wife and I hanging about your place in our spare time. I am going to try to get the General to furnish you with some Felt hounds to keep us off . . .

"Then don't forget that Felipe Carrillo expects you to be down in Yucatan for the Socialist Convention the second week in May. He does not think that he can be Governor unless you are down here.

"Our work is going on splendidly. Morones is sure a great labor leader. The so-called 'Communists' are as damnable a lot of whelps as they were when you were down here, but they do not amount to anything, and we don't pay any attention to them, anymore than does any worker. . . ." (Roberto Haberman to Mother Jones, copy of undated letter, sent from Apartado 1855, Mexico, D.F., Mother Mary Harris Jones Papers, Department of Archives and Manuscripts, Catholic University of America, Washington, D.C.)

Luis N. Morones led the conservative workers in Mexico in forming the Regional Confederation of Mexican Workers (CROM). Gompers established contact with Morones, who became the A.F. of L. contact in Mexico, cooperating with the Federation's leadership in advancing the aims and goals of the Pan-American Federation of Labor. (Sinclair Snow, "The Pan-American Federation of Labor," unpublished Ph.D. thesis, University of Virginia, 1960, pp. 56-67.) It is doubtful that Mother Jones realized that she was being used to advance the cause of conservative forces in Mexico's labor movement.

2. The reference is to the court case involving miners in Mingo, West Virginia. *See* pp. 330-32, 666-67.

3. The law referred to was a compulsory arbitration law enacted in 1920. It featured an Industrial Relations Court, appointed by the governor, which would settle labor disputes in certain industries and thus avoid strikes.

4. William Randolph Hearst (1863-1951) was using his far-flung newspaper empire to advocate the open-shop and attack Gompers as un-American.

To John H. Walker

Charleston, W. Va.
April 5, 1921.

Mr. John H. Walker, Pres,
State Federation of Labor,
Springfield, Ill.

Dear John:

I have just come down from Washington, I will be with you next Sunday. I have a good deal to talk to you about on the future of the labor movement. I think that there is a good deal that you ought to know. I have not been well John, since I came back from Mexico, I have had rheumatism so much, and it is kind of playing on me. I will stay two or three days with Mrs. Walker on my way to Mexico city. I'll explain matters to you when I get there.

Things does not look very bright to me John, you know every where they are passing bills to crush labor,[1] and it seems that the thing has been staged for a long time what they were going to do, I won't say much in this letter, but will talk it over with you when I see you.

I leave Thursday night sometime, and will leave Chicago Sunday morning, I will get Ed Nockles to telephone to you on Saturday. I had a letter from Ester and do you know John, it was a whole week before I could think who sent me that letter from the College, and all at once I woke up one night and it just dawned on me that it was Ester, so I wrote her a letter to let her know that I received her She is a very beautiful girl and I hope she will live to be a duplicate of her mother.

With best wishes for you and your home, I am,

Sincerely yours
Mother J

[John Hunter Walker Collection, 1911-1953, Illinois Historical Survey, University of Illinois Library.]

Notes

1. This was written in response to a comment by John H. Walker in a letter to Mother Jones: "We are having a desperate battle here. There are four bills in here that the enemies of labor are pushing strongly . Either one of them if enacted into law will do away with the present open form of trade unions in our state and compel us to go back to the meetings after midnight and try to work without being known, and there is too grave a danger of their being passed to suit me. However, we have a fighting chance to defeat them, and we are strongly hopeful of defeating them." (John H. Walker to Mother Jones, March 24, 1921, John Hunter Walker Collection, 1911-1953, Illinois Historical Survey, University of Illinois Library.) On June 6, 1921, Walker added: "We have

been able to prevent the enactment of proposed laws that were inimical to us. I think we have them all killed, but we cannot be sure until they have adjourned." (*Ibid.*)

To John Fitzpatrick

Mexico City,
May 16, 1921.

Mr. John Fitzpatrick,
President of the Chicago Federation of Labor
Ed Knockles,
Secretary of the Chicago Federation of Labor

My Dear friends:

Your very beautiful telegram of May the first reached me on May second. I don't know of anything I received in years that so deeply affected me for the time being. I hope you do not think or have the impression that I was unappreciative for your humane consideration of me in a far off city. I have no words to convey to you and your associates in the great struggle for justice the deep appreciation that I feel.

My reason for not acknowledging your message at once was that I was not well, but I am just beginning to get back my old fighting qualities. On the day your message arived, I was down in Orizaba, a strictly manufacturing town. I addressed a large meeting there with several diputados, or congressmen also. It was the most remarkable meeting I addressed in years; the spirit was so marvellously fine. The town was thoroughly organized and the spirit they possessed was an inspiration. One got new hope for the future. They had a union band with the finest music I ever heard in a labor display. The building was a municipal building, very large, tendered by the public officials to the Labor movement. There was no uniformed police there, either at the entrance or inside of the building. This was something marvellously new to me, because with us in the United States, in the great American Republic, you know the outside and the inside would have been multiplied by the uniformed representatives of the high class burglars. The meeting continued until nearly twelve o'clock. Not one human soul left the hall. All were deeply interested to my surprise, a flag representing the murder of the so-called anarchists in Chicago of '86 came marching in side by side with the national banner.[1] Everyone of you would have been put in jail for the next ten years if that occurred in Chicago. The congressmen, most all of them, referred to it in their speeches, the briute [tribute] paid to that baner as it entered that hall was the most remarkable demonstration I had witnessed in all my years in the industrial conflict. The next morning as the train pulled in and stopped on its way to Mexico City, the workers came out of the shop and jumped on the train and no one could keep them off. They came in and urged me to to come back again. I promised them to do so and fell just in fine spirit now to return to them.

After all one's life is not in vain when they witness the beautiful conception of industrial freedom that is taking the possession of the souls of the workers. Here they are making wonderful progress and they are not bothered with a lot of police and capitalist henchmen. But we have good many so-called Comminist freaks here that want to rule and dictate.[2] God help the day that those fanatics should ever get to the helm, we'd be worse off than we were under the rule of Wilson. The workers went up to the Camara of Diputados last Friday, May 13; walked into the Congressional Hall, planted the Red flag and notified the Congressmen that they were not getting a square deal from thier representatives and told them it act for the interest and honor of the Nation and the future destinies of the children yet to come. Of course the kept-press howled a little. There was no violence, nothing rough or loud — it was simply a practical and logical demand of their representatives. They returned in peace. If such a thing had happened in Washington, all the machine guns within a hundred miles would be called in and turned on them. They are making marvellous progress here in the Labor movement. If they only keep their heads level for the next few years, they will give an example to the world of what can be acquired in a peaceful manner instead of by force.

I expect to go to Yucatan inside of a week. The only one danger that there is here to interfere with their progress is that religious issue. If that can be kept out of the Labor movement, there will be marvellous progress made here.

Give my best wishes to Olander and Knockles. When you see Walker tell him I shall write to him soon.

They are going to have a Labor Convention here on the first of July. I am going to stay over for that. One of those refugees that I got out of jail during the Diaz administration called to see me and told me that the Mexican govenment would extend all the hospitality to me while I was in Mexico, and they would spare nothing to make my stay here pleasant.

I hope that things will go along smoothly. This awful unemployment question I am afraid will bring on trouble in the United States.[3] It looks as if the greed for money and power developed during the war, and they want to continue the game, but then the labor movement did not take advantage of the opportunity that they had.

Well you will hear from me again soon, and give my deep appreciation to all the delegates. Tell them the future is ours if they only stand

like men to-gether.
     With best wishes, I am

                                        Sincerely yours,
                                        Mother Jones

     *[John Hunter Walker Collection, 1911-1953, Illinois Historical Survey,
                            University of Illinois Library.]*

Notes

     1. The reference is to the Haymarket Affair resulting from the explosion of a
dynamite bomb in the midst of a squadron of police attempting to disperse a
peaceful labor meeting in Chicago, on May 4, 1886. Seven police were killed
and some sixty were wounded. During a wave of hysteria, eight men, all
anarchists and alleged anarchists, were arrested and placed on trial. Though
no evidence proved their connection with the actual bomb-throwing, they were
tried for their opinions only and condemned to death. Four were hanged on
November 11, 1887, one committed suicide in prison (or was murdered by the
prison guards), one was sentenced to 15 years imprisonment, and two had their
sentence commuted to life imprisonment. In 1893 the men in prison were pardoned by progressive Illinois governor John Peter Altgeld, who charged that
the Haymarket martyrs had been innocent and railroaded to their death because of their views and their activity in the eight-hour movement. Altgeld
earned the praise of American workers but the hatred of the established and
wealthy groups in the nation. In Mexico the Haymarket Affair is well-known
and the Haymarket or Chicago martyrs highly honored.
     2. Mother Jones appears to have been greatly influenced by the conservative
labor groups in Mexico associated with the Pan-American Federation of Labor.
     3. The Post-War Depression was intense by 1921 with widespread un-
employment. By mid-1923 the depression was over.

To John H. Walker

                                        Mexico City,
                                        May 27, 1921.

MR. John H. Walker,
Pres, of the State Federation of Labor,
Springfield, Illinois.

Dear John:
     I have been trying to write you ever since I came down here, but I
have not been very well. I wrote to Mooney[1] but the loafer has never

given me an answer yet. He sent me a copy of the Federationist. I saw where you received an invitation to address the convention in Huntington and I was glad indeed to know you were one of the crowd. I saw that Riley got elected President and he is by far the best to have that job. I was afraid one of the political crooks would get in.

Weve had some stormy times since I've been here. You know they have an element of so-called revolutionists here that are doing their best to destroy the labor movement. No they are not well on their feet yet here. They don't understand the danger they are up against with those fellows. You know as well as I do the enemy gets his tools inside our ranks and once they get their poison in it is not easy to apply the chemical to undue it. There is another phase, John that the heads of the Labor movement of Mexico do not understand the background and treachery of the common enemy. They have got good men, but you know here they have gone through a twelve yrs. turmoil, torn to pieces with scarsely no organization and no education on the industrial field. They had just entered the kindergarten when this political, this communist and religious question began to be injected into them. They got to fighting each other and you know John those freaks that see the light breaking out of heaven for their interest are the most dangerous sewer-rats we can get. They imagine God Almighty never gave any brains to anyone but them and they are going to solve the whole problem with the sole of their shoes. And even the fellows working for Jesus take a hand in the game. Last Sunday in Morelia the sky-pilot delivered a sermon after Mass and aroused the peoples' passions against the Reds in the Labor movement until the whole congreation went out, men and women and stoned the building where the socialist paper was published. That was Christ's philosophy filled up with capitalist swill. I wonder what Jesus will do to that dam pirate when he gets his claws on him — I want to be round. Unfortunately John, these poor fellows here have been crushed for centuries and they are just emerging from that oppression. It seems so sad that they should be interfered with, but such runs the stream of the vicious philosophy of the capitalist vultures.

Well I see that Brofy is coming to the front in District 2 of Penn. I wish we had more like Howwatt[2] I am going to write to him to-day. I shall see you on my way back John and tell you all and you tell that brick maker that brought that bottle of tonic when I was in Springfield that I've been praying for him ever since, If I dared to risk it I would bring him some tonic from here. Well I have a lot to tell you Jack but I am kind of tired. I am not well. I think the altitude is too high. I hope that Esther and Mrs. Walker are well. Had a good time in San Antonio. I met some of my old friends and they left nothing undoe to make it pleasant for me. But John there is no life in the movement there and the organizers and officials have no life in them. They can't stir the animal up. They are of the conservative dog type and I don't consider such people worth wasting time with. I see they are after Tobin. What in hell do those fellows know John about the great struggle. I never hac any use for him since he took that job away from that old man in Bloomington. They have lost out in Alabama entirely and I'm afraid they are going to loose out in Mingo because they haven't had the man to handle that strike at the beginning. There is an unfortunate in the Labor movement and some of the officials to-day. They like to have a slate and they think more of "my individual friend" that they do of the destinies of thousands of men, women and children.

Well I'm going to close until I find something to send you. I have a whole lot but I can't write it. Give my love to Mrs. Walker. I hope her mother is better. Try and keep your health for you will be needed in the near future.

Sincerely,
Mother Jones

[John Hunter Walker Collection, 1911-1953, Illinois Historical Survey, University of Illinois Library.]

Notes

1. Fred Mooney, UMW District 17 secretary-treasurer.
2. Alexander Howatt. Mother Jones expressed the same wish in a speech to the 1922 UMW convention. *See* pp. 348-59.

To John H. Walker

Mexico City,
June 21, 1921.

Mr. John Walker,
Pres. of the State Federation of Illinois,
Springfield, Ill.

Dear John:

I shall inclose the letter you received from the World To-morrow in a few days. I have already given a copy of it to one of the Cabinet officers. I regret very much that you were unable to attend the convention in Denver. It would have given you a chance to get next to things from the opening of the convention, because you know we never get the same grasp of any subject by merely being told of it or reading.

I see you have defeated the Hessian law, the constabulary.[1] If you didn't do anything else for the workers in Illinois, that of itself was a marvelous victory. Although Pennsylvania is the greatest industrial state in the Union, that law was passed in 1903 just after the anthracite strike and working men from Pittsburg went down and lobbied for it, and you will agree with me that in all those years they have not won a strike of any importance. They've got it in West Virginia and they have had nothing but war ever since the bill passed. But I couldn'd convince Keeney[2] at the time that if they didn't take pretty drastic steps, they'd pull that law over. But these men don't seem to have a grasp of the methods that the Capitalists use to enslave their class.

I have not been well John since I came here. I have not seen a well day in the two months that I have been here. I am leaving next Friday night for the East and I'll have to stop off at San Antonio on a mission — also at Denver. Then I shall go right on to Chicago and I want you to try and meet me there.

Those fellows are having a hard fight in West Virginia, but to some extent it is somewhat their own fault. Have not had a line from Lord since I left Washington, altho I've written to him three different times.

Things are not just as bright here as I would like to see them, John. but I hope the future will clear things up. You know they are up against it with those oil pirates and the gov't is doing all it can to render assistance to the workers. But they are up against a powerful machine.

I am going to close and I hope to see you in Chicago on my way East. Love to Esther and Mrs. Walker, and save for yourself a large portion. Remember me to the brickmaker.

With devotion to you and the cause we are both engaged in,

Sincerely,
Mother Jones

[John Hunter Walker Collection, 1911-1953, Illinois Historical Survey, University of Illinois Library.]

Notes

1. The bill enabled companies to use their own police to guard their property and enabled them, too, to employ them to break unions.
2. C. Frank Keeney was president of West Virginia District 17, UMW.

To Terence V. Powderly

Springfield, Illinois,
626 Fayett Av
November 23, 1921.

Hon. T. V. Powderly,
502 Quincy St., N.W.
Washington, D.C.

My dear Mr. Powderly:

I have been slow in writing you, but I have got a severe attack of rheumatism and I am laid up here in Springfield, Illinois. I want to go to St. Louis to a specialist there. I have been informed that he is an expert at this disease and I will go and get some treatment from him as soon as I am able to. I am suffering severely, and unable to do anything outside of moaning about my troubles.

I had a letter from Father O'Donaghue. He has a remedy he says to cure the trouble that we are going through now. I am very much afraid that it is more enthusiasm than any scientific medecine he has got. You can't remedy those troubles that exist until you destroy the system. The ulcer must be first removed, and as the moneyed power rule Washington and the government, we are going to have some job to remove the ulcer. It is going to take people of fare more experience than Father Donaghue.

This affair in Kansas is a very ugly thing. I am going to send you one of the papers from there so that you will be able to see whats going on. They have suspended the whole organization and they have put Howat in jail and his vice-president.[1]

Well it is a pretty hard problem to solve when your own natinal officers stand behind the enemy and put you behind the iron bars, it is not very encouraging for men or women either to fight the battle of labor. Makes no difference if Howat made the mistake. He was fighting the enemy of labor. He was fighting the most damnable infamous law, the Kansas strike law, that a capitalist governor had pulled over, and the conditions of that jail I am informed is terrible, and when any set of men even though Howat made a mistake, even though he is wrong, stand in line with the capitalist to crucify labor there is something rotten in the background.

It does not give very much encouragement for men to go forward when your own class stands with the common enemy and puts you behind the bar and tears you away from your family.

I received my things alright and thank Daisy very much for her kindness. I am in a terrible condition and hope to get alright soon. I hope Kerwin, Mrs. Powderly and all are well. Tell them I am coming home when the spring comes.

John Walker is down in Kansas fighting the battle of the miners. He sends you his best wishes and hopes the next time he goes to Washington to see you.

Give my love to all at home and tell Margaret I am suffering for that tonic that is in the cellar. I don't know whether I will send a special messenger after it or not, but then it will be well developed when I get back. and under no circumstances give anybody one single drop of it until I do get back. With a happy thanksgiving to everyone, Mrs. Myers and Mrs. Barret and the whole family, and tell Kerwin that I send him my best wishes. If you see Lord tell him you had a letter from me and that I send him my regards. I am, sincerely yours, in the battle for freedom.

Mother Jones

[Terence V. Powderly and Mother Jones Papers, Department of Archives and Manuscripts, Catholic University of America, Washington, D.C.]

Notes

1. Howat was jailed for refusing to obey the Kansas compulsory arbitration law.

To John H. Walker

Washington, D.C., March 20, 1922.

Mr. John H. Walker
626 Fayette Street,
Springfield, Ill.

Dear John:

I have been trying to get a chance to write to you for the last week, but I have been unable to do so. I have not been well since coming here. I expect to go to West Virginia soon. May be this week or the fore part of next week. I did not go from Chicago as I did not feel that I could do the work I wanted to do successfully. I think I will be able to make good next week.

I called the attention of a party in the office to cut the slime out of the Journal.[1] The Journal was not established for any such tactics and if he did not do it, I would make a move so that he would have to do it. The Journal was not meant for his use to send out poison ivy. I told

James if he did not stop it, I would.

Things do not look very good to me. I think the anthracite will come out all right but the bituminous fields look rather week.

Give my love to Mrs. Walker and tell her how much I appreciate her kindness to me. Tell her I will write to her soon. When you write to Esther give her my love.

I have not yet received my trunks and you know all my clothes are in them. I hope you insured them.

I was out to Lord's house yesterday.

Give my regards to Farrington. When you write to Howat tell him I am going to write to him soon.[2]

With best and warmest wishes, I am,

Yours to the end,
Mother Jones

Notes

1. *United Mine Workers' Journal.* In his reply, John H. Walker wrote: "I appreciate very much your effort to get the JOURNAL straightened out, although I have become reconciled to it now, and it don't bother me any personally, — and in the long run I think it will do more good than harm. At the same time, for the sake of the Miners organization, our official JOURNAL should not be used in that way. However, as long as we have vermin and rats acting as editor, we are going to have filth for their surroundings — that is their nature." (John H. Walker to Mother Jones, March 23, 1922, John Hunter Walker Collection, 1911-1953, Illinois Historical Survey, University of Illinois Library.)

2. In his reply, Walker noted: "Just received a card from Howat this morning. He is in Eastern Ohio at that convention and addressing meetings in that territory. He said that the officers are very sore. . . ." (*Ibid.*)

To John H. Walker

502 Quincy Street, N.W.[1]
Washington, D.C.
March 29, 1922.

Mr. John H. Walker
626 Fayette Street,
Springfield, Illinois.

Dear John:

I received your letter of the 23rd. I was more than glad to get it. You know the old-timers have a feeling for each other that no one but the old-timers can understand. Terrence V. Powderly and I spent last night going over the teriffic struggles we have left behind us but they don't compare with the struggle ahead of us, and he said, Mother, you and I have walked over the stormy days of the past and there is no one in the labor movement that understands its struggle more clearly than we do. For forty odd years, he says, I have known you and you have been up against the guns all the time. Its a sad indictment against us, John, that at this crucial hour we must be fighting each other and fighting corruption in our own ranks and the enemies' guns turned on us, but notwithstanding I think we will all come out ahead yet, right and justice must prevail.

I have had some letters from the poor fellows in Colorado, begging me to come to see them, and I had a letter from West Virginia telling me that things looked dark. Use your influence to keep Illinois within the organized labor;[2] under no circumstances let them puul away; if we are divided we are ruined. Keep up your spirits, we will yet come out victorious. I have just seen Wallace and he sends his love to you, and I send mine to Mrs. Walker, and tell her that I shall always appreciate her kindness to me; I think she saved my life. I got the trunks all right but you have not learned to be a good burglar, you could have pulled down that little clasp and thin it would fly open; I never had a key, and I thought surely you were on to the game, but the other fellow can burglarize you, and hold you up, but you don't get even with him. However, I am going to send this letter and in a week or so I am going to write you a longer letter, for I have a good deal to talk to you about.

With my love to Esther, Mrs. Walker and yourself. I am,

Always yours,
Mother Jones

The thing is so rotten I fear there is Noting

[John Hunter Walker Collection, 1911-1953, Illinois Historical Survey, University of Illinois Library.]

Notes

1. On September 20, 1922, Terence V. Powderly wrote to Ed Nockels: "My house number was changed a few years ago from 502 Quincy Street, to 3700 Fifth Street, N.W., but Mother Jones always clung to the old number." He continued: "Owing to her severe illness I did not discuss the subject matter of your telegram with her until your letter came. She is now out of danger and with good care she'll come out right. Mrs. Powderly is devoted to her and I need not say that Mother will get the best of care.

"As to her expenses, I am taking it on myself to tell you that her doctor bill, not all presented yet, will be something like fifty dollars. She had two trained nurses for about two weeks at twenty five dollars each. As to medicine etc. I don't know what it was, or will be, so that one hundred dollars will about pay her own bills.

"Now don't talk about paying me anything for what I do for Mother Jones, that's a labor of love. My home is hers and as one of the family she don't count when it comes to expenses. Her fidelity to the labor movement is her claim with me and my wife feels the same way about it.

"If you wish I shall get itemized bills of her expenses." (Terence V. Powderly Papers, Department of Archives and Manuscripts, Catholic Univesity of America, Washington, D.C.)

2. To this John H. Walker replied: "You need not be afraid of Illinois Mother. Illinois will not pull out of the labor movement, except to save itself from destruction, and I don't think that it is going to have to make that choice." (John H. Walker to Mother Jones, April 6, 1922, John Hunter Walker Collection, 1911-1953, Illinois Historical Survey, University of Illinois Library.)

To John H. Walker

Washington, D.C.
Apr. 22-1922

Dear John:

Just came back from W Va The Poison that has been Sown there against you Howat you and Farrington beat anything —[1] There is going to be Sure Terrable Squabbling at the Trial begins next Monday I cannot write all I m covered. The Main question that I went down for I did not get quite at the botton but got a promise it would be dug up. Am weak not Strong but better I left Springfield perhaps my Strength will come back Some time. My God the corruption in that State beats all I have ever Seen. I am tired can't write much. Tell Mrs Walker I will write her soon. I will remember kindness in my grave

Most Sincrly
Your Mother

[John Hunter Walker Collection, 1911-1953, Illinois Historical Survey, University of Illinois Library.]

Notes

1. In a bitter attack on John L. Lewis, John H. Walker wrote to Mother Jones: "The things they have done not only shows the inhuman cruel and unscrupulous nature of that gentleman, but it also shows how little he cares for the labor movement as well. It means nothing to him except as it may serve his

own personal purposes. . . . Howat is doing good work and may clean out our organization. I sincerely hope he does." (John H. Walker to Mother Jones, December 12, 1922, John Hunter Walker Collection, 1911-1953, Illinois Historical Survey, University of Illinois Library.)

To John H. Walker

Denver, Colo.,
June 26, 1922.

Mr. John H. Walker
626 Fayette Street,
Springfield, Illinois

Dear John:

I have been wanting to write you ever since I came out here but I haven't been able to do anything. I have a little quiet home to stay at with Mrs. Langdon's daughter[1] but I don't seem to regain any of my old time strength. I am just as weak now as I was some time ago although they are doing eveything they can for me out here. The boys are just as good as they can be. Moyer and Mills and the officers of the State Federation still I don't get back one particle of my old time strength.

That terrible blow that those idiotice brained gave me in West Virginia the work and sacrifice of years was wiped out almost over night.[2] The mines are all working nearly on a non union basis and open shop. There was no check off they have spent all the money that they could lay their fingers on.

The acquitted that fellow Blizard but there was no jury that could convict him because he didn't know what they meant by treason. If you asked him he would tell you it was some town or county in the United States some where.

But there will be some convictions overthere. I see they have already convicted the Minister and his son is going on trial now. It seems a very queer thing John to me that poor Howat and Dorchy and the Executive Board should be sent to jail for fighting the most infamouse law that could be placed on the statute books against labor.

And yet those officials that forced the men to break the contract at the point of guns there was not one word of reproach against them.

I cant understand the background of that. I wish you would find out for me whather Howat is in Columbus jail or in Girard. The miners of Herrin deserve the support of every man woman and child in the

United States they did the job and did it right.[3] They didn't spend hundreds of thousands of dollars I wish we had more men such as they have in Herrin.

I have a clipping that I must send you that I took out of the papers here. Wilkinson had to jump into the press and accuse the officials of Illinois, hold them responsible for that move.

Tell Mrs. Walker I am not an ingrate even if I have not written to her I have the most deep appreciation for her kindness to me; and always will. I suppose Esther is home from school and enjoying her Mother's Company.

She is a very beautiful girl and I know will be a wonderful comfort to you and her Mother in the years to come.

John keep your head level watch every one you talk to. You know the world is most treacherous today than it has been in all history.

I see the gang is getting after Foster. Foster is a student and a very deep one. He realizes that the make up of the labor movement has got to changes its methods or else it will be driven to the wall.[4]

You can see that the capitalists are amalgamating all their forces against us and we don't seem to keep pace with the great changes that are taking place.[5]

Write to me as soon as you get back. Give my real love to them all at home.

I am picking up notes to write my book and I want you to help me a little. I can't let that thing go. I wish you could get MacDonald over into the forces with you he is a food boy but that paper of his doesn't amount to a row of pins.

Give my love to them all at home and tell Mrs. Walker I am going to write to her some day.

I remain yours, John as in days of old a sincere friend,

Mother Jones

Notes

1. Emma F. Langdon was her mother.

2. Mother Jones may be referring to the fact that her advice that the second march from Mingo to Logan County be abandoned was rejected, and the consequences that followed continuation of the march. *See* pp. 331-35.

John H. Walker's comment on this point is interesting. He wrote in reply:

"Yes, it is bad the way things are in West Va. I saw Tom Tippett Monday and he told me that he had just gotten back from West Va., and that he had been in every district in it and practically all of the mines were working there every day on a non-union basis; that the situation there was hopeless.

"It has not alone been blunders — it has been much worse than blunders. It is no blunder what they are doing to Howat and Dorchy and the Executive Board of District 14. I think it was planned deliberately with knowledge of what it meant. I think too that they are being paid for it by the coal operators of that territory.

"Those coal operators paid one man by the name of Hazen, thirty thousand dollars according to the confession of their president under oath in court to destroy Howat. They hate him even worse now than they did then, and the thing that has been done to him is so raw, that I know no man with any intelligence would do it, that was honest and that dishonest ones would not do it unless they were paid, and of course those kind of men would not say anything to others, or about others who violated the contract, violated the law, or did anything else if they were friends personally of theirs for the time being — that is the situation as I see it." (John H. Walker to Mother Jones, June 29, 1922, John Hunter Walker Collection, 1911-1953, Illinois Historical Survey, University of Illinois Library.)

3. The reference is to the Herrin Massacre of 1922 which occurred during a severe strike in the coal mining area. After one coal miner was killed (some accounts indicate two were killed), a savage retaliation occurred as about twenty strikebreakers and mine guards were brutally slain. Over two hundred union men were indicted, but all were acquitted. Walker wrote on the event: "Very sorry for that happened in Herrin. Two of our men, defenseless and unarmed, were killed, That provoked the rest to do what they did." (*Ibid.*)

4. The reference is to William Z. Foster, who had founded the Trade Union Educational League to lead the militants in a struggle for progressive trade unionism in the A.F. of L. and Railroad Brotherhoods, and was being severely attacked by the labor bureaucrats as a Communist working in the interest of the Soviet Union. Foster was a member of the Workers (Communist) Party at this time, but the TUEL recruited non-communists in the trade unions as well as Communists. However, while Walker was disgusted with the conditions against which Foster was crusading, the fact that he was a Communist turned him off from the man and the movement he led. "I think Foster is honest," he wrote to Mother Jones, "and I think his purposes are good, but I believe that the methods he has adopted, instead of helping, are hurting." (*Ibid.*)

5. One of the key demands of the TUEL, led by Foster, was for amalgamation of the existing craft unions and industrial unionism in organizing the unorganized mass production industries.

To John H. Walker

Washington, D.C. July 27, 1922.

Mr. John Walker
626 Fayette Street,
Springfield, Ill.

Dear John:

I have a letter from those boys in the southern part of Illinois asking me to go down for Labor Day. I picked up the wrong letter this morning and as I do not remember the address, I ask you to convey to them my appreciation for the invitation and say that if my health permits, I will be glad to comply with their request, but as I feel at present, I could not promise them to be there. It would be only spending the money for nothing and increasing the wealth of the railroads.

Well, John, things do not look very encouraging as I read the papers. Lord left last night for the West. Maybe it was best. He could not do anything here and the Western Federation of Miners are practically out of business, John. As things look to me they will not get better in a hurry. They have not got the officers that will put life into them.

I hope to see you soon and that something will bring you to Washington. After I left you in Chicago, I went to Charleston. There are many things I want to talk to you about. That Blizzard has four more indictments against him, and I am a little afraid of the future trials.[1] I got next to many things when I was there. I also saw this moring in the Washington papers that Wilkinson of District 21 ordered all the pumpmen and the orders that keep things in conditions have been ordered out. If that is true he has made a blunder because the government can sue them for wilfull destroying property. That is something that should be looked after before it is acted on. In my opion it would be wiser if they had made agreements with the mine owners that were willing to meet them and then the others would soon follow. However, I hope it will all come out right in the end.

Give my best wishes to all at home. Things look anything but bright in West Virginia.

With love and devotion to the cause, I am,

Sincerely yours,
Mother

Notes

1. William Blizzard was involved in the trials in West Virginia growing out of the march on Logan County. He was dismissed by John L. Lewis from his post in West Virginia's UMW.
John H. Walker commented: "The whole thing is being made a mess of and unless they are able through some intrigue to work something out of it, I doubt that anything eill [sic] come out of it but disaster, although the men are standing firm, making a heroic fight and they deserve better things." (John H. Walker to Mother Jones, August 1, 1922, John Hunter Walker Collection, 1911-1953, Illinois Historical Survey, University of Illinois Library.)

To John H. Walker

Washington D.C.
Dec. 20, 1922

Dear John:

Got your Letter It was like a ray of Sunshine I think the world looked dark before I got it.[1] Your are the one human soul I look to when the cold world is freezing. John the Labor Movement looks dark there's nothing hardly in the best — after the lives and Money that have been spent — I am not gaining strenght as I had hoped to. The way that Mooney & Keeney treated me made a total wreck out of they are dirty and treacherous a group of vultures as could be found they would cut the throat of Jesus Christ to save themselves.[2] I wish you would see Darrow about that book he has wanted me write If will not write it let me know for 20 years he has been after me Now I am ready for I cannot do anything else[3]

I am so glad Mrs Walker on the road to health a that is home I don't like Hospitals you know she the best nurse in the country in Harret I am enclosing some mail, that will put you nex to thing but Send the mail right back to me

Let Mrs W. I wish I could spend Christmas with her kiss her for me I hope the poor Devils in Herrin will come out all right[4] it was an unfortunate affair just at the time it Hapned. I have a lot to tell you but I cannot write our organization in the A.F.L. has droped from 100,000 to 30,000. poor Jim what a cold blooded deal he got from the organization in which he was born.[5]

I would give anything to See you & I will go to Chicago

[John Hunter Walker Collection, 1911-1953, Illinois Historical Survey, University of Illinois Library.]

Notes

1. In his reply John H. Walker wrote an interesting comment: "Glad to hear from you although sorry to learn that you are not regaining your strength as it looks like you might, because you are needed worse in the labor movement than you ever were during all your life. It does look black. At the same time, one cannot tell how things are going to go. Just about the time it begins to look the blackest, usually it stirs the heards [sic] of many good men and women who, when things were going well, did not interest themselves, so that it might mean that there will be a change in time yet." (John H. Walker to Mother Jones, December 26, 1922, John Hunter Walker Collection, 1911-1953, Illinois Historical Survey, University of Illinois Library.)

2. The reference is to Fred Mooney and C. Frank Keeney, both of whom were fired from their UMW posts in West Virginia by John L. Lewis.

3. The reference is to the *Autobiography of Mother Jones* which Clarence Darrow wanted Mother Jones to write and for which he wrote an introduction when it was published by Charles H. Kerr & Co. of Chicago in 1925.

4. The reference is to the trial of the men involved in the Herrin Massacre, all of whom were acquitted.

5. The reference is to James Lord, a UMW official and head of the A.F. of L.'s mining department, who was dismissed from his position by John L. Lewis. John H. Walker commented: "It was the rottenest deal ever put over. It shows how brutal and conscienceless Lewis really is. There is not a particle of human feeling or decency in him." (John H. Walker to Mother Jones, December 26, 1922, John Hunter Walker Collection, 1911-1953, Illinois Historical Survey, University of Illinois Library.)

To Terence V. Powderly

Springfield, Ill.
March 1st, 1923

T. V. Powderly

I am going to speak at Fort Wayne, Indiana on the 7th of this month. I am feeling better, but I won't hold many meetings for I won't take any chances, but those poor shop men have been out since July and I feel if I am able to crawl I owe them a duty go give them a word of encouragement and know the sunshine of hope still throws out its rays.[1]

Take care of yourself write a line to me

[Terence V. Powderly and Mother Mary Harris Jones Papers, Department of Archives and Manuscripts, Catholic University of America, Washington, D.C.]

Notes

1. The railroad shopmen's strike began on July 1, 1922.

To Governor Ephraim F. Morgan

Chicago, Illinois,
April 16, 1923.

Governor Ephraim F. Morgan,
State of West Virginia,
Executive Department,
Charleston, West Va.

My dear Governor Morgan:

Your letter of April 10 was received.[1] I was very glad indeed for the information it conveyed — the release of those poor fellows in jail. I know that many of those men were unwilling to join that march, but were forced in against their own judgment and will. It is a good thing for West Virginia that she has a governor who looks at the human side of questions as well as the executive side.

So far as that poor fellow, Holt, is concerned, I do not believe, governor, that he is altogether right. And if the fellow is convicted, I hope you will use a little human consideration in his case. You know he blows off a lot of steam, without ever considering where it is going to land or what effect it is going to have. I know, governor, that it is not a very easy position to be governor of West Virginia. You were handed a very ugly ulcer upon your entrance into office. I perhaps know the condition of West Virginia and its elements about as well as anybody in West Virginia. I have been twenty-three years going all over that state from one end to another. I felt, governor, when I first met you that if we worked in harmony we could put the state on the map of America and remove that black spot which she has been carrying for years. I know well what you have had to go up against, and I believe you know me well enough to know that I will not stand by a governor whose interest is not in the welfare of the state and her people. I hope to live to see these disturbing elements in the state laid on the shelf. I have no ax to grind — I am not looking for any office. But I have always felt a deep interest in the state ranking as high as any state in the Union which she could have done if we had the right element on both sides.

You know, governor, as well as I do that the tyrrany of power is a dangerous thing to be in the hands of undeveloped minds. I am yet in hopes that before your term expires that you will leave a record that will live in history — a record that the children of the future may sit up and read with pleasure and gratification.

I notice they are referring to the money that was put up for your campaign. I wish you to see Duncan Kennedy, the commissioner of the Kanawha Coal Company, and get the figures of the amount of money he paid over to the people who are finding fault with you, and after you get the figures ask them what they did with that money. It didn't belong to them — it was the hard earned money of men, women and children who deprived their tables of the necessaries of life, and it was squandered for campaign purposes. Demand an investigation of that when they are attacking you.

Well, I am not going to write much. I am slowly improving in my health and hope I shall have the pleasure of seeing you and Mrs. Morgan. She is one noble, democratic woman for whom I have the deepest respect.

Believe me very sincerely yours for the welfare of the state and nation and her people,

My best wishes to your lovely boy, and tell him perhaps someday when he grows into manhood the world will be better.

With deep friendship,
Mother Jones

[Archives & Manuscripts Section, West Virginia Collection, West Virginia University Library.]

Notes

1. In his letter of April 10, 1923, addressed to Mother Jones c/o Ed Nockels in Chicago, Governor Morgan wrote: "I have made an investigation in regard to those confined in jail at Logan charged with having participated in the recent insurrection in West Virginia and find that they have all been released except three: Savory Holt, Buck O'Dell and G. C. Hickey. They have not been in very long and have not yet been indicted. I presume they will be at this term of the court and then some disposition will be made of their cases.

"You remember that Holt was one of the real active participants and made a speech at Lens Creek urging the crowd to go on after it had decided in response to your request to return to their homes.

"Hoping you are still improving in health and with best wishes." (Archives & Manuscripts Section, West Virginia Collection, West Virginia Library.) For the march to Logan, the so-called "insurrection" of the miners, and Mother Jones's role in the affair, *see* pp. 330-36.

To John H. Walker

Mr. John Hedge Walker,[1]
626 LaFayette Street,
Springfield, Illinois.

My dear John:

I received your letter yesterday.[2] It took several days for it to reach me. You can say to Mr. Palling that I am 94 years old, that I have lived in America 88 years and that never in all those years has the Government asked me to pay any tax for I have nothing to pay tax on. I have seen most every President in the last 40 years and they never mentioned it to me in the White House, nor in the War Department nor in the Department of Justice nor in any other Department that I went to for the workers. I have been with the Miners off and on for over 30 years. I never in all those years put in a single bill for salary. I did not even when I was in the Knights of Labor put in a bill for salary. I sent in a bill for expenses it went in twice a month to the Miners. When I got my return check I cashed it and paid no attention much to the amounts I am not a commercialist nor a financier. I spend it just as fast as I make it. As to the year 1921 I was here there and everywhere that duty called me and there are some that Mr. Palling refers to it was not for salary alone but as I never kept an account of what the money was for I am not able at this date to itemize. I was sick last for four months. I had to have doctors and nurses. I know nothing in the world of taxes I have nothing to pay taxes and the matter never in all my histore was referred to me before. I have been in the public eye for 50 years nearly I don't see why the matter was not brought before. It seems strange, John, that Mr. Palling should be the one to bring me to time. I did not know I had to pay taxes on my clothes. I think, though, that the matter can be clearly by William Green.[3] He can show that he hasn't from me for any services that I ever rendered to the workingclass. When I spoke in Detroit sometime ago they sent me a check for $60 I gave that to Sec. Mooney for the striking miners of Mingo. I don't know whether they ever got it or not, In fact I never gave any attention to taxes as I have no property or anything else. I think if you explain the matter to him he will readily understand it. I am staying now at the home of a man in the service of the Government for many years. I never heard anything about taxes. I never heard anything from any public official in Washington. I don't see why I should be attacked at 94 I have nothing to pay taxes on. When I was sick the Chicago Federation of Labor sent $100 to me and the Janitors organization, their National Office sent me $50. I don't whether I ought to pay taxes on that or not but I paid it over to the doctors and nurses. You explain this matter to him and I think when he gets his reply from Green he will be sort of satisfied. He might charge Rockefeller for taxes for feeding me in the Bull Pen for three months in Colorado.

Well John I will write to you soon again. I am not exploiting the workers and they and their poor wives and children are in need when I have a dollar they have ¾ of it.

With love to all at home, John, I will write you soon again. I have been suffering severely with rheumatism since I have been here. I am awfully nervous I don't think I will ever get over that attack.

I see that Harlen and Howet are going to look for the higher-ups Well it will be doubtful indeed if they ever get there. I did not have much time to talk to Nockles, I did not see Fitzpatrick, I saw Foster for a few minutes. We went out together and had dinner. They are going to get after Fitzpatrick, mind what I tell you, he is too honest a man too up-right to stoop the inner circle.

My strength is failing, John, I don't feel able to do the work I did, but the boys are good to me here they don't over work me, the fact of the matter is they let me come and go as I want to. I put in some very strenuous years for the last ten years, it has not been easy sailing for me, but however, I have lived to see things moving.

Give my regards to them at home and I am glad you have got that new stenographer in Ester. Take care of yourself, with devotion, I am

Always yours,
Mother Jones

[John Hunter Walker Collection, 1911-1953, Illinois Historical Survey, University of Illinois Library.]

Notes

1. "Glad to hear from you," John H. Walker wrote in reply. "You got my name wrong although, it is not John Hedge Walker it is John Hunter Walker, and I am not very much for hedging." (John H. Walker to Mother Jones, December 17, 1923, John Hunter Walker Collection, 1911-1953, Illinois Historical Survey, University of Illinois Library.)

2. In his letter, John H. Walker wrote: "I went over and saw Mr. Paulen yesterday, the Deputy Collector for the Springfield District of the International Revenue Department of our government. He had a copy of the statement that had been filed in which it said that you had no husband and no income for the year 1921. I explained the situation as best I could but in the face of the communication from Secretary Green, which I understand they are required yo [sic] file under oath, that you had received $2350.00 as salary for that year, there was nothing could be done except to pay it.

"For failure to pay during the period (which individuals are required under the law to pay) the penalty is from $25 to $100% [sic] He assessed the minimum penalty 25%, which made it $13.50. Then there is a fine from $5.00 to $1000.00 in casees [sic] of that character, and he asessed the lowest fine possible under the circumstances which was $5.00 I paid him $72.50. . . .

"I am very sorry that the situation developed as it did, but this was the best they could possibly be made of it." (John H. Walker to Mother Jones, December 13, 1923, John Hunter Walker Collection, 1911-1953, Illinois Historical Survey, University of Illinois Library.)

The reference to Green is to William Green, Secretary Treasurer of the UMW, who was soon to succeed Gompers as president of the A.F. of L.

3. On December 17, 1923, John H. Walker wrote: "I am enclosing copy of a letter I got from Secretary Green [*sic*] when I wrote him for information on this matter. I am almost sure it was Green that suggested that they write to you in care of me here in Springfield in the first place, and that he suggested to them that perhaps you would want me to represent you in the latter case, al [*sic*] am almost sure that that is the reason that the representative of the Revenue Department of the United States Government suggested to you that you have me act for you in this matter. I am sorry if I have made a mistake in the matter mother, but in the face of the law governing this man in this action and the information that was given to them by Secretary Green, I did not see how he could do anything other than what he did do, unless he put himself clearly in violation of the law, and liable under the law. . . .

"I agree with you that it looks mighty bad for a representative of the government to do what they did in your case; however, I know that there are a great many people in this country would like nothing better than that kind of information in connection [*sic*] with myself and I would have gone a good deal out of my way to have avoided their getting any information of that kind." (John H. Walker to Mother Jones, December 17, 1923, *ibid.*)

To John H. Walker

Washington D.C.
Dec 18-1923

Dear John

your Letters came to me you know that what ever you do is all right you know there is no power on Earth could shake my confidence in you You know I do not keep account of thing If you how much I had to give poor devils who were threand with arrest from that march I could say nothing to anyone for it get me into trouble.[1]

I did not every before know anything of Tax for I never had anything to tax where the Mexican gov gave me a little money I took care of it.

You the bills from the office were paid every fifteen day I kept no account of it

I am feeling better since I got your letter you are one Soul I would my Life with. I would give anything to see you.

Lewis-Murry were here yesterday they and Sec Davis went to see the Pres at the White House I think the Mission was to See if there could not that W. V. thrown out of Court — they had 3 or 4 concilliaters down there — Gover Hatfield that feller that kept us all in the B Pen in 1913.[2] Ill get on to the thing Latter on at the last Trial those fellows tried to Bribe the foreman of the Jury. the fellow who offered the Bribe is in Jail they tried to get the Gov to have me Superressd as a witness the Gov replied no then they would tell the world she was a Judas. She did her part had they left that women alone there have been no Trouble Now they want to Send her grave Miligned & vilified to Save themselves they have already done all they could to her

My hand Trmbles when I write I am nervous I have a lot to tell you If I could see I will you a checgh for the amount Keep what you have for me Say notthing to no one.

O God if I could only see you you and Nockels are the two I rely on I am going to close I have so much to tell you

Loyally,
Mother

[John Hunter Walker Collection, 1911-1953, Illinois Historical Survey, University of Illinois Library.]

Notes

1. John H. Walker wrote in reply: "Perhaps I should not have written the way I did, but sometimes it seems that everything goes wrong and the load just gets a little larger than my capacity to carry it. However, I was very much pleased to hear from you and to learn that you had not gotten my letters at all, and that you were simply writing out of your feelings before you got the copies of the letter from Green and a clear understanding of the situation."

"I am glad that it is definitely disposed of however. Sorry that I could not have gotten the thing adjusted in a better way, but that seemed to be the very best that he could do at that time." (John H. Walker to Mother Jones, December 27, 1923, John Hunter Walker Collection, 1911-1953, Illinois Historical Survey, University of Illinois Library.)

2. For Governor Hatfield, *see* pp. 56, 224-225. Walker's comment went: "Things seem to be in a terrible shape in that West Virginia situation. I don't know what to make out of it. . . . However, the presidential election being pending and as Colledge [*sic*] seems to be able to depend only on the national spokesmen of our organization for support from organized labor, I am rather the impression. . . . that the powers that be, may adjust matters in West Virginia and work out a general settlement. I sincerely hope so, at any rate, in the interest of our organization and the men, women and children depending on it." (*Ibid.*)

To John H. Walker

Washington, D.C.
Dec 31-1923

Dear John

I just got your letter. It made me feel the world was not so dark after all dont ever opolige to me for anything you do I know it was the best you could I know what burden you hav to meet. You & Ed Nockels are two men as long as I live I look to you. The W Va has no one to blame for the condition they are in but but the officers What the miners should do is to take them out & hang them for an example to other traitors. John I told you long ago that those fellows would never go to jail they have plaid a Shrewd game to fool the people Now they came up to the Department of Labor to send down some of Conciliators — that both sides were getting tired of giving money to Attorneys

What a Dmanable game to play on our poor men tey last time when J Le-Mur[1] called at the White House two weeks ago. [The Pres] Said I wish you Gentleman the fullest measure of Success in your honest endeaver to faithfully represent your constituents

In doing this you rely upon the justice of your cause and not on any influence that you can bring to bear from others. to not rely on Politic or Politicians only so far as you are right you can hope to *Suceed*

The last time they were in Court they hired a fellow to bribe the Jury foreman the fellow is in jail but they dont to jail who commit the crime

The strange part of it is that the National don't say word against it but they could crucify those who stand for a principle.

Lewis & Murray were here last week they and the Sec of Labor sent to see Coolidge I did not hear what for

I think you will hear of a compulsory arbitration bill brought at the next Congress There is Some thing rotten Strange that those fellows that have ruined the organization in West Va and Kentucky can go with their work of Distruction I was in W.V. a month a go If I could see you thre is Something rottin I am not well I am I look at the work of years

a happy new year love to all

Loyally
your Mother

[John Hunter Walker Collection, 1911-1953, Illinois Historical Survey, University of Illinois Library.]

Notes

1. John L. Lewis and Philip Murray.

To John H. Walker

Washington D.C.
Jan 11-24

Dear John

I am all in to day can only write a few Lines It looks as if will not get well again I had the Dr yesterday so far I have not had any relief I saw Van Bittener at the Dept. of L. yesterday Al Hamilton has all his tools in control of the miner's organization Hughs Phil Mr V. B. Zimmerman the our the West Va gang if I could see you I could tell you much more than I could write I am afraid I will have to go to Los Angeles I am all broke bones that W.V. ruined my health No Gun Man ever made the attack on me that Mooney & Keeny did[1] they would not be heard of it it were not for the work I did I saw Hoover the other day I think from what he said thing will move

Love to all at home

Loyally
Mother

[John Hunter Walker Collection, 1911-1953, Illinois Historical Survey, University of Illinois Library.]

Notes

1. Mother Jones is referring to the actions of Fred Mooney and C. Frank Kenney during the second Logan March and the incident involving the fake telegram from President Harding. *See* pp. 331-32.

To Governor Ephraim F. Morgan

Washington, D.C.,
January 31, 1924.

Honorable Governor Morgan,
Charleston, W. Va.

My dear Governor:

I have not written to you for some time knowing the responsibility you have on your shoulders and no time to be writing unimportant letters.

I had a meeting with Gov. Pinchot a few weeks ago with regard to a young fellow who is in jail in Pa.[1] He has a wife and little children and in the course of conversation, he referred to some Pa. Coal Miners who were in jail in W. Va., and I told him if he got in touch with you and there was any possibility withoin the law of pardoning them he need not fear but that you would do it. I say that in the 24 years I have gone in W. Va. and being mixed in all the industrial battles in it, I have never found a Governor more open nor more fair minded and with the high keen sense of justice of Gov. Morgan.[2] I told him I would you to be a man of honor and a man of deep thought and before you acted you gave all matters deep thought. I also said that if I could approach all Governors as I could Gov. Morgan many things would be avoided. But that many men in your position think the whole state and all in it belongs to them. One instance that convinced me of the man's grand and human instincts was in regard to a woman who came to see me when in Charleston the last time, who with tears dropping on her breast she told me her sad story. I took her to the Governor and she told the sad story to him. He gave her $20.00 and a letter to bring her husband home. The man left the state. He wanted to come home but was afraid of getting arrested but the Governor told him to come and he would see that he was protected. Those were acts that I myself witnessed convinced me that in the history of 24 years there was a man in the executive chair that would do his duty impartially, although he has been misrepresented, I have witnessed many kind human acts of his and as long as I live I shall always appreciate the deeds he did for poor suffering wretches. I told Gov. Pinchot to apply for pardon for these men and though you would grant it at once. I also had a talk with Mr. Hoover but did not go into the matter as deep as I did with Gov. Pinchot but I convinced him that W. Va. for the first time in 24 years had a real humane Governor.

I have not been well, Governor, all winter and I think I shall go West in the course of a month to a better climate. I hope you are getting a little rest and that they are not stabbing you with their slimy pens as they were doing. I still retain for you, Governor, the same deep respect that I formed you during the conflict when I had experience with you and found out of what material you were made and I was convinced that you could be approached at any time for a just cause.

I am with deep respect

Yours sincerely,

[Archives & Manuscripts Section, West Virginia Collection, West Virginia University Library.]

Notes

1. For further discussion by Mother Jones of this case, *see* pp. 666-67.

2. Governor Morgan replied: " . . . I certainly appreciate the good things you said about me to Governor Pinchot and Secretary Hoover.

"You have been a great help to me during my work and at many times a real inspiration. . . .

"I want to assure you that when I feel the facts and circumstances justify me under the law, it is always a pleasure to grant freedom to any of the poor fellows who may be imprisoned in our state institutions.

"I hope that you will regain your good health again, and that you may have many more years added to your life to bring sunshine and happiness to those who need advice and comfort." (Governor Ephraim F. Morgan to Mother Jones, Charleston, West Virginia, February 1, 1924, Archives & Manuscripts Section, West Virginia Collection, West Virginia University Library.)

To John H. Walker

February 11, 1924.

Mr. John H. Walker,
626 Lafayette St.,
Springfield, Ill.

My dear John:

I have not heard a word from you for a long time and I suppose you were at the convention, and things did not seem to me to go off very smooth there. It is an outrage the way they treated Howat, but it may react sooner or later.[1]

I wish you would write and let me know how things are getting on and how Mrs. Walker and Esther are. I need not ask how you are for I know you are worked to death.

I had a leter from Fitzpatrick and it made me feel good. The boys in Chicago have been so good to me. I expect to go to Chicago soon and look forward to seeing you. In the meantime write me a few lines.

With love, I am

Sincerely yours,
Mother Jones

[John Hunter Walker Collection, 1911-1953, Illinois Historical Survey, University of Illinois Library.]

Notes

1. At the UMW convention, February 2, 1924, Howat, defeated in a delegate vote manipulated by John L. Lewis, leaped to the stage and was thrown off bodily. (*New York Times*, February 3, 1924.) Lewis justified the use of force against Howat with the argument that by it conservative trade unionism had triumphed over communism. (Dubofsky and Van Tine, op. cit., pp. 124-25.)

To John Fitzpatrick

Washington, D.C., Feb. 29, 1924.

Mr. John Fitzpatrick,
166 W. Washington St.,
Chicago, Ill.

My dear Mr. Fitzpatrick:

I am sending you this letter to let you know that I have been working every angle that I could reach with influence for that boy in jail.[1] The matter was started going as Mr. Powderly knew the Lientenant Governor very well and got him to use his influence. I also got in touch with the Attorney-General who will use his influence and the Department of Labor took it up with President Tighe and he was up at the Department two days ago. He told them he would hire a lawyer to tend to the case and do everything he could for the boys. So you see I have left no angle untouched to get this poor fellow home to his wife and children.

I hope that things are going smoothly with you. I expect you to leave here pretty soon to go down to W. Virginia and get some poor fellows out of jail.[2]

Then I am going West to carry on my work for Smidthy. My heart aches for him and I am not going to leave anything undone to get him out until I see him home with his Mother.

Things do not look very favorable in the West for me. I had a letter from Denver, stating that things were in bad shape and I got a letter from California. The tailors had 1,200 members in their organization when I was there. They now have only 60 and all the force that was on the weekly paper had to get off. But we must keep up courage and get more life into the men in the rank and file and some of those organizers have to be retired.

I hope to hear from you soon.

Sincerely yours,

Things looks bright for that boy in Pa I have a lot to tell you

[John Fitzpatrick Papers, Chicago Historical Society.]

Notes

1. For evidence that Mother Jones succeeded *see* pp. 679-80.
2. *See* pp. 666-67.

To John H. Walker

Washington
Apr 13-24

My dear friend

I will be in Chicago on Thursday the 17. If possiable come up & see me. I do not Expect to Come back this Way We may not meet again. Some things I wish to you about

Loyally yours
Mother

Will be at the Washington Hotel

*[John Hunter Walker Collection, 1911-1953, Illinois Historical Survey,
University of Illinois Library.]*

To John H. Walker

Los Angeles Calif
July 2-24

Dear John

You no doubt think I have forgotten you. No I have not. I have been sick ever since I left you. I have been taking treatment for my rheummatism but I have not been very Successfull. Yet I thave a Little more Strenght than I had Some time ago

Well John the one faithful friend I had for the last 45 years has passed away Terence V. Powderly[1] he fought my battles for years he faced all the Slanders & boldly Deffended me Such men are scarce. You & Nockels Fitzpatrick & Jay Brown of Seattle are those I could depend on

I want to See you there is so much you should know before I pass away from this Earth.

Well they had a great Time in St Paul McDonald has Signed his Doom

I saw Germer the other day.[2] he is Sect for the oil workers he had an auto with 2000 Dol a fine pair of Silk Stockings a pair of Shoes must have cost 25 Dol the poor Devil pay the bills John the Labor Movement is fleced more than any other Institution Well I am getting tired I will close untill I see you they want me Johnson City on Labor Day[3] it may be the Last Labor Day I will see

fondly,
Mother

[John Hunter Walker Collection, 1911-1953, Illinois Historical Survey, University of Illinois Library.]

Notes

1. Terence V. Powderly died in Washington, D.C., June 24, 1924. John H. Walker commented: "I was sorry to hear of Powderly's going. I knew that you would feel it keenly, as you say, he was one of the few that could be depended upon at all times to stand for the thing that was right and they are very few these days." (John H. Walker to Mother Jones, July 7, 1924, John Hunter Collection, 1911-1953, Illinois Historical Survey, University of Illinois Library.)

2. Adolph Germer, Socialist and UMW leader in Illinois. In a tribute to Mother Jones, published in the *Illinois Miner* after her death, Germer recalled the meeting, writing: "I last saw her still full of fight in California in 1924. I took her for a long ride along the ocean front and often have I recalled her mental anguish on that occasion. She said: 'Germer I fear for the safety of our organization. Graft, corruption, deceit and debauchery are gnawing at its vitals. The Steel Trust is in control and when I think of the brave boys who have gone

to jail and who have been shot to death and the suffering of the women and children, it makes my heart ache. The gang got you, they got McDonald and they are making life miserable for 'Jack' Walker. They are driving the builders of the United Mine Workers out of the ranks, but, by God, I'll fight them 'till I die. Promise me one thing, Germer, stick to the ship until the end.' I told her: 'I will!'" (*Illinois Miner*, December 1930.)

Frank Farrington of the UMW bitterly attacked Germer for having published this conversation with Mother Jones, and asked: "Did you stick to the 'ship' as you pledged her you would do? Had you not abandoned the 'ship' long before 1924 and did you not enjoy shore leave for several years afterward? Did you not stay away from the 'ship' until it was prearranged for you to come aboard in 1930 as one of the commanding officers? Did you do anything in the meantime to publicly expose the evils you say 'Mother' told you were prevalent in our Union and gnawing at its vitals? . . ." (The original of the long letter of Frank Farrington to Adolph Germer, December 18, 1930, is in the Victor Orlander Papers, Chicago Historical Society.)

3. Hunter commented: "If you can make it to Johnston City next Labor Day, I know everybody will appreciate it very much and will be mighty glad to have you." (John H. Walker to Mother Jones, July 7, 1924, *op. cit.*)

To John Fitzpatrick

2759 Marengo Street,
Los Angeles, Calif.
July 31, 1924

Mr. John Fitzpatrick, President,
Chicago Federation of Labor
166 West Washington Street,
Chicago, Illinois.

My dear Mr. Fitzpatrick:

I have just received a letter from Mrs. Pinchot, wife of the Governor, notifying me that Mr. Dolla has been pardoned.[1] I am glad to convey this news to you, if you have not already been informed from some other source. I am enclosing the letter which she sent me, so that you will be able to see for yourself what has happened.

I shall leave for Chicago next week. I am to speak at Johnston City, Illinois, on Labor Day, and I want to have a few days to visit with you and Ed.

I hope that poor Ed. is back again at his desk.[2] It looks so lonely to go in and not find him there. I have not written to him, knowing that he has more than he is able to bear, and so long as you keep me posted about his condition, I am not going to bother him.

When you write to Jay Brown, tell him I want his address. I don't know where to locate him, consequently shall enclose letter herewith and ask you to forward it to him.

I have not been any too well, but I am going to muster up enough courage to go East.

With best of wishes to you, and devotion to the cause, I am,

Loyally yours,
Mother Jones

I see the Labor herald takes credit for Dole when you know they could not get him out in a hundred years[3]

[Original in John Fitzpatrick Papers, Chicago Historical Society; copy in John Hunter Walker Collection, 1911-1953, Illinois Historical Survey, University of Illinois Library.]

Notes

1. Gifford Pinchot (1865-1946), pioneer conservationist, was governor of Pennsylvania from 1923-1932 during which period he aided the cause of labor considerably. His wife Cornelia Bryce Pinchot, was a member of the Women's Trade Union League and personally assisted in the organization of women workers.

2. Edward Nockles, secretary of the Chicago Federation of Labor.

3. *Labor Herald* was the official publication of the Trade Union Educational League.

To John H. Walker

(5-25)

John R. Walker,
626 Lafayette St.,
Springfield, Illinois.

Dear friend John,

You are the last one on earth that I thought would neglect me. You have not sent me a line since I have been out here. You know a line from you always cheers me.

We have got great changes since I saw you. Sam went to sleep in

Smoky Hollow and Green took his place in Washington. I think, John, that Green was the best selection that they could have made. If that Matha Wall [Matthew Woll] or any of that machine got in there I do not know where the Labor Movement would drift, but I had great hopes for its future progress with Green. He is supplanted by Kennedy of district 7. Kennedy is a good fellow but he is a part of the machine and he can be handled very nicely. I noticed that Lewis did not get to be secretary of the Department of Labor. It is a lucky thing for the department that he did not get in there. His whole machine would be in there and some of the good fellows would have to take a walk. I felt quite sure, since I was in Washington last October, that there was very little hopes of his getting the position. If he got on the cabinet I do not know what we would do.

Well there are great changes taking place anyhow. I have a good deal to talk to you about when I get to Chicago and I hope that you will make it convenient to come in and see me.

John, I have not been well ever since I have been here, and I have given up all hopes of regaining my health. I am going back to stay at Powderly's. You know in Washington I get to see some of the old timers occasionally. While that does not bring back my health, still it does away with the blues.

I see that you have had a terrible time in Herrin. That fellow Young was a bad egg and it is no loss to have him out of the way. Perhaps peace may come now that he is gone. They have a hard time in Colorado. The Ku Klux control the whole state now.[1] They are putting Lindsey out of business and they will put everyone else out that does not suit them. I am afraid that they are going to create a great deal of trouble before they are done away with, not alone for the state, but for the national government as well.

I notice in the worker that you and Fitzpatrick, and Nockles are not behaving yourselves very well. If the Worker does not pursue some other tactics besides attacking the honest people in the Labor Movement I fear they will go out out of business some day. They are pursuing the very same tactics that the Socialists did, Condemning everyone that does not agree with their philosophy.[2]

Well, give my love to Mrs Walker and Esther, and I hope they are all well. With Best wishes I remain yours until I see you in Chicago. A Happy New Year to all at home.

Mother Jones

[John Hunter Walker Collection, 1911-1953, Illinois Historical Survey, University of Illinois Library.]

Notes

1. The Ku-Klux Klan was originally created to resist in the post-Civil War period civil, political, and economic rights for Negroes. During the 1920s a new movement began which borrowed the Klan's name, and some of its methods. It was, however, not confined to the South, nor was it solely confined to the Negro. It functioned in a number of states, especially Indiana and Vermont, and made inroads into the UMW in Illinois and Colorado.

2. In view of the split engineered by Fitzpatrick and Nockles at the Farmer-Labor Party convention in July 1923, where they sought unsuccessfully to exclude the Communist delegates, a step which Mother Jones opposed, it is surprising that she should have been upset that the *Daily Worker* criticized these men. *See* pp. 360-68 for the Farmer-Labor Party convention.

To John H. Walker

Washington D.C.
July 30/25

Dear friend

Owing to the Terrible condition of my Health I have to Leave this Climate I have Suffered Terrible agonny Will be in Chicago next Monday & Tuesday. We may never meet again I want to see you before I go West

I have so much tell you that you should know
Love to Mrs. W. & c
Be sure to see me

Loyally
Mother

O John I am all broke down cannot hold a pen in my fingers They are crippled

[John Hunter Walker Collection, 1911-1953, Illinois Historical Survey, University of Illinois Library.]

To Arrangements Committee, 27th Annual Commemoration of the Virden Massacre[1]

[October, 1925]

They stood bravely on the hill and told the scabs to return to St. Louis.

I wish every state would follow Illinois in organizing its workers. My heart beats today with devotion to those brave boys as it did the morning that they gave up their lives for a holy cause.

When I am called I want to take my last sleep with my brave boys in Mt. Olive. Under no circumstances would I choose to take my final rest in Sleepy Hollow with Carnegie and the rest of the capitalist exploiters.

To be with my boys both living or dead is all that life means to me now. Be it to their credit the workers have always rung true to the cause, while the same cannot be said of their leaders who in some cases have bartered their principles for a mess of pottage and prolonged the struggles of the workers instead of standing like men true to their pledge.

And now, my dear boys, I wish you success and the final triumph of labor. Stand by your guns when the cause is a just one.

[Daily Worker, *October 22, 1925.*]

Notes

1. The headline in the *Daily Worker* above the letter read: "MOTHER JONES, IN LETTER TO MINERS, INFERS SHE WOULDN'T BE FOUND DEAD WITH GOMPERS." The article opened: "MT. OLIVE, Ill., Oct. 31 — Too ill to be with her miner boys at the 27th annual commemoration of the heroic defense of Illinois unionism at Virden, Mother Jones dispatched a letter to the arrangements commitee in which she picks her last resting place and tells the rank and file to carry on." The *Daily Worker* correspondent made no mention of the fact that the Virden incident involved black miners who were imported from Birmingham, Alabama, to act as strikebreakers but who tried to resist being used in this capacity. (*See* Philip S. Foner, *Organized Labor and the Black Worker, 1619–1973*, New York, 1974, pp. 177–79.)

To John H. Walker

Washington D.C.
Nov 13 1925

Dear John

Just going to send you a line I have not heard from you so long I have not Just saw this morning that Keeney was quiting the Ill. minors Why did he not stay in W. V. and do his [illegible] perhaps John down all of history the workers have crowned their Leaders crucified her Saviors had he remained in his office when I went to Mammoth to stop that March. there would have been a different condition in W.Va., to day. he was not heard of hear of when I was facing machine guns & Bull Pens he struck me in the face I have not got over that Schock yet he never offered an apology look at the condition those poor fellows are in to day. When I went to that Women from robbing the Miners Magazine that Del Hamiton started in Indianapolis to slander you he told me to Leave her alone John L. Lewis sent her you had better watch that fellow don't be so damn easily fooled I know those Fellows John the fellows who betray you once will again it benefits their Pockets

I have so much tel tell you I am suffering with pain from Rhematism

fondly
Mother

[John Hunter Walker Collection, 1911-1953, Illinois Historical Survey, University of Illinois.]

To John H. Walker

2759 Marengo St.
Los Angeles, Cal.
Feb. 15-926.

Pres. John H. Walker,
626 LaFayette St.,
Springfield, Ill.

Dear John:

I have been on the scrap pile ever since I saw you, and I have been going to write to you time and time again but, owing to my condition I kept postponing it. I got some medicine that a Dr. in Syracuse New

York, sent me for rheumatism, It did me a wonderful amount of good, but the weather for the last week or so has been damp and unfavorable to my desease, and I am again beginning to feel the old pains coming back. My Dr here sent after some more of the medicine and when I receive it, and begin to take it, I feel I will get relief.

Well John, the Anthracite strike was to a great extent a fiesta.[1] Just think of making a five year contract after what the men suffered. The Morning Examiner here (a Huret Paper) made a statement "that the miners, when putting a man at their head should look around for a man with brains or, go over to the Operators and get one."

West Virginia is on the scrap pile from information sent to me there. Its a terrible enditment against the officers. I have some letters from there that I would like you to see but I cannot send them to you by mail. I expect to go to Washington the last of next month, and on my way will stop off at Chicago. You may come up and see me and I will let you see those letters that I have. I want to have a talk with you alone, and then with Nockles and Fitzpatrick. I wan't to arrange, legally. I want you to form a committee to handle the profits from the book I wrote, and it is to go into a fund to defend the poor wretches that are placed behind the bars by the capitalists courts, and their only crime is fighting for the bread they produce, for their children. I makes no difference to me whether they are I.W.s or A.F.of Ls, I will contribute my part to their defense.[2] I know that Mrs. Powderly will always take care of me so I am not worrying about that, but those poor fellows have no one to look out for them and their little ones crying. When I pass away the boys at Mt. Olive will see that I am laid to rest with the boys that gave up their lives some twenty years ago in Verdon Illinois. I don't want those dam Isms to get a dollar of it. I will have to get a lawyer when I go to Chicago to look into that thing for I don't trust that Charles Kerr. The book is not printed as I wrote it anyway, and I have never been satisfied with it.[3]

I see that the miners of Ziglar and Farringtons henchmen are at loggerheads with each other. I sent ten dollars John, to those poor fellows to help defend them, in Ziglar.[4] There were some mighty good boys down there. John, there seems to be some disrupting hand at work in the miners union as well as other organizations. It does not appear on the surface but the silent work is going on just the same. In 1922 tey had two Open Shop Papers, the capitalists had, now they have three hundred and thirty six open shop papers that they are circulating. The Labor papers don't seem to give any warning to the workers with regard to that. I have a great deal to talk to you about for the good of the miners organization, when I see you. I could sit here all night and write to you but I don't feel able John, to do it. When I was coming here, I don't think I would ever have gotten here if it had not been for Fitzpatrick who came to the Hotel and took me to the train and put me in. Fortunately when I got to Los Angeles I had a good place to come and stay. Miss Flaherty has taken the best of care of me notwithstanding that she is not in the best of health herself. I hope I'll get better and that I will be able to see you when I am going thru Chicago.

There is a peculiar apathy in the labor movement to day, unknown in its history before. I regret very much that Green did not give Percell, the delegate from England a more cordial reception than the papers said he did.[5] So far as I was able to read I think the delegate was perfectly right in his speech that he delivered at the convention in Atlanta. I am very much afraid that fellow Rickert[6] is going to influence Green. He was the hidden adviser of Gompers. Green is a good fellow, kind hearted and honest to the core, and well meaning but there are a lot of well meaning people in the Insain Asylum, John. Well, my love to all and write to me just as soon as you get this letter. I hope Esther is doing well and also Mrs. Walker. I will close with the old time friendship. Most sincerely yours,

Mother Jones

[John Hunter Walker Collection, 1911-1953, Illinois Historical Survey, University of Illinois Library.]

Notes

1. John H. Walker's letter in reply contained a number of comments of interest. First he observed: "Glad to hear from you and to know that you are still living and taking an interest in the movement." He continued: "Speaking of the anthracite strike, it is too bad that men have to suffer for any reason, but I am quite sure that if the anthracite strike had not been called, that we would have had a much worse situation in the bituminous industry than obtains there at the present time. I think that strike saved the bituminous situation for the time being. I don't know whether that justified the calling of the strike or not; but I do know that it meant saving things from going to the bad completely in the bituminous districts.

"The fact that the anthracite coal operators made absolutely no effort whatever to operate their mines non-union, and then they made this sort of settlement under the circumstances, has caused some gossip, but I think considering the circumstances at the time of the settlemtn [sic] being made, that the mine workers were lucky to get the settlement they did. That at least will maintain a nucleus of a national organization. The bituminous situation is such as to make me fearful for the future. I don't see how anything can be done to prevent suffering and injury to our people, and our organization, unless industrial conditions improve a great deal, and then perhaps a national strike being called on the eve of the presidential election might be successful and get a settlement that would save the situation.

"From the information I get, the organization is in bad shape in Nova Scotia, British Columbia, Washington, Utah, Colorado, Texas, Arkansas, Oklahoma,

West Virginia, Old Virginia, Pennsylvania, and portions of Ohio and Indiana." (John H. Walker to Mother Jones, February 22, 1926, John Hunter Walker Collection, 1911–1953, Illinois Historical Survey, University of Illinois Library.)

In 1926 John Brophy, president of District 2 in central Pennsylvania, joined forces with the Communists and others who opposed the Lewis machine in launching the "Save the Union" movement. The movement advocated a militant organizing drive to prevent the total destruction of the union, a labor party, nationalization of the mines, close cooperation between the bituminous and anthracite districts, and reinstatement of those expelled by John L. Lewis for opposing his policies. Brophy ran for president against Lewis in 1926 on this platform, but was defeated. He promptly charged fraud, but his charges were ignored. (John Brophy, *A Miner's Life*, Madison, Wisc., 1964, pp. 128-35.)

2. On this issue, Walker differed sharply with Mother Jones. Thus he wrote: "Now Mother, on these other matters, I dislike very much to write you, because during all our lifetime, we have agreed almost entirely on the different issues, but in this, I disagree with you. I think you had such feeling on the John Mitchell matter that you could not give it your usual calm, cool, impartial judgment; and I have as much feeling the other way. So that for that reason, I would not want to connect myself with that book. Then, there is the other reason. The uses to which you want to put these funds." Walker then went on to deliver an hysterical attack on the "so-called I.W.W.," and the "Communists organizations of today," even indicating that he would do nothing "to get them out of jail, if they are sentenced to it, by the socalled capitalistic court (and there is no one knows what these courts are, from the point of view of labor, better than I do.). . ." (John H. Walker to Mother Jones, February 22, 1926, *op. cit.*)

3. Mother Jones may have reference to the woman who helped her in the writing of her *Autobiography*. She was Mary Field Parton, a forty-four-year-old former social worker and magazine writer, the wife of Lemuel F. Parton, a former Chicago newspaperman and later a nationally syndicated columnist. Parton probably wrote sections of the book.

4. Walker did not sympathize with the effort to aid the miners at Zeigler, for he wrote: "In this particular case that you cite at Zeigler, they tried to set aside the present agreement in our state." (John H. Walker to Mother Jones, February 22, 1926, *op. cit.*)

5. The reference is to John Purcell, the fraternal delegate of the British Labor Party to the 1925 A.F. of L. convention, who proposed a labor party for the United States.

6. President T. A. Rickert of the United Garment Workers was one of the most conservative and bureaucratic A.F. of L. leaders.

To John H. Walker

3700 5th St N.W.
Washington, D.C., June 10, 1926.

Mr. John H. Walker,
Springfield, Ill.

Dear John:

I am writing you a few lines to let you know that I am still alive but I have been very sick after you left me that night, I got a sinking spell towards morning and I longed for the train to come to take me to Washington. I am feeling better and feel better today than for a long time and Mrs. Powderly has been taking the best care of me.

I have been using electric pads and I feel sure that helps me. I was afraid John that we would not meet again because I was so sick. I longed for the train to leave Chicago but I am down in Mr. Manning's office today getting a few letters written. It is a good thing that there are a few good people in the world as I do not what we would do if there was not.

I had a letter from an old friend of mine in Florida and I wish that you knew him and could meet with him. I hope that Esther and Mrs. Walker are feeling well and I do not what I would do if Miss manning was not a good friend to me and writes for me as I would not be able to write to you as I would not be able to write myself.

With love and devotion to you, I remain your friend

Mother Jones

[John Hunter Walker Collection, 1911-1953, Illinois Historical Survey, University of Illinois Library.]

To John H. Walker

Alliance Ohio
Sep 28/26

Dear Friend Walker

Just a line to let you I have not forgotten you —

I have been here with an old friend of 30 years ago. She & her Brother live together about 3 miles from town She feeds me on goats milk & fresh Eggs With care I have got I till weak & good for Nothing I will for Washington next week Mrs Powderly wants me home She is a little afraid to have me away

I spent so much for Dr with no Relief, I suffer Day Night from my keenes. John I Suffer more than I can tell you, there is a Dr here that Says he can help me but cannot cure me. I have little hopes of ever getting well again

This friend & her good Brother are getting every remedy they hear of but no relief I am So nervous, I leave here next Sunday for Washington. I get a back set that night before I left Chicago my knees began to torture me I have not got over it since nor never will I have not get Edo book yet after I read it will write he was one faithful soul good be relied

The Papers here had a Lot about Pres. Farrington he is not the only traitors the miners have[1]

Write me 3700-5th Street Washington D.C.

Love to all at Home

Loyally,
Mother

[John Hunter Walker Collection, 1911-1953, Illinois Historical Survey, University of Illinois Library.]

Notes

1. John H. Walker's comment in his reply, went: "The miners' situation looks hopeless Mother. That combination have got complete control — are going to do what they please — I don't think it is possible to do anything with them. It is going to take time and the miners themselves to cure it if it is to be cured at all, and the near future looks rather dark.

"I understand Farrington was drugged just before he left New York and that that was responsible for his signing the agreement that he did. That however hearsay, but in view of what was done to Frank Hayes, it seems rather likely. My information was that Farrington was going to fight the program that was agreed upon by the large interests who are attempting to consolidate the coal business and the getting it in the control of one concern, and that they were desperate in getting him out of the way. He was no angel, but he was a great deal better than a great many of them who were on there, and I do not know that he has done a great many good things and made a great many good fights for the labor movement. There are a lot of things he would not do. There is nothing that the men who tried to get rid of him, would not do. As between them and Farrington, he was much the better." (John H. Walker to Mother Jones, October 3, 1916, John Hunter Walker Collection, 1911-1953, Illinois Historical Survey, University of Illinois Library.)

However, when Walker wrote this, he was not aware that Farrington, who enjoyed the good life, had entered into a secret agreement in July 1926 with the Peabody Coal Company, the largest coal operator in Illinois, to serve as labor adviser for a three-year period beginning January 1, 1927, at an annual salary of $25,000. The contract, signed on July 1, 1926, including a pledge from Farrington agreeing not to run again for office in District 12. Later, however, Farrington repudiated that part of the agreement requiring him to disclaim all future office in District 12. When John L. Lewis made the terms of the contract public, Farrington's reputation among the rank-and-file miners disappeared forever. (*See* Dubofsky and Van Tine, *op. cit.*, pp. 125-27.)

To John H. Walker

December 16, 1926.

Mr. John Walker,
Springfield, Ill.

Dear John:

I am just writing to you to wish you and Mrs. Walker and Esther a Merry Christmas and a Happy New Year and hope that the incoming year will bring peace and happiness.

I will have to go back to California owing to the condition of my health and if I stop off at at Chicago I would like to have a talk with you. I have some mail that I got from W. Va. that might be of some service to you but I cannot send it to you through the mail. As soon as I arrive in Chicago I will call you up as I will have to stay there a couple of days.

With all the best wishes, and blessings of the season, I remain

Sincerely and loyally yours,
Mother Jones

[John Hunter Walker Collection, 1911-1953, Illinois Historical Survey, University of Illinois Library.]

To John Fitzpatrick and Edward Nockles

November 14, 1927.

Mr. John Fitzpatrick
and
Mr. Ed Nockels,
Chicago,Ill.

My dear old time Friends:

I have been wanting to write to you for some time, but I have been unable to do so. I have been quite sick and was in the Garfield Hospital hanging between life and death and I have not regained my strength since coming out.

I will be 99 the first day of next May and I want to live to be 100 and come to Chicago to celebrate the anniversary.[1]

I hope all is well with you both and when you see Walker tell him I would like a line from him. He has grown to be the most indifferent fellow among my friends.

I have some good friends in Washington in the Label Trades Department, Mr. Manning and his sisters. I owe them a debt of gratitude which I am afraid I shall never be able to repay.

Give my best wishes to friends and enemies alike.

With deep devotion and gratitude to you both, for the old time friendship, I remain

Sincerely yours,
Mother Jones

[Copy in John Hunter Walker Collection, 1911-1953, Illinois Historical Survey, University of Illinois Library.]

Notes

1. Mother Jones celebrated her 100th birthday on May 1, 1930, in Washington, D.C. at the home of Mrs. Walter Burgess.

On November 17, 1927, John H. Walker wrote to Mother Jones: "Glad to know that you are still with us and that you expect to celebrate your one hundredth birthday anniversary in Chicago next year, and if I am well and able to go , I expect I will be there whether you invite more or not." (John Hunter Walker Collection, 1911-1953, Illinois Historical Survey, University of Illinois Library.)

To John Fitzpatrick

December 14, 1927.

Mr. John Fitzpatrick
Chicago,Ill.

My dear Friend:
Received your letter some time ago and was more than glad to hear from you.

I understand that the Governor offered a parole to Mooney but he would not accept it. He wanted a full pardon.[1] If he does not accept a parole I am inclined to think he will spend his time behind prison bars. It is sad to think you have such men to deal with and that one has to put forth their best efforts to get their freedom, and then not to be appreciated any more than he appreciates it. If I could get Schmiddy and J. P. MacNamara out I would not bother with Mooney until he got tired of his boarding place.

I hope to be able to carry out your good wishes on my 100th anniversary, in Chicago and I shall do all I can to retain my health and strength to meet that occasion and tell Ed this letter is for both of you.

Trusting that the coming years will bring peace to you and Ed and all the boys, I remain

Most sincerely yours,
Mother Jones

[Original in John Fitzpatrick Papers, Chicago Historical Society,
copy in John Hunter Walker Collection, 1911-1953, Illinois
Historical Survey, University of Illinois Library.]

Notes

1. This is not accurate.

To John Fitzpatrick

January 11, 1928.

Mr. John Fitzpatrick, President,
Chicago Federation of Labor,
Chicago, Ill.

My dear Friend Mr. Fitzpatrick:

I am just going to write a few lines and tell you I received your letter some time ago but as I did not feel well could not answer it.

When I was coming back from Calif. I wanted to stop off and have a talk with you and Ed but I felt weak and thought I had better not stop but go straight to Washington. I was not here three days before I had to go to the hospital where I spent 4 long weeks, but fortunately I had some good friends in Washington such as Mr. Manning and his sisters in the Union Label Trades Department who were good and kind to me and so was Pres. Green.

Poor Schmiddy got turned down when he asked for parole. I think he made a mistake when he did not let some one else make the application. They are not so apt to comply with such a request as they are if it comes from some one with influence. Poor fellow, I am afraid he will not get out in a hurry. The one I feel sorry for is his poor sister. It is not often you find such a loyal sister as she has been. However, we must make the best of the worst and not give up hope.

Hope things are getting along smoothly and that Ed is in good health. Tell Ed from me I wish I was near him so I could get a little tonic when I did not feel well. Tell him I never forget him when I have a bad spell. I hope to be able to meet you all again. You know I have not given up hope to see my 100th anniversary and I will be in Chicago to feast with you. At least I hope so.

Some day perhaps I will have a chance to talk over the radio.[1]

With best wishes to all and tell them to be good that a new day will dawn.

Sincerely yours,
Mother Jones

[John Fitzpatrick Papers, Chicago Historical Society.]

Notes

1. Mother Jones did appear on Movietone News but not on radio.

To John H. Walker

Mr. John H. Walker,
Springfield, Ill.

Dear John:

Your letter was a welcome visitor. It relieved me of a great deal of worry.[1] I was limited to three dollars and hardly knew what to do. Whether to ask William Green to help me or to apply to the poor house but your letter completely settled the question. I had forgotten all about that John. It entirely changed my feeling and I am a different woman today than I was the day the letter came.

You know I do not like to sponge off any one or live like a pauper. I wish Jim Lord had your principle and paid me what he borrowed from me like a man not to rob an old woman like me. But I will make him pay that money yet some how.

With love to yourself and Mrs. Walker, I remain

Sincerely and loyally yours,
Mother Jones

P. S. The Miners are up against it.[2] That fellow Lewis was a crook the day he was born and so was Murray and Fagan. I am glad the miners are waking up to them.[3]

[John Hunter Walker Collection, 1911-1953, Illinois Historical Survey, University of Illinois Library.]

Notes

1. The letter read: "I am enclosing check for one ($1,000) thousand dollars to repay you for the loan you so kindly made me, to help me in finishing the payments on my home and for our girl's education. Everything is all right now and there is no good reason why I should keep this money any longer. I appreciate very much your loaning it to me and if there is anything that I can do at any time to show that appreciation in a more substantial way, all you will have to do is call on me." (John H. Walker to Mother Jones, August 29, 1928, John Hunter Walker Collection, 1911-1953, Illinois Historical Survey, University of Illinois Library.)

2. "Your comment in your post-script," John H. Walker wrote, "I think is correct. They have done the most terrible things to these men, women and children and to the whole labor movement and the cause of humanity that has done in our generation. I have more respect for the ordinary murderer than I have for those men who consciously did what they have done." (*Ibid.*)

3. Early in September, 1930, a little while after celebrating her one hundredth birthday, Mother Jones donated $1,000 to John Walker and the Reor-

ganized United Mine Workers of America (RUMWA) which had been organized at a convention in Springfield as part of the anti–John L. Lewis movement in the UMW. "I only hope that I may live long enough to see John L. Lewis licked," Mother Jones commented in making the contribution. She hoped the money would be used effectively "to help defend the miners against leaders who are thinking more of themselves than they are of my boys." (*New York Times*, September 6, 1930.)

To the Miners of Mt. Olive, Illinois

Chicago, Ill.,
Nov. 12, 1928.

A Special Request to the Miners of Mt. Olive, Ill.:

When the last call comes for me to take my final rest, will the miners see that I get a resting place in the same clay that shelters the miners who gave up their lives on the hills of Virden, Illinois, on the morning of October 12, 1907.[1] For their heroic sacrifice for their fellow men they are responsible for Illinois being one of the best organized labor states in America. I hope it will be my consolation when I pass away, to feel that I sleep under the clay with those brave boys.

Mother Jones

[Included in undated newspaper clipping, Mother Mary Harris Jones Papers, Department of Archives and Manuscripts, Catholic University of America, Washington, D.C.]

Notes

1. The event occurred in 1898 not 1907. Fourteen white miners were killed and twenty-four wounded in the gun battle between the miners and deputies guarding black strikebreakers being brought on the train to Virden.

Founded in 1898, the year of the Virden Massacre, the Union Miners' Cemetery in Mount Olive, Illinois, located about midway between Springfield and St. Louis, honors the Virden dead as well as the many activists of the Progressive Miners of America who died in scattered conflicts with company police during the 1930s. The cemetery also serves as the local graveyard for Mount Olive, a small town with a large labor heritage.

Mother Jones is buried near the elegant bronze and marble monument dedicated to the memories of scores of labor martyrs who fell in early attempts to unionize Southern Illinois coal mines. The monument's inscription reads: "WE COUNT IT DEATH TO FALTER, NOT TO DIE."

Selected Bibliography

This bibliography attempts to provide a guide for further study of the career of Mother Mary Harris Jones. Items already included in the text, such as speeches, testimony before Congressional Committees, interviews, articles, and letters of Mother Jones are not included nor are the tributes to Mother Jones. For comprehensive coverage of all aspects of the coal mining industry, readers should consult Robert F. Munn, *The Coal Industry in America, A Bibliography and Guide to Studies*, Morgantown, W. Va., 1965.

Unpublished Studies

Anson, Charles P., "A History of the Labor Movement in West Virginia," Ph.D. dissertation, University of North Carolina, 1940.

Barb, John M., "Strikes in the Southern West Virginia Coal Fields 1912-1922," MA thesis, West Virginia University, 1949.

Barkey, Frederick Allan, "The Socialist Party in West Virginia from 1890 to 1902: A Study in Working Class Radicalism," Ph.D. dissertation, University of Pittsburgh, 1971.

Camp, Helen, "Mother Jones and the Children's Crusade," MA thesis, Columbia University, 1969.

Campbell, Roy E., "History of the Development of the Coal Industry in Kanawha District, West Virginia," MA thesis, West Virginia University, 1930.

Christopulos, Diane K., "American Radicals and the Mexican Revolution, 1900-1925," Ph.D. dissertation, State University of New York at Binghamton, 1980.

Crawford, Charles, B., "The Mine War on Cabin and Paint Creek, West Virginia in 1912-1913," MA thesis, University of Kentucky, 1939.

Dunbar, John C., "Two Periods of Crisis in Labor-Management Relations in the West Virginia Coal Fields (1912-13 and 1919-22)," MA thesis, Columbia University, 1946.

Gowaskie, Joseph M., "John Mitchell: A Study in Leadership," Ph.D. dissertation, Catholic University of America, 1968.

Johnson, Alan V., "Governor G.W.P. Hunt and Organized Labor," MA thesis, University of Arizona, 1964.

Lee, Virginia, "Political and Civil Liberties during Certain Periods of Emergency in West Virginia," MA thesis, Marshall College, Huntington, West Virginia, 1942.

McGovern, George P., "The Colorado Strike, 1913-1914," Ph.D. dissertation, Northwestern Univesity, 1953.

Mikeal, Judith Elaine, "Mother Jones: The Labor Movement's Impious Joan of

Arc," MA thesis, University of North Carolina, 1965.

Posey, Thomas Edward, "The Labor Movement in West Virginia, 1900-1948," Ph.D. dissertation, University of Wisconsin, 1948.

Raffaele, Sister John Francis, GNSA, "Mary Harris Jones and the United Mine Workers," MA thesis, Catholic University of America, 1964.

Shyder, Betty Hall, "The Role of Rhetoric in the Northern West Virginia Activities of the United Mine Workers 1897-1927," MA thesis, West Virginia University, 1950.

Trail, William R., "The History of the United Mine Workers in West Virginia, 1920-1945," MA thesis, New York University, 1950.

Whittaker, William G., " 'Mother' Mary Jones and Mexico: The Defense of the Mexican Exiles, 1907-1910," unpublished paper delivered at Northwest Labor History Conference, Seattle, 1971.

Walsh, William J., "The United Mine Workers of America as an Economic and Social Force in the Anthracite Territory," Ph.D. dissertation, Catholic University of America, 1957.

White, Elizabeth, "Development of the Bituminous Coal Mining Industry in Logan County, West Virginia," MA thesis, Marshall College, Huntington, West Virginia, 1956.

Willis, Edmund P., "Colorado Industrial Disturbances 1903-1904," MA thesis, University of Wisconsin, 1955.

Books and Pamphlets

Ambler, Charles and Festus P. Smmers, *West Virginia, The Mountain State*, Englewood Cliffs, N.J., 1958.

Atkinson, Linda, *Mother Jones: The Most Dangerous Woman in America*, New York, 1978

Bernstein, Irving, *A History of the American Worker, 1920-33: The Lean Years*, Boston, 1960

Blaisdall, Lowell L., *The Desert Revolution*, Madison, Wisconsin, 1964.

Brody, David, *Labor in Crisis: The Steel Strike of 1919*, Philadelphia, 1965.

Beshoar, Barron B., *Out of the Depths: The Story of John R. Lawson, A Labor Leader*, Denver, 1958.

Brophy, John, *A Miner's Life*, Madison, Wisconsin, 1964.

Chaplin, Ralph, *Wobbly: The Rough-and-Tumble Story of an American Radical*, Chicago, 1948.

Coleman, McAlister, *Men and Coal*, New York, 1943.

Colorado State Federation of Labor, *Militarism in Colorado*, Denver, 1914.

Corbin, David, *The Socialist & Labor Star*, Huntington, W. Va., 1971.

Corbin, David Alan, *Life, Work, and Rebellion in the Coal Fields: The Southern West Virginia Miners, 1880-1922*, Urbana, Illinois, 1981.

Cornell, Robert, *The Anthracite Coal Strike of 1902*, Washington, D.C., 1957.

Evans, Chris, *History of the United Mine Workers, 1860-1900*, Indianapolis, 1918 (2 vols.).

Dubofsky, Melvyn & Warren Van Tine, *John L. Lewis: A Biography*, New York, 1977.

Fabela, Isidro, editor, *Documentos históricos de la revolución mexicana*, Mexico City, 1966, vol. X.

Featherling. Dale, *Mother Jones The Miners' Angel*, Carbondale, 1974.

Fink, W.H., *The Ludlow Massacre*, Denver, 1914.

Foner, Philip S., *History of the Labor Movement in the United States,* vol. 1, New York, 1955; vol. 3, New York, 1964; vol. 4, New York, 1965; vol. 5, New York, 1980; vol. 6, New York, 1982.

————, *Women and the American Labor Movement: From Colonial Times to the Eve of World War I,* New York, 1979; *From World War I to the Present,* New York, 1980.

Foster, William Z., *The Great Steel Strike and Its Lessons,* New York, 1920.

Frost, Richard H., *The Mooney Case,* Stanford, Cal., 1968.

Gentry, Curt, *Frame-Up: The Incredible Case of Tom Mooney and Warren Billings,* New York, 1967.

Ginger, Ray, *The Bending Cross: A Biography of Eugene V. Debs,* New Brunswick, N.J., 1947.

Gluck, Elsie, *John Mitchell, Miner,* New York, 1929.

Harris, Evelyn I.K. and Frank J. Krebs, *From Humble Beginnings: West Virginia State Federation of Labor, 1903-1957,* Charleston, W. Va., 1960.

Harvey. Katherine S., *The Best Dressed Miners: Maryland Coal Region, 1835-1910,* Ithaca, N.Y., 1969.

Hinrichs, A.F., *The United Mine Workers of America and the Non-Union Coal Fields,* New York, 1923.

Hudson, Harriet D., *The Progressive Mine Workers of America, A Study in Rival Unionism,* Urbana, Illinois, 1952.

Jensen, Vernon H., *Heritage of Conflict: Labor Relations in the Non-Ferrous Metals Industry up to 1930,* Ithaca, N.Y., 1930.

Lane, Winthrop D., *Civil War in West Virginia: A Story of the Industrial Conflict in the Coal Mines,* New York, 1921.

————, *The Denial of Civil Liberties in the Coal Fields,* New York, 1924.

Long, Priscilla, *Mother Jones, Woman Organizer,* New York, 1976.

McGovern, George and Leonard Guttridge, *The Great Coalfield War,* Boston, 1972.

McLaughlin, Doris B., *Michigan Labor: A Brief History from 1918 to the Present,* Ann Arbor, Michigan, 1970.

Mooney, Fred, *Struggle in the Coal Fields,* Edited by James W. Hess, Morgantown, W.Va., 1967.

Murdoch, Angus, *Boom Copper,* Calumet, Michigan, 1954.

Nash, Michael, *Conflict and Accommodation: Coal Miners, Steel Workers and Socialism, 1890-1920,* Westport, Conn., 1982.

Raat, W. Dirk, *Revoltosos: Mexico's Rebels in the United States, 1903-1923,* College Station, Texas, 1981.

Rankin, Robert S., *When Law Fails,* Durham, N. Car., 1939.

Rochester, Anna, *Labor and Coal,* New York, 1931.

Roy, Andrew, *History of the Coal Miners in the United States, from the Development of the Mines to the Close of the Anthracite Strike of 1902,* Columbus, Ohio, 1907.

Snow, Sinclair, *The Pan-American Federation of Labor,* Durham, N. Car., 1964.

Suggs, George G., Jr., *Colorado's War on Militant Unionism,* Detroit, 1972.

Thoughts of Mother Jones: Compiled from Her Writings and Speeches, Morgantown, W.Va., 1978, pamphlet.

Vorse, Mary Heaton, *Men and Steel,* New York, 1970.

Weinstein, Irving, *Labor's Defiant Lady,* New York, 1969.

Weinstein, James, *The Decline of Socialism in America 1912-1925*, New York, 1967.

Yellen, Samuel, *American Labor Struggles*, New York, 1936.

Articles

Blizzard, Wm. J., "The Battle of Paint Creek," *The Mountain Messenger*, Peytona, West Virginia, September, November 1973.

Chaplin, Ralph, A., "Violence in West Virginia," *International Socialist Review*, 13 (April, 1913): 729-30.

Corbin, David A., "Betrayal in the West Virginia Coal Fields: Eugene V. Debs and the Socialist Party of America, 1912-1914," *Journal of American History* 64 (March, 1978): 987-1009.

Dix, Keith, "Mother Jones," *People's Appalachia*, 11 (June-July, 1970): 6-13.

Eklund, Monica, "Massacre at Ludlow," *Southeast Economy and Society* 14 (Fall, 1978): 26-31.

Green, Archie, "The Death of Mother Jones," *Labor History* 1 (Winter, 1960): 68-79.

Jensen, Billie Barnes, "Woodrow Wilson's Intervention in the Coal Strike, of 1914," *Labor History* 15 (Winter, 1974): 67-77.

Keiser, John H., "John H. Walker: Labor Leader from Illinois," in Donald F. Tingley, *Essays in Illinois History*, Carbondale, 1968, pp. 113-42.

⸺ , "The Union Miners' Cemetery at Mt. Olive, Illinois," *Journal of Illinois State Historical Society*, Autumn, 1969, pp. 14-23.

Leeds, Joseph, "The Miners Called Her Mother," *Masses & Mainstream*, March, 1958, pp. 45-49.

Lynch, Lawrence R., "The West Virginia Coal Strike," *Political Science Quarterly* 29 (December, 1914): 626-63.

McCarthy, Colman, "The Ardor of Mother Jones," *Washington Post*, September 16, 1975.

McCormick, Kyle, "The National Guard of West Virginia during the Strike Period of 1912-1913," *West Virginia History* 22 (October, 1960): 34-45.

McFarland, C.K., "Crusand for Child Laborers: 'Mother' Jones and the March of the Mill Children," *Pennsylvania History* 38 (July, 1971): 283-90.

McLean, Louis Clenes, "Looking Back at Mother Jones," *Beckley (West Virginia) Post-Herald*, May 30, 1972.

⸺ , "Mother Jones, The Miners' Striking Spirit," *Pittsburgh Press*, January 20, 1974.

⸺ , "Mother Jones in West Virginia," *Goldenseal* 4 (January-March 1978): 15-21.

⸺ , " 'I'll Teach You Not to be Afraid,' Mania Baumgarten Rembers Mother Jones," *Goldenseal* 6 (January-March, 1980): 20-23.

Marcy, Mary E., "The Hatfield Whitewash," *International Socialist Review* 14 (July, 1913): 54-55.

Michelson, Miriam, "Sweet Land of Liberty," *Everybody's Magazine*, 28 (May, 1913): 615-28.

Smith, Russell E., "The March of the Mill Children," *Social Service Review* 41 (September 1, 1967): 298-305.

Spargo, John, "Child Slaves of Philadelphia," *Comrade*, August, 1903, p. 253.

Speidel, Mary, "Mother Jones — Labor's First Lady," *Huntington (West Virginia) Herald-Advertiser*, August 15, 1971.

Steel, Edward M., Jr., "Mother Jones in the Fairmont Field, 1902," *Journal of American History* 57 (September, 1970): 290-307.

Suggs, George S., "The Colorado Coal Miners' Strike of 1903-1904: A Prelude to Ludlow" *Journal of the West* 12 (1973): 36-52.

Sullivan, William A., "The 1913 Revolt of the Michigan Copper Miners," *Michigan History* 43 (September, 1959): 300-310.

Sunseri, Alvin R., "The Ludlow Massacre: A Study in the mis-employment of the National Guard," *American Chronicle*, January, 1972, pp. 20-32.

Thompson, Fred, introduction to *Autobiography of Mother Jones*, Chicago, 1972 and revised in edition of Chicago, 1974.

Thompson, W.H. "How a Victory Was Turned into a 'Settlement' in West Virginia," *International Socialist Review* 14 (July, 1913): 12-17.

Wells, Merele W., "The Western Federation of Miners," *Survey* 30 (April, 1913): 37-50.

Wiebe, Robert H., "The Anthracite Strike of 1902: A Record of Confusion," *Mississippi Valley Historical Review*, September, 1961, pp. 229-51.

Index

703

split with Ricardo Flores Magón, 583-86; battle with J. Mahlon Barnes in Socialist Party, 567, 568; becomes organizer for United Mine Workers, 52; belief in socialism, 360, 499, 511; birth, 47, 51; bitter attacks by on Socialist Party leadership, 225, 569-70, 572, 574-76, 577-78, 612-13; blames Rockefeller interests for "Ludlow Massacre," 535; blames Rockefellers for strikes, 250-51; breaks with Ricardo Flores Magón, 531, 580-86; buried in Union Miners Cemetery, 58, 695; called anarchist, 34; called champion octogenerian traveler, 515; called conservative at time of death, 24, called "female anarchist orator," 253; called Jekyll-Hyde, 502; called no revolutionist, 25; called "most dangerous woman in America," 34, 49, 162; called "traitor," 332; called "woman Demosthenes of the American Labor Movement," 253; calls for a class-conscious proletarian party, 93; calls for complete overthrow of capitalistic system, 455; calls for eight-hour day, 522, 552-53; calls for public works to meet depression, 534-36; calls for six-hour day, 203, 519-20; calls for solidarity of all workers, 106-8; calls for support of I.W.W. prisoners, 321; calls for union shop, 376; calls for unity of non-Communists and Communists and Farmer-Labor Party convention, 361-64; calls for unity in United Mine Workers, 311-13; calls for unity of labor movement, 321-22; calls foreign miners peaceful, 397; calls Judge Jackson a scab, 80-81 calls on women to help men organize, 284-89; calls removal of gunmen key to peace in coal struggles, 93, 389-91, 395-96; calls John L. Lewis a crook, 694; calls self a Bolshevik, 25, 318, 364; calls self more radical than ever at 100th birthday, 535; calls self a Socialist, 249, 521; calls self a social revolu-

tionist, 491; calls situation in West Virginia military despotism, 586; calls Woodrow Wilson another Lincoln, 258; campaigns for re-election of Governor Hunt in Arizona, 474-79, 609; cared for by Emma Powderly, 688; celebrates one hundredth birthday, 58, 69; challenges Governor Peabody, 557; charges against J. Mahlon Barnes dismissed, 574; charges U.S. capitalists behind imprisonment of Mexican revolutionists, 122, 125; cites labor's progress, 506; claims *Autobiography* not published as she wrote it, 685; close relations with Debs, 558-59; condemns American society, 635-36; condemns Baldwin-Felts guards, 183, 191-95, 199, 209, 211, 212, 224, 231-33, 243; condemns Canadian authorities for preventing her from entering, 514; condemns capitalism, 200-14; condemns capitalists in last interview, 535; condemns Andrew Carnegie, 171; condemns child labor, 41-42, 54, 92-93, 100-3, 201, 407-8, 504, 552-55; condemns class-collaboration labor leaders, 22, 127, 134, 139, 147-48, 178, 277; condemns corruption in labor leadership, 657; condemns Porfirio Díaz, 41, 160, 462-65; condemns government by injunction, 187-88; condemns labor bureaucrats, 627, 635; condemns John L. Lewis leadership of United Mine Workers, 58, 359, 643; condemns military despotism, 433-35; condemns militia, 164-65, 283-86; condemns ministers who support employers, 456; condemns missionaries, 166, 185; condemns John P. Mitchell, 112; condemns National Civic Federation, 139, 142, 147, 148, 174, 178; condemns private ownership of industry, 443; condemns Rockefeller church fund, 636; condemns society ladies, 84, 98, 181, 209, 366, 468-74, 571-72; condemns treachery of labor leaders, 620; condemns treatment of

ganizes on behalf of Western Federation of Miners, 43-45, 55-56; organizes oil workers, 624-26; organizes miners' wives, 56, 151, 407, 408, 417, 441-42; participates in founding of I.W.W., 55, 111; pays tribute to Italian miners, 109-11; pays tribute to Woodrow Wilson, 296; permitted to enter British Columbia, 252; placed in hospital, 241, 429; placed under quarantine, 221; plans to educate John D. Rockefeller, Jr., 263; plays about, 30, 48; pleads for imprisoned miners, 332-33; pleads for Mexican revolutionists, 120-35, 369-75, 464, 529; poems, 472-73; political philosophy, 360; praised as speaker, 36-37; praised by William Z. Foster, 317; praises A.F. of L., 326; praises black miners, 89; praises William E. Borah, 287; praises Eugene V. Debs, 599-60; praises William Z. Foster, 660, 662; praises Alexander Howat, 646-47, 675, 676; praises Governor Hunt, 474-79; praises Governor Pinchot, 674; praises Francisco Madero, 580, 582; praises John P. Mitchell, 558; praises I.W.W. for organizing unorganized, 499-500; praises Pan-American Federation of Labor, 321-22; praises Pancho Villa, 262; praises Woodrow Wilson, 268, 523, 524; praises women, 342; praises women of San Francisco, 622-23; predicts great oppression after World War I, 618, 620; predicts new day breaking for workers, 625; predicts people will own all industries; 536; prevented from entering British Columbia, 251-52, 514; problems with income tax, 668, 669, 670; proposes government take over all industries, 512; publishes first article in *International Socialist Review*, 54; quarantined, 415, 531; quits United Mine Workers in dispute with John P. Mitchell, 55; raises funds for Mexican revolutionists, 120-35; raises threat of

machinery, 444; reads forged telegram, 331-32; reads resolutions to West Virginia strikers, 191-92; reads Victor Hugo's works, 191; receives some money from Mexican government, 670; refuses to put up defense before military court, 60; refuses any longer to support Ricardo Flores Magón, 584; relations with blacks, 337; relations with William Z. Foster, 305-6; relations with miners' wives, 26-29; 56, 269, 362-63; released from military prison, 161, 604; requests be buried in Union Miners' Cemetery, 695; rescues Manuel Sarabia, 55, 370-74, 460-61; resents attack on her, 673; returns to Mexico for Pan-American Federation of Labor convention, 643, 644, 647, 649-51, 652-54; returns to United Mine Workers as organizer, 56; returns to West Virginia, 331; role in formation of Farmer-Labor Party, 360-65; role at founding convention of I.W.W., 18-20; role in Haywood, Moyer, Pettibone case, 118, role in freeing Manuel Sarabia, 55, 370-74, 460-61; role in freeing Mexican revolutionists from U.S. prisons, 143-45, 370-74, 460-61; role in 1897 coal strike, 73-76; 45, 370-74, 460-61; role in 1899 coal strike, 405-6; role in coal strike of 1900, 77-78, 405-7; role in coal strike of 1902, 49-51, 54, 78-100, 387-89, 408-9, 419-24, 481-83; role in coal strike of 1903-4, 55, 412-17, 557; role in coal strike of 1912-13, 54, 56, 156-222, 223-25, 231-321, 493-500, 587-88; role in copper strike of 1913, 69, 160, 229; role in coal strike of 1913-14, 226-68, 376-405, 425-37; role in railroad strike of 1877, 51, 404-5; role in steel strike of 1919, 303-19, 628-32; role in streetcar strikes of 1916, 287-90; role in West Virginia's bloodiest mine war, 329-48, 639-40; saddened by imprisonment of Eugene V. Debs, 640; salary as United Mine Workers organizer,

718

Walker, John Hunter, anti-Communism of, 662, 687-88; biographical sketch, 559; charges elections in United Mine Workers stolen, 624-25; helps Mother Jones with tax problems, 669, 670, 671; in Kansas, 656; letters from, 49, 619, 620-21, 625, 632-33, 634, 637, 638, 640, 644-45, 657, 658, 659-60, 661-62, 664, 668-73, 678, 679, 680-82, 684-88, 686-87, 689-90, 691; letters to, 16, 557-60, 618, 617-21, 623-26, 631-40, 643-49, 651-53, 656-65, 669, 670, 671, 673, 675, 677-78, 680-90, 694-95; opposes John L. Lewis, 352; organizes with Mother Jones, 334-35, 545; praises Mother Jones's fearlessness, 545; returns $1000 loan to Mother Jones, 694

Walker, Ryan, editor of New York *Call*, 593; letters to, 629-30, 641-42

Walker, Mrs. Ryan, letters to, 593-94

Walker, W.E., 253

Walsh, Frank P., asks Mother Jones questions before U.S. Commission on Industrial Relations, 403-47; and defense of Tom Mooney, 615; forces John D. Rockefeller, Jr. to face facts, 264; exonerates Alexander Howat, 607

Wanhope, Joshua, 222-23, 224, 489

Ware, Norman J., 139

War, against Filipinos, 93, 94

War Labor Board, 303, 304

War with Spain, 116

Warden, S.P., 53

Warren, Fred, 140, 149, 152, 572, 600, 601

Washington, George, 295, 307, 330

Washington Agreement, 350-51, 620

Washington Times, 316

Wayland, Julius A., 52-53, 62, 572, 593, 594, 600, 601

Wayland, Walter, letter to, 621-22

Webb, Beatrice, 47

Weinberg, Israel, 615

Weinstock, Harris, 441-42, 444, 448

Weinstock, Irving, 22

Weitzel, E.H., 227

Wellborn, J.F., 227

West, George P., deplores life of

Mother Jones not better known, 21; exposes John D. Rockefeller, Jr. company union plan, 267-68; Mother Jones pay tribute to, 614; nominates Mother Jones for list of greatest American women, 45; tribute to Mother Jones, 65-66

Western Federation of Miners, asks President Roosevelt to intervene in Colorado, 111; interest in Mexico, 30; Mother Jones cooperates with, 105, 106; Mother Jones organizes for, 112-15, 130-31, 412-13; Mother Jones says no difference between and United Mine Workers, 259; Mother Jones's respect for, 112; Mother Jones says is practically out of business, 663; Arizona copper strike, 474, 608; Michigan copper strike, 262; official organ, 468; role in founding of IWW, 118

West Virginia, bloodiest mine war in, 329-48; conditions in, 33-34, 132, 152-62, 332-36, 494-95; Congressional investigation of conditions in, 161, 162; effect of World War I on, 329; finally organized by United Mine Workers, 333; march of miners in, 58; martial law in, 157, 159, 210; murder of miners in, 97-98, 100, 115, 183, 310, 411-12; slogan of, 168; Socialist Party of, 218-19; strikes in, 78-100, 156-222, 231-34, 387-89

West Virginia Labor History Society, 29

West Virginia State Federation of Labor, 293

West Virginia University, 22, 162

Wheeler, Hoyt N., 46

Whitaker, Robert, 67

White, David H., 503, 510

White, John P., asks Mother Jones to help in Governor Hunt's campaign, 608, 609; asks Mother Jones to help stop strike-breaking, 239, 383; forces settlement upon striking miners, 162; joins Fuel Administration in World War I, 349; Mooney complaint against, 615; Mother Jones challenges, 281; Mother

723